Collins
dictionary of
Social Work

William Collins' dream of knowledge for all began with the publication of his first book in 1819. A self-educated mill worker, he not only enriched millions of lives, but also founded a flourishing publishing house. Today, staying true to this spirit, Collins books are packed with inspiration, innovation, and practical expertise. They place you at the centre of a world of possibility and give you exactly what you need to explore it.

Collins. Do more.

Collins
dictionary *of*
Social Work

Principal editors
John Pierson and Martin Thomas
Staffordshire University

Contributing editors
Rhoda Castle, *Staffordshire University*
Jim Radcliffe, *Staffordshire University*
Brian Williams, *de Montfort University*

Collins

HarperCollins Publishers
Westerhill Road, Bishopbriggs,
Glasgow G64 2QT

www.collins.co.uk

First published 1995
Second edition 2002
Reset edition 2006

A catalogue record for this book is available from the British Library

ISBN-13 978-0-00-721478-5
ISBN-10 0-00-721478-2

Typeset by Davidson Pre-Press Graphics Ltd, Glasgow
Printed and bound in Great Britain by Clays Ltd, St Ives plc

Using the Dictionary

Much has happened within the world of social work since the first edition of this dictionary was published in 1995. Social workers must now contend with many new statutes, new central government guidelines, new ideas for practice and a wide range of policy innovations.

Social workers are now found in many new areas – whether advising young people in the Connexions service, working in neighbourhood-based renewal projects or as members of multidisciplinary teams such as youth offending teams – even if these practitioners go by a different name. We intend the dictionary to be used by all such practitioners as well as social workers and social care workers in local authority social services, the probation service and voluntary organizations, large and small, who would naturally turn to it for updated information and guidance. We have also made this edition even more useful for students in social work education.

To make the vast range of social work terminology accessible for all readers, we have defined and explained each entry in as straightforward and concise a way as possible. Each entry is defined so as to stand on its own. We have, however, included within many entries one or more cross-references. The reader is encouraged to follow these through in order to reach a full understanding of the subject under discussion. Wherever appropriate, we have discussed implications for social work and social care practice under the individual entry. Thus readers will not find a separate entry 'social work with older people' but will find that information under **older people**. Readers should also note that we use the words 'client' and 'user' to denote the person who uses or receives social work or social care services. Although the latter term is now the more widespread, each is found in different areas of practice and we have sought to use the term that is the most appropriate for the area under discussion. Since the terms are used so frequently we have not cross-referenced them in each instance. Finally, readers will find all entries to do with welfare benefits under the series of **welfare rights**' entries. This enables the important links among benefits to be made more easily than if they were individually found in their alphabetical order.

Entries in the dictionary are of three different levels:

1. All entries have a short definition of the term;
2. Many entries consist of this short definition plus a longer summary of what the term means, usually of up to half a page;
3. Still other entries consist of the short definition, the summary and a more detailed discussion of the topic, of about two pages.

Where appropriate, further reading is cited below the entry.

Contributors

Helen Barnes, *Staffordshire University*
Suzy Braye, *University of Liverpool*
Tina Davis, *Staffordshire University*
Annette Gurney, *University of Central England*
Jo Hutt, *Staffordshire University*
Pauline Ing, *Staffordshire University*
Bernard Moss, *Staffordshire University*
Julie Pryke, *Bradford College*
Keith Puttick, *Staffordshire University*
Adrian Randall, *Birmingham Asylum Seekers Team*
Alison Read, *Staffordshire University*
Sue Wainwright, *University of Birmingham*
Ben Whitney, *Staffordshire Education Department*
Claire Worley, *Staffordshire University*
Nevil Wyatt, *Staffordshire University*

Dedications

John Pierson: To Terry Philpot,
For all the years of friendship, encouragement and collaboration

Martin Thomas: For my mother, Evelyn

Acknowledgements

We are grateful to Joan Deakin and Melody Butters for their hard work in preparing the manuscript for publication and to Clare Crawford for so manifestly improving the consistency and accuracy of the volume.

Aa

able-bodiedism the assumption that the bodily characteristics of non-disabled people are superior to those of disabled people, who should accept an inferior social status as a result.

Disabled people may have physical, sensory or psychological attributes that differ from what is most common in the general population. The definition of certain attributes as 'normal', however, suggests that they are not only the most common but also the most desirable. This approach is associated with systems of classification for people who deviate from the norm in particular ways. Some of these have resulted in pejorative labels such as 'cripple' and 'spastic'. Although these terms are no longer socially acceptable, assumptions about bodily inferiority affect the way non-disabled people interact with disabled people. Sometimes this takes the form of pity or fear. Able-bodiedism is also associated with a tendency to attribute any difficulties experienced by disabled people to bodily inferiority and to design social and physical environments to suit non-disabled people.

abortion the loss of a foetus through planned termination or miscarriage.

Abortion applies to the termination of an unwanted or unplanned pregnancy. It became legal in 1967 in England, Scotland and Wales (although the Infant Life Preservation Act, 1929, had made it legal for an abortion to be carried out if it were to save the life of the mother). Abortion is now legal up to twenty-four weeks into pregnancy. The Human Fertilization and Embryology Act, 1990, permits an unlimited extension to this period if there is a substantial risk of physical or mental ill health to either the woman or to existing children of her family. Most abortions are carried out in the first twelve weeks of pregnancy, either by the NATIONAL HEALTH SERVICE (or its agents) at no cost to the individual or at a clinic or private hospital where the patient bears the expense. Over half the women seeking abortions are not able to get NHS treatment, according to the British Pregnancy Advisory Service whose clinics charge a non-profit-making fee to cover the cost of treatment. For an abortion to be legal under the Abortion Act 1967, two doctors must agree on the grounds, including risk to the life of the woman, risk to her own or her existing children's physical or mental health and risk of serious abnormality to the foetus. In emergencies, abortions can be carried out to save the woman's life or to prevent permanent injury. If the woman is under 16 years old, the doctor will usually need her parents' consent; however, doctors can use discretion and make exceptions if the young woman refuses to give the information.

Although most women feel physically fine within a day or two, some feel emotionally 'low' after an abortion. The effects of an unplanned pregnancy are many and varied, and women therefore react in a variety of ways to their abortion. The range of emotions may include relief, euphoria, depression, grief, anger, sadness, guilt and numbness – all appropriate responses to a difficult life crisis. Severe DEPRESSION after abortion is rare but most likely to affect women who are very young, lonely or unsupported, or those who have a late abortion or a history of depression. Women facing unplanned pregnancies may need the opportunity to talk to someone, such as a pre-abortion counsellor. Some women certainly have difficulties in coming to terms with the idea of an abortion, perhaps because they have been pressured into having one or because of their or their families' beliefs. If they make considered decisions to go ahead with an abortion they often benefit from the time and support offered by post-abortion counselling.

Although abortion is legal, some people oppose it for religious or moral reasons. Some disability groups also object to one of the 'qualifying' criteria for abortions of 'abnormality to the foetus', because they believe this devalues the existence and life experiences of disabled people. They argue that more resources should be made available to disabled people and their carers in society so that women do not feel that abortion is the only option. Pro-choice groups, on the other hand, argue that it is essential for abortion to remain legal if we are not to return to the days of backstreet abortions and self-induced methods of ending unplanned pregnancies.

abuse intentional, purposeful acts or acts of omission leading to a person being hurt, injured or killed. Attention has focused mainly on CHILD ABUSE, more recently on adult abuse, including ELDER ABUSE and abuse of people with mental health problems or disabilities, including learning disabilities. 'Spouse abuse' is more commonly referred to as DOMESTIC VIOLENCE.

Particular environments can be abusing (for example, to be a child in any society where there is violent conflict or extreme poverty). In most industrialized societies, however, abuse is thought of as a non-accidental act perpetrated by an individual, family or group, or as something that an individual, family or group fails to prevent. Individuals are therefore held to be responsible, although mitigating circumstances related to abusing environments may be accepted. While most accounts now distinguish between PHYSICAL, EMOTIONAL and SEXUAL ABUSE, different forms of abuse may overlap or interact with each other. Physical abuse is likely to be accompanied by emotional abuse; sexual abuse is likely also to involve emotional abuse; emotional abuse can occur independently of the other two forms. Historically, physical abuse was the first to be recognized. Social work services and public awareness have focused on this form of abuse for some decades. The 'discovery' of sexual abuse is relatively recent in Britain, but it has attracted considerable attention in the last ten years. Emotional abuse is the most likely form to pass unrecognized unless associated with other forms of abuse.

Definitions of abuse are highly value-laden, and for this reason attempts to define abuse are usually couched in fairly general terms. In relation to physical abuse, for example, when does the physical chastisement of a child constitute abuse? Or in relation to neglect (acts of omission), to what extent must a child's development be impaired for the situation to be considered unsatisfactory and to warrant intervention? Some cultures are very indulgent of their children – among the Turks, emotional abuse is said to take place if young children are forced to sleep alone – while others encourage considerable emotional control at an early age. Sexual abuse is frequently couched in terms of a more mature person in some sense exploiting a dependent and developmentally immature person in a sexual act that the immature person perhaps does not fully understand and could not give informed consent to. How understanding and informed consent are to be interpreted are clearly matters of delicacy. Some societies define the age of sexual consent as low as 12, others as high as 18.

Definitions of abuse may simply utilize a medical model, listing injuries or deficits in relation to behaviour that cannot be explained by natural events or accidents. Or they may emphasize the circumstances in which care and protection outside the family will be required. Some definitions take a more general approach, seeking to describe the difference between the optimal development of children and their actual achievement. Others try to give shape to the needs they believe all children have and then ask what it is about a particular child that prevents the fulfilment of those needs. These attempts at definitions have helped to establish a substantial consensus that appears to 'fit' most children in most circumstances, but for many children in certain situations the problem of interpretation will be difficult.

Abusive relationships between adults are usually characterized by the misuse of power against a vulnerable person. Difficulties can arise in trying to label any behaviour as abusive if the abused person's experience of life suggests that such behaviours are 'normal'. The same issues arise in structurally unequal societies that may be patriarchal or dictatorial.

The search for predictors of abusive behaviour has been long and, so far, inconclusive. Research has concentrated both on groups of factors (explanations rooted in environmental issues, in family dysfunction, in parental characteristics and in the children themselves) and on combinations of what might be precipitating factors. No single explanation or apparent combination of explanations has to date revealed reliable predictors of who will and who will not abuse others. Clearly there are combinations of factors whereby the incidence of abuse increases. For example, a couple living in poverty, with debt, who are poorly housed, are inexperienced parents, have a poor marital relationship and have a demanding child to look after are more likely to abuse their child than a couple who do not experience these difficulties. But not all couples in these adverse circumstances will abuse their children; indeed, most will not.

Abuse in all its forms is to be found in most societies where research has been completed and in all social classes. As to its incidence, there have been widely varying estimates of the extent of sexual and physical abuse. Sources of information are confined to current cases of substantiated abuse and adult survivors who are willing to reveal their experiences. The former source overlooks undetected abuse and the latter those unwilling to share their histories with researchers; both are probably substantial groups. (See also CHILD PROTECTION.)

access the extent to which disabled people can use the services and public amenities enjoyed by non-disabled people.

Access to public buildings, work places, educational establishments, public transport and leisure facilities is necessary if disabled people are to be included within the mainstream of society. The CHRONICALLY SICK AND DISABLED PERSONS ACT first made it a requirement for new public buildings to be accessible, but there are many older public buildings to which disabled people have limited access. This can also limit their access to services. Since THE DISABILITY DISCRIMINATION ACT (1995), access to public buildings and services has been improved.

accommodation a family support service in which a child is cared for away from home for 24 hours or more by mutual agreement between parents and a local authority.

Accommodation is part of the wider range of services that a local authority can offer to families and parents. In using it, parents do not lose their PARENTAL RESPONSIBILITY, nor are they placing their child 'in care'. The use of accommodation should not be taken as a sign of parental inadequacy. Under section 20 of the CHILDREN ACT, the local authority has a duty to provide accommodation to any child in need who appears to require it, either because the child is lost or abandoned, there is no one with parental responsibility or because the person who has been caring for the child is prevented for any reason from providing suitable accommodation or care. As a service to families, accommodation can be used flexibly to include short-term and RESPITE CARE or longer periods when a child has to live away from home for whatever reason. Even where a child is abused, social workers should explore the possibility of accommodating that child on a voluntary basis.

Parents (or others with parental responsibility) retain control over the use of this service. A local authority may not provide accommodation for a child if a person holding parental responsibility (usually a parent) objects and is at the same time willing and able to provide accommodation or to arrange to have it provided. The only occasion when this power of 'veto' does not apply is if a person with a RESIDENCE ORDER for the child agrees to the child being accommodated. In this case, the parent without the residence order could not veto the child's being accommodated. Any person with parental responsibility (usually a parent) may remove the child at any time; the Act does not require notice of any kind – although how and when a child is to be removed from accommodation would be covered in the written agreement that must accompany any placement. The Act also requires prior consultation with the child. A young person 16 years and over may consent to accommodation against parental wishes. (See LOOKED AFTER.)

accountability the principle and process of ensuring that public-sector officials and elected representatives are responsible for their actions.

Liberal democracies must ensure that civil servants and other appointed officials are accountable to the people whose interests they are intended to serve. Accountability is the idea that office-holders must not abuse their positions for corrupt or irresponsible purposes. Accountability is also meant to guarantee that decisions and policies made on behalf of the public by its elected representatives are in the public interest and are actually carried out. Traditionally this has meant that most bureaucracies are based on a rigid hierarchy, with rules and regulations to ensure that officials comply with policy decisions and that their actions are recorded in detail. Accountability flows upwards, to ministers in central government and to the full council at local government level, and this results in a tendency for decision-making also to flow upwards. Some would argue that this form of accountability also includes working in accordance with the law. Others have held that social work organizations might not always honour their legal mandate or that the legal mandate can be variously interpreted in relation to 'powers' (things that local authorities might do) but also sometimes in relation to 'duties' (things that local authorities have to do). Hence it is probably worth distinguishing bureaucratic accountability from legal accountability, although they should more or less coincide.

In the case of social workers and other professional officers, accountability operates in two additional ways. First, it may flow downwards to the client or user of the service. Officials may therefore see their actions as determined by their relationship with and responsibility to the individual client, since they are advocates for that person's interests. As a result, they may sometimes find themselves in conflict with the more traditional form of accountability, which operates upwards in the social services department within which they are employed. Second, social workers and other professionals may identify a further form of accountability towards their profession: the need to behave in an acceptable professional manner, particularly in their relationship with other social work colleagues and in relation to other professional groups, such as the Probation Service and the police. Finally, some have it that professionals or, indeed, any worker can be accountable to his or her own principles and moral precepts, including religious convictions. Such convictions could have a profound effect upon how social workers advise service users on, say, issues such as abortion, marital problems or family obligations. This fivefold process of accountability creates a permanent source of tension for social workers as well as a framework for understanding their roles in their work.

R. Pyper, *Aspects of Accountability in the British System of Government*, Eastham, Tudor Business Publishing, 1996.

Acheson Report see HEALTH; HEALTH INEQUALITIES.

action plan order a sentence for YOUNG OFFENDERS under THE CRIME AND DISORDER ACT that imposes requirements to be carried out by the young person within three months of the making of the order under the supervision of a member of A YOUTH OFFENDING TEAM.

Requirements can include attending an ATTENDANCE CENTRE, reporting, taking part in specified activities, staying away from specified places, attendance at court, and REPARATION.

addiction the condition when an individual uses a substance (legal or illegal) regularly and has developed a dependence on it. Addiction often harms the individual, his or her family and society. Because the term is value-laden, the alternative term DRUG 'use' or drug 'dependency' is often preferred.

additional educational needs a broader term than SPECIAL EDUCATIONAL NEEDS, which identifies those children who require extra educational attention because of a wide variety of factors that may affect their learning.

This group approximately equates to those seen as CHILDREN IN NEED under the CHILDREN ACT 1989 and are a key focus for the duties of local education authorities (LEAs) and schools in promoting the EDUCATIONAL INCLUSION agenda. It includes children, for example, whose family life is disrupted, who are young carers or the victims of abuse as well as those with an identified LEARNING DIFFICULTY.

ADHD abbreviation for ATTENTION DEFICIT HYPERACTIVITY DISORDER.

adolescent support team a multidisciplinary team that diverts young people from the care system and works to keep adolescents at home in families with high levels of conflict.

Adolescent support teams have developed rapidly since the early 1990s. In general they provide a short-term intensive service that helps families defuse problems in relationships that might otherwise lead to an adolescent leaving home prematurely, with the risk of homelessness. Most of the families that such teams work with already have a high degree of conflict or parental mental health problems or domestic violence. Such problems are frequently intertwined with the behaviour problems of the adolescent. As many as half the young people such teams work with have suffered abuse, neglect, placement in care or social services involvement.

The practice of adolescent support teams is preventive and based on intensive, time-limited TASK-CENTRED WORK. Their approach is to start work on the problems identified by the young person, setting out aims to be worked towards in order to overcome these problems. The aims are achieved by working on small steps, or 'tasks', that both the young person and the worker review on at least a weekly basis. Much of the team's intervention involves negotiation and mediation between young people and parents.

adoption the process by which the legal relationship between a child and his or her birth parents is severed and a new legal relationship established with adoptive parents.

Adoption was introduced into English law in 1926 to clarify the position of children brought up by adults other than their own parents, in particular to ease concerns that such children would be taken back by their parents. Until that year it was impossible to transfer PARENTAL RIGHTS permanently, although in practice *de facto* adoptions did occur. Adoption creates a new legal relationship nearly identical to that between a child and his or her natural parents. When a child is adopted, all the powers, duties and rights of the natural parents in relation to the child cease and are transferred to the adopting parents.

Social workers' views on adoption were traditionally dominated by the intention of creating a completely new family for the adopted child, with no ties to the old one. The objective was to provide a permanent, secure and loving home for children whose parents were unable or unwilling to look after them. The common image of an adoption involved placing an infant with a childless couple who were complete strangers to the child's parents. The natural parents did not know the identity of the adopters and lost all right to see the child. To avoid stigma for the child, and to protect mothers of non-marital children, secrecy concerning the child's origins was strictly maintained throughout childhood and beyond. In this view, adoption was supposed to provide permanent security for children in public care who otherwise might have drifted from one foster home or children's home to another.

This perspective changed from the 1980s on. Studies confirmed that the secrecy surrounding adoption often led to confusion and unhappiness for adopted people. Lack of information about their natural parents and the mystery surrounding their family background frequently produced distrust and bitterness as the adopted child grew older. Consequently, adoption law was changed, making it possible for adopted people aged 18 and over to obtain access to their birth records and to search for their natural parents if they wished. Moreover, the value of continuing CONTACT between natural parents and the adopted child was recognized as helping to dispel confusion over identity and to stabilize the adoption placement. Courts can in fact make a CONTACT ORDER, under section 8 of the Children Act, in favour of the natural parents at the same time as making an adoption order (see OPEN ADOPTION).

The old view was also modified because, with the advent of widespread birth control and less social disapproval of 'illegitimacy', the number of babies placed for adoption fell dramatically. Now adoption is increasingly used to secure a family for older children with SPECIAL EDUCATIONAL NEEDS who may require considerable care that their natural parents are unable or unwilling to provide. Local authorities may pay adoption allowances in such cases. Step-parents have also used adoption in greater numbers to secure parental responsibility for a child of their new partner.

Who can adopt? Under the Adoption Act 1976 both married couples and single people can make an application to adopt a child. Cohabiting couples, at the time of writing, may not although there has been vigorous debate around this in discussions of the ADOPTION AND CHILDREN ACT 2002. High divorce rates and the increasing instability of families headed by a married couple have softened, but not eliminated, the legal bar on gay or lesbian couples adopting. It is possible, however, for one person of a cohabiting couple to adopt a child and a RESIDENCE ORDER under the Children Act be made to the other partner, thus at least conferring PARENTAL RESPONSIBILITY. Step-parents may also adopt but, because of the court's presumption against excluding a parent from the child's life because of adoption by a single person, they often do so jointly with their spouse, that is, the child's other natural parent. Half of all adoptions are in fact by step-parents.

Who can be adopted? Under the Adoption Act 1976 any child under 18 can be adopted but must be at least 19 weeks old and have been placed with prospective adopters for a continuous period of at least 13 weeks before an adoption order is made. Under the Adoption Act 1976, the child's wishes should be ascertained by the CHILDREN'S GUARDIAN or reporting officer as well as reported on by the social worker from the adoption agency. Various suggestions for requiring the consent of the child if over age 12 have not been taken forward in the Adoption and Children Act 2002, but that proposed legislation does give the child's opinion more formal footing in the adoption process.

Social workers have a number of tasks during the adoption process. They must obtain consent from the child's natural parents, explaining to them the effect of the adoption on their parental rights and responsibilities. They must also explain what each stage of the process involves. Such work may be extremely fraught, since parents of a child to be adopted may change their mind several times. Sometimes when parents refuse permission and the local authority concludes that adoption is the only long-term arrangement able to promote the welfare of a child in its care, the social worker has to persuade the court to dispense with parental consent (see ADOPTION HEARING).

Social workers must also gather information and write detailed reports. Because a child may be placed for adoption only by an ADOPTION AGENCY after a properly constituted ADOPTION PANEL has met to consider the decision, a social worker has to provide the adoption panel with a report covering a range of information concerning the natural parents, the child and the adopting parents. Such reports involve considerable skill in the presentation of information, based on lengthy interviews on often sensitive topics – for example, about when the prospective adopters would propose to reveal to the child the fact of their adoption. Other tasks include SUPERVISION of the child placed for adoption but not yet adopted and going to court on behalf of the adoption agency to explain why this irrevocable step needs to be taken.

Continuing professional support for adoptions has become critical. Thirty years ago virtually all adoptions were of 'relinquished infants'; now most adopted children have spent substantial time within the care system with experiences of frequent moves and perhaps abuse or neglect in their histories. Many prospective adopters are unaware of the range of circumstances that may compromise a child's health and development; according to the British Agencies for Adoption and Fostering, some 40 per cent of children placed for adoption in 1999 had developmental or learning difficulties or medical problems. In this context adoption should be seen as a lifelong service to children, with the need for close support from health, education and psychological services. There is also a historical division between fostering and adoption that may now be obsolete. Recent evidence from the USA shows that foster carer adoptions have increased dramatically, as have kinship adoptions, accounting in all for some 80 per cent of adoptions from care.

Perhaps the most recent development for practitioners is the increased emphasis on making adoption a child-centred process, proceeding strictly along the line of what is in the child's welfare and to make the child's own wishes and feelings paramount. Some children's advocates are urging that children over 12 be given the right to consent or object to their own adoptions.

Both the process and function of adoption have been under constant review since the passage of the Children Act in 1989, and adoption remains a controversial and sensitive area of policy and practice. Because it requires terminating the rights, responsibilities and relationships of birth parents and transferring them to a new set of parents it links with other powerful issues around fairness, social inequalities, religion, 'race' and gender. The Labour government elected in 1997 has placed adoption high on its agenda as a solution for children who, for whatever reason, cannot return to their parents. To make adoption somewhat easier it has attempted to loosen some of the adoption regulations – making it easier for a wider range of would-be adoptive parents. The ADOPTION AND CHILDREN ACT (2002) has introduced significant changes to the adoption process.

A. Douglas and T. Philpot, *Adoption: Changing Families, Changing Times*, London, Routledge, 1999.

adoption agency an organization approved by the Secretary of State at the Department of Health to undertake adoption services. Local authorities and diocesan adoption societies are both examples of adoption agencies.

One of the main tasks of an adoption agency is to oversee arrangements for the adoption of children. This includes selecting prospective adoptive parents, placing and supervising children for adoption and providing post-adoption services such as counselling for birth parents who have had children adopted. Increasingly, local authorities as adoption agencies are being encouraged by central government to compare the quality of their service to those in the independent sector.

Adoption and Children Act 2002 legislation that introduces both significant changes to the ADOPTION process and greater legal oversight for the way LOCAL AUTHORITIES implement their CARE PLANS for individual children.

This new legislation make the child's welfare the paramount consideration in all decisions concerning the adoption of a child, thus bringing it into line with the CHILDREN ACT, and introduces a WELFARE CHECKLIST of matters that the court or ADOPTION AGENCY must consider closely. These include the child's wishes and feelings regarding the adoption, the effect on the child throughout her or his life, the relationship the child has with relatives as well as any harm that the child may have suffered. Adoption agencies must also have regard for the child's religious persuasion, racial origin and cultural background. Another major change requires that adoption agencies place a child for adoption only where the parents of the child have given their consent or a *placement order* has been obtained. The grounds for dispensing with parental consent now are:

1 if the parent cannot be found or is incapable of giving consent; or
2 if the welfare of the child requires that consent be dispensed with.

In other words, dispensing with parental consent is to be judged only in the light of what is in the child's interest. This is a shift from previous adoption law, which allowed a parent's consent to be dispensed with by the test of 'unreasonableness', that is, that the parent was acting unreasonably in withholding consent. This was sometimes invoked by the court after a prolonged period in care (for whatever reason) and was a source of dispute – and often considerable grief – for the parents of the child.

Finally, a special form of guardianship is introduced for those children for whom adoption is not suitable but who cannot return to their birth families.

Under the national standards for adoption launched in association with the Act, LOOKED-AFTER children are entitled to have adoption considered as a means to give them a secure and permanent home. Under these standards, within six months after a child has been deemed to be 'continuously looked after' a decision regarding a permanent home should be made. If adoption is the plan, a decision in principle should be made within six weeks with suitable prospective adopters identified within six months. National standards also require that looked-after children be well prepared before joining a new family while the prospective adoptive family should reflect the child's birth heritage as long as this does not introduce undue delay.

The Act also puts the implementation of local authority care plans for individual children under greater official scrutiny. It does this by establishing the role of *independent reviewing officer*, who will carry out review meetings on the progress of individual care plans for children looked after by the local authority. Where the local authority has failed to carry out key parts of the plan, the reviewing officer will be able to take the case to the CHILDREN AND FAMILY COURT ADVISORY SERVICE.

adoption contact register a national register of names of people adopted as children and willing to be contacted by their birth parents or other relatives. The register also lists the names of parents and relatives wishing to contact children who were adopted and who have reached 18 years of age.

The function of the register is to facilitate contact between both sides of the original family. The setting up of the register is further recognition that the secrecy that used to surround adoption and the finality of the separation that occurred between adopted children and their birth parents often caused distress to both sides, and, in the case of the children, could lead to confusion as to their identity and background.

adoption hearing the proceedings in court that determine whether a child is to be adopted. Applications by prospective parents for an ADOPTION ORDER are heard in magistrates' courts but more usually in county courts and are always in private.

Information placed before the courts at an adoption hearing is strictly confidential. If the natural parents of the child have not given their consent to the adoption, the hearing is usually in two parts. First, the court considers whether grounds exist for overriding the requirement for each parent to agree to the adoption. Under the Adoption Act 1976 this can be done, for example, if the child has been persistently ill-treated and a return home is unlikely, if parents withhold agreement unreasonably or if one or both is incapable of giving agreement. The legal representatives of the agency, the CHILDREN'S GUARDIAN and the child's parents are represented and place their arguments before the court; the prospective adopting parents are not in court at this stage. The second stage follows if the court decides to dispense with parents' consent. (Alternatively, if both parents have given their consent, the hearing starts at this point.) In this second stage the court focuses on the merits of the application and whether the adoption is in the child's best interests. The would-be adoptive parents are usually in court at this stage and the natural parents are not.

If the child has been in the care of a local authority and adoption is seen as the best way to secure a permanent home for him or her, social

workers may be called to give evidence in support of the application
at either stage of an adoption hearing. Social workers' evidence is often
crucial to the outcome, so command of the facts and circumstances
of the case, and the reasoning behind the application, is essential.
In reaching any decision, the court's first consideration is the need to
safeguard and promote the welfare of the child throughout childhood,
that is, until the child reaches 18. Social workers' arguments to the court
must bear this long-term perspective in mind. The court will also take
into account the wishes and feelings of the child if it is practical to do so.
The child's wishes in the matter are set to become even more influential
following the passage of the ADOPTION AND CHILDREN ACT, which
incorporates a WELFARE CHECKLIST similar to section 1 of the CHILDREN
ACT that requires the child's wishes and feelings to be taken into
consideration in light of his or her age and understanding.

The ADOPTION AND CHILDREN ACT 2002, when implemented, will
change certain key aspects of the hearing. For example, the order 'freeing'
a child for adoption currently available under the Adoption Act 1976 vests
PARENTAL RESPONSIBILITY in the adoption agency and terminates any
pre-existing parental responsibility. Once it is made (either with the
parents' consent or by dispensing with that consent), the birth parents
of the child will not be included as parties to any subsequent adoption
application. Under the Adoption and Children Act 2002 the freeing order
is replaced by a *placement order*, which can be made only if the child is
subject to a CARE ORDER or the court is convinced that the conditions for
a care order are met. The placement order also requires parental consent
unless the court is satisfied that their consent should be dispensed with.
It can only dispense with that consent if the parent cannot be found or is
incapable of giving consent or that the welfare of the child requires that
consent to be dispensed with.

adoption order a court order that transfers legal responsibility for a child
from his or her birth family to the adoptive family.

Following an ADOPTION order, all the rights, duties and responsibilities
of the natural parents in relation to the child cease and are assumed by
the adoptive parents. Occasionally courts will also order that some form
of CONTACT between the child and the birth parents should continue.
More usually, the adoptive parents agree to afford contact to members
of the birth family and the need for a CONTACT ORDER is avoided.

adoption panel the panel constituted by each ADOPTION AGENCY that
authorizes the decision to place a child for adoption by that agency.

In deciding whether a child should be placed for adoption, the panel
considers whether the adoption is in that child's best interests and whether
a particular child should be placed with particular adoptive parents.
Panels also decide whether individual applicants should be approved as
prospective adoptive parents. Would-be adopters may include single people
or a gay or lesbian couple since the ADOPTION AND CHILDREN ACT 2002

was passed. The panel is made up of lay members, such as doctors, local councillors and parents, and is usually chaired by a senior member of the adoption agency. The panel officially makes only advisory judgements, with final decisions left to the agency, but its decisions are almost always respected in practice.

adult family placement a service for vulnerable adults who live with families that are not their own.

The service is often provided for adults with LEARNING DIFFICULTIES or with MENTAL HEALTH PROBLEMS. The families who provide the placements are usually recruited and supported by an adult placement scheme organized by the local authority SOCIAL SERVICES DEPARTMENT. The general expectation is that the vulnerable person lives as part of the family and that the family (referred to as 'carers') is paid a fee in return for providing appropriate support. Such placements assist in overcoming the isolating effects of institutional or semi-institutional accommodation in which vulnerable individuals may have been living. They are quite distinct from the board and lodging arrangements or small GROUP HOMES that were offered to vulnerable adults in the past. They also provide short breaks for regular carers.

Such placements need to be carefully planned, with any particular family 'rules' discussed and explained before the placement begins. In general the adult on placement should have accommodation and facilities that allow for privacy, personal keys that convey the freedom to come and go (with some attendant risk perhaps), and access to transport. Reasonable levels of weekly allowance and holidays are also of great practical significance and need to be agreed in advance.

adult protection the system devised by public services to provide an immediate response to ensure protection and support for adults at risk of abuse.

Adult protection services are provided by the police and health and social care working in partnership with other relevant agencies. Although in the UK there is no specific legislation to protect adults, central government guidance has increasingly acknowledged the importance of good multi-agency co-ordination and clear systems of accountability. The No Secrets guidance document, in particular, urges that social care staff should be adequately trained.

Department of Health, *No Secrets: Guidance on developing and implementing multi-agency policies and procedures to protect vulnerable adults from abuse*, London, The Stationery Office, 2000.

adult training centre a day service for people with learning disabilities, typically providing on-site training in work and daily living skills.

Adult training centres originally sought to simulate the conditions of 'real' work by organizing service users to undertake contract industrial tasks in supervised workshops. Criticisms of this approach focused on tokenistic levels of pay and the repetitive nature of the tasks. Developments in day services since have emphasized training and education relevant to the needs of service users. However, the segregation of adults with learning disabilities in day centres away from non-disabled people has also been a source of criticism. More recent policy has been to increase the use of mainstream leisure and educational facilities by service users. Day centres are now usually referred to as 'day services', which indicates that not all services are to be provided on a segregated site and that staff should support people to gain access to leisure facilities, further education courses and supported employment schemes in the outside community. Practices vary, however, and some people with learning disabilities still spend the greater part of the week within the day services site.

advice the process by which people with expert knowledge, or with considerable experience of a problem and its potential solutions, indicate how a problem might be solved or eased.

Advisers are found in many guises. They include advice centre workers, solicitors, social workers, youth workers, probation officers, general medical practitioners and specialists working in particular fields, such as Aids counsellors, consumer advisers and child guidance workers. Many advice workers continue to be VOLUNTEERS. In addition, advice can be offered by people who have experienced a certain problem or still experience it. In this context, SELF-HELP can be the method of working among those who have the same difficulties, with professional advisers expressly excluded from the process.

In the late 1990s attempts were made to give the 'advice-giving industry' more coherence in relation to both service provision and the education and training of advice workers. First, the government established the COMMUNITY LEGAL SERVICES Commission and gave this body the responsibility for creating a quality assurance framework for all advice services and agencies. This framework distinguishes between different levels of advice-giving, namely, *information-giving, information-giving with assistance, general help, general help with casework* and, finally, *specialist help*. The first two levels involve the provision of information in some kind of centre or website: in information-giving, no adviser is available to help the person with the problem to access the information, whereas in information-giving with assistance help is provided by somebody to assist the person to find information but it is up to that person to determine how useful the information is. General help is where an adviser does actually advise, and general help with casework is a level of service where the adviser can take on some or all of the responsibility for progressing a problem. Specialist services are those dealing with issues that generalist advice agencies cannot deal with because of their complexity or because the problem is highly specialized or rare. The Commission awards a Quality Mark to those advice agencies that satisfy the specification for each level of advice-giving. In addition, agencies have to be able to meet clear requirements for advice-giving on particular subjects or in fields such as WELFARE RIGHTS or debt. Each area now has a local committee that has the task of trying to establish a range of services in any community that will meet the needs of the community.

In relation to the education and training of advice workers, a Lead Body for Advice, Guidance, Psychotherapy and Counselling has been established, and this body has developed a framework of competences at NVQ levels 2, 3 and 4. Although some commentators have accepted that these four professional activities have much in common, they have also suggested that the remit for the Lead Body may be too wide. Nevertheless, this initiative has enabled many experienced advice workers to give value to their experience and to the range of short courses that they may have attended to develop and consolidate their advice-giving. The market leaders in advice work, namely the National Association of Citizens' Advice Bureaux, has also been active in developing its own in-house training programme, which shadows key aspects of the Community Legal Services Commission's framework. Higher education is also now beginning to take an interest in this 'industry'.

advice services or **advice centres** services or centres located within the statutory sector or the voluntary sector that seek to offer either general or specialized ADVICE for people with problems.

Advice services have grown significantly in recent decades, and most provision is in the voluntary sector. The best-known advice organization is the Citizens' Advice Bureau (CAB), each of whose offices is staffed by at least one paid organizer and trained volunteers. This model of staff organization and service delivery is commonly found in the voluntary sector. The CAB has developed expertise in relation to WELFARE RIGHTS, debt, consumer problems, housing, employment, and personal and family difficulties. Specialist voluntary advice and counselling services tend to focus on a single issue, such as homelessness, rape crisis, immigration (including asylum seekers and refugees), welfare rights, mental health problems, mediation or marriage guidance. They are to be found in most British cities and towns. In addition, some local authorities have built up networks of neighbourhood offices offering advice on housing, social services, environmental services, public health, and so on. This form of local authority provision, particularly when integrated into the major service-providing departments, helps to make services more accessible. It can also facilitate useful preventative work on problems that might otherwise become more serious. Such centres may also devote resources to taking up campaigns in relation to welfare benefits, home insulation or home security in localities where burglary is a major issue, and other similar matters.

Studies have often made use of advice services as centres for the systematic collection of information about problems faced by residents within a particular locality. Such information has subsequently been used to trigger community action or at least to encourage a collective approach to community problem-solving. Advice-giving, because it is essentially a one-to-one, individual process, can be limited in its objectives. However, a whole housing estate complaining together about a problem – say, damp dwellings – will be more persuasive in relation to a reluctant local authority than the same individuals complaining separately.

Democracy is said to depend heavily on good information about the law and individual rights. Advice services can act as a major source of useful and disinterested information for citizens, information that will help to solve or ease problems as well as encouraging participation in social and political life. With these objectives in mind, some advice and counselling services seek consciously to develop the social skills of service users so that they can tackle the next problem themselves. In this sense, advice-giving can become an educational process regardless of whether it is dispensed by professionals or by 'amateurs' on a SELF-HELP basis.

advocacy exerting influence on behalf of certain groups or organizations within political and legal power structures.

The idea of advocacy originated in the USA, with parents of children with disabilities voicing their concern: 'What will happen to my child when I'm gone?' Their overriding concern was to ensure that children were not disadvantaged after the loss of their parents. Reinforcement of this concept came with the United Nations Declaration on the Rights of Disabled Persons. Both these initiatives embody the principles of equality, integration and rights of the individual, including the right to access services appropriate to needs and access to legal protection from abuse.

Within the concept of advocacy there are a number of different models. *Legal advocacy* is where a lawyer or individual with legal knowledge acts on behalf of an individual. Legal advocates act on the individual's instructions. *Professional advocacy* – where professionals are paid to offer support and advice to individuals; these include WELFARE RIGHTS workers, service brokers and CHILDREN'S GUARDIANS. *Self-advocacy* – where someone speaks or acts on his or her own behalf, literally 'speaking up for oneself'. *Citizen advocacy* – where a private citizen enters into a relationship with, and represents the interests of, another individual; an example are the trained independent selected volunteers who speak for adults with learning difficulties. *Collective, class or group advocacy* – where a group of people collectively speak out about issues that affect more than the individual member of the group. *Peer advocacy* – where a self-advocate with skills speaks out on behalf of his or her peers, e.g. user committees. *Patients' advocacy* – this aims to provide patients with information and support within acute health trusts. *Informal advocacy* – unrecognized informal advocacy through families, friends and neighbours.

Through advocacy individual service users can develop skills and gain confidence to express their own feelings and wishes or voice their collective concerns. Increasingly, primacy is given to self-advocacy, as it raises self-esteem by empowering individuals and increasing their capacity. For particularly vulnerable or excluded groups, however, such as children or people with mental health needs, citizen advocates can enable the development of relationships through one-to-one support, thereby reducing social isolation.

Neil Bateman, in *Advocacy Skills for Health and Social Care*, has laid down six principles for advocates to follow. First, act in the user's best interests. Practitioners can face competing pressures from their managers and have to continually remind themselves who they are acting on behalf of. Second, act in accordance with the user's wishes and instructions. This is fundamental: while the advocate can identify facts, options and remedies, the advocate's actions have to be driven by what users want. Third, keep the user properly informed. The user must know all the essential facts related to his or her situation without being snowed under by an information deluge but must also be kept informed of all actions taken on his or her behalf. Fourth, carry out instructions with diligence and compromise. Advocates need to know their limits and should not undertake that for which they are not prepared or competent. Fifth, offer frank, independent, impartial advice. This sometimes means confronting representatives from other organizations or, indeed, the practitioner's own. A co-operative relationship based on 'partnership' with the agencies against whom a practitioner is advocating is not appropriate. Sixth, the advocate should maintain the rules of confidentiality. Users must feel completely secure in the knowledge that what they say remains confidential.

N. Bateman, *Advocacy Skills for Health and Social Care*, London, Jessica Kingsley Publishers, 2000.

age appropriateness the notion that people with LEARNING DISABILITY should dress, behave, take part in activities and be treated in ways suitable to their chronological age. This notion is often associated with NORMALIZATION.

The principle of age appropriateness suggests, for example, that adults with learning disability should not play with children's toys, although the toys might be apparently suited to their developmental level. The rationale for this approach is that such behaviour is at odds with social norms, is undignified and is unlikely to gain respect from other people.

ageing the process of physically growing older, usually associated with chronological age but not always identical.

Problems of defining ageing are rooted in the linking of *time* with *development*, when there is considerable diversity between time and development in human populations. Ageing as a variable is most frequently used to explain other phenomena, for example patterns of physiological and behavioural change in people, but ageing is itself much affected by social conditions and by the regard with which people are held. Thus older people may be old in years but vigorous in behaviour, whereas others, because of major difficulties in their lives, may be 'old before their time'. People with learning disabilities may also have difficulties behaving in an AGE-APPROPRIATE manner, although contemporary social work practice encourages age-related treatment of such people. In other contexts, ageing may have gender dimensions – for example, that girls mature more quickly than boys and that women live longer than men.

ageism the discriminatory behaviour towards OLDER PEOPLE stemming from the socially constructed attitudes and beliefs that growing old is accompanied by loss of competence and intellectual deterioration.

Underlying ageism is the fear of growing older with the inevitable link to mortality; those who are younger seek to distance themselves by creating a distinct 'otherness'. Ageism encompasses a set of ATTITUDES that assume and maintain powerlessness in old people. It is used to legitimate the 'rearranging' of power relationships between people who are young and old, which results in older people being alienated from other social groups. Ageism is apparent in the 'splitting' of images of older people – for example, perceiving them as a 'burden' contrasted with images of 'kindly' grandparents. In Britain there is no legal ban on age DISCRIMINATION when advertising for employment. It is also significant that, to date, there has been no legislation in the UK to protect adults, as is the case of specific child protection duties incorporated into the CHILDREN ACT 1989.

Substantial differences exist in the attitudes to older people from one society to another, some clearly venerating and valuing old people while others perceive them as economically unproductive and thus as a burden. ANTIDISCRIMINATORY PRACTICE includes countering ageist attitudes.

B. Bytheway, *Ageing*, Buckingham, Open University Press, 1995.

aggression action or an ATTITUDE intended to impair, injure or destroy another person's or group's physical or psychological wellbeing (see also VIOLENCE).

Aids see HIV/AIDS.

aids and home adaptations equipment and alterations to the home that enable disabled people to live more comfortably in environments that were not originally designed with their requirements in mind.

The provision of aids and adaptations is primarily the responsibility of local authority social services departments, although some equipment is also supplied by the NHS. It is also possible for disabled people to buy their own equipment privately. Aids include kitchen utensils, mobility aids, handrails, bath seats and hoists to assist with lifting. Equipment can also be provided to meet the requirements of people with sensory impairments. Adaptations to the home may include the provision of ramps for wheelchair users, structural alterations to allow access to bathrooms and toilets, the extension of homes to provide more ground-floor living space, the installation of stair lifts and the refitting of kitchens so that equipment is at a suitable height.

Under Section 2 of the CHRONICALLY SICK AND DISABLED PERSONS ACT (1970), local authorities have a duty to provide aids and adaptations where there is a need. Need is established through a specialist assessment, usually carried out by an occupational therapist. At first aids and adaptations were provided free, although limited budgets meant that disabled people often had to wait. Now there is usually a charge, and service users are means-tested by local authorities. Housing adaptations are most often provided through local authority housing departments, under Part 1 of the Housing Grants, Construction and Regeneration Act (1996). Disabled people may apply for a Disabled Facilities Grant to cover the costs of the adaptations they need. Housing departments consult with an occupational therapist from the social services department on whether the adaptations are 'necessary and appropriate'. Grants for some purposes are discretionary rather than mandatory. For example, adaptations to provide a safe play space for a disabled child attract only a discretionary grant. Disabled Facilities Grants are means-tested on the basis of the size of the loan that the applicant can afford to repay from her or his weekly income. Recent research has highlighted the effectiveness of well-planned adaptations in promoting the capacity of disabled people to gain control over their own daily lives.

The system for the provision of aids and adaptations has been criticized by disabled people because of delays and resource constraints that reduce its effectiveness. However, commentators have also referred to injustices in the 'structure of aiding', whereby the equipment needed by non-disabled people is easily accessible at reasonable cost while disabled people are subject to gatekeeping processes, including means testing, professional assessment and administrative delay.

F. Heywood, *Money well spent, The effectiveness and value of housing adaptation*, Bristol, The Policy Press/Joseph Rowntree Foundation, 2001.

alcohol a colourless liquid that acts as a central nervous system depressant and sedative, taken by mouth, usually in the form of beer, wine or spirits. It is a legal substance, although it cannot legally be sold to people under the age of 18.

Alcohol in moderation does not appear to have harmful effects. The suggested weekly maximum is 14 units for a woman and 21 for a man – one unit is a glass of wine, a measure of spirits or half a pint of ordinary-strength beer. If this level is increased on a regular basis, both psychological and physical ADDICTION are a possibility. Short-term effects include a reduction in anxiety and tension, drowsiness, increased confidence and impairment of judgement, depending on how much is consumed. The physical harm that can result from excessive alcohol use includes liver and heart disease, high blood pressure, strokes, stomach ulcers and dementia. Pregnant women run the risk of foetal abnormalities and low birth weight and mental retardation of the infant. It is important to monitor the progress of infants of mothers with an excessive alcohol intake both before and after birth, applying the normal criteria for good parenting and liaising where necessary with other professionals. It is an offence to be in charge of a vehicle while 'unfit to drive through drink or DRUGS'. *Alcohol hallucinosis* is a psychotic frame of mind often accompanied by auditory hallucinations (hearing voices). Feelings of fear and persecution are also common. This is frequently a symptom of withdrawal in acute drinkers who suddenly give up or reduce intake. *Alcohol psychosis* is a group of mental disorders resulting from the excessive use of alcohol, such as delirium tremens, Korsakow syndrome and acute hallucinosis. In such cases dysfunction or damage to the brain will be present.

alcoholism the extreme psychological and physical ADDICTION resulting from the consumption of excessive ALCOHOL over a lengthy period of time.

Alcoholism is commonly defined as a chronic illness characterized by depression of the central nervous system and liver damage. Other medical effects may include stomach and heart problems, peripheral neuropathies and auditory hallucinations. Alcoholism can also result in psychological and social difficulties, with friends and relatives becoming increasingly frustrated by their inability to affect any change in the alcoholic's behaviour. It is important for them to know whom to approach for help when the alcoholic is at the stage of wanting such assistance. Usually a general medical practitioner will be able to provide direct help or referral to a specialist agency. As alcoholism is an addiction, withdrawal will result if supplies are abruptly stopped. Withdrawal symptoms include sweating, trembling, hallucination, nervous system dysfunction and seizures. The extreme form of alcohol withdrawal is known as *delirium tremens*. When a person is in this state, confrontation is best avoided – a calm, quiet approach is preferable, with talking through problems or attempts at relaxation if appropriate. There is considerable debate as to whether alcoholism is inherited or environmental for it often clusters in particular families.

allocation the process whereby tasks are distributed among workers within a social work team. This process is undertaken sometimes within team meetings, sometimes with individual team members on an *ad hoc* basis and sometimes by a combination of both practices.

Allocation within team meetings has the advantage of conveying to all workers what each is undertaking in relation to the quantity and range of cases and to other kinds of work. Such a system may help build or develop teams by giving members information about how the team is functioning. Knowledge of colleagues' work can facilitate the sharing of tasks. Clearly some work, such as dealing with emergencies, must be allocated quickly by team managers. Allocation should be closely related to WORKLOAD MANAGEMENT and SUPERVISION to determine that work is being done well and that workers are not overwhelmed by the quantity and the demands of their tasks.

alternative dispute resolution (ADR) sometimes referred to as **appropriate dispute resolution** a non-adversarial method of tackling disputes across a wide range of issues.

This method of tackling disputes has begun to feature strongly in a wide range of areas, including separation and divorce, neighbourhood disputes, and industrial and employment disputes. ADR is also found in educational settings where peer mediation is used to help students of all ages to resolve difficulties.

Fundamental to the process is a third party whose role is to help those in dispute – first to explore their difficulties in a safe environment and then to work together towards a mutually acceptable solution. Several methods are used in this work. Mediation (see FAMILY MEDIATION) places the emphasis and responsibility upon the disputants to arrive at mutually acceptable solutions. Arbitration puts the onus upon the third party to decide the outcome, and in CONCILIATION an impartial third party helps people in dispute by hearing both sides and then offering an opinion on settlement.

There is strong encouragement coming from government to encourage much wider use of ADR in order to reduce the pressures on the court system and to help people in dispute to 'own' the resolution process more effectively.

M. Doyle, *Advising on ADR: The essential guide to appropriate dispute resolution*: Advice Services Alliance, 2000.

Alzheimer's disease an organic age-associated disorder typified by progressive brain degeneration, named after the neurologist Alois Alzheimer who first described it in 1907.

It affects around 500,000 people in the UK and is the most common dementia illness, characterized by 'plaques' and 'tangles' that develop in the structure of the brain, leading to loss of brain cells. No one single factor has been identified as causing Alzheimer's disease since it is likely to stem from a combination of factors such as age, genetic inheritance, environmental factors, diet and general health. However, age is the greatest risk factor for dementia, which affects one in 20 over the age of 65 and one in five over the age of 85. Fewer than 10 per cent of people with Alzheimer's are under the age of 65. People with Down's syndrome are more at risk of early onset because of their chromosomal make-up, and in fewer than 5 per cent of all cases, there is a form of Alzheimer's known to be entirely inherited.

The disease affects a broad range of mental and physical functions; memory loss and recall difficulties occur, and learning, perception, attention and recognition are all impaired. Rapid forgetting is evident. Disorientation and confusion are usually present, combined with a phasia (loss of words) and agnosia (loss of recognition of objects). Other characteristics include mood swings, irritability, over-activity and stereotyped movements. Depression, apathy and lethargy may also be observed.

There is no cure for Alzheimer's although there are a number of drug treatments available, such as Aricept, Exelon and Reminyl, that can delay the onset of symptoms for some people in the early to middle stages.

Good social care practice aims to maintain a PERSON-CENTRED APPROACH when working with people with Alzheimer's in order that the person does not become lost behind the condition. The goal for rehabilitation is that of helping an individual to adapt to the difference between his or her desired role and what is achievable. In spite of maintaining physical independence, such as walking or climbing stairs, many people with Alzheimer's become physically inactive because of poor social engagement. More attention also needs to be paid to aphasia, which is often assumed to relate to mental impairment, thus resulting in loss of civil liberties. Crucial to good practice are clear agency risk management policies that ensure practitioners have an informed conceptual understanding of 'risk', the balance between rights and 'risks' and an awareness of the value of 'risk-taking'.

Practitioners also need to take account of the needs of carers and to mediate any conflict of interest between the rights and needs of an individual and those of the carer. (See also DEMENTIA, MULTI-INFARCT DEMENTIA, RISK, RISK ASSESSMENT.)

M. Nolan, S. Davies and G. Grant, *Working with Older People and their Families*, Buckingham, Open University Press, 2001.

anal dilatation a clinical diagnosis that observes whether the involuntary muscles controlling the sphincter are open.

As the sphincter is normally closed, a sphincter that is open can be an indicator that a child has been sexually abused. The diagnosis was used extensively by the paediatricians involved in diagnosing the children thought to have been abused in Cleveland in 1986 (see CLEVELAND INQUIRY). The subsequent inquiry concluded that while anal dilatation suggested that penetrative SEXUAL ABUSE could have occurred, its presence was not in itself sufficient to make a certain diagnosis. This method, while still used, does not play nearly as prominent a part now in the diagnosis of sexual abuse as it once did since dilatation can occur for reasons other than penetrative sex.

anger management a systematic set of techniques to encourage an individual's self-regulation of his or her own anger.

Broadly the techniques for anger management are drawn from the wider field of COGNITIVE BEHAVIOURAL THERAPY. These techniques do not seek to prevent feelings of anger but to provide ways for the person to regulate it through increased self-control. Often an anger-management programme will be part of the rehabilitation of violent offenders in an effort to promote nonviolent ways of dealing with frustrations they encounter. Typically, a programme will have three components:
1 preparation to educate the person about the effects on others of his or her anger;
2 acquisition of skills in which particular coping strategies such as relaxation or asserting oneself in socially acceptable ways are taught;
3 application in which these skills are used by the individual in role play or monitored social settings.

anorexia nervosa severe and persistent weight loss in a person as a result of actions that that person has taken, such as minimal intake of food, regular vomiting and excessive exercise.

Anorexia arises from a number of causes, such as having a distorted self-image and seeing the self as fat or having strong fears of becoming fat. Other reasons have been linked to the need to feel in control of one's body and to try to conform to the images of thinness that predominate in the media and advertising. Experiences of abuse are frequently associated with the condition, and some feminist and psychodynamic perspectives recognize anorexia as a form of defence and a way of coping with the loss of control over the body as a result of abuse. The group most frequently identified as susceptible to anorexia are adolescent females, but it is found in young males and older females. In men or older women the condition can be misdiagnosed simply because it is not associated with such groups. Older people can re-experience abuse memories in later life, which also can lead to anorexia at that point.

Anorexia is a serious condition. It can lead to malnutrition and the cessation of menstruation and after a prolonged period of many years can result in death. The World Health Organization includes it within a group of NEUROSES, while feminist explanations suggest that anorexic behaviour develops as a symptom of women's powerlessness. Initial treatment is often provided as an inpatient in hospital with a focus on nutrition and therapeutic interventions involving the family. In extreme cases a person can be detained under the MENTAL HEALTH ACT because of the threat to life. Practitioners adopt one of several approaches when working with someone with anorexia. These include a COGNITIVE BEHAVIOURAL approach, when the internalized beliefs that the person holds about herself (or himself) are explicitly adjusted, and a radical feminist perspective that attempts to locate the sources of the person's sense of powerlessness in social and family structures.

R. Shelley, *Anorexics on Anorexia*, London, Jessica Kingsley, 1997

antidiscriminatory practice a term used to describe how practitioners seek to reduce individual and institutional DISCRIMINATION, particularly on grounds of race, gender, disability, social class and sexual orientation.

Antidiscriminatory practice refers to social work that is specifically aimed at the unfair, discriminatory treatment experienced by specific groups in society. The three areas that law attempts to address are RACE discrimination, SEX discrimination and discrimination against those with DISABILITY. Antidiscriminatory social work aims to support individual users and to assist them to tackle discrimination in their own lives as well as to challenge discrimination when found in the media, in local communities and in public stereotypes. Such a practice places demands on both social work agencies and individual practitioners. For example, monitoring all social work processes connected with groups suffering discrimination will provide critical information about the local patterns of discrimination that the agency has to confront. Recruitment of people in greater numbers from discriminated groups to positions of power within social welfare systems may help their cause, provided they are not required to work with discriminatory policies. (See also ANTI-RACIST PRACTICE, DISABILITY, SEXUALITY, AGEISM and SOCIAL CLASS.) But other groups are discriminated against in a way that is not always covered by law. For example, the relationships of GAY and LESBIAN people cannot be formally consolidated in law and in the eyes of the state, as can those of heterosexuals. OLDER PEOPLE also face a range of discriminations, whether in employment or in the covert rationing of health services.

Antidiscriminatory practice is often used interchangeably with ANTI-OPPRESSIVE PRACTICE; indeed, the latter has tended to subsume and replace the former. Some distinction, however, is still evident. The former addresses those areas where users face discrimination as well as challenging public stereotypes and prejudices experienced by specific groups. Anti-oppressive practice, on the other hand, focuses on the extreme differences in power between service users and those in dominant positions in service provision and decision-making about services. It therefore has a broader, but perhaps less focused, set of objectives.

N. Thompson, *Anti-Discriminatory Practice,* Basingstoke, Macmillan, 2001.

anti-oppressive practice social work practice that aims to counter the sources of OPPRESSION in society, whether public stereotypes, discrimination, social and economic disadvantage or unequal distribution of power.

Social work moved from concepts of ANTIDISCRIMINATORY PRACTICE to anti-oppressive practice principally because it unified the different forms of discrimination within a single theory embracing PATRIARCHY, RACISM, ABLE-BODIEDISM and AGEISM. Anti-oppressive practice begins with the recognition that individuals' lives are enmeshed in social relationships shaped by structures and attitudes that are embedded in society at large. This recognition marks the beginning of the capacity to change both those same social structures *and* individual lives. Making this connection between their personal condition and wider social forces enables a critical understanding – to define the oppression and to tackle its causes. Anti-oppressive practice asks that the social worker encourage this process of users' self-understanding as well as challenging the forms of oppression that face the users they work with. Stimulating people to define their own oppression, to look at the sources of their own disadvantage, unemployment or prejudice that they face, is a starting point. Sharing a commitment to change those circumstances, to make links between personal, social and political structures, is fundamental. Part of any social work assessment should uncover the sources of oppression that disempower particular users and lay the basis for challenging those barriers that restrict service users' freedom to act.

Challenging the many forms of oppression is difficult because of the somewhat limited tools at social work's disposal. Society is skilful at hiding its oppressive ways as the dominant groups – adults (over children), the able-bodied, men, white people, straight people – with their leverage in the media, thus setting public attitudes, succeed in creating universal definitions of normalcy that only confirm their advantages. One aspect of practice has been to challenge the language (and hence the stereotypes) that are routinely used. Language itself is never neutral but reflects dominant interests. Some words are derogatory and insulting, others exclude in more subtle ways. Anti-oppressive practice attempts to reshape the discourse around the specific oppressed groups that social workers and other professionals work with.

Using the law to break down discriminatory barriers is another feature of anti-oppressive practice, and, where effective legislation does not exist, to campaign in favour of such statutes. Proponents of anti-oppressive practice have noted that the law has slowly been reflecting an enhanced role for users in decision-making and combating discrimination in their lives, so mastery of particular statutes and the specific uses to which they can be put is essential.

There are criticisms of anti-oppressive practice. First, it often pays scant attention to poverty, the power of social class and the means for improving income. Second, anti-oppressive practice is suspicious of notions of NEIGHBOURHOOD and COMMUNITY because it regards them as masking difference and therefore as sources of oppression. But 'neighbourhood' is precisely where many initiatives to tackle social exclusion are unfolding. Third, anti-oppressive practice places a premium on language as the medium through which oppressive ideologies are cemented in place, and the social work practice it promotes requires close examination of language to reveal the extent of oppression. (See also EMPOWERMENT.)

S. Braye and M. Preston-Shoot, *Em-powering Practice in Social Care*, Buckingham, Open University Press, 1995.

J. Dalrymple and B. Burke, *Anti-oppressive practice: Social Care and the Law*, Buckingham, Open University Press, 1995.

anti-poverty strategy addressing specifically and systematically the poverty of service users, whether through local campaigns or maximizing their income through benefits or advice on employment and training.

Historically, social workers have sought answers to the personal problems facing service users through their professional relationships with users, through advice and guidance and, where necessary, legal intervention. Practitioners' awareness of how poverty increases stress and stress-related difficulties has been correspondingly low. Yet the common thread in so many users' lives is the fact that they are poor. An anti-poverty strategy places a focus on user poverty as central to social work practice and, wherever possible, works to maximize the income available to users, often with guidance and help on claiming benefits but also in relation to employment or preparation for employment. Such a strategy generally requires work at several levels within the social work agency. It should encompass, for example, launching local information campaigns on matters such as benefits or access to child care for low-income families as well as having the expertise to work with individual users on money matters. Any strategy will use a variety of methods to reach service users – whether through drop-in advice, publicity campaigns in general practitioners' surgeries or libraries or by ensuring all practitioners examine jointly with individual users their sources of income.

Poor people do not need social workers to obtain benefits, but when in contact with families and individuals, practitioners should be able to point them on the right path. The benefits system is complicated, with annually changing rates and the introduction of new, often targeted, benefits, and social workers should not be expected to know that system in detail. They should be informed, however, to the point where they are able to help families to get the benefits those families are entitled to. This might entail going through the range of the users' possible entitlements to determine whether they are claiming all that they can and securing back payments of benefits. Some knowledge of the difference between MEANS-TESTED BENEFITS and both contributory and non-contributory benefits and which specific entitlements are available within each is also critical. The structure of benefits is explained in several excellent handbooks, one of which is cited at the end of the entry.

It is important to hold on to two or three main objectives in working with users or families to maximize income. One is to be able to look across the whole benefit system to pick up linked entitlements. A claim for one benefit suggests eligibility for others. People can qualify for some non-means-tested benefits and as a result be eligible for means-tested benefits. For example, if a young mother is under 16 she cannot claim income support or income-based jobseeker's allowance but can claim child benefit as well as exemption from certain health charges such as prescriptions or for dental work.

Since the advent of welfare reform, which broadly means linking aspects of the benefits system to encourage taking up paid employment, practitioners should have some understanding of the interrelationship between benefits and work. For example, TAX CREDITS are designed to help people in low-paid work to get a minimum income but this may raise difficult issues – such as whether to encourage a person to take up employment when he or she has caring responsibilities for young children which would be undercut by that employment.

There are issues that social work organizations need to pay attention to in developing an anti-poverty strategy. Having a person in the agency specifically responsible for detailed knowledge of debt and benefits is important as a source of advice and expertise for other practitioners.

Local authority social services departments should also be aware of how its CHARGING POLICY for care services can be used creatively to reduce users' poverty. TAKE-UP campaigns seek to maximize benefit claims across a whole area through a concerted effort to remind those eligible for particular benefits to claim them. Organizing take-up campaigns is generally productive both for the user and local authority social services departments. Requests for SINGLE ASSESSMENTS for COMMUNITY CARE offer the opportunity to ensure that those approaching a social service department – carers, older people, disabled people – to review the range of benefits that they may be eligible for. (See also POVERTY.)

M. Dowling, *Poverty: A practitioner's guide*, Birmingham, Venture Press, 1998.

anti-racism the attempt to confront and eradicate any view that encourages a belief that one ethnic group is biologically superior to another ethnic group.

RACISM can take many forms. Racist attitudes can be personally held views or they can be the result of official policies or, in some circumstances, both. A social work or social welfare organization seriously wishing to confront racism must develop policies and practices that work at both the personal and institutional levels. Racist acts by staff should be clearly denoted as serious matters for both disciplinary and grievance procedures. Comprehensive training programmes accompanied by induction packages for new staff should convey to all employees the commitment of the organization to the eradication of racism in staff relationships and employment practices. In relation to issues of service delivery, particular policies are required to consider the anti-racist issues. For example, if it can be demonstrated that more black juveniles receive custodial sentences than white offenders for comparable offences, then appropriate anti-racist practice might usefully include ethnic monitoring of all the critical decision-making processes, the development of triggers to ensure that people in the justice system are aware of the potential problems, the recruitment of more black people to the justice system, the addition of black advisers' views to reports and many other possibilities. Broadly, the same processes could also be incorporated into work in the field of MENTAL HEALTH to ensure an anti-racist stance. In other circumstances, it is the under-use of social work and social welfare facilities that is notable in relation to ethnic minorities. Examples include the use of facilities for people with learning disabilities and for older people. In these circumstances, dialogue with ethnic-minority communities about their needs, explanations of the functions of particular services, the provision of good INFORMATION for ethnic minorities in appropriate languages and the employment of ethnic-minority workers can all be part of a committed anti-racist strategy.

In sum, anti-racism starts from an assumption that Britain is a racist society. Progress has been made in some areas but has been very uneven, and in some quarters the patterns of DISCRIMINATION remain remarkably persistent. Any social work practice must therefore be rooted in a recognition and acceptance of racism. Such recognition is the first necessary step towards an effective anti-racist strategy. Policies that confront both employment practices and issues of service delivery have then to be developed. It seems likely that an organization that is serious about anti-racism will attempt to make policy in both areas, and the one will undoubtedly inform the other. (See also ANTIDISCRIMINATORY PRACTICE, EQUAL OPPORTUNITIES POLICIES, ETHNICALLY SENSITIVE PRACTICE, RACE RELATIONS ACT 1976, TRANSRACIAL ADOPTION.)

L. Dominelli, *Anti-Racist Social Work*, Basingstoke, Macmillan, 1988.

antisocial behaviour a term that includes a range of specific activities such as hanging out in gangs in public places, verbal intimidation of others, fighting, public drunkenness, vandalism and creating high levels of noise.

Antisocial behaviour can be distressing for residents of a particular area to the point that the quality of life is severely curtailed. 'Nuisance neighbours' who play loud music in the middle of the night or adolescents with menacing behaviour have a disruptive and frightening impact on local residents such as older people or young children. Many local authorities now expel from their council housing tenants who engage persistently in antisocial behaviour towards neighbours. From 1997, the Labour government together has introduced a number of initiatives to control such behaviour in relation to young people. (See CURFEW, ANTISOCIAL BEHAVIOUR ORDER.)

Antisocial behaviour of young persons and how to control it have been the source of intense debate within professional and government circles. In its influential report *Misspent Youth*, the Audit Commission makes several points that social workers should bear in mind. It concluded that COUNSELLING, CASEWORK, FAMILY THERAPY and PSYCHODYNAMIC APPROACHES in general, which emphasized disruptive young people gaining 'insight' into their behaviour, did not work. But the report also highlighted a number of promising approaches, including:

1 behavioural and COGNITIVE BEHAVIOURAL methods;

2 community-based work that uses local resources and nearness to the offender's home environment to affect real-life learning;

3 matching level of risk of offending posed by a given individual with the level of intervention;

4 role play and modelling, which focus on skill acquisition, problem solving and social interaction;

5 employment-based programmes through which offenders can progress to real jobs.

Audit Commission, *Misspent Youth*, London, The Stationery Office, 1996.

antisocial behaviour order an order available under the CRIME AND DISORDER ACT, made by a magistrates' court in England and Wales or by a sheriff in Scotland at the request of the police or a local authority for a period of at least two years, which prohibits a person over the age of ten years from any kind of ANTISOCIAL BEHAVIOUR specified in the order.

Breaches of such orders are punishable by fines or imprisonment. Courts have rarely used them because of concerns about their enforceability and about human rights.

anxiety a high level of fear, tension and sense of imminent danger in direct response to an experience felt to be threatening. Anxiety involves both subjective feelings and bodily reactions that are uncomfortable and distressing.

Mental health problems often have both physical and emotional and cognitive components, and anxiety is a prime example of this. Anxiety involves reactions that anyone may experience in a threatening situation. The subjective experience is one of fear, dread, apprehension, panic and physiological reactions, including palpitations, gastric upsets, headaches, lack of concentration and faintness. It is also the case that some physical conditions, for example an overactive thyroid, asthma or heart problems, can produce the same symptoms of anxiety – palpitations, dry mouth, rapid breathing or hyperventilation. Accurate medical assessment of the causes of anxiety is therefore needed to determine the sources of such symptoms. Diagnosis is even more complex given the consideration that symptoms of anxiety are often experienced alongside those of schizophrenia or other PSYCHOSES and DEMENTIA.

The prevalence of those suffering anxiety is approximately 10 per cent of the population while those in devalued social groups, such as black people, older or disabled people, can experience it at twice that rate. Whether anxiety takes the form of stress or a NEUROSIS, the consequences can be serious. Accidents are a danger, because of lack of concentration, and young children can similarly be put at physical risk. Tension leads to irritation, family conflict and disturbed relations with children. Physical exhaustion and discomfort may also prevent the person from fulfilling role expectations. Besides resentment on the part of spouses or partners, this may lead to employment difficulties and to condemnation from relatives and friends, because of lack of recognition of the anxiety as a legitimate 'illness'.

Anxiety often occurs with depression. The combination of anxiety and depression has been found particularly where someone has experienced trauma, for example in an incident of DOMESTIC VIOLENCE. Anxiety in this connection also forms part of the wider experience of POST-TRAUMATIC STRESS DISORDER, which may even relate to events from many years previously. But recent investigations have also indicated the social sources of anxiety. Some 25 per cent of sufferers have experienced some social stressor involving feelings of fear in the weeks preceding onset while long-term difficulties, such as housing or finance as well as conflict in personal relationships, are found in three out of four persons suffering long-term anxiety. An important factor making a person more vulnerable to anxiety is poor care as a child and particularly abuse.

The social worker's role in dealing with anxiety and other mental health problems has been outlined in the National Service Framework for Mental Health. The framework requires practitioners to engage in mental health promotion. Broadly, they may provide access to social supports, act preventatively to forestall, for instance, an eviction from a tenancy and impart improved coping skills so that a person may deal with social stresses more effectively. Government policy in the 1999 white paper *Saving Lives* and in *Making It Happen* in 2001 has recognized in particular the importance of social cohesion in preventing anxiety and depression. Local authority social service departments have a role in this – working to raise levels of participation in communities and in building social support networks. This can be achieved in families of different cultures through an appropriate understanding of and respect for the family's expectations, values and beliefs. Often such work needs to be carried out in partnership with PRIMARY CARE TRUSTS and other local authority departments.

Specific interventions range from medication, in the form of antidepressants, and COGNITIVE BEHAVIOURAL THERAPY to more general BEHAVIOURAL approaches that help to teach people to manage their anxiety as well as self-help groups that offer shared experience and support in overcoming difficulties. Medication aims to block the physical symptoms of anxiety in the belief that this will relieve the subjective feelings. While ideally this should form part of a broader approach, women are particularly likely to be prescribed medication by general practitioners without referral to other professionals. The FEMINIST approach to anxiety understands it as a natural response to women's powerlessness in their relationships with male partners, to the stressful tasks of caring for dependent people, to their socialized inability to be effectively assertive and to financial pressures (women, particularly black women, are poorer than men). Intervention here would seek to help the woman – as a member of a group of other women with similar experiences or through one-to-one discussion with the (female) worker – develop an understanding that the roots of these problems lie in society. This is regarded as the basis on which a woman can start to take control of her life, perhaps developing skills such as assertiveness through assertiveness training, thereby relieving the anxiety at its source.

B. Everett and R. Gallop, *The Link Between Childhood Trauma and Adult Mental Illness*, London, Sage, 2001.

appeal the process whereby a defendant can complain about and seek remedy for a court decision that he or she considers unjust.

In criminal cases in England and Wales, appeals against conviction or sentence in a magistrates' court are heard in a Crown Court, and appeals against decisions made in a Crown Court are heard in the Court of Appeal (Criminal Division) or, finally, the House of Lords. A Crown Court has the power to increase as well as reduce a sentence, but the Court of Appeal does not have this power. However, a sentence may be increased by the Court of Appeal if it has been referred by the Attorney General as being unduly lenient, although this is not (technically) an appeal (see CRIMINAL COURTS). In civil cases, appeals are dealt with in the HIGH COURT and the Court of Appeal (Civil Division) (see CIVIL PROCEEDINGS, FAMILY PROCEEDINGS).

appeal tribunal see WELFARE RIGHTS 1.

applicable amount see WELFARE RIGHTS 5.

appropriate adult a person appointed to safeguard the interests of vulnerable people while they are questioned by the police.

For these purposes, everyone under the age of 17 and everyone with learning difficulties or mental illness are regarded as vulnerable. In most areas of England and Wales, local authorities train appropriate adults and maintain a rota so that the service is available around the clock. Parents or relatives are likely to be the first people approached by the police to attend interviews, and they count as appropriate adults under the legislation. They may not, however, be the best people to fulfil this role, which requires some knowledge of the criminal justice system and a degree of assertiveness if it is to be performed well. Unfortunately, even qualified appropriate adults intervene only in a minority of cases of inappropriate questioning, according to the only research conducted in this area.

The concept of the appropriate adult was created because of a number of miscarriages of justice in which vulnerable suspects admitted offences that they could not have committed but were nevertheless convicted and in some cases imprisoned. Appropriate adults have the right to stop an interview if they are unhappy with the way it is being conducted, but in most cases their role is more facilitative. They help the person being interviewed to understand the process, do what they can to assist communication between the police and the suspect, and ensure that the suspect's rights are protected. They can speak to suspects without police officers being present and may insist on solicitors being involved if this is in the suspects' interests.

In the case of young people, the appropriate adult service is part of the REMAND management strategy of the YOUTH OFFENDING TEAM, and teams are required by national standards to provide such a service. The appropriate adult will often be the first representative of the youth offending team to come into contact with an alleged young offender and, as such, has an important role that can lay the groundwork for an effective intervention. In some areas, the EMERGENCY DUTY TEAM or members of the youth offending team act as appropriate adults, but specially trained volunteers or sessional staff may be better able to provide a professional service.

R. Powell, *Child Law: A Guide for Courts and Practitioners*, Winchester, Waterside Press, 2001.

appropriate dispute resolution see ALTERNATIVE DISPUTE RESOLUTION.
approved social worker (ASW) the specially qualified social worker who
must by law be involved in the decision to detain a person compulsorily
in a psychiatric hospital.

The approved social worker has overall responsibility for co-ordinating
the ASSESSMENT of a person who, because of severe mental illness, may
require compulsory admission to psychiatric hospital under the MENTAL
HEALTH ACT 1983. Such an assessment will consider first and foremost
whether a person's mental illness poses risks to his or her own health
and safety or to that of other members of the family or public. Before a
decision is reached, many factors must be taken into account, including
the nature of the mental illness, any behaviour disorders the person is
showing, the person's own views as to what should happen, the
effectiveness of any proposed treatment and the impact on the person
of compulsory admission.

To obtain the information needed to make this decision, the ASW
must interview the person in a suitable manner. The code of practice for
the Mental Health Act 1983 emphasizes the manner in which this crucial
interview is conducted. It should, for example, be with the person on his
or her own unless doing so presents a risk of physical harm to the social
worker. It should not take place through a window or closed door. Every
effort should be made to facilitate the communication of the person by
providing an interpreter if the person is deaf or if English is not his or
her first language. If the person is sedated or unresponsive, the ASW
should make attempts to get his or her views by interviewing others who
might be familiar with the person. The views of the nearest relative must
also be obtained but are not binding on the ASW. Often the ASW acts as
the applicant for the compulsory admission of the person involved
although not in cases where the nearest relative has decided to do so.

The decision to admit a person compulsorily to psychiatric hospital
can be finely balanced and is never taken lightly. It is always made jointly
with a consultant psychiatrist or general practitioner so depends on the
mutual goodwill and respect between these professionals. The decision
depends in part on whether the person is in need of psychiatric
assessment or treatment in hospital. That judgement rests largely with
the consultant psychiatrist. If the decision is taken to admit, the ASW
is responsible for assembling the documentation and making
arrangements to transport the person to hospital in a manner that
takes his or her needs and wishes into account. Transport is often
by ambulance and never by the ASW acting as lone driver.

The work of the ASW is frequently conducted in an atmosphere of
crisis. It can be the focus of pressure from other professionals, such as
general practitioners and psychiatrists, who, from the perspective of
their medical training, may believe that hospital presents a quick
solution to problems posed by a person's difficult behaviour. For the

same reason, the ASW may come under pressure from family members to act one way or another. Nevertheless, the ASW has to retain a clear view of what his or her role and function are. The ASW must try to strike a balance between the short-term interest of the person, when protective considerations may predominate, and the long-term interest, when considerations of a person's social effectiveness and autonomy, which could be undermined by a period of hospitalization, are important.

ASWs are usually members of social work teams specializing in mental health. As such, they will share the work of that team, which includes assessments under the NATIONAL HEALTH SERVICE AND COMMUNITY CARE ACT of people with varying degrees of mental illness and arranging the services that provide support and assistance in their day-to-day life. This may include purchasing a place at a local day centre for adults with mental distress, arranging for a COMMUNITY PSYCHIATRIC NURSE to provide fortnightly injections of a prescribed medication and regular visits to check on progress. The work can also involve running special groups that teach participants SOCIAL SKILLS TRAINING or ASSERTIVENESS training. ASWs also have a vital preventative role in working to develop strategies and policies locally for improving services to people with mental illness. This can include, for example, working to establish facilities such as day centres that can help support an individual sufficiently so that periods of hospitalization are not necessary, explaining the nature of mental illness to other professionals and to groups of carers, and improving communication with hospitals and medical personnel.

Under proposed reforms of the Mental Health Act social workers will not have the exclusive role of contributing the non-medical perspective in the assessment process. While they will still fulfil the important tasks as the current ASW they will lose the ASW title while other non-medical professionals will also be able to execute them as well. Whoever takes on that role, recent research has highlighted two points that are important for non-medical practitioners to bear in mind. One is that the current ASW has been found to lack a supportive team framework or professional network committed to developing alternatives to admission to psychiatric hospital and, as a result, overwhelmingly agree to compulsory admission under the Mental Health Act in virtually every case. The second is that some 46 per cent of people compulsorily admitted to hospital experience POST-TRAUMATIC STRESS SYNDROME *following* the admission process. This points to the abrupt nature of the current way hospitalizations are conducted and the impact of having one's rights removed.

M. Barnes and R. Bowl, *Taking Over the Asylum: Empowerment and Mental Health*, Basingstoke, Palgrave, 2001.

area child protection committee the joint forum for developing, monitoring and reviewing CHILD PROTECTION policies in a given area.

Area child protection committees were first established in 1974 as a way of co-ordinating policies and practices between those bodies primarily involved in child protection work. Senior representatives from the medical profession, the social services, the police and major voluntary organizations all sit on these committees.

Arnstein's ladder a way of mapping out the different degrees of PARTICIPATION by local residents and users in the services or community projects that affect them.

The tool literally uses the shape of a ladder with the highest degree of participation on the top rung and the lowest degree at the bottom rung. At the higher end of the ladder citizens exert maximum power and control over a project or service. At the lower end are forms of participation that are manipulative and something of a sham. From the highest rung in descending order are citizen control, delegated power, partnership, placation, consultation, informing, therapy and manipulation. Because social work is committed to EMPOWERMENT in principle, practitioners may be tempted to think that in their work they automatically should aim for the levels of participation at the top of the ladder. But other legal obligations and the dictates of the social work agencies' policies might point otherwise. Each project or service should be looked at carefully to determine what level of participation is both desirable and realistic.

assertiveness behaviours and thoughts that have at their root a concern to establish interests and needs either of oneself or of others.

Many people experience difficulties in social situations that arise directly from lack of assertiveness. This might mean that, in a work setting for example, a person is assigned too much work, too little work or inappropriate work – all situations that are individually and organizationally counterproductive – and they feel unable to seek to alter the situation. Or in a social or family setting it may mean giving a high priority to what others want but not reaching a balance with the person's own needs and wants in those situations. In such cases, the non-assertive person denies his or her own interests. Assertion strategies encompass a set of objectives that people should attempt to develop into verbal and nonverbal strategies for stating their position. Essentially these have to do with seeing that to assert one's own interests is not selfish or self-centred but the reasonable and even sociable thing to do, something that others do all the time. Some of these thought strategies include the following:

1 the conviction to state one's own needs and set one's own priorities, and for those needs and priorities to be considered as important as others';
2 the conviction to be treated with respect as a capable human being;
3 the approval to express one's feelings, opinions and values;
4 the right to make mistakes and to change one's mind;
5 the right not to understand something and to seek information;
6 the right to ask for what one wants;
7 the right to refuse responsibility for others.

It is important to maintain a distinction between assertion and AGGRESSION. The former can be learned; the latter, which involves the denial of rights to others, needs to be unlearned. There are many assertiveness exercises that people can carry out, such as to practise saying 'no', to role-play worrying situations or to re-enact past events in new ways. The objective of such skill development is to act assertively and to feel good about oneself and others. An assertive person maintains good eye contact with others, sits comfortably and talks in a strong, steady voice, giving clear messages and responding actively to the other person.

C. L. Cooper, R. D. Cooper and L. H. Eaker, *Living with Stress*, London, Penguin, 1988.

assertive outreach a highly user focused approach for people with MENTAL HEALTH PROBLEMS that maintains intensive contact in their own environment.

First developed in the USA, assertive outreach attempts to ensure that those who require medication or support services receive it no matter where they are – at home or on the street. Assertive outreach workers offer a broad range of services, from advice to help with shopping. They maintain frequent contact, perhaps four times per week, and are committed to the long term. Their aim is to prevent crisis situations from developing, such as hospital admissions, evictions or offending. The National Service Framework for Mental Health includes a commitment to invest in assertive outreach teams in England and Wales and aimed to have them established by 2003. There is debate, however, around how fully such teams are reflecting the objectives of outreach. Two models of practice are emerging. One focuses on keeping in contact with people, ensuring compliance with medication and reducing hospital admissions. The other focuses on a person's network – on quality of life, social interactions, leisure and occupation.

assessment the process by which judgments are made about an individual or family and their environment in deciding what their NEEDS are.

Social workers have in the past regarded assessment as their exclusive professional task, akin to a medical or psychiatric diagnosis. The wide scope of social work assessments – covering many dimensions of a person's life, such as state of mind, family relationships, physical capabilities, housing conditions, and income in relation to basic needs – involves too many complex variables for diagnostic certainty to be achievable. Moreover, the new emphasis on users' PARTICIPATION in their own assessment means that assessment is no longer under exclusive professional control. Practitioners have come to recognize that assessment is a continuous process, mixing professional appraisal and user viewpoint and reflecting the VALUES of both. An assessment contains at least four elements: *description*, for example of the service user's living conditions, behaviour or the nature of family relationships; *explanation*, suggesting possible causes of any problems and probable consequences of unmet needs; *identification*, for example of problems to be resolved and the individual's or family's strengths or weaknesses in solving those problems; and *evaluation*, for example of how a person's needs might most effectively be met.

The objective of most assessments is to discover to what extent a child, adult or whole family is in need. This requires social workers, almost always with clients' consent, to gather important information about clients' recent past, health, social contacts, capacity to look after themselves, strengths, the degree of safety in their present circumstances and the resources at their disposal. The kind of assessment undertaken depends on who the service users are and what problems they wish to address or others would wish to address on their behalf.

Generally the approach to assessment takes on a different form depending on whether the service is for a child (and his or her family) or an adult. One of the common assessment tasks is to decide whether a child is in need, since a local authority can arrange services for children and their families if this applies. This may require only a brief assessment to determine whether, for example, the child might have needs that can be met by a funded place at a playgroup. Such an assessment could occur quickly, informally and with the involvement of the whole family, soon after that family contacted the social services. An authoritative guide issued by the Department of Health in 2001, *Assessing Children in Need and their Families*, lays out the requirements for more complex assessments of children (see FRAMEWORK FOR ASSESSMENT OF CHILDREN IN NEED).

Black practitioners and social work academics in the United States and Britain have developed an assessment approach that specifically takes into account environmental pressures and historical considerations in assessing a family (see BLACK PERSPECTIVE). They have been concerned to reverse prevalent notions within the social work profession of stereotypical weaknesses in black families and have accordingly developed a framework that looks at family strengths in coping with the racist environment in which black people live. It has been suggested that the following factors be included in the assessment of a black family: *the person* – what specific life-cycle tasks does each child and adult in the family face, and to what extent does the black experience influence these tasks?; *the environment* – what are the stresses, demands, rewards and attitudes in the family's environment?; *the family* – what are the nature of the relationships within the family and its coping strategies, particularly when confronted with demands from an antagonistic culture of the white majority? The FRAMEWORK FOR ASSESSMENT OF CHILDREN IN NEED places great emphasis on the importance of assessing black children and systematizes much of this work.

When assessing the needs of adults who may require COMMUNITY CARE services, such as older people or people with LEARNING DISABILITIES, the Department of Health has explicitly outlined the steps through which every assessment should progress. First, the scope of every assessment should be individually negotiated with the individual concerned. Second, it should take place in a setting where the interviewee feels most comfortable. Third, practitioners should ensure that users understand what is involved in the assessment process, the timescale, the possible outcomes and what authority or powers the practitioner holds. Fourth, the practitioner must define the cause of any difficulty, since without this it will be difficult to select the appropriate service to meet the defined need. The Department of Health makes a crucial distinction between using assessment as an instrument of social support and using it for social control, the former offering 'choices to the user' while the latter 'imposes solutions'.

Two trends are evident in the current development of assessments. The first is the increasing participation of the user, carer and their families in their own assessment. To enhance participation, individuals need more information about services and whether or not they might be eligible for them. This is precisely the kind of information that social service agencies would not make publicly available in the past. Individuals being assessed also require appropriate ways of expressing their points of view and having influence on the assessment decisions. This is particularly important for people with a DISABILITY or for whom English is not their first language. The second trend is the increasing emphasis on MULTIDISCIPLINARY assessment. The task of a social worker often requires the co-ordination of vast amounts of information, with the person's consent, on many aspects of his or her life, including health care, income, housing, mobility, social contacts and mental health. Such information can be obtained only from other professionals and is almost always recorded on lengthy assessment sheets or computerized records.

In the *questioning model* of assessment, the practitioner gathers information from the 'client' and others such as carers and family members before reaching a judgement or 'assessment' on what his or her needs or problems are and the solution to them. The practitioner's conduct is based on asking questions, processing the answers and using the responses to make a decision about the level and nature of care to be offered. It is a model that reflects the agency's objectives, which links client need to pre-set categories and budgets within the agency.

The *exchange model* takes a different approach. It focuses on the exchange of information between practitioner and all others involved. The objective is to engage family members and other significant members of a network. The perception of the situation, the inherent strengths and weaknesses, the definition of problems and their possible solution derive as much from the user and his or her family as from the practitioner. In this model the social worker is a resource, an enabler, not a conductor of the outcome. Communication across ethnic, racial, class and gender boundaries is also made easier because preconceived agency categories and solutions are not subtly framing the interaction. (See also NEEDS-LED ASSESSMENT, SINGLE ASSESSMENT).

Assessment and Action Records part of the system for gathering information, making and reviewing plans and monitoring the progress of LOOKED-AFTER children.

The records are six age-related schedules that guide practitioners in determining whether children are making progress while being looked after by a local authority. The need for the records arose in part because of accumulating evidence that local authorities acting as corporate parents were poor in following their responsibilities. The records track the experiences of children necessary for satisfactory development in seven areas: health, education, identity, family and social relationships, social presentation, emotional and behavioural development, and self-care skills.

The Assessment and Action Records were launched in May 1995, together with the rest of the Looking after Children package of Essential Information Records, Care Plans, Placement Plans and Review Forms and training materials. By 1998 over 90 per cent of local authorities in England (and 100 per cent in Wales) had signed up to use them. They were renamed in 2002 as the Assessment and Progress Records, with the intention that they be used primarily with children who are looked after for at least six months and for whom there is no identified date for their return home. Their content was also changed to encourage children to contribute as much as possible to discussions about issues that are central to their wellbeing while at the same time ensuring that the progress of each looked-after child is adequately monitored.

assessment centre a residential establishment where service users are placed for a specified length of time so that an ASSESSMENT can take place. The assessment usually includes factors such as family relationships, health, behaviour, educational attainments, parenting skills and risk. Client groups that have been placed for residential assessments include children (especially young offenders), sex offenders, parents and people with enduring mental health problems.

The concept of the assessment centre in relation to children and parents has come under increasing attack. Research has indicated that, for example, to remove a child from home or a parent from his or her normal environment only for the purposes of assessment gives a distorted picture of the child or parent. Further, since the assessment process at such centres is dominated by psychologists, social workers and senior child-care staff, little scope is left for PARTICIPATION by the child or other family members in the process. Others have held that it is possible to compensate for such artificialities and that the intense scrutiny that is possible if workers are, in effect, observing service users on a full-time basis over many weeks will often lead to a spirit of co-operation and problem-solving. In the case of very difficult groups like paedophiles the only alternative would be to work with them in secure units.

Association of Black Probation Officers a nationwide group of black members of the PROBATION SERVICE who believe that all those involved in the criminal justice system should provide an ANTIDISCRIMINATORY service to all clients in Britain's multiracial society.

The association seeks to contribute a BLACK PERSPECTIVE to professional issues and service delivery. A network for black probation officers is maintained to support individual professionals, especially if they are isolated from black colleagues in their day-to-day practice. It is also interested in promoting ethnically sensitive services and a rigorous ANTI-RACIST perspective in a system that members firmly believe to be both racist and discriminatory. Practical activity includes direct contributions to probation training courses and to the wider debate on criminal justice issues.

Association of Directors of Social Services an umbrella organization that brings together the directors of all the SOCIAL SERVICES DEPARTMENTS in England, Wales and Northern Ireland.

Membership of the association is strictly limited to directors of social services departments. Its major role is to act as a forum for heads of departments to exchange ideas and to develop policy initiatives at a national level. The association's other roles include: consultation with civil servants, ministers and Opposition spokespersons on social services issues; to meet regularly with other professional and managerial groups to discuss common issues of concern; to provide information to members and facilitate research initiatives; to give evidence to relevant parliamentary select committees; and to provide information to the press and other media.

Association of Directors of Social Work an organization representing the directors of social work departments in Scotland.

The association's activities are comparable with those of the ASSOCIATION OF DIRECTORS OF SOCIAL SERVICES. However, the social work departments of the unitary authorities in Scotland also have responsibilities associated with probation, court services and parole. This gives directors of social work a wider area of concerns than that of their English, Welsh and Northern Ireland counterparts.

ASW abbreviation for APPROVED SOCIAL WORKER.

asylum seekers and refugees an asylum seeker is a person who has applied for refugee status in the UK and is still awaiting a decision. A refugee is a person given INDEFINITE LEAVE TO REMAIN in the UK.

During 2002 the procedures for dealing with asylum seekers changed so that every applicant has an initial interview with the Immigration Service that takes their application. Many asylum seekers are destitute when they arrive in the UK so they need to apply to the NATIONAL ASYLUM SUPPORT SERVICE.

In relation to refugees, under the terms of the UN Convention on Refugee Status, 1951, a person will qualify as a refugee if he or she is unable or unwilling to return to his or her country of nationality because of a well-founded fear of persecution for reasons of race, religion, nationality, social group or political opinion. A person accepted as a refugee in the UK is entitled to benefits and social housing, like any member of the indigenous population, and can also apply to bring over dependants under the family settlement rules. Each year between 10 per cent and 20 per cent of people applying for asylum are given refugee status (10,000 in 2000) but others are given EXCEPTIONAL LEAVE TO REMAIN.

Asylum seeking has been a long-standing social phenomenon in many parts of the world for centuries, driven often by the persecution of minority religious and ethnic groups. Anti-Semitism in Germany and Russia in the 20th century (leading to Jews settling in the UK and the USA) and the persecution of Puritans in England in the 18th century (migrating to what became the USA) are well-known historical examples. In the last years of the 20th century and the first years of the 21st century the 'problems' of asylum seekers and refugees have again achieved a high political profile as international migration, fuelled by conflicts and the dissolution of empires, has gained momentum. A significant amount of this migration, although not all, has been from relatively poor countries to comparatively affluent democracies. These democracies have varied in their responses to both asylum seekers and refugees, many containing factions who are unsympathetic to the claims of those wishing or needing to start new lives in a new country. Unsympathetic groups claim that asylum seekers are often in fact economic migrants seeking a more affluent lifestyle, that the difficulties in the asylum seekers' countries of origin are much exaggerated, that the host society lacks the jobs, accommodation or the capacity to absorb alien peoples, or that other countries are better placed to take more asylum seekers. At the other end of the continuum are factions who are more inclined to accept the asylum seekers' accounts of their problems and are thus predisposed to offer meaningful support in a more trusting manner.

The support tasks for workers supporting asylum seekers and refugees are wide ranging. First, there are issues about securing a 'fair hearing' for applicants for asylum, both in relation to initial applications and to appeals. In this context there can be complications around the issue of whether people present themselves as asylum seekers at the point of entry to the UK (as official policy requires) or whether they gain entry on some other pretext before declaring themselves to be asylum seekers. Illegal entry is perhaps understandable, as it appears that claims for asylum at the point of entry are frequently unsuccessful. Regardless of where a claim for asylum is registered, there is equivocal evidence about how 'just' the vetting processes are. There can be major difficulties for asylum seekers in proving persecution when they have left countries where official records are unlikely to support their allegations. These problems can be compounded when claims are being made through interpreters, when asylum seekers are disoriented because of stressful and sometimes life-threatening experiences and do not understand the host country's systems and processes.

Second, if asylum is granted there is the issue of helping people to settle in a strange land. The characteristic problems are those of income, accommodation, reunification with family members who may still be in danger in the country of origin, education and/or employment as well as personal and social support in communities that may be hostile to strangers or even overtly racist. The British government has a policy of dispersal of refugees so that costs and pressures are shared by local authorities across the country. This policy has created problems for some because of inappropriate placements of people in sometimes shared accommodation, a lack of support services and poor quality housing in depressed communities because these areas are the only places where accommodation is available. Unaccompanied children pose additional difficulties, as do people who have been through traumatic experiences, such as torture, or where they have had close relatives killed or relatives have disappeared without explanation.

attachment a long-lasting emotional bond between two individuals, involving their seeking proximity to each other and having pleasure in each other's company. Typically, attachment is developed by infants towards their principal care-givers, but it may also characterize feelings between other people, or between a person and some object.

While in adults the term 'love' would be appropriate, 'attachment' is usually reserved for the bond between infants – human and animal – and their care-givers, usually the mother. Close proximity of infant and care-giver ensures that the former's biological needs are met and that both partners build up trust and satisfaction through a close social relationship. Such is the importance of an early relationship of this kind that biologists have suggested that the conditions for its formation must be innate. For example, newly hatched ducklings will follow the first moving object to which they are exposed – a phenomenon called 'imprinting'. Some child psychiatrists have suggested that the responses of a baby to its mother, such as smiling, are human examples of imprinting. Both psychologists and psychiatrists have modified their viewpoints in recent years, taking into account evidence that some mutual instrumental learning is also involved in mother-infant interaction. Mothers 'reinforce' the behaviours that they enjoy from their babies, and these behaviours, in turn, reinforce mothers' care-giving.

Whatever the relative importance of innate and learned factors in the development of attachment, its significance is universally acknowledged. Infants who are securely attached are more confident in exploring their environment, using their mothers as a base. They are also more confident in responding to the overtures of strangers, again using their mothers as a secure base. It has been suggested that babies who have not built up secure attachments in early life are more at risk of emotional disorders in later life than securely attached infants; also that parents who have not had an opportunity to form strong attachments to their children are more likely to abuse them.

Social workers must be careful not to interpret attachment as something that happens once and for all to newborn babies. Such an interpretation has been used to justify the permanent removal of children from families where separation between infant and care-giver (usually the mother) took place, for example as a result of that person's hospitalization or where the infant's care-giver did not form a close relationship with the infant in the first weeks of life. This narrow conception of attachment viewed children as unable to form attachments either later in their childhood or to more than one person. Such was the importance that social workers placed on attachment that rating scales were devised to help them judge the quality of attachments formed between particular children and their care-givers.

Recent research conducted by psychologists now suggests that attachment is a continuous process that passes through different phases, so that if there is disruption, even early on in the relationship between mother and child, this does not mean that attachment will not take place at all. Social workers have also learned to use the concept more flexibly, as one of many aspects they consider when forming a view of the strength of a relationship between a child and its parents.

attendance allowance a benefit for people over 65 who need assistance with personal care. See WELFARE RIGHTS 3; WELFARE RIGHTS 8.

attendance centre order a sentence for young offenders convicted of an imprisonable offence, requiring the young person to attend for up to 36 hours and take part in activities as instructed.

Most centres are run by police officers, usually at weekends, and the activities include physical exercise and work. Attendance centre orders are often used to deal with young people convicted of vandalism and of antisocial behaviour at sporting events. Breach of an attendance centre order, either by failing to attend or by misbehaving at the centre, can be dealt with by a fine or by revoking the order and imposing a fresh sentence for the original offence.

attention deficit hyperactivity disorder (ADHD) a cluster of learning and behaviour problems in children that includes poor self-control, physical restlessness, poor concentration and short-term memory, and failure to follow instructions.

The full range of behaviours can seriously interfere with learning and building social relationships. Children with ADHD may be impulsive in behaviour, such as speaking and acting without thinking, interrupting others, rushing school work and being accident prone. They may insist on doing things their way, act in a silly way in a crowd and be continuously restless and fidgety. In school they may be inattentive, prone to distraction and uneven in their work.

ADHD is difficult to diagnose since there is no clear distinction between those children who are 'normally' active, impulsive and inattentive and those with ADHD. Generally, psychiatrists would argue that if a majority of symptomatic behaviours are evident out of a list of nine associated with ADHD a child may be said to suffer from it. Others would debate such an approach and would want to ensure that any child said to have ADHD was not simply an overly lively pre-schooler finding it difficult to sit still in the increasingly academic classrooms of primary schools. They would want to examine, for instance, the possibility of developmental delays arising from other causes, the parenting the child received and any degree of family dysfunction before arriving at a diagnosis. Equally, the 'cause' of ADHD is a subject of debate, with parental behaviour, food additives and brain function all mentioned as possible causes. There is now increasing consensus within the medical profession that points to some genetic association and to small but perceptible differences in brain function of children with ADHD. The latter finding has led to widespread prescription of medication, especially Ritalin, to children with a view to stimulating the concentrative functions of the brain. The results have been subject to vigorous debate, with many voices asserting that more damage than good arises from such treatment.

attitude an habitual way of responding to, or thinking about, people, groups and objects in a generally favourable or unfavourable manner.

Attitudes influence both people's behaviour and the way they interact with the world around them. Attitudes are mental states that carry evaluative elements and behavioural tendencies; they provide ready explanations for social events and, as a consequence, may assist in the management of ANXIETY. Attitudes may be understood as mental short cuts in the processing of information, providing a framework that permits a person to make a rapid assessment of social events based on earlier experiences. Stored in memory, attitudes influence behaviour only when recalled by situations. Whatever their strength, attitudes remain undisclosed if no situation occurs for their translation into behaviour. Attitudes are developed by a person from peer-group influences, direct experience, early learning, the media, membership of social groups and social interaction. Once acquired, attitudes interact with each other and with beliefs that are already part of the person's mental processes. Attitudes seem to be most strongly held when they have been acquired by repeated experiences.

Attitudes have two components: the way an event is perceived and feelings about the event. They may vary in the intensity in which these components are present and in the intensity with which each attitude is held. A person is likely to hold several attitudes towards a person, object or event, with a corresponding choice of behaviours and actions. It is possible for a person to have one attitude and yet behave in a manner that suggests another. People may hold contradictory attitudes and, as a result, may experience the emotional and intellectual discomfort known as cognitive dissonance. A person may be motivated to resolve this conflict by changing or modifying his or her attitudes. Similarly, if a person is compelled to behave in a way that conflicts with held attitudes, then those attitudes may change.

People hold central attitudes or beliefs about such things as freedom, equality and the challenging of oppression, with such attitudes interacting closely with behaviour. Attitudes are fundamental in the way a person understands and interprets the social world, linking the person into social groups. Hence attitudes may carry social rewards or punishments for individuals by ensuring membership of, or exclusion from, social groups.

Attitudes and attitude change are key aspects of social work. They can be the root of a problem – for example, in racist or sexist behaviour, or in a negative view of one family member by another that is wholly unjustified. Determining precisely the nature of people's attitudes and the willingness or ability of people to change them is central to the social work task. (See also ABLE-BODIEDISM, RACISM, SEXISM, STEREOTYPE.)

audit the annual examination of the financial accounts of an organization aimed at independently establishing the probity of its records and expenditure. Audit is particularly important in public-sector organizations, where expenditure involves the use of public money; it is therefore related to the public ACCOUNTABILITY of such organizations.

In local government, annual audits are performed by auditors contracted by or working directly for the AUDIT COMMISSION. This is an independent organization established by the government to examine the accounts of local government and, more recently, the NATIONAL HEALTH SERVICE, to establish whether these bodies have spent money economically and efficiently. The accounts of the authorities have to be published in annual reports, and auditors can refuse to sign the accounts if they believe these do not reflect the true situation or if there are doubts concerning particular areas of expenditure. More recently, the government has expanded the role of the audit to cover the effectiveness of local government spending. This has brought the Audit Commission and the role of the audit into a more sensitive area of study. The concern with 'value for money' has led the commission to expand the role of the audit to include the identification of ways in which local authorities can make policy implementation more effective. There have been doubts, however, as to whether this is an appropriate role for the audit, given that there may be several political perspectives on what constitutes effectiveness.

Audit Commission a central government agency whose task is to AUDIT the activities of LOCAL AUTHORITIES and the NATIONAL HEALTH SERVICE on the basis of economy, efficiency and effectiveness.

Established under the Local Government Finance Act 1982 and operational in 1983, the commission took over from the District Audit Service responsibility for approving the accounts of local authorities for their annual reports. At first its remit was concerned with ensuring that the accounts had been appropriately drawn up, that there was evidence of probity in financial dealings and that spending was in line with statute. In addition, it was to provide advice on economy and efficiency in the provision of services. The commission's remit has since been widened and now includes another element in 'value for money' auditing: effectiveness. This has led the commission into a wider role of providing more direct guidance to authorities on the management of services. In doing so, it has sometimes challenged the methods employed by service professionals in service provision. The commission should not, however, be seen as a mouthpiece for central government policy. It has at times been highly critical of government, most notably with regard to the way the block grant system of local government finance was operated and how this mitigated against appropriate levels of planning for services.

In the area of personal social services and social work activities, the Audit Commission has produced major reports that are central to the development of government policy on care. The most significant such document was probably *Making a Reality of Community Care* (1986); this pointed out the lack of progress in implementing COMMUNITY CARE, conflicts in planning arrangements between local authorities and health authorities, and the anomaly of the social security system promoting residential rather than community care. In addition, the report recommended that an independent inquiry be established, which led to the white paper, *Caring for People*. Another influential report, *Misspent Youth*, paved the way for current approaches to youth offending.

Of particular note has been the role of the Audit Commission in drawing up PERFORMANCE MEASUREMENTS for a variety of local authority services, including the personal social services. These general reports are promoted very effectively as guidance to all local authorities, but much of the groundwork emerges from more specific investigations by district auditors into individual authorities. Working within guidelines from the commission, a district audit team may be made up of commission employees or private-sector firms. The results of these investigations are open to the public and may be widely disseminated.

While the Audit Commission has done important work, the extension of its remit to cover the issue of effectiveness has been open to criticism. Issues of effectiveness involve more contentious areas of management and service delivery that may overlap with policy decisions. These, it can be argued, are more legitimately the concern of elected representatives. Further, the fact that issues are perceived from an accounting viewpoint also results in a particular managerial perspective that may be challenged by other professionals and from alternative political positions.

Audit Commission, *Managing the Cascade of Change*, London, HMSO, 1992.

B*b*

backdating see WELFARE RIGHTS 1.

bail the system by which courts release an alleged offender pending his
or her trial. Bail may be unconditional or subject to sureties and/or
specified residence. The term also applies to the money used as security
binding the released person to appear in court and forfeited if he or she
does not appear.

The Bail Act 1976 requires bail to be granted unless there is reason
to believe that the alleged offender will fail to appear for trial or will
reoffend or interfere with witnesses. The term *police bail* refers to the
process of releasing a person following charge at a police station, prior
to court appearance. *Bail hostel* accommodation provided by the
PROBATION SERVICE and some organizations in the VOLUNTARY SECTOR
enables homeless offenders to be remanded on bail rather than be sent
to PRISON while awaiting trial. (See also REMAND.)

bail information/bail support see REMAND.

Barclay Report the report published in 1982 by a committee set up
by the government to examine the state of social work and chaired
by Peter Barclay. The report's formal title was *Social Workers: Their Role
and Tasks*.

The Barclay Report provided a valuable analysis of what social workers
actually did in their work, showing that CARE PLANS had become a major
component. The report stressed the importance of RESIDENTIAL CARE at
a time when it had fallen from favour among professionals, and it used
the phrase 'the continuum of care' to describe the evolving community-
based and residential options open to people needing care. Among the
report's recommendations it called for less bureaucratic service
organizations and for the devolution of decision-making to team level.
It further urged the development of more grass-roots-level COMMUNITY
SOCIAL WORK to strengthen CLIENTS' own networks as a key resource.

baseline data or INFORMATION that records behaviour or frequency of
a problem at the start of a service intervention or project against which
comparisons are later made within a set time frame to judge whether
the intervention or project has had a positive impact.

The concept of baseline data was originally developed within BEHAVIOURAL ASSESSMENT. There it is a record of the frequency in which an individual engages in a particular kind of behaviour before any programme of help begins. Obtaining this record usually depends on some form of direct observation – such as reports from the CLIENT, from other family members or by the general practitioner – in which the results have been recorded at timed intervals. Keeping track of the number of tantrums a child has during a week is an example. Such a record is used to help measure subsequent progress after intervention begins and almost always forms part of a behavioural assessment. Recently the concept of baseline, or *start point data* as it is sometimes now called, has been applied to a number of multidisciplinary projects in which social workers are involved, including SURE START, REGENERATION efforts and YOUTH OFFENDING TEAMS. Such data describes a set of social conditions or problems prior to the project starting its work. Such projects invariably have to set targets that improve on the baseline, for example reducing the number of young offenders in an area, improving the GSCE results of young people in care, or reducing the number of low birth-weight babies.

BASW abbreviation for BRITISH ASSOCIATION OF SOCIAL WORKERS.

battered baby the term first used by paediatricians in the 1960s to indicate that an infant had been injured by its parents or by other adults.

Before the 1960s the medical profession did not recognize that deliberate injury to infants was occurring. As a result, doctors were often unable to account for multiple injuries suffered by some children, such as old unexplained fractures. The term was a first step in the recognition of CHILD ABUSE as a widespread problem and of its many forms. (See ABUSE, EMOTIONAL ABUSE, PHYSICAL ABUSE, SEXUAL ABUSE.)

battered wife see DOMESTIC VIOLENCE.

BCS abbreviation for BRITISH CRIME SURVEY.

bed and breakfast a form of temporary accommodation for families considered to be homeless by local authorities.

Under the Housing (Homeless Persons) Act 1977, local authority housing departments became responsible for HOMELESSNESS in relation to 'vulnerable groups'. Vulnerable groups, in the main, were to be understood as families with dependent children, pregnant women, women in fear of violence and others considered to be vulnerable. The 'others' were never specified, which has meant that services to other people considered to be vulnerable across the country have been very uneven. The 1996 Housing Act encouraged the use of temporary accommodation by local authorities (mostly in the private sector), and although the Homelessness Act 2002 has repealed these clauses, there is still widespread use of temporary accommodation across the country, especially in urban areas.

Bed and breakfast is widely used as a form of temporary accommodation. In 2002 the homelessness charity Shelter estimated that around 11,000 families were being accommodated in bed and breakfast at any point and that the numbers of dependent children associated with these families number many more. Refugees figure prominently in this group. The problems associated with living in bed and breakfast hotels and boarding houses are numerous. There is often overcrowding, with families sharing a bedroom. Kitchen, toilet and bathroom facilities are likely to be shared. Such multi-occupied dwellings are frequently in poor condition, sometimes with structural damp and inadequate heating. Not surprisingly, people living in these conditions are vulnerable to depression and other mental distress. There is compelling evidence to show that accessing schools, health services and other key services, including housing and welfare benefits, can be difficult, especially if families are mobile. There is a strong association between being housed in such temporary conditions and poor school performance and non-attendance at school. Success in securing employment for this group is also poor.

To date people living in bed and breakfast facilities have been less visible than rough sleepers. The Homelessness Act, 2002, however, requires local authorities to develop a coherent strategy to deal with and prevent homelessness in partnership with other housing providers. In relation to this new duty, Shelter has proposed that local authorities should seek to increase the supply of good-quality temporary housing, including the long- and medium-term leasing of private sector housing to local authorities or other social landlords and to improve financial support for temporary housing by improved housing benefit processes and improved financing of short-life temporary housing to make them habitable for the short and medium term.

At the moment there is no clear mechanism for social work departments to be informed about the presence of homeless families living in bed and breakfast accommodation in their area. Yet the children of such families are clearly 'CHILDREN IN NEED', although the evidence seems to suggest that statutory child care authorities rarely get involved unless a CHILD PROTECTION issue comes to light (see also FAMILY SUPPORT).

P. Vostanis and S. Cumella, *Homeless Children, Problems and Needs*, London: Jessica Kingsley, 1999.

behavioural (and emotional) difficulties a defined category of SPECIAL EDUCATIONAL NEEDS (SEN) or LEARNING DIFFICULTY in which children's educational development is significantly impaired as a result of emotional and social factors. This may be in addition to issues affecting cognitive or sensory development. Not all children who misbehave or who are subject to EXCLUSION FROM SCHOOL have 'behavioural needs' under SEN procedures. Where problems in learning persist as a result of behavioural problems, schools should take action under the SPECIAL EDUCATIONAL NEEDS CODE OF PRACTICE, as either SCHOOL ACTION or SCHOOL ACTION PLUS. The child's INDIVIDUAL EDUCATION PLAN should address his or her behavioural needs in addition to any other learning difficulties.

behavioural assessment observation and detailed recording of the behaviour of a person, with the aim of understanding why he or she engages in it.

A behavioural ASSESSMENT begins with an exploration of problems. In doing this, it is important to acquire as much information as possible regarding the behaviour that is considered difficult. The aim is to describe a selected behaviour in as much detail as possible: what it is, who is doing it, the conditions under which it occurs and whether it is to be increased or decreased. Behavioural assessment avoids vague formulations and judgmental statements, such as 'He is badly behaved.' Instead, the assessment should include specific and descriptive statements, such as 'The boy scatters the pots and pans over the kitchen floor approximately four or five evenings a week.' It is critical to establish a BASELINE – the number of times a person engages in the particular problem behaviour – before any intervention is organized. The final element of a behavioural assessment is FUNCTIONAL ANALYSIS, which attempts to discover the purpose that the behaviour serves for the individual who engages in it.

As with other forms of social work assessment, it is acknowledged that the person being assessed, his or her family members and other people such as carers must take part to the fullest extent possible in the assessment and be a party to any decisions taken.

behaviourism a theoretical approach to explaining human development and activity, the central belief of which is that behaviour is the outcome of learning.

Behaviourism is a school of PSYCHOLOGY that considers humans as biological organisms reacting to stimuli in the environment. It argues that internal states such as thoughts, intentions and feeling are not observable and replicable, hence not amenable to scientific analysis, nor the data of a valid science, preferring instead to study human behaviour in terms of stimulus and observable response. (See also BEHAVIOUR MODIFICATION.)

behaviour modification a method of teaching people to change their behaviour by the systematic use of reinforcements and, infrequently, low level forms of punishment. It is based on LEARNING THEORY.

In general, behaviour modification programmes aim to reduce unwanted behaviour – such as tantrums, acts of self-mutilation or dependency on alcohol – and to increase positive or socially appropriate behaviour in its place. Several points are fundamental to behaviour modification:

1 all behaviour, even extreme problem-behaviour, is viewed as serving a purpose for the individual who engages in it;

2 strong emphasis is placed on defining problems in terms of behaviour that can be observed rather than looking for psychological roots of a problem in the person's past;

3 the CLIENT can learn other, more effective behaviours;

4 the behaviour to be reduced, along with the behaviour to be increased, must be measurable, since measurement is the best indicator of the extent to which a problem is being resolved.

The simplest way to increase particular behaviours, according to learning theory, is to reward, or reinforce, the person engaging in that behaviour. A *reinforcer* can be something *tangible*, such as toys, trips, preferred activities or preferred foods, or *intangible*, such as attention, praise, a hug, personal satisfaction or increased effectiveness in completing a task. A reinforcer is particular to an individual, however, and may not resemble a typical reward; one cannot assume that what acts as a reinforcer for one person will do so for another. For example, for some children a reprimand acts as a reinforcement rather than a punishment and increases rather than decreases the possibility that the behaviour that caused the reprimand will happen again. So behaviourists define a reinforcer as anything that increases the likelihood that the behaviour in question will be performed again.

Part of any effective behaviour modification programme relies on discovering what it is that acts as a reinforcer for each individual. Once identified, any reinforcement should be made immediately after the selected behaviour occurred and should be applied consistently and with conviction. The approach can be particularly effective in working with children with behaviour problems. For example, the parents and teachers of a seven-year-old boy report that he is unable to sit still for more than a few seconds. Because of this it has been impossible to teach him to read, to sit for meals or to use the toilet. They agree that teaching him to sit still is the target behaviour, since other activities will follow from that. They further agree to teach the boy to sit still for one minute and listen to instructions. Reinforcers are chosen that are attractive enough to override the boy's continuous motion. In a room free of other distractions, the boy is asked to sit down and is then held and seated on a chair. Immediately he is praised and given a crisp and a cuddle. The process continues in short sessions of no more than ten minutes with some ten to twenty attempts at the task, each similarly reinforced.

Behaviourists have also used punishments following unwanted behaviour. These have tended to fall into one of four categories: physical punishments, reprimands, TIME OUT, and 'response costs' whereby the person who engages in unwanted behaviour loses a specified reinforcer. Punishments are used less and less, however, as behaviourists realize that they present considerable ethical dilemmas and are much less effective than reinforcement. Only time out is used with any frequency, particularly in work with children. In behaviourist language, it means 'time out from positive reinforcement' and involves removal of the child to a neutral space for no more than two to three minutes where he or she receives no stimulation or reinforcement, social or otherwise, but can still be kept in view. Parents of children with behaviour problems are often taught how to administer time out rather than to use physical punishment or shouted verbal reprimands.

The use of reinforcers and punishers has attracted much criticism from non-behaviourists, since their use seems to imply a mechanical and crude view of human nature. Bestowing reinforcers creates an imbalance of power that can be used for ends other than changing behaviour. For example, in the 1950s and 1960s token economies were introduced into wards in mental hospitals. This system allowed patients to 'earn' tokens for specified behaviours, the tokens being redeemable in terms of specific goods or privileges. In fact, token economies often encouraged psychiatric nurses to act as behavioural engineers and had more to do with controlling the patient population than with teaching more effective behaviour to individuals. Behaviourists now acknowledge that the techniques were often employed by under-trained staff and used for purposes other than what they were designed for. The use of punishments, such as electric shocks, ammonia vapours and prolonged tickling, has left a legacy that behaviour modification has found hard to live down.

Behaviour modification has proved particularly effective with people with learning disabilities and with children with conduct disorders. It has also been used in treating people with addictions and in assisting people to cope with specific anxieties such as fear of open spaces (agoraphobia).

B. Sheldon, *Behaviour Modification*, London, Tavistock, 1982.

behaviour support plan a programme of action drawn up by a local education authority (LEA) in consultation with other agencies that sets out the strategies to be employed to improve children's behaviour and to support schools in addressing their needs.

The plan will also include provision from outside schools and will outline the role of support agencies such as the EDUCATION SOCIAL WORK (or education welfare) service.

behaviour therapy the treatment of a psychological disorder by altering a person's perception of the consequences of a certain type of behaviour.

Behaviour therapy is based on the theories of BEHAVIOURISM, which states that certain types of behaviour (such as phobias) can be acquired as maladaptive learning responses. The types of treatment that can be described as behaviour therapy are diverse, including systematic DESENSITIZATION and MODELLING.

Benefits Agency the executive agency of the DEPARTMENT FOR WORK AND PENSIONS responsible for the adjudication and payment of social security benefits. See also JOBCENTRE PLUS.

bereavement the LOSS of a close and personally significant relationship through death.

Bereavement is often one of the most traumatic and personally disorientating experiences that can happen to people. It can lead to feelings of acute sadness and social isolation, and can often undermine the survivor's sense of meaning and purpose in life. For some, suicidal thoughts may feature strongly in their reactions.

The impact of bereavement will depend to a considerable extent upon the significance of the relationship to the person who survives. The closer the relationship, and particularly the extent of dependency of one upon the other, the greater the impact of the loss is likely to be.

Bereavement throws into sharp relief the 'belief system' of those who survive. People who belong to faith communities, for example, may find comfort in a set of beliefs that suggests a spiritual continuity beyond death. Others may find that the experience of death challenges them profoundly about what they believe, and throws up complex issues about whether or not life for them has a meaning and purpose. These can be highlighted by the decisions that have to be made for the funeral and other rites of passage.

Different cultures respond to bereavement in different ways. The stereotypical white British male response of not showing emotion publicly – of keeping responses to grief hidden and private, as illustrated by the monarchy for example – contrasts vividly with Black African/Caribbean or Middle Eastern responses, which are openly expressive of grief in a shared communal way. It is significant, however, that in recent years major events – such as the death of Diana, Princess of Wales in 1997, and the September 11 disaster in 2001 – released far more spontaneous and openly expressive reactions in many people than had previously been seen in the UK. These events may well have contributed to some movement away from the death-denying culture that commentators had previously noted.

By contrast, some people feel socially excluded from expressing their grief. Disenfranchized grief, for example, refers to people whose relationships cannot be publicly owned – some gay relationships, or people having secret affairs. In these situations, reactions to bereavement may be exacerbated.

Individual reactions to bereavement have been widely catalogued in the literature and may include feelings of shock, disbelief, anger, pain and depression, although for some there may also be feelings of relief, and even euphoria, at the ending of a particularly stressful or oppressive relationship.

Recent writers in this field are now emphasizing the complex and varied ways in which individuals respond to bereavement. The DUAL PROCESS MODEL, for example, highlights ways in which bereaved people can move constantly between dealing with their 'hurting losses' and 'getting on with their lives'.

Bereavement has attracted a variety of theoretical responses and 'models' of understanding. 'Illness' models talk in terms of the symptoms and the 'management' of bereavement. Biological explanations identify changes in cardiovascular and immune system functioning, and point to the enhanced activity of respiratory, endocrine and autonomic systems during acute grieving. 'Pyschodynamic' models focus on the slow and painful removal of libido (life energy) from the lost person and its attachment to someone or something new. ATTACHMENT theories talk about the instinctive responses that take place in times of bereavement and suggest that loss of an attachment figure precipitates crying, longing, searching, withdrawal, apathy and anxiety in attempts to recover the lost person. (See also GRIEF.)

Although bereavement as a result of death can provoke the most acute responses, other (seemingly) less significant events can produce similar feelings. Such events include divorce, serious illness and unemployment or redundancy.

N. Thomson (ed), *Loss and Grief – A Guide for Human Services Practitioners*, Basingstoke, Palgrave, 2002.

bereavement allowance see WELFARE RIGHTS 2.

Best Value a central government direction concerning the framework through which local government services should be evaluated and developed.

Best Value was established by the NEW LABOUR government as a replacement for Compulsory Competitive Tendering (CCT) and Value for Money Auditing. The aim of the process is to provide a framework for local government to develop services aimed at increasing the efficiency and effectiveness of provision. The process involves the need to consider four key processes when reviewing existing provision and service developments. These key processes are identified as Contrast, Consult, Compare and Compete. At the heart of this process is the need to examine services in the light of information about how other local authorities are performing, with the idea that good practice will be disseminated and the weakest authorities will improve their services. In addition, consultation with the public and service users is seen as a core feature of this approach. Through their involvement the value of services is identified and associated with meeting the needs of users and, therefore, increasing ACCOUNTABILITY to users and the electorate as a whole.

As part of the process, the AUDIT COMMISSION plays a role in identifying performance measures, and local authorities utilize these to establish whether they have attained the TARGETS they have set themselves. In practice, however, the emphasis is centred on the management objectives of economy and efficiency. There has been only limited evidence of increased consultation of users and the public, while central government is making use of information about social services to develop league tables on performance.

G. A. Boyne, *Managing Local Services: From CCT to Best Value*, London: Frank Cass, 1999.

better-off test see WELFARE RIGHTS 1.

Beveridge Report the official report of the wartime committee on social insurance chaired by W. H. Beveridge. Entitled *Social Insurance and Allied Services* and published in 1942, it is still regarded as providing the foundation for the modern WELFARE STATE.

Beveridge identified five major problems to be tackled in post-war Britain: 'want, disease, ignorance, squalor and idleness'. The report sought to address the first of these by introducing a comprehensive system of income maintenance. The report recommended the introduction of a social insurance scheme to cover loss of income resulting from unemployment, sickness and retirement. Benefits were to be paid at a flat rate, regardless of other forms of income, and were to be financed by flat-rate insurance contributions. Additional amounts were payable for dependants, mainly wives and children. The scheme also proposed the introduction of maternity grants and widows' benefits based on a husband's contributions, and death grants and maternity benefits for women who had paid contributions in their own right. Benefits were to be paid at a subsistence level. Although Beveridge intended the scheme to cover the majority of situations in which someone was unable to work, he recognized that there would be a need for a system of means-tested social assistance to provide a safety-net for people whose circumstances were not covered by the insurance scheme (see NATIONAL ASSISTANCE ACT 1948).

From the outset, Beveridge was clear that his social security scheme could succeed only if it were supported by other related areas of policy. He therefore recommended the introduction of child allowances to be paid for the second and subsequent child where parents were in work but to include the first child where the parents were in receipt of an insurance benefit. These allowances were intended to eliminate family poverty without undermining incentives to work or causing wage inflation. The system was to be further underpinned by a system of comprehensive health care and the avoidance of mass unemployment.

The Beveridge proposals were accepted almost without change with the passing of the Family Allowances Act 1945, the National Insurance Act 1946 and the National Assistance Act 1948. There were, however, a number of significant departures from the plan that had implications for its success and can still be felt today. First, the government rejected the proposal that the retirement pension should be phased in over a period of twenty years but allowed individuals to claim much earlier. The resulting loss in revenue meant that the levels of all benefits were much lower than Beveridge had envisaged. Second, entitlement to unemployment benefit was limited to one year rather than being paid indefinitely. Third, Beveridge's plan for a scheme of benefits to be paid on separation was rejected totally. The implications of these changes were that far more people were dependent on means-tested National Assistance than Beveridge had anticipated. The low rates of insurance benefits meant that many people had to claim National Assistance to cover their housing costs. Beveridge also made assumptions about the nature of family life and the position of married women in society that meant that their needs were inadequately catered for, while the growth and continued existence of high rates of unemployment have also exposed weaknesses in the plan. Failure to address the needs of LONE PARENT FAMILIES and people with sickness and disability who never work has also meant that these groups remain disadvantaged today. Reform since 1945 has attempted to fill some of these gaps but within the framework set by Beveridge.

bipolar disorder see MANIC DEPRESSION.

black perspective a view of issues that contains and reflects the reality of the experience of black people in Britain.

In Britain in the 1970s and 1980s many black commentators argued that the experiences of black people were not being heard or sought in relation to policy formation in the social welfare and justice systems. Often black history was not acknowledged at all, rendering black people marginal or anonymous even where, as in Liverpool and many other British seaports, they have formed part of the community for a very long time. More recently, black activists have been able to demonstrate that black people's concerns were not being recorded, let alone acted upon. The term 'black perspective' incorporates and acknowledges the different experiences and needs of black people living in Britain. Fundamentally, it includes bringing black people's knowledge, aspirations, analysis and developments to bear on issues faced by black communities and individuals, and also illuminating them for white communities. A key part of this process is to dislodge white people from positions of power and authority where they apparently speak for black people. The black perspective is motivated by a sense of current injustice for black people in Britain.

One of the key issues concerning the black perspective relates to how it is to be determined and expressed in social and political life. Does there need to be, for example, black representation in key political and policy-formation processes? Within a social work context, should black workers' groups be invited to give a black perspective on all issues or should the 'normal' democratic representational procedures be relied on to deliver a black view? How, in effect, is the 'tyranny of the majority' to be avoided and how can weight be given to minority views? (See also ETHNOCENTRISM, RACISM.)

B. Ahmed, *Black Perspectives in Social Work*, Birmingham: Venture Press, 1990.

Black Report see HEALTH; HEALTH INEQUALITIES.

blind and partially sighted registration social services departments keep a register of blind and partially sighted people living in their areas or ensure that this is done on their behalf.

The registration of people with VISUAL IMPAIRMENT is voluntary. While registration may still be required in order to access services from some local voluntary groups, to participate in some employment training schemes and to gain some financial concessions, most services and benefits are available without registration. The main purpose of registration is to assist in service planning.

The registration of blind people predates local authority registration of disabled people generally and was originally intended to identify potential claimants of financial benefits. Only people who have been examined by a consultant opthalmologist (eye specialist) and certified as blind or partially sighted can be registered. The National Assistance Act (1948) defines blindness as 'being so blind that they cannot do any work for which eyesight is essential'. However, a person need not be completely without sight to be registered blind. Generally, registration as blind is considered if a person can see at 3 metres what a 'normally' sighted person can see at 60 metres. This is referred to as 3/60 vision. Registration may also be considered for people with 6/60 vision if they have a restricted field of vision. Partially sighted people are defined for registration purposes as 'substantially and permanently handicapped by defective vision, caused by congenital defect or illness or injury'. Registration as partially sighted is considered for people with a visual acuity between 3/60 and 6/60 with a full field of vision or for people with very limited fields of vision. On receipt of the certification form, known as a BD8, from the consultant opthamologist, the social services department should make contact to find out whether the person would like to be included on the register and whether services are required. However, service users have reported long delays between certification and the assessment of their needs, and shortcomings in the services that are eventually offered. The experience of sight loss, medical diagnosis and certification can raise significant anxieties about the future, so prompt provision of support, information and services is crucial.

The Improving Lives Coalition, *Improving Lives: Priorities in health and social care for blind and partially sighted people*, London: RNIB, 2001.

Bliss symbol communication system a system of symbols that facilitates communication for people with limited speech and physical impairments.

Bliss symbols provide a means for people with multiple impairments to make their wishes known to care staff and informal carers. They are designed to be quick and easy to draw, and can be set out on conveniently placed communication boards. They do not rely on reading skills, but words can be added to the symbols so that they are easily understood by any staff who are not familiar with the system. People need to be able to indicate a symbol, but this can be done in a range of ways, including eye gaze.

Bliss symbols were originally created in 1949 by Charles Bliss, who believed that the development of a common world language would improve international understanding and make war less likely in the future. The language was first developed for disabled people in Canada in the 1970s. Although it has been associated with people with communication, language and learning disabilities, it allows for varying levels of abstraction and can be appropriate for people with a range of intellectual abilities. More applications for Bliss symbols have been devised as computer technology has developed. They have been used with speech synthesizers and incorporated within computer software. The latter has been particularly important since the development of the Internet, which has facilitated the use of Bliss symbols in international communication in line with the original aims of Charles Bliss. The advocates of Bliss symbols believe that disabled users are in a position to assist speaking persons to discover the benefits of communication between people who use different languages.

Braille a system of raised dots embossed onto paper that allows visually impaired people to use their fingers to read script. It is named after Louis Braille, who invented the system.

There are two levels of Braille. One spells out each word fully and the other uses abbreviations for recurring groups of letters or words. Braille texts tend to be bulky, however, which restricts the volume of material that it is practical to produce. Many visually impaired people prefer other means of reading text. About 19,000 visually impaired people use Braille, which is a minority of those registered as blind. Braille texts are usually produced by a transcription agency, but it is now possible to obtain computer software to convert word processing files into Braille.

breach proceedings legal proceedings whereby an offender placed on a COMMUNITY SENTENCE who fails to meet the requirements of the order may be returned to court for a fine or warning or to be re-sentenced.

breakfast clubs informal sessions prior to school each morning that provide children with breakfast and some activities before the start of the school day as well as care.

There is strong evidence to support the effectiveness of breakfast clubs. Children in a given area may be coming to school tired or hungry and unable to absorb the ideas or have the concentration for learning, no matter how good the teaching at school. Breakfast clubs meet a number of important objectives simultaneously:

1 they help to overcome 'food poverty' for families by providing a balanced meal at the beginning of the day;

2 they ensure that children start the school day on time, feeling well nourished and settled;

3 they enable parents to reconcile family and work life through the provision of a safe, supervised environment before school starts; they form part of the network of out of school child care that is vital support for families with school-age children;

4 they overcome educational difficulties arising from erratic attendance and poor concentration and behaviour, especially in the first years of primary school.

Breakfast clubs usually run from 7.30 or 8.00 a.m. until school begins. Children may attend one, two or more days a week depending on the working patterns of their parents or carers. The clubs can take place in schools or community centres and usually combine the opportunity to eat with other activities, whether free play, arts or homework, depending on the age of the children. They may be organized by the local authority, voluntary agency, local businesses or by schools themselves.

N. Donovan and C. Street, *Fit for School: How breakfast clubs meet health, education and childcare needs*, London: New Policy Institute, 1999.

British Association of Social Workers (BASW) the main professional body representing the interests of social workers in Britain.

The British Association of Social Workers is a relatively new professional association, having been founded in 1970. This was the result of a fairly long period of discussion between various social services associations under the auspices of the Standing Conference of Social Workers, established in 1963. Before 1970 social workers were organized in associations based on client or functionally related areas. These included the Association of Child Care Officers, the Association of Family Case Workers and the Institute of Medical Social Workers. The move towards a single professional association was stimulated by the recommendations of the SEEBOHM Committee for comprehensive social services departments in local authorities and by the trend towards generic social work rather than client-based approaches.

BASW now has a membership of approximately 9,000 professional social workers and in 1992 established a set of core purposes. According to its annual review for 1993, these purposes are: to promote and provide a focus for social work activities throughout the United Kingdom and through the International Federation of Social Workers; to promote rights, participation and partnership in the practice and development of social work services with the people who use them; to promote anti-oppressive policies and practice, and equality of opportunity, in social work activity and in the affairs of the association; to lobby and liaise on social policy and campaign to influence government and others; to promote BASW membership and local, regional and national activities; to promote the BASW code of ethics; to provide support services, advice and representation to all BASW members; and to develop and support staff care policies.

As the main representative body for social workers, the association plays an important part in the development and scrutiny of policy issues. It actively responds to policy proposals and guidelines emerging from the DEPARTMENT OF HEALTH and other government departments, and is regularly invited to give evidence before parliamentary select committees. BASW also employs a parliamentary adviser to brief Members of Parliament and Members of the Lords on social work issues. These pressure group activities are in addition to the association's role in supporting members in their relations with employers.

British Crime Survey (BCS) a survey carried out regularly by HOME OFFICE researchers by interviewing a large sample of people about their experiences as VICTIMS of crime.

The data collected by the survey illustrate the need for more than one source of information about the crime rate. Victim surveys of this kind invariably show that crime is under-reported and that particular kinds of crime are especially unlikely to be reported. BCS researchers have used computer-assisted interviewing techniques in an attempt to encourage discussion of sensitive offences, and extra samples of members of minority groups have been used to improve understanding of their experiences as victims.

British Sign Language (BSL) a visual language that is indigenous to the UK and used by members of the DEAF community.

British Sign Language is one of the languages used by deaf people. It is usually associated with movements of the hands but also comprises a range of gestures involving the arms, head and body, and also facial expression. BSL is not based on English spelling or grammar so has its own structure. It is estimated that BSL is the first or preferred language for 70,000 people. Organizations of deaf people seek official recognition of BSL in order to promote the rights of the deaf community.

'broken windows' see ZERO TOLERANCE.

budgeting loan see WELFARE RIGHTS 8.

bulimia an eating disorder involving periodic bouts of bingeing and dieting. Attempts to lose weight can include self-induced vomiting, going without food for lengthy periods and the excessive use of laxatives and dieting pills.

The condition seems to be particularly associated with women. Treatment includes trying to help women develop more positive views of themselves and to resist, as feminists see it, oppressive stereotypes of women's bodies.

bullying harassment, threats, intimidation or physical violence shown to a child by one or more other children, in school or elsewhere.

Bullying can include name-calling, text-messaging, racist and sexually motivated ABUSE, AGGRESSION and extortion of money or property as well as actual violence. Surveys suggest that large numbers of children are subjected to various forms of bullying at both primary and secondary schools. All schools should have policies and procedures designed to combat bullying and for dealing with incidents. There is often a strong association between bullying and other educational issues such as SPECIAL EDUCATIONAL NEEDS and TRUANCY. All local education authorities (LEAs) should have advisers to assist schools in developing appropriate responses. These may include classroom work and involving pupils through initiatives such as school councils and 'circle time' as part of the citizenship agenda or through personal, social and health education.

Cc

CAFCASS abbreviation for CHILDREN AND FAMILY COURT ADVISORY AND SUPPORT SERVICE.

capacity building developing the means to help residents in a local area to take control of their own affairs and to take a lead in solving their own problems.

Capacity building means teaching or creating the skills within local residents groups and organizations that enable them to engage in consultation, planning and implementation of new services. A local area's capacity to solve its own problems, however, depends also on the strength of its organizations, the levels of residents' participation and engagement in local affairs and the skills of local leaders. Knowing how to acquire and use political power and to engage in PARTNERSHIPS is therefore also part of the picture. Capacity building includes training, personal development, mentoring and peer support, based on the principles of empowerment and equality provided they ultimately benefit the neighbourhood. If capacity building can be reduced to one phrase it would be 'learning to acquire and to use power and influence to secure certain democratically determined objectives'.

Example of capacity building initiatives can include: development of vision and action plans, negotiating a written service agreement between the locality and the agencies involved, ensuring local representatives chair and have the majority of places on partnership boards and other forums, resident-led consultation, including street meetings, door-to-door surveys, and local planning events, resourcing and supporting resident involvement in developing new local organizations, such as credit unions, to the point where they manage the project and assets.

S. Skinner, *Building Community Strengths: A resource book on capacity building*, London, Community Development Foundation, 1997.

care component SEE WELFARE RIGHTS 3.

care management the process of identifying the social and health care needs of individuals in the community, together with the planning and delivery of integrated programmes designed to meet those needs.

Care management, or *case management* as it is often called, evolved, in the 1970s in the United States, where services are provided across numerous health and welfare organizations and the need for coordination is especially pressing. The concept was introduced into Britain in the 1980s in the form of pilot projects in certain health authorities and was subsequently given prominence by the Department of Health as the most effective way of overseeing individual CARE PLANS for people in the community. It has become popular because it seems to meet two different requirements: the effective coordination of services, and the containment of costs. Care management is a means to coordinate health and social care services to a named CLIENT; without such coordination, services from different providers with differently trained staff would be fragmented and not suited to the needs of the client.

The range of care management functions, undertaken by a *care manager* or *case manager*, varies with the agency and client group involved. There are, however, a number of functions in common. First is the initial ASSESSMENT OF NEED, involving service user, carer and other professionals, who reach agreement, with the care manager, on how needs will be met. Second is the drawing up of a plan, also agreed by all parties. Third is the negotiation of agreements, or contracts, with organizations providing the required services. Fourth is the monitoring of the plan through regular CASE REVIEWS to ascertain whether the agreed services are having the desired effect and, if not, to see how far the person's needs may have changed and require different services.

The aim of care management is to help stimulate a wider choice of services from both the statutory and the independent sectors. The interests and responsibilities of the care manager and associates who purchase the service are separate from those who provide it. The former are able to offer a NEEDS-LED ASSESSMENT and then to commission the services that the assessment has identified. But care management also includes responsibilities for cost containment, and local budgets will not necessarily cover the purchase of whatever services are required. As a result, there is considerable disagreement over how an individual's need that cannot be met should be recorded, if at all (see UNMET NEED).

Department of Health, Social Services Inspectorate and Scottish Office Social Work Services Group, *Care Management and Assessment Practitioners' Guide,* London, HMSO, 1991.

care order a court order under section 31 of the CHILDREN ACT directing a local authority to take into care a child named in the order. Only the local authority or the National Society for the Prevention of Cruelty to Children, as an 'authorized person', may apply for a care order.

For a care order to be made, the applicant must convince the court that the child is suffering, or likely to suffer, SIGNIFICANT HARM, and that this harm can be attributed to a standard of care falling below what a parent

could be reasonably expected to provide or to the child's being beyond
parental control. The applicant must also show the court how the care
order will benefit the child, by outlining a plan for the child and showing
why other alternatives, such as providing support services to the family,
will not work. Once an order is obtained, the local authority acquires
PARENTAL RESPONSIBILITY for the child, who then passes into its care,
although the necessity continues for parents and the local authority to
work in PARTNERSHIP. A care order lasts until the child is 18, unless the
order is discharged earlier by a court. An order cannot be made on a
young person who is 17 or who is 16 and married. Applying for a care
order is an extremely serious step that should be taken only after other
alternatives such as support services have failed.

The court will reserve the care order for the most serious cases where
the probability of significant harm to the child's health or development
is high and the willingness of parents to cooperate is low. Such an order
does not give the local authority the power to do whatever it likes with
the child, and parents do not lose their parental responsibility. The
authority may restrict the parents' exercise of their responsibility only
when it is satisfied that this is necessary to safeguard or promote the
child's welfare. Other sections of the Children Act require joint planning
and decision-making with parents, as well as consultation with the child
before a placement is made with FOSTER CARERS or in a CHILDREN'S
HOME. Throughout the duration of a care order the child's circumstances
must be regularly reviewed to evaluate whether the plan for the child is
working. The parents and others important to the child should be able
to visit at reasonable intervals or have other forms of CONTACT with the
child. Parents, the child or the local authority may appeal against a
decision to the HIGH COURT or apply for a discharge of a care order.

Department of Health, *Guidance to the Children Act. Vol. 1, Court Orders*,
London, HMSO, 1991.

care plan a written statement specifying the objectives for the future,
agreed by practitioners and users and their carers or family, outlining
the means by which those objectives are to be met.

Historically social work placed little emphasis on planning and, in
particular, on written plans; instead, it tended to put faith in the strength
of relationships between CLIENT and practitioner and in the latter's
counselling skills as the primary means by which obstacles and
difficulties, often primarily of an emotional nature, for the client would
be overcome. Plans, certainly written plans, were not deemed necessary
for such CASEWORK objectives. Even as social workers became more
involved in protective work with children, child-care plans, if they
existed at all, were rudimentary This lack of planning was critically
highlighted in a summary of research published by the Department
of Health (DoH) in 1986 as a chief reason why children were often the
subject of erratic decision-making by local authorities.

The DoH now requires local authorities to draw up substantial plans for adults who receive their services under COMMUNITY CARE arrangements and for children who are being LOOKED AFTER by the authority. For adults such a plan would usually begin with a statement of what the person's needs are, following ASSESSMENT. Although there is no one prescribed format for care plans for either adults or children, DoH guidance for both the CHILDREN ACT and the NATIONAL HEALTH SERVICE AND COMMUNITY CARE ACT has laid down what should be included in such plans. For children being looked after by the local authority, the DoH has developed the ASSESSMENT AND ACTION RECORDS, an effective and comprehensive format now widely in use.

care plan for older people the formal agreement reached as a result of an assessment of need within the framework of the NATIONAL HEALTH SERVICE AND COMMUNITY CARE ACT 1990.

It is a part of the care management process instigated by *Care Management and Assessment: Manager's Guide* in 1991, the government guidance that was central to how the reforms of the 1989 white paper *Caring for People: Community Care in the Next Decade and Beyond* were to be implemented. Following an assessment, a care plan is drawn up within the budget set by local authorities. The cost limits of a care plan relate to the local authority's definition of 'need' and the care for which it will take responsibility, which it sets out in its overall community care plan and which may vary significantly between local authorities. Good practice dictates that the plan should give specific details of what will be provided when and by whom, giving information about key personnel and how they can be contacted. It should also take account of the support that comes from family, informal networks and community resources and be regularly reviewed.

The thrust of changes in community care policy and legislation have been to make services more responsive to individual need. There was the hope that this would take a more holistic view of the service user and produce better outcomes. For some younger adults in the community, a person-centred planning approach to assessment and care planning does take account of educational, employment and leisure needs. For many older service users, however, the care plan does little more than document the input that will be made by the local authority to maintain physical daily living skills. Thus, for many older service users the social and emotional dimension of their lives is not addressed.

carer a person – often but not always a relative – responsible for looking after another person who cannot look after himself or herself in some or all respects. The care provided is likely to take place in domestic settings and to be largely without monetary reward.

The term describes a range of relationships whereby one person cares for another, sometimes solely, sometimes in conjunction with others. The level of dependence of the cared-for person varies enormously, from people largely able to look after themselves – except for, say, shopping – to others requiring almost constant attendance. Care involves a wide range of physically and emotionally tiring activities: bathing, assistance with basic bodily functions, help with personal hygiene, feeding, containment, home nursing, the management of personal finances, and organizing or liaising with health and social services. The care given may or may not be supplemented by DOMICILIARY and DAY CARE services provided by social welfare and health agencies. It is difficult to estimate the exact number of carers since it is not clear-cut the point at which informal 'helping' becomes caring. Research suggests that at least 70 per cent of carers are women, the remainder being men and children. Caring often imposes a financial cost for items such as extra heating, lighting and laundry. A limited number of carers are able to claim welfare benefits in recognition of their caring duties, but most are ineligible for help from the state. To care for someone means, in many instances, giving up the chance of paid employment, and such 'opportunity costs' are incalculable. Sadly, the government's National Carers Strategy, launched in 1999, simply did not address this issue. Carers are characterized as wanting 'the wellbeing of the cared for person; freedom to have a life of their own; to be able to maintain their own health; to have confidence in services and a say in service provision'. On the issue of income, the strategy had little to offer and fell significantly short of acknowledging the poverty that many carers face.

It was the NATIONAL HEALTH SERVICE AND COMMUNITY CARE ACT 1990 that brought the first official recognition of the needs of carers. The white paper preceding the Act, the Act itself and subsequent government guidelines made it clear that statutory service providers should do everything reasonably possible to assist and support carers. Further, there was an understanding that the needs of cared-for people and of carers may differ or even conflict; in these circumstances separate ASSESSMENT of NEED was perceived as a requirement, and this was subsequently legislated for by the Carers (Recognition and Services) Act 1995. This Act gave two new duties to local authorities: first, to assess the needs of carers if they (the local authority) were also undertaking an assessment of the needs of the 'cared-for' person and, second, to take account of the carer's assessed needs when making decisions about the services that may be offered to the person cared for. The Act did not permit a separate assessment of a carer's needs if the cared-for person did not want any services from social services departments. As a result, and because there was mounting evidence of relatively few carers in fact having their needs assessed (research conducted by the Carers National Association), pressure mounted for some more comprehensive legislation, culminating in the Carers and Disabled Children Act 2001. This Act now permits carers to have an independent assessment of their needs irrespective of the wishes or needs of the 'cared-for' person.

There are difficulties with the words 'care' and 'carer'. Both assume or imply that the domestic environment is a place of warm or loving reciprocal relationships between kin. Such connotations can disguise the feelings of duty and obligation that may be involved as well as the considerable levels of stressful work. Carers usually provide care because of a pre-existing relationship with the cared-for person; such relationships may contain a range of emotions, from hostility (including ELDER ABUSE) to affection, and from satisfaction to guilt. Feminist arguments indicate that assumptions about the loving nature of caring may be exploitative of carers in general and coercive in relation to people who are reluctant to undertake the task. It is suggested that a distinction can usefully be made between 'caring for' and 'caring about', the former implying the labour involved and the latter acknowledging the love or affection. Other criticisms of the term come from service users, particularly in the disability movement, who argue that it can diminish the reciprocity of relationships even where there is a need for physical care. Those who are cared for can also be care-givers, giving emotional support to partners and friends, and those who are carers have other dimensions to their lives that can be overlooked. Some assert the right to be cared for by people with whom they are not in a relationship, thus challenging the current policy emphasis on informal care. Recent research, *Without Us*, published by the charity Carers UK, claims that to replace existing carers with paid staff would cost the country the equivalent of a second NHS.

A key anti-oppressive task for social and health service workers is to create a climate in which it is possible for potential carers to reveal feelings about the extent to which they are willing, if at all, to undertake caring tasks and responsibilities.

Carers' support groups have burgeoned in the last few decades. Sometimes such groups are supported directly by social workers and by financial help from statutory sources; other such groups are organized on a SELF-HELP basis. There is no doubt that current statutory provision for vulnerable people rests upon the assumption that families and relatives will undertake the bulk of caring activities. The relief provided to carers under considerable stress is often negligible. Local authority assessments of carers' needs are heavily influenced by available resources, such as day-care centres, rather than by the actual needs of the individual carer. With more women working and with the increasing divorce rate – hence a potential loss of the daughter-in-law as carer – the assumptions held by the statutory services will have to be adjusted if current provision is to be maintained, if not improved.

The experience of Asian and Afro-Caribbean carers appears to be broadly similar to those of white British carers, except that there is generalized evidence that ethnic minority families use social services less than white British people (such as respite services), are even less likely to have their needs as carers assessed, experience greater poverty and, more likely in the case of Asian carers, spend more time in the caring role.

B. Bytheway and J. Johnson, 'The Social Construction of Informal Carers' in A. Symmonds and A. Kelly (eds) *The Social Construction of Community Care*, Basingstoke, Macmillan, 1998.

carer's allowance SEE WELFARE RIGHTS 3.

Carers and Disabled Children Act 2000 legislation that strengthens the right of carers to an assessment of their needs and extends the groups to which local authorities may make DIRECT PAYMENTS for community care services.

Under previous legislation, an informal carer could request an assessment of her or his own needs only if the person 'cared for' had agreed to being assessed for community care services. In some cases, this led to carers having no access to support services. The Carers and Disabled Children Act 2000 entitles carers aged over 16 who are caring for someone over 18 to request an assessment in his or her own right irrespective of whether the person 'cared for' has been assessed. Services can be provided directly to the carer, and this can be done in the form of direct payments. These direct payments, however, must concern the carer's needs and not services to meet the needs of the 'cared for' person. The Act also amends the Children Act 1989 so that local authorities can make direct payments to parent-carers as an alternative to providing services to the *child*. To encourage independence during the transition period, the Act extends direct payments to young disabled people aged 16 and 17 in lieu of all or some of the services they may need. However, parent-carers and young people are not allowed to use the direct payments in order to purchase services from relatives living in the same house. The Act also provides a system of vouchers that carers and disabled people who are assessed as in need can use in order to 'purchase' short-term respite breaks. It is envisaged that this will provide more flexibility as to when and where these breaks are taken.

The Carers (Recognition and Services) Act 1995 includes adult carers caring for adults, young carers under the age of 18 and parent-carers of disabled children in the groups whose needs can be assessed and taken into account when decisions are made about services for the 'cared for' person. However, the Carers and Disabled Children Act does *not* offer an enhanced right to assessment to any carer aged under 16 or to parent-carers of disabled children. Organizations representing the interests of carers have been critical of this and have pointed out that reliance on the Children Act is likely to lead to insufficient emphasis on the needs of carers.

Carers (Recognition and Services) Act 1995 an Act that provides CARERS with a statutory right to an ASSESSMENT of their NEEDS by the local authority.

In reforming the arrangements for community care provision in the early 1990s, the government recognized the substantial contribution made by unpaid carers to the care of those with needs arising from age, disability or illness. Following sustained advocacy by carers' organizations, there was formal recognition that such care was often provided at considerable personal cost and that carers' needs should be taken into account. The Carers (Recognition and Services) Act 1995 provides that when an assessment of need is taking place under section 47 of the NATIONAL HEALTH SERVICE AND COMMUNITY CARE ACT, anyone providing a substantial amount of care for the service user on a regular basis (excluding professional, paid carers) is eligible for a carer's assessment. The carer must request the assessment. This provision gives carers a statutory right to an assessment of *their* needs, and those needs must be taken into account when making decisions about what services might be offered to the service user. However, it places no obligation on the local authority to provide services. The legal mandate for services to carers is found in the CARERS AND DISABLED CHILDREN ACT 2000, which also allows a carer's assessment to take place in the absence of a community care assessment.

The needs of carers of disabled people are also covered by section 8 of the DISABLED PERSONS (SERVICES, CONSULTATION AND REPRESENTATION) ACT 1986, which requires a carer's ability and willingness to care to be taken into account when deciding on service provision for the disabled person under section 4. The duty arises whether or not the carer has requested such consideration.

Department of Health, *Caring For People: Community Care in the Next Decade and Beyond*, London, HMSO, 1989.

Care Standards Act 2000 legislation that brings together government proposals for improvement in social care. Essentially the Act is concerned with social care standards both in the workforce and in statutory, private and voluntary sector provision.

In relation to improving workforce standards, the Act set up a new body in October 2001, namely the GENERAL SOCIAL CARE COUNCIL (GSCC). This has responsibility for regulating the social care workforce by setting high standards for education and training, registering the trained workforce and setting codes of conduct and standards of practice. It also deals with matters of serious misconduct.

Other main provisions of the Act are to ensure that there are systems in place to monitor standards of care in children's homes and homes for vulnerable adults, in both the public and private sector. This remit also applies to non-NHS hospitals. Standards for domiciliary care to people living in their own homes and arrangements for fostering and adoption are also subject to monitoring. To support these developments a National Care Standards Commission has been set up whose key aim is to establish and maintain similar standards throughout the UK, and a new power for ministers allows statutory guidance to be issued on charges for residential care.

The Act also passed local authority responsibility for the regulation of child-minding and day care for under fives to the Early Years Directorate, a new branch of Ofsted (Office for Standards in Education).

case conference a formal meeting of representatives from different professions called to decide a course of action in relation to a particular person or family with whom they have been working.

Case conferences are often used where the client or service user concerned is in some degree of risk and there are a number of professionals involved with that person. Each case conference has a formal agenda, with a chairperson to manage proceedings. Its purpose is to exchange information, to discuss plans of action and to coordinate services in relation to the particular client or family. Typically, there may be from six to ten professionals present at a case conference, all of whom should have direct dealings with the service user(s) concerned. Workers attending may include the health visitor, the social worker and the social worker's line manager, who may well be the chair of the conference. Case conferences are particularly important in CHILD PROTECTION work, where representatives from the police and the local education authority are also usually present as well as the child's doctor. Such conferences can be either initial meetings or review meetings. Initial meetings are those that are triggered by some serious concerns about a child; review meetings are designed to chart progress in respect of some agreed CARE PLAN. The chief task of a child protection case conference is to decide whether to place the name of the child on the CHILD PROTECTION REGISTER after considering the child's circumstances and weighing the risks. Such conferences also may decide what course of action should be taken in relation to the child (for example, whether the social services department should apply for a CARE ORDER), but such decisions are only recommendations and not binding on the individual agencies participating in the conference.

Wherever possible, the conference should include members of the client's or service user's family or, indeed, the client or service user himself or herself, unless it is clearly not in his or her interests to be present. The decision to exclude a service user or child should be made consciously and explicitly recorded in order that such a decision might be challenged by the family or significant other. Parents of the child concerned (in the case of child protection case conferences) are frequently present for some of the conference although this is still a relatively new practice and many authorities have been slow to include parents in any decision making. Best practice certainly suggests that service users should be properly briefed about the functions and procedures of case conferences, that support should be provided by either the key worker or some other ADVOCATE to ensure that the service user is able to represent himself or herself adequately and to be able to question any of the participants to the conference.

case history a historical account of a person and his or her family, emphasizing significant events or factors that appear to 'explain' the individual's or family's problems. Some social welfare agencies prefer the term 'social history'. Health authorities use the term 'medical case records'.

Trends in relation to the RECORDING of case records have sometimes
stressed full case histories, at other times brief notes on the individual
and the family background. The consensus until the late 1960s, influenced
by therapeutic models of social work practice, was to keep full case
histories. Since then recording has become relatively brief and focused.
Recent research sponsored by the Department of Health, however, has been
critical of the lack of family background information in relation to children
in care. For long-term cases at least, the current practice is to keep fuller
accounts of case histories. Major practice dilemmas concern the keeping
of records and the issue of access. Regarding the former, the concern is
whether records should be kept for each individual in a family and whether
there should be a family file. With the latter the issue is who should have
access to the records and whether information might be kept confidential.
caseload management a system for monitoring cases allocated to a social
worker, adviser or counsellor. The concept is allied to the notion of
WORKLOAD MANAGEMENT, which differs only in that its primary concern
is all work and not purely CASEWORK.

Caseload management entails the supervision of cases to ensure that
workers deliver a good service. A supervisor will be concerned about
the quantity and range of a practitioner's work. A caseload should be
appropriate to the worker's experience, skills and interests, and it should
take account of the morale of the practitioner and any personal stress
he or she may be experiencing. An undiluted caseload of challenging
or distressing cases consistently allocated to somebody under pressure
is likely to lead eventually to a poor service and a less effective worker.
case management see CARE MANAGEMENT.
case review/case review system a process by which work by social welfare
workers is reassessed, taking stock of work done since the case was
opened or since the last review. If new problems emerge or earlier plans
have proved unhelpful, a new plan should emerge from the review.

A *case review* is a key event in a piece of long-term CASEWORK. Reviews
offer an opportunity for a further appraisal of the effectiveness of work
undertaken to date and a chance to devise and implement new plans if
necessary. They should prevent drift in casework and ensure that long-
term work continues to have a focus. Long-term goals can usefully be
broken down into shorter-term objectives. Like case conferences, reviews
should involve as far as possible all concerned parties, including the focal
person and his or her family unless there are exceptional reasons for
exclusion. The spirit of user involvement in social work currently makes
such PARTICIPATION more likely.

The *case review system* determines the frequency with which cases are
to be looked at anew. Some systems have fixed intervals between reviews;
others are more flexible, with the interval decided according to the
merits of the case. Review system can have other functions, including
the collection of critical data about an organization's work.

casework a way that social workers, advisers and counsellors work with individual people and families.

The term was widely used among social workers in the 1950s and 1960s, when all casework was thought to entail the giving of support to the person or 'ego' and/or seeking to help him or her achieve insight into problems and effect permanent change. The work could be undertaken in families or with individuals. Social work as therapy, with the social worker as therapist, was the model, influenced by PSYCHOANALYSIS. The problems experienced by the person or family were considered amenable to the influence of the social worker (therapist), and external factors (such as poor housing or debts) were regarded as less important in unravelling the difficulties.

Casework later came to include additional aspects, such as liaising with other organizations with whom the service user had a problem. For the worker to act as an advocate was seen as consistent with casework, as was mediation and the giving of technical advice. Thus casework came to acquire a wider meaning, although it was still regarded as work with individuals and families. It also came to be seen as one form of social work among many, including GROUPWORK and COMMUNITY WORK. Problems might now be solved or eased by non-therapeutic methods or combinations of methods.

The RADICAL SOCIAL WORK movement of the 1970s was extremely critical of the casework method, which it perceived as rooted in the belief that problems were to be explained by personal or individual failure rather than by wider social causes, such as unemployment, poor housing and poverty Casework was thought to actively inhibit the service user from understanding the structural origins of his or her problem. However, a radical form of casework is currently considered possible, with individual work in a variety of guises now deemed necessary in some circumstances (such as feminist COUNSELLING in relation to domestic violence or rape) as a prelude to understanding wider issues. Casework in this sense has a secure place in social work, ADVICE and counselling practice, although it no longer has its former monopoly.

J. G. Barber, *Beyond Casework*, Basingstoke, Macmillan, 1991.

catharsis the revealing and re-experiencing of unresolved emotions that accompanied past traumatic events in order to bring them to resolution.

The process of catharsis assumes that past traumatic events and the feelings engendered by them have not been resolved and that unresolved emotions are affecting current behaviour, thoughts or feelings. Catharsis occurs where the re-experiencing of past events and associated emotions leads to a resolution of the person's difficulties (see CRISIS INTERVENTION).

caution an alternative to charge and prosecution, replaced in England and Wales by REPRIMANDS and FINAL WARNINGS under the 1998 CRIME AND DISORDER ACT.

A formal caution is intended to divert offenders who admit their guilt from the court process. Although this was a successful way of keeping offenders out of the criminal justice system, it was replaced in England and Wales with the more interventionist system of reprimands and final warnings, administered by the police, in 2000. Final warnings now include a referral to the YOUTH OFFENDING TEAM (YOT) in the case of offenders under the age of 18. The YOT must consider providing a programme of intervention in all such cases. Some police services operate 'restorative cautions' where the victim is not present but an attempt is made to ensure that the young offender comes to understand the victim's perspective.

In Northern Ireland and Scotland, different arrangements apply. In Northern Ireland, the police are able to give 'advice and warning' to young people misbehaving or committing offences, and also formal cautions. The latter can include restorative cautions. Around one in 20 adult criminal cases is deal with by means of caution. In Scotland, the police and prosecutors have the power to give warnings, and the term caution is not used.

centile chart a chart on which the growth in height and weight of a child are plotted and compared with national averages.

Children tend to grow at a regular rate, and this simple fact is used to assist in recognizing when a child has suffered some disturbance. Depending on weight and height at birth, a child should proceed to grow along a recognized curve, or centile, which is simply the average for a child of similar height and weight at birth. But a child may stop growing in some way when emotionally upset over a long period of time or inadequately fed or ill. An unexplained change in the rate of growth can be a sign of the child's FAILURE TO THRIVE. To be of use, the charts require regular measurement of the child in question. Young infants are usually measured by HEALTH VISITORS at specific intervals. School-age children for whom there might be concern can be monitored by the school doctor. Social workers often use this information to help them to decide whether a child is being abused or not.

chaining a method of teaching a person a new skill or activity by breaking it down into small steps or behaviours and reinforcing the mastery of each part until the entire chain is learned and the skill or activity can be performed.

Chaining is frequently used in work with people with LEARNING DISABILITIES who need to learn ordinary skills of day-to-day living, such as dressing themselves, eating with utensils, shopping or using public transport.

challenging behaviour a broad spectrum of behaviours that can be aggressive, unpleasant or highly attention seeking and can adversely affect the health and safety of those who engage in it and their carers.

Challenging behaviour includes self-injury, destructiveness, verbal threats, screaming and tantrums, inappropriate sexual conduct and physical aggression such as biting or pinching. The term originally referred to behaviour displayed by some young people and adults with LEARNING DISABILITY that was dangerous to themselves or other people, or was sufficiently unacceptable to limit significantly their opportunities for living in the community or going out into public places. Treatment was usually a form of BEHAVIOUR MODIFICATION, which often proved at least partially effective although in some programmes interventions were unacceptably punitive. Other interventions included the use of psychotropic drugs, methods encouraging relaxation and attempts to improve the person's communication skills.

More recently the term has been used in relation to behaviour by other groups of service users including young offenders and young people who are in SECURE ACCOMMODATION, adults with MENTAL HEALTH PROBLEMS and confused OLDER PEOPLE. In each case the behaviour poses dilemmas for social work and social care professionals. How far, for example, can the actions be tolerated of an older confused male resident who repeatedly throws his dinner at residential staff? How often can a young male with mental health problems living in a small GROUP HOME be allowed to verbally abuse others living in the same home or in the neighbourhood? The key issues for social workers are the same across all users who engage in challenging behaviour: the degree to which the person's behaviour is a threat to himself or herself or others and how far other people are willing to put up with that behaviour, which can be extremely disruptive.

E. Emerson, *Challenging Behaviour* Cambridge, Cambridge University Press, 2001.

charging policy the policy followed by a LOCAL AUTHORITY with regard to charges for its services. Authorities have significant discretion in this area.

In the field of social services, charges for RESIDENTIAL CARE are controlled by statute. By contrast, charges for DOMICILIARY SERVICES are governed by the Health and Social Services and Social Security Adjudication Act 1983, of which section 17 allows an authority 'to recover such charge (if any) for a service they consider reasonable'. A reasonable charge relates to the cost of providing the service and to the means of the service user. Although this is a matter for individual consideration in each case, authorities will sensibly devise a charging policy that provides an immediate assessment in the majority of cases. Authorities concerned with ANTI-POVERTY issues generally devise a policy compatible with the rules of MEANS-TESTED BENEFITS to ensure that charges do not form a barrier to service use.

charity a non-profit-making organization registered with the Charities Commission that seeks to dispense services and sometimes grants to people in need.

Charities have different practices and different terms of reference. Some deal directly with potential recipients of their services and/or grants; others deal with intermediaries such as social workers; yet others work only through other organizations. Some charities are extremely modest, with very specific objectives within perhaps a very small area. Others are immensely rich, with wide terms of reference and perhaps serving an area as large as the whole of Britain. Many VOLUNTARY organizations are also charities.

Social workers and others working in social welfare are often employees or members of management committees of, or VOLUNTEERS with, charities. More frequently, perhaps, social workers make appeals to charities on behalf of service users in need. Many workers feel uneasy about this practice, especially if the need arises from poverty or disability This unease rests upon the view that, first, the state ought to meet these basic needs and, second, the kinds of account of CLIENTS' difficulties that charities find persuasive smack of the 'deserving poor'. Some also make the point that the use of charitable funds or services inhibits the realization of a more just society because ideas of charity and of discretion obscure the need for basic rights in relation to, for example, an adequate income for all or the ability of a disabled person to participate in society on equal terms with able-bodied people. Workers prepared to appeal to charities on behalf of people in need argue that present problems need present solutions and that they wish to deal with a problem immediately in order to enhance people's LIFE CHANCES.

A charitable organization is one that is designed to provide something of benefit, in cash or in kind, to people. The Charities Act 1993 provides the legislative framework for agencies to be registered as charities. The established categories of charitable objectives are the relief of poverty (and the associated relief of unemployment), the advancement of religion, the advancement of education, and other activities beneficial to the community (including urban and rural regeneration).

Many social work and social welfare agencies in the voluntary sector are charities. In fact, their legal status can vary substantially, from unincorporated associations to companies limited by guarantee and other legal entities. The advantages of charitable status include tax relief of various kinds; the disadvantages for some will be the restriction on political activity since charities cannot be involved in party political activity. They can, however, be involved with politics in order to further their own agency's objectives or to provide information to groups and parties explicitly involved in politics (such as parliamentary briefings).

A new Charities Bill has been considered by the House of Lords and will be discussed by the House of Commons in 2006.

J. Reason, R. Hayes, and D. Forbes, *Voluntary but not Amateur*, London, London Voluntary Service Council, 2000.

child abuse physical or psychological harm done to a child through a deliberate act or neglect.

Social workers have to work with several forms of child ABUSE. PHYSICAL ABUSE is the intentional use of physical force to hurt, injure or kill a child. Social workers are not expected to diagnose with certainty whether a child has been abused or not, but they are expected to be alert to suspected cases of abuse so that they can initiate a CHILD PROTECTION investigation. To do this, they require some familiarity with injuries that might have been deliberately inflicted on a child (often called 'non-accidental' injuries). Some knowledge of the difference between accidental bruising and non-accidental injury assists in this recognition. The former usually occurs where bone is close to the skin, such as the forehead, shins or knees. The latter is more frequently present on soft parts of the body, such as the cheeks, buttocks, upper legs and mouth. Bruises caused by an adult slapping or grabbing a child often leave a distinctive mark, such as several finger bruises. Burns, particularly cigarette burns and scalds from hot liquids, and frequent fractures are other injuries deliberately inflicted. Social workers also encounter children harmed through neglect: the persistent lack of attention paid to the child's needs by his or her parents or carers. Pre-school children are most vulnerable to neglect, which can take the form of injury in repeated accidents, for example burning a hand in an unguarded fire, weight loss or abnormally slow growth rates (see FAILURE TO THRIVE). Social workers also work with children who have been sexually abused. Child SEXUAL ABUSE can take several forms: exposure, such as the viewing of sexual acts, pornography and exhibitionism; molestation, that is, the fondling of genitals, either the child's or the adult's; sexual intercourse – oral, vaginal or anal – without the use of force and over a period of time; and rape, that is, intercourse achieved by use of force.

Although injuries to an abused child can be extreme, detection of abuse is rarely easy and is usually achieved only by the pooling of knowledge and expertise by both professionals and lay people. Health visitors, pre-school playgroup assistants, teachers, general practitioners and medical staff at hospital emergency units as well as paediatricians, social workers and police all play important roles in this task. Often the children's own willingness to speak to someone confidentially about the abuse happening to them or the observations of non-abusing parents are critical to detection. Children's accounts of the experience of abuse have in the past been treated sceptically by many child-care professionals, but it is now commonly recognized that children often do tell the truth, and each child's account is taken seriously. The social worker's task is to assemble all the information and opinion. Frequently a child protection CASE CONFERENCE, attended by professionals and others who work with the child, as well as by the child's parents, will be held to appraise precisely the nature of the abuse that has taken place.

There has been some attempt to develop 'indicators', factors that, when present in a child's life, might suggest an increased likelihood of abuse of that child. Such indicators usually include a young (teenage) mother without support, an infant who was premature or of low birth weight, a previous history of violence in the family, alcoholism, and one parent who was abused as a child. Indicators have been heavily criticized by feminist practitioners as apparently laying the responsibility for abuse with the mothering of the child and ignoring the fact that the great majority of abusers, particularly child sex abusers, are male. Others have argued that heavy emphasis on child abuse and child protection has seriously skewed the nature of social work, which has become excessively cautious and defensive as a result, relying more on compulsory legal action than on the development of preventive and support services for families. It is important to underscore that the incidence of child murders has fallen dramatically in the United Kingdom since 1973, with the biggest drop being among infants. For all the publicized failures of SOCIAL SERVICES DEPARTMENTS to protect certain children, children are relatively more protected now than they were twenty years ago.

H. Owen and J. Pritchard (eds), *Good Practice in Child Protection: A Manual for Professionals*, London, Jessica Kingsley, 1994.

child abuse inquiries public inquiries held to examine why particular children were assaulted or killed when SOCIAL SERVICES DEPARTMENTS were involved in the cases.

There have been a number of major inquiries as to why children have been harmed or killed by adults in the family while the children were either under the direct supervision of social workers or known to a social services department. Some of the inquiries investigated the way certain residential children's homes systematically abused children in their care, such as those in Leicestershire, Staffordshire and North Wales. Others examined the cases of children killed by parents, step-parents and partners in the family, and why social workers and other professionals failed to protect them even when their circumstances were familiar to those professionals. This second group includes the inquiries into the deaths of Kimberly Carlisle, Jasmine Beckford, Lucy Gates and Tyra Henley. Each inquiry in this group published detailed reports that gave precise accounts of what happened, including the day-to-day actions of the social workers involved and their immediate line management. They often made stinging criticisms of the conduct of both social workers and their departments. Both the hearings and the reports themselves were extensively covered in the media, partly because of the distressing nature of the children's deaths and partly because of the heavy criticisms directed at the way the professionals working with the children failed to take sufficient protective action in time. A third group of inquiries dealt with instances where social services departments were deemed to have overreacted and removed children from families unnecessarily (see CLEVELAND INQUIRY).

The inquiries were usually conducted along quasi-judicial lines, either formally or informally, with a prominent barrister or judge overseeing the accumulation of evidence and testimony and writing the report. Most of the reports offered important recommendations regarding changes in the law, social work practice and communication between professional agencies. In general, the reports focused on the particular circumstances of the family concerned and paid little attention to the effects of environmental disadvantage on the family and on the behaviour of the abuser. The inquiry into the death of Tyra Henley was a notable exception, as it also looked at the impact of poor housing conditions on the family. The inquiries also concentrated on the family as recipients of a service, so many of the recommendations have to do with improving inter-agency communication as a means of enhancing that service rather than with wider issues of social policy.

The inquiry in 2002 into the death of Victoria Climbié the year before re-ignited the concerns that child protection systems were still overly prone to error and lapses in communication.. Victoria was a black girl from West Africa who died in 2000 at the hands of private FOSTER PARENTS after a prolonged period of physical abuse. The case triggered one of the longest and most contentious inquiries into the death of a child while under supervision by a social services department. The long-running hearing of evidence exposed a story of evasion of responsibility, ignorance of procedures and extremely poor communication skills among managers, health authority and local authority social workers alike. In the course of the inquiry a number of issues came to light. The practitioners and managers from the London social services department involved in Victoria's case revealed a picture of disengagement and failure to follow through with concerns passed on by other agencies. The picture was complicated, however, by the fact that both the field social worker and the police constable involved in the case were black, as were Victoria's African-Caribbean foster parents. This resulted in charge and counter-charge of racism. It was alleged that the black social worker made an assumption on the basis of skin colour alone, and on this basis decided that Victoria was in safe hands. (The social worker admitted at the inquiry that she had not known that Victoria was from the Ivory Coast so had not picked up the profound cultural difference between the child and her foster parents.) But the inquiry also showed that senior managers had emphatically distanced themselves from taking any responsibility for Victoria's death (and were promoted to better jobs) while the local council members had slashed the spending of the authority by some 40 per cent the year before, leaving the department seriously under-funded. The results of the inquiry point to a general failure of the system and highlight the extreme reluctance of all the major protagonists to assume any responsibility for the tragedy.

Department of Health, *Child Abuse: A Study of Inquiry Reports 1980–1988*, London, HMSO, 1991.

child assessment order an order under section 43 of the CHILDREN ACT requiring any person in a position to do so to produce the child named in the order for ASSESSMENT.

To obtain a child assessment order, the applicant, which may be the local authority or the NSPCC, must have reasonable cause to suspect that the child is suffering or is likely to suffer SIGNIFICANT HARM, that assessment of the child is necessary in order to establish whether that harm has occurred or is likely to occur, and that the required assessment would be unlikely to take place without the order being made. If the court grants the order, it can also direct where, when and how the assessment will take place. Only very rarely will the assessment involve the child in an overnight stay away from home. The maximum duration of the order is seven days from the date specified in the order. The child can refuse to undergo the arranged assessment, since the Children Act allows children of sufficient age and understanding to refuse medical or psychiatric examination although the court can, and has, overruled the child's refusal. Since the passage of the Children Act over a dozen years ago social workers have sought very few such orders.

child benefit see WELFARE RIGHTS 5.

child guidance a service for school-age children with emotional, behavioural or educational problems (or some combination of these problems). The service is provided by education departments of LOCAL AUTHORITIES, although such services often work in close collaboration with SOCIAL SERVICES DEPARTMENTS.

Child guidance clinics provide MULTIDISCIPLINARY teams of social workers and EDUCATIONAL PSYCHOLOGISTS with access to psychiatric services. REFERRALS are usually from general practitioners, schools or social services departments, although other routes are possible. Clinics often offer FAMILY THERAPY services too, given that many problems of children are located within families rather than solely in the children themselves.

child-minders people who look after children for reward, in domestic premises, usually their own homes, during the day. Child-minders must be registered with, and approved by, the LOCAL AUTHORITY under the CHILDREN ACT.

Child-minders – almost always women, often with children of their own – look after pre-school and school-age children up to the age of eight. The local authority will inspect the premises for safety and to see that they provide a stimulating environment. A good child-minder will play with the child, provide intellectual stimulation, companionship, food and warmth, and take the child on excursions. Child-minders and parents should work in collaboration to ensure agreement on all important matters affecting the child as well as establishing a clear understanding regarding fees, hours of attendance and sickness and holiday arrangements. Child-minders are expected to share with parents any important information about the child that they pick up while with the child. They may be deregistered by their authorities if the care they give is seriously inadequate with regard to the child's racial origins or religious or cultural needs; the authority can provide training on these and related matters. The extent to which child-minders may discipline children in their charge has become a hotly debated issue, with one minder taking her local authority to court to establish her right to smack a badly behaved child. The importance of child-minding as a family support service has been under-scored by the Children Act's emphasis on day care for CHILDREN IN NEED.

child poverty the particular impact that poverty has on children's lives, especially in terms of their social, emotional and intellectual development.

The numbers of children in the UK affected by poverty are among the highest in the developed world. Recent studies have shown that Britain has the third highest proportion of children in poverty overall and the highest of any European country. In 1998–9 a record four and a half million children were living in households with less than half the average national income after housing costs. By this standard, one in three children were living in poverty, twice the rate in France or the Netherlands and over five times that in Norway and Sweden. The realization that poverty in childhood increases the likelihood of exclusion in later adult life only further underscores the costs of childhood exclusion. While the Labour government elected in 1997 has estimated that specific new measures will lift over a million children out of poverty, this will merely bring the number of poor children roughly into proportion with the number of poor adults. The Joseph Rowntree Foundation has developed several indicators for computing the number of children living in poverty and SOCIAL EXCLUSION. Among them are:

1 the number of children living in workless households;
2 children living in households with below half-average income;
3 low birth-weight babies – revealing persistent inequalities in health;
4 births to girls under the age of 16.

Practitioners can assist families in poverty by INCOME MAXIMIZATION, arranging DAY CARE for children and other FAMILY SUPPORT services, and working with residents of low-income neighbourhoods to improve the level of services.

Joseph Rowntree Foundation, *Poverty and Social Exclusion in Britain*, York, 2000.

child protection action taken by social workers and others to safeguard children from harm.

Child protection is the general term for the measures, steps and procedures taken when an initial assessment has determined that a child is suspected to be suffering or is likely to suffer SIGNIFICANT HARM. Although social workers play a lead role in individual cases, steps to protect a child are almost always the result of intensive collaboration between SOCIAL SERVICES DEPARTMENTS – including management, doctors and paediatricians, health visitors and police. Generally, the more complicated the case and the graver the ABUSE of the child, the more intensive is the collaboration among professionals.

There are a number of steps involved when there are suspicions of significant harm. If a social services department has reasonable cause to believe that a child is suffering or is likely to suffer significant harm, it must carry out inquiries under section 47 of the CHILDREN ACT to determine whether it should take any action to safeguard or promote the child's welfare. The FRAMEWORK FOR ASSESSMENT OF CHILDREN IN NEED provides a structured approach for gathering and analysing the appropriate range of information required. It also guides practitioners in preparing to make the difficult decision on how to intervene, if at all. The inquiries must be carried out by a social worker from the local authority social services department after it receives a REFERRAL or has cause for suspicion. Such referrals come from doctors, teachers or playgroup assistants but can also come from neighbours or members of the child's family. The information includes obtaining the child's views on the situation, interviewing the child where appropriate and exploring with the parents the circumstances in which the alleged abuse took place. Other information is obtained from professionals already working with the child or family. Even this early stage of the work poses difficult decisions for social workers, since to begin such an investigation means accumulating information on the child and the family and beginning discussions with the child's parents about the alleged abuse. Most families find such an investigation intrusive, so a decision to begin investigation has to be taken carefully.

The aim of any child protection inquiries under section 47 is to judge whether or not immediate action must be taken to protect the child. Where there is a risk to the life of the child or a likelihood of serious immediate harm, action must be taken urgently to secure the safety of the child. This is done through an EMERGENCY PROTECTION ORDER (EPO) by one of the three agencies empowered by law to do so: the social services department, the police or the NSPCC. Emergency action can be necessary at any point in involvement with the family even before section 47 inquiries have been completed. The decision to take immediate action will be based on the nature of the cause for concern and the parents' reaction to it; the child's age or vulnerability; the knowledge of, and whereabouts of, an alleged perpetrator; past knowledge of the family; and the capacities of the parents. Obtaining such information can take place in a tense, or even hostile, atmosphere and requires social workers to be skilful in their interviewing techniques, careful in their recording of the information and calm in the face of considerable pressure.

The Department of Health guidelines on the conduct of child protection inquiries, *Working Together to Safeguard Children*, published in 1999, states that planned emergency action should normally take place following an immediate *strategy discussion* between police, social services and other agencies, such as the NSPCC and a senior medical practitioner if they are involved. If action must be taken urgently this discussion on strategy should follow as soon as possible to plan the next steps. In addition to the EPO, practitioners can also consider the use of EXCLUSION ORDERS under the FAMILY LAW REFORM ACT 1996 or rely on POLICE PROTECTION powers under section 46 of the Children Act. Social workers should obtain legal advice before taking any legal action.

The strategy discussion should determine whether section 47 inquiries should be initiated, plan how they should be conducted, including the need for medical treatment, and determine what information about the strategy should be shared with the family. The strategy discussion also determines who should be interviewed, by whom, for what purpose and when. These are vital matters, particularly when a crime may have been committed, since they have important implications for gathering evidence. (See INVESTIGATIVE INTERVIEWING.)

Following section 47 inquiries, the social worker and agency have several courses of action available to them. One is to determine that the concerns over the likelihood of significant harm are not substantiated so no further action is needed. This is the outcome in the great majority of referrals. However, because a large number of children subject to child protection inquiries fall within the definition of CHILDREN IN NEED, there may be reason to provide FAMILY SUPPORT services, such as a place at a FAMILY CENTRE. Another outcome is the conclusion that while the child has been thought to have suffered significant harm, he or she is not in continuing risk. The parents may be cooperative in taking action to ensure the child's safety, a perpetrator of abuse may have left the household or other family members or, indeed, the child's own view of the situation may shape this outcome..

If, however, the child is judged to be at continuing risk, long-term planning, possibly involving court orders, is required. If so, it is necessary to call a child protection CASE CONFERENCE in order to get a multi-disciplinary view on matters such as the child's health and development, parental capacity to ensure safety and future action, including the long-term removal of the child. (See also FAMILY GROUP CONFERENCE.)

Child protection work can also mean working long-term with the family of the abused child. This may include drawing up a written agreement with the family specifying the plan for the child's return and how the family will then work to safeguard the child's welfare, plus arrangements for monitoring, such as attending a family centre. This work may involve the social worker in providing family support services or guidance to the family on matters of discipline. It can also entail arranging for more specialist work to be undertaken with the abuser, such as techniques for controlling anger or containing sexual impulses.

No aspect of social work has caused more controversy with the public or stress for practitioners than child protection work. Collaborative work is essential at every stage, and particular care is needed to ensure good communication between the various professionals involved in the case and within the social services management team. Often the social worker takes an important role in seeing that this is done. Social workers are selected for child protection work on the basis of a range of skills and experience that enable them to gather information and make decisions under extreme pressure, to work with parents and other family members following physical assault by those same people, to present testimony to court and to record their interviews and decisions meticulously.

Child advocates have noted that the child protection process still pays scant regard to the issues of child empowerment. The child at the focus of intervention remains emphatically in an adult world of legal procedure and subject to the demands of obtaining evidence for a possible crime. Although social workers have seen themselves as advocating the child's best interest, they have proven unreliable in this role primarily because of the counter-demands that an investigation of abuse places on them. Currently children have little chance within the process to call on an advocate. Increasingly, child advocates argue that space be made within formal procedures for children and young people to insert their opinion if they wish and with greater responsiveness to the child's perception and experience. (See also CHILDREN'S RIGHTS.)

Department of Health, *Working Together to Safeguard Children*, London, The Stationery Office, 1999.

child protection conference see CASE CONFERENCE.

child protection inquiry a legal obligation on local authorities, under section 47 of the CHILDREN ACT, to investigate where they suspect a child is suffering or might suffer SIGNIFICANT HARM and to determine whether action is needed to promote and safeguard the welfare of the child concerned.

Department of Health guidance encourages social workers to take a broad perspective when pursuing such inquiries by following the approach outlined in the FRAMEWORK FOR ASSESSMENT OF CHILDREN IN NEED. Determining the child's needs and the capacity of parents and family to safeguard the child's health and development depends on many factors, with information drawn from a number of sources. Social workers should always interview the child separately, since he or she is the key source of information as to what has happened, especially in instances of child SEXUAL ABUSE. Everything should be done to enable the child to participate in such an interview and to keep any possible distress for the child to a minimum. Children need time to develop the trust to express their views. Special consideration must be given to facilitating interviews with very young children or children with communication difficulties or children who do not speak English. If children are too young to be interviewed, other ways should be devised for obtaining the child's perspective. Under the Children Act 1989, other agencies such as health or education must help with the inquiry. In return, social workers have to be able to explain why the inquiry is taking place and why the inquiry process will achieve a better outcome for the child involved. All individuals who are interviewed should be helped to participate in the inquiry process as fully as possible.

They include those who are personally or professionally involved with the child or parents. As part of the process an examination or assessment of the child may be carried out by paediatricians or psychologists. An inquiry must be alert to the needs of other children in the household.

If the child concerned has been the victim of a crime, it may be necessary to undertake an *investigative interview*, the object of which is to gather evidence for criminal proceedings. If the interview is to be videotaped for evidential purposes, it should be conducted by those with specialist training and experience in interviewing children and should follow the guidelines outlined in the *Memorandum of Good Practice on video recorded interviews for child witnesses* (currently being revised at time of publication of this dictionary).

Accumulated research has shown that social workers are prone to a number of errors of judgement when making such an inquiry. Too often they do not give sufficient importance to the information provided by family, friends and neighbours as well as from the child or other children in the family. Practitioners are also tempted to lay too much emphasis on the most pressing problem of the moment and thereby miss other signs that things are not right. They have a tendency to form assumptions about families that lead to a distortion of their decision-making process and to misinterpret parent behaviour, whether that is cooperative or not. Research has also highlighted that even initially hostile and uncooperative parents prefer openness, honesty and a social worker who shows concern and listens to their point of view. Such basic principles are an essential requirement in helping parents engage in a relationship with professionals focused on concerns about their child or children. Initial decisions about immediate action to protect the child are likely to be based on limited information. In consultation with management and others with knowledge in the professional network, the social worker is likely to base such decisions on the nature of the cause for concern and the reaction of the parents to it; the child's age or vulnerability; knowledge, and whereabouts, of an alleged perpetrator; past knowledge of the family and parental personalities; and the current initial assessment of the parents.

Department of Health, *Working Together to Safeguard Children*, London, The Stationery Office 1999.

child protection register the central list of all children in an area who have been considered by a CASE CONFERENCE to be likely to suffer SIGNIFICANT HARM or who have actually suffered or are suspected of having suffered significant harm.

It is the sole responsibility of a CHILD PROTECTION case conference to register (or deregister) particular children. The register is usually kept by the local SOCIAL SERVICES DEPARTMENT, which is able to respond quickly to bona-fide queries, for example from a doctor, as to whether a child is on the register or not. The purpose of the register is to alert other professionals to the fact that the child listed has already been discussed by a case conference and may well be receiving services.

Children Act 1989 the single most important piece of legislation concerning children, providing a wide-ranging framework of responsibilities and duties for parents, courts and local authorities for safeguarding and promoting the welfare of children.

The Act came into effect in October 1991. Its central principle is that children are best looked after within their own families, with both parents playing a full part. The concept of PARENTAL RESPONSIBILITY, which replaces the notion of PARENTAL RIGHTS over children, reflects this. Both parents, if married, have parental responsibility for their child automatically, and both retain it should they divorce or the LOCAL AUTHORITY looks after the child for a period of time. Unmarried fathers acquire parental responsibility either through a court order or by agreement with the child's mother. The Act places a primary duty on the local authority to promote the upbringing of children in need by their families as long as this is consistent with the children's welfare. Children in need are defined as those whose development and health would be impaired if they did not receive support services or who are disabled. To carry out this duty, the authority must identify children in need in their area and offer a range of support services to them, including nursery places, child-minding, family aides, home help and laundry services, and ACCOMMODATION either in a CHILDREN'S HOME or in FOSTER CARE. Other services include financial help in exceptional circumstances, guidance and counselling, holiday arrangements, and cultural or educational activities. (This is a general duty, however, so any individual child does not necessarily have a right to these services.) The authority is not expected to provide all such services itself and may assist VOLUNTARY SECTOR organizations in providing them. Other family members may be the recipients of these services as long as it can be established that provision of service will assist the child in need to remain with his or her family. For example, an adolescent who shoulders a large role in caring for a younger sibling with a severe physical disability may be supported in this through regular leisure opportunities arranged by the authority.

To ask for support services is not a sign of parental inadequacy and should be agreed on the basis of PARTNERSHIP between parents. Local authority services, including accommodation, are provided after negotiation and agreement with parents in order to help the parents to meet their responsibilities towards their children rather than as a substitute for them. The family's racial origin and cultural and linguistic background are considerations that the authority must take into account when making plans with parents for their children.

The Act recognizes, however, that support services are not always enough to protect the child from harm. For instance, parents may be uncooperative and refuse services, or the child may be subject to abuse by a parent or another person in the household. In such cases the local authority can apply to the courts to take further action under one of several orders. A SUPERVISION ORDER places the child under the responsibility of a social worker or a probation officer who has the power to lay down certain requirements for the child or young person to follow. A CHILD ASSESSMENT ORDER requires the parents to cooperate in the assessment of their child. Alternatively, the local education authority may apply for an EDUCATION SUPERVISION ORDER to help ensure school attendance.

In more extreme cases the local authority may apply for a CARE or SUPERVISION ORDER. To obtain either, it must convince the court that the child is suffering, or is likely to suffer, SIGNIFICANT HARM because of a lack of reasonable standard of parental care or because the child is beyond control. In addition, the authority must demonstrate to the court that making an order will be better for the child than not making it, by explaining the plans it has in mind for the child in question. Although the grounds for a care order are exactly the same as for a supervision order, the courts will in practice grant a care order only in the most serious circumstances, where other alternatives have been tried and have failed to safeguard the child from significant harm. A care order lasts until the child is 18 years of age, unless discharged earlier, and, more importantly, gives the local authority parental responsibility and, with it, decision-making powers over the plan for the child.

Not only does the Act govern court proceedings between local authority and parents, it also introduces new orders for use in disputes between parents over their children. The Act does not use the concept of custody of the child, which often results in a bitter contest between parents, but provides four orders that take their name from the section of the Act in which they appear: SECTION 8 ORDERS. Each of the four orders is intended to resolve disputes over practical arrangements concerning the child, such as who is to see the child and where the child is to live, and to encourage both parents of the child to work out these arrangements between them. The two most important of these are the RESIDENCE ORDER, which designates with whom the child is to live, and the CONTACT ORDER, which establishes the frequency of contact between the child and parents or others in the family (see also PROHIBITED STEPS ORDER, SPECIFIC ISSUE ORDER). The courts have great flexibility in using these orders in both matrimonial and care proceedings. For a child subject to care proceedings, the court may decide to combine a residence order, to a grandparent for instance, with a supervision order to the local authority instead of granting a care order. Children are also able to apply for these orders and have done so in well-publicized cases where they wish to separate from one or both of their parents.

When a child is involved in any FAMILY PROCEEDINGS, that is, proceedings for care or supervision order or matrimonial proceedings, the Act stipulates that the child's welfare is the court's paramount consideration. To underscore this, the WELFARE CHECKLIST lists a number of factors that the court must bear in mind when making a decision on the case before it.

Whether a child is accommodated with the agreement of the parents or subject to a care order made by the courts, the Act considers that child as LOOKED AFTER by the local authority, which then has the responsibility of placing the child with FOSTER CARERS or in a CHILDREN'S HOME. The authority must try to place the accommodated child as near to home as possible and to consult the child about the placement decision. If the child is accommodated by agreement with the parents, the arrangements must be covered by a WRITTEN AGREEMENT covering such matters as the continuing role of the parents in the life of the accommodated child and when the placement will end. The authority must still attempt to work in partnership with the parents of any child it is looking after, but it is recognized that after contested care proceedings, for example, parents may continue to dispute the local authority's plans for their child. In exceptional circumstances the local authority may limit the parents' exercise of parental responsibility in relation to their child as long as that child is subject to a care order. Detailed regulations covering plans, written agreements and reviews for children looked after by the authority are covered in the Arrangements for Placement of Children Regulations accompanying the Act.

The Act also sets out how the local authority, the police or the National Society for the Prevention of Cruelty to Children should respond when they believe that a child may need emergency protection. Where the local authority has reasonable cause to suspect that a child is suffering from significant harm, it has a duty to investigate the child's circumstances. The objective of that inquiry is to enable the authority to decide whether it should apply for an EMERGENCY PROTECTION ORDER or take any other action under the Act, such as offering support services to the family in question. The emergency protection order should be made only in extremely urgent cases, where the child's safety is under immediate threat. The order allows the authority either to remove the child from home or other place of danger, or to retain the child in a safe place, such as a hospital, for a maximum of eight days, with a possible extension of up to another seven days in exceptional circumstances.

Taken together, the major reforms initiated by the Children Act made a sharp break with earlier child-care law and practice. The Act seeks to avoid bringing children before the court, but if this has to happen, it ensures that the child's voice is heard in public law proceedings although not in private law proceedings such as divorce and that parents have an opportunity to be represented at every stage. It also underpins the importance of the parents' point of view in planning for children in need with the local authority. Making this partnership work, often in the most difficult and stressful circumstances, is the most important challenge the Act presents for social work professionals.

Department of Health, *An Introduction to the Children Act*, London, HMSO, 1989.

Children and Family Court Advisory and Support Service (CAFCASS)
a child-focused service representing the needs, wishes and feelings of children involved in family proceedings.

CAFCASS replaced the previous provision by the Family Court Welfare service, guardians *ad litem*, and the Official Solicitor's office. The single, national service covering England and Wales reports to courts on children's views in contested divorce cases and supports parents who are in conflict over finances or arrangements for children.

children in need a central concept in the CHILDREN ACT 1989 on the basis of which local authorities are able to offer family support services.

According to section 17 of the Act, a child is 'in need' if he or she is unlikely to achieve or maintain a reasonable standard of health or development *without* support services from the local authority. Should the child fall sufficiently below this 'reasonable standard', in either health or in developmental progress, or if the child's development is impaired to the point that services are required, that child is deemed as 'in need' in contrast to children who attain a reasonable standard of health and development. Since the passage of the Children Act, there has been a gradual broadening of the factors that social workers should take into account when trying to determine whether a child is in need. These include looking at how the whole family may be struggling to cope on its own, particularly with low income or other factors to do with SOCIAL EXCLUSION. (See also FRAMEWORK FOR ASSESSMENT OF CHILDREN IN NEED.)

Children (Leaving Care) Act 2000 an Act that stipulates the responsibilities and tasks that a local authority has to undertake in preparing a child or young person for leaving its care.

The Act lays important duties on the local authority in relation to young people leaving its care. These include the duty:
1 to assess and meet the needs of eligible people aged 16 and 17 who are in care or are care leavers and to remain in touch with all care leavers until they are 21 regardless of where they live;
2 to have a clear 'pathway' plan mapping out a route to independence for every eligible young person when he or she turns 16 for whom local authorities must provide the personal and practical support;
3 to provide each care leaver with an adviser who will coordinate provision of support, with particular emphasis on education, training and employment;
4 to introduce new more straightforward financial arrangements that offer comprehensive support, especially with education and employment, up to the age 21 and beyond if necessary.

Local authorities have had a variable record in the past when acting as the parent for LOOKED-AFTER children. The child, whether accommodated with the agreement of her or his parents or subject to a care order, rarely has an advocate equal to his or her parents or other family relations. The instability of their experiences prior to coming into care means that as a group they are beset with difficulties. Young people in public care are well below average in educational attainment, in acquiring basic skills and in health or social relationships, and yet their ability ranges match national averages. The under-achievement at school goes hand in hand with much higher rates of truancy and exclusion. The effects of this experience take their toll in later life: a higher than average level of looked-after children are unemployed and homeless, and engage in criminal and abusive behaviour. Among homeless young people, young offenders and the prison population, the proportion of those who were in care is extremely high: roughly some 30 to 40 per cent of each population.

In assisting in the transition to adulthood of a young person in care, there are a number of matters that have to be dealt with. *Accommodation* may involve initial moves to interim forms of housing, such as hostels, lodgings or staying with friends, which are often followed up by moves to independent tenancies in the public, voluntary or private sectors. *Life skills* include budgeting, negotiating with officials, landlords and employers, and practical skills such as self-care and domestic skills such as cooking, laundry and cleaning. *Social networks, relationships and identity* are other facets of leaving care that both the young person and practitioner have to come to grips with. Even if family links had not been positive, retaining them was important and lent symbolic certainty to their lives. Those that did not have even this lacked self-esteem, were less confident and less assertive.

A full 70 per cent of looked-after children have no qualification on leaving school. In recent years only three in a hundred care leavers obtained five or more GCSEs at Grade C or above, compared with 60 per cent of their peers. The guidance on family placements (foster care) and residential care already recognizes the extreme disadvantages experienced by most looked-after children. The *Looking After Children* ASSESSMENT AND ACTION RECORDS used by most local authorities indicate the specific questions that need to be asked to ensure that a child's education is supported and promoted. But beyond this, the full range of educational visits, school trips and spare-time activities need to be supported. Motivation needs to be encouraged and nurtured. Too often in the past residential care provided an anti-intellectual environment, with no study facilities, reference books nor understanding of what is required in general for a young person to be able to engage in intellectual activity.

The object of the Act is to achieve what has been so elusive for local authorities: effective 'corporate parenting' in which the local authority and all professionals involved with a young person leaving care can act as effective advocates in the areas of life that really matter. A 'pathway plan' for each care leaver should be based on the extensive involvement of the young person and should look ahead at least to his or her 21st birthday. It should pick up and extend the dimensions covered in the FRAMEWORK FOR ASSESSMENT OF CHILDREN IN NEED. The young person's health needs, future education and supporting family relationships all form part of it. Accommodation needs should be carefully looked at before young people leave care and arrangements made for joint-assessment between social services and housing authorities. Sources of income and avenues to employment must also be considered.

Children's Fund a programme set up by central government in 2001 to provide local networks with the funding to engage in PREVENTIVE WORK with children between the ages of 5 and 13 who are at risk of SOCIAL EXCLUSION.

The preventive element of the fund is directed at services helping children and their families suffering from the consequences of poverty. It is seen as bridging the gap between SURE START for pre-school children and the CONNEXIONS service for the over-13s. The fund works through local area partnerships, embracing voluntary organizations, community and faith groups, statutory agencies and young people, that can plan and develop such services. Local partnerships carry out an assessment of existing needs and existing preventive services and then decide which types of services are priorities in their areas. The fund can support a wide range of projects as long as their key focus is helping to prevent children and their families from suffering the consequences of poverty and that the proposed services are new in each area and distinct from what is already offered by mainstream services. Projects fall well outside the usual social services remit and may include arts, counselling, sport, family support, literacy and health awareness.

One of the central threads of each local partnership is the PARTICIPATION of children and young people within the planning, delivery and evaluation of policies and services relevant to them. Equally, local groups, whether voluntary, community or faith-based, must play an influential role in shaping plans within the partnerships.

children's guardian (guardian *ad litem*) a trained social worker selected from a local panel to provide an independent social work opinion to a court about what is best for a child's welfare during proceedings for an ADOPTION ORDER, a CARE ORDER, an EMERGENCY PROTECTION ORDER or a SUPERVISION ORDER.

The children's guardian makes a full assessment of each case by interviewing the child and his or her family, as well as any professionals such as health visitors and teachers who are involved with the child. The guardian also has access to records kept about the child. On the basis of this assessment, the guardian reaches a decision about what he or she thinks best serves the child's welfare. At all times the guardian represents the child and, if necessary, instructs a solicitor on the child's behalf. The management of children's guardians is administered by the CHILDREN AND FAMILY COURT ADVISORY AND SUPPORT SERVICE (CAFCASS).

children's home a residential unit that provides 24-hour care for children and young people.

The Department of Health guidance on the CHILDREN ACT refers to several different types of children's home:

1 community homes maintained, controlled and assisted by the LOCAL AUTHORITY;

2 homes run by VOLUNTARY-SECTOR organizations;

3 registered children's homes run by private organizations;

4 independent schools accommodating between four and 50 boarding pupils and not approved under the Education Act 1981.

The Act further defines a children's home as a place providing care and accommodation for more than three children.

Each home must register under the Act and issue a statement of purpose and function describing what the home sets out to do for children and the manner in which care is provided. There is a diversity of services offered by children's homes, including emergency PLACEMENT, short-term or respite placement, bridging placements (for example, between a child's own home and a foster placement), SECURE ACCOMMODATION and long-term placements that may incorporate some therapeutic provision. Increasingly, children's homes are aiming to meet specific needs of children at particular phases of their lives, such as preparing children for long-term foster care or helping young people to prepare for living on their own.

It is legally possible for some voluntary children's homes or registered children's homes to apply to the Secretary of State for Health for a certificate that allows them to provide a refuge for children who appear to be at risk of harm. This exempts the home from offences under the Children Act, such as harbouring or abducting children. The significance of such status lies in the fact that it recognizes that some young people do require a legitimate breathing space where refuge workers can help them return to parents or local authority care or to sort out some other arrangements if appropriate.

Following the CARE STANDARDS ACT, 2000, the Department of Health introduced National Minimum Standards and Regulations in respect of Children's Homes, published in March 2002. These regulations and accompanying guidance aim to eliminate the institutional abuse that has been evident in a number of children's homes throughout England and Wales over the past 20 years.

children's rights claims to treatment, benefits or protection made by, or on behalf of, children on the basis of law, code of practice or declaration.

Historically, children had no RIGHTS separate from their parents or guardian. They were viewed as the property of their father, who enjoyed complete freedom in how he raised them. Fathers always gained custody in courts when disputes arose. Increased concern over poverty and extreme examples of neglect in the late 19th century began to produce a change in the law to permit legal intervention in family life to prevent the worst excesses of cruelty. For the first time courts could award mothers custody of their children. The National Society for the Prevention of Cruelty to Children was established in 1882 – ironically, some years after the first animal protection legislation.

Children still lacked recognisable rights at this time, however, mainly because of the prevailing view of them as immature, self-centred and requiring strict discipline. To confer political and social rights on children was held to be unfair, burdening them with responsibilities they could not cope with. This view endured for many years, even among professionals working with children. During the last twenty years, however, a vigorous and expanding discussion of the nature of children's rights has had an increasing impact on the law, on parents and on professionals working with children. The debate has changed, with the realization that children have significant capacities for decision-making and self-expression, combined with arguments that children should be able to decide some things for themselves or at least express their opinion on key decisions taken on their behalf.

There are three broad areas of children's rights: rights to protection and the safeguarding of their welfare; rights that give greater choice and autonomy; and procedural rights through which children have a say in decisions affecting them. The first area is now largely enshrined in the CHILDREN ACT. Measures developed in the wake of the CLEVELAND INQUIRY balance the need to protect the child with some of the problems found in child abuse investigations, when children were often kept away from home for lengthy periods and with no contact with their parents.

Considerable changes have also occurred recently in relation to children's rights to decide things for themselves. The House of Lords' ruling in GILLICK v. *West Norfolk Health Authority* implied that the child's capacity to make decisions was not tied to a specific age and that if the child sufficiently understood the issues he or she should be able to contribute to decisions affecting him or her, and in certain matters have his or her wishes prevail. The Lords' ruling in the Gillick case directly influenced the drafting of the Children Act, in which, for example, children have the right to withhold their consent regarding medical or psychiatric examination or social work ASSESSMENT, even when they are being checked for possible signs of abuse. Children may begin certain legal proceedings on their own initiative, such as applying for a discharge of a CARE ORDER. They can also initiate complaints about services that they are receiving from the local authority, including the quality of residential care if they are in a children's home. Perhaps most importantly, if they are to be LOOKED AFTER by the local authority, that authority must find out the child's wishes and feelings about any possible PLACEMENT and give them due consideration.

Other positive rights for children have been established in relation to education and health. Children have the right to see their school records, the power to take action over discriminatory practices and policies, and the right to free medical and dental checks through local education authority schools. Schools may no longer use corporal punishment as a method of discipline.

Many children's rights activists believe that such rights as outlined above are too narrow and are only the start. There are still many areas of a child's life in which they think a child should have a far greater say, such as schooling. In particular, they consider that children of 12 and over have far greater powers of understanding and judgement for choosing courses of action than hitherto recognized. In addition, there are a number of positive rights, such as the right to health, to a safe environment, to adequate play areas and pre-school services, and to a standard of living adequate for their physical, mental and social development, that have still to be won for children.

The notes to the United Nations Convention on the Rights of the Child created a significant impact on constructions of children and their needs and created a minimum standard for children's rights around the world. Various articles within the convention strive for children and the protection of their rights.

In the UK, the Children Act 1989 clearly laid down that before a local authority made any decisions with regard to looked-after children and young people, it should take account of their wishes and feelings.

Within the context of welfare, children's rights are often located in the debate between needs and rights, that is, adult obligations and a set of enforceable children's rights, such as a right to decent services, a right to protection, a right to be heard and a right to be consulted. The debate is premised on the fundamental right of children to have rights as a framework in which their lives and needs can be located. Critics of this view argue that allowing children rights allows them complete freedom and control, and may ultimately place them at risk of danger. The balance of children's rights, freedom and autonomy, therefore, continues to be a source of tension. (See also CITIZENSHIP.)

children's rights officer an officer, appointed by the local authority, whose job is to ensure that children and young people with whom the authority is working are able to exercise their RIGHTS and seek redress if necessary.

Local authorities have laid increasing emphasis on the rights of children in their care, particularly after numerous recent examples of physical and mental cruelty at the hands of staff to children in residential care. The rights in question may relate to confidentiality of personal information, consultation in decisions affecting them, contributions to CASE REVIEWS and CASE CONFERENCES and access to information so that they can make informed choices about their future. (See also CHILDREN'S RIGHTS.)

child support the policy of ensuring that both parents, in particular absent fathers, contribute to the financial maintenance of their child or children.

The Child Support Act 1991 introduced radical changes in the area of child maintenance following relationship breakdown. The Act introduced a standard formula to assess how much the 'absent' parent should pay and established a new executive agency of the Department of Social Security, the Child Support Agency (CSA), to assess, collect and enforce these payments. The initial assessment formula was relatively complex, since it sought to balance the needs of the children and the parent with care against the needs of the absent parent and any second family. Many complaints by absent parents over the years have resulted in some amendments to further protect their income. Even after these changes the formula has produced figures several times higher than those previously awarded by the courts.

The Child Support Agency has to rely on the parent with care providing information to help trace the absent parent. To encourage this cooperation in cases where the parent with care is in receipt of benefit, a reduction lasting up to 18 months may be made if she or, rarely, he does not provide appropriate help. The requirement to cooperate will be waived if there is a risk of the parent with care or any child suffering harm or undue distress. Although there is no widespread evidence of the use of the benefit deduction, it is feared that it might lead some mothers to cooperate inappropriately and put themselves in danger When the Child Support Act came into effect, changes were made in the rules for means-tested benefits to enhance work incentives. However, for the majority of LONE-PARENT FAMILIES who remain on income support there is no gain in the arrangements.

Court orders and voluntary agreements need not be disturbed unless one party seeks to vary a court order or the parent with care claims income support or other benefit. Voluntary agreements are likely to be less stable in the future, because the services of the CSA will be relatively accessible. Although increased payments under the agency's assessment will sometimes be phased in over 18 months, the assessment takes no account of previous maintenance agreements. 'Clean-break' agreements, where in the past (typically) the absent parent transferred equity in a home to the parent with care, would be ill-advised in future because the child support assessment will take no account of such transactions.

Although the British public largely accepts the idea of PARENTAL RESPONSIBILITY for child maintenance, the Conservative government's motivation for change was almost certainly to limit the level of social security expenditure, a view that was endorsed by the Labour government after 1997.

Child Support Agency see CHILD SUPPORT.

child tax credit (CTC) see TAX CREDIT; WELFARE RIGHTS 5; WELFARE RIGHTS 9.

Chronically Sick and Disabled Persons Act 1970 legislation that sets out the duties of LOCAL AUTHORITIES in respect of providing the support necessary for disabled people to live in the community.

This is one of several Acts of Parliament under which COMMUNITY CARE services are provided. It relates solely to disabled people who fall within the definition of DISABILITY provided in section 29 of the NATIONAL ASSISTANCE ACT 1948. Because of the link with this definition, it falls within the definition of community care services in section 46 of the NATIONAL HEALTH SERVICE AND COMMUNITY CARE ACT 1990, but it is important to note that the Act applies equally to disabled children.

The Act requires local authorities to maintain a register of disabled people and also specifies services that should be provided for disabled people where need has been established. There has been disappointment about the impact of the Act in practice, but it did considerably strengthen the existing responsibilities of local authorities to provide support for disabled people in their own homes. The Act is still the basis for the provision of many aids, adaptations and services for older and disabled people.

This was the first social care legislation to focus on disabled people specifically. Disability is age-related, however, and the Act has therefore also proved significant for older people. It differs from previous legislation, which focused primarily on making provision for residential services, by laying out the duties of local authorities in respect of supporting disabled people in the community. The Act imposes a duty on the local authority to inform itself of the number and needs of 'handicapped' people in its area and to publicize available services. Section 2 lists the services that local authorities should provide to those whose need for them has been established by an ASSESSMENT. These include practical assistance in the home, recreational facilities, travel, adaptations and 'special' equipment, holidays and the provision of meals. Although the National Health Service and Community Care Act 1990 brought about changes in the way that needs are assessed and social welfare services delivered, the duty of local authorities to provide these particular services to those in need still stems from the Chronically Sick and Disabled Persons Act. Initially, the passing of this act led to optimism about future provision, and some commentators described it as 'a charter for the disabled'. Its focus on entitlement to services in the home was thought to exemplify an acceptance of the social rights of disabled people and a changed attitude towards their presence in the community. The Act did not live up to these expectations, however, with many local authorities being inadequately funded to fully comply with it. Assessments were often delayed, as authorities could then claim ignorance of the needs they were failing to meet. It was not until the DISABLED PERSONS (SERVICES, CONSULTATION AND REPRESENTATION) ACT 1986 that the duty of local authorities to carry out an assessment when requested to do so by a disabled person was clarified. The extent to which local authorities had a duty to provide services irrespective of resource constraints has been unclear. In 1990, the National Health Service and Community Care Act stipulated that all community care services must be provided within budgetary limits. There have been a number of legal test cases since, however, in which the courts have supported local authorities' right to restrict access to services for budgetary reasons.

Current Department of Health Guidance, *Fairness in Access to Care Services* 2002, stresses that resources can be taken into account. The Chronically Sick and Disabled Persons Act has also been criticized for its lack of potential for choice and service user self-determination. However, it remains a landmark in that it acknowledges a collective responsibility for the support that disabled people need in order to live in the community.

The House of Lords (*R* v *Gloucestershire CC and Another ex p Barry* [1997] 2AllER1) has determined that the local authority may take resources into account when assessing the needs of a disabled person when deciding whether it is necessary to make arrangements under section 2 of the Chronically Sick and Disabled Persons Act 1970 and when determining how those needs will be met. However, the judgement does not give local authorities licence to take decisions on the basis of resources alone. They must still take account of all other relevant factors and must not act in an arbitrary or unreasonable way. Once the local authority has decided that it is necessary, in order to meet the needs of a disabled person, for it to arrange a service listed in section 2, then it is under a duty to arrange it. Lack of resources cannot be used as a reason to limit implementation of this duty. Where the local authority wishes to change the service provision a reassessment of need must be undertaken in respect of each individual service user.

Under section 17 of the Health and Social Services and Social Security Adjudications Act 1983, local authorities may, if they choose, charge service users for the services provided.

M. Oliver and B. Sapey, *Social Work with Disabled People*, second edition, Basingstoke, Macmillan, 1999.

citizenship legal, social and political status conferred by a state on individuals in which certain RIGHTS, duties and obligations are placed on both the state and the citizen.

In effect, citizenship is legal membership in a nation state. It emerged as a concept in the 17th and 18th centuries with the consolidation of strong centralized state authorities in Europe and in the wake of the English, French and American revolutions, which called into question the limits of that authority in relation to individuals. Citizenship was underpinned by the idea that states should be founded on the will of the people, involving a contract of mutual rights and responsibilities.

One of the most influential interpretations of citizenship has been that of T. H. Marshall, who broadly linked citizenship with the acquisition of rights over the last three or four hundred years: legal rights, such as the right to property and freedom from arbitrary arrest; political rights, such as the right to assembly and to vote; and social rights, such as health care and welfare benefits. In Marshall's view, citizenship in our own time has come to include economic welfare and security for each citizen as well as the right to live life according to the standards prevailing in the society

A number of factors have undermined Marshall's progressive concept of citizenship. Much of it was based on the presumed permanence of a thriving welfare state providing a range of entitlements and a safety net for the poorest. Financial limits placed on welfare spending and the widespread retrenchment of the welfare state have called into question the inevitability of this concept of citizenship. The political philosophy of the NEW RIGHT, which emphasizes responsibilities rather than rights and believes in the MARKET as a way of allocating services, has also introduced new elements into discussions of citizenship. Feminism contests such an understanding of citizenship and its gender neutrality, and challenges the inherently male precepts of citizenship. Feminists argue that such a concept is defined by male interests and concerns, and needs transformation to include the development of feminist political and social theory.

It is being increasingly recognized that citizenship may also contain negative connotations and include restrictive citizenship, as defined within the UK immigration laws and restrictive practices within the European Union.

R. Lister, *Citizenship: A Feminist Perspective*, London, Macmillan, 1997.

civil proceedings court proceedings that do not involve criminal matters. The HIGH COURT deals with many aspects of civil law in England and Wales, but the civil proceedings most relevant to social workers and probation officers are those relating to FAMILY PROCEEDINGS under the CHILDREN ACT and those relating to DOMESTIC VIOLENCE. Most civil proceedings start in a magistrate's court or county court; they may be referred to the High Court or the Court of Appeal (Civil Division) on appeal. (See also CHILDREN AND FAMILY COURT ADVISORY AND SUPPORT SERVICE.)

classical conditioning the process of transferring the automatic response of the nervous system to one stimulus to a different stimulus, by repeated associations.

The process of classical conditioning involves a basic technique for adapting reflexes, which are part of the nervous system. For example, a squirt of lemon juice in the mouth will stimulate salivation; if the lemon juice is squirted into a person's mouth on a number of occasions at the same time as a bell is sounded, salivation will occur at the sound of the bell alone. Classical conditioning describes this process as the pairing of an unconditioned stimulus (lemon juice) with a neutral stimulus (the bell) to produce a conditioned response (salivation). Salivation at the lemon juice alone would be an unconditioned response. The discovery and terminology of classical conditioning are credited to the Russian psychologist Ivan Pavlov. The technique is used in BEHAVIOUR MODIFICATION.

Cleveland Inquiry the judicial inquiry set up by the government to examine how certain suspected cases of child SEXUAL ABUSE were dealt with in Cleveland in 1987. The inquiry was headed by Lord Justice Butler-Sloss, whose 1988 report was praised for its analysis, balance and advocacy of reforms.

Between February and July 1987, 121 children were diagnosed by two consultant paediatricians in Cleveland as having been sexually abused. The paediatricians relied heavily on a method of diagnosis called ANAL DILATATION. The majority of the children were compulsorily removed from home or kept in hospital under court orders. The crisis became heated and aroused a national debate when parents began to complain vigorously about the allegations of abuse levelled at them and about the way they and their children were treated: removal of children without prior notice, restrictions on their visiting the children, lack of consultation and information, and the impossibility of appeal. The involvement of the local Member of Parliament on the parents' side highlighted a breakdown in confidence in the local social services department.

The report principally recommended that in future cases of suspected abuse the child should not be subjected to repeated medical examinations and that interviews with children should not use probing or confrontational methods; the Cleveland children investigated had been subject to both. Butler-Sloss considered the examinations and interviews with the children as forms of abuse in themselves and reminded practitioners that 'the child is a person and not an object of concern'.

Lord Justice Butler-Sloss, *Report of the Inquiry into Child Abuse in Cleveland*, London, HMSO, 1988.

client a term used to designate a person receiving a social service. The word 'client' was originally intended to convey an emphasis on the quality of the relationship between the individual recipient of a service and his or her social worker, home carer, occupational therapist or other social services professional. It was also intended to avoid any connotation of a patient in need of treatment. The term applied equally to those who sought out a service and those who were compelled by law to submit to it. Thus probationers, adolescents on supervision orders and parents whose children were compulsorily removed could all be referred to as clients, as could an older person requiring short-term care.

From the beginning the word 'client' acquired a meaning opposite to the one that was understood by other professions, such as in law or architecture, where the relationship with the client is based on a contractual obligation to provide specialist services for a fee. In social work the relationship was intended to be based on empathy, warmth and understanding freely given on the part of the social worker. Problems in using the term gradually multiplied, and in the 1970s, when SYSTEMS theory first made an impact on social work thinking, the client could be seen as more than one person. The first question for a practitioner to ask was, Who is the client? Often it became clear that more than one client was involved in a given case, each with individual, even competing, objectives. It made more sense to speak of the 'client system' – the person, family, group, organization or community that engaged the services of the worker and was the presumed beneficiary of the services.

Also at that time the first studies were published of clients' views on the quality of services; it was a measure of how little the client actually counted in social work thinking that this had not been done before. From these studies the general conclusion emerged that while clients valued the quality of the relationship they also wanted help with practical and material problems. Modest as these conclusions seem now, they were a challenge to the long-held view that the helping relationship itself was of primary importance and that environmental problems were secondary.

RADICAL SOCIAL WORK also began to highlight the class element common to social services clients and to show that economic disadvantage played a powerful role in shaping their 'problems'. The picture of the client that emerged was of a powerless, unwilling but dependent recipient affected by social and economic forces beyond their control. The word in its original meaning hardly did justice to the real nature of the relationship between the social services professional and the receiver of a service. The term continued in use, however, if only for the practical reason that alternatives were unsatisfactory. The BARCLAY REPORT (1982) decided on 'client' and specifically rejected the alternative term 'service user' because it did not carry the notion that social work is a personal service to meet individual needs, still less that some who receive services are subject to measures of control. The universal use of the term has come under fresh pressures from the perspectives of PARTNERSHIP and EMPOWERMENT theory, which have served notice that people receiving services will no longer be passive recipients but are joint participants in arranging those services. The word 'USER' has been adopted primarily by ADVOCACY and SELF-HELP groups, particularly in the fields of MENTAL HEALTH, DISABILITY, LEARNING DISABILITY and child care, to convey their message that there is a chasm between the quality of services offered and what people expect of those services. The pressure is having effect, and 'user' is increasingly being taken up by professionals inside the service.

Something of a division of terms has emerged. 'Service user' describes those who are voluntarily in touch with services and 'client' those who, under law, are compelled to receive a service. A disabled person asking for a home care service is a user; the parents of a child taken into compulsory care are a client. Thus 'client' has come full circle; originally coined to de-stigmatize, it is now increasingly linked to those who have little choice but to be the targets of intervention. The trend over recent years has been to adopt the term 'service user' as a generic term for all who are in receipt of social work services, whether they wanted such services or not.

S. Croft and P. Beresford, *Citizen involvement: A Practical Guide for Change*, Basingstoke, Macmillan, 1993.

client system the immediate social and family SYSTEM of which the CLIENT is part.

Because all parts of the client system are interrelated, there may be more than one person asking to be considered as a client within that system. The intention of analysing a client system is to see how the relationships inside it are shaped by other parts of that system. A client's 'problems' may arise as a result of the way the system functions as a whole rather than being the result of one person's behaviour. This can be particularly true in families, and it forms the basis of FAMILY THERAPY. The social worker may intervene within the system to improve aspects of support for the client or to try to change the way the system responds to the client. In the terminology of the 'unitary method', if the social worker intervenes within the client system it also becomes the TARGET SYSTEM.

closed-end question a question used in an INTERVIEW framed in such a way as to require a specific answer. Such a question does not encourage the client to respond more fully with his or her own opinions, information or feelings.

Principles of good practice suggest that closed-end questions be used only occasionally, especially when interviewing a child who may have been abused.

CLS abbreviation for COMMUNITY LEGAL SERVICE.

code of ethics see ETHICAL CODE.

cognitive behavioural therapy an approach to group and individual therapy that aims to change the ways in which people think about themselves and their environment.

The approach, which grew out of BEHAVIOUR THERAPY, stresses that thought patterns are crucial to the ways in which a person views his or her own behaviour. Changing such thought patterns can be important in the resolution of problems such as DEPRESSION and in ANGER MANAGEMENT. People are taught to monitor their 'self-talk' for entrenched lines of thought, interrupting these destructive ways of thinking and replacing them with strategies ('thinking skills') taught as part of the therapy. Successful experiments with these new strategies are reinforced by more positive responses from other people, thus maintaining the changed approach. If one learns to handle anger effectively, for example, one gets a better reaction from other people, which may reinforce one's use of the new skills.

Since the late 1980s, cognitive-behavioural work has become increasingly popular in group work with adult offenders, particularly in the PRISON and PROBATION services. This approach concentrates upon helping offenders to face up to the consequences of their actions for themselves and others, to understand their own motives and to develop new ways of controlling their behaviour. Cognitive-behavioural methods are often successfully combined with other approaches such as SOCIAL SKILLS TRAINING, for example in the case of group work with SEX OFFENDERS. There are, however, potential ethical problems in requiring members of captive populations to restructure their thinking processes if they are not in a position to give fully informed consent.

Offenders need to be allocated to programmes according to their individual needs and learning styles, and staff delivering such programmes need rigorous training. The Home Office has established an accreditation process aimed at ensuring that these standards are met. (See also EFFECTIVENESS.)

J. Vennard, D. Sugg and C. Hedderman, *Changing Offenders' Attitudes and Behaviour: What Works?* Research Study 171, London, Home Office.

cohabitation two adults living together in the same domestic unit. The couple may be in a heterosexual or a homosexual relationship.

Cohabitation is widespread, with one quarter of all children born to cohabiting couples. Reasons for cohabiting differ considerably. For some couples it is not the result of a clear decision but a gradual process that in the end has the partners living together. But research also indicates that a sizeable majority of those cohabiting view cohabitation as an equivalent to marriage, requiring a commitment to the relationship over a lengthy period of time. At the same time, cohabitation allows for greater honesty and individual freedom within the relationship as well as commitment to egalitarian gender roles. Formal ties, sanctioned by the state, are viewed as a relic of a more religious and even oppressive past. The sexual behaviour of individuals who are cohabiting is closer to that of persons who are single, divorced or separated rather than that of married couples.

In some important areas cohabiting couples have different rights from those of married couples – for example, in relation to tenancies, INJUNCTIONS and welfare benefits. For the purposes of means-testing, 'a couple' is defined as two partners, over 16, married and living in the same household or, if not married, 'living together as husband and wife' in the same HOUSEHOLD. Gay and lesbian partners do not count as a couple and must claim as single persons. Often there is widespread ignorance of the law among cohabiting couples themselves. In certain areas when a relationship breaks down partners do not enjoy the same rights as married couples. For example, mothers who have given up work to raise children cannot assume rights to any claim on the father's pension or ownership of the house. A recent change in the law now gives an unmarried father PARENTAL RESPONSIBILITY for any children of their relationship as long as both parents have signed the child's birth certificate.

The relationship of cohabiting couples is approximately four times more likely to break down than married couples', according to contemporary statistics. As with married men after separation, cohabiting fathers' contact with their children drops dramatically even when they had been the child's primary care-giver. (See MARRIAGE.)

cold weather payment a payment to cover extra domestic heating costs during exceptionally cold weather. See WELFARE RIGHTS 8.

Commission for Racial Equality (CRE) the body established by the RACE RELATIONS ACT 1976 with primary responsibility for the elimination of racial DISCRIMINATION, the promotion of 'equality of opportunity and good relations between people of different racial groups' and keeping the workings of the 1976 Act under review.

The CRE has the power to carry out formal investigations into any circumstances covered by the Act where racial discrimination is suspected. Such investigations can require organizations to produce information. If the CRE decides that discrimination has occurred, it can produce reports and make recommendations. The major mechanism for this process is the issuing of 'non-discrimination notices', which spell out in what manner the person or organization has contravened the law and gives instruction about the changes required to bring any policy or practice into line with legal requirements. Other major areas of work for the CRE include the publication of investigations and suggestions for good practice, as well as much advice and counselling to individuals. The CRE has attracted considerable criticism, especially on the part of radical blacks who maintain that the British approach to eliminating racial discrimination lacks vigour and commitment. Its defenders hold that the CRE is constrained by being part of the government and by the limited powers conferred upon it by the 1976 Act. Researches, however, are consistent in their findings that little progress has been made in the last two decades in eliminating racial discrimination in Britain.

communication the giving or exchange of INFORMATION through a variety of media.

In social work and social welfare agencies, good, clear, accurate communication is essential in several contexts. First, all organizations should provide quality information about the services that they offer, which should be widely accessible. This will involve not only a range of languages relevant to their local community but also in electronic, Braille and perhaps taped formats. Secondly, all workers need to develop appropriate communication skills both for face-to-face and for written communications. The ability to avoid jargon and to communicate in good clear English is of paramount importance. When using other languages, it is equally important that the clear meaning is fully communicated. Workers also need to consider the context in which they are required to speak and to write, and to ensure that they develop a style that is appropriate and relevant for their audience.

Thirdly, some people have very specific communication needs. People who take pride in belonging to the DEAF community, for example, need to be offered trained competent BRITISH SIGN LANGUAGE (BSL) interpreters so that they can communicate clearly in their first language. Some people who have serious communication problems as a result of DISABILITY may require specialist support for communication (see BRAILLE, LOW VISION AIDS, MOON). Fourthly, agencies that are closely collaborating on projects, working in partnerships or negotiating service level agreements need to develop effective channels for communication in order to enhance collaboration. Fifthly, with the developing emphasis upon a research culture in social welfare, workers need to be able to communicate clearly with funders, research colleagues and research participants in order to produce high-quality results and be able to disseminate their findings clearly and imaginatively in order to improve practice. Finally, communication has a non-verbal dimension. Workers need to be aware of body language, and the importance of LISTENING skills, as part of their effective communication repertoire.

G. Hopkins, *Plain English for Social Services – a guide to better communication*, RHP, 1998.

communitarianism a philosophical approach that emphasizes the importance of the family and other social networks in maintaining s ocial order and argues that individuals should be encouraged to pay as much attention to their social responsibilities as they do to their rights.

Some communitarian writing is distinctly authoritarian, but other writers in this tradition argue that it is social exclusion and DISCRIMINATION that destroy communities. What they have in common is a desire to restore civic virtues of reciprocity and neighbourliness and to encourage individual commitment to moral behaviour and a responsible role in the community. This has been criticized for sentimentalizing a mythical past and for failing to recognize the potentially oppressive nature of informal social control networks such as the family.

Communitarian philosophy, particularly the writings of American sociologist Amitai Etzioni, has significantly influenced European criminal justice legislation and practice. Obvious examples are the PARENTING ORDER and CURFEW, which seek to involve the parents of young people more fully in their supervision and to educate them about their responsibilities. Another is the spread of REPARATION and greater attention to the needs of the VICTIM: this approach provides scope for informal community-based solutions to crime that nevertheless involve censure and REINTEGRATIVE SHAMING.

A. Etzioni (ed), *New Communitarian Thinking*, London, University Press of Virginia, 1995.

community a group of individuals with associated interests and/or common goals; the concept also describes social relationships within groups or territorial boundaries.

Many writers in the social sciences have sought to analyse the concept of community, offering numerous definitions. It has been suggested that attempts to make sense of the concept fall broadly into three groups: community as geographical locality; community as a collection of related interests; and community as relationships or as particular qualities to relationships. Geographical proximity, interests and relationships may coincide, and often do, but there is no necessary overlap between them.

Community defined by geography may appear to be easily identified (for example, a parliamentary ward, an inner city housing estate or a village). However, the assumption of consensus, of common goals or even of relationships cannot be made in these examples. Communities can be relatively anonymous. Even where people live in close proximity, it cannot be assumed that they have similar interests or that they will have any kind of meaningful relationship. When an issue or common cause arises, however, then the 'community' may begin to self-identify, to campaign together to achieve an improvement, for example, in poor-quality housing, or to prevent chemical waste being disposed of in the locality. Thus the geographical community is transformed into a community of interest(s), the second meaning of 'community'. If the common cause has facilitated the development of personal and/or social relationships, then community becomes, in part, an expression of relationship or the achievement of a particular quality of relationship, the third meaning of 'community'.

There is perhaps an implied notion in the way that the idea of community is used in discourse. There appears to be an assumption that to have community is better than not to have it. Yet some have argued that rural communities, for example, can give rise to parochial, conservative and confining relationships. Urban settings, by contrast, because they can be more anonymous and contractual, have the potential to be liberating because they reflect what people have become rather than the limitations and constraints of birth or origin.

Community or neighbourhood can also be the 'unit of analysis' and thus the unit of intervention for some social welfare work. COMMUNITY WORK certainly takes the view that communities can have a major impact upon the experience of individuals, families and peer groups in important ways and that communities can be mobilized to bring about improvements in the quality of life for residents. In addition, community is used as a way of characterizing some statutory services, such as community care services, community health services or community policing, where services are organized around a designated area. Community can also describe services delivered by members of a community (as in community support or network) in contrast to those offered by professional agencies. Finally, community could also describe services delivered to people in their own homes (in effect, domiciliary services) or to community facilities within a locality by contrast with services delivered in residential or institutional settings. In sum, the word 'community' is capable of many shades of meaning.

G. Crow and G. Allen, *Community Life: An introduction to local social relations*, Hemel Hempstead, Harvester Wheatsheaf, 1994.

community advocacy a process utilized by community SELF-HELP groups to campaign or intervene in response to events and policy decisions affecting their particular interests. Current examples include activities by women trying to effect reconciliation in areas of major factional or ethnic conflict, such as in Bosnia-Herzegovina or Croatia, or following 'riots' or civil disturbance in inner city areas of the UK and protests by the Disabled People's Direct Action Network (DAN) against the unsatisfactory Disability Discrimination Act 1995.

community care the provision of care services and social support for people living in the COMMUNITY, usually in their own homes.

It is worth noting that the term 'community care' is a contested one and encompasses debates about the relationship between the individual citizen and the state and the responsibility for care. At the heart of such debates are concerns about whether, as a society, we endorse collective responsibility for providing care or whether responsibility lies with individuals and families. In government policy the term is used to describe a range of care services provided for people in NEED who continue to live in the community. Usually this means that the people in need remain in their own homes, but sometimes they live in a house or flat shared by others who have similar needs. The objective of providing such services is to enable a person to continue to live in familiar surroundings rather than in an institution such as a hospital or residential home. The services most commonly associated with community care are personalized services such as meals on wheels and assistance with bathing, but they also include those provided nearby and outside the home, such as at DAY CARE centres. Other services linked to community care are those that enable a person to develop social, leisure or educational interest. Still other services focus on the needs of CARERS, such as arranging for cared-for people to spend a few days in RESIDENTIAL CARE so that the carers have time to themselves.

The term 'community care' was first used in the 1960s to describe the policy of relocating people from psychiatric hospitals into less institutionalized surroundings. It is now used in relation to all adult clients of social services, such as people with learning disabilities and older people. In this sense the term is now used very loosely to describe any policy or service designed to help people stay out of institutional care, including residential homes and hospitals. (See also CARE MANAGEMENT, DOMICILIARY SERVICES, NATIONAL HEALTH SERVICE AND COMMUNITY CARE ACT.)

Audit Commission, *The Community Revolution: Personal Services and Community Care*, London, HMSO, 1992.

Community Care (Direct Payments) Act 1996 an Act of Parliament that permits local authorities to give money directly to service users who then purchase their own services.

Under this Act, a local authority may provide cash payments to service users where, following assessment under section 47 of the NATIONAL HEALTH SERVICE AND COMMUNITY CARE ACT 1990, it has determined that services should be provided to meet assessed need. The cash must then be used by the service user to arrange his or her own care.

Whilst the original provision related to disabled people aged between 18 and 65, this was extended in 2000 to people over 65. The CARERS AND

DISABLED CHILDREN ACT 2000 further extended the facility for direct payments to carers, including 16–17-year-olds, for services to meet their own assessed needs as carers, and to 16–17-year-old disabled children for services to meet their own needs.

There are certain exclusions, notably for people subject to compulsory orders under the MENTAL HEALTH ACT 1983, people on probation with requirements for psychiatric treatment, and people who cannot manage the payments even with assistance. Certain services may not be purchased: residential care exceeding four weeks in any one year; services provided by the local authority; help from close relatives or other residents of the household; health care; housing.

Direct payments can make an important contribution to promoting autonomy, flexibility and choice, to the benefit of people who use care services. As originally conceived, the mandate leaves local authorities with discretion about whether to operate such a scheme, but in 2002 the government signalled its intention to make direct payment schemes mandatory.

community care grant see WELFARE RIGHTS 8.

community care plan a three-year plan produced by SOCIAL SERVICES DEPARTMENTS, covering community care provision in their area.

The NATIONAL HEALTH SERVICE AND COMMUNITY CARE ACT established the requirement for local authorities to produce community care plans. The aim, according to the 1989 white paper *Caring for People*, was to increase public accountability by requiring local authorities to publish their proposals for future provision. These plans should also involve other core agencies, including health authorities, housing authorities, and the voluntary and private sectors. The aim is to ensure that plans made by the various agencies involved in community care do not conflict with each other. According to the government, plans should cover a three-year period and include issues such as the development of the local authority's own services, what services are to be purchased from the private and voluntary sectors, proposals for individual case management and the development of complaints procedures. In addition, plans are published to ensure improvements in the public accountability of local authority services, and it is emphasized that they should be written in an accessible manner.

The 1989 white paper approach recommended that community care plans cover specific matters such as: assessment of NEED in the local authority population; strategic objectives for the service; the development of information systems; systems for purchasing services; plans for improvements in domiciliary care; and coordination with other agencies. The DEPARTMENT OF HEALTH has an important role to play in the planning process, in that all community care plans require its approval to establish that they are in line with national government policy. Critics have therefore contended that, while there is an emphasis on decentralizing services to ensure flexibility and tailor services to individual needs, in reality there is a much greater degree of centralization involved through a more interventionist Department of Health and a more powerful Social Services Inspectorate.

community care worker a person in a social services department who undertakes relatively simple ASSESSMENTS of adults, such as frail older people or people with a learning disability, who may require services under the NATIONAL HEALTH SERVICE AND COMMUNITY CARE ACT.

The community care worker is usually a member of a FIELDWORK team, does not hold a social work qualification and will have some limited authority to negotiate and purchase services for a client, such as day care, up to a preset limit.

community development see COMMUNITY WORK.

community drug team a multidisciplinary team that delivers a range of local drug services. Such services include needle exchanges and other harm-minimization services for drug users, including steroid and sports drug users, work within prisons and for those leaving prison, arrest referral schemes where offenders with drug problems are encouraged to take up treatment options under the CRIME AND DISORDER ACT 1998, day services with links to training and employment, counselling, mandatory treatment and testing (under the Crime and Disorder Act), setting up rehabilitation centres and outreach work with young people.

M. Bloor and F. Wood (eds), *Addictions and Problem Drug Use*, London, Jessica Kingsley Publishing, 1998.

Community Legal Service (CLS) an inclusive legal service that provides information, advice and legal representation for all sections of the community, including those who cannot afford legal costs.

The CLS, set up through the Access to Justice Act 1999, works through local partnerships that include solicitors, law centres and funders of legal services as well as information providers such as libraries and post offices. All legal assistance in civil matters, including representation for those who could not otherwise afford it, is now provided by the CLS. Its priorities include cases of child protection, domestic violence and abuses of human rights. It replaced the earlier arrangements for legal aid and aims to provide a more universal and general service.

community profiling a systematic and comprehensive description of the needs of a particular local area defining itself as a COMMUNITY and the local resources available for tackling any problems identified.

Essentially the profile is a catalogue, or audit, of the needs of the local area as experienced by residents. Such needs may be numerous, whether overcrowding in homes, poor housing infrastructure, not enough activities for young people, local shops that overcharge. But they also may be reported in ways that do not simply echo existing services but express the difficulties that residents have in living their everyday lives. Reports of feeling endangered on the streets may be a generalized fear built on the fact that shops have closed down, there are no police patrols on foot or gangs of young people are simply hanging about. A community profile will also include the resources at hand to deal with social problems – whether the level of skills, the strength of local institutions such as churches or mosques or the effectiveness of local NETWORKS. In addition, a community profile is carried out, with local residents playing an active part from the beginning in the range of activities required to complete the profile and also involved from the beginning in putting together an action plan – how to overcome the problems uncovered with the resources available.

Any community profile requires careful planning. Profiling can be time-consuming to plan and carry out, can absorb a group's attention and divert time and energy from other main tasks, produce poor-quality information that in the end is unusable and perhaps raise expectations that the findings on their own will lead to change. Forming a steering group with high levels of resident participation and developing a management structure are essential first steps. At this stage there are key questions that any profiling effort should answer before starting to collect information: What is the purpose of the profile? How will the information be used? Will it be used to: lobby within your own or other service organizations to improve the level of provision? Present to the media or use at a public meeting in order to raise public awareness or support? Develop better relations with neighbourhood residents and activists who want to move on some issues?

Gathering data may involve different forms of information-gathering, such as observation, description of existing services, case studies or public opinion surveys. Data and information may be quite technical and will certainly be comprehensive. In general, there are important categories of data to pursue: land use, the condition of public spaces, the environment and degrees of pollution, population statistics, types and quality of housing, the state of the local economy, including employment, the availability and quality of local services, the communication networks and media, and the local power structure.

In drawing up plans for data-gathering there are a few rules to remember amidst the complexity: try to keep it simple – a lengthy questionnaire will put residents off. It must be easily understood by all who come in contact with it; collect all relevant information, *especially* that which might run counter to what you expect or want to get out of it; use sound research methods that cannot be easily dismissed when used to back up the action plan for improvement.

M. Hawtin, G. Hughes and J. Percy-Smith, *Community Profiling auditing social needs*, Buckinghamshire, Open University, 1994.

community psychiatric nurse (CPN) a person employed by the NATIONAL HEALTH SERVICE to work with people with MENTAL HEALTH PROBLEMS in the COMMUNITY.

Community psychiatric nurses have traditionally worked with any person in the community referred by the psychiatric services. In practice, this can include people attending a psychiatric hospital or a psychiatric wing of a general hospital as outpatients, people attending community mental health facilities or people in their own homes. More recent developments have included a limited number of attachments to general practitioners' surgeries. The work of CPNs can be varied, ranging from administering medication to long-term mentally ill people to counselling on problems of living. With people suffering neuroses, CPNs are often involved in conducting anxiety- and stress-management groups; in the case of people with long-term psychoses, domiciliary visits for monitoring and assessment purposes constitute a major role. Joint work with social workers is increasingly common, both in community mental health teams and in joint care planning for psychiatric patients who are to be discharged into the community and have problems of accommodation, income or social supports.

community punishment and rehabilitation order a COMMUNITY SENTENCE that combines the requirements of a COMMUNITY PUNISHMENT ORDER and a COMMUNITY REHABILITATION ORDER, requiring an offender to do unpaid, supervised work and also to report regularly to a probation officer and fulfil any other conditions added to the order (previously known as a combination order).

community punishment order a COMMUNITY SENTENCE under which an offender aged 16 or over is required to do unpaid, supervised work for between 40 and 240 hours (previously known as a community service order). The work is normally required to be completed within 12 months.

A community punishment order may be combined with other sentences. When combined with a COMMUNITY REHABILITATION ORDER, it is known as a COMMUNITY PUNISHMENT AND REHABILITATION ORDER. Community punishment orders are administered and supervised by the PROBATION SERVICE and governed by NATIONAL STANDARDS FOR YOUNG OFFENDERS. Offenders who fail to carry out the work or who behave inappropriately on work sites can be taken back to court under BREACH PROCEEDINGS, which may result in the order being allowed to continue, usually with an added FINE for breach, or in re-sentencing. This can include imprisonment.

Community punishment orders were introduced in the 1970s, originally as a direct alternative to imprisonment but more recently as sentences in their own right made for imprisonable offences. Although initially intended to be indirectly reparative, the popularity of the sentence with the courts meant that streamlined methods of supervising offenders were required, including workshops where large numbers of people could work off their hours. The probation service increasingly found itself in competition with other providers of free labour for the work opportunities required. Nevertheless, opportunities remain for individual as well as group placements, and a small number of offenders do still undertake work for the benefit of the community, which has some obvious connection with their offences.

Community punishment orders appeal to courts because they combine punishment with at least a symbolic element of REPARATION, allowing the offender to remain in the community, permitting rehabilitation and instilling the habit of working. They appeal to offenders because they allow them to remain at liberty, allow them to make amends for the offence and can stimulate satisfaction at a job well done. However, the orders have also been criticized on a number of grounds. They were originally designed to avoid substituting for paid employment, but some community projects have become increasingly dependent upon free labour from groups of offenders. Some offenders needing help are sentenced to community punishment orders when they might benefit from the making of a community rehabilitation order. In some areas, the orders have developed a very male, macho image that can exclude female offenders. The probation service is increasingly alert to this criticism, however, and has taken steps to ensure that a range of projects, and childcare facilities, are available. The research that has been undertaken suggests that there is a high level of satisfaction among the beneficiaries of the work of offenders serving community punishment orders. It is periodically proposed that community punishment orders should be 'toughened up', but the authorities in the UK have so far resisted following the example of some states in America, which require offenders undertaking their community work to wear uniforms.

A. Worrall, *Punishment in the Community: The Future of Criminal Justice*, London, Longman, 1997

community rehabilitation order a COMMUNITY SENTENCE requiring an offender to be supervised by a probation officer for up to three years (previously known as a probation order).

A community rehabilitation order may be made on any offender over the age of 16, although the juvenile equivalent, a SUPERVISION ORDER, remains an available sentencing option for 16- and 17-year-olds. Courts decide which order to use with this age group according to the young person's maturity and whether they wish them to be supervised by probation officers or social workers, although this is less of an issue since the establishment of YOUTH OFFENDING TEAMS.

The community rehabilitation order has a long history, dating back to the Probation of Offenders Act 1907. The name was changed in 2001, although the objectives of such orders had been changing since 1992 when the order became a sentence in its own right rather than an alternative to sentencing. Traditionally, the order required a probation officer to 'advise, assist and befriend' the offender with a view to rehabilitation. This aim is now supplemented by protecting the public and preventing re-offending, and these have gained greater importance and emphasis than rehabilitation, despite the name of the order. The conduct of community rehabilitation orders is governed by NATIONAL STANDARDS. Orders can be made for periods between six months and three years.

Offenders subject to such orders are required to report to their supervisors regularly and to notify the probation officer of any change of address or employment. If they fail to meet these requirements they may be subject to BREACH PROCEEDINGS.

Courts can add a variety of conditions to a community rehabilitation order, including residence (in a hostel, a treatment facility or as directed by the supervisor), specified activities (including group work, attendance at an approved centre) or treatment for a mental condition or for drug or alcohol dependency. The order can also be combined with unpaid work in the community by means of a COMMUNITY PUNISHMENT AND REHABILITATION ORDER (formerly known as a combination order).

Increasingly, the probation service *manages* community rehabilitation orders rather than directly providing all the services an offender is assessed as needing. There is increasing emphasis on confronting offending behaviour by getting offenders to understand the damage they have done and what they need to do to avoid re-offending.

D. Faulkner, *Crime State and Citizen: A Field Full of Folk*, Winchester, Waterside Press, 2001.

community sentence a term introduced by the CRIMINAL JUSTICE ACT 1991 to describe the tier of sentences between financial penalties and custodial sentences, which courts in England and Wales can pass if the offence is considered to be 'serious enough'. Further community sentences were added to the courts' sentencing powers under the CRIME AND DISORDER ACT 1998.

Community sentences are designed as restrictions on offenders' liberty short of custody, and in some cases they can be combined with one another. The following community sentences are available: ATTENDANCE CENTRE ORDERS, ACTION PLAN ORDERS, SUPERVISION ORDERS, COMMUNITY REHABILITATION ORDERS, COMMUNITY PUNISHMENT ORDERS, COMMUNITY PUNISHMENT AND REHABILITATION ORDERS, CURFEW ORDERS, DRUG TREATMENT AND TESTING ORDERS. Of these, the supervision order and the action plan order are available only in respect of offenders under 18, and the attendance centre order only for under-21s. The operation of all these sentences is governed by NATIONAL STANDARDS, with punishments available for BREACH.

As a tier of sentences, community sentences come above fines and discharges and below custodial sentences in seriousness. As such, the phrase 'serious enough' in the 1991 Act contrasts with the test that judges and magistrates have to use to justify passing custodial penalties, that is, whether the offence is 'so serious' that no community sentence is justifiable. This was partly intended to prevent inconsistent and discriminatory sentencing by imposing standardized tests of seriousness upon the courts, but it has been largely unsuccessful in this respect, as shown by the continued over-representation of black people in custodial institutions. However, the notion of community penalties has institutionalized the requirement to consider whether a sentence is proportionate to the harm done by the offender.

A. Worrall, *Punishment in the Community: The Future of Criminal Justice*, London, Longman, 1997.

community social work an approach to social work that seeks to promote or maintain COMMUNITY-based supports for people already providing care and help to others.

The premise of community social work is that people in difficulty most often receive help from other individuals within their social NETWORKS and recognizes that mainstream social services are peripheral to many people's lives. For example, the care of vulnerable adults is largely undertaken in the community by family, relatives or friends and not by public services. Community social work's objective is to ensure that these informal sources of support function well and, where a person with needs does not have a network of supports to call upon, to help develop one. Community social work begins with the problem affecting an individual or group and then seeks to support and promote the networks of formal and informal relationships to help resolve those problems. Its style of working is decentralized and local, relying on people's own initiatives and capacities to do what in an earlier time social work itself would have tried to do (but less satisfactorily) with service USERS. Community social work requires social workers to see service users not just as family members but as part of a wider social network and to focus upon the links that exist in practice or could potentially be developed for that person. These links are based on family networks and neighbourhood contacts and interests shared between people, such as having a common problem to deal with.

While community social work's greatest influence was in the 1980s, most notably within PATCH teams, it has had lasting influence in the way that social workers now pay considerably more attention to the support systems around families, carers and clients. The planned involvement of family members in care and in coordinating neighbours and volunteers to provide direct care, buttressed by specific services such as DAY CARE and short-term RESIDENTIAL CARE, reflects something of what community social work intended to achieve. Its main concerns are still acutely relevant: the emphasis on social problems, interest in networks, the need to 'go local', formation of partnerships, the requirement for practitioners to be 'bridge-builders' between service systems and different interest groups (especially those without resources).

In framing its practice, community social work avoids the alternative of intervention in the 'community' or with the 'individual'. Community social work teams engage in a whole spectrum of activities and see *both* as legitimate, each requiring planning and resources. For its foremost proponent, Gerald Smale, community social work includes *direct intervention*, or work carried out with individuals, families and their immediate networks to tackle problems that directly affect them; *indirect intervention*, or work with wider community groups and other professionals and agencies to tackle problems that affect a range of people, including the individuals involved in the direct work; *service delivery activity*, providing services that help maintain people in their own homes, to reduce risks to vulnerable people, and to provide relief for overloaded parents and carers. Finally, *change agent activity* seeks to change the ways that people relate to each other that are responsible for social problems, whether at individual, family or neighbourhood levels. It has to do with reallocating resources, such as staff, time and money, in different ways to tackle social problems. This includes making such resources available to neighbourhood residents and organizations and joining with other agencies in holistic solutions.

G. Smale, G. Tuson and D. Statham, *Social Work and Social Problems*, Basingstoke, Macmillan, 2001.

community work a wide-ranging set of practices designed to improve the quality of life for individuals within designated areas, geographical localities or communities. Community work can entail work with individuals, groups and communities, but the key indicator of success for community work activity appears to be whether conditions, social relationships and 'social capital' in a locality are improved. Enhanced 'social inclusion' of people previously marginalized could also be regarded as a key objective.

Community work may be construed as an alternative or additional form of social work. Work can focus upon individuals, families, groups or larger collectives within an area. Work with individuals is regarded as important in its own right, but such work can also contribute to group and community goals. Experiments in the 1970s and 1980s in Britain witnessed attempts to solve individual and family problems through collective work rather than the individual or family casework approaches that had previously dominated social work activity. Instead of being treated as separate 'cases', with sometimes an implied suggestion that the individual or family was to blame for their malaise, individuals and families were invited to join community groups designed to address problems experienced by many people within a locality. Such an approach was thought to be appropriate for apparently personal problems like domestic violence, alcohol dependence or confidence building as well as problems construed as external to individuals or families, such as housing conditions, refuse clearance or the absence of a community nursery on a patch. (See FAMILY SUPPORT.)

Community work seems to fall into three broad groups of activities or theoretical perspectives, namely community development, community action and community service delivery. In practice, it is often difficult to distinguish the perspectives from each other, and many community workers are eclectic in their working practices. There are, however, some discernible differences or emphases.

Community development had its roots in a broadly based movement to try to encourage better living standards in colonial societies, especially after the Second World War, when literacy programmes and schemes to promote citizenship were prominent, especially in countries where there were different ethnic groups trying to develop ways of co-existing peacefully. Since then community development, at a basic level, has been loosely applied to activities promoting the generation of community contacts where there are none or where they are poorly developed, such as in new towns or in localities where people do not linger, like 'hard to let' or 'sink' estates. Later, with the Home Office's ambitious Community Development Programme (CDPs), community development acquired more ambitious operational objectives. These projects entailed a series of well-funded experiments designed to tackle areas of multiple deprivation in both inner-city areas and areas of rural poverty. Home Office funding was used to improve 'infrastructure', such as renovating housing stock and community facilities, enhanced staff-pupil ratios in primary schools (in order to try to help children to compensate for the negative impact of their depressed communities on their school performance) and the provision of resource centres to assist people in relation to welfare benefits advice and job creation. The central focus of the Home Office's conception of community development, however, appeared to be to determine how much communities could mobilize to help themselves. Researchers evaluating the CDPs found virtues in locally based initiatives but considered that improvements to neighbourhoods and communities would always be seriously constrained by wider economic and political forces, such as industrial decline, rising unemployment or a decrease in the value of state benefits. As some commentators pointed out, if General Motors or Ford (based in the USA) sneezed, then areas where there are car production plants in the UK would catch colds or even pneumonia. Similar arguments have been cited in relation to the closure of coal mines or shipyards. The final CDP reports were critical of government policies that sought to tackle poverty solely through local activity. The Home Office abandoned the schemes in the mid-1970s. Nevertheless, similar approaches have been taken by a number of both government and voluntary initiatives across the country since that time.

The term *community action* has been used rather more specifically to describe attempts to secure additional resources for a locality, to achieve a measure of political participation for marginalized groups or perhaps to defeat some proposal thought to be against the interests of those living within the locality. Hence, groups have campaigned to have high-rise blocks demolished because they were damp, expensive to heat and inappropriate for young families. Others have worked collectively to prevent, say, the building of a highway through a neighbourhood. The achievement of change or, paradoxically, its prevention, are usually the focus of community action. There is also a sense in which community action implies that campaigners will use rigorous if not combative methods to try to achieve their goals. The activities of 'eco-warriors' in relation to the Newbury bypass in Berkshire and the second runway at Manchester Airport are examples of this kind. The various professional and qualifying bodies representing community workers have always dissociated themselves from any activities that involve violence, but aggressive 'civil disobedience' has always been regarded as a legitimate tactic. Other less combative forms of community action have involved petitioning, demonstrations, rent strikes, the use of the media and lobbying of political institutions, either locally or nationally. The latter raises interesting issues about identifying appropriate targets for campaigners. Sometimes activists have to decide whether the target is to be local government, for example when regarding some local facility, or whether to try to influence central government if it is construed as a problem of national government starving local government of much needed resources.

The third perspective, *community service delivery*, focuses on the provision of community services. It aims to restructure the delivery of services to make them more responsive to community needs. In this respect it is argued that real community involvement is fundamental. A further element of this perspective is a requirement that all services that have a stake in a problem should seek to collaborate effectively, again taking into account a community's views of its needs. While mostly a 'top-down' approach that seeks to encourage community consultation and participation in developing responsive services, the community service delivery model has been adapted by community workers to try to develop a more 'bottom-up' approach, an approach that can challenge the 'professional-bureaucratic ethos'. The model takes the view that those in need of services are most able to identify that need. In this view the role of the community worker is to assist communities in articulating their needs. Partnership between communities and the service providers is also perceived as key. An example of good practice is perhaps Women's Aid, an organization that has a strong track record of involving service users in management committees and of employing previous service users. The organization has also played a major role in bringing relevant agencies together and in supporting women in violent relationships so that they can shape the very services that are supposed to help them. Difficulties can arise if agencies bring hidden agendas and competing aspirations to consultations with service users. In these circumstances, it is the task of the community worker to facilitate mediation and negotiation between service users and relevant agencies to effect agreements in the service users' interests.

Community work does not imply a particular political perspective, although in practice many community workers tend to be 'left of centre'. More significantly, there is usually a connection between a community worker's analysis of the origins of social problems and the community work methods adopted by a worker. Thus, there can be community workers who stress individual responsibility for behaviour or personal difficulties, thereby emphasizing the importance of responsibilities as well as rights (see COMMUNITARIANISM). Others will take the view that articulating community needs and interests and mobilizing problem solving are the two key dimensions of the role. Significant difficulties can arise when there are fundamental differences between what a community wants and the beliefs and values of the community worker. For example, a community may not wish to have a facility to support refugees sited nearby while the community worker has considerable sympathy for this vulnerable group.

R. Martin (ed), *Learning for Action: Community Work and Participative Training*, London, Federation of Com-munity Work Training Groups, 1991.

H. Butcher, 'The Concept of Community Practice' in L. Haywood (ed), *Community, Leisure and Recreation*, Oxford, Butterworth-Heinemann, 1994.

compensation a financial payment made either by a criminal court or by the Criminal Injuries Compensation scheme to pay victims of crime in order to make amends for loss or damage or to recognize it symbolically.

Courts are required to consider making compensation automatically in relevant cases and to give reasons if they do not award any. Court-ordered compensation is usually restricted to damage or loss that is proved on the day the case is heard, and in practice it is collected only in cases where the police or the prosecution have gone out of their way to obtain the necessary evidence. It is required to be paid to the victim before any fines or costs also ordered by the court, but it may nevertheless be paid in small amounts over a long period if the offender does not have the means to pay outright.

Criminal injuries compensation is paid only to victims of violent crime (and the survivors of murder and manslaughter offences). The amount paid is fixed according to a tariff of injuries, and payments may take months or years to be decided upon and made. VICTIM SUPPORT assists victims in making claims.

complaint and complaints procedure a grievance or accusation and a formal mechanism for hearing the complaint and making recommendations.

Both the CHILDREN ACT (section 26) and the NATIONAL HEALTH SERVICE AND COMMUNITY CARE ACT (chapter 6 of the policy guidance on COMMUNITY CARE) require LOCAL AUTHORITIES to establish complaints procedures. Complaints are construed widely to include comments on the way that a particular case is being handled rather than simply a negative view of events. In adult services, complainants may include users and their carers and representatives. In children's services, complainants can include the child or his or her parent, a person who has PARENTAL RESPONSIBILITY for a child, a foster parent or, finally, any person considered by the local authority to have a legitimate interest in the welfare of the child.

The policy guidelines recommend that a senior officer in any SOCIAL SERVICES DEPARTMENT be given overall responsibility for the complaints procedure. All staff, however, need to be committed to the policy in order to deal with complaints effectively at an early stage or to help complainants shape up a formal complaint if the difficulty cannot be resolved informally. Leaflets in various media need to be devised (for example, for the BLIND, for members of ethnic minorities and for children), and careful thought needs to be given to distribution. Procedures for dealing with complaints require clear timescales and must be clear to all, and the whole operation should be closely monitored, with annual reporting of the nature of the complaints and the quality of the organization's response to them. It is also recommended that all authorities have a designated complaints officer and some independent member on the complaints committee. Random inspection of services and the use of lay visitors can help ensure that staff operate the scheme positively. Any formal complaint should receive a written answer within a few weeks, including a decision about the validity of the complaint and, if justified, any remedial or compensatory action proposed. Another possible channel for complaints is to use the Parliamentary Commissioner (Ombudsman), who has responsibility for investigation of any alleged maladministration on the part of a local or POLICE authority The police also have their own internal mechanisms for dealing with complaints by the public, including by people in custody.

Department of Health, *Right to Complain: Practice Guidance on Complaints Procedures in Social Service Departments*, London, HMSO, 1991.

compulsory competitive tendering SEE BEST VALUE.

compulsory school age the ages of children within which parents are required by law to ensure that they receive full-time education, either at a school or 'otherwise' under sections 7 and 8 of the EDUCATION ACT 1996.

The period begins at the start of the term following a child's fifth birthday. It ends, for all children, on the last Friday in June in the school year in which the child becomes 16. It does not end on the child's actual 16th birthday, which may be several months earlier. This definition affects all other definitions used in education, for example those relating to the EMPLOYMENT OF CHILDREN. In this context, the term 'young person' is applicable only to those who have completed compulsory education. A parent does not have to send their child to a school to meet the legal requirement. Education can take place in other ways, such as tuition at home by a parent or private tutor, a further education college or a self-help school. In this case the provision will be subject to inspection by officers of the local education authority (LEA).

conciliation a process in which an impartial third party helps the people in conflict to resolve their dispute by hearing both sides and then offering an opinion on settlement. See FAMILY MEDIATION.

concurrent jurisdiction the competence of two or more courts at different levels of the court system to hear the same case.

The concept of concurrent jurisdiction is relevant to proceedings involving children under the CHILDREN ACT, whereby an application for a care order may be sought from either a FAMILY PROCEEDINGS COURT, where proceedings will be heard by MAGISTRATES, or a county court, where the proceedings will be heard by a judge. The decision as to which court a particular case should go is generally taken by the clerk to the family proceedings court; most cases start there. More complex cases go to the county court.

conditional response now usually referred to as 'conditioned response'. See CLASSICAL CONDITIONING, OPERANT CONDITIONING.

conditioning any form of learning about the dependence of one event on the occurrence of another. See CLASSICAL CONDITIONING.

conduct disorder a term used in behavioural PSYCHOLOGY to refer to any of a broad range of serious and persistent antisocial behaviours in children that result in significant impairment of a child's everyday functioning to the point that the behaviours are considered unmanageable by parents, care-givers, teachers or others in the child's life.

Estimates vary as to the number of children who show conduct disorders, which include hitting, setting fires, stealing, truancy and running away, and range from 4 per cent to 10 per cent of the child population. But among those children referred to clinical services for help, the proportion may be as high as 50 per cent. There is widespread agreement that conduct disorders are becoming more prevalent and are creating a need for specialist services in education, clinical psychology and social services that far exceeds available staff and resources. Conduct disorders in children have proven difficult to change, and studies of some children have shown a link with problems in later life. Certain approaches focusing on the child's behaviour or on the behaviour of that child's parents or other care-givers, however, have begun to indicate some hopeful ways of tackling the problem. One of these is parent training, where the parents of the child are taught to observe and identify behaviours in new ways and in particular to reward sociable behaviours and to avoid the unwitting rewarding of antisocial behaviours by shouting, counter-aggression and escalation of conflict.

confidentiality the safeguarding of privacy in relation to INFORMATION about service users.

Social welfare agencies are much concerned about issues of access to CLIENT information. There are several senses in which confidentiality is an issue. First, service users are concerned that information about them is not freely shared with third parties. Second, workers may wish to protect the identity of people who help to reveal, say, CHILD ABUSE or some other criminal offence. Third, there may be information on social work or other files to which access by the service user is denied. Fourth, information divulged to a worker by a service user may not in some circumstances be kept confidential.

Many of the issues surrounding confidentiality are complex in practice. Information about a service user is habitually shared with other agencies with welfare issues as the justification. Thus a case of alleged child abuse may involve a social worker in inquiries with the family doctor or HEALTH VISITOR or at the child's school. Should such inquiries be initiated only with parental permission (which may be withheld)? Or are the interests of a possibly abused child sufficient to override such concerns? Similarly, should there be a confidential section on social work files to which the service user has no access, because such information may be upsetting to the focal person or involve sensitive material about third parties? Should social workers at least provide information about the kinds of information held in the confidential section of a file in order that the service user or client might challenge a decision not to allow him or her access to such material? Finally, can a social worker ever guarantee confidentiality when such information may concern his or her statutory duties?

Connexions a central government programme that provides personal advisers for all young people to assist them in the transition from school and adolescence to employment and adulthood.

Connexions is designed to overcome the divisions between services for young people principally between housing, employment and education which makes the transition to adulthood so difficult for young people, particularly those from a disadvantaged background. The personal advisers are central to helping individual young people make sense of these services. They are drawn from a range of agencies including the youth service, youth offending teams, and social workers and are seconded to a variety of locations such as schools and further education colleges. Their role is to befriend and support individual young people while identifying what their particular needs are – and to increase their employability. Personal advisers will ensure school attendance prior to the age of 16, provide information regarding future learning and work opportunities, conduct basic skill assessments, provide support in gaining access to education and training and broker work placements. For LOOKED-AFTER young people and CARE LEAVERS the assistance of Connexions has much to offer.

There are a number of competing strands within the Connexions programme, including a strong emphasis on getting ready for work and on the responsibilities and obligations of CITIZENSHIP. There is less emphasis on issues such as self-fulfilment and identity and on ensuring that individual young people understand the social, ethnic and familial forces that have shaped them.

constant attendance allowance see WELFARE RIGHTS 3.

consultation a lower level form of PARTICIPATION in which the opinions of local service users are sought by service managers on a few carefully selected issues.

Consultation provides people with a limited role and choice at the planning stage of a new community project or service. A typical format for consultation would involve service management presenting at a public meeting two or three options as to how a project or service might develop and then listening to feedback and comment from the floor. Within such a consultative process there is no requirement that management take opinions obtained in this way into account before proceeding. Practitioners involved in consultation are not looking for service users' involvement in implementation, but they are hoping that the service or project will enjoy the consent of those consulted. Social work uses consultation widely to improve services and to win support from users when options are limited and the overall aim is already in place. Consultation is not appropriate when practitioners are seeking to empower local interests or are not in a position to take up the suggestions put forward. The main methods for consulting are: carrying out local surveys and questionnaires, forming consultative committees, and consultation days with presentations and the discussion of scenarios and feedback built in.

In a consultative process, practitioners should be clear about their own role and who ultimately will take decisions and how this will be done. They also should be clear about how realistic the different options are that they present and ensure that they are conveyed in a way that is understood. If a task force or local forum is formed to aid the consultative process, its terms of reference should be clear. Thought also has to be given to how feedback from those being consulted will be handled, and the means by which it will be logged or recorded. Perhaps the most challenging question for practitioners engaged in consultation is whether they are really just seeking endorsement of current plans that are essentially unchangeable or they are actually prepared to change those plans in response to feedback.

P. Beresford and S. Croft, *Citizen Involvement: A practical guide for change*, Basingstoke, Macmillan, 1993.

contact the different means by which a child keeps in touch with family members when away from home.

A child living away from home, for example in local authority care, or not living with one of his or her parents following separation or divorce, can maintain links with people such as parents, siblings and grandparents in a variety of ways, including visits, telephone calls, cards, e-mails, letters and gifts. Maintaining contact for a child being LOOKED AFTER by the local authority and his or her family is a matter of great importance to social workers. Research has shown that the consistency and degree of contact between a child in care and his or her parents is one of the best indicators as to whether the child will return home successfully or not. Because of this key finding, the CHILDREN ACT pays a great deal of attention to contact.

Section 34 of the Children Act requires that children subject to a CARE ORDER have 'reasonable contact' with their parents or other member(s) of the family as long as this is in the welfare of the child. The Act does not define what is 'reasonable' but leaves this to the parties concerned to work out, including the child, if old enough, the parents and other important family members. The Act also lays a general duty on social workers to facilitate contact for children whenever they are away from home, a duty that must receive the social workers' priority. Facilitating contact is not always easy. Difficulties in the parent–child relationship, distance from the child's placement and resistance of the child's foster carers are all factors that can adversely affect the frequency of contact. Nevertheless, social workers are expected to commit considerable resources, in terms of their own time or in offering to pay fares, to ensure that contact comes about. The frequency of contact and how it will be undertaken form an essential part of any CARE PLAN for a child. Only if the welfare of the child is jeopardized may the local authority ask the court for a CONTACT DIRECTION, restricting contact or even terminating it altogether. Similarly, parents may ask the court for such a direction for increasing contact.

Some feminist researchers have uncovered the less positive side of presuming contact between a non-resident father and his child when violence and abuse have characterized the relationship of the child's parents. Contact between father and child, they argue, offers only further opportunity for the violent father to continue his intimidating, controlling and abusive behaviour. (See also CONTACT ORDER, REUNIFICATION, FEMINIST SOCIAL WORK).

contact direction stipulation by a court regarding the degree of CONTACT to take place between a child in the care of the LOCAL AUTHORITY and other members of the family.

Under section 34 of the CHILDREN ACT, the court making a CARE ORDER may also specify the degree of contact that the child may have with those who have PARENTAL RESPONSIBILITY for him or her, or any other person the court deems relevant, such as siblings. It may do this at the time the care order is made or at any time afterwards. Any party to the proceedings may ask the court for such a direction. This includes a local authority that wishes to terminate all contact between a child in its care and his or her parents, or a parent of a child in care who wishes to visit his or her child more frequently. If no such direction is made, the Children Act assumes that 'reasonable contact' will take place between the child in care and the parents.

contact order a court order under section 8 of the CHILDREN ACT determining the frequency and kind of CONTACT that a child will have with a parent or others with PARENTAL RESPONSIBILITY for the child in private law proceedings.

Contact orders are generally used to settle differences of opinion as to how often the child should see one or the other of the parents in matrimonial disputes. An order can also be used in relation to a child who goes to live with other members of the family, such as grandparents, including a child who might otherwise have come into local authority care. The order should not be confused with a CONTACT DIRECTION, made by a court to regulate contact between a child in local authority care and the parents or other family members.

contributory benefits see SOCIAL SECURITY; WELFARE RIGHTS 1.

controlled drugs policy policy shaped by central government designed to roll back the number of people becoming dependent drug users.

There are two major elements in policy to control drug dependency. First is law enforcement. Drugs thought to have dangerous consequences have been made illegal, so people using or supplying them have been convicted as criminals. Second is treatment, originally exclusively under the medical or biological model but now with nurses, psychologists and social workers also playing key roles. The treatment role led to drug and alcohol dependency units in psychiatric hospitals, staffed by these different professionals. These have largely given way to COMMUNITY DRUG TEAMS, but still hospital in-patient treatment (usually DETOXIFICATION) takes place.

Controlled drugs policy became important in health and welfare policy in the 1970s as a result of the big increase in drugs misuse. A concept from those years still governing the treatment aspect of policy and services is that of the 'problem drug user'. This notion held that people with drug problems did not just become dependent upon one drug but were likely to be 'poly-drug' users. The problem was therefore less about the physical craving for particular drugs and more about psychological dependency on substances. Particular people were dependent upon substances, it was thought, because they lacked the capacity to cope with the stresses in their lives and were unable to shoulder the responsibility it took to develop this capacity because of their vulnerability.

Treatment approaches now include developing the individual's capacity for responsibility and coping, along with rehabilitation in residential drugs units and community drug teams. The objective has been to foster responsibility rather than dependency and passivity linked to hospitalization and to an overemphasis on medical interventions.

Social workers contribute to this in their CARE MANAGEMENT role, mainly in assessing for entry to, and funding for, residential rehabilitation, but there is the potential for social care intervention to play other important roles in the reduction of drug problems.

The white paper *Tackling Drugs to Build a Better Britain*, published in 1998, laid out three objectives for a ten-year strategy:

1 to help young people resist drug mis-use and achieve their full potential;

2 to protect communities from drug-related antisocial and criminal behaviour;

3 to help people to overcome drug misuse and to live healthy and crime-free lives.

Policy now aims to meet the spectrum of need, with an awareness that drug problems are part of SOCIAL EXCLUSION as well as a distinctive pattern of acquisitive crime to fund the purchase of drugs in the illicit market. These considerations have led to policies within the drugs strategy and in different policies, requiring partnership between key agencies such as health, social services, criminal justice, YOUTH OFFENDING TEAMS and housing to prevent drugs misuse in the community. The idea is that each agency addresses an aspect of social exclusion leading to drugs misuse. By preventing drugs misuse, other aspects of social exclusion are prevented, such as crime, unemployment, EXCLUSION FROM SCHOOL and poor parenting.

Social workers will help implement this policy through a number of channels. They include youth offending teams involved in community safety policies, SOCIAL SERVICES DEPARTMENTS charged with preventing drugs misuse in the community, and CARE MANAGERS who are required to assess and provide services for dependent drug users. With regard to the latter role, many users receive assessment and funding for rehabilitation or other services under a DRUG TREATMENT AND TESTING ORDER. As a result, any relapse is notified to the authorities, with PRISON as the consequence. Social workers are also involved in mental health promotion linked to substance misuse, as 30 per cent with DEPRESSION and ANXIETY in primary care misuse substances, and parental mental health problems and SUBSTANCE MISUSE increase the risk of children and young people offending, misusing substances and being excluded from school.

councils of voluntary service the major coordinating bodies for VOLUNTARY-SECTOR organizations within particular geographical areas. Some rural areas are able to sustain a council, but predominantly they are located in large towns and cities. Most such councils receive their funding from local authorities.

Following the publication of the Wolfenden Report on the future of voluntary organizations in 1974, many councils of voluntary service were established. These either replaced the former councils of social service or were entirely new creations. Their functions include the development of voluntary activity in the locality, often through the provision of volunteer bureaux to recruit VOLUNTEERS to affiliated organizations; the provision of information about local conditions and needs; the coordination of effort and policy among voluntary bodies; and sometimes the direct delivery of services to the public and to voluntary organizations (for example, printing and distribution of newsletters, or training of volunteers including management committee members). Councils of voluntary service have in recent years been active in opposing cuts in public expenditure. Given that many voluntary organizations work with vulnerable and marginalized groups, the councils are in a unique position to offer opinions about how such groups are faring in relation to government policy. The councils have also been particularly active in promoting harmonious race relations.

council tax benefit see WELFARE RIGHTS 6.

counselling the process whereby a trained professional counsellor gives another person support and guidance in an individual or group setting.

Counselling provides one form of assistance when a person experiences stress in his or her life as a result of traumatic life events, such as rape, DOMESTIC VIOLENCE or BEREAVEMENT, or because of the effects of general circumstances – for example, an unhappy marriage, BULLYING or work-related stress. Counselling may also involve ADVICE-giving, as in careers guidance or Citizens Advice Bureau work, although many would argue that counselling does not or should not involve advice. Despite the breadth of use of the term, however, the core of its current meaning is the enabling of the counselled person to take control of his or her own life through greater understanding and a realistic assessment of his or her current emotional and interpersonal experiences. Counselling is a rapidly expanding field and is becoming professionalized. The British Association of Counselling approves and accredits courses that meet the standard requirements.

Although Freud's 'talking cure' (see PSYCHOANALYSIS) set the stage for the development of counselling, the crucial theorist is Carl Rogers, who introduced client-centred therapy as a method. He believed that the counselled person is helped primarily through the quality of the relationship with the counsellor, who must provide the three 'core conditions' of empathy, genuineness and unconditional positive regard. Some counselling methods, however, are more directive; for example, COGNITIVE-BEHAVIOURAL methods aim to shape thinking behaviour towards greater realism, while the PSYCHODYNAMIC APPROACH proceeds by looking to childhood experience to explain current emotional states and the resolution of these problems through CATHARSIS. Evaluation studies of counselling suggest that these diverse theoretical approaches and their associated methodologies have preferred application in different client groups and at different stages of the counselling process. An eclectic approach is therefore often preferred by practising counsellors. (See LISTENING, PERSON-CENTRED COUNSELLING.)

J. McLeod, *Introduction to Counselling*, Buckingham, Open University Press, 1993.

CPN abbreviation for COMMUNITY PSYCHIATRIC NURSE.

CPS abbreviation for CROWN PROSECUTION SERVICE.

credit union a group of people, with a common bond, who save money together in order to build up sufficient funds to make low-interest loans available to participants in the union. Credit unions in Britain are governed by the Credit Union Act 1979.

The credit union movement is long established and international. Popular and successful unions exist, for example, in Ireland, the Caribbean and South Asia. Poor people often do not have access to 'mainstream' credit facilities because credit agencies, such as banks and loan and insurance companies, will not lend to them. Facilities that are available to them, such as local moneylenders, invariably charge very high rates of interest or operate other constraints, such as the requirement that goods are purchased from certain stores.

Credit unions must comprise people who have a 'common bond' – for example, people who all live in the same neighbourhood, belong to the same church or work for the same company. Members save and, once a personal target and a collective target have been reached, can borrow. Loans are usually modest and rates of interest low. In Britain, interest rates must not exceed 1 per cent per month (annual percentage rate 12.6). Credit unions have grown significantly over the last ten years.

Crime and Disorder Act 1998 a law that came into force in 2000, introducing a new sentencing framework in respect of offenders in England, Wales and Scotland and new arrangements for inter-agency crime prevention and for racially aggravated offences. The Act complements the criminal justice act 1991, which was the previous statement of a sentencing framework and parts of which remain in force.

The 1998 Crime and Disorder Act made changes to the range of sentences available, and to the administration and philosophy of the youth justice system in particular. In addition, it introduced statutory CRIME AND DISORDER PARTNERSHIPS that give local authorities a responsibility to coordinate the preparation and implementation of crime reduction strategies.

In respect of adult offenders, the Act introduced SEX OFFENDER ORDERS, prohibiting sexual offenders from acting in defined ways. It also introduced extended supervision periods for violent and sexual offenders released from custody. It introduced DRUG TREATMENT AND TESTING ORDERS. It clarified the law on RACIALLY AGGRAVATED OFFENCES, allowing courts to sentence more severely when it has been established that offences of assault, criminal damage, harassment and public disorder are racially motivated. It restricted the availability of BAIL in serious cases.

The Act introduced a range of new sentences for young offenders (see ANTISOCIAL BEHAVIOUR ORDER – also applicable to adults – and

PARENTING ORDER, CURFEW, REPRIMAND, FINAL WARNING, ACTION PLAN ORDER, REPARATION ORDER, DETENTION AND TRAINING ORDER, applicable only to young offenders). These new sentences are intended to ensure that courts have a wide range of possible responses not only to crime but also to disorderly behaviour by young people, and that the relevant authorities intervene early enough to have an impact on such behaviour. It also made a number of changes to the SUPERVISION ORDER. More importantly, it defined for the first time the aim of the youth justice system, established the national YOUTH JUSTICE BOARD and required local authorities to set up multi-agency YOUTH OFFENDING TEAMS. A particularly controversial change was the abolition of the legal assumption that young people under 14 are less likely to be able to tell right from wrong than older people (see DOLI INCAPAX).

The principal aim of the youth justice system is defined in the Act as 'to prevent offending by children and young persons'. This deceptively simple statement masks an extremely complex reality. The new youth offending teams had to introduce all the new court orders at the same time as establishing ways of bringing a range of agencies with differing philosophies and purposes together at a time when the government was also introducing FAST-TRACKING procedures to speed up the system. The focus on preventing offending was not altogether new, but it was intended to remind all the agencies concerned that young offenders should have their offence-related needs met first. They were to be seen as offenders first and as children in need second – although this has remained a controversial and contested view and the provisions of the CHILDREN ACT 1989 remain applicable to young offenders. The previous social services-run youth justice teams were seen by the government as overly concerned with the welfare of young offenders and insufficiently focused on carrying out the sentences of the courts. Youth offending teams, incorporating staff from a wider range of agencies including the police, probation, health and education workers, were seen as heralding a new culture of youth justice work. Numerically, however, the teams were predominantly made up of social workers from the previous youth justice teams, and not all the other staff welcomed the new arrangements wholeheartedly. Many staff saw the new court orders as having a NET WIDENING effect, drawing more young people into the formal criminal justice system and increasing the severity of courts' responses, including a greater use of custody and secure care. Change was increasingly driven by centralized initiatives from the youth justice board and by the detailed requirements of its NATIONAL STANDARDS.

Another cultural change for youth justice arose from the introduction of action plan orders, reparation orders and, under subsequent legislation, REFERRAL ORDERS. These orders all create possibilities for REPARATION whereby young offenders make good the damage done by their offence, and this requires youth offending teams to consult

VICTIMS of crime. While this was not new to some probation officers or most police officers, other members of youth offending teams had rarely had occasion to contact victims of crime, and this necessitated a substantial programme of staff training.

B. Goldson (ed), *The New Youth Justice*, Lyme Regis, Russell House, 2000.

crime and disorder partnerships multi-agency groups, set up under the CRIME AND DISORDER ACT 1998, that exist to formulate and implement crime and disorder strategies that set and monitor local crime reduction targets.

The government's stated aim in setting up these groups was to empower local people to take a fuller part in fighting crime and disorder. Partnerships are required to include the police, probation and health services under the coordination of the local authority and to report regularly to the HOME OFFICE on their targets and achievements. The government's guidance to local partnerships emphasized the need to involve young people in consultations, treating them as a resource rather than a problem, and stressed the necessity of involving 'hard to reach' groups, such as ethnic minorities and gays and lesbians. How far this has been achieved in practice is unclear, but the partnerships need not consist only of statutory agencies. Such corporate partnerships, however, have often been dominated by the most powerful partner agency, the police, whose priorities tend to prevail. Nevertheless, policing strategies and local authority policies have certainly changed in some areas in response to consultations.

crime prevention any of a variety of interventions aimed at addressing the mechanisms that cause crimes, ranging from educational initiatives to the use of closed circuit TV cameras in public areas.

Although the term 'crime prevention' has been criticized for its vagueness, it is useful in describing a wide range of interventions. It covers both the precautions taken by individuals and businesses to protect themselves and their property from crime, and the steps taken by local authorities, the police and other agencies to prevent crime. Individuals and businesses can choose to fit burglar alarms, bolts and bars to property or to employ private security companies; the police can decide to give priority to potential cases of repeat victimization or to neighbourhood watch and other inter-agency activities in preference to conventional policing.

Many agencies are now required by law to prepare crime and disorder reduction strategies under the CRIME AND DISORDER ACT 1998, and these are likely to include 'situational' crime reduction measures as well as social policies. Situational approaches include making the prospective targets of crime, such as homes, less inviting, reducing the prospect of opportunistic crime through measures such as the visible introduction of closed-circuit TV cameras, placing security staff in car parks or improving street lighting. At an earlier stage, prevention also includes approaches to architecture and planning aimed at 'designing out crime', for example by ensuring that public areas of housing estates are all overlooked by someone's windows. Crime reduction also relies on the use of social networks, including neighbourhood watch schemes, community REPARATION projects, measures to support people repeatedly victimized, racial harassment and other VICTIM SUPPORT projects. Other such efforts include educational programmes with schoolchildren and others, publicity programmes (such as the ZERO TOLERANCE campaigns in a number of cities) and a range of inter-agency community safety initiatives.

A distinction is often made between primary and secondary crime prevention, and some writers also refer to tertiary prevention. *Primary prevention* concentrates on the general public or the environment and tends to involve educational and situational work. It attempts to prevent crime by raising awareness and by improving security of homes and business premises. *Secondary prevention* pays attention to people seen as being at risk of offending or becoming victims, and as such it includes many of the social approaches to crime prevention described above. *Tertiary prevention* involves working with people who are already identified as victims or offenders to prevent repeat crimes, and is the business of agencies such as PROBATION and the voluntary VICTIM SUPPORT sector as well as the police and local authority agencies such as housing departments. (The three categories are defined differently by different authors, and tertiary prevention is included within secondary prevention by some.)

A. Crawford, *Crime Prevention and Community Safety: Politic, Policies and Practices*, London, Longman, 1998.

criminal court a court dealing with the prosecution of people accused of breaking the law. Criminal courts deal with behaviour considered harmful to society as a whole, as opposed to civil courts, which deal with legal disputes between one private interest (whether an individual or an organization) and another.

The main criminal courts in England and Wales are the MAGISTRATES' courts and the *Crown Courts*. Magistrates' courts deal with the great majority – around 98 per cent – of criminal cases. They hear the facts of a case, make decisions about guilt or innocence and give sentences. *Lay* (unpaid volunteer) *magistrates* are ordinary members of the public, appointed by the Lord Chancellor, and they have the power to impose any sentence up to the legal maximum for the offence, except that the maximum prison sentence they can impose is six months for one offence or a total of twelve months for more than one offence. Increasingly, lay magistrates are being supplemented or replaced, particularly in busy urban courts, by *district judges*, professional magistrates previously known as *stipendiary magistrates*. Small rural courts are also being closed and replaced by modern buildings in urban centres. Although these may be better equipped (often with separate waiting rooms for VICTIMS and witnesses), they are not always welcome replacements for rural courts on the part of magistrates, victims and witnesses who consequently have further to travel than previously. If magistrates consider that an offence requires a greater punishment than they have powers to inflict, they must commit the defendant to the Crown Court for trial and sentencing by a judge and jury. Some offences – *summary offences*, such as criminal damage – can be dealt with only in magistrates' courts, whereas very serious *indictable offences* (such as murder and rape) can be dealt with only by the Crown Court. Most offences, however, are triable either way, allowing the defendant or magistrates to decide whether the case is dealt with in the magistrates' court or the Crown Court. Many defendants elect for a Crown Court trial because they believe they will have a better chance of acquittal. The appeal process starts at the Crown Court, which hears appeals from magistrates' courts, and may proceed to the Court of Appeal, the High Court and ultimately the House of Lords.

The process whereby an offender comes to court is complicated. A person arrested by the POLICE who admits to committing an offence may receive a formal CAUTION, with matters being taken no further. A young person may receive a REPRIMAND, which has a similar effect, or a FINAL WARNING, which involves referral to the local YOUTH OFFENDING TEAM. If the defendant denies committing the offence, or if it is considered too serious for a caution or warning, the police report the matter to the CROWN PROSECUTION SERVICE, which decides whether or not to prosecute. The police may release the accused person on BAIL to appear later at court, or simply agree to send them a summons; or they may keep the person in CUSTODY at a police station, in which case they must take them to court within a specified period of hours. The permission of the MAGISTRATES must be obtained before defendants can be detained beyond the specified period (see REMAND). The accused person can be transferred to a remand prison until his or her case can be dealt with.

Magistrates' courts are relatively local and open to the public. They have existed in one form or another for over 650 years. They cover several hundred small geographical areas known as *petty sessional divisions*, although they are being concentrated in larger groups of divisions in rural parts of the country. *Lay magistrates*, or *justices of the peace*, sit in panels, usually of three, known as benches. They undergo basic and ongoing training but are not legally qualified. They have legal advisers and court administrators, known as *justices' clerks*. They are meant to be representative of the local community, and recruitment has become a more open process in recent years. They nevertheless tend to be predominantly middle-aged and middle-class. In urban areas, there are often also *district judges*, professionally qualified magistrates who sit alone. Magistrates sometimes adjourn a case for two or three weeks to obtain PRE-SENTENCE REPORTS or medical reports before passing sentence on a defendant. There are separate magistrates' courts for young people under 18 years of age, known as YOUTH COURTS, where proceedings are intended to be less formal and from which members of the public are excluded; the press are admitted but may not normally publish defendants' names or addresses.

The right to trial by jury is seen as a fundamental constitutional right in England and Wales, although there has been debate about restricting this right in order to reduce the burden on Crown Courts and the subsequent delays in bringing cases to trial (see FAST TRACKING). Crown Courts have existed only since 1972, when they replaced *quarter sessions* and *assize courts*. Depending on the seriousness of an offence, the Crown Court is presided over by a *High Court judge* (for the most serious), a *circuit judge* (most cases) or a part-time *recorder*, all of whom are experienced barristers. Like magistrates' courts, Crown Courts are open to the public. If a defendant pleads not guilty, the decision about his or her guilt or innocence is made by a jury of twelve lay people, selected at random, after they have heard all the evidence from the prosecution and defence lawyers and the witnesses. After the jury has delivered its verdict, it plays no further part in the proceedings; it cannot influence the sentence, which is the decision of the judge.

The Crown Court acts as an appeal court against both conviction and sentence in the magistrates' court. It can impose any sentence that could have been imposed by the magistrates, whether harsher or more lenient than the original sentence. All appeals against conviction or sentences passed in the Crown Court are heard by the *Court of Appeal*, which does not hear witnesses but considers only written material. It also has the role of interpreting the law if it is unclear and setting precedents to be followed by the lower courts. Other courts can also be involved in appeals: where a point of law is at issue in a magistrates' court, the *Queen's Bench Division* of the High Court hears the appeal. The highest court of appeal is the *House of Lords* or, more accurately, the nine or ten law lords who sit in panels of five to hear cases granted leave to appeal by the Court of Appeal.

Although there is no written British constitution, there is a basic assumption that the criminal courts are independent of Parliament and local government and not subject to political influence.

M. Berlins and C. Dyer, *The Law Machine*, fifth edition, London, Penguin, 2000.

Criminal Defence Service the service that replaced criminal legal aid and aims to provide quality defence services for those accused of a criminal offence. It was established by the Access to Justice Act 1999 and, in parallel with the COMMUNITY LEGAL SERVICE, incorporates legal aid in criminal proceedings for those who are eligible.

Criminal Justice Act 1991 an act that established a number of important principles in sentencing offenders, including the seriousness of the crime and a positive view of community sentences.

It laid down a requirement that courts sentence in a way that reflects the seriousness of the offences committed ('proportionality'), although it was subsequently amended to allow offences committed while the defendant was on BAIL to be treated more seriously. The Act drew a distinction between property offences and those against the person, with the latter to be considered as more serious. Where a prison sentence is passed for an offence of violence, the need to protect the public from serious harm can help to determine its length. The Act recognized that community sentences constitute a sentencing band (see below) in their own right, providing a degree of restriction of liberty commensurate with the seriousness of the offence. Such sentences were no longer to be seen as 'alternatives to custody' but rather as the appropriate response to offences of a particular level of seriousness. The Act also required (in section 95) that the criminal justice system be administered fairly, efficiently and without discrimination, and the Secretary of State is required to publish relevant information about the attainment of these objectives annually. These provisions of the Act remain in force following passage of the CRIME AND DISORDER ACT 1998.

crisis intervention an attempt to understand the nature of episodes that people find extremely difficult or impossible to handle and to understand how services might be organized to help people through such events.

Crises are precipitated by hazardous events, which may be a single catastrophe or a series of mishaps. They may be brought about by something external to the person or by something that appears to be rooted in him or her (although on further investigation an external cause may be revealed, such as an earlier trauma or crisis). The same hazardous event may bring about a crisis for some people but not for others – although some events (for example, the unexpected death of a loved one) bring about a state of crisis in most individuals. The hazardous event is likely to disturb the person's 'balance' and arouse feelings of extreme vulnerability. Most people attempt to deal with such difficulties by employing their usual coping mechanisms. If these coping mechanisms do not help, the person may employ rarely used emergency methods as a measure of desperation. If the problem persists and cannot be alleviated or avoided, the person is likely to enter a period of acute discomfort. This period is thought to be the state of *active crisis*. The interval between the onset of a crisis and its resolution will vary, but the active state of crisis is unlikely to last more than four to six weeks.

As individuals experience a crisis, and during the early stages of conflict resolution, they are especially amenable to help. They may even embrace help that they had earlier rejected. Minimal focused effort at this time, because of emotional accessibility, may bring about a substantial change. As the person recovers, new 'ego sets' and adaptive styles may be learned that may enable the person to cope with future crises. Complete, rather than partial, recovery seems to be dependent upon a 'correct' understanding of the event. Thus, a woman who has been raped needs to understand that she was in no way responsible for the event and that she has been a victim of a man's abuse of power. Services dealing with crises have to be able to give the time to help people through these events. Intensive support is required, and services need to be organized so that an appropriate response is possible. Rape crisis centres and women's refuges, for example, are in some measure organized in the expectation of crises, but other services clearly are not. Children are often rescued from abusive situations, yet services are rarely mobilized to help them cope with their crises in the aftermath.

K. O'Hagan, 'Crisis Intervention: Changing Perspectives' in C. Harvey and T. Philpot (eds), *Practising Social Work*, London, Routledge, 1994.

crisis loan see WELFARE RIGHTS (8).

Crown Court see CRIMINAL COURT.

Crown Prosecution Service (CPS) in England and Wales the national service of solicitors and barristers with responsibility for deciding whether a case should be brought to court and for conducting the prosecution in court.

The decision to prosecute taken by the CPS is based on the evidence gathered by the police but is completely independent of the police. Generally any decision to prosecute follows:

1 an examination of the evidence, and

2 whether a prosecution is in the public interest.

A critical factor in any decision is whether the crime involved racial hatred or other discrimination and whether the victim is vulnerable in some way. The CPS also makes recommendations about remanding defendants on BAIL or in CUSTODY. The service may also decide to discontinue a prosecution if it considers that there is insufficient evidence or that it would not be in the public interest to continue.

CTC abbreviation for child TAX CREDIT (see WELFARE RIGHTS 5, WELFARE RIGHTS 9).

culture of poverty a term devised and developed by sociologists and anthropologists to describe the existence of poor people, with the suggestion that people living in long-term POVERTY develop a particular way of life, passing on that way of life to future generations. The term is closely allied to the ideas of a CYCLE OF DEPRIVATION, UNDERCLASS and SOCIAL EXCLUSION.

The anthropologist most closely associated with the idea of a culture of poverty is Oscar Lewis. He believed that his researches in both developing and advanced capitalist societies revealed a complex culture of interlocking behaviours, beliefs and attitudes that characterize poor people. Thus, a strong present time orientation, the cult of machismo, matriarchal family structures and a sense of fatalism all appeared to be widespread features of the lives of poor people. Additionally, the inability of the poor to become involved in institutions such as trade unions, political parties and 'normal' economic activity was thought to add to their marginality and to confirm their membership of an underclass. Lewis has been criticized because there is a sense in which he seems to blame the poor for their own poverty. If culture is a set of responses for coping with immediate circumstances, the critical issue is how much those attitudes and values rooted in the experience of poverty may prevent a person or community from responding to improved circumstances. Lewis has it that the culture of poverty will inhibit ANTI-POVERTY STRATEGIES, whereas others have argued that if life chances are significantly improved for poor people, they will quickly respond.

Many professionals working in social welfare have been dismayed at what they perceive as the inability of the poor to respond to help offered. Others take the view that social welfare workers, in the main, have little to offer poor people in relation to an improvement in LIFE CHANCES. On the contrary, most social welfare workers, they argue, endorse the *status quo* and in that respect become agents of social control. COMMUNITY DEVELOPMENT programmes, designed to improve the lot of poor communities, have been criticized because they do not acknowledge the importance of structural inequality and therefore must be regarded as superficial. Although the idea of the culture of poverty is perceived as flawed by its critics, its influence is still acknowledged as substantial. Many social workers probably see at least some individuals, families and communities in terms that imply a view of poverty consistent with that of Oscar Lewis.

D. Moynihan (ed), *On Understanding Poverty*, New York, Basic Books, 1968.

curfew order an order requiring a person or group of people to remain at home during specified hours.

Under the CRIME AND DISORDER ACT 1998, child curfew schemes enable local authorities to ban all children under ten years of age from being in a specified place at specified times. Courts have made little use of this provision. Individual young people aged up to 17 can also be made subject to curfews under the Powers of Criminal Courts (Sentencing) Act, 2000. These can last up to six months, for up to 12 hours per day, and may be combined with ELECTRONIC MONITORING, which requires the young person to wear an electronic 'tag'. Where the young person is under 16, courts are required to obtain information about the family circumstances and the likely impact of such an order upon the family, usually by means of a PRE-SENTENCE REPORT.

The term 'curfew' is also used colloquially to refer to BAIL conditions, which can require defendants to remain at home between specified hours.

custodial sentence see CUSTODY.

custody imprisonment, including being held by the police on remand.

Adults are held in PRISON, while young offenders are held in a range of secure institutions, including the equivalent of prisons, known as YOUNG OFFENDER INSTITUTIONS (YOIs), youth treatment centres and secure training centres (see SECURE ESTATE). Strictly speaking, only YOIs are custodial institutions, although the other centres are also total institutions whose inmates have little freedom of choice or movement.

There are many offences that can, in law, attract a custodial sentence, and these are referred to as 'imprisonable offences'. This does not mean that anyone convicted of such an offence is bound to be sent to prison. With the exception of murder (for which a LIFE SENTENCE of imprisonment is mandatory), all offences can be dealt with by non-custodial measures such as a fine or a COMMUNITY SENTENCE.

Courts are required by law to pass prison sentences only when one or more of the following grounds applies: the offence(s) before the court is so serious that only a prison sentence is appropriate; the offence is violent or sexual and the public must be protected from serious harm from the defendant; the defendant has refused to consent to a community sentence, which requires consent; the defendant has breached a community sentence where this is an imprisonable offence; or, in the case of 12–14 year-olds, the defendant meets the seriousness criterion and is a persistent offender. Imprisonment is a sentence of last resort. Before a sentence of imprisonment is passed, the court is required to give its reasons for doing so. State-funded legal representation must be offered to the defendant, and a PRE-SENTENCE REPORT must normally be obtained. A sentence of imprisonment can be suspended for up to two years in the case of adult offenders but not young offenders sent to YOIs. Suspended sentences can be given only in exceptional circumstances, and they mean that the offender does not go to prison unless a further offence is committed during the period of suspension.

The length of a prison sentence is a matter for the court's discretion, although higher courts have laid down guidelines. Maximum sentences are laid down in law for every offence, but these are not often relevant in routine sentencing because maximum sentences are used very sparingly. The length of time that an offender spends in custody will not be the same as his or her stated sentence because, under the arrangements for EARLY RELEASE, a proportion of the sentence is served in prison and the remainder in the COMMUNITY, sometimes under supervision. During that time, however, the offender is at risk of being returned to prison to serve the remainder of the sentence if a further offence is committed.

Imprisonment is a sentence of last resort because it is expensive, damaging to the individual offenders and ineffective in reforming their behaviour. Almost three-quarters of young offenders and almost half of adults sentenced to imprisonment are re-convicted of another offence within two years of their release, according to HOME OFFICE statistics.

Women and black people are disproportionately likely to be sentenced to imprisonment, despite legislation outlawing discriminatory sentencing (see CRIME AND DISORDER ACT 1998). A high proportion of serving prisoners have mental illnesses, and a large minority have a history of drug misuse. Conditions in overcrowded British prisons are not conducive to rehabilitation, and the rate of SUICIDE and self-harm is high. Nevertheless, prison has become part of the rhetorical armoury of populist politicians who are content to claim, without any supporting evidence, that it 'works'.

D. Faulkner, *Crime, State and Citizen: A Field Full of Folk*, Winchester, Waterside, 2001.

cycle of deprivation an explanation for the persistence of POVERTY that focuses on how attitudes, values and behaviours are passed on from one generation to the next, mainly through the family but also through communities.

The notion of the cycle of deprivation achieved considerable political prominence at the hands of Keith Joseph, Minister for Social Services, in 1972. It is closely linked to the theories of the CULTURE OF POVERTY, developed in the 1960s by, among others, the North American writer Oscar Lewis, the concept of the UNDERCLASS and some current ideas about SOCIAL EXCLUSION. Governments in Britain and the United States, particularly in the 1960s and 1970s, were influenced by ideas that have roots in the concept of a cycle of deprivation. Attempts to tackle urban poverty, especially in inner-city areas, have often focused upon early education (for example, Educational Priority Areas, pre-school provision and the US Headstart programme and most recently in Britain with the ambitious SURE START programme) in an attempt to improve the LIFE CHANCES of young children from poor homes. Critics of these schemes have argued that wider forces, such as SOCIAL CLASS, RACISM and GENDER stratification (and indeed capitalism in general), cannot be so easily overcome.

Dd

dangerousness the potential to cause physical or psychological harm to others. The term is used in the courts in the offender sections of the MENTAL HEALTH ACT 1983, referring to some people who are convicted of an offence and who are also mentally disordered (see MENTALLY DISORDERED OFFENDERS). The term now has wider applications.

If the court considers, on psychiatric evidence, that a person is 'dangerous', he or she will be sent to a special hospital offering secure psychiatric provision. He or she will also be placed on a restriction order under the Mental Health Act, which means that he or she will be detained until considered by psychiatrists to be no longer dangerous. The concept is used also in relation to families or individuals who may be abusing children. 'Dangerous families' are those in which the pattern of interaction between partners, the degree of VIOLENCE and conflict or the presence of an unstable and aggressive individual exposes the children of that family to physical harm. Social workers try to gauge the potential for causing physical or psychological harm in the behaviour of both individuals and families (see RISK ASSESSMENT). They do this in a number of situations, such as with an older person who may have been assaulted, a child who may have been sexually abused or a psychiatric patient who may attack others. Social work has attempted to gauge the 'dangerousness' of an abuser more accurately by developing 'indicators' such as psychological portraits of child abusers and of partners who collude in the abusive acts.

The concept of dangerousness has many critics. In relation to working with children in particular, such critics have pointed out that focusing on dangerousness reflects a drift from a rehabilitative model of child-care work to a more coercive way of working. The social work role becomes more narrowly protective by swiftly distinguishing and removing children from the truly dangerous families as opposed to those that are not so dangerous, with which children are safe. In working with people defined as 'dangerous' by the courts or other professionals, practitioners need to be aware of the public STEREOTYPES of dangerousness – how these are based on images of wild animals and of badness fixed in the person's character. These can lead to perceptions of the person's character being wildly exaggerated, which results in the worker feeling extremely anxious. This in turn makes the building of a relationship or the carrying out of social work tasks such as ASSESSMENT highly fraught.

Some have now included the behaviour of social workers as being capable of dangerousness. Dangerous practice includes taking unacceptable risks, bowing to pressures from aggressive or violent service users or their carers or of claiming to practice in an ethnically sensitive way and in fact ignoring child or adult protection issues.

A. Aleszewski *et al, Risk, Health and Welfare,* Open University Press, Milton Keynes, 1998.

Data Protection Act 1984 legislation designed to restrict the possibility of individuals being harmed by the abuse of personal data or information and to enable the United Kingdom to satisfy the Council of Europe Convention.

The Act gives people (*data subjects*) the right to know what is being stored about them on computers and aims to protect the individual by laying certain duties on organizations (*data users*) that keep information on computer. There are eight principles that data users must follow:

1 information must be collected and used fairly and lawfully;

2 data users must register the purpose for which information is held;

3 the information cannot be used or disclosed except for those purposes;

4 data users can hold only information that is relevant to their purposes and cannot hold more than is needed;

5 the information held must be accurate and, where necessary, up to date;

6 the information held must be kept no longer than necessary for those purposes;

7 the information must be accessible to individuals and correctable or erasable if appropriate;

8 data users must have appropriate security against unauthorized access, disclosure or destruction and against accidental loss or destruction.

The Act gives data subjects five rights:

1 to know if any organization keeps information about them on computer;

2 to see a copy of the information, except if this is being held to safeguard national security, to prevent or detect a crime, to catch or prosecute offenders or to assess or collect tax or duty;

3 to make a complaint to the Data Protection Registrar if a person does not like the way a data user is collecting or using personal information about him or her;

4 to have inaccurate records erased or corrected;

5 to claim compensation through the courts if the person has been hurt by the loss or destruction of personal data through an improper disclosure or because of inaccuracy.

day care a variety of caring facilities for people in need who are still living predominantly in their own homes.

Day-care facilities have been devised for virtually all client groups where people are regarded as at risk or have a condition or problems that would benefit from contact with others. Such facilities may focus upon rehabilitation, monitoring or respite care to give CARERS a break or to supplement their efforts or as a social focus for isolated and vulnerable people. Day care figures in statutory, voluntary and private agencies. Programmes of work in day-care centres reflect these differing objectives. Some facilities are specialized, for example ADULT TRAINING CENTRES for people with LEARNING DISABILITY; others may be multipurpose, where there is an attempt to meet the needs of all client groups. The other major client groups for day-care provision include people with enduring mental health problems, the dying, elders, physically disabled children and adults, and pre-school children. Many facilities that have residential provision as their major focus also have day-care services, for example, residential homes for old people and HOSPICES. Day care is seen as a very important part of COMMUNITY CARE provision.

DDA abbreviation for DISABILITY DISCRIMINATION ACT.

deaf-blind being both deaf and blind; this refers both to people who were born with one or more sensory impairment and to those who become deaf and/or blind through illness, injury or ageing.

In practice, the term 'deaf-blind' is used interchangeably with 'dual sensory impairment'. Recognition of a person as deaf-blind does not require clinical diagnosis of total blindness and total deafness. There may a degree of residual vision and/or hearing. The Department of Health stresses that ability to function can vary and that people whose 'combined sight and hearing impairment cause(s) difficulties with communication, access to information and mobility' can be regarded as deaf-blind. Deaf-blind people communicate in a range of ways, depending on preference and any abilities developed before the onset of acquired dual impairment. Some may use methods adopted by blind or deaf people, while others may use methods based on touch. Estimates of the prevalence of deaf-blindness vary widely, but it is at least 40 people per 100,000 population. Although there are deaf-blind people of all ages, about 75 per cent are aged over 75 and have acquired rather than congenital impairments. There is no form of registration particular to deaf-blindness, and, until recently, no formal system for recording the identity and numbers of deaf-blind people. Deaf-blind children and adults are often not identified or offered appropriate services by local authorities. Many are not recognized as deaf-blind, as staff awareness of deaf-blindness can be 'masked' by other impairments that are regarded as the primary reasons for service provision. However, mainstream services or those for either deaf or blind people may not be suitable. In 2001 the Department of Health issued statutory guidance requiring local authorities to 'identify, make contact with and keep a record of deaf-blind people in their catchment area'. The guidance aims to increase the involvement of specialist staff in assessments under the Children Act and community care legislation, and to provide more widespread access to trained one-to-one support workers when needed.

deaf/Deaf people *deaf* – the audiological condition of not hearing; *Deaf people* – those who identify themselves as part of a linguistic and cultural minority group. (The lower- and upper-case d/D is increasingly used in the USA and Britain to make this distinction.)

A construction of deafness from the perspective of Deaf people, based on their experiences in a predominantly 'hearing' society, is in the early stages of articulation. This perspective describes a group of people who share a common language, that is, sign language (see BRITISH SIGN LANGUAGE), and whose culture is historically created and transmitted across generations. Being Deaf usually means the person has a hearing loss, but the degree of loss is not in itself a criterion for being Deaf. There is also the common notion of deafness as a sensory impairment, that is, lack of hearing. This view of deafness as a physical deficit has dominated most professional discourses (such as medical, audiological, educational and welfare services) and lay discourses (such as film and fiction). Deafness is seen as a deviation from the so-called 'normal healthy state', and emphasis is placed on normalization and cure. In psychology, deafness has been seen as a defining characteristic of a deaf person. The two main models of deafness are therefore the clinical/pathological model, which focuses predominantly on audiological factors, and the cultural model, which emphasizes social factors.

Social work with Deaf people has its origins in the missions or welfare societies that were established for social and religious purposes through-out Britain during the 19th century. In common with many social welfare services, the missions were church-based organizations concerned with the religious and moral affairs of Deaf people. These organizations were developed initially by people who had some contact with Deaf people but were rarely Deaf themselves. Their motivation was compassion, charitable concern and a response to Deaf people's desire to meet together. As the societies developed and became more complex, they became the centre for social, educational and vocational activity for Deaf people. A person, usually male, was appointed to carry the responsibility of organizing activities and fund-raising. This person was the missioner, the predecessor of the social worker with Deaf people. The work of the missioners included visiting and advising, job-finding and interpreting, while at the same time managing and organizing the society. They concentrated on adult Deaf people who were users of sign language. In the 1920s in-service training was offered to people working in the societies, a large part of which was the development of sign language and interpreting skills. Missioner were involved in the daily life of

Deaf people, available day and night for preaching or interpreting at church services, and interpreting at job interviews and doctors' appointments. They had the opportunity to develop sign-language skills and to understand Deaf culture in a way that is perhaps unavailable to some present-day social workers with Deaf people. Some Deaf people view the time of the missioner positively, as they had ready access to sources of help, while others see it as a time of oppression when the missioners' involvement in so many aspects of Deaf people's lives created dependency on the mission.

The services of the missions constitute almost the only welfare service provision for adult Deaf people for over a century. The first statutory funding became available in 1933, and services became mandatory in 1960 following the Younghusband Report in 1959. From this time, local authorities took a more direct interest in the welfare of Deaf people by funding either their own services or those of a voluntary agency.

The majority of social workers with Deaf people are employed by local authorities offering direct services, and a minority of workers are located in voluntary organizations that provide services on behalf of their local authority. Despite reports highlighting the need for skilled workers, social workers with Deaf people are less likely than their generic colleagues to have a social work qualification. Even more rarely do they have the dual qualification of basic social work and a post-qualifying certificate in the specialism. Only a small percentage of social workers have the requisite signing skills to practise, as recommended by the Social Services Inspectorate report *Say It Again* (1988). In some local authorities there are no services at all, with posts vacant or filled by unqualified people. About 20 per cent of social workers with Deaf people are deaf themselves. It has been argued that section 11 funding (Local Government Act 1966) could be used to ensure that posts are designed for Deaf people themselves to work with their own community group. Yet this would require a shift in thinking on the part of the policy-makers towards the view of Deaf people as a cultural minority group rather than as disabled (that is, dependent). Similarly, the numbers of black social workers with Deaf people and black Deaf social workers are small. The city of Bradford has been referred to as an example of emerging good practice – it employs an Asian social worker to work with Asian deaf families. Overall, however, there has been a decline in the provision of specialist social workers employed to work with Deaf people, as there has been a move towards setting up separate interpreting services and employing technical officers to deal with environmental equipment.

Social services departments provide services to all 'hearing-impaired' people, which includes people who are audiologically deaf but do not identify with Deaf culture. Greater emphasis may be placed on their actual hearing loss, adjustment to it or management of it when referral is made to social services. Some local authorities and their agents' services for Deaf people are provided by social workers with Deaf people (SWDPs), who have particular information and knowledge about deafness, but others are not. This results in a distinction between service providers who are employed to work bilingually and trans-culturally with people from a minority group – that is, Deaf people – and mainstream social workers who, with information and appropriate communication skills, work with people whose hearing is 'impaired', that is, deaf people. Both Deaf and deaf people do share, however, experiences of oppression and DISCRIMINATION in a society that seeks to 'normalize' those who are seen as 'deficient' (see DISABILITY, IMPAIRMENT).

Social workers with Deaf people have inherited the role of the missioners, and whether they should or should not interpret is probably the single biggest issue of debate in services to Deaf people. That interpreters are required is not in question, but responsibility for the funding and provision of such services is. Where social workers with Deaf people work in isolation, are 'hearing' people and have sign-language skills, they have often been expected, by the employing body and by Deaf service users in that area, to carry the interpreting role. Some have done this willingly and have not accepted the argument that a social work role is, in the main, in conflict with that of an interpreter. For example, interpreters follow a code of practice that includes not offering personal opinions or advice and keeping all matters confidential, which would be inappropriate for a social worker to adhere to. It has been argued that combining the social work and interpreting roles actually oppresses Deaf people by denying their rights of 'self-determination, independence, choice and equality'. Some local authorities, responding to opinion from both service user groups and some service providers, recognized the need for separate interpreting services and are acting accordingly. The provision of equipment for daily living has been another task that social workers with Deaf people have traditionally undertaken. It is an important service in terms of quality of life for service users, but because of the high demand, it is also very time-consuming. In many areas, this is now being undertaken by technical officers as part of the overall service offered to Deaf people.

Some social workers with Deaf people argue that, without the demands of interpreting and assessing for equipment, they could concentrate on areas of work that have, in some areas, been neglected and that require a high standard of social work skill, a sound understanding of Deaf culture and British Sign Language, and a commitment to anti-oppressive practice. These areas of work include sexual abuse of deaf children, working with Deaf people with mental health problems, and working with deaf-blind people and those with other disabilities. In common with other social workers in the mainstream, some social workers with Deaf people are concerned at what they see to be the decline in preventive work. Some local authorities have responded to this in a positive way by creating a development worker's post and appointing Deaf people to this position to work in partnership with service users, as part of their commitment to services that value Deaf people's skills, resources and lifestyles.

So far reference has predominantly been made to Deaf people – those who, regardless of their degree or age of onset of hearing loss, identify with Deaf culture and use British Sign Language. Such people are frequently referred to in social services departments as 'profoundly, pre-lingually deaf' or 'deaf without speech'. These categorizations are misleading and often inaccurate, but they reflect the model of deafness predominating in service provision, namely the medical model of deafness as a deficit rather than the recognition of Deaf people as a minority group. As service users, Deaf people may present the same problems as other service users, including child-care issues, debt or housing problems, and mental ill-health, which are not directly related to their 'hearing loss' but will be influenced by the fact that they are from a minority group in a society that does not widely recognize sign language and devalues the experience of Deaf people.

Although Deaf people share experiences around 'being Deaf', the Deaf 'community' also reflects the wide variety of human beliefs, lifestyles and attitudes. Deaf people are therefore of all ages and ethnic origins, male, female, gay/lesbian, bisexual, heterosexual and mentally or physically disabled. Prejudice is evident in the Deaf community as in any other, and some Deaf people are marginalized and have different experiences of using social services. For example, from a study of the experiences of both Deaf/deaf people from ethnic-minority groups, it was concluded that black Deaf people are isolated and generally receive poor services. Other reports suggest the same is also true for deaf-blind people (see DEAF-BLIND).

Deaf people are not often born into Deaf culture but rather they acquire it, as the majority of Deaf people have hearing parents and families. As such, it is difficult to describe a deaf child as culturally Deaf before he or she has developed a self-identity as a Deaf person by mixing with other Deaf people, using sign language, etc. Given the general lack of awareness about Deaf issues, parents sometimes find it difficult to take on board the idea that their child will become a Deaf adult. Also, the place of sign language and the role of Deaf people in the education of deaf children are part of an ongoing controversial debate that again highlights the different ways of understanding deafness. These issues have influenced the provision of social work services to deaf children and their families.

S. Gregory and G. Hartley (eds), *Constructing Deafness* London, Open University and Pinter, 1991.

debt advice see MONEY ADVICE.

decentralization the transfer of staff out from social services headquarters to local and COMMUNITY-level offices.

Decentralization has become an increasingly important approach to the delivery of social services by local authorities. The aim is to establish a closer link between officials and the local community they serve. The main services affected by decentralization are those of housing and social services, although some authorities are experimenting with a wider range of services. The introduction of decentralization has been associated mainly with Liberal Democrat local authorities and Labour authorities, particularly those of the Left. It has been noted that decentralization is principally of three kinds: *departmental decentralization*, in which departments are reorganized into neighbourhood or community-level teams; *corporate decentralization*, where a range of services are decentralized into what are often termed 'mini-town halls', with the aim of providing almost the full range of services at community level within easy reach of local people; and *political decentralization*, where local-level committees of elected representatives are also devolved to advise the neighbourhood offices. With the latter approach, the aim is to provide a political reform that encourages local groups to become more involved and to increase levels of participation; emphasis is often placed on those groups who are most often excluded from the traditional networks of representation, including the disabled, ethnic-minority groups and women.

While decentralization approaches have sometimes proved very successful, they have also resulted in opposition. In particular, corporate and political decentralization has proved to be expensive, and in periods of financial constraint there has been some retrenchment. Costs have been high because of a number of factors – first, there is a need for training as junior officers are given greater responsibility; second, there is some capital cost in setting up neighbourhood offices; third, the relative success in the area of housing has led to an increase in demand from the public for services. However, departmental decentralization in the provision of social services has been maintained, as the development of community care has often been seen as more effective within a decentralized structure. Also, many senior managers have seen the devolution of some day-to-day management responsibilities as a way of freeing themselves to concentrate on more strategic planning of services. In addition, the AUDIT COMMISSION is promoting decentralization as a way of challenging entrenched power structures within local authority SOCIAL SERVICES DEPARTMENTS. The Audit Commission has argued that these vested interests mitigate against the interests of service users; in particular, the commission sees the need for budgets to be devolved so that decisions on the level of service provided for an individual can be made as close to the client as possible.

decision-maker see WELFARE RIGHTS 1.

deferred sentence a decision by a court to postpone sentencing for up to six months to enable a defendant to demonstrate motivation to reform –

for example, by obtaining employment, making reparation to the victim, responding to treatment or making other positive changes.

A sentence can be deferred only once in respect of a particular offence, and courts cannot impose any other requirements or restrictions on the defendant at the same time as the deferment. If the offender re-offends during the period of the deferment, the court can re-sentence for the original offence as if the deferment period had expired. If the period of deferment is successfully completed, a more lenient sentence is usually the outcome.

de-institutionalization a policy of moving residents in large care institutions, such as mental hospitals, to places of a smaller scale in the community, such as shared flats, foster homes or independent accommodation.

The policy gathered support after research had indicated that living in large institutions led to passive and dependent behaviour on the part of many residents. The policy has been criticized on the grounds that people have been poorly prepared for living in the community. Critics cite evidence, for example, that people who have previously lived in large children's homes or mental hospitals make up a disproportionate number of homeless people. Thus, if the policy is genuinely to benefit those service users at whom it is aimed, it has to be more than relocation. It should take account of the processes through which individuals can be integrated into their community with the same opportunities and choices about how they live their lives as other citizens.

dementia a progressive and irreversible decline in intellectual abilities, usually of gradual onset, affecting all areas of the brain. The disorder is usually associated with old age.

At age 75, the proportion of all people of that age who are affected is approximately 10 per cent. The prevalence doubles with every five years of increasing age so that it can be calculated that by age 85, as many as 40 per cent of this age group has dementia, whereas at age 65 the risk is only at 2.5 per cent. Dementia can also appear in middle-aged people, however, when it results in more rapid deterioration. Indications of dementia are impairment in short- and long-term memory and in judgement, inability to learn new information, to remember past personal information or facts of common knowledge, to perform routine or basic tasks, or to make and carry out plans. In addition, there may be significant changes of personality and major disorientation in time and place. There are differences in the degree of symptoms, however. Those with mild dementia have some impairment of social activities, although the individual retains adequate control over tasks associated with daily living. Sufferers of moderate dementia require some supervision of daily tasks, while the activity of those with severe dementia is so impaired as to require constant supervision or institutional care.

Definitions of dementia have become much more precise over the last twenty years in terms of the clinical features by which it should be identified. Other causes of impairment, such as general medical illness or drug toxicity, must be excluded. There are also distinctions made between different sub-types of dementia.

ALZHEIMER'S DISEASE is the principal, but not the only, cause of dementia, accounting for some 55 per cent of all cases. Other causes include minor strokes, degenerative disorders such as Parkinson's disease, ALCOHOL toxicity, head injuries, infections of the central nervous system and transmittable diseases such as Aids and Creutzfeldt-Jakob disease. Whatever the cause, the condition results in emotional, motor and behavioural problems, which often require interdisciplinary care from both health and social services, including the services of consultant geriatricians, community psychiatric nurses, social workers and domiciliary carers. Assessment of need under the NATIONAL HEALTH SERVICE AND COMMUNITY CARE ACT 1990 sought to promote interdisciplinary work and to involve service users and their carers to the fullest extent possible.

Care of people with dementia should take account of the clinical features presented, the personality prior to outset and any subsequent changes, accompanying medical conditions and the psychosocial pressures on the person and carers. Dementia may be accompanied by anxiety, sleeplessness, agitation, paranoia, depression and apathy. While medication may relieve some symptoms, careful assessment should identify whether any of these relate to a monotonous environment. Sufficient levels of stimulation in the person's immediate environment have proved to be a critical factor in maintaining optimal mental functioning.

C. Cantley (ed), *A Handbook of Dementia Care*, Buckingham, Open University Press, 2001.

Dementia in Focus: Research, Care and Policy into the 21st Century, Blackwell.

Department for Education and Skills (DfES) the government department that deals with all matters relating to education, including schools and lifelong learning (previously the Department for Education and Employment).

Department of Health (DoH) the main central government department responsible for personal social services and policies affecting social work.

The Department of Health was created in 1986 with the dismantling of the Department of Health and Social Security. Its responsibilities include the NATIONAL HEALTH SERVICE (NHS) community care policy, implementation of major parts of the CHILDREN ACT, the operation of the SOCIAL SERVICES INSPECTORATE and health promotion. As with all other central government departments, the DoH is headed by a secretary of state, who sits in the cabinet as a senior minister. This cabinet minister is accountable to Parliament for the policy of the DoH and sits on the government's front bench. Legally and constitutionally subordinate to the secretary of state is a group of ministers responsible for aspects of the department, served by a group of senior civil servants who provide advice on health and social services policy and manage the department's business. Within the department, there is a National Health Service Management Executive and a National Health Service Policy Board. These are responsible for NHS organization and policy matters and report directly to the secretary of state through the NHS chief executive.

In respect of social work activities, the Secretary of State for Health has been given important powers under the NATIONAL HEALTH SERVICE AND COMMUNITY CARE ACT and the Children Act. The first requires all local authority social services departments to develop community care plans, which have to be submitted for approval to the secretary of state. The second has given the secretary of state power to have DoH officials enter and inspect all premises where children are kept under the Act and the children in these premises. The department also communicates policy guidance to local authority social services through a series of circulars and ministers' letters. These follow up on points of detail to clarify aspects of government legislation but do not necessarily have the same force as Acts of Parliament. They are influential, however, and allow the government to work towards national standards in the application of legislation. The use of other agencies including the Social Services Inspectorate and the Health Advisory Service also helps to communicate policy guidance to providers as well as furnishing the department with information on the response from providers to legislation.

Ministers respond to questions on policy on the floor of the House of Commons as well as through a spokesperson in the House of Lords. Both ministers and civil servants respond to parliamentary questioning in front of PARLIAMENTARY SELECT COMMITTEES. The DoH also works closely with other departments on the development of aspects of policy, notably with the DEPARTMENT FOR WORK AND PENSIONS on issues relating to benefit systems. At the same time, the department is often in competition with other departments for resources from the Treasury to try to pay for new and continuing policies.

Department of Health, Social Services and Public Safety, Northern Ireland
the department responsible for health, social services and social security within the province of Northern Ireland.

This department coordinates all health and personal social services work in association with four boards. It is headed by a junior minister, who in turn is responsible to the Secretary of State for Northern Ireland. The Northern Ireland Office is itself seen as temporary, having been established in 1971 when direct rule from London began. The explicit intention is that at some stage control will return to the devolved government of the province. According to the official expenditure plans in 1993, the Health and Personal Social Services wing of the department is responsible for hospital and community health services, personal social services for the most vulnerable members of the community, family health services, centrally financed services for training and research, and administrative support. The Health and Personal Social Services wing is divided into a series of policy divisions covering the development of policy and legislation across a wide range of services. These divisions include the Health Policy Division, Family and Child Care Division, Social and Community Division, Client Groups, Social Legislation and the Strategy and Intelligence Group.

Department of Health, Social Services and Public Safety, Northern Ireland, *Northern Ireland Expenditure Plans and Priorities*, London, HMSO, 1993.

Department of the Working Age see DEPARTMENT FOR WORK AND PENSIONS.

Department for Work and Pensions (DWP) the central government department responsible for the regulation of welfare benefits, pensions and employment services.

The creation of the DWP in 2001 was a clear signal in the development of NEW LABOUR policies towards welfare benefits and issues concerning rights and responsibilities. Increasingly, there has been much debate about the role of the benefit system and the levels of dependency of people on the state. This originally was associated with the NEW RIGHT and authors such as the American, Charles Murray. They argued that the WELFARE STATE had undermined the independence of increasing numbers of people who had become more and more reliant on the benefit system. This UNDERCLASS was increasingly separated from the rest of society and gave rise to the concept of SOCIAL EXCLUSION. New Labour identified social exclusion as being a key issue it wished to tackle as well as the problems associated with an increasing level of expenditure on social security, which had become the largest area of public spending in the UK, as in many other European welfare states.

The creation of the DWP aimed to directly link employment services and the benefit system with the aim of ensuring that the receipt of benefits is tied into pressures to accept employment, with the removal of benefits from those who do not accept work offered. The first of these initiatives was targeted at single parents, with the idea that there was a significant section of the population who would benefit from access to employment. The relative success of this policy in the government's view led to the restructuring of the department to promote further the link between benefits and work.

The DWP incorporates two executive agencies: The Pension Service and Jobcentre Plus. The *Pension Service* looks after benefit issues for the retired and those who are planning retirement. The *Department of the Working Age* is responsible for people of working age and will be serviced by the new *Jobcentre Plus* network, which was phased in to replace the BENEFITS AGENCY and the Employment Service from April 2002.

depression feelings of hopelessness, sadness, tearfulness and intense ANXIETY.

Depression is the most common of all psychiatric disorders, with a high reported incidence throughout the population, of between 10 and 15 per cent. It is twice as common in women as in men and is more prevalent in lower socioeconomic groups. Depression affects people in different ways. A person suffering from depression can feel sadness, low self-esteem, hopelessness or something more extreme, such as feelings of total despair, complete worthlessness, intense guilt and constant irritability. Tasks require extra effort; thinking becomes more difficult, and thoughts can centre on SUICIDE or be preoccupied with fears of serious illness. Speech and particularly physical movements can be slowed drastically, while at the same time the sufferer is tense and restless, with pronounced interruption to sleep patterns. Depression is frequently classified as *endogenous*, which means 'arising from within', when it seems to have no specific cause, or *reactive*, when it is a result of specific events, such as bereavement, in a person's life. Reactive depression is generally viewed as the milder form, from which the sufferer may recover spontaneously over a period of time.

The causes of depression are much debated. Certain social and economic factors have been highlighted. In a famous study in the late 1970s it was noted that of 500 women in an inner London suburb some 33 per cent experienced some degree of depression. Against a background of bad housing and unsatisfactory marriages, the authors noted four vulnerability factors:

1 three or more children aged under 14 living at home;
2 lack of an intimate or confiding relationship;
3 loss of mother in childhood;
4 lack of employment outside the home.

Certain psychological explanations have also been advanced, centring on the concept of LEARNED HELPLESSNESS – certain individuals believe that they have no control over their environment and that any effort on their part is bound to be ineffective. This state of mind leads people to view problems in their lives as the product of long-standing personal inadequacies and not as the result of specific situations that can be resolved.

Many people who are depressed are diagnosed as such by a medical practitioner, including their own general practitioner, and receive some form of medication, such as anti-depressants or major or minor tranquillizers. But in many cases, social work practitioners and counsellors are able to offer assistance that enhances personal effectiveness. This has proved particularly so in the case of ASSERTIVENESS training, often provided for a group of depressed people, in which people are encouraged to express their opinions and feelings in a direct and appropriate way. Social workers have also been effective in running all-women groups, which often provide a therapeutic and support element as well as some assertiveness training. Conversely, practitioner and sufferer may decide that individual COUNSELLING, particularly grief counselling, is the most effective way to help the person find an alternative response to the loss that she or he has suffered and to which the depression is a reaction.

Corob, *Working with Depressed Women*, Aldershot, Gower, 1987.

desensitization a principal component of BEHAVIOUR THERAPY, involving the gradual substitution of a relaxed response for an anxious response in relation to an event, object or thought that a person finds anxiety-provoking.

Desensitization is usually achieved by combining relaxation techniques with visualized images of the thing that is feared. The technique is often used in relation to PHOBIAS such as fear of open places or flying.

designated teacher a term widely used in schools to identify the person responsible for CHILD PROTECTION issues. It may also refer to the person responsible for children who are LOOKED AFTER (often the same person, especially in primary schools).

detention the process of a defendant being held in a police station for a limited period under the provisions of the police and criminal evidence act 1984 (see also APPROPRIATE ADULT). The term is also used in relation to custodial sentences (see DETENTION AND TRAINING ORDER).

detention and training order (DTO) a custodial sentence given by a youth court in England and Wales.

The custodial part of a DTO is served in a YOUNG OFFENDER INSTITUTION or in another establishment set up for the purpose of holding young offenders in secure CUSTODY. A DTO can be given only when a court is satisfied either that the offence is so serious that only a custodial sentence can be justified or, where the young person is being sentenced for a violent or sexual offence, the court decides that the public needs to be protected from serious harm from the offender. Such orders can be in respect of any imprisonable offence committed by people aged 12–17, but only those defined by courts as persistent offenders can be given DTOs if they are aged under 15. A DTO is served half in the custodial establishment and half in the community under the supervision of a YOUTH OFFENDING TEAM. Orders are made for fixed periods of 4, 6, 8, 10, 12, 18 or 24 months. Time spent on REMAND prior to sentencing is taken into account.

The DTO was created by the CRIME AND DISORDER ACT 1998 and led to a substantial increase in the use of custody in relation to young offenders.

detoxification the process whereby a person dependent on DRUGS stops using the substance to the point that the body no longer requires it.

Detoxification often involves receiving other medication under medical supervision to help with the physical discomfort as the body adjusts to the absence of the drug. Detoxification itself does not deal with psychological dependency, which often has to be addressed afterwards. Social services, under the NATIONAL HEALTH SERVICE AND COMMUNITY CARE ACT, are involved in assessing for and funding the rehabilitation services needed for this phase of the work. In general it is assumed that there is no point in attempting rehabilitative work unless detoxification has taken place.

An alternative to detoxification is a *maintenance prescription* (known as a 'script') where the person is stabilized on a regular dose of the drug or drug substitute, for example methadone in place of heroin (although heroin itself is now prescribed because it is more effective in stabilization. This also avoids the user falling back on the illegal market.

D. Hammersley, *Counselling People on Drugs*, London, Sage, 1995.

deviance a sociological term referring to behaviour perceived to deviate from socially constructed and accepted norms and role expectations. It may also be described as social 'rule-breaking' or a breach of social order.

Deviant behaviour need not be criminal (for example, mentally ill people are often classified as deviant), but explanations or THEORIES OF CRIME are frequently regarded as specific examples of more general theories of deviance. Deviance tends to be studied in two ways: as an objective reality or as a subjective experience. Those who view deviance as an objective phenomenon argue that there is widespread consensus on norms and values in society and that this basic agreement makes it relatively easy to identify deviants. Standard negative sanctions can then be imposed, and this act of punishment or control reaffirms for the group that it is bound by a set of common values and norms. Those who view deviance as a subjective experience are concerned with its social definition. They are concerned to examine how particular people are identified and set apart and what the consequences are both for such people (in terms of developing a deviant identity) and for those who impose the label of deviance.

devolution the process by which key aspects of government have been decentralized to the nations that make up the United Kingdom and Northern Ireland.

Northern Ireland has seen the development of an elected power-sharing executive where different sides of the sectarian divide between Catholics and Protestants (or Republicans and Loyalists) are included on the basis of proportional representation. This is a very specific form of devolution that is part of the Northern Ireland Peace Agreement.

In Scotland and Wales different arrangements were made in line with the specific relationship that had existed between these two nations and England. Scotland has an elected Parliament with specific powers of legislation and taxation, which has led to some important decisions in the area of social care. It is important to note that this is largely because Scotland has for a long time operated with its own laws in key areas of education and health, which make it different from both England and Wales. Wales, however, has an older formal relationship with England and is a principality with a legal and administrative system much more in line with England's. As such, Wales has an elected Assembly rather than a Parliament, and this Assembly has very limited powers compared with the Scottish Parliament. This has led to a belief amongst Welsh Nationalists that there is still a very long way to go in terms of devolving real power to Wales.

Devolution can have a significant impact in the area of health and social care in Scotland, which can lead to debates between the new Parliament and the central government in London. The most contentious has been that over payments for nursing care and social care.

The Department of Health has determined that there is a significant difference between nursing care, which responds to the needs of the sick, and social care, which is used for people with long-term disabilities or social needs such as home helps. The Department of Heath has determined that nursing care is a health issue and therefore comes under the remit of the National Health Service and is free at the point of demand. Social care is about daily living and, as such, comes under the remit of Social Services – as a result, local government social services departments may charge for these services. In Scotland the devolved Parliament has seen the issue differently and has decided that both nursing and social care should be paid by the state and therefore be free at the point of demand. This has lead to pressure from support groups, particularly of the elderly, on central government and the Department of Health to follow suit. At present, however, the government is holding out against such a change. What this does show is the potential for significant differences to emerge in service delivery between different parts of the United Kingdom as a result of devolution.

R. Hazell, *The State and the Nations: The first year of devolution in the UK*, Thorverton (Devon), Imprint Academic, 2000.

DfES abbreviation for DEPARTMENT FOR EDUCATION AND SKILLS.

diagnosis a term used originally within medicine but now with a wider use to describe a professional's action in identifying and solving an individual's problems.

Diagnosis refers to the part of the professional role concerned with identifying the problems to be solved. This involves classifying the problem – understanding its nature and what the first steps are towards solving it. Diagnosis and intervention are both founded on a professional knowledge base – understanding the nature of the problems in the particular professional domain and how they can be solved.

The most widespread use of diagnosis in the MEDICAL MODEL refers to the use of a knowledge base to identify the presence of a particular illness in a person. Illness is thought to be an abnormality or pathology in the person's physiological processes so diagnosing the presence of illness means identifying an abnormality. Because of its origins in this meaning, diagnosing a MENTAL ILLNESS in a person conveys the message that he or she is abnormal.

Although it is primarily a medical term, psychologists also use 'diagnosis' in relation to personality problems, which are not seen as illnesses but are regarded as being fixed and as 'real' as illnesses. This kind of diagnosis lies behind the definition of MENTAL DISORDER, for example in the MENTAL HEALTH LAW REFORM. In medical and psychological use, therefore, the diagnosis of a person conveys a pathology rather than finding what may be an intelligible and meaningful response that a person is making to his or her particular circumstances. Earlier critics of the medical model, particularly in relation to mental health, have therefore stated that diagnosis is only the elevation of a judgement of one person by another into a scientific category and that the potential of this for the person's loss of rights is immense.

Nevertheless, diagnostic procedures are quite stringent. Doctors are not expected to reach a diagnostic conclusion, so label someone without going through specific steps of clarification first. International disease classifications spell out the 'symptoms' and 'signs' (see MEDICAL MODEL) related to particular diseases, and a substantial number of these symptoms and signs are required to be evident before a particular diagnosis is applied. In both mental and physical ill-health, however, the process of making a diagnosis involves the medical professional making an interpretation of the person's experiences and behaviour from her/his position of expertise rather than taking into account the service user's understanding of these. Good practice will take account of the latter, but the routine expectation is that it is the doctor who can classify the person's responses, not the person.

The diagnostic process also involves identifying whether a *syndrome* and a *course* of a disease are present. The syndrome is the combination of symptoms present – different illnesses are defined as having different combinations of symptoms. The course is the pattern and outcome of the illness and predicts the likely prospect of recovery, duration and relapse. If the syndrome or course turn out to be not what was expected in relation to a given diagnosis, the diagnosis would have to be changed – that is, the assumption would be that the person did not have that particular illness.

With mental health problems recent research has suggested that people given particular diagnoses, such as schizophrenia, do not share the same combination of symptoms, nor do they share the same course of illness. Equally, medication for anxiety, for example, can be effective with schizophrenia. Such findings have led to a questioning of current practice, with the suggestion that diagnoses be restricted to particular symptoms, such as identifying hallucinations or a depressed mood. This would encourage biological, psychological and social problems to be treated more specifically rather than the person being given a more general treatment that may not be related to her/his particular combination of symptoms.

Although diagnosis, particularly in MENTAL ILL HEALTH, has thus been questioned, both in value terms and in terms of scientific validity, there is merit in identifying a problem because intervention can then be tailored to it. If an individual experiences a problem, and there is already established evidence that there are specific difficulties associated with that problem, a sensitive diagnosis can help lay out the range of responses required.

The diagnosis of an illness does confer on the person some rights – to sympathy, treatment, time off work and intervention intended to be in her/his best interests. This is in contrast to, say, a criminal conviction where the public interest has priority over the convicted person's best interests. Psychological/personality diagnoses (see PERSONALITY DISORDER) do give that priority to the public interest in the last resort.

S. Williams and J. Gabe, *Health, Medicine and Society: Key Theories and Future Agendas*, London, Routledge, 2000.

Diploma in Probation Studies (DipPS) the basic qualification for probation officers in England and Wales, introduced by local consortia of probation services in collaboration with universities, in response to criticism of the previous route to qualification (the diploma in social work).

The Diploma in Probation Studies is an intensive two-year course leading both to a degree and to a National Vocational Qualification. It is approved and delivered on a regional basis by a combination of groups of employing probation services and one or more universities. Probation officers in Northern Ireland and criminal justice social workers in Scotland continue to qualify using the DIPLOMA IN SOCIAL WORK.

The DipPS curriculum focuses more closely upon offending and working with offenders than social work training, although the latter has specialist routes to qualification for working with young and adult offenders on some programmes. The DipPS curriculum emphasizes the need for students to acquire skills, knowledge and VALUES, including the ability to deliver ANTIDISCRIMINATORY practice.

The decision to discontinue probation training in England and Wales was a political one, taken as part of a drive to divorce probation from social work. The DipPS was partly a pragmatic response to the need to devise a new qualification that achieved this separation and allowed qualifying training to come back into existence after a period during which none existed. Universities and consortia work closely together to implement the prescribed curriculum, and the probation service employs PRACTICE DEVELOPMENT ASSESSORS to supervise students' professional practice.

Diploma in Social Work (DipSW) the qualifying award for social workers up through 2002. A new degree for social workers becomes the qualifying award, replacing the Diploma in 2003.

direct action challenging methods adopted by campaigners who feel all other avenues open to them have been utilized to little effect. Direct action is usually community action based on the key principle of peaceful protest. There is widespread agreement that direct action cannot be regarded as COMMUNITY WORK if violence is involved. Theorists such as Alinsky, Gandhi and Freire advocate explicit challenge to the powerful and the decision-makers. Communities and community workers can engage in conflict or challenging behaviour, but the principle of non-violent action remains core in most cases, with genuine self-defence, perhaps, as the sole exception. Martin Luther King, a follower of Gandhi, summed the issue up by stating: 'Non-violence is the answer to the crucial political and moral questions of our time: the need for man to overcome oppression and violence without resorting to oppression and violence. Man must evolve for all human conflict a method which rejects revenge, aggression and retaliation.' (See also COMMUNITY WORK.)

Martin Luther King Jr, *Where Do We Go from Here: Chaos or Community?* New York, Harper and Row, 1967.

direct payment (community care) a regular payment made by a local authority to a person assessed as needing community care services so that he or she can purchase services on her or his own behalf.

Under the Community Care (Direct Payments) Act 1996, local authorities are permitted to make direct payments to service users instead of purchasing services for them through the care management system. Initially, this was available only to younger disabled adults, but direct payments can now be made to older people as well. The Carers and Disabled Children Act 2000 has extended direct payments to carers who have been assessed as needing services in their own right, including parent-carers of disabled children, and to disabled young people aged 16 and 17.

The introduction of direct payments followed sustained criticisms of community care provision by disabled service users, who considered that they would be better able to achieve flexibility and autonomy if they had control over their own services. Services provided as a result of care management were seen as inflexible and restrictive, and service users also complained of poor coordination between National Health Service and social care services. Although local authorities were officially prevented from making direct payments, some set up schemes in which payments were made to organizations managed by disabled people. These organizations provided varying levels of support to disabled people so that they could be as involved as they wished in managing the money and employing staff. Now that direct payments are encouraged by the government, most local authorities have either developed an 'arm's-length' unit for supporting direct payments' recipients or have nominated an independent organization to do this. Levels of satisfaction with direct payments are high, with many service users reporting that they are more able to control the way that they live and engage in activities they enjoy. The use of direct payments has been associated with a change in the relationship between service users and paid workers. Service users are now employers, and many prefer to refer to 'personal assistance' rather than 'care'. This emphasizes that control lies with the older or disabled person, in contrast with the authority exercised by some carers in the past.

Access to direct payments is more problematic for people with LEARNING DISABILITY, as legislation requires that they should be able to manage direct payments (albeit with assistance) and to consent to receiving the payments instead of services. In practice, some local authorities have used these conditions to debar people with learning disability from their schemes. The government has now made it clear, however, that blanket exclusions such as this are unacceptable. Organizations such as Values into Action have campaigned for access to direct payments for people with learning disability and argue that tests of mental capacity are not appropriate in determining whether a person should have access. They have pointed out that, with the right support, everyone can make decisions, including people with multiple disabilities including communication impairments. It is argued that a model of SUPPORTED DECISION MAKING, in which decision making is seen as an ongoing process, should inform policy in this area.

C. Glendinning *et al, Buying Independence: Using direct payments to integrate health and social services*, Bristol, The Policy Press, 2000.

disability social oppression on the basis of physical or mental IMPAIRMENT. Disability is increasingly recognized as those disadvantages, restrictions and exclusions that arise as a result of the failure of society to take into account the requirements of people with impairments when determining social and environmental arrangements.

The notion that disability is socially constructed is relatively recent, and it is still commonly assumed to be an individual attribute. Exclusion from the mainstream of social life and reliance on segregating forms of welfare were considered inevitable consequences of the need for assistance with 'normal' activities of daily living. It was not until disabled people themselves identified that there was nothing inevitable about such exclusion that dominant assumptions were challenged. An important tool in this struggle has been the redefinition of disability as a form of social oppression and exclusion, and the development of a social model of disability.

Disabled activists have challenged the World Health Organization International Classification of Impairments, Disabilities and Handicaps, which defines disability as 'any restriction or lack (resulting from an impairment) of ability to perform an activity in the manner or within the range considered normal for a human being'. This definition has had a long-standing influence on policy, practice and research, and implies that the inability of many disabled people to gain paid work, engage fully in social life and maintain autonomy results directly from their impairments. Disabled activists have pointed out that many of the restrictions disabled people experience are imposed by disablist attitudes and practices based on dominant notions of normality. Disablism is based on the assumption that the abilities of people with impairments are inferior to those of 'normal' people and that this is a legitimate reason for the restriction of their rights. It does not appear only in individual attitudes and behaviour but also in the wider policies and practices of societies. The social model identifies that social and physical environments have been constructed so as to systematically exclude disabled people. It is argued, therefore, that disability is not a medical or individual matter but a social construction. In practice, the barriers faced by disabled people include individual prejudice, inaccessible transport and public buildings, segregated education and employment, and welfare regulations and practices that restrict autonomy. The extent to which discrimination against disabled people is enmeshed within the policies and procedures of government, private sector employment and the provision of goods and services suggests that it is institutionalized. Disablism is a factor in the multiple oppression experienced by particular groups, in particular older disabled people, disabled women, disabled people from minority ethnic communities, and gay and lesbian disabled people. Policies and services often take little account of the particular needs of these groups, whose access to support and to mainstream social life can be even further restricted as a result.

There was a long struggle on the part of disabled activists to achieve full civil rights for disabled people. The legislation that was eventually passed fell far short of guaranteeing access to full participation in society, but the disability discrimination act (1995) does provide for the first time a degree of protection against discrimination in employment and access to goods and services. The definition of disability in the Act, however, corresponds closely with that of the World Health Organization, being based on the inability to carry out 'normal' activities.

Social care legislation defines disability in terms of individual impairment. The definition first used in the National Assistance Act (1948) is still used with minimal adaptation in both adults and children's legislation, and refers to 'the blind and partially sighted, the deaf and hard of hearing, the dumb, persons who suffer from any mental disorder, and other persons who are substantially or permanently handicapped by illness, injury or congenital deformity'. Entitlement to services is grounded in this Act, and also in the CHILDREN ACT 1989, the CHRONICALLY SICK AND DISABLED PERSONS ACT 1970, the DISABLED PERSONS (SERVICES, CONSULTATION AND REPRESENTATION) ACT 1986, the NATIONAL HEALTH SERVICE AND COMMUNITY CARE ACT 1990, and the COMMUNITY CARE (DIRECT PAYMENTS) ACT 1996. Despite the medical and individualized definition adopted in legislation, guidance issued to social workers by the Central Council for the Education and Training of Social Workers suggests that practice should be based on the social model of disability. The focus of this should be on the rights of service users, with a consequent emphasis on choice and autonomy. Commentators on disability policy have identified that these principles may be inconsistent with a system in which 'need' is based on a professional assessment and purchasing decisions made without any service user involvement. Research evidence suggests that some disabled people do not gain access to assessment and that care packages are often restricting rather than enabling. Professional education, however, emphasizes the way that needs-led assessment and care planning can be undertaken in more empowering ways in which the perspectives of disabled service users are at the fore. Social workers need to develop skills in negotiating packages of care that reflect the needs and aspirations of disabled people in working with other agencies to deliver these, and in fully involving service users in the whole process of care management. Until 1996, social services departments were not permitted to make payments to service users so that they could purchase services of their own choice. Since the Community Care (Direct Payments) Act, such payments have been allowed. They are reported to increase the flexibility of care packages and the degree of autonomy experienced by disabled recipients.

Services for disabled children are provided by children and families teams, and disabled children are regarded as 'children in need' under the Children Act. Services should be provided to minimize the effect of disability and facilitate 'normal' life. The Act emphasizes that disabled children are 'children first'. In meeting the needs that arise from disability, social workers should ensure that needs as a child are given priority. As a result of this philosophy, far fewer disabled children now live in permanent residential care and the emphasis is on family support. The transfer of support services for disabled children and their families to Children and Families Teams, however, meant that in some local authorities these services had to compete for staff time with Child Protection and were regarded as low priority. There are now more specialist teams working with disabled children, and the increased emphasis given to family support in the recent Framework for Assessment of Children in Need is likely to benefit this group.

M. Oliver, *Understanding Disability: From Theory to Practice*, Basingstoke, Macmillan, 1996.

Disability Discrimination Act (DDA) 1995 legislation that aims to combat discrimination against disabled people in the fields of employment, education, the provision of goods and services and the buying or renting of land or property.

Since the passing of the Disability Discrimination Act in 1995, several important changes have been made to its provisions and operation as a result of the recommendations of the Disability Rights Task Force, a body set up by the Labour government on its election in 1997. Originally the DDA included very limited coverage of education, but this has now been amended by the passing of the SPECIAL EDUCATIONAL NEEDS and Disability Act 2001. The DDA's provisions in respect of education are now similar to those covering other areas. The other major change since the passing of the DDA is the establishment of the DISABILITY RIGHTS

COMMISSION (DRC) to oversee the operation of the Act. Originally there was no independent organization responsible for advice, conciliation and enforcement, which marked out the DDA as noticeably weaker than corresponding legislation of 'race' and sex.

The DDA still differs considerably from other antidiscrimination legislation, as it covers discrimination against *disabled people* rather than discrimination on the *grounds* of disability. It is not enough to show that discrimination took place for reasons associated with disability; the individual discriminated against must meet the Act's definition of disability. Disability is defined as 'a physical or mental impairment which has a substantial and long-term adverse effect on his [*sic*] ability to carry out normal day to day activities'. 'Long-term' refers to conditions lasting at least a year and 'substantial' to effects that are more than minor or trivial. 'Mental impairment' refers to both LEARNING DISABILITY and mental disorders that are recognized by established medical opinion.

Although there has been criticism of the restrictive nature of the DDA definition of disability, it covers a wide range of long-term medical conditions and mental impairments as well as the mobility and sensory impairments more commonly associated with the term 'disability'. It also covers progressive conditions in which the effects might initially be minor but are likely to become more substantial. The effect of medication or equipment that helps a disabled person to overcome the effects of an impairment is ignored in determining whether the person can be considered as disabled under the Act. The definition is based on functional deficit in individuals, however, and takes no account of the disadvantages that people may experience as a result of prejudice and discrimination. The only exception to this is its inclusion of people with facial disfigurements.

Rather than identifying direct and indirect discrimination, the Act defines discrimination as treating a person 'less favourably' because of her or his disability and/or failure to make 'reasonable adjustments'. Discrimination against a job applicant, therefore, might not only result from employers' decisions to deliberately exclude disabled people but also from failure to ensure that selection procedures are adjusted to take account of applicants' impairments. Once a disabled person is employed, failure to make 'reasonable adjustments' to enable her or him to do the job would also be regarded as discrimination. In service provision, discrimination involves refusing to provide a service, providing it on worse terms or providing a lower standard of service. There is guidance for employers and service providers on the type of adjustments that might be regarded as 'reasonable' and, conversely, those that might be 'unreasonable'. In addition, service providers and employers can claim that less favourable treatment or failure to make adjustments is 'justified' in some cases. Justification has to be relevant to the particular circumstances and substantial. Critics have argued, however, that direct

discrimination can never be 'justified' and that this provision should
be removed from the Act. Other contested provisions of the DDA are
the exemption granted to employers of fewer than 15 people and the
exclusion of the uniformed public services from its provisions.

The provisions of the DDA have been phased in gradually, with the
employment rights coming into force first in 1999. Most rights regarding
access to goods and services have now also come into force, and these will
be followed by the new provisions giving disabled people protection against
discrimination in education in September 2002. The 'final rights of access',
which will require service providers to make necessary changes to buildings
in order to facilitate access for disabled people, come into force in
October 2004. Individuals who consider that they have been discriminated
against can complain to an employment tribunal, a county court or a
special educational needs tribunal, depending on which section of the Act
applies. The Disability Rights Commission (DRC) also has a wider
enforcement role and can carry out investigations, issue non-discrimination
notices and apply for injunctions in cases of failure to comply.

Research into the operation of the DDA during its first 19 months
of operation found that almost 2,500 employment cases were brought,
which was substantially higher than the equivalent period for other
antidiscrimination legislation. However, only 22 per cent of cases were
actually heard at a tribunal. Others were either settled in other ways or
withdrawn. Of the cases heard at tribunal, the applicant was successful
in only 16 per cent. Recruitment cases were less likely to succeed than
dismissal cases. It was found that applicants who were legally represented
were more likely to win their cases and also that people with sensory
impairments were more successful than those with physical or mobility
impairments. Levels of compensation ordered by tribunals were
significantly lower than those awarded under the Sex Discrimination
and Race Relations Acts. At this stage, very few cases had been brought
in relation to the provision of goods and services, and the researchers
identified significant barriers for potential applicants. The inaccessibility
of court premises and lack of disability awareness among the judiciary
were noted in some cases; it was also apparent that applicants were
heavily reliant on voluntary sources of advice and representation. Since
the DRC commenced work in 2000, applicants have had better access to
advice, support and legal representation.

In its final report "From Exclusion to Inclusion' (1999), the Disability
Rights Task Force made a number of additional recommendations on
which action has not yet been taken. The government's response,
however, indicates willingness to widen the definition of disability in
the DDA to include people with cancer and HIV. They also intend to
dispense with the provision that allows employers to 'justify' failure to
make reasonable adjustments, as this is already covered by the concept
of 'reasonableness'. Other Task Force proposals on which government

intends to act include: dispensing with the exemption of small employers, the uniformed public services and voluntary workers from the DDA; extending the coverage of the DDA so that it includes most public sector functions; and placing a duty on public bodies to promote equality of opportunity for disabled people. Many of the Task Force recommendations have anticipated the provisions of the European Union Employment Directive, on which agreement was reached in 2000. This covers protection against discrimination in employment on a number of grounds, including disability. In order to comply with the Directive, the government intends to extend the provisions of the DDA in areas such as vocational training, employment services, occupational pensions and performance pay, but does expect to fundamentally alter the Act. There has been criticism of government response to the EU Directive, however, with the DRC expressing the opinion that more wide-ranging change is indicated. In particular, it is argued that the EU Directive calls for changes to the way that discrimination is defined, a more comprehensive scope, and for employers to be required to anticipate the adjustments that potential employees might need rather than waiting until a disabled person applies. This would merely extend to the employment sections of the Act the anticipatory requirements that exist in the section on provision of goods and services.

The DDA continues to be strengthened incrementally in response to pressure from disabled people and from European regulation. There is evidence, however, that it is still weaker than legislation on 'race' and sex and that the rights it offers are more equivocal.

C. Bourne, *The Discrimination Acts Explained*, London, The Stationery Office, 2000.

disability living allowance a benefit for people under 65 who need assistance with mobility or personal care or both. See WELFARE RIGHTS 3.

Disability Rights Commission (DRC) an independent body set up under the Disability Rights Commission Act 1999 to promote the rights of disabled people, work towards eliminating discrimination and advise on the effectiveness of antidiscrimination legislation.

The Disability Rights Commission operates in England, Wales and Scotland. In Northern Ireland, the Equality Commission for Northern Ireland has similar functions in respect of disability. The four main functions of the Commission are: to work towards the elimination of discrimination against disabled people; to promote the equalization of opportunities for disabled people; to encourage good practice in the treatment of disabled persons; and to keep under review the workings of the DISABILITY DISCRIMINATION ACT (DDA) 1995 and the Disability Rights Commission Act (DRCA) 1999. These functions are similar to those of the EQUAL OPPORTUNITIES COMMISSION in respect of gender and the COMMISSION FOR RACIAL EQUALITY for 'race'.

The DDA 1995 deals with discrimination against disabled people in the fields of employment, the provision of goods and services, and the management, buying or renting of land and property. Originally its coverage of education was much more limited, being restricted to the requirement for educational establishments to provide information. Since the passing of the SPECIAL EDUCATIONAL NEEDS and Disability Act (SENDA) 2001, this section of the DDA has been amended to make the coverage of discrimination in education similar to the provisions of the Act for employment and access to goods and services.

Originally, the arrangements for the enforcement of the DDA were weak, and the onus was on individual complainants to bring cases to county courts or employment tribunals. The Labour government elected in 1997 set up a Disability Rights Task Force to consider the effectiveness of the legislation and the enforcement arrangements. Following the recommendations of the Task Force, the government introduced legislation to create a body to oversee and enforce the Act. The DRC can now provide advice to disabled people and also legal representation in cases where no other source of funding is available. However, the DRC stresses its commitment to first working with all parties in a non-confrontational way in order to offer information and advice. This may apply to particular cases but is also part of its wider educational role of encouraging good practice. In connection with this, the DRC publishes information leaflets and codes of practice for employment and the provision of goods and services. Draft codes of practice for education have recently been produced. The DRC also provides conciliation but can also carry out formal investigations. These may be general investigations of a particular service or employment sector, be in response to complaints about particular organizations or individuals, or be a check of compliance with a non-discrimination notice it has previously issued. Non-discrimination notices identify aspects of an organization's policy and practice that are unsatisfactory, and specify what must be done to comply with the law. If this is not done, a court injunction can be sought. The DRC also commissions and publishes relevant research.

Other important elements that affect the rights of disabled people are the HUMAN RIGHTS ACT and the European Directive on equal treatment in employment. The former includes provisions on the rights to life, education, non-discrimination, marriage and having a family, as well as freedom from degrading treatment. This is likely to have considerable impact on the way that public services interact with disabled people. The DRC has asked the government to expand its role so that it can assist disabled people in bringing cases under the Human Rights Act, but so far this request has been refused. The recent EU Employment Directive means that the UK government will have to end the exemption of employers with fewer than 15 employees from the employment provisions of the DDA. It also means that the UK can no longer exclude certain occupations from the provisions of the DDA. The DRC has been

involved in consultation with the government over the implications
of the EU Directive for UK law and also over its plans in respect of the
remaining recommendations of the Disability Rights Task Force. While
there are many areas of agreement, there remain matters on which the
government is reluctant to legislate despite the views of the Task Force
and the DRC.

disability service team a team, usually based in a Job Centre, that provides
advice, training and job placement for disabled people.

Disability service teams include specialist disability employment
advisers (DEAs) whose task it is to offer individual advice and support to
disabled job seekers. They may offer access to training courses and assist
in identifying suitable job vacancies. DEAs may negotiate with potential
employers and seek ways of overcoming obstacles to the employment
of the disabled applicant. They may also gain access to funds for the
purchase of equipment that enables the applicant to do the job through
the Access to Work scheme or advise some applicants of suitable
SUPPORTED EMPLOYMENT schemes.

Disabled Persons (Services, Consultation and Representation) Act 1986
an Act of Parliament that provides a right of assessment of individual
needs if requested by a disabled person or his or her carer.

This Act was intended to achieve improvements to the position
of disabled people in relation to three areas. First, it gave the right
to assessment of individual needs: section 4 of the Act provides for
assessment of need on request by any disabled person or his or her carer.
This was intended to plug the loophole left by the rather weaker section 2
of the CHRONICALLY SICK AND DISABLED ACT 1970, which stopped short
of conferring an assessment duty. In providing for assessment on request,
it confers the strongest kind of mandate for assessment, that of an
absolute duty. Even so, it remained necessary for disabled people to
know of their right to request an assessment in order to activate the duty.
This loophole was eventually closed by section 47 of the NATIONAL
HEALTH SERVICE AND COMMUNITY CARE ACT 1990, which requires a local
authority, if undertaking a community care assessment of someone who
then appears to be disabled, to inform the individual of his or her rights
under the 1986 Act and to undertake a concurrent assessment under
section 4 of the Disabled Persons (Services, Consultation and
Representation) Act 1986. This is important, because this section 4
assessment is specifically for services under section 2 of the Chronically
Sick And Disabled Act 1970, which the local authority is bound to provide
once it has identified that the individual has needs and that it is
necessary to meet these needs.

Second, it provided for coordination of services for young people at
the point of transition to adults' services: sections 5 and 6 require local
authorities to identify and assess disabled school-leavers and to ensure
smooth transition to adult service provision. Under the Act local

education authorities must also notify social services of all potential school-leavers who have STATEMENTS OF SPECIAL EDUCATIONAL NEEDS. Social services must then determine whether these children are disabled (within the meaning of the definitions within section 17 of the CHILDREN ACT 1989 and section 29 of the NATIONAL ASSISTANCE ACT 1948). For those who are disabled, social services must ensure that appropriate assessment of their potential needs as adults is undertaken.

Third, the Act requires the publication of information about services, and section 10 requires consultation with organizations of disabled people in relation to appointments to public bodies. Sections 1 to 3 of the Act, providing for advocacy and representation, have never been implemented.

Section 8 of the Disabled Persons (Services, Consultation and Representation) Act contains provision for carers. This is not as extensive as in the later CARERS (RECOGNITION AND SERVICES) ACT 1995, in that it stops short of a full carer's assessment, but it nevertheless requires a carer's ability and willingness to care to be taken into account when deciding on service provision for the disabled person. The duty arises whether or not the carer has requested such consideration.

disabled person's tax credit SEE WELFARE RIGHTS 3.

disablement benefit SEE WELFARE RIGHTS 3.

disbenefited case the term to describe those instances where ASYLUM SEEKERS who have been entitled to Social Security benefits and social housing lose these entitlements when they get a first negative decision on their applications.

Under the Asylum and Immigration Act 1996 persons who sought asylum at their port of entry were entitled to social security benefits until their first negative decisions only. If they appeal they can be supported by the NATIONAL ASYLUM SUPPORT SERVICE (NASS) during this period. Local authorities have been asked to try to maintain existing tenancies for families in these circumstances and claim the costs from NASS. Single asylum seekers must claim support from NASS using a special procedure.

disclosure when a child tells or otherwise represents that he or she has been sexually abused.

Setting the right conditions for interview in which a child may say that he or she has been sexually abused is among the most difficult of all social work skills and one for which considerable training is required. The child may be in distress and reluctant to say that perhaps his or her father or some other trusted adult abused him or her in some way. Talking about this may take some time and require a number of different forms of communication, such as drawings or play. At the same time, the social worker may be working with police officers to gather evidence for a criminal investigation that involves technical equipment such as video-taping. Some social workers and paediatricians have been criticized for conducting 'disclosure interviews' with children, on the grounds that because they have presumed that abuse has happened they encourage, even pressure, children to provide these admissions. Such presumption heavily influences the style of questioning and, at its worst, can lead to prolonged and insistent questioning until the 'right' answer is obtained, so the term 'disclosure interview' is no longer used. The Memorandum of Good Practice (see INVESTIGATIVE INTERVIEWING), issued by the government, makes it clear that interviewing styles based on the presumption that children will disclose eventually are impermissible.

Department of Health and Home Office, *Memorandum of Good Practice*, London, HMSO, 1992.

discretionary housing payment see WELFARE RIGHTS 6.

discrimination see ABLE-BODIEDISM, ANTIDISCRIMINATORY PRACTICE, EQUAL PAY ACT 1970, FAIR EMPLOYMENT COMMISSION, GENDER, HOMOSEXUALITY, RACISM, SEXISM.

district nurse a registered nurse employed by a district health authority or NATIONAL HEALTH SERVICE TRUST to provide nursing care in patients' homes, health centres and general practitioners' premises.

diversion a variety of ways of dealing with offenders without using the courts and, in general, keeping them out of the criminal justice system.

Diversion from prosecution enables the criminal justice system to avoid unnecessarily LABELLING people as offenders when they have committed only minor or one-off offences. The evidence is that most offenders who are diverted do not go on to reoffend whereas formal prosecution can reinforce a sense of DEVIANCE and is also costly and time-consuming. Diversion takes a variety of forms in the different countries of the UK. In England and Wales, REPRIMANDS and FINAL WARNINGS are used with young people as well as REFERRAL ORDERS for first offences. With adults, the CAUTION allows the police to divert minor offenders and those with mitigating circumstances such as certain types of disability. In Northern Ireland, the caution is used extensively with young offenders (including restorative cautioning) and with adults as an alternative to prosecution. In Scotland the police and prosecutors have the discretion to issue warnings as an alternative to prosecution.

In addition to these various means of processing offenders without recourse to criminal courts, it is also possible to refer offenders to various agencies for assistance rather than criminalizing them. The police have discretion in certain circumstances to take 'no further action', and this is often used, for example, to deal with offences committed by people suffering from mental illness or severe stress. Rather than simply letting the matter go, there would normally be an expectation that the person concerned seek assistance from psychiatric services, housing or social work agencies.

divorce the legally sanctioned dissolution of a marriage, often preceded by a period of separation that may also be legally ratified.

In recent years widespread concern has been raised by government, welfare and religious agencies about the high rate of divorce in the UK. Approximately one marriage in three ends in divorce, with second marriages being twice as likely to fail as first marriages. In relation to children, about one child in twenty experiences his or her parents' divorce by age five, and one child in five by age 16.

Attitudes to divorce in the UK have changed significantly over the last few decades. Generally speaking, there is less social stigma attached to divorce, particularly as society adjusts to a much more complex understanding of what it means to be a family. Single parents and reconstituted or blended families are recognized by many as part of an enriched social family structure. This is not to say that there is no opposition to these developments. Many religious groups, and some secular organizations, remain strongly opposed to divorce.

The concern about rising divorce statistics in the UK led to the FAMILY LAW ACT 1996, which removed the concept of 'fault' in divorce proceedings but also introduced a more reflective requirement to the divorce process in the hope of 'saving' at least some marriages. The Act has not yet been fully implemented and illustrates the complex nature of family law and divorce reform.

The impact of divorce upon adults can be traumatic and involves several layers of adjustment. These are likely to happen at different paces if one of the partners has moved into a new relationship, thereby leaving the other partner feeling abandoned. By contrast, some-one moving out of a relationship as a result of domestic violence may feel a huge sense of relief, thereby being able to get on with the rest of his or her life.

Researchers have distinguished several elements to a divorce in terms of social and personal implications. First, there is the emotional and sexual separation and uncoupling; secondly, the issue of child custody and continuing parenting arrangements; thirdly, the settling of material issues, including maintenance and pension rights, and the disposal of property; fourthly, the rearrangement of social, community and official relationships; and fifthly, the complex issues for each of them to move on into a new future, which may for some be painful and complex (see BEREAVEMENT).

Studies of the impact of divorce upon children can be difficult to interpret because the emphasis is often upon negative reactions. It is difficult to estimate how many children live through the divorce of their parents relatively unscathed emotionally and developmentally. Some researchers on re-ordered families suggest that the better the lines of communication between separating parents and their children, the better the chance of the children coping successfully with the transition. However, a 25-year longitudinal (see RESEARCH) study by Wallerstein and Lewis, *The Unexpected Legacy of Divorce*, published in 2001, highlighted some serious issues in this field. Adults reflecting back over the past

25 years on their parents' divorces reported a high level of not being consulted or listened to, either by their parents or by the 'divorce court professionals'; considerable emotional turmoil that affected their emotional and physical health, and their educational performance, and a significant level of painful, re-stimulated memories at key anniversaries extending over a period of 15 to 20 years.

The role of professionals in this field has continued to be important, especially from the child's perspective when parents decide, for whatever reason, that they have to have their day in court in order to resolve their divorce disputes. The Divorce Court Welfare Officer (DCWO) has always played a key role in providing expert opinion and assessment for the court, and this frequently involves talking to the children, especially when they are deemed old enough to be able to express an opinion. DCWOs became independent from the Probation Service and were reconstituted as the CHILDREN AND FAMILY ADVISORY AND SUPPORT SERVICES for England and Wales (CAFCASS) together with the former guardian *at litem* and Reporting Officer Service, and the Children's Divisions of the Official Solicitor's Department. Other professionals include those working in FAMILY MEDIATION, which has become increasingly centre stage since the FAMILY LAW ACT 1996. Family mediators seek to enable disputing and separating adults/parents to negotiate their own agreements, which subsequently can be legally ratified. Alongside these professionals is a relatively new organization, introduced by the Lord Chancellor's Department in 2001, the Family Advice and Information Network, which seeks to provide a single reference point for divorcing and separating parents to access a wide range of help, support and advice.

E. Walsh, *Working in the Family Justice System – A guide for professionals*: Family Law, 1998.

DoH abbreviation for DEPARTMENT OF HEALTH.

doli incapax (from a Latin legal phrase meaning 'incapable of evil') the legal convention that a child aged under 14 was not legally capable of committing a crime unless it could be proved that he or she fully understood the difference between right and wrong.

This convention, or rule, was legally abolished when the CRIME AND DISORDER ACT 1998 came into force. Its abolition was controversial because it was seen as likely to lead to the criminalization of ever younger children without their rights being appropriately safeguarded. The 1991 Criminal Justice Act had encouraged courts to inquire into the maturity of young offenders in reaching decisions about how to deal with them, but the 1998 Act moved away from this approach. By abolishing the *presumption* of *doli incapax*, the 1998 Act put the burden of proof on the young person's defence lawyer to show that it is relevant to particular cases. However, defence lawyers are still able to use *doli incapax* as an argument that an individual young person did not understand that what he or she did was wrong.

domestic violence a term that usually refers to the physical, sexual and emotional ABUSE of women by their male partners or ex-partners. Such abuse on the part of the man can include social isolation, intimidating, bullying and belittling behaviours as well as economic deprivation.

The term and its definition are controversial. Some feel that the term 'domestic' implies a cosiness that detracts from the seriousness of the VIOLENCE and prefer the term 'partner abuse'. Terms such as 'marital violence', 'spouse abuse' and 'battered wives' imply that the couple must be married when many are not. It has also been pointed out that the terms 'battered wives' and 'battered women' divert attention from the key issue, which is one of violent behaviour by male partners. Others have used the term 'family violence', which appears to group many different kinds of inter-relationship violence, including CHILD ABUSE, ELDER ABUSE and sibling abuse. Violence can clearly occur between any two or more members of families or cohabiting people. It can also refer to violence between couples who are lesbian or gay and to relationships where the abuser is a woman. Convention seems to have established that the term 'domestic violence' is restricted to those who are, or have been, in a close, sexual, cohabiting relationship where the abuser is a man and the abused a woman.

The term includes violence in cohabiting relationships that have only recently been established, relationships that have lasted many decades as well as relationships that have been terminated and where the couple no longer cohabit. In this respect violence in the relationships of elders who have been together for a long time should properly be characterized as domestic violence rather than elder abuse. Similarly, domestic violence is not confined to the home but may occur in many locations, including public places. Given the complexities of all these issues, it is clear that the term is by no means watertight and that it lacks clarity at the 'edges'.

Attempts to understand domestic violence have been wide-ranging. At first commentators emphasized pathological aspects of men's behaviour, arguing that domestic violence is perpetrated by very damaged individuals or those whose personalities are somehow warped. Pathologies of this kind were thought initially to be rare. Such explanations have essentially been undermined by compelling evidence that domestic violence is widespread in many societies and in all ethnic groups and social classes. In the same vein, others have suggested that there are continuities between the attitudes and values of non-violent men with violent men. Biology has been thought of as offering another plausible explanation. Men, it has been argued, are predisposed biologically to be aggressive. In this context high levels of testosterone in men have been held responsible for their violent behaviour. Critics of this theory have pointed out that any 'natural' drive does not compel a man to be violent. Any predisposition to behave in a particular way can be diverted, modified or even denied. There are, after all, many people who have sexual instincts but do not choose to express them. To further undermine this theoretical perspective, others have pointed to studies that have found no discernible differences in the levels of testosterone in violent men compared to non-violent men.

Other theorists have focused on accounts given by many women that appear to associate violent events with alcohol. Many men, it is alleged, are violent only when under the influence of alcohol, as if the man could somehow be 'other than himself'. This theory has been criticized on the grounds that although some men are violent in a generalized way after taking alcohol, most men 'under the influence' are able to confine their violence to their partners or ex-partners or possibly other family members lacking power.

Social stress is another alleged cause of domestic violence. Theorists who favour this kind of explanation have tried to link structural inequality with an increased propensity for men to be violent. Thus, unemployment, poverty, poor housing and, in general, few life chances are thought to be instrumental in creating social stress, which is more likely to be expressed in violence to women. Others have argued that the evidence is equivocal. First, middle-class women are to be found in REFUGES, although, in absolute terms, in lower numbers. Second, more middle-class women, because of their comparative wealth, are likely to have more options when trying to leave an abusive relationship. Third, analyses of accounts of violent relationships by survivors and by their children have revealed that domestic violence is widespread in all social strata.

Some have perceived domestic violence as a problem caused by family dysfunction. These theorists perceive families as social systems that have structure, reciprocal relationships, boundaries and that seek to maintain some kind of equilibrium. Any family's equilibrium can be affected if the structure, reciprocal relationships or boundaries are disturbed. Violence in this context is regarded as evidence of something fundamentally wrong with any of these features of the system. Thus, if the established roles and responsibilities that brought about equilibrium are challenged or changed, then families can develop negative relationships. Critics of this approach point out that families are not systems where power is distributed evenly between members. Usually it is the man who is the dominant actor, and it is the abuse of power on the part of the man that explains the unhappiness within families rather than a 'neutral' system that has somehow become unbalanced.

Feminists have provided the most persuasive critiques of the perspectives outlined above. They believe that the issue of domestic violence is best understood by analysing the patriarchal relationships that seem to characterize most societies. Domestic violence, they argue, is part of a generalized oppression of women. Men occupy most of the significant positions of power in economic, religious, political and social institutions. This dominant position is maintained through men's control of ideas or, more broadly, of ideology, reinforced by violence or its threat. Women are in effect covertly persuaded to adopt attitudes and values that are instrumental in their own oppression. Thus, pornography, the perception of women as sexual objects, child bearers and carers, and as having primarily domestic roles with few claims on resources (both within society and within families) are all indicative of a patterned inequality and a subservient position for women. Feminists acknowledge that there are stresses within society, within communities and families, and that these stresses can be severe for individual men and women too. In this sense women are not being idealized. The key question for feminists is 'why do men feel that it is reasonable to use violence?' For them, the answer is that a patriarchal culture legitimates unequal power and the use of force to maintain such inequality.

Records of the police, health and social welfare agencies, organizations dealing with victims/survivors and the British Crime Survey have consistently found that domestic violence is the most common form of interpersonal violence. Although estimates from these diverse sources vary, it is now generally accepted that domestic violence is a serious social problem. The CRIME AND DISORDER ACT 1998 now requires local authorities to establish a community safety strategy, which among other duties requires estimates of the incidence of the problem to be established within communities. This new duty will, in due course, provide more accurate data.

Various estimates have also been made of the costs to the public purse of the problem. These estimates have included the costs incurred in intervening with victims, children and perpetrators by helping and justice agencies, such as the police, social services, probation services, health services, WOMEN'S AID, voluntary advice and counselling services, housing agencies and the BENEFITS AGENCY. Domestic violence often leads to the separation of partners, child-care support issues, rehousing, including relocation to other areas, loss of jobs, landlords having to find new tenants (and possible loss of rent), individuals becoming reliant upon benefits, and many other social costs. It may be that the recognition of the costs of domestic violence both to individuals and to statutory and voluntary services has led to a renewed interest in how best to coordinate the services currently delivered by many agencies.

There is compelling evidence that domestic violence is connected to child abuse. First, children living in households where a woman is being abused can be 'indirectly' abused emotionally. Second, abusers of women are often intentional abusers of children. There is also evidence that domestic abuse is a common ingredient in the backgrounds of women with mental health problems. Similarly, it is now known that older people and people with disabilities are especially vulnerable to domestic violence. Despite this evidence, surveys of social services departments' policies and practices across the country have revealed very patchy provision and a lack of clarity about what abused women can expect by way of support and resources. There are similar findings in relation to the police, the probation service, legal practices, housing and refuge services, counselling and victim/survivor support services. Some have argued that the problem of domestic violence is so important and so widespread that a major government initiative is warranted that should prescribe which agencies must have responsibility for the problem and how such agencies should work together in multi-agency partnerships. To date, Women's Aid has probably been the lead agency, but many have argued that in matters of personal safety and of the human rights of both women and children, that statutory agencies should be the key players.

The social work task in relation to domestic violence has many dimensions. Assessing the needs of potentially vulnerable children and adults is core, including securing the immediate and future safety of a woman and any children, enabling a woman to make considered decisions about her future, and helping both woman and children to recover from the trauma of violence. In this context there are many practical and legal problems that may have to be considered, including the custody of children, issues of income and shelter, and long-term protection from a man who may be intent on further violence.

Audrey Mullender, *Rethinking Domestic Violence: The Probation and Social Work Response*, London, Routledge, 1996.

Cabinet Office (Women's Unit) and the Home Office, *Living Without Fear: An Integrated Approach to Tackling Violence Against Women*, London, Central Office of Information, 1999.

domiciliary care personal care services provided to help service users accomplish daily living tasks. Domiciliary care has replaced what was known as the Home Help Service, and the change in name has brought a change in emphasis to the nature of the work. The latter largely provided domestic help and help with practical tasks such as shopping, cooking and cleaning. The new service is targeted more towards adults with personal care needs, and although some shopping, cleaning and cooking may be part of the overall remit, such services would not be provided unless there were also other more complex needs. Many local authorities will provide assistance to service users who are not eligible for domiciliary care but request domestic help to make their own private arrangements.

domiciliary service any social welfare or health provision taken to the recipient in his or her own home.

The justification for such services are many and include: the idea of 'aftercare' for those who are still vulnerable after discharge from hospital; provision for those who could not reasonably get to a service based in a hospital or in the community, such as a person with a disability; and provision for somebody in a frail state wishing to stay within his or her own home rather than being cared for elsewhere. Such services include community psychiatric nurses, family aides, HEALTH VISITORS and HOME HELPS (or COMMUNITY CARE WORKERS). Domiciliary services are related in intent to the idea of OUTREACH. Similarly, many believe that the success of COMMUNITY CARE will in part depend on the comprehensiveness or otherwise of domiciliary services.

DRC abbreviation for DISABILITY RIGHTS COMMISSION.

drug an ingested substance that alters an individual's emotional and/or psychological state, physical state and/or behaviour. Drugs include legal and socially valued drugs as well as illegal drugs.

Drug misuse affects and can harm health and mental physical functioning, and this applies to all categories, whether pharmaceutical and prescription drugs such as valium (through over use or side-effects), legal leisure drugs such as alcohol or tobacco, physique-enhancing drugs such as steroids, or volatile substances such as glue. There are different patterns of drug or alcohol misuse. These include *experimental use*, or one-off usage; *recreational use*, where use is controlled and interferes minimally with ordinary living; and *dependency*, where use is beyond the person's control and has a pervasive impact on the person's life. Drugs are not easily distinguished one from another – illegal drugs, such as marijuana, can alleviate psychological or physical pain while legal pharmaceutical drug can create DRUG DEPENDENCY. All drugs have benefits and disadvantages. Leisure drugs can have as harmful effects as illegal drugs.

Drug misuse is linked closely to major social work tasks. It can figure prominently in CHILD PROTECTION cases where parents have a drug dependency that seriously impairs their capacity to parent, in the behaviour of young offenders, and in mental health cases, either through dependency on prescribed drugs or in the use of mind-altering drugs. The latter often arises through a need to 'self-medicate', either to relieve symptoms and distress or to minimize uncomfortable side effects from prescribed drugs.

Intervention is generally provided by a specialist COMMUNITY DRUG TEAM, but GPs are also often involved. The common assumption informing treatment originates in historical ideas about substance misuse being a 'choice' and therefore 'self-inflicted'. Thus, treatment and other services are usually offered only if the person is deemed 'motivated'. Some services have a broader idea of motivation, however, recognizing that if users' basic needs are met, for example housing or regular income, they can more easily sustain that motivation. This is supported by research findings indicating that approximately 70 per cent of dependent users positively wanted to become drug-free; the fact they had not been able to showed the presence of other barriers apart from individual motivation.

Services to tackle drug misuse include:

1 psychological services predominantly geared to change in motivation, including COGNITIVE BEHAVIOURAL THERAPY, 'motivational interviewing', and counselling;

2 medical services including DETOXIFICATION, which addresses the physical dependency on drugs and alcohol;

3 maintenance prescriptions offered prior to detoxification if the person is unable to come off at a given point in time, although this approach has stirred public debate and even led to prosecutions of staff in hostels for drug rehabilitation.

4 residential rehabilitation can follow detoxification; this service is an intensive opportunity for the person to unlearn old lifestyles and identities and learn new ones. It is considered important for the rehabilitation to be residential, as the person can be drawn back into misuse if remaining in her/his community;

5 arrest referral schemes and prison programmes for offenders.

Social workers are involved in providing services for people with serious drug misuse problems receiving treatment. Under care management, social workers are often involved in assessing for and funding rehabilitation, but there is also opportunity for provision of follow-up support, such as access to supported housing, in partnership with the health authority. Providing supports, for example child care for a drug dependent parent, can make a difference to that person's motivation. Another less recognized role is to link people to counselling and therapy services that address childhood sexual and other abuse. Mainstream services tend to ignore the high rates of earlier abuse amongst dependent users of both drugs and alcohol.

P. Emmett and G. Nice, *Understanding drugs: A handbook for parents, teachers and other professionals*, London, Jessica Kingsley, 1996.

drug action team an inter-agency team established to provide services to drug misusers and to prevent the further misuse of drugs.

Drug action teams were formed in England and Wales as part of the strategy set out in the government's *Tackling Drugs Together* policy in 1995. They attempt to combine treatment and prevention services in community settings. They have been involved in the delivery of DRUG TREATMENT AND TESTING ORDERS since the implementation of the CRIME AND DISORDER ACT 1998. They represent a community crime prevention model of controlling the misuse of drugs, attempting to minimize problems with drugs and crime by providing community services and supervising drug misusers in their own areas, as well as bringing the responsible agencies together to devise and implement local drug control strategies.

In Scotland, there is more emphasis upon HARM MINIMIZATION than on prevention.

drug or alcohol dependency broadly, a social threshold defined by 'problem drug use', that is, relying on a DRUG as a response to stress that people exhibit who are unable to cope with social or life demands that various social services are able to deal with.

Such a definition moves the notion of dependency beyond that of addiction and disease (arising from childhood or genes), which was how such dependency was previously understood, and places it in a social context. The World Health Organization recognizes a number of criteria for making a diagnosis of dependency. These include:

1 more of the substance taken than intended;
2 the desire to cut down but unable to control use;
3 large amount of time expended in substance-related activity;
4 frequent intoxication or withdrawal symptoms when the person is expected to function, for example at work or in a physically hazardous activity such as driving.

Other criteria for dependency that WHO specifies are drug use replacing social, leisure and work activities, physical tolerance of large amounts of the drug and use of the substance to relieve or avoid withdrawal symptoms.

An old stereotype held that drug dependency often followed experimental use of hard drugs, such as cocaine or heroin, but recent investigations have established other more powerful causes. For example, a majority of dependent users have experienced physical or sexual abuse as children. Domestic violence is also a frequent contributing factor particularly affecting women. For social workers, such findings mean that dependent persons cannot easily become drug-free given earlier traumatic episodes. Thus the decision to come off and stay off can be a long process requiring continuing support, both practical and therapeutic.

Social workers face many problems associated with drug misuse. For example, it is estimated that some 60 per cent of child abuse perpetrators have drug misuse problems, while drug or alcohol dependency is strongly linked to violent offences (and is particularly high among those with diagnosed serious MENTAL HEALTH PROBLEMS). High proportions of those with drug dependency are also found with those suffering from depression (30 per cent), with PSYCHOSES (50 per cent) and some 20 per cent of older people and disabled people with depression. Drug dependency in mothers is also associated with a range of further difficulties in health, relationships and money, although their sense of commitment to their children is not diminished.

There is evidence to show that social workers, in common with other professionals, can have negative attitudes towards drug users, especially parents. They can see them as deceitful, manipulative and criminal in motivation. As a result, they miss the potential of collaborative work and partnership with those who are drug-dependent and move quickly instead to coercive forms of intervention.

R. Hampton, *Substance Abuse, Family Violence and Child Welfare*, London, Sage, 1998.

drug treatment and testing order (DTTO) a court order requiring an offender who misuses drugs and is susceptible to treatment to submit to such treatment and to mandatory drug testing and other conditions.

A drug treatment and testing order can be made on any offender aged over 16 who meets the criteria above. Offenders who fail to comply with DTTOs can be fined or the order can be varied or revoked. When an order is revoked, the offender can be re-sentenced for the offence in respect of which the order was made. Orders can last for between six months and three years, and standard conditions include compulsory drug tests and regular reviews in court. The orders are administered by the probation service, usually in collaboration with drug treatment agencies, and can be made alongside COMMUNITY REHABILITATION ORDERS and SUPERVISION ORDERS. Probation officers are required to prepare written reports for review hearings, including the results of drug tests. DTTOs can only be made with offenders' consent, although there is usually no alternative other than a custodial sentence.

DTTOs are intended to offer an intensive programme of supervision, treatment and testing for persistent offenders who are seriously drug-dependent. Such offenders often commit numerous property offences to fund their drug habits, and the intensity of DTTOs, combined with the ability of DRUG ACTION TEAMS to obtain speedy access to treatment and other resources, are intended to ensure that these offenders receive serious official attention. The element of compulsion sits uneasily with treatment and prevention approaches, however.

DTO abbreviation for DETENTION AND TRAINING ORDER.

DTTO abbreviation for DRUG TREATMENT AND TESTING ORDER.

dual diagnosis a term used to describe people with serious MENTAL HEALTH PROBLEMS who also have DRUG OR ALCOHOL DEPENDENCY.

Both these broad conditions are classed as illnesses in the International Classification of Diseases by the World Health Organization. Thus, 'dual diagnosis' is taken to mean two illnesses, with their separate diagnoses, existing alongside each other. In some ways this is helpful, as it signals a need for services that can address both conditions simultaneously. It marks an advance of a sort for, until recently, drug services would not provide for people with serious mental health problems, and mental health services would not treat substance misuse. Today there are three different approaches to 'dual diagnosis':

1 drug and mental health services treat the person simultaneously but separately;

2 consecutive treatment, one after the other;

3 integrated service, addressing both conditions and how they interact with each other.

On the other hand, the idea of 'dual diagnosis' can be misleading. There are well-researched links between serious mental health problems and substance misuse. The combination of these conditions is common – amongst 60–70 per cent of people with serious mental health problems – because people with serious mental health problems experience extreme inner distress and disturbance alongside powerful stressors in their social environment. Substance misuse can be a way of relieving this stress – a form of 'self-medication'. Side effects of anti-psychotic medication (see PSYCHOSES) can also be very hard to live with, and substance misuse is therefore often used to combat these. Integrated services try to address these links and offer, necessarily, a 'biopsychosocial' service that looks at the medical issues in psychosis and drug dependency, social stressors that trigger both misuse and psychotic relapse and psychological coping strategies.

Social workers often encounter people with 'dual diagnosis' when working with people with mental health problems who are receiving community care services. They may be case managers, coordinating a care plan or contributing to multi-agency assessment and care planning. It is important for them to be aware of the way in which social stressors and social care needs can trigger substance misuse and psychotic relapse and also of the implications for social isolation through homelessness.

P. Kearney, *Alcohol, Drugs and Mental Health Problems – Working with Families*, London, National Institute of Social Work, 2000.

dual process model a model of understanding GRIEF and LOSS that emphasizes constant movement between 'loss orientation' and 'restoration orientation' for people who are grieving.

dual sensory impairment see DEAF-BLIND.

DWP abbreviation for DEPARTMENT FOR WORK AND PENSIONS.

dying the sudden or gradual cessation of all physiological and mental processes in a person.

This definition of dying, simple and clear, could cause offence to many people, because Western societies have traditionally been death-denying societies. Reluctance to employ direct language to describe death – the use of such euphemisms as 'going to heaven', 'going to God' and 'falling asleep' – may indicate people's feelings about dying. People may change the subject or joke, or consider talking of dying as morbid. Often dying people are denied the opportunity to talk about what is one of the most significant events of their lives. Dying people may feel isolated from their carers.

The reluctance to deal openly with death and discussion of death makes it difficult for people who are dying to express their needs in personally meaningful ways. In her work on the subject, Elizabeth Kubler-Ross notes that a patient dying of cancer in a hospital was prevented from saying how good it felt to be dying: the care she received, the relief from pain, the new friendships with hospital staff and the acceptance of the fact of death by Kubler-Ross all helped ensure that for her dying was a peaceful, shared and comfortable experience. The reluctance towards, or taboo against, discussion of dying means that many people do not receive the support and help they need, as in the case of a nurse who, when dying, was permitted to share her feelings with others only by writing them down.

Many people have difficulties when the fact of a person's dying needs to be communicated to the dying person and to others. It has been suggested that this is linked to the fear of dying that most people have and to the belief that others have the same fear. Although there may be a fear of dying in most people, possibly shared by people who 'manage' death professionally (such as medical personnel), it has often been argued that the experience of dying should be shared. Many people when told initially that they are dying may deny or ignore the information. Working effectively with dying people requires a recognition of social taboos on talk about dying and the willingness of a worker to break that taboo if a dying person desires it. Working with the dying means offering an accepting and supportive relationship, responding honestly to cues that the dying person may give as to the direction he or she wishes discussions to take.

In a multicultural and multi-faith society it is important to recognize that death and dying can mean different things to different people. Some believe in a life after death; others believe in reincarnation, while still others are convinced that death is the absolute and total end of a human being's existence. People's beliefs and attitudes towards death and dying will often provide a sense of meaning and purpose for the living, and it is important for social workers to be sensitive to this. (See PALLIATIVE CARE.)

E. Kubler-Ross, *On Death and Dying,* London, Routledge & Kegan Paul, 1970.

E*e*

early release arrangements for early release from prison, including PAROLE.

Sentences of CUSTODY are served partly in PRISON and partly in the COMMUNITY. Adult prisoners serving determinate short-term sentences may be released early under a CURFEW with ELECTRONIC MONITORING. If the person breaches the curfew or leaves the specified address, his or her early release licence can be revoked and he or she is then liable to be returned to prison. Parole applies only to longer sentences and life imprisonment.

early years the term now used to denote children under five and the services provided for them.

The importance of a child's pre-school experience cannot be overestimated. Recent studies have revealed several pointers for practice. First, children from 0–4 need a variety of learning experiences that are active, relevant and enjoyable throughout that entire period. Second, education and care should be integrated in a well-planned, stimulating and healthy environment. Third, an appropriate curriculum should encourage active learning and 'purposeful play', and fourth, a partnership between parents and educators is essential to make that curriculum work.

Despite the emphasis on FAMILY SUPPORT in the CHILDREN ACT 1989, most local authorities continued to operate a deficit model for children's services well into the 1990s, giving highest priority in terms of resources to CHILD PROTECTION. By the late 1990s, the convergence of evidence and a number of voices were urging the creation of an integrated early years service as a way of moving local authority social work practice beyond the single concern with risk. Persuasive data from the United States also demonstrated that for every dollar invested in early years, there was a long-term net return of at least seven times that amount. With the election of the Labour government in 1997, each local authority was asked to develop early years' partnerships, now called *early years' forums*. The forums oversee service integration for children under five at ground level. Nursery schools, playgroups, child minders, family centres and social services all combine care with pre-school educational opportunities to promote the development of young children and offer practical support to parents.

The aims of such partnerships are:

1 to enhance the care, play and educational experience of young children;

2 to be directed by the diverse needs and aspirations of children and their parents;

3 to pay attention to the support of families;

4 to build active partnerships that can bring together enough members to ensure coverage of all relevant local initiatives.

A. Jamieson and S. Owen, *Ambition for Change Partnerships, children and work*, London, National Children's Bureau, 2000.

earnings disregard SEE MEANS-TESTED BENEFIT; WELFARE RIGHTS 9.

eating disorders SEE ANOREXIA NERVOSA, BULIMIA.

ecological approach a perspective in social work that emphasizes the adaptive and reciprocal relationship between people and their environment.

The perspective sees a person's social environment as a set of concentric circles through which it is possible to picture how institutions, social attitudes and family dynamics promote or curtail the opportunities and wellbeing of individuals. Individuals develop within the *microsystem* of home, the *meso-system* of school, neighbourhood, and other local institutions such as churches, clubs and associations, and the *exo-system* through which more distant but powerful institutions and practices bear on the individual's life. For a child such institutions may be the parent's workplace (and its level of pay and working conditions), the conduct of local agencies such as youth clubs or something as everyday as the local public transport system. For a young adult it may be how information regarding job opportunities or skills training is transmitted. For a person with disability it may be the attitudes of local employers or the supported employment opportunities or more skills training.

Finally, there is the *macrosystem* – a large field embracing the cultural, political, economic, legal and religious context of society. It includes social attitudes and values that, although not always perceived in daily life, have a huge impact on individual lives. For example, our dominant images and opinions on GENDER, OLDER PEOPLE, HIV, crime and punishment emerge often from the macrosystem.

The ecological approach helps social workers to highlight a range of factors that might otherwise have be overlooked in understanding the problems and needs of a person, family or local community. These include the importance of income and concrete resources, like child care and employment opportunities, and better coordinated services around health, education and housing. It also shows the changes that can be achieved only by community building where the capacities of local people and neighbourhood organizations are developed.

G. Jack and D. Jack, Ecological Social Work: 'The application of a systems model of development in context' in P. Stepney and D. Ford, *Social Work Models Methods and Theories*, Lyme Regis, Russell House Publishing, 2000.

ecomap a diagram used by a variety of social welfare workers to describe the focal person's social situation. It could typically include family or kin (see GENOGRAM) but also other people significant to the person. In many situations significant or influential people can come from outside the family, such as a teacher or family friend. Some problems are now seen as at least partly soluble by mobilizing potential helpers from outside the family.

EC Social Security Directive 79/7 a directive setting out the then European Community's (now European Union's) objective for sex equality in SOCIAL SECURITY.

The directive stated that 'there shall be no discrimination on grounds of sex either directly or indirectly by reference in particular to marital or family status'. Member states were supposed to abolish discriminatory laws and practices by 1985. The directive applied to the 'working population', but this included people whose work was interrupted by ill-health or involuntary unemployment, people who were retired and people looking for work. Women who gave up work to care for children were not covered, but women who gave up work to care for a person with a disability were. Benefits covered included those relating to sickness, invalidity, old age, unemployment and industrial injury. Income support paid, for example, to an unemployed person was covered, but housing benefit and family credit were not.

Education Act 1996 the current framework for most educational provision, which has replaced the previous core Education Act of 1944.

The Act consolidated earlier legislation on the education of children. Under it, the local education authority (LEA) has a duty to provide education and parents have a legal obligation to secure their child's education. If a child is not registered at a school and the LEA is satisfied that the child is not receiving a suitable education at home, it may serve a School Attendance Order on the parents. The failure to comply with such an order is a criminal offence. The Act also defines SPECIAL EDUCATIONAL NEEDS, which call for special provision where a child has LEARNING DIFFICULTIES. The latter are established when the child has significantly greater difficulties than the majority of children of that age or has a DISABILITY that prevents or hinders her or him from making use of the education facilities provided for children of the same age.

educational inclusion a term used by the Office for Standards in Education (Ofsted) to describe educational processes, structures and policies that promote more effective outcomes for children who are currently marginalized from learning or facing EXCLUSION FROM SCHOOL.

Many of these children will be CHILDREN IN NEED as defined by the FRAMEWORK FOR ASSESSMENT OF CHILDREN IN NEED and will therefore be receiving services from a variety of agencies. Guidance from Ofsted for school inspectors talks of the importance of LEA and school staff identifying those at risk of missing out and taking positive steps to promote their involvement. Many local education authorities will be promoting the interests of such children through their EDUCATION SOCIAL WORK (education welfare) service or other staff appointed to combat SOCIAL EXCLUSION. Schools will also be developing their own responses, such as the appointment of staff to follow up children who are absent or in-school learning support units.

Department for Education and Skills Circulars 10/99 and 11/99, *Social Inclusion: Pupil Support*.

educational maintenance allowance see WELFARE RIGHTS 4.

educational psychologist a teacher with additional qualifications in psychology, responsible for conducting a STATUTORY ASSESSMENT OF SPECIAL EDUCATION NEEDS to determine whether a child with SPECIAL EDUCATIONAL NEEDS requires a STATEMENT.

Educational psychologists also devise packages to assist learning, to support parents and school staff, and to facilitate behaviour change. If provision within a school under SCHOOL ACTION AND SCHOOL ACTION PLUS is not meeting the child's needs, they may be asked to assess the child with a view to more specialized provision, either in a mainstream or special school. (See also STATEMENT OF EDUCATIONAL NEEDS.)

education clothing grant see WELFARE RIGHTS 4.

education social work or **education welfare** a form of social work that supports the education of vulnerable and marginalized pupils and combats SOCIAL EXCLUSION.

Education social work is one of the oldest forms of public welfare provision, dating back at least to the Education Act 1870 and the extension of compulsory education through local school boards. Whether such work is 'social work' is a matter of some debate, not always resolved by the title chosen by the local education authority (LEA) for its particular service. There is no national standard or qualification. Formal social work qualification is not a requirement in most current services, although some LEAs seek to appoint only such staff. 'Attendance officers' were historically responsible for identifying children in their areas who were not registered at any school or receiving education in some other way and establishing whether they should be enrolled. Much of this work involved seeking to assist children who could not attend school because of poverty, supervising children at work and protecting children found to be at risk. These duties still form the core of such officers' responsibilities.

The traditional perception of the role of attendance officers as based essentially on legal enforcement does not do justice to what were quite sophisticated attempts to approach the work from a 'welfare' perspective. Although the failure of parents to ensure that their children are 'properly educated' has always been an offence (currently with a maximum fine of £1,000 for a first offence and up to £2,500 subsequently), contemporary commentators noted that as early as the beginning of the 20th century these officials were acting as the 'children's friend and the parents' adviser' rather than relying too much on their power to prosecute.

With the provision of financial assistance for meals at school from 1902, as well as the administration of charitable funds for clothing and footwear, the welfare of children at school formed a much wider agenda than simply forcing children to attend.

With the Children Act 1948 much of this wider responsibility passed to the children's committees and then to SOCIAL SERVICES DEPARTMENTS. Since then education social work has tended to be seen as of lower status than other forms of local authority provision. The major focus has continued to be school attendance, (CHILDREN ACT 1989, section 36; EDUCATION ACT 1996; EDUCATION SUPERVISION ORDERS) although education social workers (ESWs) and education welfare officers (EWOs) also have a statutory duty for monitoring the EMPLOYMENT OF CHILDREN, assisting children with SPECIAL EDUCATIONAL NEEDS and participating in CHILD PROTECTION procedures. They may also have other roles defined in the local education authority's BEHAVIOUR SUPPORT PLAN.

With a continuing debate about the future of local education authorities, their declining role in the day-to-day management of schools and the growing emphasis on delegating resources to local schools, education social workers still face an uncertain future, as they have for several years. Some ESWs and EWOs feel that recent changes have tended to undermine their traditional role of being independent advocates for children and have made them more accountable to head teachers than they would prefer.

The Ralphs Report of 1973 highlighted the nature of the tasks as being substantially the same as other forms of social work, but governments have increasingly taken the view that their role should be more 'educational' and less 'social work' in focus. In many situations it will now be a teaching or non-teaching member of the school staff who should be the first point of contact when a child has a problem rather than the ESW/EWO. Many schools are appointing their own staff, such as attendance officers or home/school liaison officers. These have taken over much of the work previously done by ESWs/EWOs who may in future concentrate more on statutory work, data analysis, specialist advice and assistance in policy development rather than casework. All schools will normally have a named officer, however, usually working with the school under a service level agreement that defines the role and the time available in which to do it.

education supervision order (ESO) provision under the CHILDREN ACT 1989 (section 36) whereby a local education authority (LEA) may apply to the FAMILY PROCEEDINGS COURT to have a child who is not being 'properly educated' placed under the LEA's supervision, initially for one year. The order may be extended for up to three years.

As with all Children Act orders, an ESO must be considered to be better for the child than making no order. In practice, these powers have been used to only a very limited extent, largely because LEAs lack the necessary resources to ensure effective involvement but partly because making an order, in itself, will often not resolve the problems of a child who is not attending school. An ESO places a parent under a significant duty to follow the 'directions' of the supervisor, usually a member of the EDUCATION SOCIAL WORK (or education welfare) Service. This is likely to be helpful only where parents are failing to act responsibly or where a child has complex needs, including SPECIAL EDUCATIONAL NEEDS. An ESO is unlikely to be very helpful in addressing the needs of a young person who is disaffected with education or beyond the control of his or her parents. SOCIAL SERVICES DEPARTMENTS have a duty to assess whether other services and orders may be needed in the event of the child failing to follow reasonable directions.

education welfare see EDUCATION SOCIAL WORK.

effectiveness ways of working with offenders that succeed in reducing re-offending (often referred to as 'what works').

The national Probation Inspectorate has, since the mid-1990s, exhorted staff to concentrate on working with offenders in ways that have been shown to reduce re-offending. The CRIME AND DISORDER ACT 1998 made prevention of offending by young people the principal aim of the youth justice system. Both services have tended to assume that the research evidence shows that the most effective ways of reducing offending and re-offending involve COGNITIVE BEHAVIOURAL approaches to offender supervision. Although this is an over-simplified reading of the research, it has had profound consequences on the ways in which work with offenders is organized.

Research has shown that some traditional approaches to offender supervision are unlikely to be successful in reducing re-offending. In particular, punishment does little to change offenders' attitudes for the better, especially imprisonment or institutionalization, and unstructured counselling is unlikely to be effective. This is not to say that there is no place for counselling, but it needs to be combined with other approaches and planned as a response to particular needs.

Much of the effectiveness literature stresses the importance of concentrating supervisory attention on 'criminogenic need'. This means giving precedence to the needs presented by the offender that relate to their offending or make re-offending more likely if not addressed. In one sense, this is obvious – but it is sometimes interpreted as meaning that staff should not concern themselves with 'welfare' needs, which would seem to be a misinterpretation of the research. Clearly, staff should concentrate upon working with those needs that they are in a position to address and refer service users to other agencies when appropriate. There is also good research evidence that effective supervision depends upon a constructive and respectful relationship between offenders and their probation officer or youth offending team (YOT) worker, and a powerful tool in building positive relationships is helping offenders with the problems that they choose to present. It would be churlish to refuse assistance on the ground that the need was not criminogenic enough, particularly if the help given makes it easier to engage with other aspects of the offender's behaviour. Unmet needs are also likely to get in the way of effective supervision.

Effective work with offenders begins with a full assessment, and this should include assessing the level of RISK presented by the individual. This is an inexact science, like establishing 'what works', but it is important because intensive intervention can exacerbate the problems presented by an offender if it is inappropriate. Low-risk offenders should receive less intensive attention. This principle of parsimony can come into conflict with a desire for early intervention in order to 'nip in the bud' antisocial behaviour, but the research suggests that excessive early intervention is likely to be counter-productive. Offenders' learning styles should also be routinely assessed, so that any intervention leads to effective engagement (the 'responsivity principle'). Many, perhaps most, offenders prefer an active and participatory approach, suggesting that group work should use few 'chalk and talk'-style presentations and concentrate upon group and individual activities, role play and exercises.

The research literature emphasizes 'programme integrity', which essentially means that interventions should be delivered in the way in which they were planned. Without attention to programme integrity, 'mission drift' can occur as workers make unplanned changes to the programme to suit their own style or preferences. Staff need to be properly trained and supervised, and programmes need to be evaluated. The need for programme integrity can be exaggerated, however. Workers reading from a manual are unlikely to deliver group work in a lively, engaging, manner.

Research suggests that many effective programmes include attention to thought patterns that lead to offending. These cognitive-behavioural approaches are best seen as part of a supervisor's professional repertoire: no single approach fits all cases. However, they have become the mainstay of practice in the PROBATION SERVICE in England and Wales. Programmes are centrally accredited and evaluated, and there is pressure to put large numbers of offenders through them in order to meet performance targets. Some observers feel that this is in danger of suppressing the creativity and spontaneity of staff.

P. Raynor, D. Smith and M. Vanstone, *Effective Probation Practice*, Macmillan, 1994.

elder abuse the mistreatment of an older person, either continuously and systematically or as a single incident.

Elder abuse usually occurs in the context of long-standing relationships and often, though not always, at the hands of the person who has the main care of the older person. It is also known to have occurred in residential institutions. Both older women and men may experience abuse. Abuse takes many forms, but psychological distress is always a feature of it. The abused person experiences hopelessness, fear, anxiety, insecurity and loss of self-respect. Abuse may lead to confusion in an older person, which may in turn lead to further abuse.

Elder abuse manifests in a number of ways, and older people may encounter any one or several types of abuse. These include:

1 *physical abuse*, such as hitting, burning, restraint, injury, forcible feeding, the withholding or overdosing of medication, and confinement to bed;

2 *psychological and emotional abuse*, such as shouting, harsh language, threats, ridicule, swearing, ignoring, rejecting and isolation;

3 *financial abuse*, such as stealing or exploitation of property, values and assets, misappropriation of the pension or bank book, and denying money for personal use;

4 *sexual abuse*, such as assault, rape and coercion into sexual activity without consent.

They may also suffer forms of severe *neglect*, such as abandonment, starvation, preventing or not enabling access to needed public services, and of hygiene routines. Other forms of abuse include *neighbourhood abuse*, such as harassment and scapegoating; and *domestic violence*, such as a long-standing history of violence in a relationship that has become increasingly dangerous because of the frailty of older age.

Abuse usually occurs in a domestic setting, which makes the incidence difficult to identify, and research has usually focused on abuse within families. However, abuse can occur in hospital, day care, nursing homes and care homes. The abuser is likely to be known to the abused person, perhaps as daughter, granddaughter, daughter-in-law, son, grandson or son-in-law – the most likely abuser being the main carer. Frequently such situations are reflections of desperation on the part of care-givers, who often feel quite hopeless. Although abuse may be taking place, it is often mixed with other, more positive feelings for the cared-for person, and in these circumstances the abuser may indeed feel that he or she has failed as carer.

Theoretical explanations for why abuse occurs are various. Some use a social construction analysis, arguing that ageism and able-bodiedism result in attitudes that disempower older people. Physical and/or mental disability may result in loss of respect and render the person vulnerable to abuse. Other explanations draw on psychological theories to provide a range of perspectives. Abuse may be a spontaneous response to a stressful situation or may arise from long-standing difficult domestic interactions. Sons and daughters may resent caring for a formerly dominant parent and retaliate for past suffering.

Abusive carers may be sadistic, gaining pleasure from the abuse – something that has been seen in both domestic and institutional environments. Or they may be overwhelmed by what seems an unending burden, exacerbated by social isolation, loss of control and resultant depression. Carers may be angry and frustrated at the high levels of dependency of the old person. They may additionally experience feelings of revulsion at the person soiling, vomiting or eating rubbish. Bizarre behaviour may occur, notably if DEMENTIA is present, raising anxiety throughout a household. Family members may also resent the changes brought about by the need to care for an old person.

Currently within the UK there is no specific legislation to protect older people such as is in place to protect children. Legal protection is available through both criminal and civil courts if a person is able and willing to take action. Both physical and sexual abuse could lead to criminal action on the basis of actual harm to the person under the Offences against the Person Act 1861. The restriction of a person's movements may be actionable under the tort of false imprisonment, and where financial abuse occurs, prosecutions for theft and/or fraud can take place. It is possible to bring an action for negligence where it can be proved that the carer has a duty of care and that duty has been broken. All such actions require that the older person, or possibly his or her advocate, will make the appropriate complaints. In practice, this is very rare, as older people are unwilling to risk offending family members and possibly jeopardizing the limited amounts of care that they have. Both the National Assistance Act 1948 and the Mental Health Act 1983 allow for an old person to be removed from home if mentally ill and considered to be neglected or ill-treated. Certain forms of abuse may also be remedied under the Domestic Violence and Matrimonial Proceedings Acts and the Sexual Offences Acts. Although criticisms have been made of the current potential of the existing law to protect older people, there has been a marked shift in policy during the latter part of the last century to acknowledge the prevalence of elder abuse. This new emphasis is reflected in the Department of Health's guidance, *No Secrets: The Protection of Vulnerable Adults: Guidance on the Development and Implementation of Multi-Agency Policies and Procedures.*

P. Decalmer and F. Glendenning (eds), *The Mistreatment of Elderly People*, second edition, London, Sage, 1997.

O. Stevenson, 'Old People at Risk' in Phyllida Parsloe (ed), *Risk Assessment in Social Care and Social Work*, London, Jessica Kingsley, 1999.

electronic monitoring the practice of electronically 'tagging' offenders to check their compliance with CURFEWS and other restrictions ordered by courts.

Electronic monitoring began in North America in the 1980s. Since the passage of the Criminal Justice Act 1991, it has been possible to make offenders subject to electronic monitoring in the UK, but the practice was slow to become established, partly because of persistent problems with the technology. These have now been surmounted, and 'tagging' has become an important aspect of criminal justice policy. Initially, tagging was introduced as part of the conditional release of long-term prisoners, but it was then made available as a sentence in its own right and more recently as a condition of bail, at first with adults and then with young offenders.

The equipment involved has got smaller since the 1990s and now consists of a transmitter about the size of a wristwatch, which is attached to the offender's wrist or ankle in such a way that it cannot be removed without this being detected. Equipment is also installed at the offender's home, requiring a telephone line, and this sends signals to a computer at the offices of the private company that runs the monitoring arrangements. Offenders can be ordered to comply with a CURFEW or to stay away from certain places as part of the conditions of electronic monitoring.

Many criminal justice practitioners had severe reservations about the introduction of electronic monitoring, feeling that it would threaten the rights and dignity of offenders and also that privatization might threaten their jobs. There remains considerable concern about the implications of ordering an offender to remain in his or her home, not least because this may constitute a form of punishment for others living there who have not been charged with any offence. In practice, however, it has often been welcomed as a lower level of intrusion than the alternative, imprisonment. It is questionable, though, whether it has always been used as a direct alternative to custody. Its EFFECTIVENESS with less serious offenders is poor: research shows that it increases re-offending. It is more effective with more serious offenders, particularly when combined with other forms of intervention. In North America, its increased use coincided with increasing prison numbers, and the same has happened in England and Wales.

From 2002, tagging has been available for serious young offenders over the age of 12 in parts of England and Wales under the provisions of the Criminal Justice and Police Act 2001.

D. Whitfield, *Tackling the Tag: the Electronic Monitoring of Offenders*, Winchester, Waterside Press, 1997.

eligibility criteria the criteria established by local authorities to determine who is in NEED and may receive services under the NATIONAL HEALTH SERVICE AND COMMUNITY CARE ACT.

Eligibility is a central feature of the systems developed for the arrangements for assessment and care management. To avoid demands for services that local authorities would be unable to meet, in 1992 the Audit Commission advised them to make their definition of 'need' clear to the public. This was further refined so that the relative priority of need could be assessed through criteria that deemed individuals eligible for services in accordance with their perceived degree of dependence and risk. Most local authorities' eligibility criteria are set so that those who are most likely to receive services are those considered in danger and without personal support networks.

Eligibility criteria are an aspect of the tensions that arise from conflicting social policy aims but which frontline social care practitioners are required to manage. On the one hand, the aims of the 1989 white paper *Caring for People* require that practitioners respond to an individual's perception of his or her own needs rather than rely on well-established service definitions of need. On the other hand, 'need' is defined by the local authority, as are the criteria that decide who will be eligible for services. Thus, expectations raised by the rhetoric of individually tailored responses to assessment are counterbalanced by the rationing agenda or, as it is now familiarly known in SOCIAL CARE, *targeted resources.*

Some of the earlier research into the impact of the new reforms suggests that, for some frontline workers, the development of these processes has reduced practice to a more technical and bureaucratic exercise in which assessment is confined, first, to consideration of whether individuals are eligible and, then, for which services. Changing the culture to a 'needs-led' service requires frontline workers to look beyond those services and supports in a locality for which the local authority has direct budgetary responsibility and to consider the resources of other statutory and voluntary agencies along with informal networks. Rationing has always been an aspect of social care, however, and it can be argued that this serves to make the process more open to scrutiny, promotes equity and makes the local authority more accountable. Nevertheless, the focus on 'dependence and risk' as the main criteria for access to assessment and service sits uneasily with the rhetoric of promoting 'independence'.

M. Langan (ed), *Welfare: need, rights and risks,* London, Routledge, 1998.

emergency duty team a team of local authority social workers providing social work services when offices are closed overnight, at weekends and during holidays.

Generally the team covers a large geographical area, such as an entire county, and responds only in urgent situations. These critical situations include when a person may have to be detained in mental hospital or a child may have to be removed from his or her parents to avoid further abuse. Members of the team are experienced practitioners skilled in working with psychiatrists and the police who will frequently be present when they are called out.

emergency protection order (EPO) an order under section 44 of the CHILDREN ACT allowing a local authority social worker (or a National Society for the Prevention of Cruelty to Children officer) to remove a child from his or her parents or other adults, or to retain the child in a safe place, such as a hospital, if the worker has reasonable cause to believe that the child is suffering or is likely to suffer SIGNIFICANT HARM.

The order may also be applied for if the social worker is unreasonably denied access to a child who is likely to suffer significant harm. It is usually obtained by the worker's application before a magistrate without other parties to the case, such as the child's parents, present (see EX-PARTE). The application must outline the circumstances in detail, including why the child is likely to suffer significant harm. If the social worker thinks that entry to the home where the child is living will be refused, he or she can ask the court for a warrant to enter the premises and for a police officer to assist in this.

The order lasts for eight days, with a possible seven-day extension in exceptional circumstances. During this time the local authority must decide on the course of action it is to take, such as returning the child home or preventing the child from going home by asking the court for a CARE ORDER. If at any time while the order is in force the authority thinks it is safe to return the child home, it must do so. Parents, the child or anyone with whom the child was living before the order was made may apply for a discharge of the order after 72 hours if the original order were made ex-parte. As long as the order is in force, parents and their representatives enjoy reasonable CONTACT with the child, unless the court has made a specific direction to the contrary. One of the main objectives of the Children Act is to ensure that local authorities remove children only when this is necessary in order to protect life and limb. In this it has succeeded: the number of emergency protection orders taken by authorities has fallen significantly compared with emergency removals of children under previous child-care law. Department of Health guidance says that authorities should try to secure the child's safety through other measures, if at all possible, such as providing FAMILY SUPPORT services.

Department of Health, *Guidance to the Children Act. Vol. 1: Court Orders*, London, HMSO, 1991.

emotional abuse and neglect terms used rather loosely by many writers to describe negative psychological effects on people resulting from the damaging behaviour of others.

'Neglect' is a term suggesting systematic or major inattention by a carer or significant other. Emotional abuse has been considered by some to be an active process and neglect an act of omission, but this distinction is hard to sustain and is probably not useful. Emotional abuse and neglect clearly overlap.

Emotional ABUSE can be a result of physical or sexual abuse, or it can be a consequence of other behaviours rooted in sustained unpleasant and unhappy transactions between two or more people. In social work most recent attention on this issue has focused on children, although emotional abuse can relate to adult relationships within whole families or specifically to vulnerable elders, adults with disabilities and to marital and partner relationships. Some writers prefer the term 'psychological abuse' because they regard emotional reactions as properly the province of psychology. Others differentiate between matters pertaining to the mind as against issues of feelings or emotions. Clinical psychologists would regard the distinction as unsustainable, arguing that feelings and emotions are the concern of psychology and provide crucial evidence of personal adjustment or maladjustment. The distinction, in their view, possibly originates in a confusion about means and ends. Physical, sexual or emotional abuse can all, singly or in combinations, lead to psychological maladjustment. Different forms of abuse (means) may result in psychological problems (ends).

Whatever term is used, there is some consensus about the kind of behaviour that can be described as emotionally abusing. Intimidating behaviour, deprivation of a carer or loved one, loneliness and isolation, withholding approval or a consistent negative response, constant refusal to recognize someone's needs or worth and the encouragement of negative or antisocial behaviour can all be usefully cited. Physical and sexual abuse can be emotionally damaging too. To have been physically or sexually assaulted, and perhaps to live in fear of it happening again, is almost certainly to experience at least some of the circumstances described above. The severity of the abuse depends on a number of factors, including its duration, the age and maturity of the abused, and the degree of power exercised by the abuser.

In relation to children, it is comparatively rare for social welfare agencies to intervene on the basis of emotional abuse alone. Even with children who are clearly very unhappy and are displaying major indicators of psychological disturbance, the chances of compulsory intervention are slight unless sexual or physical abuse is present too. Explanations for this worrying situation are varied. The problem of proof seems to be more elusive than for sexual or physical abuse, partly because there are competing psychologies of human development. Social workers and health professionals are not at ease in this field even where they are sure that emotional abuse is visible and substantial. Some critics have suggested that there has been a fundamental failure to recognize the emotional abuse involved in removing children from their homes as a result of, for example, physical abuse – further evidence, perhaps, of social workers' inability to handle emotional issues with confidence. Others have suggested that whereas sexual and physical abuse can be understood by the public, emotional abuse is difficult to comprehend. Intervention by SOCIAL SERVICES DEPARTMENTS, already viewed critically by the world at large, would almost certainly not have unequivocal public support. In the meantime, many children are being irreparably damaged because their abuse is not being heeded. (See also CHILD PROTECTION, PHYSICAL ABUSE, SEXUAL ABUSE.)

Social workers appear to be more confident about dealing with neglect. For children to develop normally, they require regular stimulation for them to become emotionally, intellectually, physically and socially mature. Neglect can lead to ill-health because of a failure to provide a child with appropriately nutritious food or an unwillingness or inability to keep them reasonably clean. Some diets can make children listless and lacking in energy, and thus lead to a lack of curiosity. Significant under-stimulation of children can have similar effects, leading to poor development of intellectual capacity, and if there is lack of interaction with other children or adults, then social abilities and skills will be stunted too.

The key issue for both emotional abuse and neglect in relation to children is whether the SIGNIFICANT HARM test is satisfied and whether convincing evidence of the cause of that significant harm can be marshalled. In terms of process, similar thresholds must be passed if any emotional abuse of adults is to be proven. Adult protection teams are now beginning to be established, and they will increasingly have to make these kinds of judgements. A similar test is applicable, say in cases of domestic violence where a man is stalking his estranged partner.

K. O'Hagan, *Emotional and Psychological Abuse of Children*, Buckingham, Open University Press, 1993.

O. Stevenson, *Neglected Children: Issues and Dilemmas*, Oxford, Blackwell, 1998.

employment of children part-time employment of school-aged children. The employment of children is subject to regulation and inspection by the local education authority (LEA) in accordance with national legislation and local bylaws.

The primary legislation affecting child employment, the Children and Young Persons Act 1933, is badly in need of reform. Although new bylaws were introduced in 1998, many elements of the primary legislation remained unchanged. These regulations cover only employment in any undertaking carried on for profit, whether or not the child is paid. Consequently, jobs such as babysitting or washing neighbours' cars are exempt, but newspaper delivery, shop work, waitressing and so on must all be licensed. No child can be employed at all under the age of 13, before 7.00am or after 7.00pm on any day or for more than two hours on a Sunday. A child (defined as all those still of COMPULSORY SCHOOL AGE even if they are already 16) may not be employed for more than 12 hours in any week (including the weekend) in which he or she is also required to attend school. There are various other limits on the number of hours for which a child may be employed and a wide list of prohibited employments. Thirteen-year-olds can only do jobs on a 'specified list'. There are widespread breaches of the law. Research shows that most children work and that most work illegally, but prosecution is rare, partly because of the antiquated nature of the regulations, which do not command widespread public support. Some local education authorities are more vigilant than others, and there is some concern at the level of injury and exposure to risks by children in the workplace which is largely tolerated. Different regulations govern 'work experience' as part of an approved educational programme, and there are also rules relating to the protection of children who take part in professional entertainments.

empowerment any process whereby those lacking, comparatively, in power become or are helped to become more powerful. The acquisition of power is thought appropriate to them as citizens, consumers or service users. There are both personal and political dimensions to the concept.

Empowerment implies a kind of 'power deficit' theory, very much in the same territory as the SOCIAL EXCLUSION paradigm. Empowerment can refer to, for example, self-help, to community action, to an involvement in a political process but also to any transactions between a service user and a social worker or helping professional. In relation to the latter 'micro' definition, empowerment means that service users can become more powerful as a result of engaging with helping professionals in particular ways in attempts to solve their problem(s).

Empowerment can be regarded as liberational in intent. In relation to service users it is concerned with several inter-related issues. First, many service users do not understand their own needs or problems or they have an incomplete understanding of them or, indeed, they have attributed their problem incorrectly to a particular cause. Further, some may have an understanding of their needs or problems but find it difficult to articulate them. Finally, many do not know how to solve their own problems or, if they do know how, lack the confidence to initiate action.

These kinds of problems of disempowerment may have their roots in low levels of education, including illiteracy, in problems of confidence or self-esteem, in difficulties of communication, such as English being a second language or in being profoundly deaf and without access to an interpreter or someone conversant with British Sign Language, in having lived a marginalized life in which decisions or even opinions were not required.

Professionals in helping and caring occupations believe that it is possible to empower service users by working with them in open, transparent and non-oppressive ways. In this context, minimizing the 'social distance' between professional and service user is thought to be crucial, as is working to the service user's agenda, facilitating understanding, supporting or sharing problem-solving activities, being prepared to review problems and tasks, building social skills and, in general, trying to increase the service user's abilities to deal with his or her own problems. In sum, this view of empowerment embraces the idea that people can acquire more power and, crucially, be able to use it effectively in meeting their needs and problem solving.

Other writers have perceived SELF-HELP activities as having great potential for empowering service users. This view of empowerment emphasizes the importance of not involving professionals and of learning from experience with others who have or have had the same problems. Empowerment is thought more likely to come about because the learning experience will be more profound, service users will be able to act more freely in exploring the utility of problem-solving activities and, if resources are delegated to service users (as with DIRECT PAYMENTS), they will be able to have control over which services are purchased. This view of empowerment rests upon a view that service users are, in a sense, experts in their own problems or needs, or at least that their experience of their problems or needs is valuable in deciding how best to develop services.

RADICAL SOCIAL WORK has taken the view that the key issue in empowerment is to explicitly connect 'people with problems' with the political process. Regardless of whether the impetus to connect the personal to the political is driven by professional advice or self-help, the crucial issue is to uncover the political nature of health and social welfare services and of the political structures within which they operate. In this context the point is not that service users should be 'consulted' but that they should be a core and necessary part of the political process.

Empowerment is thus a concept that invites analyses of professional-service user relationships, of how power unavoidably colours that relationship, of how that relationship might be reconfigured to make it more equal (and by so doing, empower both service user and professional) and of how power imbalances characterize the relationship between service users/citizens and social institutions, including political institutions and agencies concerned with health and social welfare. In sum, empowerment admits of the possibility of change in both key personal relationships and in the relationship between people and social and political structures.

enabling authority the concept of local authorities providing an environment that enables consumers of services to exercise choice and encourages the development of the private and voluntary sectors.

Under the concept, the role of local authorities is no longer that of the primary or sole service provider but rather to ensure that the services are available in their area, no matter from what source. The enabling authority is more of a regulator and purchaser of services, through contracts and contract enforcement, than the direct provider of services such as residential accommodation or home helps. Such a change of role results in the reduction of local authority services and may also lead to a changed role for many officers, including social workers.

G. Wistow, M. Knapp, B. Hardy, C. Allen, *Social Care in a Mixed Economy*, Buckingham, Open University Press, 1994.

encopresis the passing of stools into clothing or in other inappropriate places by a child who has reached an age at which this is no longer socially acceptable.

There are several different definitions of encopresis. US definitions are broader and tend to cover all possible causes of 'soiling', while in the

UK definitions have been restricted to those cases in which the causes are psychological and where the child has physical sensation and control. This is further complicated by the fact that children may experience emotional distress and other psychological reactions as a *result* of encopresis, whatever its cause. The age at which 'soiling' can be regarded as encopresis is not clear. Some definitions place this as low as four but also emphasize that 'soiling' should be regular and of at least one month's duration in order to be regarded as encopresis. In practice, parents may seek help when the child reaches school age if the encopresis is causing embarrassment to the child and adverse reactions from staff and other children. Specialist treatment may be available from paediatricians or Child Guidance Clinics and usually includes behavioural approaches and support for parents. In some cases treatment is effective only temporarily. However, some children with encopresis improve without professional intervention.

enuresis involuntary wetting during the day or at night by non-disabled children aged five years or over.

Enuresis has been more specifically defined as the 'involuntary discharge of urine by day or night or by both, in a child aged 5 years or older, in the absence of congenital or acquired defects of the nervous system or urinary tract'. Night-time 'bedwetting' is the more common form, and it is found more frequently among boys. A number of factors are involved, such as delayed physical maturation, stressful life events or infections in the urinary tract. Enuresis may be a source of unhappiness for children and in their relationship with their parents. It can bring with it a loss of confidence and affect social life, such as overnight stays. There are also practical problems to consider – increased washing and cleaning and the financial costs of these. Treatment responds to a child's individual needs: these can be established only by a detailed assessment, including a medical examination. The child should be encouraged to actively participate in any programme aiming to tackle it. Treatment is frequently behavioural, including star charts, bladder training and using an alarm system to wake the child before wetting at night.

EPO abbreviation for EMERGENCY PROTECTION ORDER.

Equal Opportunities Commission an official body created as a result of the SEX DISCRIMINATION ACT 1975 with primary responsibility to eradicate gender DISCRIMINATION in Britain.

The duties of the Equal Opportunities Commission are to enforce the law in relation to the Sex Discrimination Act and the EQUAL PAY ACT 1970. In this respect, the commission has the power to investigate any case of alleged discrimination. In some circumstances it can require organizations to provide information, even if they are reluctant to give it. Where discrimination is proved, the commission can issue a non-discrimination notice, requiring the organization to mend its ways in some defined respect. The commission also helps individuals in some legal cases, especially where there is an important point of principle or perhaps a significant test case. Individual advice and counselling are a major area of work, as is the provision of information and educational programmes.

equal opportunities policy a statement of intended practice adopted by an organization to confront DISCRIMINATION in relation to both the employment of staff and the delivery of services.

Equal opportunities policies are usually prefaced by a guiding statement of principle. Such statements indicate which groups are recognized by the organization as experiencing discrimination within the wider society. Thus GENDER, 'RACE', marital status, DISABILITY and religious commitments are invariably found in such statements. Age, ex-offenders, SOCIAL CLASS or social status and sexual orientation or preference are mentioned less often, especially the latter.

In relation to employment practices, some social welfare employers operate procedures that are more rigorous than they once were. Thus, job descriptions, person specifications, interview schedules and formal decision-making procedures have been adopted as good practice by many organizations. The willingness of organizations to adopt additional procedures to address revealed discrimination within their organization is much more limited. Monitoring of applications, the effectiveness of targeted advertising, appointments, promotions and uptake of training opportunities are indicators of organizations' willingness to identify problems and to take POSITIVE ACTION to address them.

All organizations ought to be able to present annual reports in which they can specify progress made in relation to agreed policy targets. For example, a report should be able to indicate how many employees with disabilities are currently part of the workforce, what efforts have been made over the past year to increase the numbers of disabled workers (if, indeed, this had been an acknowledged problem in the previous year), an evaluation of those efforts and finally an action plan for the forthcoming year. The organization's plan should include all groups experiencing discrimination.

With reference to issues of service delivery, social welfare organizations' performance has been very uneven. A full and comprehensive equal opportunities policy should contain an analysis of ANTIDISCRIMINATORY measures needed with every client (service user) group. Thus with older people, as a user group, the needs of black, poor and disabled elders should all be separately identified, as should those who have a religious affiliation or are gay or lesbian. Where little is known about a particular group's needs, plans should be devised to collect critical information. Also, action plans need to be drawn up to address particular policy objectives. An example will serve to illustrate this sequence. It may be noted, as a result of monitoring processes, that no black elders use social service DAY-CARE facilities, and it is not known why this is so. A plan to

consult black community organizations is devised. Offers are made
to arrange visits to day-care centres for individuals, families and
community groups. Critical information leaflets are translated into
the appropriate languages, and efforts are made to highlight the services
with other key social welfare personnel such as doctors and other
support health workers.

Such a process shows the link between reviews of policies, monitoring
and planning. Sometimes, however, it is possible to have policies in
place, but an organization may make little progress in relation to
antidiscriminatory practice. Researchers have sought to understand
this problem by looking at the organization's culture or climate. Where
people are actually involved and committed to policies they are more
likely to work in practice. In this respect, it is likely that a commitment
to equal opportunities in relation to service delivery will enhance an
organization's commitment to equal opportunities in employment
practices. An organization that actually employs disabled people, has
women in senior positions and has black people at all levels is more
likely to deliver services that promote equal opportunities.

Equal Pay Act 1970 an Act of Parliament that seeks to deal with
discrimination against women specifically in relation to pay.

Under the Act a woman is entitled to the same pay when she does work
that is the same or very broadly the same as that undertaken by a man.
Subsequent legislation has included the provision of equal pay for work
of equal value. Employers have over a very long period of time sought
to exploit women by giving them lower pay and inferior conditions of
work to men. Justifications – or, more accurately, rationalizations – for
this behaviour have included the excuses that women work only for
pin money, that they are temporary employees only and that men are
breadwinners. Since many women work on a part-time basis, other
dubious practices have limited the payment of bonuses to full-time
workers only. Some employers have women do virtually the same job
as men in most respects but have used the minor differences between
men's and women's jobs to justify major differences in pay. Under the
legislation women can ask for job evaluation exercises to determine the
value of their jobs in terms of some agreed criteria about responsibility
and skill Although not without their difficulties, such exercises have
helped women in some important cases. Despite the legislation, the
EQUAL OPPORTUNITIES COMMISSION estimates that women still earn
significantly less than men in comparable jobs across the whole
occupational spectrum.

ESO abbreviation for EDUCATION SUPERVISION ORDER.

ethical code a body of guiding principles or value statements for
professional organizations to set the standard for good practice in
relation to service delivery, relationships with clients, or service users,
and professional relationships including relationships with other

occupations and the 'world at large'. Codes should also be seen as binding on research, evaluation and any consultative processes.

The British Association of Social Workers has produced a code of ethics that has become influential within the occupation, regardless of whether practitioners are members of the association or not. The code has been drawn up to be consistent with the Ethics of Social Work: Principles and Standards devised for the International Federation of Social Workers in 1994. The British statement has been revised several times, most recently in 2002. The United Nations Universal Declaration of Human Rights 1948 has also been influential in the drafting of the British code. The British version has much in common with that produced by the Australian Association of Social Workers and emphasizes the importance of five basic values, namely, 'human dignity and worth', 'social justice', 'service to humanity', 'integrity' and, finally, 'competence'. Each of these guiding principles is discussed further in the document with some acknowledgements, here and there, about potential problems of using them in practice. For example, the statement on 'human dignity and worth' has it that all human beings have intrinsic value and that everyone has a right to 'well-being, self-fulfilment and to as much control over their own lives as is consistent with the rights of others'. The commitment to 'social justice' brings with it some strong statements about a 'fair and equitable distribution of resources', 'fair access to public services', 'equal treatment and protection under the law' and 'advocating strategies for overcoming structural disadvantage'. The latter is very interesting given that there is evidence to suggest that social workers on the whole are not involved in explicit political activity either through political parties or pressure groups, and that the gains made by social workers on behalf of service users tend to be essentially modest. In regard to the principle of 'service to humanity', the commitment to contribute 'to the creation of a fairer society' is repeated along with the view that the fundamental goals of social work are to, first, 'meet personal and social needs' and, second, to enable people to meet their potential. The commitment to integrity is every bit as demanding. The code states that 'integrity comprises honesty, reliability, openness and impartiality' and that it has a primary place in underpinning social work practice. Finally, social workers need to be competent, and this umbrella statement brings with it a need to continue personal development, use supervision appropriately, take proper steps to deal with personal ill health and stress among many other exhortations to work to a high standard.

The second half of the code explores many of these guiding principles as they may be implemented in practice. There are strong sections on dealing with conflicts of interest, promoting self-determination and the ability of service users to reach informed decisions and that action will not be taken, unless required by law, without the 'informed consent' of service users. Similarly, in relation to cultural awareness, social workers should 'acknowledge the significance of culture in their practice', 'obtain a working knowledge and understanding of service users' ethnic and cultural affiliations and identities' and, ideally, 'communicate in a language and by means which they understand, using a qualified interpreter where appropriate'.

The code does not really address the issue of potential conflicts between ethnically sensitive services and human rights or, indeed, whether cultural relativism needs to be measured against any 'universalistic framework'. The final section provides cogent advice for researchers working in the social welfare field if they are intent on ethical research. Here the code underlines the duty of social work researchers to 'maintain an active, personal and disciplined ethical awareness and to take practical and moral responsibility for their work'. Secondly, 'the aims and process of social work research, including choice of methodology, the use made of findings, will be congruent with the social work values of respect for human dignity and worth and commitment to social justice'.

The British Association of Social Workers' code of ethics is in many respects an impressive statement of good practice underpinned by key principles that most people would feel able to support. The code places a duty on individual practitioners (and, it is hoped, their employing organizations) to work in ways that safeguard the interests of vulnerable people, support competent service delivery and seek a substantial redistribution of society's resources in order to combat structural oppression. These are laudable objectives, but it is hard to accept them as a reflection of what social workers actually do, especially in relation to structural inequality.

ethnically sensitive practice social work practice based on a recognition of the cultural traditions of a particular group of people, including family patterns, lifestyles, language and culture.

The problem for social work practice is that services may often be undertaken with scant knowledge or understanding of minority client groups, as the ASSOCIATION OF BLACK SOCIAL WORKERS and allied professions has argued with regard to black and other ethnic-minority communities. Some commentators hold that the provision of an ethnically sensitive service is not simply a matter of adjusting social work practice to take into account cultural differences, with the applicants being the passive beneficiaries, but should instead be a two-way process, with black families actively involved in and contributing to the social work service offered. The notions of 'ethnicity by consent' and 'compulsory ethnicity' have been used to distinguish between individuals' differing abilities to reject or adopt a specific ethnic identity. Compulsory ethnicity refers to the institutionalization of ethnic identification as a basis for the assertion of collective claims concerning the distribution of scarce resources. Additionally, many clients have interpreted the cultural pluralist approach of social services departments as an attempt to impose a form of compulsory ethnicity, with efforts to provide a more 'ethnically sensitive service' serving as a further instrument of oppression rather than redressing the balance of past injustices. The provision of an ethnically sensitive service should be seen not as 'extra' or 'special' but as a basic client entitlement.

While the importance of such ethnically and linguistically sensitive practice has to be recognized, however, it should not be allowed to overshadow forms of anti-racist practice. That is, while ethnically sensitive practice recognizes the importance of cultural difference, anti-racist practice goes a step further in recognizing the significance of assumed cultural (or 'racial') superiority. The significance of racism in the lives of black people will, of course, have an influence on their experiences of the life course and its various points of transition. (See ANTI-RACISM.)

L. Robinson, *Psychology for social Workers Black Perspectives*, London, Routledge, 1995.

ethnocentrism an ideology that produces a strong orientation towards the norms, values, history and beliefs of a particular ethnic group, so that the interests of that group are always or frequently placed above the interests of other ethnic groups in the attitudes of both individuals and institutions of ethnocentric societies.

Ethnocentrism exists in any society where the dominant ethnic group seeks to persuade others that there is only one ethnic group, which has a monopoly of ideal and desirable attributes, or is more 'civilized' than others. This is based on the assumption that it is both possible and desirable to define that which is 'ideally human' or more worthy of belonging to humanity than other ethnic groups. Ethnocentrism assumes that the culture, values and moral standards of the dominant group are necessary to the wellbeing of people in other ethnic groups. Ethnocentrism discourages efforts to maintain or promote the history, language, religion or customs of ethnic groups outside the dominant culture if they go beyond the limits of that which the dominant group has defined as acceptable or appropriate.

The influence of EUROCENTRICISM is culturally pervasive. It shapes opinion. The 'values' of British society are essentially based on Christian ethics and Western European philosophy. Eurocentricism features in the way history is written and the perspective from which it is taught. It is part of the socialization of children, the production and transmission of images and language. It is an omnipresent feature of human communication and relationships. Ethnocentrism must therefore be continually challenged and questioned simply in order to recognize the extent of its influence on society and on the thought processes of individuals.

N. Begum, M. Hill and A. Stevens (eds), *Reflections: Views of Black disabled people on their lives and community care*, London, CCETSW, 1994.

Eurocentrism a form of ETHNOCENTRISM that involves understanding and interpreting the world exclusively, or nearly so, through the experiences and perspectives of (white) Europeans.

A Eurocentric perspective, which by implication places Europe at the centre of the world, may be detected in such apparently 'objective' activities as the presentation and interpretation of historical events and definitions of 'correct' methods of child rearing and organizing family life. Eurocentric textbooks, teaching methods and underlying philosophies reinforce negative perceptions of many non-European peoples and fail to inform about the diversity and strength of the many cultures, languages, ethnic communities and religions that enrich and make positive contributions to human society.

European Union funding the provision of finance for services and economic development from the European Union.

The European Union (EU; European Community prior to the enactment of the Maastricht Treaty) provides a series of grants to various services and projects under a broad range of different headings. These cover issues such as education, social policies, and urban and regional economic development.

The most significant areas are covered by grants under the European Regional Development Fund (ERDF) and the European Social Fund (ESF). The ERDF supports infrastructure projects and productive investment, including urban improvements. The ESF is concerned with training and employment measures for the long-term unemployed and young people. Both these are designated as structural funds and aim to counter the effects of industrial decline and unemployment. They are also concerned with helping in the promotion of rural development and promoting new ideas for changing agricultural structures. Other important EU initiatives include funds such as Now and Horizon. Now is an initiative concerned with equal opportunities for women, including financial aid for employment assistance in the creation of new businesses and cooperatives run by women; financial assistance may also be available for training advice and the development of child-care facilities. Horizon is a similar initiative aimed at people with disabilities. The aim of this programme is to prevent people with disabilities being marginalized in society; it provides financial support for the development of information exchange networks concerning good practice in respect of disability, vocational training and funding for small businesses and cooperatives run by people with disabilities.

Chartered Institute of Public Finance and Accounting, *Achieving Better Value from European Community Funds* London, CIPFA, 1996.

euthanasia the term used to describe the act of ending a person's life who has chosen to die because of intense pain or complete incapacity, derived from the classical Greek word meaning literally a 'good death'.

For the first half of the 20th century 'euthanasia' was associated with programmes to kill people with mental and physical disability, most notably in National Socialist Germany 1933–45 but also in other countries, such as Sweden, at the same period. New trends have now brought the question of the deliberate ending of life to the fore in a different context, one in which a person, in the midst of acute suffering and without the prospect of recovery, chooses to die. This new context has emerged from changing patterns of how we die, at least in the developed countries. Once infectious diseases brought life abruptly to an end for great numbers of people, but now, in the developed countries, we die from more prolonged degenerative diseases such as cancer. Equally, medical technology is now able to prolong life for people with degenerative diseases or total incapacity whereas previously they would have died fairly soon. Finally, there is a new emphasis on patient autonomy and control, allowing the person to make substantial choices about their treatment, quality of life and, perhaps, death.

The issues are morally and legally complex and understandably arouse great feelings about the nature of disability, the degree of pain a human being should be allowed to tolerate and religious convictions about the sanctity of life and the deliberate act to end life. Broadly, those who argue in favour of euthanasia and PHYSICIAN-ASSISTED SUICIDE do so on the following grounds:

Autonomy: just as a person has the right to determine the course of his or her own life as much as possible, so a person has the right to determine the course of their own dying.

Mercy: no person should have to endure pointless suffering as they are dying; if there is no other way to avoid the suffering, that person should have the right to end his or her life in a time and place of his or her choosing.

Social burden: the social, psychological and economic costs of sustaining a person in an intolerably painful, fatal condition or in a prolonged coma are immense, both to society at large and to family and care-givers.

Those who oppose euthanasia generally argue along the following lines:

Human life is sacred: life is of absolute intrinsic value to many of the world's religions and it is always wrong to put an end to it no matter what the circumstances are.

Slippery slope: any legal justification or court decision permitting a person to be killed, no matter how tightly worded, will by degrees and in time lead to persons being killed against their will.

Amelioration of pain: pain management has advanced in recent years to the point where virtually no person has to suffer needlessly; intense pain over a long period of time, therefore, should not be a reason for ending life.

Among the strongest opponents of euthanasia are religious institutions and adherents, disability advocates and those from the

HOSPICE movement who believe that proper PALLIATIVE CARE removes
the need for the deliberate ending of life.

M. Otlowski, *Voluntary Euthanasia and the Common Law*, Oxford,
Clarendon Press, 1997.

evaluation the process through which information is obtained and
judgements made on whether an intended course of action is producing
the desired results.

Evaluation is a main source of evidence through which social work
agencies decide whether their programmes and practices are effective
or not. Historically, social work as a profession has not readily embraced
evaluative methods for its own work. Now, however, it is an inescapable
means of accountability to users and the public and is applicable for
virtually any kind of programme or intervention that social work is
involved in. Such programmes may have to do with reducing the number
of children in care, improving the time in which older people are
discharged home from hospital or running a group on parent education.
Or they may be the more collaborative multi-agency programmes such
as a neighbourhood-based intervention for children under five. All such
programmes should be evaluated.

Although often relying on a distinctive set of concepts, such as inputs
and outputs or bench marks and indicators, evaluation is really about
one question: is effective work being done? To answer this question,
some notion of a starting point, or *baseline*, has to be established,
that is, what is the current state of affairs that an intervention proposes
to change. Let the baseline be the number of children on the CHILD
PROTECTION REGISTER or the number of adults with LEARNING
DIFFICULTIES in employment (with the intervention proposing to reduce
the first or raise the second). *Indicators* – or yardsticks for measuring
progress – also have to be determined. Often this is done by negotiation
among all the key stakeholders in a programme. Once a baseline and
indicators have been established, the evaluation task then requires
information to be gathered on a regular basis and assessed. Gathering that
information requires planning. What kind of information is needed – for
example, is it in the form of statistics or opinion? From whom should
information be obtained, for example from users, local residents or
community representatives? Once these issues are decided, information
can be obtained by *observation* – that is, having an observer present when
key events occur either as a participant-observer or as non-participant;
by asking questions – through questionnaires, face-to-face interviews,
consultations or focus groups.

Some models of evaluation essentially deploy four variables: inputs,
processes, outputs and outcomes. *Inputs* are the range of resources and
tools available to the programme, such as practitioner's skill level, the
quality of management and the resources available. *Processes* are defined
as those actions that need to take place to direct inputs towards specified

outcomes. *Outputs* are the product of community empowerment, the specific actions that relate to economic, social, environmental or political issues of the locality. These outputs may include social service development, a safe and healthy community or increased citizen control over services and political developments. *Outcomes* are the consequences of the outputs relating to the improvement in the quality of life of the locality.

Social work initiatives are complex and often have significant social objectives that call on a range of actions and resources the results of which are often difficult to track. Take, for example, developing a more effective FAMILY SUPPORT programme or devising a seamless service for older people between social care and health authorities. Each will draw on a range of inputs from different agencies, will include user perspectives in devising the programmes and rely on a number of different resources and professional and voluntary activity to reach the desired outcomes. Most evaluative efforts are now participatory and involve all stakeholders from the beginning. These stakeholders include managers and practitioners, service user groups, users themselves and their families, and local residents, and all have different interests and commitments.

As a result, it often takes time to reach agreed standards for evaluation, frequently described as the tension between 'process' and 'product'. Process refers to building participative structures, agreeing the rules of the game for partners, establishing the authority within the initiative and building trust among collaborating organizations. This takes time and does not easily yield to deadlines. Product refers to the specific outcomes sought – the number of young offenders brought successfully through a local final warning scheme or increasing the number of disabled adults in work. Managers, councillors, funders, even elements of the neighbourhood itself, will be more interested in product while users would find an excessive emphasis on product disempowering. Taking time to establish participatory channels and to equip users to participate in a specific programme are part of 'process', which can be undermined by tight deadlines and constant emphasis on concrete outputs.

Certain ethical principles should inform any strategy for programme evaluation. These include:

Consent: gaining the informed consent of people involved in the evaluation process is of paramount importance. All the people participating in the evaluation will be given accessible information for them to keep about the nature of the evaluation.

Confidentiality: all information gathered in the process of the evaluation will be anonymous, and no information about sources will be available outside the evaluation team. Any personally identifying information will be held securely and destroyed when it is no longer needed and, in any case, at the end of the evaluation. No individual participant will be identified in written reports, articles or presentations. The only exception to this will be information leading to concerns about the safety of any individual child, which will be reported to the appropriate party in the local authority concerned. Participants will be made aware of this at the time of the evaluation.

Equal opportunities: the evaluation team is committed to ensuring that research undertaken incorporates the perspectives of groups who have experienced social exclusion and discrimination, and contributes to promoting their interests. In order to promote participation, we will strive to meet communication needs such as for those who speak little English.

Dissemination: as the evaluation process itself should be accountable we will strive to find the means and format to make our conclusions as widely available as possible. Such findings will be disseminated locally via a research report, findings document and, perhaps, a conference presentation.

R. Berk and P. Rossi, *Thinking About Programme Evaluation*, London, Sage, 1999.

eviction the process by which people living in a dwelling, legally or illegally, are required to give up possession of the property.

Grounds for eviction include rent or mortgage arrears, illegal occupation of the property, and unacceptable behaviour. In some circumstances a property may have to be sold to release capital to pay off a debt. Social work tasks involve helping a tenant or owner-occupier attempt to retain tenancy or ownership of the dwelling and may entail advocacy with landlords, building societies and the courts. With problems concerned with rent or mortgage arrears, the central objective is to come to an arrangement that is considered feasible and manageable by landlord or building society, tenant or owner, and, if involved, the courts. A critical component of this problem can sometimes be that tenants run the risk of being labelled INTENTIONALLY HOMELESS. If a family is so labelled, the local authority is not required to rehouse them. In relation to alleged unacceptable behaviour, the social worker's or housing adviser's task may be to challenge the accuracy of the evidence. Hostile landlords sometimes manufacture evidence if they wish to have occupancy of the property for their own purposes – perhaps to increase rents, or because of their racial or sexual harassment of the tenant. Harassment and unlawful evictions are criminal offences and should be preventable under the Protection from Eviction Act 1977 (amended by the Housing Act 1988).

evidence written documents, verbal statements or exhibits presented in court to support or refute accusations against an alleged offender.

There are strict legal rules governing what is and what is not admissible as evidence. Several notable miscarriages of justice have hinged on the inadmissibility of confessions believed to have been made under duress. It was to counter such allegations that the POLICE AND CRIMINAL EVIDENCE ACT 1984 was passed, requiring the police to record interviews of suspects. The CRIMINAL JUSTICE ACT 1991 recognizes the particular problems faced by child victims and witnesses in giving evidence, and it makes provision for children to give evidence to courts on videotape recordings in certain circumstances.

exceptional leave to remain leave to remain in the UK for a limited period, usually between one and four years.

Asylum seekers who are refused refugee status may be given 'exceptional leave to remain' if it would be unsafe for them to return to their home country but their application for asylum is not based on a 'convention reason' (see ASYLUM SEEKERS and refugees). People given exceptional leave to remain can work, claim benefits and access social housing like any member of the indigenous population. They cannot, however, bring dependants over to join them. Before their leave to remain expires they can apply for INDEFINITE LEAVE TO REMAIN.

exceptionally severe disablement allowance see WELFARE RIGHTS 3.

exclusion from school the correct term for what is usually called 'suspension' or 'expulsion'. A child is officially prevented from attending school, usually following unacceptable behaviour.

There are only two types of exclusion from school: *fixed term* (which can amount to no more than 45 days in total in the same school year) and *permanent*. Headteachers cannot exclude children indefinitely or remove them from the admission register without formal procedures. Unless an incident is extremely serious, schools are expected to have already tried every possible attempt to meet a child's needs in other ways, for example by use of a PASTORAL SUPPORT PROGRAMME, before permanent exclusion becomes appropriate. Detailed guidance on procedures, which are statutory, can be found in the Department for Education and Skills (DFES) circular 10/99, 'Social Inclusion: Pupil Support'. In recent years local education authorities have had targets to meet for the reduction of permanent exclusions, but these have now been reached and no further targets have been set. Parents have the right to make representations about exclusions to the discipline committee of the school's governing body, which has the power to reinstate. In the case of a permanent exclusion only, they may then appeal to an independent panel, whose decision is binding. There are financial incentives for schools not to exclude permanently. Local education authorities have a duty to make alternative full-time provision within 15 days. Except in the case of children who have been permanently excluded more than once, this will normally be in another school, but provision may be through alternatives such as vocational/home tuition or a PUPIL REFERRAL UNIT.

ex-parte hearing the legal phrase for a court hearing that is held without all the parties to the case being present, *ex parte* literally meaning 'without the parties'.

Social workers are most likely to come across ex-parte hearings when applying for an EMERGENCY PROTECTION ORDER in relation to child-care issues or an INJUNCTION in relation to the problem of DOMESTIC VIOLENCE. With the first example, these can be heard ex-parte, without the parents or the child present, and usually involve a single magistrate, the magistrate's clerk and the social worker on the case. The aim of such a hearing is speed, since time may be short to protect the child concerned. Ex-parte hearings can be organized quickly and sometimes occur in a magistrate's own home if out of hours. In cases of domestic violence, the term is used where one party, usually the woman, seeks an injunction to prevent something happening. The injunction will be in force without the defendant being present and until such time as a full hearing can be arranged.

expert witness a person who, by virtue of training, qualification or experience, is regarded by a court as capable of supplying expert opinion in criminal or civil proceedings.

The chief function of an expert witness is not to support one side or the other in contested hearings but to make his or her knowledge and judgement available to the court so that it is able to reach the best decision. In an application for a CARE ORDER for a child that is opposed by the child's parents, a psychologist or paediatrician often appears as an expert witness to help the court decide what solution is best for the child's welfare.

expulsion see EXCLUSION FROM SCHOOL.

extended sentence a period of imprisonment longer than the period that is proportionate to the seriousness of the offence.

The extended sentence, previously known as 'preventive detention', was formally abolished when the provisions of the CRIMINAL JUSTICE ACT 1991 came into force. However, that Act also provided for brief extensions to the supervision period of sexual offenders after serving periods of imprisonment. The CRIME AND DISORDER ACT 1998 built upon this principle by creating extended sentences for serious sexual and violent offences in England, Scotland and Wales. There is also provision for an extended licence period when the time served in prison is likely to be too short for effective treatment to be given. Under these arrangements (which apply both to young offenders and to adults) possible supervision periods after offenders are released from custody can last for several years. The additional period of supervision renders the offender liable to recall to prison if his or her behaviour gives cause for concern and the imprisonment period is then reviewed only annually. The PROBATION SERVICE and in some cases YOUTH OFFENDING TEAMS are encouraged by HOME OFFICE guidance to consider the implications for post-release supervision when preparing PRE-SENTENCE REPORTS on serious sexual and violent offenders. Reports need to consider an assessment of the likelihood of re-offending, the degree of RISK to the public and the possible value of an extended period of supervision for participation in longer treatment programmes.

The law is complex, and sentencing procedure in these cases is subject to guidelines laid down by the Court of Appeal.

'Extended sentence guidance' in *Probation Journal*, March 2002, pp. 63–4.

extroversion–introversion a description of personality characteristics based on certain kinds of personality tests. Extroversion describes a personality type more concerned with external reality than with inner feelings, and introversion its opposite.

The extrovert dimension embodies TRAITS of sociability, impulsiveness, assertiveness and sensation-seeking, while the introvert dimension describes the opposite traits of lack of sociability, anxiety and social withdrawal. Extroversion is now seen as a major influence behind those with severe behaviour problems such as severe antisocial PERSONALITY DISORDER and ATTENTION DEFICIT HYPERACTIVITY DISORDER (ADHD). Introversion is linked to depression and anxiety. Although the extroversion–introversion dimension is a means of describing and categorizing personalities, it does not explain why people are this way. Some theorists think that such dimensions are genetically transmitted; others argue that biochemical processes inhibit reception of stimuli in for example ADHD. PYSCHODYNAMIC explanations of extroversions suggest they arise from defence mechanisms against trauma.

F*f*

failure to thrive the term applied to children who are not receiving adequate nutrition to achieve normal growth.

One common form of measuring whether a child is failing to thrive is through a CENTILE CHART, which plots the child's weight, head size and height against national averages. If a child falls below the third centile in one or more of these for a period of time, this is an indication of failure to thrive. Certain factors in a child's background are associated with, but not the cause of, failure to thrive. These are POVERTY, which may severely restrict the child's diet, social isolation of a parent and the child's having severe behavioural problems. Failure to thrive is rarely the product of deliberate parental neglect. Support for the parents is usually given in the form of guidance on diet from HEALTH VISITORS and doctors. In extreme cases, brief periods of hospitalization or ACCOMMODATION help the child to gain weight and size.

Fair Employment Commission established by the Fair Employment (Northern Ireland) Act 1989 with the primary duty to eliminate DISCRIMINATION in Northern Ireland in the employment of Catholics and Protestants.

Employers in Northern Ireland, depending upon their size, are required to undertake various procedures to encourage fair employment. They have to register with the commission and are expected to monitor their workforce and regularly review all practices concerned with recruitment, training and promotion. If employers are found to be discriminatory in their practices, they can be required to take affirmative action by setting targets within specified time limits. Comparatively substantial financial penalties – fines of up to £30,000 – and economic sanctions may be used against organizations that do not make reasonable progress or are found to be discriminatory in their policies and practices. For example, government grants may be denied to such organizations, and government may not purchase goods and services from them. Many commentators have compared provision in Northern Ireland to eliminate discrimination with the relatively ineffective powers and sanctions of the COMMISSION FOR RACIAL EQUALITY.

faith-based services welfare services provided either by religious institutions or by persons motivated at least in part by tenets of a religious faith or denomination.

There is considerable debate over whether religious institutions or religiously motivated people can provide useful and effective social services. Such services have both positive and negative characteristics. In general they are delivered by institutions, such as mosque, church, synagogue or temple, that are embedded in their localities and have an allegiance, at least among local adherents, of the particular faith organizing that service. They also are motivated by a strong sense of mission but are willing to operate on small budgets, often through a dedicated volunteer staff. They frequently provide practical, informal services that carry out care tasks and give informal support for those residents who are among the most rejected and excluded within a given locality.

On the other hand, such services are often confined to one group, that is, provided for those who share the particular faith of the providers. They are frequently difficult to evaluate in even a most basic way because they rely on informal organizational and management styles. Social work discomfort in working with such movements and institutions has resulted in its keeping its distance from institutions that have strong roots in local communities and a long record of service provision, some of it quite innovatory. Social workers were suspicious partly because of the profession's strong secularist orientation and partly from a deeper appreciation of how many religious institutions restrict and confine the role of women and may be hostile to other groups such as gays and lesbians.

This should not obscure the vital role that faith communities of all kinds – Islamic, Jewish, Sikh, Catholic, Evangelical Protestant – have played in the past and the important role they still must assume. There is an evident dedication to maintaining some voice, often in the poorest neighbourhoods, and links with some of the most excluded and unwanted individuals. At a time when other institutions no longer maintain a neighbourhood presence, churches, mosques, temples and synagogues have maintained an involvement. The tenets of faith do provide sources of energy arising from bearing witness, working with the poor and prophetic action. Catholic social doctrine, liberation theology, church action on poverty, Jewish and Islamic dedication to service are all articulate sources that ground such energy. Among the newer ranks of faith-based action are black majority churches, Pentecostal and independent evangelical institutions. It is also important to recognize that changes in how doctrine is understood are under way while at the same time there is a growing understanding of the commonly accepted broader principles and practice of community development toward inclusiveness. Faith institutions are increasingly aware of their shortcomings and recognize that they cannot 'do' community development on their own but must work with partners.

A recent survey by the Shaftesbury Society provides some interesting considerations for faith-based work. The survey found that:

1 deeply held moral convictions mean that there is often unease about homosexuality, and it is less likely than other factors to be covered in equal opportunities monitoring;

2 faith-based community work continues to be distinctive from secular community development because of its theological foundation and values;

3 projects highly value their informality and open personal relationships. There is some apprehension among those involved in faith-based projects that a more formal management style will distance them from members of their community and will be perceived by local residents as more bureaucratic in approach;

4 faith-based community work tends to be broad and to have generic goals. A majority of projects surveyed had taken action on between two and six major social problems.

Shaftesbury Society, *Faith and Community Development Work*, London, 2000.

Family Advice and Information Networks see DIVORCE.

family assistance order an order under section 16 of the CHILDREN ACT available in matrimonial disputes involving children and where the court may be considering a SECTION 8 ORDER that allows the court to appoint a probation officer or local authority social worker to advise, assist and befriend any person named in the order.

The aim of the family assistance order is to provide short-term help in 'exceptional circumstances' to resolve conflict between parents or to help overcome problems associated with their separation or divorce. The work is often undertaken with the parents rather than with the child, although the court's main concern in making the order is the child's welfare. The order lasts for six months and may be made only with the consent of every person named in the order (other than the child). Social workers have found it difficult to use the order effectively. Judges are uncertain about what the order actually means and what constitutes 'exceptional circumstances', while local authorities have no specifically designated resources for practitioners to carry out the work. Nevertheless, it has some potential as a consensual platform for offering guidance and help to a family experiencing separation or divorce.

family centre a unit run by either a local authority or a voluntary organization that works with both children and their parents to achieve such objectives as teaching improved parenting skills or reducing family conflict.

Family centres provide a safe environment in which to show parents how to play with their children and build a more positive relationship with them. They may be intensively therapeutic or more in the nature of local drop-in centres. Centres run by large voluntary organizations or local authorities generally work with the families of children who have suffered some ABUSE or severe emotional disturbance. Local authority family centres are often former day nurseries, but some have overnight accommodation for use in family crises.

T. Smith, 'Family Centres, Children in Need and the Children Act', in J. Gibbons (ed), *The Children Act 1989 and Family Support: Principles into Practice*, London, HMSO, 1992.

family, children and young people's benefits see WELFARE RIGHTS 4.

family group conference a meeting of the extended family and adults significant to a child who it is thought may have been abused.

Such a conference or meeting is called together to work out a plan to protect the child, if this is what is required, and is given powers and responsibility to make the necessary plans to protect the child. In New Zealand, where the concept originated, the family group conference has replaced the CHILD PROTECTION CASE CONFERENCE, thus marking a significant reallocation of power between professionals and family members. The group conference takes place in two stages: during the first stage, the family meets together to develop its own plans to protect the child; in the second stage, social workers or other professionals are called in to provide advice or to help secure resources. Although the concept is viewed with some suspicion by social work professionals in Britain because it accords the family considerable new powers and status to make decisions, it is gaining adherents as a way to develop protection plans that are both effective and tend to include arrangements for keeping the child within the extended family.

Family Law Act 1996 a major contribution to family legislation that encourages parties to end a marriage that has irretrievably broken down with a minimum of distress.

The Act relies on the no-fault notion of 'irretrievable breakdown' of the marriage but does not require any of the five 'facts' – such as adultery or unreasonable behaviour – to be established.

Although widely welcomed and having cross-party parliamentary support, this legislation has run into several difficulties that have prevented its full implementation. These include an ambivalence among the general public about FAMILY MEDIATION, and some results from pilot projects which showed that the concept of compulsory Information Meetings was proving difficult to implement. One response to this was the introduction of Family Advice and Information Networks in 2001.

Since the Act has not been implemented, in the meantime the MATRIMONIAL CAUSES ACT 1973 still governs the DIVORCE process.

family literacy a programme that encourages whole family involvement as children learn to read.

There is a positive correlation between levels of parental education (often the mother's) and a child's proficiency in literacy skills. There is also voluminous evidence to suggest that the involvement of parents in their child's education fosters that child's achievement. Yet children from low-income backgrounds are less likely to have the advantages of living with highly educated adults and tend to perform less well on measures of reading comprehension. One way of encouraging this is through family literacy schemes. These involve family members in supporting the development of their child's reading, writing and talking. But they achieve more than that. They increase parental confidence and break a cycle of destructive and overly disciplinary styles of parenting through increased parental control and improved self-esteem. They also have been shown to break the cycle of disadvantage by removing some of the risk factors that may predispose young males toward crime as they grow older.

Parents will play an active part by reading or learning to read themselves alongside their children, carrying out library visits, or writing shopping lists and notes. Expectations and attitudes towards literacy, family routines and resources of information and experience form a kind of social capital that the family can provide and that will affect the child's literacy development. In such schemes, however, it is easy to slip into paternalistic habits. Parents may associate school with failure and feel inadequate and not want to repeat the experience. The use of volunteers, perhaps retired people or those from a different social or ethnic background, may be perceived as condescension, while attempts to develop charts and targets could be misunderstood and resented.

Those schemes that take place within primary schools (as opposed to nurseries, playgroups or local colleges) have been judged most effective principally because of the involvement of the head teacher who drives the project forward. While teaching staff may play a prominent part in selecting children, if the scheme is collaborative selection should be a joint process. Suggested criteria for family literacy include children roughly between the ages of 7 and 9 who show signs of school failure, particularly in literacy, and who also demonstrate emotional and behavioural problems. Parents who would benefit include those who need to acquire literacy skills themselves, are reluctant to become involved in school activity but do seem to value education for their children.

Crime Concern, *Families in Schools: Best practice approaches for family literacy and positive parenting programmes*, Swindon, Crime Concern, 1999.

family mediation a non-adversarial method of helping divorcing and/or separating couples to negotiate decisions and agreements about residence and contact issues for their children and about maintenance, pension rights and property.

Family mediation has been available for over 30 years as an ALTERNATIVE DISPUTE RESOLUTION, but it has come into prominence only following the central role assigned to it by the FAMILY LAW ACT 1996. Central themes include a trained, impartial mediator who works with the parties in dispute and helps them to develop PARENTING PLANS and strategies that will help them to maintain their parenting roles following the dissolution of their own relationship. Mediation is legally privileged, which means that the content of discussions cannot be brought by either of the parties into any subsequent legal complaint or proceeding against the other. It is also essential that both parties enter the process voluntarily.

The Family Law Act 1996 hoped that mediation would become a popular and cost-effective method of encouraging separating and divorcing couples to plan their futures in a less adversarial way than going immediately into the court system. Pilot studies have revealed, however, that the majority of couples still prefer the traditional approach. Undoubtedly, there seems to have been resistance to the idea that couples would be required to go to mediation as a precondition to receiving financial help with their divorces. This militates against the voluntary nature of mediation. Mediation can only work effectively if there is a reasonable measure of mutual trust between the parties to implement the agreements they reach. Consequently, in cases where serious DOMESTIC VIOLENCE has featured, it is highly unlikely that mediation can be effective because of the abuse of power of one party over the other.

Mediators often struggle to find the most appropriate way of involving the children's perspective in the future arrangements being negotiated by the parents. A common starting place is to assume that the parents are the experts when it comes to the best interests of the child, but this view is being challenged by a movement to 'hear the voice of the child' wherever possible (see ADVOCACY and CHILDREN'S RIGHTS). Mediators are therefore actively exploring ways of consulting children, where appropriate, as part of the mediation process.

Family mediators are rigorously trained and supervised by their 'parent bodies', such as the National Family Mediation, the Solicitors' Family Law Association (SFLA), and the Family Mediators' Association (FMA), all of which now belong to the UK College of Family Mediators, which operates high standards for selection, training and supervision.

Directory and Handbook of the UK College of Family Mediators, London, Sweet and Maxwell, published annually.

family proceedings a group of court proceedings involving disputes about children.

Family proceedings are defined under the CHILDREN ACT 1989 as including most proceedings that originate in that Act, such as those for CARE ORDERS, SUPERVISION ORDERS and SECTION 8 ORDERS. They also include proceedings under other laws, such as divorce proceedings, adoption proceedings and INJUNCTION and non-molestation proceedings between married or unmarried couples. By designating this range of proceedings in this way, the Children Act allows courts greater flexibility in dealing with cases before it. (See FAMILY PROCEEDINGS COURT).

family proceedings court created under the CHILDREN ACT 1989, this court deals with non-criminal matters relating to children, such as care proceedings, adoption, child protection, and residence and contact following divorce (see CRIMINAL COURT). It is staffed by lay MAGISTRATES who have undertaken additional training to fulfil this specialist role.

family reunification returning children to their family after they have been LOOKED AFTER by the LOCAL AUTHORITY for a period of time.

The conclusion of much research in the 1980s was that children who were looked after by the local authority away from home for a period of time easily lost touch with their family – the longer the period of separation, the greater the likelihood that the child would remain in the long-term care of the authority. To successfully reunite a looked-after child and his or her family means consciously planning for this from the very beginning of the PLACEMENT. To do this the social worker and foster parents or residential care staff facilitate CONTACT, such as visits and exchange of letters and gifts. The intention is to keep the parents and family involved in the life of their child and allow them to make as many decisions affecting their child as possible.

The concept of reunification, therefore, has to do both with the planned return as well as with the actual return of the child to members of his or her family. The family is understood in the extended sense – for example, the child may be returned to relatives such as grandparents or adult siblings. For many years the word 'rehabilitation' was used to denote the process of returning the child home, but this implied that parents had to overcome certain personal defects and thereby 'earn' their child's return. This approach has now been firmly discarded. 'Reunification' acknowledges a far greater responsibility resting with the local authority social worker, who often has to work intensively with parents in setting up plans and facilitating home visits to ensure that the child's return home takes place quickly and effectively.

S. Millham, A. Bullock, K. Hosie and M. Haak, *Lost in Care*, Aldershot, Gower, 1986.

family support a range of services to support children and their families where the children are 'in need' as defined by the CHILDREN ACT, 1989.

Local authorities are required to offer a range of services for children 'in need', where need is rooted in concerns about CHILD PROTECTION, child development, juvenile offending, disabled children and a range of additional issues where children's developmental needs might be significantly affected. Research in the mid-1990s suggested strongly that much child-care social work was couched in terms of child protection issues, even though compelling evidence revealed that the vast majority of child protection investigations did not result in children being placed on CHILD PROTECTION REGISTERS. In addition, such investigations did not lead in many cases to the provision of services even though families were often seen as needing significant help. These findings suggested to many commentators that there needed to be a fundamental reconfiguration of child-care services to emphasize support and prevention rather than close monitoring and policing of parenting and children's development.

Nearly a decade on, the child protection versus family support debate is seen by many as a false dichotomy. First, family support should properly be seen as child protection, albeit in a particular form. Second, it is possible to work with families, even where there are issues of child protection, in ways that emphasize partnership in a belief that families and parents have strengths and thus an ability to contribute to problem-solving. Third, as a backdrop to these debates, there is a much more frank acknowledgement of the negative impact of the 'care experience' for children. The courts have become used to asking some difficult questions about whether removing a child from parents will actually improve a child's life chances or development. Fourth, some have argued persuasively that some shift of resources from the investigatory functions to family support is warranted because there is also evidence that support services can help marginal parents to do better and can help to maintain the morale of parents in often adverse circumstances.

Some of the work of agencies like the Family Service Units and Barnado's has shown that a community development approach to neighbourhoods where there are significant problems of child care within a context of general deprivation can have better results for children than a heavy CASEWORK approach that relies almost solely upon monitoring parenting standards. The key theme is a view that stresses the importance of addressing the problems that affect the morale of parents, such as poverty, indebtedness, poor-quality housing, poor-quality community resources and SOCIAL EXCLUSION. Improvements in the wellbeing of parents, it is argued, will increase their chances of responding to encouragement to do better by their children.

This thinking has lead to the diversification of some statutory child-care services. Many social services departments have invested resources in FAMILY CENTRES, family aides, day-care services of various kinds, respite care services and child and adolescent mental health services. However, a number of SOCIAL SERVICES INSPECTORATE (SSI) reports, specifically about the provision of family support services, have suggested that many statutory social work agencies could do much more. A consistent message from the SSI is that a number of problem areas in relation to parenting and child care are appearing again and again across the country. These problems are, first, DOMESTIC VIOLENCE and its impact upon children; second, the quality of child care where parents are drug abusers (both substances and alcohol); third, child care where parents have significant or enduring mental health problems; fourth, parents with learning disabilities; fifth, the parenting of children with disabilities and/or with significant health problems; sixth, the parenting of persistent young offenders; and, finally, child care where parents have separated or divorced. In addition, there was substantial evidence of uneven and often poor services for ethnic minority families and their children.

The SSI reports indicated that statutory authorities needed to complete an audit of provision within their areas of responsibility and to match provision with realistic estimations of need. One of the telling criticisms in the reports was the finding that sometimes local authorities had little idea of how many disabled children were in a defined area or how much domestic violence figured on their patch or the incidence of other identified problem areas. There were sometimes similar findings about social work departments' knowledge of the work being done by other statutory and voluntary agencies. Services, of course, might be offered by a variety of statutory agencies, such as health authorities, the police, education, housing, social services, youth offending teams, youth services, CAFCASS and the probation service in addition to a wide variety of voluntary agencies. More recent government initiatives, such as SURE START, CONNEXIONS, supporting people and FOYERS, all have the potential for supporting children in need and their families. A key issue for social work departments, according to the SSI, was that they should be encouraged to use their pre-eminent position to forge meaningful inter-agency partnerships and rationalized provision to meet clearly identified needs. This was regarded as essential, especially for those problems that were multi-faceted, such as domestic violence where many agencies have to be involved.

Department of Health, Social Care Group and Social Services Inspectorate, 1997, *Responding to Families in Need*, London, 1997.

M. Little and K. Mount, *Prevention and Early Intervention for Children in Need*, Aldershot, Ashgate, 1999.

family therapy a range of techniques and strategies for helping families to resolve relationship problems, attain goals and function more harmoniously.

There are many variants of family therapy. Most of them work on the central premise that relationships between family members can become rigid, so that behaviour between members tends to repeat compulsively a familiar destructive pattern. This pattern may involve blaming or scapegoating a particular member of the family or coercive behaviours such as shouting, physical ABUSE, isolation and withdrawal. Such patterns provide a kind of 'solution' – the family survives but in a way that prevents further development and often at immense cost to the individuals.

The central insight of family therapy is drawn from the SYSTEMS APPROACH, namely that relations between family members are circular – how each member behaves affects the way everyone else behaves, and so on. An oft-cited example is where a parent continually criticizes an adolescent, who withdraws from family life but who then elicits more criticism, only to withdraw even more. The therapist or social worker begins with the assumption that no one is to blame. The therapist's role is to provide an outside view of the way the family interacts as a whole and to try to minimize the 'blame games' that inevitably occur in a family deeply at odds with itself. Maintaining a position of neutrality, the therapist explores with the whole family how to achieve a different overall pattern and how to view behaviours more positively. By doing so, the therapist enables the family to change attitudes, viewpoints and behaviour.

M. Preston-Shoot and D. Agass, *Making Sense of Social Work*, Basingstoke, Macmillan, 1990.

far Right part of the political spectrum that is heavily racialized in its campaigns and propaganda and often deploys intimidating and violent tactics against individuals and groups, particularly if the latter are perceived to be from 'outside', as a means of arousing conflict and disorder on the streets of the locality where they are active. Gays and immigrant groups are favourite targets for their strategy. See also HATE CRIME.

fast tracking arrangements for speedier sentencing of offenders in order to avoid unnecessary delay.

Courts have recently been encouraged to reduce delays and to process cases more quickly, partly in order to reduce re-offending while on bail and the length of time spent by offenders on REMAND, awaiting trial. Statutory time limits and case management techniques have been introduced in order to cut delays, with a view to ensuring that young offenders in particular are dealt with while the offence is still relatively fresh in their minds, preserving a link between the offence and the sentence.

Fast tracking in youth justice coincided with the creation of YOUTH OFFENDING TEAMS and the new court orders introduced by the 1998 CRIME AND DISORDER ACT. This led to criticisms that speed was being given greater priority than justice, particularly where the arrangements for consulting VICTIMS were concerned.

feedback written or verbal comment given to others about how well they performed a particular task.

The term originally came from SYSTEMS theory, where it referred to part of a system's output being 'fed back' into the system itself, which was then able to evaluate it and undertake necessary modifications to improve its output. 'Feedback' is now used much more generally to include any comment or judgement given to a person or group of people.

femininity a term that describes the way gender roles of women are socially constructed.

Notions of femininity are therefore experienced differently in different groups within society. Concepts of *appropriate* femininity vary according to social differences of age, class and ethnicity etc. For example, in relation to differences of ethnicity and race in differentiating norms of femininity, black feminists have suggested that the cultural construction of femininity among African-Caribbean women differs immensely from the forms of femininity surrounding white women. Rather than adopting a EUROCENTRIC understanding of gender roles based on the distinction between male and female abilities with regard to the labour market, the black women in some studies had adopted a model of femininity based less upon such distinctions and more upon notions of equality.

Indeed, such concepts of masculinity and femininity are essentially culturally defined and refer specifically to the way people believe that they and others *should* behave in terms of their biological sex. Placing emphasis on the word 'should' here highlights that values are integral to these concepts, thereby producing ideas that are necessarily subjective. Gender roles, therefore, can be said to represent ideological frameworks that exist both to tell us how to behave appropriately in terms of our biological sex and, most importantly, represent a form of social control since they lay down guidelines for people to follow.

While this is the common understanding of gender roles, post-structural theorists have increasingly challenged this dichotomous understanding of masculinity and femininity. For example, Judith Butler has argued that we act out our gender roles through a 'gender performance'. The ultimate question is what form that gender performance will take. Essentially, the argument is that by adopting different performances, we might work to disrupt existing gender norms. (See also GENDER, MASCULINITY, POSTMODERNISM, QUEER THEORY.)

Gender Trouble: Feminism and the Sub-version of Identity, London, Routledge, 1999.

feminism a theoretical perspective, social movement and ideology that has at its core a recognition of gender equality, especially in relation to women's subordination to men.

Feminism, especially in the context of political struggle, has a long history. Most accounts of feminism, however, have focused on western conceptions despite the fact that women in former colonial states played an active part in challenging both their gender subordination and colonial rule. In the west feminism as a social movement and ideology is commonly divided into two distinct periods. The first 'wave' is usually located towards the late 19th century and early 20th century, from the writings of Mary Wollstonecraft through the Suffragette movement to the enfranchisement of women. The second 'wave' emerged during the latter half of the 1960s alongside the emergence of the New Left. While feminism is separated in this way, it may be more useful to think of feminist thought in terms of a continuum that has arisen and developed alongside other social movements, including anti-slavery campaigns and the fight for black civil rights. Feminist theory has informed practice, from fighting for civil rights to votes for women and the development of women's refuges and rape crisis centres.

While it is useful to talk of a 'universal' feminism, it is nevertheless vital to recognize that this is in itself an umbrella term used to group together different strands of feminism. These include:

Socialist-Marxist feminism: this prioritizes social class as the prime factor in determining the place of women within capitalist societies. Consequently, this approach relies heavily on the work of Marx and Engels and argues that gender inequality is a product of capitalism and class oppression. It is critical of the essentialism inherent within radical feminism and also challenges the ahistorical approach to patriarchy.

Liberal feminism: the suffragette movement of the early 1900s was founded on the concept of basic equality and justice and rose from the abolition of slavery and equal rights through to the civil rights movements in the USA. Liberal feminists view the route to equality through the mechanism of the state, i.e. legislation to prohibit discrimination on the grounds of gender. In this respect, liberal feminists can be seen to have achieved some progress, most evident in the 1975 Sex Discrimination Act, which outlaws direct and indirect discrimination in employment on the grounds of gender, and the 1970 Equal Pay Act, which stipulates that women and men must receive equal pay for equal work. Numerous studies have challenged the effectiveness of this legislation, however, pointing to the continuing inequalities between women and men in the labour market.

Radical feminism: radical feminism is characterized by the belief that patriarchy is the universal cause of women's oppression. As a result, radical feminists focus on power and the unequal power between men and women. Radical feminists' central argument has at its core the notion that all women are subordinated by male oppression (patriarchy), which is exercised through institutions such as marriage and the family. For example, radical feminism particularly focuses on accounts of violence against women in the home to greatly inform the wider women's refuge movement in both the USA and the UK. An important offshoot of the radical feminist movement, lesbian/separatist feminists, provided a useful critique of the notion of compulsory and/or institutionalized heterosexuality.

Black feminism: developed during the 1980s in response to the universalized discourse of feminism as a whole, black (and 'third world') feminists challenged white/Western feminism for ignoring issues of race ethnicity in women's experiences of oppression and for focusing largely on the lives of white Western women in their accounts, thereby denying and excluding the voices and experiences of black women.

While these strands of feminism are central to the concept of feminism, this list is not exhaustive. Additional elements include academic feminism, cultural feminism, psychoanalytic feminism and political lesbianism.

Christine Hallett (ed), *Women and Social Policy*, London, Prentice Hall/ Harvester Wheatsheaf, 1995.

Adrienne Rich *Compulsory Heterosexuality and Lesbian Existence* London Only Women Press 1980

H. S. Mirza (ed), *Black British Feminism: A Reader*, London, Routledge, 1999.

feminist social work a diversity of social work approaches that have as their common element recognition of women's oppression and the aim of overcoming its effects.

Feminism regards all aspects of social relations as being shaped by the great inequality of power held by men over women in all aspects of life:

in the family, in the professions, in politics, in work and employing organizations, in purchasing power and in community institutions. Feminist social work begins with this fundamental perspective and develops a practice that attempts to address this inequality. When women social workers are working with women as clients, it adopts strategies of EMPOWERMENT. This often places it at odds with the traditional role of social work, which seeks to control difficult or poorly adapting individuals or to regulate families in difficulty. A significant part of feminist social work takes place in the small local organizations that have developed as responses to male violence, including DOMESTIC VIOLENCE: rape crisis centres, women's refuges, incest survivors' groups among others.

Feminist social work places heavy emphasis on the role that the oppression of women plays in creating the very problems that social work deals with. One notable example is in the field of child SEXUAL ABUSE, where much of the conventional analysis from both inside and outside social work assigned the 'cause' to distorted family relationships and implicitly blamed poor mothering. Conventional analysis ignored the fact that by far the greater number of abusers were men and that this rested on the extreme differences of power held by men and others in the family. This analysis applied to much of social work with children, where the content of case records, court reports and CASE CONFERENCES blamed women as individually poor mothers rather than focusing on poverty and lack of material resources. Feminist social workers have also looked more closely at the behaviour of the male abuser, have called attention to the secrecy that male abusers demand and have called for protective solutions that remove the abuser, rather than the child, from the family (see OUSTER ORDER and INJUNCTION).

One of the major concerns of feminist social work is the inequality based on gender within social services organizations themselves, particularly in the management structures of those organizations, which are dominated by men although women form some 80 per cent of employees overall. How to structure management jobs so that they are more appealing to women, as well as allowing more flexible working arrangements, including part-time and job share, are objectives that feminists have at least succeeded in having social services organizations discuss, if not put into practice. It is argued that greater representation of women in social work agencies will likely lead to a more effective 'woman-centred' practice.

A. Hudson *et al*, 'Practising feminist approaches', in C. Hanvey and T. Philpot (eds), *Practising Social Work*, London, Routledge, 1994.

fieldwork social work undertaken in the COMMUNITY, most frequently in people's homes, with an area or district office as administrative centre.

Field social work is the principal way of organizing local authority social work. Other ways of organizing, such as RESIDENTIAL WORK and HOSPITAL SOCIAL WORK, are not nearly as common. Field social workers are invariably based in teams at a local authority social services office. From there they undertake the many administrative tasks associated with social work, such as recording and writing reports for court and developing CARE PLANS. They often also see clients at the office, meeting in rooms specially designated for INTERVIEWING. The defining element of fieldwork, however, is precisely that some of the social work tasks are undertaken 'in the field', in the homes and neighbourhoods where clients live. There are many different kinds of fieldworkers: they may be specialist, such as those working only with children and their families or with adults with LEARNING DISABILITIES, or they may be generic, that is, general social workers with different client groups on their caseload. Over the last twenty years and more since the SEEBOHM REPORT, the trend in fieldwork has been steadily in the direction of relatively specialist teams, who are likely to focus on adult services (and sometimes subdivisions into services for disabled people, older people, people with mental health problems) and children's services. Occasionally social services departments devise sensory impairment teams to offer a service to blind and deaf people.

Because fieldworkers visit service users in their own homes, as opposed to undertaking social work tasks only in the office or in a residential or day-care establishment, they have a number of difficult roles to merge. On the one hand, they are entering the user's personal space and property, and should do so with the same respect and consideration as anyone would (for example, only after making an appointment first, unless there are overriding issues of protecting a child). On the other hand, they are also local government officers, with authority and legal powers, charged with undertaking certain tasks and responsibilities. Fieldworkers carry out the main functions of social work, such as ASSESSMENT, care planning, arranging family support services, ADVOCACY and COUNSELLING, within this difficult framework. Issues of the field-worker's personal safety also increasingly arise.

J. Hillman and M. Mackenzie, *Understanding Field Social Work*, Birmingham, Venture Press, 1993.

final warning an alternative to court proceedings in relation to offences admitted by young people, introduced by the Crime and Disorder Act 1998.

A final warning may be used where a young person has previously received a REPRIMAND for a minor first offence, or it may be given for a somewhat more serious first offence. These decisions are at the discretion of the POLICE. Final warnings and reprimands may be cited in court in the same way as previous convictions.

After receiving a final warning, the young person will be referred to a YOUTH OFFENDING TEAM so that a rehabilitation plan can be drawn up, aimed at preventing further offending. The plan may include an element of REPARATION to the VICTIM of the offence if the victim has agreed to this.

foster care the placement of a child with a family or lone carer who is able to offer the child full-time day-to-day care in place of the child's natural parents. It is sometimes referred to as substitute family care.

There are many possible fostering arrangements and, with the exception of PRIVATE FOSTERING, they are regulated by the CHILDREN ACT and national standards for foster care. A child may be placed in foster care by a parent, by anyone with PARENTAL RESPONSIBILITY for the child or by the local authority where the child is normally resident. Foster care usually refers to a placement with local authority foster carers or with foster carers from recognized fostering agencies (again with the exception of private fostering), who are recruited and trained by local authorities or the recognized agencies. Financial maintenance of the child is through a fostering allowance paid by the local authority to foster carers at a locally set scale of payment. Alternatively, the local authority may pay a fee to a fostering agency that in turn makes monthly payments to its own foster carers while a child is in placement. Foster care is the preferred way of providing care and nurture for children who need to be LOOKED AFTER by a local authority because it provides family-based as opposed to institutionally based care. Foster care has enabled local authorities to develop flexible patterns of care for the children they look after. There are different kinds of local authority foster placements, as follows:

(1) *Short-term placements*: the child is placed with foster carers who take care of them on a short-term basis until long-term plans are made for the child. The range of goals for a short-term placement can include 'shared' or relief fostering, holiday fostering, emergency protection, assessment of needs, a bridge to a long-term placement and pre-adoptive fostering. There is no universally agreed duration for short-term placements, which can last from days to months, depending on the child's situation. Research indicates that short-term foster placements become long-term placements with variable success. It is generally agreed that it is poor practice to let a short-term placement drift into a *de facto* long-term placement with no agreed long-term plan.

(2) *Bridging or link placements*: these are used when a child's long-term placement has broken down or the short-term foster carers cannot continue to look after the child and a long-term placement has yet to be found. Some children are placed in bridging placements after a period in residential care. The task then is to help the child to readjust to family life. The duration of the bridging placement varies according to the child's situation and the speed at which suitable long-term carers are identified for the child.

(3) *Long-term placements*: the child is placed with foster carers on a planned long-term basis; this is sometimes referred to as a permanent foster placement. The intention is that the child will live with his or her foster family until ready to live independently. It is an alternative to adoption for some children, taking into account factors such as the

child's age, any special needs, the level of ongoing contact with family of origin and the child's wishes. Studies indicate that long-term fostering is less successful than adoption. It is recognized in current child-care practice that children need a sense of permanence and a sense of identity if their developmental needs are to be met. This is more difficult to achieve in long-term foster placements because the foster carers do not acquire parental responsibility for the child, and a sense of insecurity may result from the involvement of the social worker in supervising the placement and in the way reviews and medicals are carried out.

(4) *Respite or shared care*: this arrangement involves the day-to-day care of the child being shared between the family of origin and foster carers. This kind of placement may be offered if the child has special needs or if the quality of the care available at home can be enhanced. It enables the child and the family to have regular breaks from each other and provides the child with additional caring relationships outside the family. It is good practice to ensure that the same respite foster carers look after the child on each occasion and that respite care is offered on a planned, predictable basis rather than only in response to a crisis. Specialist placements are designed to meet the needs of a child with specified special needs in accordance with a scheme set up by a local authority or voluntary agency to provide a family-based alternative to residential care. Each scheme recruits foster carers to look after children who are deemed hard to place by reasons of their age, disability or behaviour. Foster carers involved in these schemes receive special training and are often referred to as 'professional foster carers'. They are paid enhanced fostering allowances in recognition of the skills they offer and the additional costs incurred in caring for children with such special needs.

(5) *Fostering with a view to adoption*: a child may be placed with foster carers who are recruited as prospective adopters. This enables the placement to be tried before a decision is taken to make an adoption order. It is possible for short-term or long-term foster carers to apply to adopt their foster child. In these instances, the foster carers have to be reassessed as prospective adopters by an ADOPTION AGENCY (usually the child's local authority).

(6) *Foster placements with relatives*: a child who is unable to live with his or her birth parent may be placed with an extended family member. A relative can become a local authority-approved foster carer for a particular child. The local authority has the same legal obligations in respect of a child fostered by a relative as to any child in a local authority foster placement. This includes the payment of a fostering allowance. Research suggests that long-term placements with relatives are among the most successful for children. Relatives can care for a child without the need for them to become approved foster carers. The local authority has the discretion to provide financial support under section 17 of the Children Act or through payment of a RESIDENCE ORDER allowance if the relative acquires a residence order under the Act.

Guidance under the Children Act, together with a more recent code of practice issued by the Department of Health in 1999 and National Standards, now govern the placing of children with foster carers by the local authority. The foster carers (except private foster carers) have to be approved by the authority. This process usually involves lengthy discussions as to what the responsibilities of fostering are and why they want to become foster carers. Authorities now also have to make rigorous checks when recruiting to ensure that paedophiles do not gain approval. From 2001 assessments have included police checks on all people over age 10 in the foster household. Additionally, adults will have to account for all their time since leaving school and for all their addresses and will be probed on their views on discipline and sexual attitudes.

Foster carers are expected to meet the full range of day-to-day needs of the child placed with them, such as supporting the child's progress through school or undertaking all health and developmental checks. The National Standards now require that foster children receive encouragement to develop their talents and interests, that they participate in decisions related to their care or their future and are provided with advocacy and support where necessary to exercise these rights. The children, their birth families and foster carers should have a copy of the CARE PLAN within two weeks of the placement beginning, with a WRITTEN AGREEMENT based on the plan also provided.

Matching the child with an appropriate family is also an important social work task. The written agreement should contain, according to National Standards, specific references to the elements of matching taken into consideration for the child concerned. There is strong evidence to show that a child's identity is best preserved when the foster carers share the same ethnic and cultural origins as the child. As a result, many authorities have policies stipulating same-'race' placements wherever possible and actively engage in recruiting foster carers to reflect the diversity of the community they serve. The National Standards also now require, for transracial placements, that the foster family be given additional training, support and information. They also stipulate that children be equipped to deal with all forms of discrimination and that black and minority ethnic children are helped to develop specific skills to deal with racism. Children with disability should be helped to maximize their potential, including any necessary equipment or adaptations to the foster homes.

Recruiting foster carers and finding appropriate placements for the children who need them is a perennial problem. The reasons for this are well known: the needs of the children requiring foster care have increased and are more diverse and perhaps more difficult for families to respond to. At the same time, changes in women's working patterns and families' expectations about their lifestyles have reduced the number of prospective carers coming forward. Local authorities themselves have not always nurtured and supported foster carers nor given sufficient thought to remuneration packages. As a result, carers have moved increasingly to independent fostering agencies. To tackle these difficulties, local authorities have been encouraged by the Department of Health to examine closely how their services measure up to other competing independent agencies – whether in unit costs, timescales for approving carers, the responsiveness in matching children with carers, which includes race, language and religion. They have also been urged to provide fees and allowances that recognize the time and skills demanded of carers and offer support 24 hours a day throughout the year. (See also LOOKED AFTER.)

Department of Health, *Fostering for the Future – Inspection of Foster Care Services*, London, DoH, 2001.

foyer a form of transitional accommodation for young people, linked to training/employment and social support.

Foyers embrace a range of activities and rationales. The provisions and services offered through foyers can also vary dramatically from purpose-built buildings with good leisure facilities, such as cafés, information centres and gyms, to modified older buildings with little more than a residents' lounge, laundry, games machines and communal kitchen. In general, foyers offer a single room in a facility that also has some staff to provide help with personal problems and advice on work, searching for jobs and finding training courses. They are different from hostels in that residence is conditional on joining a training scheme or jobs club.

C. Worley and J. Smith, *Moving Out and Moving On from Foyer Accommodation to Independent Living*, London, Housing Corporation and West London YMCA.

Framework for Assessment of Children in Need and Their Families the systematic approach to assessing vulnerable children, issued by central government.

The framework, published jointly by the Departments of Health, Education and Employment and the Home Office in 2000, must be complied with by all social workers in virtually all circumstances when assessing children and their families who may be in NEED. The framework replaces the earlier assessment criteria of the late 1980s, which emphasized the task of protecting children from risk and were familiarly known to a generation of practitioners as the 'orange book'. The framework draws heavily on recent advances in our knowledge of children's development and significantly extends the social factors on which social workers must gather information when engaged in assessment.

The framework covers a wide range of factors that should be taken into account in any assessment into three domains and maps them out on the three sides of a triangle. One side has the child's *developmental needs*, which includes the child's health, education, emotional and behavioural development, family and social relationships, self-care skills and identity. On the second side is the *parents' capacity* to provide basic care, ensure safety, emotional warmth, stimulation, guidance and boundaries. On the third side are *family and environmental factors*, which include community resources, the family's social integration, the family's employment and income, housing and family functioning.

The framework explicitly adopts an ECOLOGICAL PERSPECTIVE that focuses on the interaction between the characteristics of the particular family of the child, the wider neighbourhood institutions and the social and cultural influences of the area. As a consequence, the impact of specific social factors, including housing and economic disadvantage, is given relatively greater prominence than in child assessment approaches of the past. The framework also explicitly addresses the assessment of black and disabled children and provides ways that it expects social workers to use in assessing each of the three main domains in relation to black or disabled families with children in need. This multiplicity of factors is explained in considerable depth in official guidance issued alongside the framework.

The framework distinguishes between an *initial assessment* and a *core assessment*. An initial assessment should address the dimensions of the framework but is brief and should be completed at the most within seven working days of the social services department receiving the REFERRAL. Its objective is to determine whether the child is in need, what services may be provided and by whom, and whether a more detailed core assessment is needed. An initial assessment may include interviews with the child and family, if appropriate, as well as contacts with other agencies that might be involved in the child's life for the purposes of gathering information. A record of the decision of any further action, or, indeed, no action, must be made and communicated in writing to the family and the agencies involved.

A core assessment is lengthier and in greater depth. It considers the most important elements of need in the child's life and looks more closely at the parents' capacity to respond to these needs as well as the context of the wider family and community in which the child lives. A core assessment is led by practitioners from the social services department but will draw on the work of specialists from other fields who may undertake assessments of their own. Planning the assessment is crucial to its outcome. Matters such as who will undertake the assessment, what resources are needed to do so, which family members will be included, what methods for collecting information will be used, how the assessment will be analysed must be thought through in advance. At its conclusion, the core assessment should provide an understanding of the child's needs and circumstances and underpin the further provision of services and the expected objectives of the work. The assessment should be completed within, at most, 35 working days, with the first day marked by the end of the initial assessment or the point at which a *strategy discussion* has decided to initiate a CHILD PROTECTION INQUIRY.

The process of assessment – how and in what manner relationships are developed, especially with the family – is as important as the information sought. The framework lays great stress on explaining the assessment process to family members in both oral and written communication. It particularly calls for communication and direct work with children, especially if there are child safety issues to be addressed. It stipulates that any assessment must include seeing the child, however young and under whatever circumstances. Practitioners must also develop a relationship with children – enabling them to express their thoughts, concerns and opinions. Talking to children, the framework makes clear, requires time, skill and careful preparation and takes culture, language and other communication needs into account. The framework also draws on research that shows that parents seek clear explanations even in the most trying circumstances and want to be treated with openness, honesty, respect and dignity at all times. It is one of the positive elements of the framework that it provides examples for practitioners to emulate, for example in explaining the assessment process to family members.

The objective of an assessment is to produce an improvement in the wellbeing of the child. The final stage, then, is the analysis of the child's needs, a decision about what intervention is required and devising a plan that details who is to take what action, with a timetable and a process for review. Along with the framework, to help practitioners with such an analysis the DoH has issued a number of scales and questionnaires that correspond to the kinds of information the assessment will have gathered.

Department of Health, *Assessing Children in Need and their Families: Practice Guidance*, London, The Stationery Office, 2000.

free nursing care an outcome of a recommendation by the Royal Commission on the Long Term Care of the Elderly in 1999 making nursing care free in all settings.

This includes nursing care in older people's homes, in residential settings and in nursing homes. A distinction is made between nursing care – care related to a specific medical condition – and personal care, which is related to help with daily living tasks and involves the direct touching of a person's body. Not all the recommendations of the commission were implemented. A radical proposal to split the costs of long-term care between living costs, housing costs and personal care costs was made. Personal care should be available after assessment according to need and be universally free. This was rejected in England, although accepted by the Scottish Parliament. Means testing should apply to living and housing costs only.

free prescriptions the availability of free drugs on prescription to a number of different targeted groups.

People entitled to free prescriptions include those getting income support (see WELFARE RIGHTS 5) or income-based jobseeker's allowance (see WELFARE RIGHTS 5), people aged under 16 or under 19 and in full-time education, women over 60 and men over 65, pregnant women and those who have given birth within the past twelve months, and people suffering from listed conditions, including epilepsy, colostomy and diabetes. It is also possible to obtain an exemption certificate on the grounds of low income. (See also HEALTH BENEFITS.)

free school meals see WELFARE RIGHTS 5.

functional analysis a way of analysing the purpose of a particular behaviour, developed within BEHAVIOUR MODIFICATION.

Much behaviour that is considered abnormal does in fact serve a purpose for the person who engages in it, but it is not always easy to discover what the purpose of a particular behaviour is. Functional analysis begins by closely defining what behaviour is to be analysed. The practitioner or carer, or the client, notes carefully what happened before the person engaged in that behaviour (the *antecedents*) and what happened as a result of that behaviour (the *consequences*). The information is usually logged on an ABC (antecedents, behaviour, consequences) chart, which logs time, antecedent, behaviour and consequences in parallel columns. In practice, the observer's recording often begins when the behaviour is observed. The consequences are noted with a view to isolating those that act as *reinforcement*, such as gaining attention or relief from a task. The last step usually is to try to recall the antecedents – what was happening before the behaviour took place.

From a behavioural point of view, all behaviour, even seemingly destructive behaviour, that is repeated must be receiving reinforcement and must therefore serve some purpose for the person who engages in it. The point of functional analysis is to understand how the behaviour is reinforced and how it is triggered in the first place. For example, a young adult with LEARNING DISABILITY regularly throws tantrums (behaviour) at the training centre that he or she attends. Observation indicates that the tantrums frequently happen after he or she has been asked to undertake a complex task for which there has been no training (antecedent) and result in the person having the task taken from him or her (consequence) – a response that removes anxiety.

Functional analyses have also been used to deconstruct what social workers do or should do. Such analyses have been helpful in devising training programmes and in the development of social work competences. (See NATIONAL VOCATIONAL QUALIFICATIONS.)

funeral expenses payment see WELFARE RIGHTS 8.

Gg

gatekeeping the controlling of access to services so that, out of all those people who seek the service, only those who most require it will receive it. The assumption is that many more people will ask for the service than can be provided for.

gay the term used to describe a political identity based on sexual preference. Post-civil rights movements of the late 1960s/1970s saw the emergence of a gay social movement with a public voice and presence, which had previously been silenced. The gay community was particularly significant given the impact of HIV/Aids on gay men in terms of their political efforts to challenge the myths surrounding HIV and Aids and also to provide a source of community for gay men.

The gay movement has been criticized, however, for not being fully inclusive and not providing space for lesbian voices or minority ethnic groups. (See also HOMOSEXUALITY.)

R. Chapman and J. Rutherford (eds), *Male Order: Unwrapping Masculinity*, London, Lawrence & Wishart, 1988.

gender the social and psychological characteristics attributed to men and women.

Social scientists maintain that whereas sex is determined by biology or anatomy, gender is determined by social processes that can vary significantly between social groups and historically within societies. SOCIALIZATION is regarded as the key process by which gender characteristics are conveyed to individuals, a process that can be much influenced by social class, membership of ethnic groups and other factors. There is still a substantial debate concerning the issue of whether there are any biological bases to behaviour that are rooted in biological differences between the sexes. For example, does a woman as child-bearer have a biological predisposition also to nurture that is different from that of a man? Most social scientists now believe that such behaviour is a matter of social expectation, pointing to major differences between societies with regard to parenting.

Increasingly, however, the understanding of gender has become more subtle and complex. Theorists have pointed to the need to see gender as constructed through and in relation to other differences such as race, ethnicity and class. The issue of what we call 'gender' is fundamental to all social analysis not just in isolation but rather as integral to all other aspects of identity. This has wide implications for social care practitioners who need to recognize how gender intersects with other aspects of identity such as ethnicity, age, and sexuality. At other situations however they should see that gender might not appear to be important, for example in cases of homelessness, mental health and substance misuse where the primary concern maybe meeting those immediate needs. Thus practitioners must be aware of how issues of gender both impact and differentiate such experiences. This points towards the need for practice and service provision which is gender-specific and gender aware to best meet the needs of service users, both male and female. (See also FEMININITY, MASCULINITY, POSTMODERNISM, QUEER THEORY.)

E. Spelman, *Inessential Woman*, London, The Woman's Press, 1990.

gene a piece of code in DNA (deoxyribonucleic acid), passed on from parent to offspring, that determines certain physical attributes and capacities and that perhaps shapes behaviour as well.

Genes can be thought of as instructions that shape the formation of any one individual in ways that have only recently become clear. Up to a point, the more complex the life form is, the greater the number of genes. Viruses have the fewest: the influenza virus, for example, has eight genes; bacteria have several thousand, flowering plants about twenty thousand and humans some sixty thousand, roughly comparable to those of fish and mice. More important than the number of genes, however, are the *instructions* that those genes carry out. The sophistication of such instructions is crucial to producing the complex, thinking behaviour that we associate with human beings.

It is in the area of 'gene copying' that much attention and debate are now focused, inasmuch as that this is the source of both inherited disability and the capacity of some genes to duplicate themselves within the same organism. The more complex the organism, the greater the number of permutations and also the greater possibility of 'message decay', that is, genetic instructions being wrongly copied. Biologists estimate that perhaps as many as 50 per cent of human fertilized eggs have 'chromosome errors'.

Recent advances in the knowledge of genes have presented individuals – and society – with complex difficult decisions. Genetic counselling and genetic testing are expanding rapidly and assisting couples in a range of matters, such as overcoming various genetically transmitted conditions, for example, cystic fibrosis and sensory impairments and infertility. Controversy arises when disability advocates see yet another means by which disabled people will be viewed as unwanted and now avoidable by gene selection. It also arises with the notion that a new division will emerge in society at large: the 'gene rich' who can afford genetic manipulations for their would be offspring and the 'gene poor' who cannot.

general practitioner (GP) a qualified and registered doctor who holds a contract to provide general medical services to the public.

General practitioners services are now located in PRIMARY CARE TRUSTS. They are independently contracted by the NATIONAL HEALTH SERVICE and receive a fee based on the number of people registered with them. General practitioners often refer patients to the social services department of the local authority for COMMUNITY CARE and are often involved in the multidisciplinary ASSESSMENT of needs. Medical practices can also be a locus for social work services, if only on a part-time basis. As such they are important colleagues of social workers and social care professionals.

General Social Care Council an agency of the Department of Health established to regulate the social work workforce and register social workers.

Established under the General Standards Act 2000, the purpose of the Council is to ensure that the social care workforce is of an appropriate standard, and it does this by setting codes of conduct and practice as well as regulating and supporting training. As part of this role, it is establishing a register of social care workers, a new degree in social work to replace the diploma and regulating professionals and their employers in social care.

generic 'general, unspecialized': a generic social work service deals with all or most client groups and their problems, as do generic workers.

In the pre-SEEBOHM period, social work training courses and social work services were specialized. The profession distinguished between work in the child-care field, in mental health and in welfare (the latter dealing in the main with people with disabilities and old people). During the 1960s and earlier, some practitioners and commentators stressed the common elements to these branches of social work and called for both common training and a unified service. With the establishment of SOCIAL SERVICES DEPARTMENTS, generic services replaced specialized provision as the dominant model in England and Wales (in Scotland, the PROBATION SERVICE was also added). Generic services are now much less common. In the 1980s they came to be viewed as uneven in their responses to different client groups. Priorities for generic teams seemed always to be statutory child-care and emergency mental health work, with other service users receiving comparatively short shrift. Many social services departments have now been restructured into adult services and children's services, in effect encouraging specialisms again. Some have noted that specialisms can bring limitations and a loss of skill where family problems bridge adult services and children's services. For example, concern about a child might be rooted in the mental health problems of a parent. A few departments have retained INTAKE TEAMS, where generic workers handle all initial work for a short period before passing it on to specialist teams. Another reason for the demise of genericism is continued growth in the range of duties that social workers are expected to discharge. Professional training courses can no longer pretend to be other than basic, with many specialist skills added as a result of post-qualifying or advanced training. The advent of COMMUNITY CARE work is also significantly changing the focus of some parts of social work, stressing MULTIDISCIPLINARY WORK. It is unlikely that genericism will re-emerge unless the social work role contracts or, as in many European countries, education and training are considerably extended.

genetic counselling a medical service providing information to potential parents about the likelihood of their conceiving a disabled child.

People referred for genetic COUNSELLING are those with a disability or who have a close relative who is disabled. Information about the probability of certain conditions occurring or recurring can be offered. This form of counselling is likely to play an increasing part in medical practice.

genogram a diagram used by social workers, mediators and therapists to describe a family tree.

The convention is to depict females with circles and males with squares, with a cross through the square or circle if the person is deceased. Horizontal lines indicate marriage or a cohabiting relationship. A vertical line with squares and circles beneath describes the children of a relationship. Additional information can be added, such as dates of birth, marriage or cohabitation, divorce or separation, deaths, major illnesses and other critical events. Problematic relationships can be indicated with wavy lines. Such visual representations of families can help in the ASSESSMENT of family problems because significant events and relationships can be described briefly on one piece of paper. Genograms are especially useful in LIFE STORY BOOKS to indicate to children something about their background when they have lost touch with their birth family (see also ECOMAP).

geriatrics the branch of medicine concerned with the health or ill-health of OLDER PEOPLE.

The Royal College of Physicians recognized geriatrics as a specialist area of medicine in 1977. The distinguishing aspects of geriatric care are accurate diagnosis, careful identification of problems, judicious medical intervention and the management of sickness in old age through multi-agency care teams.

gerontology the MULTIDISCIPLINARY study of the ageing of OLDER PEOPLE.

Gerontology embraces biological, psychological and social theories in its understanding of older people. Biological theories suggest that changes occur in older adults' ability to adapt and interact with their environment. Psychological theories focus on older adults' self-concepts, and sociological theories examine the nature of older adults' social relationships and of the position of older people in society.

Gestalt 'a whole, a good configuration': a German term that is difficult to translate so has entered English usage.

The original Gestalt psychologists, working in the early decades of the 20th century, argued that reducing perceptual phenomena to simple elements loses the meaning of the total configuration; that is, the whole is greater than the sum of its parts. They formulated laws, such as that items that are similar and items that are close together tend to group, and that wholes that have a part missing will still be perceived as wholes. The essence of this perspective is that the appropriate level of analysis is holistic, whereas a reductionist analysis is generally inappropriate. If this argument is transferred from physical perceptual phenomena to the perception of people and their relationships, the individual is seen as a complex whole, existing in the present context, but composed of past and present influences plus plans and aspirations for the future. It is also evident that the emphasis could be on patterns or behaviour, perhaps at the level of the family rather than the individual, and the individual will be seen as part of a network of wider social relationships.

Gestalt PSYCHOLOGY was used in the 1940s and 1950s as the theoretical basis to develop Gestalt therapy. With an emphasis on the 'person as a whole', driving towards greater fulfilment through becoming more complete, or self-actualized, this therapy was very much part of the larger movement, termed the 'third force' in psychology – the humanistic movement – which developed as a counterbalance to psychoanalysis and behaviourism. The Gestalt therapy of its most celebrated practitioner and advocate, Fritz Perls, aims to assist individuals to complete those aspects of themselves that seem incomplete and restrict their personal growth. There may be 'unfinished business' with a parent or sibling as a hangover from the past; there may be a current situation that does not 'make sense', and clarification may come through action or understanding. The form of therapy may be individual or group work. It is primarily aimed at helping those involved to become aware of themselves as functioning organisms – a psyche and a body that form a whole. This awareness must include the context of this functioning organism, that is, social and cultural pressures that influence and are influenced by it. These features – of holism and of the total 'field' – are the essence of Gestalt theory and form the underpinning of Gestalt therapy. The actual methodology may vary among practitioners but is humanistic in that it recognizes self-actualization as a basic drive, and self-healing as a possibility.

The social worker may find this a useful theoretical position in that it emphasizes the necessity of seeing the person as a unique whole but also as part of the sociocultural context. Therapeutic insights may be gained by considering how clients may have interpreted past experiences inappropriately through their effort to make a Gestalt (for example, if a child is abused, he or she 'makes sense' of this by feeling responsible or guilty). A new, more appropriate understanding is necessary for the individual to move on from current problems resulting from this.

Gillick-competent the term used to describe a child under 16 years old who is deemed legally competent – that is, has sufficient understanding to consent to all forms of medical treatment, including psychological assessment.

The term originated from the decision in the 1986 case of *Gillick v. West Norfolk Area Health Authority*, in which Mrs Victoria Gillick tried to show that it was illegal to offer contraceptive treatment to her daughter, who was under 16, without her parents' consent. The House of Lords decided that a child under 16 could consent to medical treatment, provided he or she could demonstrate 'sufficient understanding to make informed decisions'. The ability to consent is still linked to chronological age in the sense that the Law Lords recognized that competence was a developing capacity but that the rate of development between children varied. The decision about whether a child is competent is decided by the doctor responsible for treatment. If a child is deemed to be 'Gillick-competent', the doctor can treat the child without the consent or knowledge of the parents.

The principle of Gillick competence was incorporated into the CHILDREN ACT. A child who is subject to a CHILD ASSESSMENT ORDER, an EMERGENCY PROTECTION ORDER, an INTERIM CARE ORDER or a SUPERVISION ORDER can refuse to submit to a medical or psychiatric examination or other assessment if he or she is able to demonstrate sufficient understanding to make an informed decision. This applies even if the examination has been ordered by a court. Further case decisions since the Children Act came into force have made the issue of consent less clear cut, however. A person with PARENTAL RESPONSIBILITY, or the High Court in exercising its powers, can override a child's refusal to consent to treatment, including where the child is over 16 years of age, provided the decision is deemed to be in the child's best interest. At the same time, however, the concept has been extended to other areas of the child's life. Notably, solicitors will ask if a child is 'Gillick-competent' to instruct them.

Government Offices of the Regions organizations that have been established to coordinate the work of key government departments at the regional level within England.

They bring together responsibility for the environment, transport, trade and industry as part of the overall aim of ensuring a coordinated regional response to economic development. They are strategic organizations whose remit is affected by the work of the REGIONAL DIRECTORS OF HEALTH AND SOCIAL CARE who will aim to ensure that the Office of the Regions takes into account the health and social care needs of the region in their development plans.

graduated pension see WELFARE RIGHTS 8.

grave crime a serious offence that can trigger long custodial sentences for young offenders under the law in England and Wales.

Originally intended only for the most serious offences, this provision has increasingly been used to sentence young offenders to long periods in CUSTODY or the SECURE ESTATE. Scores of young people were sentenced for grave crimes in the early 1990s, but a decade later this had increased to several hundred. This was mostly because such crimes were not defined in law, and young people committing an increasingly wide group of offences were sentenced under this provision, including those found guilty of domestic burglary.

grief intense sorrow or mental and emotional suffering arising from the loss of someone or something precious.

Grief must always be understood as being something intensely personal to the individuals who have experienced the loss. Only these people will fully understand the emotional impact of their loss, because only they will fully appreciate what their relationships meant. Furthermore, each individual will have inherited a set of understandings about how people deal with grief, which will have an almost unique feel. This will be built upon how the individual's parents, for example, dealt with grief, and how people of the same, and different sex, handle it.

We all tend to absorb certain messages about how women and men deal with grief and often base our own behaviour upon these 'models'. The cultural groups to which we belong can also determine how we feel we should, or should not, deal with grief, especially the extent to which grief should be a private or public matter. We will also be strongly affected by other factors, including disenfranchized grief, and whether or not there are complicating factors, such as a disaster, or a sudden or violent death, for example. All these factors can heavily influence how we as individuals undertake the complex journey of grief and the extent to which we 'get it right' for ourselves, irrespective of how others seem to be handling these painful and disorientating events.

Despite (or perhaps because of) the uniqueness of this human experience, workers and researchers in this field have demonstrated a fascination for the subject and have developed models for seeking both to understand grief and also how most appropriately to respond to it. One widely used model has been the 'stages' model of grief, which suggests that the commonly experienced reactions of shock, denial, numbness and anger can somehow be systematized into an almost linear progression until people eventually emerge from a dark tunnel into a new future without the deceased. Unlike the perceptive and experienced developers of such models, popularizers can frequently interpret this model in a far more mechanistic (and to bereaved people themselves often insensitive) way.

People in grief rarely move in straight lines. More recently, therefore, more sophisticated models have been introduced, although they are not necessarily incompatible with the notions of stages of grief. The 'tasks of grief' model, for example, suggests that people need to 'work at the tasks' of accepting the reality of the loss, experiencing the loss, adjusting to the loss, before finally investing energy into new relationships and activities. It is not suggested that these tasks are either self-contained or are to be tackled in a strict order of progression – in some ways anyone experiencing grief tackles some of these tasks simultaneously to a greater or lesser degree.

A further model emphasizes the importance of 'meaning" and suggests that the key task for people who are grieving is to learn how to 'reconstruct' whatever has previously given meaning and purpose to them, now that their loved one has died. A similar approach emphasizes the importance of learning how to reshape the story of the person suffering the loss in the light of his or her bereavement. This allows the individual to put the life of the person who has died into some sort of new context so that he or she can move to the next phase of life.

A common feature of many models seems to be the notion that in due course people will 'get over it' and put the grief safely behind them. In many ways this is true, of course – people do move on and develop ways of living where the sharpness of grief abates. The DUAL PROCESS MODEL, however, has made a significant impact upon our understanding of grief precisely because it emphasizes that people have to live with two apparently contradictory but very powerful realities – the experience of loss and the adjustment to the future. These are called 'loss orientation' and 'restoration orientation', and this model highlights the ways in which grieving people regularly move in and out of these 'orientations', sometimes on a hourly, let alone daily, basis. As time goes by, the 'loss orientation' may fade, but it will never completely disappear – there will always be sharp reminders that take people back into their feelings of loss, sometimes perhaps many years later.

It is important to bear in mind that most early work in this field was undertaken from a white Eurocentric perspective and that it is crucial for a multicultural and multi-faith perspective to be brought to bear upon these very important issues.

N. Thompson (ed), *Loss and Grief – a guide for Human Services Practitioners*, Basingstoke, Palgrave, 2002.

group home a very broad term to indicate a type of service provision utilizing ordinary houses and other domestic settings to provide a home for small numbers of service users.

Commonly the term is used for homes for groups of about four people, but it has also been employed to describe accommodation for considerably larger groups. This pattern of service provision is often used for people with LEARNING DISABILITY and people with MENTAL HEALTH PROBLEMS. Staffing levels vary according to the need of service users and may range from no permanent staff at all to staff being on duty at all times.

groupwork a range of activities, including a method of social work intervention, that can enable individuals and groups to develop problem-solving skills to address both their own concerns and those of members of the wider COMMUNITY (see also FAMILY THERAPY).

Evaluation of the groupwork method in social work relies predominantly on subjective accounts of group members' experiences and on observations of group leaders or facilitators. Such accounts seem to point to the potential effectiveness of working with groups in all areas of social work, statutory and voluntary field and residential. Although it is widely accepted that individual behaviour and attitudes are influenced by groups, it does not automatically follow that groups formed by social workers will achieve their aims. It is appropriate, however, to look at the possible advantages and disadvantages of this method and at the skills and knowledge required by workers who may wish to include groupwork in their repertoire of responses to problems presented by service users.

A way of classifying the different models of groupwork is by looking at the aims of groups under broad headings such as the following: alleviating isolation; promoting social learning and maturation; preparing for an approaching crisis or other life change; solving or clarifying problems at the personal/familial level; solving or clarifying problems in the members' environment; and achieving insight. In practice, groups may combine these aims or start with one and develop into another during the life of the group.

Models of groupwork are influenced by theories from a range of disciplines, such as sociology, social psychology and criminology, that have contributed to our understanding of behaviour in groups. These theoretical frameworks inform the worker's practice and influence and shape the methods used in groupwork. Values are also important, in that they affect how the social worker plans and facilitates groups. Groupwork practice is never value-neutral, so workers need to be clear about their own values and the principles on which they base their practice. For example, in the 'self-directed' groupwork model, which emphasizes ANTIDISCRIMINATORY PRACTICE and EMPOWERMENT, five practice principles may be outlined:

1 all people have skills, understanding and ability;
2 people have rights;
3 the problems that service users face are complex, and responses to them need to reflect this;
4 practice can effectively be built on the knowledge that people acting collectively can be powerful;
5 practise what you preach.

An essential part to planning when using this model is the worker's recognition of these principles. Whatever model or approach group-workers choose to use, they need to consider the difficulties and circumstances of individual group members and their public and political context rather than having a narrow focus on just one of these areas.

What are some of the possible advantages and disadvantages of using groupwork? Groups cannot offer exclusive individual attention. This can be positive, however, for some service users who find a one-to-one relationship too intense and are therefore more comfortable in a group setting. Being able to put aside personal considerations at times may be necessary since members will need to work cooperatively to achieve the aims of the group. Any benefits of groupwork may not be immediately apparent because it takes time for a collection of people to start to function as a group. Confidentiality can be difficult to maintain; information about individuals is often shared with other group members, who may not be bound by a professional ethic. In groupwork, the roles of client and worker are not clear-cut – members may develop skills of leadership, for example –so it can be a democratic, participatory and empowering method of social work.

For groupwork to be antidiscriminatory in practice, leaders or facilitators need to be prepared to challenge oppression on the grounds of age, gender, race, sexual orientation, class and disability. This means that workers and co-workers will have explored and defined their own values before planning a group and will have thought in advance about how issues are to be dealt with. A worker's commitment to anti-oppressive practice will involve learning about lifestyles different from his or her own and about the way DISCRIMINATION impacts on people's lives. In practice, this can mean having to make some difficult decisions about whether a group should proceed at all if crucial questions about the group's racial and gender mix or access requirements cannot be adequately addressed. Further essential considerations for groupwork practice are supervision or consultation, recording and evaluation. Each of these issues needs to be looked at in some depth, and all groupwork publications stress their importance.

Overall, groupwork is demanding on a worker and requires a great deal of commitment in terms of time and effort to plan and resource any initiative. As groupwork is more 'visible' than individual work and the worker is more exposed as a person, this may increase the level of anxiety. However, working with groups of people in ways that develop their potential can be a rewarding experience.

guardian *ad litem* see CHILDREN'S GUARDIAN.

guardian's allowance see WELFARE RIGHTS 5.

guardianship a legal arrangement whereby one person looks after the affairs of another who cannot act for himself or herself. Guardianship is based on the common law concept of *parens patriae* (literally 'the state as parent'), whereby a guardian looked after and cared for those who could not attend to their own needs.

Within the current legislative framework of England and Wales, 'guardianship' has two distinct meanings, one in relation to children and the other, less commonly, in relation to adults who are incapacitated in some way. Guardianship in respect of children is governed by the CHILDREN ACT. The effect of guardianship is that the person or people appointed as the child's guardian(s) acquires PARENTAL RESPONSIBILITY for the child. A person may apply to the court to be appointed as a child's guardian if the child has no living parent with parental responsibility or if a RESIDENCE ORDER has been made with respect to a child in favour of a parent or guardian who died while the order was in force. The court's decision concerning the appointment of a guardian must be in the child's best interest. A parent with parental responsibility or a guardian can appoint an individual to be a child's guardian in the event of his or her death without recourse to court, provided the appointment is made in writing.

Guardianship in respect of adults is governed by section 47 of the NATIONAL ASSISTANCE ACT 1948, where the person in need suffers from 'grave chronic disease' or is 'aged, infirm or physically incapacitated', and by sections 7 to 10 and 37 of the MENTAL HEALTH ACT 1983, where the person in need suffers from a MENTAL DISORDER. The powers of guardianship in respect of adults are more limited than those in relation to children. If the criteria laid down in the National Assistance Act are fulfilled, a local authority may apply to a court for an order to remove the person from the place where he or she lives to a suitable hospital or other premises. This provision is intended to be used where an adult is unable physically to care for himself or herself or is not receiving adequate care from someone else so is living in insanitary conditions. The provision under the Mental Health Act is intended to enable any mentally disordered person aged 16 or over to receive COMMUNITY CARE where it cannot be provided without the use of compulsory powers. Technically, this may be used where the person has either a mental illness or a learning disability, but because of the definition of mental impairment in the Act, the latter group are largely excluded.

The powers of guardianship in this context can restrict the liberty of the person to ensure that various forms of treatment, social support, training, occupation or education are undertaken. A guardian cannot, however, consent to medical treatment on behalf of a person. Guardianship can be granted by application to the local authority by an approved social worker or a nearest relative supported by the written opinion of two registered medical practitioners. The local authority or a private citizen may be appointed as the guardian. Courts in criminal proceedings may, in certain circumstances, make guardianship orders as an alternative to a penal disposal for offenders who are mentally disordered at the time of the sentence. Guardianship in relation to adults is rarely used; some commentators argue that this is largely because of the resource implications involved and the limitations imposed on the powers of the guardian.

H*h*

habitual residence test a test to determine whether a new arrival to the UK is entitled to MEANS-TESTED BENEFITS such as income support, income-based jobseeker's allowance and housing and council tax benefits.

A person is assessed as habitually resident by having regard to his or her intention to settle and the nature of any connections remaining (for example, family or property ownership) with the country he or she has left. The test was introduced by Peter Lilley, Conservative minister, to remove benefit entitlement from 'Italian backpackers' who, he alleged, came to the UK to holiday and claim benefits. In reality, those most often affected are British citizens and those with settled status who go abroad for extended periods. In common with asylum seekers left destitute, under the Immigration and Asylum Act 1996, local authorities may have a responsibility to support those left destitute.

hallucination a false perception of the senses that occurs in the absence of any external stimulus. *Simple* hallucinations may take the form of noises, such as buzzing, banging or sounds of shuffling, while *complex* hallucinations involve a combination of sounds such as voices or music.

Auditory hallucinations are commonly experienced as voices that may convey a message or may be unintelligible. Such voices, if intelligible, are experienced as directing the person to do something or as 'running commentary' in which the person's activities are discussed. *Visual* hallucinations are commonly experienced in the form of people, objects or animals, symbols or flashes of light. *Tactile* hallucinations are experienced as sensations of touch, such as the feeling of insects crawling on the skin or of another person's fingers touching the body.

handicap a term that has been used to describe both DISABILITY and its associated social disadvantages; it is now used less frequently and is rejected by many disabled people.

The term is still used in some official publications, including a question in the Census designed to enumerate the prevalence of disability, but is discouraged in most social work texts and government guidance on health and social care. It is explicitly defined in the World Health Organization (WHO) international Classification of

Impairments, Disabilities and Handicaps, where it is described as a disadvantage that limits or prevents an individual fulfilling 'normal' social roles. While this has something in common with the way 'disability' is defined by supporters of the SOCIAL MODEL OF DISABILITY, the WHO definition attributes the cause of any disadvantage to individual IMPAIRMENT and/or the inability to carry out 'normal activities'. This approach to causation, and also the association of the term 'handicap' with limitation, means that the term is rejected by disabled self-advocates. However, it has not disappeared from everyday speech, and is sometimes used to signify a more severe impairment or disability. This reflects usage of the term in OPCS surveys of disability in the early 1970s.

harassment see VIOLENCE.

harm minimization a term employed in relation to the use of (mainly illegal) substances to mean reducing the social, medical, legal and psychological harm surrounding the taking of such DRUGS.

When taken under medical supervision, diamorphine (HEROIN), for example, will not cause any harm to the body and may be used safely over a considerable period of time. In its illegal state, however, it is likely to be mixed with adulterants that can be harmful, especially if injected. It is expensive, which often leads the user to indulge in criminal activities, with all the social and psychological consequences this can entail. COMMUNITY DRUG TEAMS often prescribe METHADONE as a substitute for heroin, thus enabling the user to stabilize his or her life, avoid the black market and use the drug of ADDICTION safely. If the user is injecting, a supply of clean needles/syringes is made available to reduce as far as possible the harm surrounding drug use.

HAS abbreviation for HEALTH ADVISORY SERVICE.

hate crime a criminal offence that is motivated by prejudice or negative attitudes on the grounds of race, religion, disability, gender or sexuality.

The term 'hate crime' is American and has no legal status in the UK. However, it usefully describes a range of possible motivations for offences against the person or property, some of which have recently been recognized in law as aggravating factors to be taken into account in sentencing.

From the VICTIM's point of view, this type of crime can be particularly demoralizing and distressing. Offenders often commit numerous relatively minor offences that are unlikely, individually, to attract much police attention but the cumulative effect can be serious. For example, racist ABUSE of Asian shop workers makes them feel ashamed and degraded, and may mean that they feel they have to change their lifestyles to avoid further victimization, but it can be difficult to get the authorities to take it seriously. Neighbour disputes based on prejudice can also go on for lengthy periods without effective official intervention. Only when the police and local authorities decide to take a pro-active approach can such offences be dealt with effectively.

Some types of hate crime arise from perpetrators being in a position of power over potential victims. Examples include institutional abuse of older people and people with disabilities, and financial and sexual abuse of vulnerable people in their own homes. Not all commentators accept the use of the term 'hate crime' to describe such offences, but others argue that the use of phrases such as 'neglect' or 'sexual exploitation' to describe offences against vulnerable people in their own homes belittles the problem. While perpetrators may not actively hate members of oppressed and vulnerable groups, they take advantage of their vulnerability and low social status to offend against them with a lower chance of detection and prosecution. To some extent, the emergence of the concept of hate crime represents an attempt by the victims', anti-racist, women's, gay and lesbian, older people's and disabled people's movements to put the issues on the map.

In some states in the USA, legislation requires that statistical information on hate crimes be collected and published regularly, and this process has assisted in substantiating the claims of the victims' movement. In England and Wales, limited information on discrimination on race and gender grounds is published as a requirement of the 1991 Criminal Justice Act, but it has been produced selectively and its influence has been more limited. In some areas, practice has changed since the publication of the report of the STEPHEN LAWRENCE INQUIRY, which made detailed recommendations about improved treatment of victims of racially motivated crime. One response was the introduction of new offences of a RACIALLY AGGRAVATED nature in the 1998 CRIME AND DISORDER ACT. Under these provisions, courts are empowered to take account of racial or religious prejudice on the part of offenders convicted of assault, criminal damage, harassment and public order offences in England, Scotland and Wales. This can lead to more severe sentences.

B. Williams, *Working with Victims of Crime: Policies, Politics and Practice*, London, Jessica Kingsley, 1999.

health in medical terms, the absence of illness.

On the basis of the MEDICAL MODEL, illness can be regarded both as an individual phenomenon and as something that occurs naturally. Illness can, of course, be induced by people, as with SUBSTANCE MISUSE, but in the main, according to this view, biology provides the best explanation for illness. Using the social or environmental model, health is seen in the context of particular societies. Thus, 19th-century Britain gave rise to particular epidemics because of problems of sanitation, poor diet and poverty. The social model does not entirely reject biological explanations, for even in the healthiest societies people grow old. This model, however, has to be supplemented by an appreciation of wider forces, including the physical environment and social relationships.

These differing definitions of health have major repercussions for the way health services and social services are organized. If the medical model is adopted, then the means of treatment are primarily drugs and surgery. If the social definition is used, then health becomes the concern of a wide range of people other than medical staff. The Black and Acheson Reports, in 1980 and 1998 respectively, reflecting upon different patterns of mortality and illness in Britain in relation to SOCIAL CLASS, came to the conclusion that ANTI-POVERTY STRATEGIES were as, or more, important than putting more resources into health provision and reorganizing such services.

Sociologists have revealed interesting connections between health and other factors. Unemployment and ill-health appear to be strongly associated, although this association is not a simple one. Poverty is often also a feature of unemployment, whereas in other circumstances (such as early retirement) unemployment can be viewed positively if there is no hardship. In terms of access, the poorer sections of the population clearly use health services less than the better off. People from ethnic minorities see themselves as poorly served by the NATIONAL HEALTH SERVICE, particularly in relation to MENTAL HEALTH. Although many health workers are from ethnic minorities, they rarely have power over decision-making or the development of policy. Similarly, the major critique of the health and social services from a feminist perspective is that it has a mainly female workforce and yet mostly male management. The assertion is that women's problems have been unnecessarily 'medicalized' and that the process is a form of control exercised by men over women (see HEALTH INEQUALITIES).

Health Advisory Service (HAS) an independent agency of the DEPARTMENT OF HEALTH concerned with all aspects of the organization of the NATIONAL HEALTH SERVICE.

Established in 1969, the HAS frequently works with the SOCIAL SERVICES INSPECTORATE (SSI) in looking at services for specific client groups, evaluating these services and providing advice on improving them. HAS advice includes considering issues of patient care organization and management, education and training, and cooperation between agencies, particularly in joint planning of services. As with the SSI, the role of the HAS is both to disseminate good practice and to provide a monitoring service to government on the impact of service provision on users. Unlike the SSI, however, the HAS is independent of the Department of Health and is headed by a clinician or other medical specialist, not by a civil servant; staffing is largely made up of professionals working for the HAS on a temporary basis. In relation to social work, the main role of the HAS is to collaborate with the SSI in promoting effective cooperation between health authorities and social services departments, which is of particular importance in relation to the development of COMMUNITY CARE. In 1986 the HAS also established the Drug Advisory Service to help advise district health authorities on the development of services for drug users in their area. The HAS has fought hard to maintain its independent status and sees itself not as an inspectorate but rather as a professional consultancy. Its ability to maintain this level of independence reflects the greater power of clinicians as a profession compared to social workers and their determination to maintain professional and clinical freedom. In order to gain the cooperation of clinicians, the HAS emphasized its advisory role and the idea of professionals in dialogue rather than appearing to be a mouthpiece for the Department of Health.

P. Day and A. Klein, *Inspecting the Inspectorates*, York, Rowntree Trust, 1990.

health benefits benefits associated with the NATIONAL HEALTH SERVICE, including FREE PRESCRIPTIONS, free dental treatment, free eye tests, vouchers towards glasses, fares to hospital appointments, wigs and fabric supports, free milk tokens and free vitamins.

Free milk tokens and free vitamins are available to expectant mothers and children under five getting income support/income-based jobseeker's allowance. The other benefits listed are available to people on income support/income-based jobseeker's allowance and to others on low incomes who satisfy a separate means test that is similar to, but marginally more generous than, that for income support. Under this low-income scheme, people can qualify for partial help towards dental treatment, eye tests, glasses, fares to hospital, wigs and fabric supports, as well as being eligible for free services. Although all the other services can be provided completely free, since the introduction of the 'vouchers for glasses' scheme, many income support claimants find it impossible to obtain glasses without contributing to the cost themselves. People who want to apply for help under the means test can get forms at local Department for Work and Pensions offices. People who are already authorized through their receiving income support can apply for the free service directly to the pharmacist, dentist, optician or hospital.

health inequalities differences in life expectancy (mortality) and illness (morbidity) that are persistent and appear to be related to socio-economic and structural features of society, including social class, gender and ethnicity.

Death rates have been falling in the UK over the last century, and life expectancy has increased for all social groups. There are differences in death rates, however, and in the incidence of illness between social classes, and these differences are increasing. Social class in this context is denoted by occupation. Thus class I includes professional occupations, such as those of accountants, doctors or architects. Class II comprises managerial, technical and intermediate occupations, such as those of teachers, nurses, computer programmers. Class III includes both manual and non-manual skilled occupations, such as those of carpenters, plumbers or bank clerks. Class IV comprises occupations such as those of farm workers, machine tool operators or caretakers, and, finally, class V comprises unskilled occupations such as those of labourers, cleaners or factory packers.

A series of government reports that have appeared over the past 25 years (notably the Black Report, 1980, and the Acheson Report, 1998) have found that health inequalities have been remarkably persistent and that in some respects such differences are widening. For example, as the Acheson Report states, 'in the late 1970s death rates were 53% higher among men in classes IV and V compared with those in classes I and II. In the late 1980s they were 68% higher. Among women, the differential increased from 50% to 55%.' In relation to morbidity (the incidence of diseases), there are similar differences. For example, there is an increased incidence of depressive illness and anxiety disorders, lung cancer, coronary heart disease, stroke and respiratory disease from social class I to social class V, and these significant differences have also widened over the past 20 years.

Explanations for the higher incidence of death rates and poor health among social classes VI and V in particular are to be found in a constellation of factors – low incomes, unemployment, low educational achievement and poor housing. Poor dietary habits, in part influenced by low incomes, less usage of health services and increased smoking in particular, were also cited as contributory factors in the maintenance of health inequalities. As a result, many of the recommendations of both the Black and Acheson Reports focused on anti-poverty strategies, increased employment opportunities and improved housing as well as restructured health services to involve more people, especially older people, mothers and children in order to increase usage of health services, including preventive services.

The social work task in relation to health inequalities, often discharged in conjunction with health service professionals, is multi-faceted. Work in relation to income maintenance, such as an involvement in benefit take-up work, work to encourage the provision of public services without charge or at low cost, encouraging a healthy diet for service users, support for teenage parents and their children, child protection activities, work with people with significant and enduring mental health problems, support for vulnerable older people, activities associated with improving housing, including work to secure more appropriate housing to meet individual need, and many other areas of work impact upon health. As successive governments have encouraged cooperation between health and social work/care professionals through new structures such as PRIMARY CARE TRUSTS, health action zones and SURE START, there is an increased likelihood of a 'seamless' service that acknowledges the complexities and interrelationships between social and economic factors and health outcomes.

D. Acheson (chairman), *Inequalities in Health*, The Stationery Office, London, 1998.

E. McLeod and P. Bywaters, *Social Work, Health and Equality*, London, Routledge, 2000.

Health Services and Public Health Act 1968 an Act of Parliament that allows local authorities to arrange services for older people.

This is one of several acts of Parliament under which COMMUNITY CARE services are provided. Under the Act, local authorities may make arrangements for promoting the welfare of older people. The services might include information, meals, recreational activities, assistance with travel, assistance with finding accommodation, social work support and advice, home help, home adaptations and warden costs in sheltered housing schemes. Because the mandate consists of a power rather than a duty, the local authority retains discretion over exactly what is provided and to whom.

The Act does not define who qualifies as an older person, but the provision is intended to apply to people whose needs arise through age rather than other factors such as disability or illness. Its provisions are similar to those provided for disabled people under the NATIONAL ASSISTANCE ACT 1948 and the CHRONICALLY SICK AND DISABLED ACT 1970, and for people who are ill under the NATIONAL HEALTH SERVICES ACT 1977.

Under section 17 of the Health and Social Services and Social Security Adjudications Act 1983, local authorities may, if they choose, charge service users for the services provided.

health visitor a registered nurse who is also qualified to provide regular home health check-ups at specified intervals for infants and young children.

Health visitors are generally employed by a PRIMARY CARE GROUP and based at a health centre or general practitioner's surgery. They are often viewed as a source of support, advice and guidance in the care and upbringing of children, and because of this they may play an important role in assessing whether a child has been abused or neglected, sometimes representing health services rather than general practitioners. Most district health authorities also employ GERIATRIC health visitors, whose principal concern is the care and welfare of older people in their own homes. Sure start programmes have given health visitors an enhanced role in relation to pre-school children.

Her Majesty's pleasure some very serious offenders could at one time be sentenced to imprisonment 'at her majesty's pleasure', meaning that they were released only when the monarch consented.

In recent years, European human rights rulings and the HUMAN RIGHTS ACT 1998 have replaced this provision with a system whereby HOME OFFICE ministers are publicly accountable for their decisions about LIFE SENTENCES for adult prisoners and young people sentenced for 'GRAVE CRIMES'. In practice, decisions were taken by the Home Office rather than the monarch. Indeterminate sentences for serious offences can still, nevertheless, be very lengthy, and a small minority of life-sentenced prisoners spend the whole of their remaining life in custody.

heroin a sedative DRUG processed from the opium derivative morphine; opium grows mainly in the Middle East and Far East. Heroin is also known as 'smack', 'H', 'scag' and 'junk'.

Heroin in its pure pharmaceutical and legal medical form is a white powder, called diamorphine, that is used to alleviate extreme pain. By the time illegal heroin reaches the streets, it is very low in purity and has been adulterated with other similar looking substances. It is a brownish, off-white powder usually sold in small 'wraps' of paper. Street heroin is either smoked ('chasing the dragon') or injected. Both routes can lead to physical and psychological ADDICTION. Injectors also run the risk of infections such as septicaemia, abscesses, hepatitis B and HIV. Heroin is a class-A drug and attracts the most severe penalties under the Misuse of Drugs Act 1971, ranging from a fine for possession to life imprisonment for supplying.

The effects of taking heroin on a regular basis are wider ranging than the actual physical effects on the body. Physical effects include a slowing down of the body's activities, such as breathing and heart rate. Those new to the drug usually experience nausea as well as varying states of 'intoxication'. The initial 'high' is a feeling that users try to repeat, but TOLERANCE to the drug builds up and more is increasingly required to give the same effect. After the initial feeling wears off, varying degrees of sedation follow ('nodding off'), which may culminate in an overdose if too much is taken or if the purity is higher than expected. Because the drug is expensive and tolerance increases, funding the habit can become a problem, with all the social and legal implications that may follow. Users who are addicted to heroin may be offered a METHADONE prescription by their general practitioners or COMMUNITY DRUG TEAMS as a way of stabilizing their lives. Giving up a heroin addiction, as with any other entrenched habit, is not easy and entails DETOXIFICATION. Some users decide to go on to a RESIDENTIAL REHABILITATION house to complete the process of staying off.

heterosexism the standard against which difference in sexuality is measured. Heterosexuality becomes the desired 'norm', whilst other forms of sexuality, such as lesbianism, become the 'abnormal'. Evidence of heterosexism is most clearly demonstrated through statements like 'It's not normal' or 'It's not natural' to love or be attracted to someone of the same sex.

High Court a collective term for four different divisions of court with different functions: Queen's Bench Division, Family Division, Chancery Division, and Divisional Court of the High Courts.

The largest division of the High Court, the *Queen's Bench*, is concerned with civil disputes involving greater sums of money than can be dealt with in the MAGISTRATES' courts. It also has a general role of protection against the abuse of power, so that it is concerned with a range of matters such as libel, habeas corpus (issuing writs for the release of someone unlawfully detained) and the judicial review of government and local authority decisions. The *Family Division* is concerned with disputes about children and family property, covering matters relating to DIVORCE, ADOPTION and wardship (see FAMILY PROCEEDINGS). The *Chancery Division* deals mainly with matters of taxation, wills and company disputes.

The High Court also has an appeals function. Appeals from magistrates' courts under the CHILDREN ACT 1989 are heard in the Family Division. Appeals on points of law from magistrates' courts and crown courts are heard in the Divisional Court of the High Courts. (See also CRIMINAL COURT).

High/Scope an influential curriculum for, and approach to, encouraging the development of young children under five.

The High/Scope approach, developed in the USA, has had a significant impact in the UK on both the direction that EARLY YEARS' partnerships should take and their day-to-day work. It is based on several important principles. First, certain key experiences are central to young children's development, which can be grouped under various headings – social relations and initiative, creative representation, music and movement, language and literacy, classification, numbering, sequencing, space and time. These key experiences happen most often when children are actively learning through handling materials, talking about what has happened, experimenting and exploring for themselves. Second, adults should taken an interactive role by observing, supporting and extending the children's interests, knowledge, skills and understanding. Third, the learning environment should be arranged in a logical way to allow children to help themselves to what they need. Thus rooms are carefully arranged with different items labelled. Fourth, work with children includes their parents as part of the team.

High/Scope establishes a well-defined pattern to the child's day. At the beginning is 'circle time', when each child is greeted and acknowledged. Then in 'plan/do/review' sessions the main sequences of activity are planned out for the day. These are child-led, with less emphasis on keeping tidy and more on 'doing' and 'exploring'. During the day the child's experiences are linked immediately to learning by:

1 using language and literacy; reading – signs, symbols, own writing;
2 classifying, comparing and arranging things in a series or patterns;
3 explicit attention to numeracy;
4 focusing on social relations – taking care of the child's needs, expressing feelings, sensitizing the child to feelings of others, becoming used to group routines.

High/Scope has been closely evaluated, and there is evidence that it improves language deficits and behavioural problems through adherence to a daily routine of plan-do-review.

J. O'Flaherty, *Intervention in the Early Years: An Evaluation of the High/Scope Curriculum*, London, National Children's Bureau, 1995.

HIV/Aids HIV (abbreviation for human immunodeficiency virus) is the virus that may lead to Aids (acronym for acquired immunodeficiency syndrome). HIV damages the body's defence (immune) system, making it more vulnerable to the effects of opportunistic infections.

The HIV virus is spread by an inter-change of bodily fluids, which must pass from an infected person into the body of an uninfected person. The behaviour most likely to affect this interchange is penetrative sexual intercourse and the sharing of needles and other drug-using equipment. The virus may also be passed from an infected mother to her unborn child or to the child at the time of birth. The HIV antibody test shows whether or not the body has developed antibodies to the virus. If it has, this means that the body at some time has been infected by HIV, but it may take up to three months for the antibodies to develop after the virus has been contracted, so ideally two tests with 'safe' behaviour in between are necessary.

Social work has important roles to play in responding to both, whether through COUNSELLING, ADVOCACY, SOCIAL ACTION or policy development. Social work with people living with HIV and Aids has changed considerably in the last few years. Significant advances in medical treatment of the virus have been made using highly active anti-retroviral treatment that slows the impact of HIV and has extended life expectancy dramatically. This progress has added only further complexity to the social work task however. In addition to needing broad counselling skills around momentous life events – relationships with sexual partners, dying, death and bereavement – social workers now work with Aids survivors who need support in planning for their futures, becoming informed about intricate drug regimes and in returning to work or job training. In promoting empowerment, the social worker helps people to normalize HIV and to hold open different possibilities for their future, whether developing aspects of their social and sexual lives or learning to take an active role in their own medical management.

The social stigma surrounding a person with HIV or Aids, fuelled by fear, ignorance and discrimination, is still immense and requires challenging by practitioners and survivors. At the core of oppressive public attitudes are physical intimidation and violent displays of HOMOPHOBIA. Prisoners and drug-related offenders are particularly vulnerable to contracting HIV/Aids. The Prison Service has consistently refused to issue condoms to prisoners, except on home leave, or to countenance needle exchange schemes despite the prevalence of homosexuality and drug taking in prisons. Practitioners should also bear in mind evidence suggesting that families from minority ethnic communities and low income groups are less likely to seek early treatment. A culturally sensitive approach to assessment and intervention using key health providers from within specific communities is an important element of the interdisciplinary work required.

R. Furley, 'HIV and Aids: Current issues for the social work role', in *Social Work Review*, Volume 12, Number 3.

home help a person who undertakes domestic tasks, such as cooking, cleaning and shopping, for people unable to do such things for themselves by reason of DISABILITY, illness or the affects of ageing.

A home help is usually available from a private or voluntary agency, or from a SOCIAL SERVICES DEPARTMENT. Their assistance is often obtainable only through a REFERRAL. Home helps are also known as community care workers. Services are often hard pressed and, as a result, rationing on the basis of greatest need is widespread.

homelessness the condition of being without a home or shelter or of living in circumstances wholly inappropriate to personal and social needs.

Definitions of homelessness, and consequently estimations of the extent of homelessness, have varied widely in Britain. Official registers are unreliable because many people do not bother to report themselves in need of housing. Statistics usually reflect only those people who are accepted as homeless by housing departments of local authorities. However, there have been a number of initiatives that have tried to estimate the size of particular groups of homeless people, such as rough sleepers or young people. Many people who are not in priority categories do not report themselves as homeless because they believe that local authorities cannot help them. Others despair of lengthy waiting lists, often accepting poor-quality accommodation in the private sector. Official statistics therefore grossly underestimate the extent of the problem. Some analysts would add to the homeless list all those who are in inappropriate accommodation, that is, people living in hostels, BED AND BREAKFAST accommodation or in overcrowded or insanitary conditions. In addition, there are many thousands of people living in abusive relationships who warrant alternative, safe accommodation. If all these groups are admitted as homeless, then the problem is clearly substantial.

The current legislative framework for homelessness in Britain was established by the Housing (Homeless Persons) Act 1977, the Housing Act 1996 and the Homelessness Act 2002. The 1977 Act established a statutory obligation to accommodate homeless people if they were 'vulnerable'. Vulnerable groups included children, pregnant women, women at risk of violence and elderly people. Although there was also a statement in the Act about additional 'vulnerable groups' these were not specified. As a result, other groups such as care leavers, ex-prisoners, people with serious and enduring mental health problems, refugees and people with learning disabilities were sometimes helped by some local authorities, but often were not. Other key aspects of the 1977 Act included, first, a clause whereby homeless people had to establish a local connection before they could expect to be helped by housing departments, and, second, homeless people had to prove that they were not intentionally homeless. This broad framework was amended by the 1996 Act, which brought in three changes. First, the duty of local authorities towards the 'recognized' homeless was changed so that such help was to be offered for a minimum of 12 months and reviewed before two years had elapsed. Second, the duty of local authorities to provide accommodation to people in priority categories could be curtailed if the local authority in question was satisfied that appropriate alternative accommodation was to be found in the area. Such provision, of course, was likely to be in the private sector. Finally, secure accommodation was to be offered only to people who were on council waiting lists. Such lists do not usually include homeless people. The crucial issue here is that people regarded as 'queue jumpers', such as teenagers who became pregnant, were no longer to be given priority over those considered more worthy. These changes increased the difficulties experienced by homeless people and made more complex the tasks for social workers and support workers as they sought to establish 'vulnerability' and to challenge restrictive if not oppressive practices in some areas.

The Homelessness Act 2002 repealed the limitation to provide temporary housing to the 'recognized homeless' for up to two years (that is, those 'who are eligible, homeless through no fault of their own, and have a priority need'). Now 'suitable accommodation must be provided until people secure more settled housing'. The clause in the 1996 Act specifying that a local authority could discharge its responsibilities to the homeless by asserting that suitable accommodation was available in the area was also repealed. Other clauses in the Act require authorities to develop a more strategic multi-agency approach to try to prevent homelessness. This strategy must include an initial review of homelessness within a specified area within twelve months (thereafter every five years) and a plan to deal with and prevent homelessness based upon the review. A crucial element of this requirement to think strategically was that lettings policies should in the future offer more choice to homeless people in order that accommodation might meet their needs and thus lead to less social exclusion and more sustainable and settled communities.

Yet progress has been made for some vulnerable groups in some areas and recent initiatives such as SUPPORTING PEOPLE, CONNEXIONS and FOYERS promise much more. In essence, there is increasing recognition of the association between homelessness and some social problems. For example, the educational attainment for children of homeless families often suffers. This is because there are often delays in finding places in schools and because children find it difficult to adjust to new schools even if a school can be found to accept them. For families who make many moves, these problems become very difficult indeed. Both mental and physical health can be seriously affected as a result of poor or insanitary accommodation and because of difficulties in accessing health services. Other chronic problems include difficulties in claiming benefits and in securing employment. Feelings of powerlessness among homeless people are common, especially where people have been housed temporarily away from their communities of origin and their support networks in often poor-quality accommodation. In this context, oppressed groups such as single parents (mostly women) and ethnic minorities figure prominently.

S. Hutson and D. Clapham (eds), *Homelessness: Public Policies and Private Troubles*, Cassell, London, 1999.

J. Smith and S. Gilford, *The Family Background of Young Homeless People*, York, Joseph Rowntree Foundation, 1995.

Home Life see NURSING HOME.

Home Office the central government department responsible for most criminal justice policy in England and Wales.

Other important responsibilities are shared with the Lord Chancellor's Department (responsible for the courts and the judiciary) and the Attorney General, who is in charge of the CROWN PROSECUTION SERVICE, although the Home Office drafts the laws that govern the work of these law officers. The Home Office makes policy in respect of the POLICE, PROBATION and PRISON SERVICE, and issues circular instructions and NATIONAL STANDARDS to bring these into force. Through the YOUTH JUSTICE BOARD, it is also responsible for the work of YOUTH OFFENDING TEAMS. The Home Office has, since 1990, issued a series of VICTIM'S CHARTERS and has taken responsibility for steering central and local government policy on the treatment of VICTIMS of crime.

Since the 1980s, the Home Office has taken an increasingly interventionist approach to the services for which it is responsible, demanding 'efficiency, effectiveness and economy' and requiring services to reorganize and restructure themselves with this end in mind. At the same time, the Home Office has remained mindful of constitutional constraints upon government interference with the work of the judiciary and has been reluctant to fetter the discretion of judges and magistrates.

When the CRIME AND DISORDER ACT 1998 came into force, the Home Office effectively took over responsibility for youth justice policy from the DEPARTMENT OF HEALTH, although the latter continues to have some influence upon practice.

homophobia an intensely negative feeling about homosexuals and HOMOSEXUALITY.

Homophobia may be an irrational fear and possibly a deep-seated hatred of homosexuals and of what is perceived as their lifestyles. It is thought to be widespread in society, although for most people the feeling is relatively dormant, brought occasionally to life by anti-homosexual jokes. It is rare for people to be involved in active anti-homosexual politics or campaigns. Some have argued that homophobia may be evidence of repressed or latent homosexuality.

homosexuality a socially constructed term used to define same-sex desire, particularly among males.

Although same-sex desire between men has been present historically within all societies, the term gained usage within 19th century. The death penalty for 'buggery' was not abolished until 1861 in England and Wales. Yet this did not herald liberalization of the law but rather represented the tightening of its grip, and in 1885 the Criminal Law Amendment Act effectively made male homosexuality itself 'illegal'. The Vagrancy Act 1898 also criminalized homosexual soliciting and extended the meaning of homosexuality beyond buggery.

From this time and well into the 20th century, homosexuality was seen as a pathological disease that could be cured. This notion was actively challenged by the Gay movement of the 1960s, and the term 'homosexuality' itself has been transformed into a more positive affirmation of sexual desire. Under the Sexual Offences Act 1967, homosexual acts were decriminalized as long as both parties are consenting and both have reached the age of 16, as amended by the Sexual Offences (Amendment) Act 2000.

Homosexual acts are defined in law as 'buggery' or 'gross indecency'. The 1967 Act is used largely to prosecute gay men accused of 'cruising' in a public place, whether or not there is anyone else present. Such legislation relating specifically to gay men further enforces the idea that homosexuality is wrong. Similarly, section 28 of the Local Government Act 1988 states that no local authority shall either 'promote homosexuality' or 'the acceptability of homosexuality as a pretended family relationship'. A move by the Labour government to repeal section 28 as part of the Local Government Bill was defeated in the House of Lords by 270 to 228 votes at the end of July 2000. On 21 June 2000, however, the Scottish Parliament overwhelmingly passed the Ethical Standards in Public Life Bill, which included the repeal of section 28 by 99 votes to 17.

There are specific implications for social care practitioners, especially with regard to fostering and adoption. The Guidance and Regulations to the Children Act 1989 states that 'It would be wrong arbitrarily to exclude any particular groups of people from consideration.' This principle was reinforced in 1997 in a landmark decision when a judge concluded that the law 'permits an adoption application to be made by a single applicant, whether she or he ... lives alone, or cohabits in a heterosexual, homosexual or even asexual relationship ....'

While there has been a significant shift in both attitudes towards and images of homosexuality in society, in part because of the efforts of the lesbian and gay movement, in many respects it has been unsuccessful in achieving legislative social change, and discrimination on the basis of homosexuality remains, especially within the workplace. In 2005 Civil Partnerships between same-sex couples became legally recognized.

See also QUEER THEORY, GAY, SEXUALITY.

hospice care an approach to working with DYING people that combines medical interventions for symptom relief with concern for the emotional and psychological wellbeing of the dying and those about to be bereaved.

Hospice care in Britain began in the 1960s with the opening of St Christopher's Hospice in South London. Dame Cicely Saunders, a nurse, doctor and social worker, is credited with the early development of the hospice movement. Her approach was not a departure from medical modes of working with terminally ill people but an attempt to view dying people in a holistic way, acknowledging their broad spectrum of psychological, emotional and medical needs. The modern hospice movement now offers active total care (palliative care) to dying people whose diseases no longer respond to curative intervention. It is an approach that enables dying people to live with dignity until death. The hospice offers palliative care in a number of ways. Residential inpatient units offer short- or long-term care and pain management. The day hospice, usually found within residential units, offers a wide variety of activity and care to the dying person. Home care approaches offer the dying person and his or her relatives advice, support, care, and pain control in the person's own home. Home care teams may be based in the hospice or at a hospital. More recently, hospitals have been developing support care teams to bring hospice palliative care principles to the needs of dying people in hospital.

The hospice movement has recently expanded to include the needs of children and young people and their families and siblings, with specific organizations such as Winston's Wish developing support and training materials. One criticism of the movement has been its perceived neglect of the needs of minority ethnic groups, and much work is now being put into addressing this issue.

hospital social work social work services conducted in hospital and allied settings.

Although terminology varies between authorities and institutions, the label has tended to replace the competing term 'medical social work' and has displaced entirely the now defunct 'almoner'. The probable reason for the demise of the term 'medical social work' is the rejection, at least in some quarters, of the MEDICAL MODEL as the predominant explanation for social problems experienced by users of social work services. The generalized movement suggesting the social construction of problems is preferred in many medical settings. Hospital social workers are present in the whole range of hospitals and clinics and increasingly in other settings such as HOSPICES and community mental health teams. A number of specialisms are developing in particular areas of practice – for example, mental health, older people (including the elderly mentally infirm), people with DISABILITIES stemming from traumatic events like accidents or strokes, patients with kidney failure, people with HIV/Aids, DRUG abuse, profound learning or physical disability, and children with behavioural difficulties.

Although much of the work undertaken by hospital social workers is within the institution, a considerable proportion can be within the community. Thus, helping discharged patients to adjust to life in the community can be a major objective. Similarly, work, say, in relation to mentally ill people to prevent their re-admission to hospital might be a substantial part of a social worker's brief, while work in relation to people with sexually transmitted diseases can be primarily located within the community, and so on. A large part of hospital social work is conducted in teams of a MULTIDISCIPLINARY nature, with nurses, psychologists, doctors, health visitors, social workers and others often required to work together. A key issue is the extent to which such professionals are able to work together with equal status or whether the medical hierarchy dominates both the teams and the way problems are framed.

hostel a residential unit that offers a measure of support, supervision or, sometimes, protection.

Hostel facilities are often a halfway house between a long-stay institution and 'normal' community living, or they may be designed to help vulnerable people to live more independently and thus at some later stage effect a move into community living. They may offer both supervision and support to ex-offenders without family support, especially after a long prison sentence. Such facilities are often appropriate to those on PAROLE and where a conviction has included an offence against the person. Hostel accommodation, together with a PROBATION ORDER, is also increasingly offered to sex offenders as an alternative to imprisonment as part of a rigorous regime of 're-education'. Supervision and support are also pertinent to people with mental health problems, either as a temporary measure to reintroduce them into the community or, conceivably, to prevent admission to hospital, or as a long-term placement for those who cannot manage alone. Other vulnerable groups, including OLDER PEOPLE (see also SHELTERED ACCOMMODATION), people with LEARNING DISABILITIES (see also GROUP HOME), children LEAVING CARE, alcoholics 'drying out' and HOMELESS people or families (as a prelude to finding more settled and secure accommodation), have all benefited from hostel accommodation of varying kinds. Hostels differ in terms of social work support, which is provided intensively on the premises in some cases and more distantly in others, with workers visiting from time to time. (See also BAIL HOSTEL.)

household an open-ended concept used to define eligibility for certain welfare benefits.

The notion of household is left undefined in regulations. Whether two people should be considered as members of the same household depends on (sometimes quite subtle) circumstances. A house can contain a number of separate households – for example, a person living in exclusive occupation of separate accommodation, say in a self-contained flat, will be deemed a household. Nor is physical presence always essential: there must be a 'particular kind of tie' between two people together in a domestic establishment such as lodging house or hostel.

M. Wolfe, *Debt Advice Handbook*, fourth edition, London, Child Poverty Action Group, 2000.

housing association a non-profit organization involved in the building and maintenance of housing.

Housing associations are organized in a variety of ways reflected in their status, which can range from that of a friendly society through to charitable companies under the Charities Act. Under the changing legislation of the 1980s, housing associations have expanded to become an increasingly important part of public or social housing provision. As a result of this expansion, they are responsible for approximately a third of all newly built housing. This has been largely because of the way central government has aimed to reduce the role of the local housing authorities in providing and managing public-sector housing. This change has also allowed central government to have greater direct control over the housing programme, bypassing local authorities. In 1964 the government established the Housing Corporation as an agency for financing housing associations. Through the Housing Corporation the government can channel funds through a system of deficit loans that allow housing associations to engage in building new housing without being dependent on raising finance through more commercial channels such as the banks.

As housing associations have increased their role in providing new housing, so have they also established themselves as a major provider of supported accommodation for people emerging out of long-stay hospitals (including people with enduring mental health problems and people with learning disabilities) in addition to recovering alcoholics, drug users, elders and women fleeing violent relationships. SOCIAL SERVICES DEPARTMENTS have worked with housing associations in the development of new forms of sheltered and supported accommodation, often maintaining allocation rights in return for contracts with housing associations. This has enabled social services departments and health authorities to develop new initiatives, particularly in areas where the district housing authority is a limited supplier or in response to the government's emphasis on non-statutory provision. Housing associations are likely to play a major role in the government's SUPPORTING PEOPLE initiative.

P. Malpass and A. Murie, *Housing Policy and Practice*, fifth edition, Basingstoke, Macmillan, 1999.

housing authorities the housing departments of local district councils and unitary authorities, primarily responsible for the management of council housing stock.

Housing authorities are involved in the provision of public-sector housing, as both builders and managers. Within the metropolitan areas they are part of the metropolitan district council alongside SOCIAL SERVICES DEPARTMENTS. Similar arrangements are now in existence in other unitary authorities established when Local Government was last restructured in 1997. This has allowed for some close working relationships to develop, and in some authorities, including Tower Hamlets in London and St Helens in Merseyside, there has been a move towards the integration of these services as a response to the demands of COMMUNITY CARE. However, local authority housing provision has come under severe strain since 1979, when the Conservative government introduced a range of financial and statutory controls on housing finance. Most important was the introduction of the statutory right to buy in the Housing Act 1980, which resulted in approximately one and a quarter million sales of council dwellings by 1988. The financial benefit to local authorities from the sale of council dwellings was restricted because of capital controls on the use of receipts from sales. These and other controls led to a fall in capital spending on housing by local government and HOUSING ASSOCIATIONS becoming a more significant provider of public housing.

The Conservative government introduced its controls on housing finance with the stated objective of reducing the role of the state in providing public housing. The aim was to increase the role of the Housing Corporation and housing associations in public housing and to provide more incentives for the private sector both in owner-occupation and in rented accommodation. Additionally, the government introduced measures to ensure that local authority housing was provided at a price closer to its market value. Local authorities' housing revenue accounts can no longer be subsidized from other sources, so management, repair and maintenance costs must come out of the rents charged. This has inevitably resulted in an increase in rents in recent years and consequently a major increase in housing benefit payments – see WELFARE RIGHTS 6 – as tenants find rents outstripping their ability to pay.

Critics have argued that the introduction of the right to buy, allied to controls on capital spending, resulted in a reduction in the housing stock available to local authorities for housing the poor. This gave rise to an increase in the number of cases of homelessness and the use of BED AND BREAKFAST accommodation to try to resolve the problem.

With all these financial pressures, some local housing authorities concentrated more on providing SHELTERED ACCOMMODATION. The approach adopted involved the use of wardens and introduced an element of care into the service. This led to the publication of a response to the Griffiths Report by the housing authorities of the largest non-metropolitan English city councils, including Bristol and Stoke-on-Trent, who argued against Griffiths's view that housing authorities should concentrate on the 'bricks and mortar' aspects of housing management and instead emphasized their welfare role in caring for tenants. However, with the changes in government policy stressing the role of housing associations as providers of public housing, social services frequently see these as partners in providing accommodation for clients rather than the district housing authorities. The election of a Labour government in 1997 did not significantly reverse this trend in housing developments, and the emphasis remains on a mix of providers of public sector and low-cost housing.

P. N. Balchin and M. Rhoden *Housing Policy: An introduction*, fourth edition, London, Routledge, 2002.

housing benefit see WELFARE RIGHTS 6.

housing costs for families see WELFARE RIGHTS 5.

Housing (Homeless Persons) Act 1977 legislation that gave local authorities in Britain a duty to help homeless people with a priority need.

Priority need is interpreted under the Act as HOMELESSNESS as a result of a disaster (such as a fire), someone being pregnant, someone who has dependent children, and vulnerable people. People deemed to be INTENTIONALLY HOMELESS are not regarded as a priority. Homelessness is defined as a person's lack of accommodation that he or she has a right to occupy, or, if there is such accommodation it is too dangerous for the person to occupy it; a person occupies emergency accommodation; a family is living apart because its accommodation is unsuitable, the dwelling is of such a poor standard that the family could not reasonably be asked to live in it, or the family has been illegally evicted and cannot regain possession of the dwelling. Potential homelessness is defined as a situation where one of the above conditions will apply within the next 28 days.

Much depends upon how local authorities interpret the conditions outlined above, and there is in practice considerable variation from one authority to another. The idea of vulnerability in particular is used sympathetically by some authorities, but the majority, in the face of dwindling public housing stock, have little to offer ex-prisoners, the mentally ill and young people LEAVING CARE. Much of the 1977 Act has been subsequently incorporated into the Housing Act 1985. This Act issued a code of guidance that gives a generous view of local authorities' obligations in relation to vulnerable groups, but the code is not binding. The social worker's and housing advice worker's task of trying to secure accommodation for vulnerable people may find the code helpful.

housing problems a wide range of problems, involving social workers and support workers, concerning access to housing, the relationship between housing and personal needs, security of tenure, housing and community context and HOMELESSNESS.

A distinction is often drawn between a shelter and a home. The functions of a shelter are to provide protection from the elements and some measure of personal security whereas a home, additionally, includes notions of privacy and seclusion for individuals and families to express themselves in a manner that meets their personal needs and reflects the standards of the society in which they live. A home is thus a basic requirement without which people cannot adequately function in relation to their principal social roles (for example, work, raising a family or being in a married or cohabiting relationship and living in a community).

There is no universal right to a home in Britain. The state recognizes a need to house 'vulnerable' people, but housing agencies are inconsistent in the help offered to such groups (see HOMELESSNESS). In this context, as many commentators have pointed out, the number of dwellings in Britain exceeds the numbers of individuals and households needing a home. The problem has thus been construed as political. Access to housing or appropriate housing, both for people in general and for those with particular needs, continues to be a major problem that engages social workers. Research has identified young people (and especially care leavers), ex-prisoners, people with enduring mental health problems, drug abusers, older people, lone parents, ethnic minorities, people in violent relationships and disabled people as experiencing persistent problems of accessing suitable housing.

For example, the majority of ex-prisoners are released from custody to 'no fixed abode' or to accommodation of a quality inferior to what they enjoyed before being imprisoned. Given the known association between offending and homelessness and the difficulties ex-offenders experience in securing work, such a lack of support services to rehabilitate ex-prisoners to a stable environment is clearly worrying. Similar problems are faced by care leavers, who are much more likely in later life to be found in prisons, to become mentally distressed, to use drugs and alcohol, to be unemployed and to find it difficult to maintain satisfactory personal relationships. All these 'downstream' problems are related to the problem of homelessness. Care leavers are especially vulnerable among young people, but there are also substantial numbers of young people from apparently normal backgrounds who have left home prematurely as a result of abuse or family conflict. This group, too, requires special attention to meet their accommodation and support needs.

Mental health problems are now perceived as both a cause and effect of homelessness. This cause and effect is heightened if a person is drug- or alcohol-dependent. Given that some mental health problems are episodic in nature, requiring varying levels of support, suitable accommodation may be hard to access. The best-planned provision includes a range of services, with spare capacity, to meet often short-term needs. These services allow people to move between packages of care, support and accommodation as their problems improve or deteriorate. The work of assertive OUTREACH teams and active REHABILITATION teams can help to both prevent the need for moves or to make them short term. In both scenarios there is the potential for significantly increased stability for service users.

The issue of how independent or dependent a lifestyle can be sustained is also especially important to both older people and to disabled people. Britain has an ageing population, and although there is no necessary association between age and disability, some older people do acquire both physical and mental disabilities. Younger people can be physically or learning-disabled from birth or through illness or traumatic events such as accidents. Planners have devised a number of supported housing options for both groups, with varying levels of social support ranging from people living in their own homes (with visiting or domiciliary support) to clustered accommodation through group homes and sheltered accommodation to residential and nursing homes. The social and caring support needed can also be conceived of as being on a continuum from a few hours a week to 24-hour cover, depending upon a person's needs.

A different issue arises for women wishing to leave a violent partner. Women have to decide whether, with appropriate measures in place, they can seek to oust the partner or whether they need to get away to some place of refuge. Many women have felt it necessary to leave, but increasingly justice and community agencies have tried to put together a package of legal and protective measures designed to enable women and their children to feel safe in their own homes. Better that women and children can maintain important aspects of their daily lives, such as schooling, work and social supports, than to have to start all over again in another area.

Other housing problems concerning social workers and support workers involve issues that could be broadly labelled as 'neighbour relations'. This clutch of problems includes some very testing issues such as racial harassment, antisocial behaviour and the problem of housing known sex-offenders. Work on these problems requires the careful balancing of rights and risks. Black and ethnic minority groups clearly need to be able to live without fear from racists in any community, and social workers and housing workers need to act decisively in the event of racist behaviour. With sex-offenders living in the community, the issues are those of wishing to rehabilitate people but also ensuring that women or children are not put at risk. Similar issues arise in relation to people exhibiting behaviour labelled as antisocial. Social workers are required to ensure that there are good reasons why anyone should be evicted and that humane alternative accommodation is found for those so regarded.

The threat of eviction can arise for additional reasons, such as rent or mortgage arrears, from the behaviour of unreasonable landlords (especially where landlords will not make essential repairs or there are indefensible rent increases) or because of an alleged failure on the part of tenants to maintain property. Such difficulties often result from personal and relationship problems, such as redundancy, divorce and separation or financial mismanagement. Social workers can help through debt advice (see MONEY ADVICE) and negotiations with mortgagors or landlords and by sometimes helping service users to maximize their incomes.

The last decade has witnessed a reconfiguration of social work services focused on housing issues. Increasingly, social workers and social support workers are being employed by housing agencies concerned with vulnerable groups rather than being located in social work agencies and acting as advocates for service users in their dealings with housing agencies. This movement is epitomized by the SUPPORTING PEOPLE initiative, which is to be implemented in 2003. The movement is also evidence of a new thinking about complex social problems, namely, that specialist workers can most effectively work together if they work in dedicated teams within the same organization.

Housing inequalities reflect broader structural social and economic features of society. These inequalities concern not only the quality of accommodation, but also community infrastructures and, often, other 'life chance' issues such as health, education and employment. Housing is therefore an important locus for social work and community work activity and it must be seen as an important dimension of urban and rural regeneration strategies.

P. Balchin and M. Rhoden (eds), *Housing: The Essential Foundations*, London, Routledge, 1998.

human development the process of change that occurs throughout the human life cycle.

In terms of developmental PSYCHOLOGY, humans develop abilities in four domains: cognitive, social, linguistic and emotional. Development in the linguistic and cognitive domains is completed first. In terms of learning their native language, practically all children are accomplished speakers by the time they reach four years of age. In terms of cognitive development, all basic mental operations are acquired in the early years of life: a person's IQ is relatively stable after the age of 18. Cognitive and linguistic development is still able to occur throughout the life cycle, however. Social development is an ongoing process, involving how we attain and maintain a concept of self, whether we are introverted or extroverted, whether we perform well in groups and have leadership qualities, whether we need company or are content to be alone. All these qualities have their basis in childhood but are shaped by life events. The development of an understanding of emotions does not appear to begin until middle childhood, and problems with interpreting emotions persist throughout the life course. The developments that occur in these four domains do not occur in isolation, and changes in each separate domain can have profound effects on the other three.

Human development begins before the infant is born or even conceived. The foetus can detect sounds from the outside world and is affected by the mother's emotions as well as by physical agents such as drugs, alcohol or HIV. Parental expectation before conception may affect human development – for example, the desire for a child of a certain sex, with a high IQ, a special gift or the willingness to pursue a specific career. The study of human development also considers the process of ageing, dementia and so-called abnormal development, such as congenital deafness/blindness, autism and schizophrenia.

Human Rights Act 1998 a law that sets out the rights of the citizen in the UK, incorporating the provisions of the European Convention on Human Rights into domestic law.

Under this legislation, not only the courts but all national and local public bodies are required to uphold the rights set out in the Convention. This has important implications for criminal justice and for social work more generally. If courts come across potential conflicts between the existing domestic law and the requirements of the Human Rights Act, they are required to draw these to the government's attention and legislation can then be enacted to correct the anomalies. There is also a general duty to interpret domestic law in the spirit of the Human Rights Act wherever possible. These changes represent an enormous shift in the legal culture of the UK, although they are based on a limited and conditional view of citizenship. They potentially extend rights to the whole population that were previously available only to those with the resources or backing to take test cases to the European courts.

The rights protected include the right to life, the right to liberty unless this is lawfully taken away and then to a fair trial, the right to respect for private and family life, freedom of thought, conscience, religion, expression, assembly and association, the right to education and the right to marry and set up a family.

Although the European Convention on Human Rights is in many ways dated, having been drafted in the 1940s, its effects have been modified by a number of other more recent treaties and international agreements. These include provisions for young people to be dealt with differently from adults in criminal cases, under the United Nations' Beijing Rules of 1985, minimum standards for the incarceration of young people, under UN rules (the Riyadh guidelines) agreed in 1990, and rights to protection from DISCRIMINATION under a range of provisions.

hysteria a mental disorder that results in the appearance in a person of some physical ailment that has no physical cause.

Symptoms include physical ailments such as the loss of function of a limb or sense organ, combined with the absence of any detectable physical cause of such symptoms. The term 'hysteria' is derogatory in its connotations because it has been used to describe behaviour that is devalued in Western male-oriented society, which values independence and 'rationality': that is, behaviour involving the supposed expression of dependency needs in an unconscious, irrational way. Selfish motives are imputed to this behaviour: the subject may be believed to be unconsciously feigning physical illness to gain gratification and, in fact, the borderline drawn between malingering (conscious manipulation) and hysteria may be thin.

Feminist therapists reject the diagnosis as referring to any real state experienced by women. Hysteria can also be misdiagnosed by Western psychiatrists when, for example, women from other cultures follow certain culturally required expectations in their behaviour.

The traditional PSYCHODYNAMIC explanation for hysteria is one of repression. The person cannot face a particular conflict or anxiety so represses it. It then becomes unconscious and reappears as a physical complaint. Alternative explanations of the behaviour are offered by feminist psychotherapists who consider that the behaviour associated with 'hysteria' may be the result of childhood experiences of violence or sexual abuse and may be more appropriately understood as POST-TRAUMATIC STRESS SYNDROME.

There is a tendency for women to be given drug treatment only for hysteria, especially women from black and other ethnic-minority groups. Social workers are in a position, with other mental health professionals, to try to address the person's emotional needs, usually in combination, perhaps, with a medical approach. Care should be taken, however, if deeper work with the person's past experiences and pain is required, that this is carried out in a fully structured and 'safe' therapeutic relationship, either by the worker or via a referral elsewhere (see PSYCHODYNAMIC APPROACH). With people from cultures different from that of the worker, a culturally sensitive, ANTI-OPPRESSIVE approach to helping, usually involving partnership with organizations working within the person's culture and/or transcultural counselling, is necessary. It is also important to consider the possibility that the person's physical complaints may have a real physical base. Here ADVOCACY and/or liaison with the medical practitioner may be required.

Ii

ideology an organized system of ideas and beliefs concerning the political, social and cultural views of an individual or group.

For most of us, our ideas about political and social structures tend to be unformed or not fully thought through. Few people have a developed system of ideas that are logically integrated within a system and, as such, we tend to react to changing issues in an *ad hoc* and pragmatic way. Ideologies, on the other hand, are more formally established sets of ideas and beliefs that can be seen as a guide to action. Political ideologies are for the most part the classic example of sets of formulated ideas concerning behaviour, organization, responsibility and action. These often have a well-established history behind them, having been developed during the period associated with the development of popular democracy in the 18th and 19th centuries. Ideologies associated with the main political parties, including socialism, conservatism and liberalism, all emerged in the 19th century and are clearly associated with the way in which society, the economy and the political system should operate. They are also linked closely with the development of the Welfare State and debates around its future.

Liberalism and socialism were bodies of thought that identified to varying degrees a role for the state in providing support for the most disadvantaged within society, with socialism seeing the collective good of society being of greater concern than individual need. Conservatism has largely been pragmatic in its response to these developments and, until recently, has not reversed the trend towards more collectivist approaches to welfare. Within conservatism, however, there is a strong trend that believes that the role of the state should be minimal as it leads to dependency and the undermining of individual freedoms. These conflicting ideologies have been powerful forces in the development of welfare services and play a key role in debates over the future of welfare. For example, the relationship between the level of state provision and the role of the private sector in areas such as pensions, residential homes or health care insurance is a key debate where the ideologies of the main political parties ensure that such issues are always of high political importance.

Some would also argue that while most people have not formulated clearly their political and social beliefs, they still respond to issues from an ideological position. Evidence for this is that people who tend to support one issue, such as equality of treatment for women, will tend to support other related issues, such as disability rights. Indeed, pragmatism itself may be seen as an ideological position.

H. Cowen, *Community Care, Ideology and Social Policy*, London, Prentice Hall, 1999.

IEP abbreviation for INDEPENDENT EDUCATION PLAN.

Immigration and Asylum Act 1999 an Act that introduced new arrangements for providing accommodation and support for ASYLUM SEEKERS.

People seeking asylum after April 2000 are accommodated and supported by a division of the HOME OFFICE – the NATIONAL ASYLUM SUPPORT SERVICE (NASS). NASS makes arrangements by contracting with private providers and local authorities for accommodation and providing cash (previously vouchers) for daily living needs. The Act also formalized INTERIM ARRANGEMENTS whereby social services departments remain responsible for supporting people who applied for asylum before April 2000.

Immigration and Asylum Act 1999 accommodation see WELFARE RIGHTS 6.

impairment a physical, sensory or psychological characteristic or aspect of functioning that falls outside norms established in medical practice.

The distinction between impairment and DISABILITY is vital to the critique that disabled activists have developed of approaches to disability based on the limitations of individuals. Impairment has been defined by disability activists as 'lacking part or all of a limb, or having defective limb, organism or mechanism of the body', whereas disability is regarded as the social restrictions and exclusions imposed on people with impairments. These result from the way that the requirements of people with impairments are disregarded in social and environmental arrangements. Impairment can be caused by differences at birth or by illnesses and accidents. However, it is more common in later life. There are many types of impairment, and the above definition from within the disability movement does not mention mental distress or intellectual impairment, more usually referred to as LEARNING DISABILITY.

Recent discussion within the disability movement has focused on whether there should be more emphasis on impairment and the restrictions and discomfort this imposes on some disabled people. In particular, it has been argued that the movement could be more inclusive by acknowledging difficulties arising from illness and impairment. The counter-argument to this has been the danger of focusing on impairment rather than on the external barriers that can be tackled by political action. Academic critics have pointed out, however, that impairment is itself socially constructed on the basis of dominant conceptions of normality and that this should also be subject to analysis.

C. Thomas, *Female Forms: Experiencing and Understanding Disability*,
Buckingham, Open University, 1999.

incapacity benefit see WELFARE RIGHTS 3.

inclusion a general approach to the education of children with
ADDITIONAL EDUCATIONAL NEEDS and SPECIAL EDUCATIONAL NEEDS that
seeks to promote their learning alongside their peers in mainstream
schools wherever possible rather than in separate special schools or units.

This whole approach often has to be held in tension with other
educational priorities that tend to encourage selection and separation
rather than maximizing the achievement of the whole population.
Promoting EDUCATIONAL INCLUSION is a key task of all schools but is
often tempered in practice by national and local political decisions about
the organization of schools and the significance of performance tables.

income maximization assisting service users in receiving the highest
level of income available to them for any given period of time, drawing
on all possible sources such as welfare benefits, child support, paid
employment or a combination of these.

Poor people do not need social workers to obtain benefits, but when
in contact with low-income families and individuals practitioners
should be able to point them along the right path. The benefits system is
complicated, with annually changing rates and the introduction of new,
often targeted, benefits. Social workers should know enough about the
benefit system and the relationship between benefits and work to help
families to get what should be theirs but should not expect to have
detailed knowledge about specific benefits. The expertise necessary for
appearing at tribunals could realistically be expected only from a full-
time WELFARE RIGHTS officer, but practitioners should be able to
recognize when to focus on users' income improvement is essential
and know enough about the benefits system to be able to:

1 go through the range of users' possible entitlements to determine
whether they are claiming all that they can;

2 secure back payments of benefits if it can be demonstrated that a
claimant should have had a benefit earlier, had a good reason not to
claim or there was inefficiency on the part of the Benefits Agency.

Practitioners should have several objectives in working with any users
or families to maximize their income. One is to look across the entire
benefit system to pick up any entitlements that are linked to others. For
example, if a young mother is under 16 she cannot claim income support
or income-based *jobseeker's allowance* (see WELFARE RIGHTS 9) but can
claim *family allowance* (see WELFARE RIGHTS 5) as well as exemption from
certain health charges such as prescriptions or dental work. The second
is to help the user to look closely at the interrelationship between
benefits and work. For example, if a person is in full-time work with
child-care responsibilities she may qualify for a TAX CREDIT, but this may
raise difficult issues – such as whether to encourage a person to take up

employment when he or she has caring responsibilities, for example, that would be undercut by that employment. Intangible matters, such as the social contacts outside the home that a job might bring, have to be weighed against the caring responsibilities.

Child Poverty Action Group, *Welfare Benefits Handbook*, London, CPAG, 2000.

income-related benefit SEE MEANS-TESTED BENEFIT.

income support SEE WELFARE RIGHTS 5.

income support and mortgage interest (ISMI) SEE WELFARE RIGHTS 5; WELFARE RIGHTS 6.

incontinence an inability to control bladder or bowels in socially acceptable ways.

Incontinence may result from a wide range of physical, emotional and environmental causes and is a common phenomenon that may be temporary or permanent. Its incidence may be under-estimated because people affected by it are reluctant to seek help because of the STIGMA attached. Many health authorities now employ incontinence advisers, nurses specializing in this area of work who may supply relevant equipment. (See also ENCOPRESIS, ENURESIS.)

indefinite leave to remain the right of a person to remain in the UK without time limit or conditions.

Indefinite leave to remain gives a person the right to work, claim benefits and access social housing and other services. A person with indefinite leave to remain can also bring over members of his or her family for settlement under the normal immigration rules.

independent living a concept developed by disabled people involving the achievement of control over their own lives and the ability to live in settings of their own choosing.

The term 'independent' is often used by professionals in connection with the ability of a disabled person to carry out everyday tasks without assistance from anyone else. Disabled people themselves, however, have emphasized the link between independence and personal autonomy. In order to pursue personal ambitions and aspirations in the same way as non-disabled people, disabled people need to maintain control over their own living arrangements and personal assistance. For most people, this involves moving out of institutional settings and obtaining independent accommodation.

Centres for Independent Living are run by disabled people and offer information and support to those who are seeking more independence. An important factor in the development of independent living has been the opportunity for disabled people to be the employers of their own PERSONAL ASSISTANTS rather than the clients of care organizations. The wider availability of DIRECT PAYMENTS for COMMUNITY CARE services is beginning to make these arrangements more common. Social services departments may make arrangements for direct payments schemes to be run by Centres for Independent Living, which can provide support to disabled people in carrying out their duties as employers.

J. Morris, *Independent Lives: Community Care and Disabled People*, London, Macmillan, 1993.

Independent Living Fund an independent trust set up by central government in 1988 in response to criticism following the abolition of the domestic assistance addition that had been paid with supplementary benefit to give people with severe DISABILITIES financial help to remain living in their own homes.

The fund established its own criteria for awards and generated an unexpected demand for assistance. Criteria were progressively narrowed, but despite this over 20,000 people were receiving help by the time the fund closed in 1993. The wider responsibilities for funding COMMUNITY CARE taken on by local authorities in 1993 cut across the fund. Existing recipients are assured of continued, and if necessary increased, payments under the Independent Living (Extension) Fund. People can get help from the new Independent Living Fund (1993) only if the local authority already provides DOMICILIARY SERVICES valued at £200 per week or more. The 1993 fund, like its predecessor, will give money to purchase personal care and domestic assistance that are necessary for independent living. The applicant must be aged between 16 and 66, receiving disability living allowance with the higher-rate care component (see WELFARE RIGHTS 3) and have capital of less than £8,000.

independent reviewing officer see ADOPTION AND CHILDREN BILL 2002.

independent sector providers of a service from the private, VOLUNTARY and not-for-profit sectors. They are independent of the state, principally of LOCAL AUTHORITIES, although local authorities may purchase services from them.

individual education plan (IEP) an outline of the strategies being employed to ensure that an individual child with SPECIAL EDUCATIONAL NEEDS (SEN) has the appropriate learning.

The plan, the requirements for which are contained in the Department for Education and Skills circular on school exclusions, is normally drawn up by the school's SPECIAL EDUCATIONAL NEEDS COORDINATOR (SENCO). It should include information and targets, the nature of the provision being made available, success and exit criteria, and arrangements for review. All children with identified SEN should have such an individual plan.

individual racism a form of RACISM that occurs when (usually) a white person treats (usually) a black person unfairly because of his or her racial or ethnic origins.

Acts of individual racism appear to their perpetrators to confirm their underlying belief that black people are inferior to white people in relation to culture, intellect, beliefs and lifestyles. This racist ideology was developed by white people in the 17th and 18th centuries and was given credence/legitimacy by pseudo-scientists, historians, literary people, religious and missionary bodies, academics, politicians and workers in the media who supported the belief that physical criteria determine intellectual and other abilities. The core of individual racism consists of people acting as though ideas about 'race' are valid criteria for differentiating among human beings, yet there is wide support for the view that there is no adequate biological basis for believing in 'race' as a legitimate, scientifically proven term. Racism is not, however, simply individual prejudice but rather a reflection of discriminatory structures and institutional practices. The net effect of this is that racism is built into social structures and dominant social institutions. (See ANTIDISCRIMINATORY PRACTICE.)

N. Thompson, *Anti-Discriminatory Practice*, Basingstoke, Macmillan, 1993.

industrial injuries benefits see WELFARE RIGHTS 3.

information in social work, knowledge that may be acquired or transmitted about services and about legal and social work processes.

There is increasing recognition of the importance of good information about a wide range of services and transactions in social welfare organizations. The CHILDREN ACT, for example, requires that SOCIAL SERVICES DEPARTMENTS publicize their services to children in need, and often the relevant information includes details about voluntary provision where the voluntary sector works closely with the statutory services. The NATIONAL HEALTH SERVICE AND COMMUNITY CARE ACT has a requirement that COMMUNITY CARE PLANS are published for public consumption and consultation.

Organizations need an information strategy to inform potential users of all services. The strategy should include an analysis of the most likely points of contact with particular client groups and an appreciation of the forms of communication most suitable to their needs. For example, a leaflet for children might have to be written in a different way from one designed for young people or adults. Similarly, DEAF and BLIND people have very particular needs. Social work processes and clients' and parents' rights could also usefully be described in written or another appropriate form. When, for example, an EMERGENCY PROTECTION ORDER is served, parents need to be able to understand what has happened or, if invited to a CASE CONFERENCE, they need to know what might happen. Similarly, service users or their representatives will benefit from information about sources of help, if they are in dispute with social welfare agencies, or about how to make a complaint. Some agencies have made considerable progress in the development of information services, although others have not. (See also RECORDING.)

information giving the lowest level of participation in which practitioners and service managers inform users and local people about specific services or projects in their area.

Giving information to people is fundamental and a necessary requirement for any service that aspires to have user participation. Clearly, users or local residents need to know specific details of a project or service that is going to affect them in all but the most select instances. If, however, practitioners provide *only* information and seek no opinion or feedback in return, it amounts to a take-it-or-leave-it approach that may produce even more aggressive feedback. Information giving is appropriate if practitioners have no room for manoeuvre with regard to the services they are providing and must follow one course of action or if it is the start of a wider consultation process with the opportunity to participate later.

In providing information to user groups it is important to be familiar with the target audience: what do they already know and what might they expect? Practitioners should make sure that the audience understands the ideas being advanced and the language in which they are expressed. Be clear from the start about the need for providing information alone rather than consultation. The principal means for channelling information to users include leaflets, newsletters, posters and other printed material; presentations at meetings; briefing the media with press releases and conferences; advertising, exhibitions and video.

G. Chanan, *Local Community Involvement: A handbook for good practice,* London, Community Development Foundation, 1999.

initial interview the first attempt by a worker in a welfare agency to assess a potential service user's problems and the appropriateness of the agency's services for this person.

Considerable attention has been given to the issue of who becomes a service user and who does not. One of the important issues here is the quality of first contact with an agency. This first contact is sometimes with reception staff and sometimes with a duty officer. It is clear that the service user must feel some measure of welcome and interest on the part of the agency and, in many circumstances, that the agency can be trusted. With sensitive problems of a personal nature, such trust and confidence have to be established very quickly. Failure in this regard may result in the service user withdrawing from the service even when he or she patently needs it. Features associated with effective initial interviews seem to be clarity of INFORMATION about the agency's services, an inviting atmosphere, and an ability on the part of the worker to listen attentively and to clarify and summarize at intervals the nature of the problems as they emerge from the interview. How the agency can help, perhaps in conjunction with other services, and the service user's willingness to receive the service (where this is optional) need to be determined. (See also REFERRAL.)

B. Compton and B. Galaway, *Social Work Processes,* fourth edition, Belmont, California, Wadsworth, 1989.

injunction a court order that prohibits particular behaviour.

A judge or magistrate may issue an injunction order under the FAMILY LAW REFORM ACT 1996. Orders may prohibit the harassment or molestation of one person by another. An injunction order can be obtained without the respondent being present (EX-PARTE), and it can have the power of arrest attached to it so that if the person concerned ignores it the police will arrest him.

insight a new understanding of the root or origins of a problem or situation.

Insight may be gained when new information comes to light or old information is 'rearranged' to give new significance to familiar aspects. Insight is thought necessary before some problems can be solved or before people are able to 'move on' or make necessary adjustments to their lives. Historically, the idea of insight is strongly associated with PSYCHOANALYSIS, where it has the very specific meaning of discovering the influence of childhood experiences upon adult difficulties. In current usage among social workers and counsellors, the word is employed more loosely to denote an understanding of something and it is seen to apply to both recipients of services and to workers. In this more generic usage of the term, experience of class, race and gender is considered especially important, although other, more personal factors can also be critical.

inspection a process of external examination that is intended to establish whether a service is managed and provided in conformity with expected standards.

Three bodies now have inspection functions for work in the social care and social work field; these are the SOCIAL SERVICES INSPECTORATE (SSI), the AUDIT COMMISSION, and the NATIONAL CARE STANDARDS COMMISSION. Nationally the Social Services Inspectorate is the chief regulatory body in social work. The SSI together with the Audit Commission undertake a programme of joint reviews of social services departments every five years. These major inspections raise major issues about the quality of local social services. Areas of good practice are highlighted as well as areas that need to be improved or developed. In between these five-yearly joint reviews, there are usually three separate inspections by the SSI alone of first, child care services; second, adult care services; and third, an area of service provision of 'high priority'.

The National Care Standards Commission, through its regional offices, requires a wide range of services in the statutory, voluntary and private sectors to register with them. The regional body also has responsibility for the inspection of these services, including care homes, children's homes, domiciliary care agencies, residential family centres, voluntary adoption agencies, independent fostering agencies, private and voluntary hospitals and clinics, exclusively private doctors and nursing agencies. Finally, the regional bodies are also responsible for the welfare aspects of boarding schools and local authority fostering and adoption services. From April 2002 inspection services previously located in local authorities have been disbanded.

instinct an innate, biological mechanism motivating behaviour.

The behaviour of lower animals tends to be dependent on instinct, and this can be seen in the stereotyped behaviours of nest-building, courting and mating rituals, sparring, and the cooperative behaviour of insects living in communities. Human behaviour is less dependent on innate mechanisms because the cortical development of the human brain allows for much learning as the result of experience. There is debate about the extent to which human behaviour is instinctually based (for example, the presence of a 'maternal instinct'). Humans do have biological drives that are necessary for survival, such as eating and drinking, but it is inappropriate to regard any common behaviour as instinctive, for example a competitive instinct, since it is not known if there is a biological basis. Freud regarded instincts as the key motivators of behaviour, nominating sex and aggression as primary. He saw these as complementary: sex, the life instinct, Eros; and aggression, the death instinct, Thanatos. These instincts reside in the id and are unconscious. Eros involves all behaviours leading towards survival, so it is not synonymous with the sex drive, although this is central to it. Eros is creative, in contrast to Thanatos, which is destructive. Behaviours associated with Eros are life-enhancing and pleasure-seeking while Thanatos is associated not only with aggression but with denial, particularly of pleasure, and the negation of development. (See also PSYCHOANALYSIS.)

Social workers within the PSYCHODYNAMIC tradition may find the place of instincts within personality dynamics conceptually useful. The adult personality, according to psychodynamic theory, is the result of the child's experiences in learning to deal with the libido and with aggressive instincts. In general, however, it is important to be cautious about the assumptions of biological determination since this provides only a partial explanation, excuses the person of responsibility and reduces the possibility of change. The human brain allows for profound effects of experience in forming behaviour, not only in the early years but through the LIFE COURSE. Any behaviour, whether problematic or not, is the result of hereditary and environmental factors interacting. For example, it would be unwise to attribute adult aggression solely to an aggressive instinct, to frustrations in childhood or even to the observation of aggressive acts in childhood; there will also be contextual factors involved. (See also NATURE-NURTURE DEBATE, VIOLENCE.)

institutional racism the processes that lead to discrimination against members of particular racial or ethnic groups.

It has long been understood that not only individuals but also institutions can systematically discriminate against members of oppressed and excluded groups. This need not be intentional nor even as a matter of deliberate policy: an institutional practice may simply not take account of ethnic or racial differences sufficiently to prevent discrimination occurring in practice. Thus, it may be institutionally racist to fail to provide appropriate support to someone present when a murder is committed because he is a potential suspect. This is what happened in the case of Duwayne Brooks, who was a CO-VICTIM with Stephen Lawrence, a traumatized witness of a racist attack, but was not treated as such. Police procedures gave priority to trying to obtain evidence and prevent it from being 'contaminated' at the expense of providing support and information to Mr Brooks. For this and other failures of the investigation, the STEPHEN LAWRENCE INQUIRY Report found the Metropolitan Police guilty of institutional racism, incompetence and poor leadership. While there may have been no explicit racist intent on the part of individual officers, the cumulative effect was the same as if they had all been deliberately racist. The report also made it clear that part of the problem was ignorance, prejudice and stereotyping, demonstrating that the line between institutional and intentional racism is a fine one in practice. The indignant police reaction to the report tended to concentrate on the allegation of institutional racism rather than on the evidence provided of ignorance, prejudice and stereotyping.

Institutional racism can be attacked only at a systemic level: removing individual 'bad apples' from the staff of the institution makes no real impact upon it. As such, the failure of criminal justice and social services to provide appropriate professional services to black people has to be addressed at a policy level. The Stephen Lawrence Inquiry Report made recommendations in respect of the treatment of victims and witnesses of crime, and also on police training, the ways in which racist incidents should be defined and recorded, and the enforcement of the law on racial harassment and violence.

During the mid-1990s, social work training was attacked for its emphasis upon antidiscriminatory practice, but this is now becoming a more orthodox approach to professional training. Institutional racism can partly be addressed through staff training, but changes may also be required to complaints procedures, recording processes, the collection of statistics, the evaluation of services, and prosecution or administrative action against racist offenders. Public sector institutions such as the PROBATION and SOCIAL SERVICES and YOUTH OFFENDING TEAMS, as well as the POLICE, have enormous powers that can be used responsibly against perpetrators of racial harassment and violence.

C. Knight and K. Chouhan, 'Supporting victims of racist abuse and violence', in B. Williams (ed.), *Reparation and Victim-Focused Social Work*, London, Jessica Kingsley.

intake team a group of social workers who take on and work with all problems submitted to a social work agency for a limited period of time.

An intake worker might work with a family or individual for up to three months, although in some cases the work may be handed over to specialists much sooner after the intake worker has completed the emergency work. Such workers are normally GENERIC, prepared to work with the full range of problems, but, although they are not specialists, intake workers are usually relatively experienced. Many SOCIAL SERVICES DEPARTMENTS in the 1970s and 1980s had intake teams to handle initial assessments. As specialisms began to reappear (usually divided between children's teams and adult teams), intake teams were often disbanded and replaced by a duty function, sometimes run by a single individual, sometimes on a rota basis, staffed by workers from the specialist teams. Emergency duty teams covering weekends and out-of-office hours are all, in a sense, intake teams.

intellectual impairment a level of intellectual functioning that is more limited than that of the majority of the population and with norms established in medicine and psychology. People with intellectual impairment may experience barriers as the social environment has been constructed without their requirements in mind.

'Intellectual impairment' is often used interchangeably with LEARNING DISABILITY, but, strictly speaking, it has a more limited meaning that is confined to the attributes of individuals. Learning disability, however, indicates the barriers that may arise as a result of the interaction between individual ability and the social environment. The term 'intellectual impairment' does not appear in legislation. Education legislation refers to LEARNING DIFFICULTY (severe or moderate) and social care legislation to learning disability or MENTAL HANDICAP. The Disability Discrimination Act 1995 refers to MENTAL IMPAIRMENT in its list of disabilities. However, mental Impairment includes both learning disability and any recognized mental disorder.

intelligence testing forms of testing that are intended to measure people's cognitive abilities.

The first documented attempts at intelligence testing were made by the French psychologist Alfred Binet, who had been asked by the French government to devise a means of identifying those children who would not be able to cope with standard schooling. Binet assembled a number of tasks, such as digit span (the capacity to memorize a series of numbers), and introduced the term 'mental age' (MA) to refer to the level of performance expected of a child at a given chronological age (CA). Later the intelligence quotient (IQ) was devised, based on the formula: $IQ = MA \div CA \times 100$. Thus, a child of average intelligence should have an IQ of 100.

The practice of intelligence testing has been controversial for a number of reasons. First, theorists have disagreed about what constitutes intelligence and therefore about what should be contained in a test of intelligence. Second, different theorists have come to varying conclusions about whether intelligence is a single ability or a constellation of abilities; those who hold the latter view have argued that a single score, IQ, does not do justice to the complexity of intelligence.

Most tests in use today contain items that assess three abilities: verbal, numerical and spatial. More recently, cognitive psychologists have argued from an information-processing perspective that a test of intelligence should deal with each of the processes involved in reasoning. A further source of controversy has been the use of intelligence testing to compare the intelligence of different 'races'. Related to this is dispute over whether IQ is a measure of potential or of achievement. If the latter is the case, then it must be affected by experience. This has prompted the devising of 'culture-fair' tests that are meant to remove the effects of experience. Intelligence tests have also been devised for use with special groups, such as non-verbal tests for DEAF people and versions of Binet's original test for use with BLIND people. Intelligence testing is sometimes used by employers to select candidates for jobs. This seems appropriate only when the job requires the sort of skills measured by IQ tests, such as computer programming. The most appropriate use of intelligence tests is by clinical and educational psychologists as a diagnostic tool to identify the particular 'weaknesses' in an individual's reasoning.

S. J. Gould, *The Mismeasure of Man*, London, Penguin, 1981.

intentionally homeless describes people identified by a local authority as having made themselves HOMELESS by virtue of unacceptable behaviour or by giving up accommodation that might reasonably have been kept.

If a local authority has decided that an applicant for public housing is intentionally homeless, it is not required to offer that person permanent housing, although in some circumstances (if the person is in priority need) temporary accommodation may be offered. The usual criteria applied by councils in such decisions include substantial rent arrears, antisocial conduct, including criminal activity and the misuse of property. They may also decide that a person is intentionally homeless if they believe that the person has left the property without sufficient cause, as in the case of a woman who is not experiencing domestic violence. There are often major differences between housing authorities in their interpretations of the criteria and in their willingness to use the appropriate legislation. The social worker's and housing advice worker's task is often to challenge a local authority's decision and the alleged evidence upon which such a decision has been made. Since evidence from a tenant's past behaviour, often over many years, may be cited, the task of helping such tenants can be complex.

inter-country adoption the adoption of a child born and raised in one country by adoptive parents in another country.

Inter-country adoptions raise a number of issues concerning different safeguards in the adoption procedure, removing a child from his or her home culture and surroundings and the sometimes huge disparity of income between birth family and adoptive family. In inter-country adoption the children to be adopted frequently come from poor families in developing countries while the adoptive parents reside in the United

Kingdom. The disparity of personal incomes undoubtedly is a factor in the relative ease with which, until recently, would-be adopters from the UK could find and bring back with them infants from developing countries. The 'adoption' of twins who were in effect purchased over the internet from an African-American mother by a UK couple brought some of these issues into the open. The Adoption Inter-Country Aspects Act of 1999 now makes it illegal for any UK resident to bring a child into the country for adoption without first being assessed to the same standard and approved to adopt in the UK. The Hague Convention on inter-country adoption, in the process of being ratified in the UK, ensures that all inter-country adoptions are made through government-approved ADOPTION AGENCIES. It stipulates that children should be adopted by families outside their countries of origin only when there is no opportunity for those children to enjoy life in their own countries.

P. Selman, *Intercountry Adoption*, London, British Agencies for Adoption and Fostering, 2000.

interim arrangements arrangements for the continued support of ASYLUM SEEKERS by LOCAL AUTHORITIES that supported them prior to the Immigration and Asylum Act 1999, which was enacted between April and August 2000.

These asylum seekers were supported by the local authorities as a last resort because they were left destitute by the Immigration and Asylum Act 1996. The Immigration and Asylum Act 1996 removed entitlement to benefit for asylum seekers who did not apply at their 'port of entry' to the UK. It also denied them access to social housing.

After the 1996 Act, asylum seekers used the courts to establish that local authorities had duties to accommodate and support single adult asylum seekers who were destitute under the NATIONAL ASSISTANCE ACT 1948 and families with children under the CHILDREN ACT 1989. SOCIAL SERVICES DEPARTMENTS across the UK had to establish arrangements that were eventually financed under a central government grant regime. These arrangements became the 'interim arrangements' when the 1999 Act was enacted. This Act explicitly removed the duty to support asylum seekers under the National Assistance Act 1948 but established these interim arrangements, which emulated the prior arrangements. It was envisaged that the NATIONAL ASYLUM SUPPORT SERVICE would quickly take direct responsibility for these cases under the 1999 Act, but this has not happened so thousands of asylum seekers are still supported by social services departments.

interim order an order made under the CHILDREN ACT for a limited duration. A court may make interim orders in respect of care, supervision, residence or contact. When hearing an application for any of these orders, it may decide to adjourn the proceedings. To make an interim care or supervision order, the court must be satisfied that there are reasonable grounds for believing that the child in question is suffering or likely to suffer SIGNIFICANT HARM. This is a less stringent test than for a full care or supervision order, which requires the court to be satisfied that the child is actually suffering or likely to suffer significant harm. The making of an interim order should not prejudice a final hearing on the full order, as the situation may have changed considerably following a further period of ASSESSMENT and social work intervention. Interim orders when first made can last up to eight weeks and thereafter up to periods of four weeks.

The whole aim of interim orders is to provide further flexibility to the court in settling the outcomes of care or supervision proceedings. They provide a short-term legal intervention into a family's life if the situation warrants it. The powers given the local authority are the same as under a full order but they are of limited duration. The court determines how long the order is to last and may give directions to the local authority to carry out a medical or psychiatric examination or other ASSESSMENT with the child's consent. In the main, interim orders are used to follow a period of emergency protection for a child, particularly if the authority has not yet completed inquiries. If the authority thinks that direct supervision of the child and parents is required for a short time but that it does not need to obtain PARENTAL RESPONSIBILITY, then an interim supervision order is sufficient. If the authority concludes that it must remove the child and acquire parental responsibility for a limited period of time, then it will ask for an interim care order. Interim orders are commonly used during the course of care proceedings, which average between six and 12 months from initial application to final hearing.

Department of Health, *The Children Act 1989 Guidance and Regulations Vol. 1 Court Order*, London, HMSO, 1991.

internal market arrangements for different units inside large public service organizations to buy and sell services from each other.

Throughout the 1980s the Conservative government reorganized many public services so that parts of, say, the National Health Service took on the sole function of buying services from other parts of the same organization. The intention was to set up MARKET-like transactions inside the organization itself, whereby separate units buy and sell the service in question on behalf of clients or other members of the public. The aim of the reform was to compel the public services, such as local authorities and the health service, to behave as if they had to deal with market conditions. This, it was argued, would encourage them to be more responsive to the public and to provide services with greater efficiency, which are the chief characteristics of any market. These large public service organizations were in particular need of such reforms, since they had previously provided their service under monopoly conditions and grown complacent and bureaucratic as a result.

In one form or other, internal markets have been introduced into education, with the introduction of local management of schools, into local authority services, such as refuse collection, by means of compulsory competitive tendering (see BEST VALUE), and into the health service by establishing NHS hospital trusts and fund-holding general practitioners. Purchaser/provider units within COMMUNITY CARE services are a form of internal market arrangement that has affected social services agencies considerably. In each case, the aim of the policy was to achieve greater efficiency and responsiveness of the service by introducing a sense of competition and the discipline of cost control.

The proponents of internal markets hoped that they would provide a third way between forcing public service organizations into open, external markets and the old style of central control and monopoly provision. Critics argue that the introduction of internal markets so far shows little prospect of making a difference, particularly in the health service. This is because the arrangements protect purchaser monopolies, have increased administrative work and in the end still produce a heavily rationed and unappealing service.

J. Le Grand and W. Bartlett (eds), *Quasi-Markets and Social Policy*, Basingstoke, Macmillan, 1993.

intersectionality the term that covers the interlinking of different sources of identity stemming from 'RACE', GENDER, SEXUALITY and DISABILITY.

'Identity politics' promoted the claims that individual authenticity stemmed from social sources and social groups defined by the new social movements such as black consciousness, feminism, gay and disability groups. The social characteristics of an individual – whether male or female, gay or straight, disabled or able-bodied, black or white – powerfully shape that individual's perspective, primarily through the advantages or disadvantages they bring with them. In the 1980s, for example, black women were defined as suffering from the 'triple oppression' of 'race', class and gender. This framework of analysis, however, came to be seen as inadequate both theoretically and politically. Partly this was because it is conceptually difficult to rank a hierarchy of oppressions and partly because, increasingly, such notions were used in an 'essentialist' way – social characteristics seemed to trump whatever other qualities of identity an individual had. The concept of 'intersectionality' developed within black feminism in order to move beyond this difficulty and to highlight the ways in which 'race', gender, class and so on are interrelated and interdependent. This paradigm shift has resulted in an increased awareness of the need to deconstruct seemingly fixed categories of identity and called for a more fluid understanding of subjectivity and power.

R. Aziz, 'Feminism and the challenge of racism: Deviance or Difference?' in H. Mirza (ed), *Black British Feminism*, London, Routledge, 1997.

intervention a general term suggesting, in social work, a step or plan with a purpose initiated by a social worker or other welfare worker with or on behalf of a service user. The recipient of intervention might be an individual, a couple, a family or a wider group.

The term came into vogue in the 1970s, replacing the concept of 'treatment', which had strong associations with the MEDICAL MODEL. Although the word 'intervention' is still used, it has tended to be replaced by other terms that are specific to particular social work transactions, such as CARE PLAN and INITIAL INTERVIEW.

interview in social work, a purposeful exchange, usually face to face, between a social welfare worker and a service user or potential service user.

In some circumstances, interviews may take place on the telephone or via a video link. It is useful to distinguish between a planned interview with a known person and an INITIAL INTERVIEW with an unknown person. Interviews may have an information-gathering, decision-making or therapeutic focus. The interviewer has the prime responsibility for ensuring that sufficient time and attention are given to the service user so that the purpose of the interview is achieved. LISTENING and COMMUNICATION skills are crucial to success. For initial interviews, open-ended questions (for example, 'How do you think we may be able to help you?') are especially useful, both in information gathering and in determining the nature of the problems. Closed questions (for example, 'How long have you been married?') help to gather information and narrow the focus of discussion. Interviews often begin with open and broad-based questions, moving on to more closed or focused questions as particular problems and concerns are identified. Planned interviews with known service users can sometimes proceed in the same way, but it may be that an interview schedule has been prepared to some purpose. For example, a juvenile justice worker might be trying to understand why a teenager offends. Thus the interview will be focused on offence behaviour, and such an interview could entail specific questions about the circumstances in which offences are committed.

Increasingly with very important set pieces, such as initial investigations in child protection work, or the assessment of children and their families when ABUSE is known to have taken place, formal interview schedules are habitually used, ensuring that the crucial questions are covered systematically. The Department of Health's assessment guide to protecting children is one example of such a schedule. Other sensitive areas, such as the interviewing of children thought to have been sexually abused, which is to be recorded on video, or techniques in family therapy, require specialized training. (See also JOINT INTERVIEW.)

A. Kadushin and G. Kadushin, *The Social Work Interview*, New York, Columbia University Press, fourth edition, 1999.

investigative interviewing an INTERVIEW conducted with a child as part of an inquiry following concerns that a child may have been abused.

The term denotes that interviews with children are to be approached with an open mind in accordance with the three possible situations that the child faces:

1 the ABUSE has occurred and the child is speaking of it;

2 the abuse has occurred and the child is unable to speak of it or is denying it;

3 the abuse has not occurred and the child cannot speak of it.

Investigative interviews are generally jointly conducted by a police officer and a social worker specifically trained in interview techniques in accordance with the *Memorandum of Good Practice*, the voluntary code of practice on interviewing children issued by the HOME OFFICE and DEPARTMENT OF HEALTH in 1992. The interviews do not have to be recorded on videotape. If a criminal prosecution of an adult for an offence against the child is a possibility, however, a video recording is usually made unless the child is unhappy about being recorded. Further, the CLEVELAND INQUIRY recommended that children should not be subject to repeated interviews nor to probing confrontational DISCLOSURE interviews, as they are potentially damaging and represent a form of abuse themselves. Current practice interprets this as meaning preferably one interview, or at most two. Investigative interviews are particularly significant in cases of alleged SEXUAL ABUSE because forensic evidence of assault is often ambiguous or absent. In cases of PHYSICAL ABUSE there is usually an injury present that is open to forensic analysis and thus makes the testimony of the child less crucial.

The process of investigative interviewing is problematic because of the difficulty of balancing a child-centred approach to communicating with children with a need to satisfy evidential requirements if the child is to be legally protected or a successful prosecution is to be mounted. Theoretically the burden of proof is less in CIVIL PROCEEDINGS than in criminal proceedings. In practice, civil courts have applied a rigorous burden of proof when concerned with allegation of child sexual abuse, and the way the child's testimony is obtained is subject to close scrutiny. This approach is unlikely to change unless or until the Department of Health issues guidance on interviewing specifically designed to take account of the requirements of civil proceedings. Current guidance focuses on the requirements of criminal proceedings.

Home Office and Department of Health, *Memorandum of Good Practice*, London, HMSO, 1992.

involuntary client a person who is compelled to be a recipient of a social work or medical service.

Typically people become involuntary clients as a result of a court order (for example, a COMMUNITY REHABILITATION ORDER or CARE ORDER) or if they have been found guilty of particular offences or have been compulsorily hospitalized under mental health legislation. Although in some situations service users appear to lose all or most of their rights to SELF-DETERMINATION (such as under compulsory treatment in a hospital), in many circumstances they may well have some rights or some say in decisions. People on community rehabilitation orders, for example, have to agree to the arrangements. It may be argued that this is no freedom to choose when the alternative is prison, although some do prefer the custodial sentence. For those compelled to be treated in a mental hospital, the element of compulsion is removed as soon as the service user is thought responsible for his or her actions.

A core objective of good practice is to work with people in a manner that respects their person and rights and promotes self-determination and EMPOWERMENT. Where compulsion is seen to be necessary these principles do not have to be abandoned. Self-determination, for example, is not a concept without limits, for one person's actions may infringe another person's liberty. Thus, to work in partnership with an involuntary service user may be an elusive aspiration, but it should be pursued nevertheless. To consult at every stage in the work with such people, and to provide them with good-quality INFORMATION and independent help in the form of, say, advocates, are important sources of empowerment for the involuntary service user that may counterbalance the unbridled power of the professional.

Jj

Jobcentre Plus an executive agency of the DEPARTMENT FOR WORK AND PENSIONS (DWP), created from the merger of the BENEFITS AGENCY and the Employment Service to administer social security benefits and tax credits to people of working age.

Jobcentre Plus started as a pilot scheme in 17 areas offering an integrated work and benefit services and since April 2002 is being phased in nationally. The DWP anticipates that it will take several years to integrate the entire local office network of Jobcentres and Benefits Agency offices fully. During this time, services will continue to be provided in local social security offices and Jobcentres.

jobseeker's allowance (JSA) see WELFARE RIGHTS 9.

joined-up action the concept of a more integrated approach to the planning and delivery of services across government.

British government has traditionally been characterized by 'departmentalism', whereby each government department pursues its area of activity with only limited reference to the work of other departments. Ministers are seen as defenders of their departmental interests, and this has led to problems in coordinating policies across government. Similar problems exist at other levels of government and service delivery, with the area of health and social care being seen as particularly problematic. The needs of a range of user groups, such as older people and people with disabilities, cross the boundary between the NHS and social services. This organizational separation is complicated by the existence of different models of need, often identified as the social model versus the medical (or individual) model in which social workers and health care workers view the cause of problems faced by individuals with needs differently.

This complex range of barriers to effective care has been identified by government as in need of resolution, and joined-up action is one proposed solution. The approach is centred on the idea that different government departments and levels of government should work together. The aim is to provide coordinated action to tackle the needs of communities and individuals where those needs cut across organizational barriers. The identification of lead agencies, such as PRIMARY CARE TRUSTS, is seen as a way in which such problems of coordination can be overcome. These are long-standing problems, however, and the concept of joined-up action faces significant barriers to successful implementation.

joint finance health authority funding for COMMUNITY CARE projects developed with SOCIAL SERVICES DEPARTMENTS.

Established in 1976, the purpose of joint finance resources is to act as a source of 'pump priming' for new schemes in the community. These are mainly schemes managed by local authority social services departments but may be run by the health authority or the voluntary sector. A number of problems have been encountered by joint finance as funding periods have come to an end. As the Audit Commission noted in 1986, at the end of the joint funding, responsibility transfers to the main agency, and local authorities have become increasingly reluctant to accept long-term commitments implied by such funding. With the pressure local authorities felt on their finances, they sometimes saw joint funding as a way for health authorities to pass on expensive responsibilities. However, while the government recognized some of the difficulties encountered in the area of joint finance, the 1989 white paper *Caring for People* reinforced central government commitment to its continuation as an important way in which resources could be transferred from the health authorities to social services departments.

Audit Commission, *Making a Reality of Community Care*, London, HMSO, 1986. Department of Health, *Caring for People*, London, HMSO, 1989.

joint interview a formal meeting with one or more service users, conducted by two social welfare or justice workers.

Joint INTERVIEWS may achieve greater effectiveness than single-worker interviews. This may be the case in FAMILY MEDIATION work, so that each of the two workers may focus on a different parent, for example, to avoid the accusation of bias, and also to enhance the process through the two workers being able to compare notes. FAMILY THERAPY can also benefit from the joint approach. In addition, such interviews are increasingly used in initial child protection interviews, which are invariably conducted by the police, together with a social worker. The police are concerned to know whether a crime has been committed, the social worker whether a child needs protection. Where workers are threatened with VIOLENCE or AGGRESSION, joint working has clear merits.

joint planning a statutory obligation placed on local authorities and health authorities to collaborate in planning care provision for their areas.

Local authorities and health authorities have had a statutory duty to plan service provision together since 1974. The National Health Service Act 1977 expanded on this by recommending that joint planning take place at all levels within the service planning process. However, there has been frequent criticism of the operation of such planning systems. The Audit Commission noted in *Making a Reality of Community Care* (1986) that joint planning arrangements were often too complex, largely because of the number of agencies involved. Given the geographical coverage of some local authorities and health authorities, joint planning meetings could involve both regional and district health authorities as well as county and district local authorities. The number of agencies was often well into double figures, resulting in a complex series of meetings; in one case, the director of social services of one of the largest shire counties estimated that his staff had to attend 2,000 such meetings a year. With the white paper *Caring for People* (1989), the government stated its intention to emphasize joint planning agreements as a more flexible approach to try to overcome the problems experienced. However, there is still a recognized need for local authorities and health authorities to work closely together in the development of services for client groups.

JSA abbreviation for jobseeker's allowance (see WELFARE RIGHTS 9).

judicial review legal review of the legitimacy and propriety of government actions.

This is a process that involves the senior judiciary in reviewing the actions of the executive, i.e. the major government departments or other public bodies such as local government or universities, to identify whether they have exceeded the powers granted them by parliament. This involves the concept of *ultra vires*, in which the courts examine the actions of government and the statutes under a number of headings. O'Donnell (see below) has noted the idea of substantive *ultra vires*, in which actions exceed the powers given by statute, actions abuse the powers given, powers are delegated when no authority is given to do so, delegated powers are used 'unreasonably' and when a duty in law is not performed. A further form of *ultra vires* is when procedures that are mandatory are not complied with. The role of the judiciary is to examine the cases to identify whether any of these features exist within a specific action of the state. A further feature of such reviews is the role played by the concept of natural justice whereby the executive may be deemed to have infringed natural justice by acting in a biased way or having refused an individual the right to be heard.

A. O'Donnell in R. Pyper *Aspects of Accountability in the British System*, Eastham, Tudor Business Publishing, 1996.

just deserts the theory of sentencing which holds that offenders should be punished in proportion to the seriousness of their offences.

The 'justice model' of sentencing theory argues that the offender's welfare or public policy considerations, such as exemplary sentencing and deterrence, are irrelevant to individual sentencing decisions: the offender should be dealt with according to the seriousness of the current offence. While this is logical and can have a restraining influence upon political interference in sentencing, it fails to take account of legitimate considerations such as the social causes of crime. It has tended, in recent years, to go hand in hand with punitive 'law and order' approaches to sentencing policy.

justice a term that is indefinable without answering the questions 'justice for whom?' and 'justice within what context?' In the context of criminal law and legal proceedings, the simplest definition might be 'the fair treatment of offenders and victims by people given the power and authority to punish'.

Such a definition of justice recognizes the existence of power relationships, but the phrase 'fair treatment' requires further analysis. It has been argued that offenders have a strong sense of justice insofar as they expect 'fair treatment' to be based on the following principles: cognisance – that is, efforts have been made to establish guilt; consistency – people of the same status committing the same offences should be treated the same; competence – those who pass judgement should be able to justify their right to do so; commensurability – punishment should fit the magnitude of the crime; and comparison – differences in treatment between offenders of different status should be reasonable and tenable.

Sociologically, there are three broad perspectives on 'criminal justice'. A conservative or traditional approach would argue that the British criminal justice system comes close to dispensing justice most of the time. Our system of law and due process is regarded as rational, sophisticated and effective, giving appropriate weight to different PRINCIPLES OF SENTENCING and taking account of a wide variety of relevant information about the offence, the offender and, where appropriate, the victim. It is inevitable that mistakes are made from time to time, but there are sufficient checks and balances in the system to ensure that mistakes are remedied, and serious miscarriages of justice are, therefore, rare. A liberal approach would argue that the widespread existence of discretion in the system means that justice cannot be guaranteed and has to be negotiated. Achieving the ideal of justice requires individuals to interact or 'play parts' in the 'drama' of criminal proceedings. Decisions may be unduly influenced by non-rational, non-legal variables, such as discrepancies of age, class, race or gender, and between the offender and criminal justice personnel (see ANTIDISCRIMINATORY PRACTICE). To achieve justice, the use of discretion must be monitored and constrained, and criminal justice personnel must be held more visibly accountable for their decisions. A radical approach would argue that what we choose to call 'justice' is no more and no less than the product of a system designed by those in power to maintain their position. 'Justice' is a rhetoric that persuades the majority of people that the criminal justice system exists for their benefit while criminalizing the poorest and most vulnerable groups in society. From this perspective, there will never be true criminal justice without the achievement of broader social justice, which itself is dependent on reducing structural inequalities in society.

D. Matza, *Delinquency and Drift*, New York, Wiley, 1964.
justice of the peace see MAGISTRATE.
juvenile justice see YOUTH JUSTICE.

K*k*

key worker a named worker responsible for co-ordinating service arrangements for a person using residential or day-care services and who usually forms an important relationship with that person.

Originally the key worker was a named worker to whom a child in residential care could turn to discuss his or her plans and problems. Now the role includes acting as a focal point for the coordination and communication about a particular social work case. The key worker should be a competent professional known to others participating in the case and should have skills in communicating and working with other identified professional workers. The key worker, especially in CHILD PROTECTION cases, has an important role and responsibilities and is perceived by professionals in other agencies as the key person who ought to have a grip on the issues and be pursuing them actively and effectively. The key worker advises all professionals involved in the case on the methods and processes of inter-agency contact, records promptly, files all written communications and disseminates information to the relevant professionals. Additionally, the key worker keeps under review the involvement of other agencies and actively seeks information from other professionals.

L*l*

labelling (and labelling theory) the process whereby people holding positions of power or influence sometimes attribute generalized negative characteristics to particular categories of individuals, tending to produce or amplify the characteristics attributed.

Influential groups who may label include the police, judges, the communication media and social workers. As the outcome of such a labelling process, the individuals or categories of people labelled (for example, as 'drug addicts' or 'the mentally ill') tend to live up to the negative label, thus tending to confirm, reinforce or amplify the behaviour that led to the initial label. In these circumstances, it may become difficult for a person to counteract or ever escape the implications of the application of a label (see STIGMA). The people or categories of people so labelled may acquire what sociologists refer to as a 'deviant identity'. DEVIANCE has been famously described as not a quality of the act that a person commits but rather a consequence of the application by other people of rules and sanctions.

At one level, the insight of sociologists with regard to labelling may appear relatively trite, seeming to assert little more than such commonplace or folk conceptions as 'Give a dog a bad name and it will tend to live up to its reputation.' Guided by the theoretical approach in sociology known as symbolic interactionism, however, labelling theory directs systematic attention to several features of human social behaviour:

1 the way our behaviour is highly influenced by the social expectations that others have of us;

2 that, far from always successfully explaining deviant behaviour, some forms of 'scientific' (or positivistic) social science (such as would-be genetic explanations of criminal behaviour) can operate as part of the labelling process;

3 the widespread operation of 'labels' and labelling in modern societies, in which both individuals and agencies often operate on the basis of stereotypical conceptions of particular categories or groups of people (see STEREOTYPE);

4 that individuals can become caught up in an escalating process initiated by labelling that leads to an increasing exclusion from conventional social intercourse or even incarceration;

5 that institutional labellers, including social workers, and labelling state agencies, such as social work, possess considerable power to attach labels that can radically influence the lives of others.

Labelling theory can be seen as part of a distinctive social-interactionist approach to social problems. Criticisms can be directed at labelling theory: for example, that it sometimes overstates the effects of labelling while ignoring the intrinsic features of some deviant behaviour. Nevertheless, an awareness of labelling theory and the widespread operation of labelling processes is useful to social workers, first because many clients of social work can be seen as adversely affected by the application of social labels, and second because social workers must be aware of how they themselves operate as labellers. A concern to offset the more negative effects of labelling processes can be seen as central to the orientation of much modern social welfare practice, with its aim of limiting discriminatory practices both within social work and in wider society.

H. S. Becker, *Outsiders: Studies in the Sociology of Deviance*, Glencoe, Illinois, Free Press, 1963.

leading question a form of question that either suggests a required answer or is based on alleged facts that have not yet been proved. Rules of evidence do not permit information gained from leading questions to be placed before courts. The Memorandum of Good Practice provides advice to those conducting INVESTIGATIVE INTERVIEWS on how to avoid leading questions.

learned helplessness the inability of a person to act in situations in which he or she has learned previously that he or she will have no control over the outcome.

Learned helplessness has three components: an environment in which some important outcome is beyond a person's control; the already learned response of giving up; and the person's expectation that no voluntary action of his or her own can control the outcome. Learned helplessness has been implicated as a contributory factor to DEPRESSION, since one aspect of depression is the giving up of attempts to control one's own life.

M. E. P. Seligman, *Helplessness, Development, Depression and Death*, New York, W. H. Freeman, second edition, 1992.

learning difficulty a term indicating INTELLECTUAL IMPAIRMENT; this has now been replaced by LEARNING DISABILITY as the term approved by government.

The term 'learning difficulty' replaced MENTAL HANDICAP as a way of referring to people with intellectual impairments. Criticism of learning difficulty focused on the fact that there can be many reasons for difficulty with learning, not all of which result from intellectual impairment. It is still used in education, however, as part of current definitions of SPECIAL

EDUCATIONAL NEEDS. In social work and social care, the officially approved term is now LEARNING DISABILITY, but many self-advocates prefer 'learning difficulty' to this. As a result, the term is still used in some publications to which they have contributed. There have also been arguments from some social scientists that the term 'difficulty' better promotes a focus on the interaction between the individual and the social environment.

C. Goodey, 'Learning disabilities', in S. Hood, B. Mayall and S. Oliver (eds), *Critical Issues in Social Research: Power and Prejudice*, Buckingham, Open University Press, 1999.

learning disability a level of intellectual functioning that is more limited than that of most people in the general population. The government now urges professionals to give priority to capacity for communication and independent social functioning over the level of a person's IQ in determining the need for learning disability services.

The recent white paper on learning disability, 'Valuing People' (2001), defines learning disability as 'a significantly reduced ability to understand new or complex information, to learn new skills (impaired intelligence), with a reduced ability to cope independently (impaired social functioning), which started before adulthood, with a lasting effect on development'. Traditionally, social services departments have focused on people with an IQ of below 70 for the allocation of learning disability services. The white paper suggests that level of social functioning should be a more important criterion.

It is estimated that 210,000 people in England have severe learning disability, including 65,000 children. About 1.2 million people have mild/moderate learning disability; this amounts to about 25 out of every 1,000 people in the general population. Severe learning disability is fairly uniformly distributed around geographical areas and social groups, but there is a link between poverty and mild to moderate learning disability. Relatively few people with learning disability now live in large institutions. Most are either with their own families or in small residential homes and supported housing projects. Although this appears to be more inclusive, in reality most have limited access to mainstream social life. Many adults with learning disability are users of day services, being poorly represented in the labour force. Access to education and leisure is also limited.

The exclusion of people with learning disability was associated with the segregation of groups perceived as non-productive in the late 19th century. The introduction of mass education also made the intellectual limitation of some children more visible than it had formerly been. Systems of medical classification were developed for these children, and these became stigmatizing labels that diverted attention from any potential for learning. The Mental Deficiency Act 1913 reinforced these trends and created an entirely separate set of services based on institutional care. The environment in the large hospitals was very poor and was associated with institutionalization. In some cases, there was proven abuse of patients.

The move towards deinstitutionalization for people with learning disability has been influenced by a number of factors, but the philosophies that have had the greatest impact on professionals are those of NORMALIZATION and SOCIAL ROLE VALORIZATION (SRV). These have emphasized that people with learning disability should be able to live in the community and enjoy the roles and styles of living that are valued in society generally. A criticism of these approaches is that they fail to challenge the attitudes and practices of other people towards people with learning disability, as they accept uncritically that service users should adopt prevailing norms of behaviour in order to be accepted. There have also been challenges to normalization on the basis that it does nothing to expand the range of social acceptability or to ensure that services meet needs in terms of gender, ethnicity and sexual orientation. Normalization has been introduced by service providers rather than struggled for by service users. However, the principles of community presence, community participation, choice competence and respect, which are associated with normalization, have influenced the more progressive service settings to support people in making choices, gaining skills and taking part in community life. This often involves using mainstream education and leisure facilities rather than spending all the time in a segregated day centre.

Rather than providing a standard service for groups of people with learning disability, there is now individual planning. The system of Individual Programme Planning (IPP) involves regular reviews of progress towards goals and involves the service user and any professionals involved with her or him. In practice, however, this has had a strong emphasis on assessing individual competence, and many people with learning disability have found it difficult to put across their views and aspirations sufficiently assertively. PERSON-CENTRED PLANNING is intended to increase the contribution of service users and has been promoted in the white paper 'Valuing People'(2001). In order to achieve this, people with learning disability will require support in preparing for meetings, and also access to ADVOCACY and SELF-ADVOCACY in the assessment and planning processes. Citizen advocacy offers the opportunity to have an independent person to speak on behalf of those who cannot do this for themselves. Self-advocacy simply means a person speaking up on his or her own behalf. This can be on an individual basis, but the development of self-advocacy groups to take up common issues has been a strong feature in learning disability services.

Current policy stresses the principles of: rights, independence, choice and inclusion. The government has identified a range of problems with the existing system, including: the poor coordination of children's services and transition planning; lack of involvement, choice and control for service users; the neglect of health, housing and employment needs of people with learning disability; lack of attention to the needs of ethnic minorities, and poor interagency coordination. In order to tackle these, it is planned to increase access to advocacy, DIRECT PAYMENTS, and person-centred planning, to set up local learning disability partnerships with service user representation to plan and coordinate local services, to modernize day services, and to increase the support available to particular groups. These are people from minority ethnic groups, children with severe disabilities and adults living with informal carers aged over 70.

learning theory a cluster of theoretical explanations that seek to explain how experience at a particular point in development affects subsequent behavioural and mental activities. Learning theory embodies such perspectives as BEHAVIOURISM, cognitive views of conditioning, observational and ecological explanation.

leaving care the process whereby young people move from the care of a local authority into independent living. Increasingly this is a planned process that provides support mechanisms to ensure that young people leaving care are enabled to succeed during the transition into independent adulthood.

Department of Health figures reveal that at March 2001 58,900 young people were being LOOKED AFTER in England. In respect of care leavers during 2000–01, 6,500 young people left care aged 16 or older. The figures suggest a slight rise in the number of care leavers aged over 18, with the numbers leaving at 16 or 17 continuing to fall.

There has been growing concern over the outcomes for looked-after young people leaving care. These concerns include educational qualifications, emotional and psychological concerns, social skills, health issues including substance misuse, the number of young females leaving care who are either pregnant or who have children. Also recognized are the unmet needs of minority ethnic groups where the cultural needs of these young people are currently not addressed.

DoH figures also reveal the extent to which the local authority as corporate parent has failed the educational needs of young people in public care. In 2000–01 just over a third (37 per cent) of the 6,500 young people leaving care had obtained one or more GCSEs – though this is an increase on the previous year of 30 per cent. Care leavers with five or more GCSEs rose by 1 per cent from the previous year to 5 per cent (300 young people). Of 150 local authorities, only 30 reported that they had met the government's target of 50 per cent of their care leavers obtaining one or more GCSEs.

Under the 1989 Children Act an attempt was made to address the difficulties faced by care leavers, including befriending and promotion of welfare. Following the DoH report 'Me Survive Out there?' in 1999, new legislation, the CHILDREN (LEAVING CARE) ACT 2000, places the needs of looked-after care leavers at centre stage and improves the life chances of young people in care.

legal aid see COMMUNITY LEGAL SERVICE; CRIMINAL DEFENCE SERVICE.

lesbian a term used to define same-sex desire between women, partly used as a form of categorization of sexual preference and as a political label for a positive affirmation of personal identification. Female same-sex desire has been present in all societies and cultures throughout time, although in many different societies it has largely been ignored because of the patriarchal structure of social life. In the early 1990s, the mainstream media 'discovered' lesbians, and 'lesbian chic' or 'lipstick lesbians' emerged as an alternative to previous stereotypes about lesbian identities. (See also HOMOSEXUALITY.)

Lesbians and Gay Men in Probation a national support group for lesbian and gay probation officers. The group's primary purposes are to provide personal assistance to individual officers and to promote ANTI-DISCRIMINATORY PRACTICE in relation to lesbian and gay people caught up in the criminal justice system.

The group organizes training events and provides advice and counselling services, and it acts as a pressure group both within the PROBATION SERVICE and more broadly within the justice system.

LETS abbreviation for LOCAL EXCHANGE AND TRADING SCHEME.

liability order an order made by a MAGISTRATE's court confirming an individual's liability to pay council tax. It allows a local authority to use an attachment of earnings or bailiffs to collect sums owed.

libido energy arising from sexual drives that can be directed into other activities, such as artistic creativity. The term is often interpreted as meaning 'life energy' and is a key concept in PSYCHOANALYSIS.

life course the process of personal change, from infancy through to old age and death, brought about as a result of the interaction between personal and social events.

Growing interest in exploring and defining the concept of life course in recent years has been from two broad perspectives: first, the biological, which emphasizes stages in psychosocial development, the common process underlying the human life course (in this usage often referred to as the *life cycle*); second, the experiential, which emphasizes the importance of unique experience and significant life events, that is, the contrasts between lives rather than their similarities. While the biological model provides a framework, each individual life course is unique; individuals have the power to make choices, and each constructs his or her own biography within broad biological and social constraints.

Acknowledging the importance of both age and experiences when considering an individual's current concerns, a model has been proposed that describes the adult developmental process, not tied to age stages or to typical life experiences but distinguishing concerns. It describes the establishment of self-identity, the establishment of relationships, the extension of community interests, the maintenance of position, disengagement and the recognition of increasing dependency. While this may be seen as a life course process, individuals may pass in and out of these areas of major concern, become stuck in one, cope well or badly, and experience crises and development as a result of the interactions within them. Social workers and educators particularly may find this and other models of the life course useful in interpreting reactions to crises at transition points, problems of adjustment, and failures of communication between family members, and in assisting individuals to gain insight, use their experiences developmentally and improve their social relationships.

life sentence an indeterminate period of imprisonment given for serious offences that replaced the death penalty when it was abolished in Britain in 1965.

A life sentence is mandatory (compulsory) for the offence of murder and discretionary (one of a range of available options) for a number of other serious offences such as manslaughter, rape, arson and kidnapping. When giving a life sentence, judges are also required to state the tariff, which is the minimum period to be served in custody in order to satisfy the requirements of retribution and deterrence. This can be as short as two years and as long as the offender's 'natural life'. In the case of mandatory life-sentenced prisoners ('lifers'), the tariff period can be overruled by the Home Secretary. Once the tariff date is reached, prisoners are subject to periodic inter-agency reviews that assess the prospects for their release, based upon stated criteria such as their behaviour in prison, the risk to the public, and the extent to which they have shown remorse. The Parole Board then makes a recommendation for release in appropriate cases, but in the case of mandatory lifers the Home Secretary is not bound to follow this advice.

The number of life-sentenced prisoners has increased enormously, from 140 in 1957 to over 4,000, and this presents management problems for prisons. At one time lifers were subject to a special regime, but this is now more difficult to put into practice. Judges have recently become more ready to give discretionary life sentences for offences such as rape than in the past. There is also pro-vision for 'automatic' life sentences for offenders convicted of a second offence of certain crimes, such as robbery, under the Crime (Sentences) Act 1997, which may further increase the lifer population substantially unless interpreted very restrictively by the courts.

life-story book an account of a child's life, put together in terms and in media that can be clearly understood by the child. Such a document might contain written material, photographs, pictures, letters and even audio or video material.

The central purpose of a life-story book is to give shape to a child's past so that the child has a sense of his or own roots and an understanding of what has happened to him or her. Such documents are thought to be critical in helping a child to form and hold on to an identity. Life-story books have been found to be extremely helpful to children who have experienced many, and often distressing, changes in their lives. Any trusted adult may be able to help a child to construct his or her own life-story book. Social workers, foster parents or a 'significant other' could all be appropriate. The process of constructing the book can also be critical in unlocking a child's emotions, so the process must not be hurried and should be taken at the child's pace.

T. Ryan and A. Walker, *Making Life Story Books*, London, British Agencies for Adoption and Fostering, 1985.

listening the ability to hear what someone is communicating completely and accurately.

Listening skills are generally held to have cognitive and social dimensions. First, cognitive skills enable the listener to understand what has been conveyed in both detail and substance and to convince the speaker that such understanding has been achieved. Second, social skills help and encourage clients to unburden themselves in a manner that makes it more likely that the whole story will be told. Key elements to these two related skills seem to be management of body posture and facial expressions, empathy, encouragement to the speaker, accurate listening to what is really being said, patience, summarizing and checking at intervals, and monitoring and evaluating the listener's own contribution.

J. McLeod, *Introduction to Counselling*, Buckingham, Open University Press, 1993.

local authorities the democratically elected bodies responsible for providing public services at a local level.

The present local government system was established by the Local Government Act 1972, implemented in 1974 and later reformed in 1997. This created a two-tier system of shire and metropolitan county councils as the upper tier, with district (including London borough) councils as the lower tier. Each tier of government had a council composed of elected local people who are part-time councillors, increasingly members of one of the main political parties. Serving the councils are full-time officials, including general administrators and professionals such as social workers and housing officers. Services are divided between the two levels, with services deemed to require a larger geographical and demographic component to work effectively being at county level. The districts provide services that cater for more local needs. For example, large departments providing education and social services are the responsibility of the shire counties, while housing, refuse collection and street lighting are provided by the districts. The metropolitan counties operated slightly differently, as their districts had very large populations and were therefore deemed to be able to provide some of those services provided by the counties in the rural shire counties themselves, including education. However, in 1985 these metropolitan counties, including the Greater London Council, were abolished as the result of a mixture of administrative reasoning and political conflict. All their responsibilities were devolved down to the district authorities, so that in areas such as Greater Manchester, South Yorkshire and the West Midlands a single-tier system of district authorities is in operation.

The problems associated with two-tier authorities continued to exist into the 1990s and a commission was established to resolve them throughout the non-metropolitan areas. While the Conservative government of the time favoured single-tier authorities the issues of local identity proved to be more complex. As a result, when the commission finished its tour of the local authorities, their recommendations were varied and complex with some authorities emerging as single-tier systems while others retained their two-tier format. Often the restructured authorities emerged as a compromise solution combining both approaches, with single-tier cities surrounded by two-tier counties.

D. Wilson and C. Game, *Local Government in the United Kingdom*, Basingstoke, Macmillan, 1998.

local exchange and trading scheme (LETS) a scheme to benefit local communities by using indirect bartering instead of currency for an exchange of services, skills, goods.

LETS are usually supported by a dedicated community group or key worker who assist in the development and management of the scheme. LETS have also been known as Skill Exchanges. Run on a system of points, one person may offer 'baby-sitting' or 'elderly-sitting' services, others fresh vegetables from their allotments, others car maintenance, gardening, and so on. Each member begins with a credit of, say, 50 points, and a value is agreed within the scheme for each member's specific contribution. A directory identifies the goods and services on offer and appropriate contact details. On receipt of the item or service, tokens indicating payment of points are given and 'banked' (credited) with the coordinators. Money can also be exchanged where appropriate, for example, to cover the costs of car parts. Those spending points then have to earn more by providing their goods/services/skills as required to another participant in order to rebuild their purchasing power. Such schemes can be very successful in areas where money is limited and are often linked to CREDIT UNIONS. However, many of the more successful schemes operate within middle-class communities that already have substantial buying power.

lone parent family a family with one parent on his or her own raising dependent children.

Lone-parent families arise for different reasons but share similar difficulties. They include single mothers who have never married and mothers who have either separated, divorced or been widowed. Lone fathers form a small but evident percentage of all lone-parent families – approximately 8 per cent. Whatever the source of lone parenthood, over the last twenty years the number of lone-parent families has roughly doubled from about half a million to about 1.3 million. Altogether, nearly 2 million children are currently being raised by a lone parent, and lone-parent families now constitute some 20 per cent of all families with dependent children. Lone parents usually face financial hardship, having to rely primarily on income support and only to a lesser extent on earnings because employment compatible with looking after children is difficult to obtain and often poorly paid. Research indicates that lone fathers are usually better off financially because they are more likely to be in full-time employment as well as receiving higher wages than women for comparable work. Maintenance is not a major source of income for many lone parents, on average accounting for no more than 7 per cent of their income, despite the government's recent CHILD SUPPORT initiatives.

The circumstances of lone-parent families have caused unease across the political spectrum. Commentators from the FAR RIGHT are concerned that lone parenthood is a matter of individual moral failure that undermines the integrity of the family as an institution linked to the growth of an amoral UNDERCLASS. Liberal and social democratic analysts point to the fact that because most lone parents are reliant on income support, a great many children are raised in families on unacceptably low incomes. NEW LABOUR government falls somewhere in between, with a policy that encourages (but not requires) lone parents, including mothers raising young children, to find work through the *New Deal for Lone Parents*. There is wide agreement that absent fathers must acknowledge responsibility for their children by at least contributing financially to their upbringing.

The principal dilemma facing most lone mothers arises from the uncertainty in society at large over whether mothers ought to stay home to look after their children or work in order to provide them with an adequate standard of living. Lone parent families have repeatedly been shown to be worse off materially than the poorest categories of two-parent families. A large percentage of all children in poverty live in a lone parent household.

For a lone parent with young children whether to work or not, and, if so, for how many hours a week, presents a huge dilemma. In general, social attitudes now expect all adults who can work to work while central government's programme of welfare reform now explicitly encourages even mothers with young children to find work or to prepare for work through training or further education. This is yet another pressure on mothers with young children to find work and leave her children in DAY CARE.

Social workers working with lone mothers should have a good grasp on the many issues involved in finding work. A basic knowledge of benefits is important. For example, although the lone parent premium was eliminated in 1998 they are entitled to the higher rate of child benefit for lone parents if they had already been receiving it before that year. Also, the rate of personal allowance for determining income support for a lone parent 18 years or over is the same as for a single claimant aged 25 or over and thus substantially higher than for a single claimant aged between 18 and 24.

For the parent coming off benefit and going into work there can be gains in income, improved networks and wider social contacts. But such gains vary greatly from individual to individual and depend on their earning capacity. Researchers have established that to secure these gains, investing in 'human capital' – that is, qualifications, job-related training and accumulated work experience – is crucial to lone mothers' obtaining higher wages. Other barriers to work may also arise, such as cultural or social values that restrict the search for potential jobs, or lack of suitable kinds of work at local level, the prejudice of employers or the costs of transport or child care.

For a parent on her own with care for UNDER-FIVES, work can present many difficulties. It is important not to exaggerate the benefits of work. For those with low levels of skill or educational attainments and for those who, because of care commitments, can work only part-time, the work that is available is often low paid, temporary and unsatisfying.

There is some flexibility in the benefits system to help with the transition to work:

1 lone parents starting work may be entitled to up to two weeks of income support when they start and up to four weeks extended payments of housing benefit and council tax benefit;

2 they may also be eligible for single payments when starting work as a kind of 'back to work' bonus. If a lone parent begins to earn part-time and receives less in benefit as a result she can receive up to half the amount of that reduction as a lump sum when she takes up work full-time.

looked after the phrase used in law to describe a child being cared for by the local authority.

Under the CHILDREN ACT a child is looked after by the local authority if either the child has been provided with ACCOMMODATION at the request of the parents or the child is in the care of the authority. The whole point of the concept is to underscore that the responsibilities of the local authority are the same for any child, regardless of whether the child has been voluntarily accommodated or is the subject of a CARE ORDER or EMERGENCY PROTECTION ORDER. The primary duty of the authority is to safeguard and promote the welfare of children they are looking after, including taking decisions in their long-term interests. In planning the placement of children it is looking after, the authority must consult all those concerned with the children as well as the children themselves before placement decisions are reached. The Children Act also requires that the authority place children as near to their homes as practicable. The authority is responsible for drawing up a plan for the future of every child being looked after, including how long the placement will last, when that child will be reunited with his or her family and the amount of contact between child and family while on placement.

Investigations into the quality of life of children while they are being looked after as well as the conduct of the local authority itself as a corporate parent indicate a high level of variability in promoting the child's wellbeing. Whether in educational attainment, in job finding or in their life following care, children or young people who have been looked after by the local authority have often been at a large disadvantage to their peers. For example, a substantial proportion of the homeless and of the prison population have had care experiences in their past. Much effort has gone into improving the situation. The ASSESSMENT AND ACTION RECORDS from the Department of Health provide age-related checklists for continuing assessment of the child's or young person's progress while being looked after. The CHILDREN (LEAVING CARE) ACT 2000 has also specified the tasks a local authority must undertake as it prepares a looked-after young person for independence. It also stipulates that local authorities continue to support in various ways a young person up to the age of 25 if necessary.

loss the feelings and behaviours that accompany BEREAVEMENT, change and/or separation, and during the period immediately following bereavement or change.

Loss is an inherent part of many of the situations that social workers might work with. For example, children moving from home into a care environment, older people entering residential care, a person disabled by a road traffic accident, and a person experiencing insidious sensory impairment will all experience loss to a greater or lesser extent. However, not all loss is traumatic. *Developmental loss*, associated with the process of growth, of moving from one life stage to another, involves changes in appearance, in status, and so on, but may not be experienced as painful. If appropriate supports and social facilitation are present, such losses may actually be life-enhancing. *Traumatic loss* is the form of loss that accompanies traumatic life events such as divorce, death or unemployment. Some losses carry a measure of control – for example, divorce or a change of job – and the strength of control may mitigate the effects of the loss.

The feelings and sensations that typify loss vary according to a person's support systems, personality and the strategies that may have been developed in the past to manage life crises.

Prior to loss, there must be ATTACHMENT to a person, place or thing from which the separation occurs. Loss is closely linked to grieving, the latter being the process of recovery from loss. The emotions that accompany loss may include anxiety, insecurity, fear, unhappiness, bewilderment, loneliness, loss of self-esteem and hopelessness. There may be anger towards the dead person or towards others, for example medical staff. However, people may also feel relief, a sense of challenge or 'new life', depending on the nature of their relationship to the deceased or separated persons.

The behaviours accompanying loss may include crying, yearning, searching, panic, withdrawal, passivity apathy, restlessness, talkativeness, lethargy and motivational deficits. There may be a preoccupation with images or mementoes of the dead person or, alternatively, a refusal to look at photographs, etc. Physical sensations may be present: changes in heart and/or breathing rate, muscle tension, appetite disturbance, sleeplessness, hallucinations, thought blocking and monitoring the movements of others.

The wide variability of responses in loss reflects the variability of ways in which people cope with traumatic life events. A person could, in principle, exhibit all, none or any combination of emotional, behavioural and physical reactions to loss, but the majority of people are likely to experience a period of disengagement from social events and relationships. Recovery from loss is complete when the person experiences increased feelings of pleasure at the resumption of activities.

Effective social work practice with people experiencing loss should focus on permitting the person to explore the nature and extent of the loss. For example, following the death of her husband a woman may wish to talk about not simply the loss of her partner but the loss of income, of shared parenthood or grandparenting, of status, of friendship and possibly the loss of a home. Support with such practical issues as funeral arrangements, paying bills, shopping or form-filling is vital. The loss experienced by an older person entering residential care may involve support for decision-making, moving belongings, introductions to new people, enabling the person to say goodbye to familiar things in his or her home and neighbourhood, and offering emotional support as the person encounters the loss of home and independence. Black elders may experience loss and longing for a homeland they may never see again, and social workers should pay attention to the black elder's need to share memories and to reminisce with others from similar backgrounds.

Social work with loss should also seek to discover how people affected by it coped with traumatic life events in their past and how they make sense of life events. This can be effective in identifying with the person the strengths from previous situations that can be built on in this current period of loss. Alternatively, such work might indicate that a person is in need of more specialist help than a social worker can offer, such as PSYCHOTHERAPY and/or medical intervention.

C. M. Parkes, *Bereavement: Studies of Grief in Adult Life,* London, Tavistock, 1972.

low pay income that barely permits individuals and families to meet the basic requirements of life. Conventionally, low pay covers the poorest sections of the working population, although these sections will vary according to the economic climate of a country and prevailing governing economic policies.

Low pay correlates closely with POVERTY. Low-paid jobs are frequently associated with a lack of security, training and retraining opportunities and fringe benefits (including holiday entitlement and pension rights). Women, disabled people and people from ethnic minority backgrounds are significantly over-represented in the poorly paid occupations. Jobs such as bar work, cleaning, portering, shelf-filling in retail stores, labouring, agricultural working, waiting in restaurants, cleaning, car park and petrol station attending, care working and similar posts have been poorly paid for many decades in Britain.

The National Minimum Wage was introduced by the Labour Government in April 1999. From October 2006 the minimum wage has been set at £5.35 per hour for those over 22, £4.45 per hour for those aged 18–21 and for 16–17 year olds (excluding apprentices) £3.30 per hour. It is now illegal for employers to pay less than the minimum wage, regardless of whether workers are part-time, casual, temporary, agency or homeworkers.

The Low Pay Unit (LPU), one of the major campaigning pressure groups in this field, believes that governments should be committed to raising the level of the minimum wage (in relation to average wages) and to automatic uprating of the minimum in accordance with general increases in prices and wages. The LPU argues that there should be a political commitment to raise the minimum wage to the level of the Council of Europe's decency threshold (£7.60 in 2002) within 10 years. The government's Low Pay Commission, established in 1998, is currently considering these and other proposals for making work worthwhile – a key plank of new Labour's thinking.

The task of social workers and other advice workers is to ensure that people in work are claiming all the benefits (for example, housing benefits) and tax credits (especially Working Families Tax Credits – to be replaced by Employment and Child Care Tax Credits in 2003) to which they are entitled and to press for greater fringe benefits for all workers.

low-vision aids equipment to assist people with VISUAL IMPAIRMENT to maximize useful sight.

Although medical treatment may not be available for some eye conditions, much can be done to make the most of existing vision. Low-vision aids include relatively 'low-tech' solutions such as magnifiers, improved lighting, large-print books and more effective colour contrasts. There are now also text enlargement and other specialist programs for computers. Low-vision aids are available commercially but can often be provided by social services departments, voluntary organizations and hospital eye clinics.

Mm

Macpherson Report see STEPHEN LAWRENCE INQUIRY.

magistrate also called a **justice of the peace** (or **JP**) an ordinary member of the public appointed by the Lord Chancellor to preside over the lowest level of FAMILY PROCEEDINGS and CRIMINAL COURTS, dealing with 98 per cent of criminal cases.

The term was also used in respect of the lowest tier of the professional judiciary, formerly called stipendiary magistrates but now renamed district judges. District judges can sit alone in a magistrate's court, whereas lay magistrates normally sit in benches of three, with an experienced chair and two 'wingers'. See CRIMINAL COURT and YOUTH COURT.

Makaton a system of signs and symbols used to assist communication for people with learning disability who cannot use conventional speech.

Makaton originated in the 1970s in connection with a research project into communication methods for deaf adults with learning disability. Makaton signing is described as an aid to communication rather than a language, as it does not have grammar of the same complexity as BRITISH SIGN LANGUAGE (BSL). However, the vocabulary is based on BSL. Makaton symbols are designed to be easy to draw by hand and aim to represent meaning in pictorial form.

mandated problem a problem that, by law, client and social worker must address.

The term is found in TASK-CENTRED WORK, an approach that in the main focuses on problems that the client regards as a priority. 'Mandated problem' are those exceptional matters that the social worker must bring up, whether or not the client considers them a problem. For example, the social worker must raise the problem of poor parenting standards with a client if those standards are likely to cause his or her child SIGNIFICANT HARM. The worker will attempt to frame the problem in a way that the client is willing to address. If the client then refuses to acknowledge this as a problem, no further task-centred work can be undertaken with that person although the worker may have to pursue some compulsory intervention.

manic depression defined in PSYCHIATRY as an 'affective disorder', that is, a type of PSYCHOSIS, involving responses of moods and emotions that depart from cultural expectations. It is also more frequently referred to now as 'bipolar disorder'.

Extreme MOOD SWINGS are the central experience of manic depression; for psychiatry these are the main 'symptoms' of the 'disease'. Involved in these swings are 'mania' and DEPRESSION, and either may be predominant for some time. Mania is a powerful feeling of elation, which leads the person to 'speed up' all his or her responses and behaviour to an extreme degree. It involves the experience of 'flights of ideas', vigorous activity – often involving excessive drinking, spending or sexual activity, regardless of how different this may be from the person's usual values and behaviour – and a conviction that nothing can go wrong. These extreme feelings of elation thus have enormous consequences for the person and for others. Depression involves feelings of pessimism and hopelessness, sadness, guilt and low self-esteem. These feelings are likely to lead to the opposite behaviour from that following mania, that is, loss of interest and enjoyment in life, slowness and inactivity, withdrawal and tearfulness. Poor memory and weak concentration, indecisiveness and disturbance in sleeping and eating (often the person does not eat) are also likely, and there may be delusions and auditory HALLUCINATIONS, expressing the guilt experienced by the person.

The mood swings described above can be understood perhaps as reactions to each other and thus to a degree can be experienced by many people. PSCHODYNAMIC theory explains that manic feelings can protect the person from feeling depressed and depression can be a natural reaction to guilt and loss. It is the extremity of these feelings, however – and hence the person's extreme behaviour – that result in the definition of psychosis, because these responses fall outside the limits of what can be understood in the person's culture. There is evidence from recent research in psychiatry that there is a strong genetic influence upon the likelihood that an individual may develop manic depression; in as many as 70 per cent of identical twins, if one twin develops the condition, the other will too. The strength of this constitutional influence means that medication (lithium carbonate) given for the condition is particularly effective, but only if taken consistently. One difficulty for people with manic depression is that they may consider themselves 'well', when elation is approaching, and thus stop taking their medication. People are likely to develop this condition in their forties, and recovery is possible, but the existence of chronic social problems makes it likely to persist. Social work clients are, of course, particularly likely to experience chronic social problems and thus are at risk of the condition becoming long-term.

The responses of people suffering from manic depression are likely to generate serious problems for themselves and for others. Their actions when elated can result in debt, violence in the home or in public places as a consequence of drinking, disruption to neighbours (for example, playing music loudly), sexually transmitted diseases, and accidents (the latter following perhaps from drinking or from the conviction that no harm can possibly befall the person, as when driving a car very fast). Excessive drinking is also strongly linked to child ABUSE and to DOMESTIC VIOLENCE and is therefore of particular significance for social work. Additional difficulties arising from the risk and antagonism thus generated include court proceedings, family breakdown, hostility and possible refusal of services by agencies if the person harasses them as part of their mania (such as by writing frequent letters of complaint to councillors or housing departments). Depression can put the person at risk of suicide, or, in extreme cases, death can result from malnutrition or from an accident caused by poor memory and concentration. Withdrawal may lead to poor self-care and to neglect of children.

Many opportunities exist for social work involvement that can make for improvements in the situation of manic depressive people. Help to the family in understanding that the person acts thus from 'illness' rather than intention; help to the person (when recovering) and/or family in managing debts; liaison with angered agencies or neighbours to explain the situation and negotiate better relations; planning for child protection; support and access to legal help with court proceedings: all are ways in which the practitioner can assist. In relation to the person's inner world, much guilt is experienced when recovering after mania-led actions, and the worker can help alleviate this by using the 'sustaining' psychosocial approach that provides the person with a sense of personal value and security; they may also help the sufferer work towards a better future by discussing the implications of taking medication or other preventive steps the person may wish to take in the event of relapse. With depression, the worker is mainly concerned with identifying that the person has become depressed and assessing the risks (see MENTAL ILLNESS), along with alleviating any social problems and helping the family cope with the situation: again the 'sustaining' psychosocial approach is invaluable and can have a positive effect on the person's feelings of depression, perhaps increasing his or her motivation to use help.

In relation to both moods, and to the person generally, the practitioner will usually work in conjunction with the psychiatric services; he or she will thus need to develop the skills and awareness of issues relevant to MULTIDISCIPLINARY working and have a basic understanding of psychiatry. Manic depression is, among all serious mental health problems, perhaps the most responsive to medication, so the worker needs to be clear about what aspects of the person's difficulties can be helped in this way and which require social work intervention. For example, it is not helpful if the worker tries to 'cure' the condition by using PSYCHOTHERAPY or behaviourism while ignoring the person's financial debts. Monitoring is another important part of the social work role in relation to people with these difficulties, that is, the ability to assess when medical intervention may be necessary, such as when the person is becoming depressed, and perhaps not eating, or starting to become elated.

MAPPP abbreviation for MULTI-AGENCY PUBLIC PROTECTION PANEL.
marginal tax rate the percentage of additional earnings lost because
of new or increased deductions in a particular set of circumstances.

The marginal 'tax' rate refers to the rate of tax paid as income increases
– for people claiming means-tested benefits it occurs when benefits are
reduced to take account of increased income – usually in the form of
earnings. There are circumstances where additional income results in
increased 'taxation' in relation to National Insurance Contributions, personal
tax and loss of other benefits including housing benefit, council tax benefit
and possibly also loss of working families tax credit. In 1997 nearly 750,000
families faced a marginal tax deduction in excess of 70 per cent (70 pence
out of every £1 earned might be lost). By 2002 this had decreased to only
250,000, largely because of the introduction of working families tax credit.
Although it is estimated that this number has declined further since the
introduction of the new tax credits in 2003, commentators suggest that
the marginal tax rate for many families will still exceed 60 per cent or the
loss of 60 pence for every additional £1 income. (See also POVERTY TRAP.)
marital problems problems arising between two people who are living in
a committed relationship. This field of work covers people who are not
married and includes both heterosexual and homosexual relationships.
Work with such couples is often called couple COUNSELLING or couple therapy.

Our understanding of MARRIAGE in contemporary society is complex,
and although cohabiting heterosexual couples and gay and lesbian
couples may not be legally married by the law of the land, their
relationships may be just as committed as those of married couples,
and they may thus experience similar problems. Marital problems are
difficulties that either or both partners choose to define as problems;
the problems should not be defined by someone else except by agreement
and discussion with counsellors as suggested new ways of looking at
a difficulty. Social workers or counsellors need to take particular care
therefore to encourage the partner(s) to describe as fully as possible,
in their own terms, exactly what the problems are and what impact they
feel they have on their relationship.

A common theme in marital problems is the breakdown in
communication between partners, often resulting in needs not being
met and expectations not being fulfilled. The ROLES played in the
relationship by each partner may alter and develop over a period of time,
and couples may not always realize that the shape of their relationship
has been changing. Parenthood, for example, can reshape a relationship,
as can new caring responsibilities for older dependants or when a woman
resumes a career after a period of child-care. Poor communication may
result in a deteriorating sexual relationship, with either or both partners
becoming sexually unfulfilled. Some partners respond to these difficulties
by seeking other sexual partners, and many who cannot resolve their
difficulties separate and divorce.

A range of help is available to couples who are experiencing relational problems. Relationship counselling seeks to enable couples to communicate with each other about the problems they face and to work towards solutions. For some couples the problems can be tackled and their relationship deepened; for others the solution involves disengaging from the relationship, ideally in as honest a manner as possible. Relate (formerly the Marriage Guidance Council) is a national organization that offers professionally trained counselling to couples in need of help. The organization's change of name indicates its commitment to work towards solutions that are in the best interest of the couple concerned (and of any children there may be). Counselling may be with both partners or with just one, depending on the willingness of each to engage in the process. Specific help with SEXUAL PROBLEMS is also available through Relate, which trains its own sex therapists. The main focus of their work is to enable and empower a couple to deepen the quality of their physical relationship by (re)learning how to relax and enjoy each other's intimate company as a prelude to undertaking specific regimes and programmes designed to help them overcome sexual problems such as failure to achieve orgasm, premature ejaculation and general unresponsiveness. Couples who need help in greater depth may be referred to FAMILY THERAPISTS, psychologists, psychosexual counsellors or marital therapists. Couples who need specialist help during separation or divorce may be offered FAMILY MEDIATION by the CHILDREN AND FAMILIES COURT ADVISORY AND SUPPORT SERVICE as part of its divorce court welfare work, especially if the care of children is a contentious issue. There are also independent mediation services provided by the VOLUNTARY SECTOR.

Social workers should also be aware of the needs and problems of couples in a relationship where either partner or both may have a physical DISABILITY. Special care needs to be exercised to ensure that as far as possible they can meet each other's emotional and physical needs, and that they are empowered to create an environment where their relationship can develop and flourish. Specialist advice to help people with physical disabilities overcome sexual difficulties is available through organizations such as Sexual Problems of the Disabled. There is a debate about society's and social workers' response to people with LEARNING DIFFICULTIES who express a wish to live together and/or to be married. Social workers may be reluctant to face issues of emotional and sexual need and to explore ways of working in PARTNERSHIP to help people with learning difficulties overcome any problems they may have.

Particular difficulties arise where counselling is attempted with couples where violent or aggressive behaviour (see DOMESTIC VIOLENCE). Many couples' counsellors or marital therapists will not work with couples where this is an issue or will suspend any programme if such problems are current. Where violence has been an issue, and especially where couples are temporarily separated but are trying to find a way forward, contingency measures need to be in place if violent or aggressive behaviour erupts during a meeting.

A frequent criticism of agencies that offer help to people with marital problems is that their workers are predominantly white and middle class and do not meet the needs of significant minority groups. There are common STEREOTYPED assumptions about Asian families, for example, that imply that counselling and support are not necessary because their communities are self-sufficient and care for each other. There is an increasing body of evidence, however, that Asian women whose relationships have broken down experience devastating social isolation. Social workers need to be aware of this growing problem. There are now some Asian mediation services in existence, and some counselling services actively recruit counsellors from ethnic-minority groups, but in general such services are scarce.

S. Litvinoff, *The Relate Guide to Better Relationships*, London, Vermillion, 1992.

market a means through which products may be bought and sold. Markets bring buyers and sellers together in a particular place (for example a farmers' market) or through other mediums such as linked computers (the stock market). Often the word 'market' or 'marketplace' is used to denote the aggregated transactions for a given product within the country as a whole, such as the housing market. Markets are one, but not the only, mechanism for allocating goods and services in conditions where resources and personal incomes are limited but demand tends to be unlimited.

Two factors, *supply* and *demand*, are central to the functioning of a market. As consumers we have wants for goods and services but a limited income with which to obtain them. We have to make decisions as to which goods and services we should buy. *Demand* for a particular product arises from the extent to which consumers are willing to pay for it (if at all). In general, market theory holds that the higher the price for a product, the lower the consumer demand for that product will be. *Supply* is the quantity of goods or services available from its producers and, in general, depends on costs such as materials and labour; the lower the costs for producing the product in relation to the price obtained for it, the greater the supply of that particular item. To put it another way, the higher the price at which the product can be sold, the more resources producers will put into its production. Economists talk of the theory of the 'perfect' market. In reality, markets are frequently distorted by various pressures and are not necessarily stable. Supply of a particular product can remain in the hands of a few producers or even one. The latter case is called a *monopoly*, which can often result in the consumer paying an unjustifiably high price. Or the reverse can be true: too many producers produce an *excess*, or *glut*, so that quantities of goods remain unsold regardless of price; then producers suffer, since they often do not recoup their costs.

The use of a market to allocate goods and services assumes that consumers are placed in the best position to make the decision as to whether a particular good or service is worth paying for at a particular price, that is, the consumer is best placed to decide on the value of the goods or services. This finds expression in the notion that 'the consumer is sovereign' or 'the customer knows best'. In practice, there are important questions concerning the quality and accuracy of the information that consumers hold, and whether their decisions are affected by such external influences as advertising.

From roughly 1990 successive governments tried to introduce market-like mechanisms into health care and COMMUNITY CARE. Advocates of market principles note the lack of choice in the provision of services because their supply is dominated, in effect, by public monopolies – the LOCAL AUTHORITIES and the NATIONAL HEALTH SERVICE. They conclude that this fosters dependency, in as much as people do not try to provide for themselves but are forced to take what is on offer or go without the service. They view the introduction of the market mechanism into community care services as the only way to increase both choice, by encouraging other suppliers to come forward, and efficiency, by containing rising costs. Government expanded the influence of market mechanisms in determining allocation of both health and community care services, separating *purchasers* of services, who assess needs and buy the services to meet those needs for a particular individual, and *providers*, who organize and sell the services required. These two distinct roles became widespread within local government and are undertaken by different personnel in an attempt to change the culture and the way of thinking. One consequence is that local authorities have greatly reduced or abandoned their direct provision of services – such as housing or residential care for OLDER PEOPLE – and have relied on commissioners to purchase those services from suppliers from the private or VOLUNTARY SECTOR.

Evidence is mixed as to whether such reforms achieved their stated objectives of increased choice and more efficient use of resources. Competition between suppliers is essential to a fully functioning market, and in health and community care services it is assumed to lead to greater choice for consumers and greater efficiency for purchasers. Experience within the National Health Service, however, suggests that, because of the obvious need to preserve continuity of service provision, purchasing bodies may increasingly adopt a partnership model – involving long-term contracts for a wide range of services – as opposed to a competition model, and thus blunt some of the reforms' objectives. In community care services the success of the reforms will depend on whether market mechanisms will in themselves increase diversity within the private sector. In some cases, however, user choice of community care services has not expanded; indeed, in some areas the particular service contracted for by the local authority was the *only* service available in that locality. In such situations, user choice is clearly not the only important criterion in shaping purchasing strategy. The NEW LABOUR government elected in 1997 has pulled back from some of these market-oriented mechanisms. Its introduction of the BEST VALUE framework is designed to encourage certain aspects of markets into public services (value for money, designing services that people actually want) without giving markets free rein within those services. New Labour also abolished GP fundholding, a key market-inspired reform within the health service set up by previous governments.

marriage a socially acknowledged relationship or union between two adults. In the UK a legally ratified marriage must be between a male and female over the ages of 16.

Marriage in traditional or pre-industrial societies appears to serve kin interests and to be regulated by kin relationships. Marriage within capitalist or industrial societies is more likely to be a matter of choice between the two adults concerned, although choice seems to operate within a comparatively narrow range; that is, most people marry others of roughly comparable social status. In Britain individual choice seems to predominate, although there are situations where more traditional forms of marriage still occur, for example among some Muslim and Sikh groups or in some parts of rural Wales. Sociologists have noted at least two kinds of models for marriage in developed countries. One is marriage based on *functional equality*, where both spouses work, maintain separate bank accounts, pay separate taxes and equally divide household and care-giving tasks. The other is the *domestic partnership model*, which emphasizes the partners making more personal choices and rewards partners for making mutually considerate decisions on how best to use their time, resulting in varying patterns of paid and unpaid work to emerge in relation to different family needs. *Arranged marriages* play an important role within specific ethnic communities. In arranged marriages, the families of both spouses take a lead role in arranging the marriage but the choice of whether to accept the arrangement remains with the individuals. The emphasis on mutual respect and sustained lifelong support for partners and family members is often balanced by western observers with the dominance of male authority in the relationship and within the family as a whole. There is a distinction between an arranged marriage and a *forced marriage*, in which one party does not consent to the marriage and an element of duress and criminal offence is involved, including threatening behaviour, harassment, assault and kidnap. It should be noted that not all victims of forced marriages are women, with husbands forming some 15 per cent of unwilling partners.

In general, popular belief in the importance of marriage is slowly eroding in the UK. The average age at which people get married is now around 27 years old, up from 21 years in 1970. There are corresponding further delays when married couples have children. Increasing DIVORCE rates have also further clouded the image that people hold of what marriage actually means. COHABITATION before marriage is also increasing rapidly. Powerful social and economic changes have clearly weakened the once close link between marriage and parenthood. Compared with thirty years ago, it is easier for women to raise children without men and for men to escape the responsibilities of fatherhood. More women go to work so their financial need for marriage is less. One widespread view among social theorists suggests that marriage restricts self-development and individual freedom at a time when society places a strong emphasis on precisely these same values. Another locates the responsibility with the rise of 'no fault' divorce in statute and the relative ease with which marriages can now be terminated.

In the wake of such trends, proposals for the reform of marriage as an institution are pressing in different directions. Some have urged a reform of the ceremony itself, making it more meaningful and personal to the individuals concerned by permitting couples to devise their own vows and rituals that blend secular, religious and familial meanings. Others have urged a contractual approach that would underpin each marriage with negotiated pre-nuptial agreements (subject to renegotiation after ten years). In the USA in particular a counter-move has emerged to this contractual approach that seeks to re-establish the traditional submission of wife to male authority.

With the exception of marriage counselling, social workers usually work with couples (whether gay, lesbian or heterosexual) over specific tasks or problems *after* the consequences of conflict in the relationship have become acute. This includes the effects of DOMESTIC VIOLENCE on family members or instances where one spouse has MENTAL HEALTH PROBLEMS. That work often tries to reduce the risk of further physical or emotional harm, accompanied by the recognition that the marriage itself is a lower priority than the safety of individuals. Where children are involved, however, and there is no concern over their upbringing the FAMILY ASSISTANCE ORDER provides a consensual legal basis for offering guidance and support to the family as a whole across a number of matters including the parents' relationship.

masculinity concepts of masculinity and 'what it means to be a man' must be viewed as a social construct and therefore variable over time and space. Traditional traits of masculinity include strength, physical ability, autonomy and power, and ideas of hegemonic masculinity ensure the reproduction and reinforcement of patriarchy within society. More recently, however, it has been argued that it may be more useful to talk of masculinities in the plural rather than a single all-encompassing notion of masculinity. This allows for a consideration towards notions of 'difference', most specifically in relation to ethnicity, sexuality and class. In terms of practice, this can be understood as a need for recognizing the complexities of human experience as differentiated by masculinity and its relationship with other aspects of identity such as ethnicity. An example of the importance of this would be in the case of an Asian lone male parent who would need to negotiate his masculine role both in relation to the interpersonal setting, the cultural context and that of the wider social structure.

The relatively new focus upon 'men' and 'masculinity' can be said to have arisen partly in response to (or indeed as a backlash from) the 'second wave' of feminism, yet also as a result of changes in employment patterns and the make-up of the family. These developments have increasingly led to a problematization of 'man' within contemporary society, especially in response to the underachievement of boys in education and their over-representation within school exclusion rates. Current debates focus on how best to respond to this 'problem', be it via structural changes in the delivery of education or more interpersonal responses evident in schemes such as mentoring, which aim to provide a suitable role model for young men on their transition to adulthood.

R. W. Connell, *Masculinities*, Cambridge, Polity Press, 1995.

maternal deprivation a theory that has sought to demonstrate a connection between an unsatisfactory relationship between a child and its mother and difficulties for that child in later life.

Deprivation here may be understood either as the loss of a mother entirely or as her absence for lengthy (if temporary) periods, or as a mother who acts distantly or indifferently towards the child. The originator of the theory, John Bowlby, conducted research that appeared to show that maternal deprivation can lead to juvenile delinquency and to behavioural disorders in later life. Bowlby's work has been read to imply that even short and temporary separations can have profound and lasting effects upon the child's later ability to function as a mature adult. The debate on maternal deprivation seems to reappear vigorously from time to time. Some, for example, have argued that a pre-school child attending a nursery or with a child-minder should be seen as experiencing maternal deprivation. More recent considered criticism of Bowlby's ideas has it that there are many important ingredients in a (separated) relationship between a child and its mother, including the age of the child, the quality of the relationship before separation occurred, the length of separation, the quality of substitute care and the quality of maternal care after child and mother are reunited (if this happens). Where a period of separation is relatively brief, where the child understands what is happening and why, and where a warm and loving relationship exists both before and after separation, it is unlikely that any harm will come to the child. A more negative experience on any of these criteria might increase the chances of later difficulties for the child. Feminists have argued that the theory is oppressive to mothers. They argue that in times of war or periods of economic expansion, men are content to encourage women into paid employment; in periods of recession, however, women are reminded of their domestic responsibilities and especially the duties of motherhood. Government thinking in the early part of the 21st century, in its encouragement of women to work to combat SOCIAL EXCLUSION and POVERTY, is clearly convinced that adequate child-care arrangements do not lead to damaged children. The theory can be perceived as trying to control women directly and indirectly, the latter by avoiding the question of what the role of the father should be in relation to child-rearing and what consequences for the child may result from paternal deprivation.

M. Rutter, *Maternal Deprivation Reassessed*, second edition, London, Penguin, 1981.

maternity allowance see WELFARE RIGHTS 7.

Matrimonial Causes Act 1973 the main statute governing DIVORCE in England and Wales. There is now only one general ground for divorce, and this is that a marriage has 'irretrievably broken down'.

To demonstrate to a court that their marriage has failed, petitioners must show either that the other parties have committed adultery or that they have behaved unreasonably, or that they have deserted for at least two years, or that the couple have lived apart for two years and that the respondent agrees to the divorce, or that the couple have lived apart for five years (in which case the respondent's consent is not necessary). Petitioners may not seek a divorce within the first year of marriage. Judicial or legal separations are covered by the same legislation. A legal separation can be secured at any point in a marriage on the same grounds as for divorce. Legal separations are sought by people who may have a moral or religious objection to a divorce. Legally separated people cannot remarry until they secure a full divorce.

The FAMILY LAW ACT 1996 proposed a waiting period of between 12 and 18 months during which couples were expected to use FAMILY MEDIATION to settle matters in relation to children, property and maintenance. In this proposal solicitors would have played a less prominent role, although they might still have been involved in the drawing up of legal agreements to ratify any negotiated settlements that were achieved through mediation. Mediation is now provided by a range of organizations affiliated to the UK College of Family Mediators. Government and other key institutions remain very ambivalent about 'cooling-off' periods and the costs and benefits of mediation, and, in some respects, key aspects of the Family Law Act 1996 have not been implemented.

meals on wheels the provision of meals to older or vulnerable people, either within their own homes or in luncheon clubs in community facilities, by statutory or voluntary organizations.

Meals on wheels provision is increasingly offered by voluntary organizations like the Women's Royal Voluntary Service, often on a less generous basis (in terms of both cost and frequency) than before because of cuts in public expenditure.

means-tested benefit also known as **income-related benefit** a benefit where entitlement depends on personal circumstances, family structure and means (specifically income and capital).

Means-tested benefits are not linked to the payment of NATIONAL INSURANCE CONTRIBUTIONS. Eligibility is determined by a needs-resources assessment that compares the claimants' (including dependants') notional needs against the resources available to them. Each means-tested benefit has its own 'means-test' – the rules regarding how needs and resources are calculated and compared. Means-tested benefits include *income support* (also known as the *minimum income guarantee* for people age 60 plus – see WELFARE RIGHTS 5, WELFARE RIGHTS 8), *housing benefit, council tax benefit* (WELFARE RIGHTS 6), *working tax credit* (WELFARE RIGHTS 9) and HEALTH BENEFITS. A key aspect of means-tests is the way in which income is assessed. Among other things there may be an element of earnings or other sources of income that can be 'disregarded'. An *earnings disregard* is that part of earned income that does not count in full when a person's income is calculated for purposes of income support, income-based jobseeker's allowance, housing benefit or council tax benefit.

The level of disregard varies according to the claimant's circumstances – for example, a carer, person with disabilities, lone parent and people in specified occupations (firefighter, territorial army, coastguard) can earn up to £20 a week before benefit is reduced; in contrast, single people not in any of the above categories can earn up to only £5 before benefit is reduced.

In the community care services area of the welfare system, means-testing also plays a part – for example, those entering RESIDENTIAL CARE with more than the permitted amount of capital are expected to pay for, or contribute towards, their costs (at least while their capital remains above that level). Similarly, support for carers may be charged for, depending on their means, as provided for under the CARERS AND DISABLED CHILDREN ACT 2000.

medical model the understanding of a person's behaviour, difficulty or condition in terms of illness, diagnosis and treatment.

The notion of disease is used to explain both mental and physical health problems. From the perspective of the medical model, both physical ill-functioning and ill-functioning of a person's thinking, mood, behaviour or perception are seen as a result of disease in that person's physiological processes and treated by various forms of medication. Often such treatment has been administered in isolation from everyday life in an institution and within a detached impersonal relationship between physician and patient. The medical model is also associated with professionalism, which embodies an expertise that gives authority to the professional to define the problems and prescribe intervention without reference to the person's own view of his or her difficulties.

The medical model has been frequently criticized from social work perspectives, particularly in relation to mental ill health. Symptoms such as hallucinations or delusions are located in the behaviour, feelings, thoughts or wishes of the person and, from a social work perspective, can be seen as a product of social relations and social stresses rather than an illness. By seeing these as signs of a disease, their meaning is regarded as an abnormality rather than as communicative or expressive behaviour. Further social work concerns have to do with the way the medical model ignores social causes of mental distress and denies the person her/his own control over her/his experiences. This is especially so in relation to persons of minority ethnic cultures. The international classifications of disease and of mental ill health are mostly derived from the western culture of developed countries and the ill-functioning defined in relation to these norms of the culture.

These criticisms can apply also to physical ill-health. Investigation into inequalities in health show that social factors make a real difference as to whether someone becomes ill or dies young. Some recent research suggests that social causes indeed can have a great effect on physiological processes, and this has the potential to turn the medical model on its head, with 'disease entities' resulting more from social stress than biological causes. At the same time, genetic influences in shaping individual vulnerability to the effects of adversity are also evidenced. All this promises important new developments in the understanding of both mental and physical ill-health.

Whatever the subtleties of our developing understanding, medical practitioners, with their knowledge base and skills, are essential in tackling and reducing the problems of ill-health of all descriptions. Social workers are unlikely to object to medical help in understanding a physical or mental condition. Recent evidence links physiological disturbances to mental ill-health, just as to physical ill-health, and reduction of these disturbances does mean reduced symptoms, with their associated discomfort and implications for poor functioning. With policy requirements for seamless health and social care in mental and physical health services, this means that treatment for biological disturbances linked to mental distress, discomfort and poor functioning would simply be one aspect of multi-agency working. Social workers address psychosocial stressors also linked to mental and physical ill-health as part of the multi-agency team.

H. Freeman, *Handbook of Medical Sociology*, fourth edition, London, Prentice Hall, 1989.

Memorandum of Good Practice SEE DISCLOSURE; INVESTIGATIVE INTERVIEWING.

men (social work with men) social work with men and boys where ideas of masculinity, held by practitioners, service users, families, communities and society, impact upon helping objectives and processes.

Whereas sex is thought of as a biological entity, gender has been held by social scientists to be socially and culturally constructed and subject to historical change. Feminists have for several decades encouraged critical analyses of the idea of gender and, in particular, of the treatment of women in society. These analyses have been driven by both empirical research and by significant theorizing. Inevitably, the behaviour of men has come under scrutiny by feminists and others. In this context a variety of key issues concerning the behaviour of men as social workers and as service users, and in social work transactions, have preoccupied researchers and practitioners. These issues include VIOLENCE, including DOMESTIC VIOLENCE, EQUAL OPPORTUNITIES and ANTI-OPPRESSIVE PRACTICE, parenting (including CHILD ABUSE and neglect) and offending behaviour (see PARENT EDUCATION AND TRAINING).

One important issue, especially in relation to social work with children and their families, has been the relative invisibility of men unless they have been suspected of abusing their children or their partners. Where families include both a woman and a man, social work records habitually contain much more information about the woman than the man. This appears to be a reflection of social workers' predisposition to think of women as having primary responsibility for the care of children, a tendency that may lead, as some feminists claim, to 'woman blaming' when things go wrong. Some have argued, however, that social workers prefer to engage with mothers rather than fathers, even where fathers are involved with the child care. Mothers are construed as more compliant or reasonable as service users or clients whereas men are regarded as being more difficult, aggressive or even violent. Another contributory factor may be the heavily gendered nature of child care and parenting services, which are staffed almost exclusively by women. Thus there may be disincentives for fathers or male carers to participate in these. Yet the objective, perhaps, should be to involve more men in both child care and in caring services if the responsibilities of parenting are to be acknowledged by both men and women.

Those working with perpetrators of domestic violence have increasingly found it useful to deconstruct men's accounts of their abusive behaviour. This work has highlighted the tendency of men to rationalize, to minimize their personal responsibility for injuries and to redefine violence in a narrow way to exclude a variety of controlling and abusive behaviours. Rationalization includes blaming the woman for 'not having the dinner ready' or 'not controlling the kids' or 'looking at another man' or regarding the incident as essentially an accident, as in 'I didn't intend to hit her that hard' or 'I did push her, but I didn't realize she was she was next to the glass door'. Locating the problem in stress is also common, including financial pressures or unemployment. Some accounts either deny any violence at all or exclude behaviours that are not physical blows. Blocking, confining, intimidating or bullying behaviours or socially isolating a woman or denying her economic resources are all excluded from some men's idea of violence, although such behaviours are underpinned by violence or its threat. The task of social workers has been to reveal the interconnected nature of these behaviours, to demonstrate that they are essentially about the misuse of power. The key objective is to bring men to the point that they will understand their behaviour, accept responsibility for it and, by so doing, control and develop other more appropriate strategies for dealing with personal relationships.

Similar objectives underpin other kinds of work with boys, youths and men in relation to such problem areas as teenage pregnancies, adult and youth offending and residential care. One part of the strategy to reduce teenage pregnancies is to encourage what educationalists call 'personal and social education', whereby young people take responsibility for their sexual behaviour. Such programmes include contraceptive advice, advice about personal and sexual relationships and issues of parental responsibility. Although evidence suggests that teenage fathers are unpromising sources of support, services for teenage mothers rarely seek the involvement of the father, regarding them as essentially irresponsible and likely sources of additional problems. Some of this work takes place in residential child-care settings because young people in care, both males and females, are more likely than other young people to become teenage parents.

Work with both young and adult offenders includes topics and issues that concern offenders' ideas of masculinity. Victim reparation schemes, community service and offence behaviour analysis all have elements that emphasize personal responsibility for actions, developing awareness of the repercussions of offending behaviour for victims, understanding the personal and peer pressures that may lead to offences and the development of strategies for dealing with opportunities and temptations to offend.

A number of commentators have explored the issue of whether the gender of workers affects the response of male service users or clients. At times some have argued that it is the responsibility of male workers 'to deal' with the men and the boys. Yet there is compelling evidence to suggest that women are quite able to deal with offenders of all ages, including sex offenders, violent men and parenting issues, and that there are very positive reasons for not offering 'segregated' services. Problems can sometimes occur when male and female workers co-work and male clients attempt collusion with male workers, or where male workers presume the role of leader. Consciousness of these issues, together with planned strategies for dealing with them, are necessary and may be instrumental in helping males to accept a more responsible notion of masculinity.

Kate Cavanagh and Vivienne Cree (eds), *Working with Men: Feminism and Social Work*, London, Routledge, 1996.

mens rea a legal phrase, from the Latin, meaning 'guilty mind'.

Many crimes can be proved only if the legal test of *mens rea* has been successfully applied: the defendant has to be shown not only to have done something but to have done it with intent. The most common example is theft, where it is not sufficient to show that somebody took an article from a shop but also that he or she intended to deprive the owner of it permanently.

mental disorder any disorder or disability of mind with an impact on the person's mental functioning.

The concept of mental disorder is no longer linked to diagnosis and can imply a psychological PERSONALITY DISORDER as well as a type of biological or 'illness' disorder. This change in usage from that of the 1980s has important adverse implications as severe antisocial personality disorder can be classed as a mental disorder without being seen as an illness. It suggests that the person's therapeutic benefit from treatment does not have to be a consideration and that public protection can come before this, which is precisely what the white paper *Reform of the Mental Health Act* or *No Secrets*, published in 2000, suggests.

mental handicap a term referring to intellectual impairment; it has now been replaced by the term LEARNING DISABILITY.

The term 'mental handicap' is regarded as offensive by many self-advocates and tends to be associated with long-stay hospitals and segregated services.

mental health absence of MENTAL ILLNESS, referring to an individual's personal and social wellbeing, as reflected in both inner experience and outer behaviour.

Western culture locates health conditions in 'body' or 'mind', hence giving rise to the concepts of mental and physical health. In other cultures this distinction may not be so important, but in most there is a concern with something similar, although the emphasis on inner experience or outer behaviour will vary. Ideas of wellbeing express the social values of importance in the person's culture and thus differ between cultures. For example, contributing to group harmony may constitute positive mental health in Eastern cultures, as opposed to individualism in the West. It is therefore likely that service users will hope to realize such values as a result of social work intervention, not only with MENTAL HEALTH PROBLEMS as such, but generally. Anti-racist workers consequently need to be responsive to these value differences, both in their individual interventions and in the promotion of culturally sensitive services. Failure to do this may compromise the service user's cultural identity, which is a form of racism.

The World Health Organization has defined HEALTH in general, including mental health, as 'a complete state of physical, mental and social well-being, not merely the absence of illness'. This definition incorporates two different perspectives on mental health that are currently being debated and have major implications for service provision.

The first of these perspectives – mental health as the 'absence of illness' – is associated with Western PSYCHIATRY. From this perspective, a significant departure from the state of personal and social wellbeing that constitutes mental health is understood as a state of illness, that is, any inner experiences that are subjectively unhappy and any outer behaviours that contravene social values in particular ways are defined as mental illness.

The second perspective – defining mental health as 'mental wellbeing' – is more likely to be found in non-Western cultures, but it is also associated with both conservative and more radical approaches to mental health concerns in Western social work and health-care thinking. From this viewpoint, most forms of mental distress or socially unacceptable behaviour may be understood as being within the range of 'normal' human functioning and therefore not indicating the presence of the 'abnormal' state of illness, although in most cultures some experiences or behaviour will be defined in these terms. This position is adopted by 'anti-psychiatry' theories – especially in the ideas of Thomas Szasz – and by radical social theory, which provides the theoretical basis for radical and anti-oppressive social work. Szasz defines most departures from the state of personal and social wellbeing conservatively as 'problems of living' that are an essential and 'normal' part of human life; in radical social theory they are understood as the products of oppressive social, economic and political conditions. From these viewpoints, then, mental health is regarded as a consequence of resolving these problems – for Szasz involving the individual in developing ways of coping with 'problems of living', and in radical social theory through the reduction of oppression in society. Both approaches consider mental health to be neither automatically present nor the product of medical treatment; rather, it depends on the powers of the individual and/or of the collective to achieve personal and/or social growth. This gives the key role in promoting positive mental health to social workers, service users and non-medical professionals instead of to health professionals working within a medical model; hence. community care policy gives priority to social care in the provision of services to people with mental health problems.

Social work approaches to promoting positive mental health are outlined in EMPOWERMENT theory and FEMINIST and ANTI-RACIST theories, and they involve enabling people to take control of their inner and outer lives collectively and individually.

S. Fernando, *Mental Health, Race and Culture*, second edition, Basingstoke, Macmillan, 2002.

Mental Health Act 1983 legislation that governs the ASSESSMENT and treatment of people with MENTAL DISORDER, including the conditions under which a person can be compulsorily detained in a psychiatric hospital.

The Act sets out four specific categories of mental disorder. Three of the four – mental impairment, severe mental impairment and psychopathic disorder – all share similar characteristics: incomplete development of the mind, which may include significant impairment of intelligence and social functioning and is associated with abnormally aggressive behaviour or socially irresponsible conduct. The fourth and most important category, MENTAL ILLNESS, is left undefined in the Act. Consultative documents issued by government at the time the Act was passed, however, defined mental illness as having the following characteristics:

1 persistent interruption of intellectual functioning as indicated by a failure of memory, orientation, comprehension and learning capacity;
2 persistent alteration of mood to such a degree that it gives rise to the patient making a delusional appraisal of his or her situation;
3 the presence of delusions or other persecutory or grandiose beliefs;
4 thinking so disordered as to prevent the person from making a reasonable appraisal of his or her situation.

Section 2 of the Act provides for a person to be admitted to hospital for psychiatric assessment for up to 28 days if he or she is suffering from a mental disorder (that is, one of the categories above) to the extent that detention is justified and that the person ought to be detained in the interests of his or her own health or safety or that of others. Compulsory admission for assessment can take place only on the recommendation of two registered medical practitioners. After the 28 days have elapsed, the person must either remain in hospital as an 'informal' – voluntary – patient or be detained for treatment under section 3. An order for the person's discharge may be made at any time during the 28 days. The person may seek his or her own discharge by making an application to a mental health tribunal within 14 days of admission.

A person may be detained under section 3 of the Act for treatment on the grounds that he or she is suffering from mental illness, severe mental impairment or psychopathic disorder to the degree that it is appropriate for him or her to receive medical treatment *and* it is necessary for the health or safety of the person or others that he or she receives treatment that would not otherwise be received without detention. Again, the application for compulsory treatment requires the written recommendation of two medical practitioners.

The Act also allows for compulsory admission for assessment for 72 hours in cases of emergency. An emergency application may be made by a person's nearest relative or by an APPROVED SOCIAL WORKER and the written recommendation of a medical officer who is familiar with the person in question. The application cannot be renewed at the end of the 72-hour period.

The Act also allows for the appointment of a guardian for people over the age of 16 who are suffering from mental disorder to a degree justifying the appointment. The guardian is usually a local authority social services officer, who can require the person to live at a specified place, to receive specified medical treatment and to permit access by a medical practitioner or approved social worker. The value of guardianship has been the subject of considerable debate, since it contains no powers of enforcement and must rely on the cooperation of the person.

Department of Health Mental Health Act Code of Practice, second revised edition, London, HMSO, 1993.

mental health law reform the substantial reform of existing mental health legislation proposed by the Labour government in 2002.

The proposed reforms represent a continuation of the RISK ASSESSMENT policies of the 1990s, which followed the recommendations of public inquiries in connection to homicides committed by people with PSYCHOSES, or serious MENTAL HEALTH PROBLEMS. In recent years, homicides by PAEDOPHILES have led to additional concerns about public safety, and the reform proposals have sought to address these too. At the same time, the proposed reforms seek to incorporate the HUMAN RIGHTS ACT 1998 and to promote social inclusion of people with severe mental health problems. Provision for long-term mental incapacity, for example people with DEMENTIA and LEARNING DISABILITIES, which aims to increase both the users' rights and the public's protection are also included in the proposals.

Within the proposed reforms, the need for compulsory admission to psychiatric facilities lies squarely with the person – that is, if someone is 'unable or unwilling' to comply with treatment. This does not address the responsibilities of the various mental health services themselves for contributing to a context of risk, which may be considerable. In a recent study, a quarter of the people who committed suicide after discharge from a psychiatric unit had not been followed up, and this was because they were assessed as not being at risk. It also ignores the contribution that wider social stressors and inequalities can make to MENTAL ILLNESS.

The reforms proposed in the white paper *Reform of the Mental Health Act,* 2000, are divided into Part I and Part II. Part I concerns compulsory treatment for people with serious mental health problems and provisions for long-term mental incapacity. Part II is a set of proposals targeted at people diagnosed as having severe antisocial PERSONALITY DISORDERS, a group that for the first time has special provisions under mental health legislation.

Among the proposals from Part I are a new definition of MENTAL DISORDER, which is no longer linked to a psychiatric diagnosis, unlike previous mental health legislation, but has a much wider definition, including psychological conditions not classed as 'illnesses' and can include personality disorder. Persons falling within the definition of mental disorder *and* at 'significant risk of serious harm' would be liable for compulsory intervention under the Act. They would be assessed by a psychiatrist and a non-medical mental health professional who may or may not be a social worker. On the basis of this preliminary assessment, compulsory action could be taken for a further 28-day assessment order involving either admission to psychiatric hospital or a compulsory treatment order, which may be implemented in the community and lasts for six months. The treatment order is a multi-agency CARE PLAN that the person is compelled to comply with. It makes provision for treatment and service interventions, expected to minimize the risk of harm that the person might commit. The individual concerned has a right to independent ADVOCACY and can appeal to an independent tribunal made up of experts who are obliged to consider the least restrictive alternative available.

The person with severe antisocial personality disorder, if also considered to 'present significant risk of serious harm' to others, can be indefinitely detained. This is regardless of whether or not he or she has committed any offence.

The person will receive a compulsory treatment order, primarily geared to 'behaviour management'. There is an important distinction between this and the order relating to people under Part I. In Part I, the care plan is designed for the person's therapeutic benefit, but under Part II, this can be waived – the person will be required to receive the 'behaviour management' he or she is assessed as needing, regardless of how beneficial this is to the person, if it is thought to be the best way of preventing risk to the public. That person's rights are the same as those outlined above for the treatment order. The proposed legislation was dropped in 2006.

mental health problems problems identified, in Western cultures, with the 'mind'.

From the time of Descartes in the 18th century, 'mind' has been defined as the workings of a person's 'consciousness', including perception, thought and judgement, emotions and behaviour. Thus, in Western society mental health problems are located in both a person's inner thinking, feelings and experience and in his or her outer actions, and this means that the person's social as well as psychological functioning is affected, as most behaviour takes place in a social context. Most cultures have a similar concern with this area of personal and social functioning but may not make such a strong distinction between 'body' and 'mind'; instead, they may experience mental health problems holistically – as expressed in descriptions such as 'my heart is squeezed'. In white culture, too, physical illness and aches and pains accompany these problems.

Range of mental health problems: psychiatry and Western culture divide mental health problems into the following categories: stress, POST-TRAUMATIC STRESS (for example, among adult survivors of child SEXUAL ABUSE), NEUROSES or 'minor psychiatric disorders' (ANXIETY, DEPRESSION, EATING DISORDERS, HYSTERIA, obsessions, PHOBIAS, psychosomatic illness), PSYCHOSES or 'major psychiatric disorders' (MANIC DEPRESSION, schizophrenia), PERSONALITY DISORDER (including psychopathy and seven other categories), and organic diseases of the brain (such as the DEMENTIAS).

In the discussion of MENTAL HEALTH it is shown that mental health problems can be understood either as 'illness' or as psychological or social difficulties and distress. There is broad agreement that the 'major psychiatric disorders' and organic disease of the brain may be understood as 'illnesses', which is reflected in findings that most people with these conditions are referred to the psychiatric services. At the other end of the scale, stress represents psychological and social difficulties, and most sufferers are not referred. There is great disagreement, however, over the classification of neuroses or 'minor psychiatric disorders' – known from the 'health' perspective as 'mental health problems' – and reactions to extreme experiences, and a substantial minority of people with these problems are referred.

What are mental health problems? These conditions are understood to have varying causes. Stress is seen as the human and appropriate response to adverse circumstances, but discomfort may cause physical and psychological distress. Organic diseases of the brain have been found to have physical origins and may possess the characteristics of 'illness', but only in the case of psychoses is there any evidence of a physiological component. With neuroses and personality disorder, PSCHODYNAMIC theories suggest that causes may lie in early parent-child relationships, and LEARNING THEORIES see these problems as learned behaviour. It is of particular significance to social work, however, that social factors have been found to have strong links with neuroses and psychoses, in that people in disadvantaged circumstances, without confidants and experiencing low self-esteem, are more likely to experience these conditions on a long-term basis, and stress generated by life events can trigger their onset. Members of oppressed groups are therefore especially vulnerable as a result of structural oppression. The explanation given by psychiatrists is that social factors may 'trigger' a 'predisposition' to the condition, but writers on EMPOWERMENT theory consider social disadvantage and oppression to be sufficient causes of depression and anxiety through the experience of LEARNED HELPLESSNESS and of psychoses as extreme distress.

Consequences of mental health problems: although the risks of psychoses and organic disease (see DEMENTIA) are well known, there may not always be an appreciation of the consequences of less serious mental health problems such as ANXIETY, NEUROSES, stress, POST-TRAUMATIC STRESS SYNDROME and PERSONALITY DISORDER (see also MENTAL ILLNESS).

Responses to mental health problems: large numbers of social service clients experience mental health problems – perhaps 60 to 70 per cent, and 80 per cent of mothers of black children in care – yet workers are often not aware of these problems unless they are the subject of the referral. Most of these people experience the less severe conditions, the neuroses of anxiety and depression, for which they are unlikely to be referred to the psychiatric services, and therefore they do not have a mental health 'label' to draw workers' attention to these problems. In other cases, perhaps where psychosis, personality disorder and even post-traumatic stress syndrome are involved, where the person has been referred to a psychiatrist, it has been shown that workers are ill-equipped to respond to these difficulties if the mental health problem is not the reason for referral.

Social workers work with people with mental health problems in a variety of ways. They offer assessment and care management under the NATIONAL HEALTH SERVICE AND COMMUNITY CARE ACT. This entails the purchase of social care services, such as supported accommodation, daytime activities, access to employment, home care and support for CARERS, which maximize the person's independent functioning. For people with long-term serious mental health problems, social workers develop care plans alongside health services, addressing matters like managing a budget, capacity for self-care, housing and social isolation. These become critical matters when the prospect of eviction, homelessness or offending heightens the risk to the individual and, possibly, the public. Mental ill health also is prominent in work with children and families. At least a third of mothers on social work caseloads experience DEPRESSION; some receive treatment for this from their GP. Mothers with depression may also experience a range of social difficulties, whether financial debt, domestic violence or social isolation. There are risks – both to the mother and child – as a result of maternal depression, among them self-harm and poor concentration or involvement in parenting tasks. Finally, poverty and the effects of mental distress intermesh for a high proportion of service users, particularly for disadvantaged or devalued groups such as OLDER PEOPLE or black people. Practitioners need to be sensitive to such sources of mental distress, which may not be immediately apparent.

V. Coppock and J. Hopton, *Critical Perspectives on Mental Health*, London, Routledge, 1992.

mental illness traditionally, 'disease' of the mind and of reasoning faculties that distorts a person's thinking, perception of reality and problem-solving capacity.

Although both physical and mental illness have been seen within the MEDICAL MODEL as involving a disease rooted in the person's biological functioning, mental illness has also been viewed as having a completely different component. It has been thought that the symptoms and experiences of someone with mental illness do not involve 'real' concerns around pain or discomfort or poor functioning; rather they are regarded as simply distortions produced by the mind. Physical illness, on the other hand, has been thought to involve real suffering, discomfort and effects on functioning. Part of the stigma attached to people with mental health problems stems from this – it is thought they cannot be taken seriously and that their symptoms are simply meaningless.

Recent thinking and research show, however, that mental and physical illnesses have certain similarities in that they both involve biological disorders that affect physical and mental functioning to a greater or lesser degree. Mental illness, therefore, like physical illness does involve real suffering and real effects on functioning of its own distinct kind, and this needs to be taken into account in work with people with mental ill health.

Mental illness is, like physical illness, strongly linked to social stress, social exclusion and inequalities of income. Life events such as trauma, bereavement or pressure from high expectations frequently precede the onset of both. Prolonged social stress has distinct biochemical effects, leading to both physical and mental ill health. Long-term social exclusion, with its loss of networks, unavailability of employment and low levels of social support, again prolongs both mental and physical illness. There are significantly higher rates of both among low-income and devalued groups.

There is considerable public concern over people who experience symptoms of mental illness. Because the person's self-control is thought to be undermined, the fears of risk, danger and incompetence associated with people with mental illness are great and, particularly in the case of the chance of physical harm, massively exaggerated. Although symptoms do affect functioning, and at times present a risk to the public, it cannot be assumed that there is no 'person' there striving to cope and manage that risk. Yet the public often perceive in the person's emotional and behavioural responses, actions and activities that fall outside conventional norms. Such norms often derive in western cultures from the idea of *personhood*, a notion that conveys independent functioning, capacity to work, self-discipline, and control over impulses and emotions. Since personhood also underpins notions of citizenship with its rights and responsibilities, being diagnosed as mentally ill means losing some or all of a citizen's rights, especially if compulsorily detained under MENTAL HEALTH LAW REFORM. It also brings with it a major STIGMA, leading to forms of SOCIAL EXCLUSION and discrimination.

P. Bean, *Mental Disorder and Community Safety*, London, Palgrave Macmillan 1996.

mental impairment a generic term that appears in the DISABILITY DISCRIMINATION ACT 1995 and includes both LEARNING DISABILITY and any recognized mental disorder.

mental incapacity long-term irreversible difficulty in performing mental functions.

Those with mental incapacity, including people with DEMENTIA and LEARNING DIFFICULTIES, are thought to have an irreversible condition as opposed to those with MENTAL ILLNESS. Persons defined as 'without capacity' are those who, when a decision is to be made, are unable by reason of mental disability to make a decision or communicate a decision. There has been rising concern about the many forms of abuse of mentally incapacitated service users at the hands of formal and informal carers. Part of the MENTAL HEALTH LAW REFORM is to give such persons some legal protection and to ensure that they have rights in long-term care given that they lack capacity to protect themselves. The discussion of such reforms include several principles:

1 the scope of any definition of incapacity should be linked to specific decisions that the person is unable to make;

2 practitioners and others should assume the person has capacity unless proved wrong;

3 the person should not be regarded as being incapable of making or communicating decisions unless all practical steps to enable her or him have been taken without success.

Good practice acts in the interests of persons so defined, which means taking into account their ascertainable wishes and feelings. It also means acting for these people in such a way as to encourage them to improve their ability to participate in any decision affecting them as fully as possible.

Mental incapacity is an important criterion for deciding whether or not practitioners are empowered to act against the person's wishes in order to protect her/him from adult abuse. People who may be victims of abuse would be assessed for mental capacity only if they are defined as 'vulnerable adults'. Vulnerable adults are defined in the white paper *No Secrets* as any person of 16 or over who is or may be in need of community care services by reason of mental or other disability, age or illness and unable to take care of himself or herself, or unable to protect himself or herself against significant harm or serious exploitation.

Johns R. Sedgwick, *Law for social work practice – working with vulnerable adults*, Basingstoke, Macmillan, 1999.

mentally disordered offenders offenders defined by the courts as suffering from a mental disorder and therefore subject to hospital treatment or community supervision.

Mentally disordered offenders are defined as those who display 'abnormally aggressive or seriously irresponsible conduct'. Many offenders who might be so defined are not recognized as suffering from a mental illness and are sent to PRISON. Those who are categorized as mentally disordered may be held in secure institutions or supervised in the community.

Although there is widespread public concern about mentally disordered offenders living in the community, they are at greater risk of self-harm than of behaving violently against others. While there is certainly some overlap between mentally disordered offenders and people with learning disabilities, those with learning disabilities who commit serious offences are relatively rare. The most common offences are sexual assaults and fire-setting.

Social work practice with mentally disordered offenders involves the continual assessment and re-assessment of RISK. This needs to be done with care and objectivity, not least because of the over-representation of black people and women in secure hospitals. Assessments are made as an aid to sentencing, as part of treatment and in the course of preparation for release, which also needs to take account of the VICTIM perspective.

Work with mentally disordered offenders is challenging, not least because it sits uneasily on the boundary between a medical model of behaviour and a criminal model, neither of which offers a full understanding of the offender's behaviour. There are ethical dilemmas involved in working between these two competing ways of understanding behaviour, especially when so much of the professional knowledge involved is disputed. There is a growing tendency to manage this work in an inter-agency way.

H. Prins, *Will they do it again? Risk assessment and management in criminal justice*, London, Routledge, 1999.

mentoring the process whereby someone with experience in a particular situation offers advice or support to others in a similar position.

Mentoring is increasingly being used in work with young offenders. Mentors are adult volunteers, who have usually received specific preparatory training to assist with the supervision of young people who are contact with YOUTH OFFENDING TEAMS. They are not usually ex-offenders, but they are recruited because they can engage with young people and spare the time to give intensive supervision.

methadone a synthetic OPIATE available in liquid, tablet or ampoule form, in varying strengths, commonly used as a clean alternative in the treatment of people addicted to opiates (see also COMMUNITY DRUG TEAM).

Methadone is available on prescription only and is a class-A drug under the MISUSE OF DRUGS ACT 1971, with a fine and/or imprisonment for unlawful possession or supply. Vehicle drivers may be at risk if they are apprehended and a sample of urine taken shows the presence of methadone; their driving licence may be withdrawn, and their vehicle insurance invalidated. Effects of methadone vary according to whether the person is a regular user of opiates or not. Like HEROIN, it is a sedative and could have fatal effects on someone unaccustomed to its use, depending on the amount used. However, the correct equivalent dose for a user with a high TOLERANCE to opiates will have the result of preventing WITHDRAWAL, enabling the user to maintain a normal lifestyle. People on a methadone prescription can work and bring up families without anyone knowing that they are addicted to opiates. The advantage of prescribing methadone over heroin in a treatment setting is that it is twice as long-acting and therefore does not need to be taken so often. In common with other opiates, methadone may cause users constipation, depression of respiration and a suppression of coughs. Because the liquid form is 50 per cent syrup, it may lead to tooth decay. It is not easy to come off methadone, and users need considerable support for some time after they have stopped.

MIG abbreviation for minimum income guarantee (see WELFARE RIGHTS 5; WELFARE RIGHTS 8).

milk tokens see WELFARE RIGHTS 7.

Minicom a brand name for a type of textphone used by deaf people; it is often used as a generic term for textphones.

Textphones enable deaf people to communicate with other textphone users by typing messages. They have a keyboard and a screen, which allows received messages to be displayed. It is possible for textphone users to communicate with people who use standard telephones through the Typetalk service, operated by BT and the RNID. Messages are channelled through an operator who can receive and transmit both speech and text.

minimum income guarantee (MIG) see WELFARE RIGHTS 5; WELFARE RIGHTS 8.

minimum intervention the principle that it is better to avoid unduly early or intensive work with young people (especially young offenders) if this may lead to NET WIDENING.

Minimum intervention (also sometimes called *parsimony*) is based on research evidence that shows that young minor offenders are less likely to re-offend if they are not subjected to unnecessarily intensive intervention by the courts and the youth justice system. Inappropriate intervention can lead to LABELLING and reinforce deviant identities. The opposing school of thought favours early intervention on the grounds that misconduct ought to be nipped in the bud by teaching pro-social behaviour at the earliest opportunity. The disadvantage of minimum intervention as it was practised in the 1980s and 1990s was that the repeated use of the CAUTION caused many observers to believe that youth crime was being condoned by a system that repeatedly failed to intervene. Rather than intervening only when appropriate, the professionals making the decisions were criticized for taking a *laissez faire* attitude, literally 'leaving the kids alone' when some response to offending and disorder was required. Youth justice workers put a great deal of energy into managing the system in such a way as to divert young people from court and from formal intervention. They saw the criminal justice system as the focus of their intervention rather than individual young people. The pendulum has now swung the other way since the implementation of the CRIME AND DISORDER ACT 1998, with first offences often being dealt with by means of REPRIMANDS and first court appearances by making REFERRAL ORDERS. These normally involve interventions by YOUTH OFFENDING TEAMS, bringing young minor offenders into extended contact with the formal criminal justice system on a larger scale than ever before.

minor mental illness any of a less serious array of symptoms and mental health problems. See NEUROSES.

Misspent Youth an influential report on the YOUTH JUSTICE system that was published by the AUDIT COMMISSION in 1996.

The report highlighted a number of areas of youth justice that, it argued, needed reform. The system was too slow, which meant that young people saw little connection between their offending and the sentence given months later. Youth justice workers spent too little time with young people and too much on paperwork. The system failed to address the underlying causes of youth crime and did not work in a 'joined up' way, wasting resources. Too little use was made of the CAUTION and other forms of DIVERSION. The report's recommendations were very selectively implemented in the shape of the CRIME AND DISORDER ACT 1998.

Misuse of Drugs Act 1971 the major piece of legislation in Britain concerning the use and misuse of DRUGS.

The Act lists numerous drugs, not all of which have medicinal purposes, and divides them into classes A, B and C, depending on how harmful the drug is perceived to be. Those in class A – for example, OPIATES, cocaine and some hallucinogenic drugs – carry the most severe penalties, ranging from a fine to life imprisonment. It is illegal to possess, supply, produce or let premises to be used for the use of these drugs. Any drug that is injected is placed automatically in class A. The vast majority of prosecutions for drug use (and the police may stop and search if they have reasonable suspicions) in the recent past were for possession of cannabis during the time when a considerable lobby developed for its legalization. In 2002 the Home Secretary made the decision to reclassify cannabis as a C category drug.

mixed economy of care the provision of services from a variety of sources, including the statutory agencies and the private and voluntary sectors.

Many policy analysts, both inside and outside the Conservative Party, believe that the provision of welfare services purely by the state sector reduces choice for individual users, undermines efficiency through monopoly and benefits welfare professionals and local bureaucrats rather than those in need. An important core belief of Conservative ideology is that choice equals freedom and that by opening up the provision of care to a greater variety of providers more choice will be available to users of services, who will therefore experience greater freedom. The Conservatives also argued that through the existence of what is largely a state monopoly there is inevitably more chance of inefficiency and waste. Some analysts see the state as being too insulated from the 'discipline of the MARKET' because it does not suffer the threat of bankruptcy that the private sector experiences, which in their view acts as a spur to efficiency. Thus, they argue that there is a need to open up the state sector to competition from the non-state sector and to introduce an INTERNAL MARKET through identifying purchaser/provider roles within SOCIAL SERVICES DEPARTMENTS. In addition, the private sector has complained that the criteria that local authorities use to register private residential accommodation are more rigorous than those used for their own in-house provision. Consequently, the Conservative government increased competition through encouragement of the mixed economy made up of both the private and voluntary sectors.

The development of the mixed economy of care should not be identified solely as a cost-saving exercise. The belief that the private and voluntary sector can provide care at a lower cost played an important part in the policy. Privatization and competitive tendering were seen as ways of reducing public expenditure and the power of public-sector trade unions. The fiscal crisis of the state, emerging out of welfare commitments and the changing demographic structure, put pressure on governments to seek ways of reducing the role of statutory provision. Local authority social services departments, however, still retain a core regulatory role and involvement through the purchase of services. The NATIONAL HEALTH SERVICE AND COMMUNITY CARE ACT placed local authorities at the centre as enabling bodies that purchased services from the private and voluntary sector in competition with their own in-house providers. The contractual relationship created between the state and the non-state sector was aimed at ensuring that users were provided for and that the level and quality of provision would be guaranteed and open to scrutiny.

While the Labour government elected in 1997 has argued and legislated against the maintenance of competitive tendering as a compulsory element in public sector provision, it still has a place for the private and voluntary sectors. Its commitment to the mixed economy of care can be identified through the role of BEST VALUE and the questions asked of local government providers through that process.

mixed-parentage or **mixed-heritage** a term used to describe first-generation offspring of parents of different 'races'.

Like 'mixed race', the terms typically describe individuals of black and white racial parentage but are not limited to this combination. The topic of racial/ethical identity in mixed-parentage children has received increasing attention in recent years, spurred by demographic trends that indicate a rapid increase in the numbers of people with mixed parentage and by the acknowledgement that there is little well-defined research and theory in this area.

Reviews of the research suggest that few children seem to experience their situation as a painful clash of loyalties between black and white. There are some mixed-parentage children, however, whose experiences give cause for concern. These are the children who are two and a half times more likely than other children to enter local authority care. Studies have shown that some mixed-parentage adolescents in local authority care exhibit identify confusion and low self-esteem. Some authors argue that mixed-parentage youngsters should be classified as black and that they should see themselves as so: the argument is that society sees them as black and that they will be better off if that is their self-perceived identify. Although mixed-parentage children encounter problems faced by most minorities, they must also figure out how to reconcile the heritage of both parents in a society that categorizes individuals into single groups. Thus, the development of a health biracial identity means not only the minority and majority community, but having the flexibility to accept that others may identify them as minority, majority or biracial.

mobility the ability of people to get around indoors and to get to places they want to go. The term can be used in connection with individual capacity for movement or with the skills and facilities that are needed in order to negotiate the physical environment.

Mobility impairments are bodily characteristics that restrict the capacity of individuals to move around without personal assistance or aids. People with VISUAL IMPAIRMENT, however, also experience difficulties in getting around, and rehabilitation programmes emphasize the skills needed to avoid hazards in the physical environment. Mobility goes beyond individual abilities and skills, and involves access to transport and the places to which people want to go. For example, many disabled people have limited choice of employment or leisure because they are restricted by the limited transport or assistance available. Much public transport is inaccessible for disabled people, and this has been identified as an issue for action by the DISABILITY RIGHTS COMMISSION.

mobility component see WELFARE RIGHTS 3.

modelling essentially, learning by example, a therapeutic technique in BEHAVIOUR MODIFICATION.

The person being treated watches another person coping appropriately with an ANXIETY-provoking stimulus, including anything from a social event to spiders. He or she thus learns the inappropriateness of his or her own reactions and more effective ways of responding. Many studies have confirmed that modelling is a speedy and effective treatment method.

modernization the government objective of improving the delivery of health and social services through a range of key initiatives.

Firstly, the government identifies the need to identify and spread best practice in central government activities, including the joint training of ministers and civil servants to support JOINED-UP ACTION. Secondly, such joined-up working should also be evident at the local level and include increased responsiveness of services to users and the public. As part of this process, all services are to be reviewed once every five years to identify if the public sector is the best provider or whether the private sector should considered. New TARGETS will be provided and performance will be monitored to identify failing services.

Two key documents for social services were published in 1998, 'Modernizing Social Services' and 'Modernizing Health and Social Services'. In these documents the respective roles of health and social services in the areas of provision, including child care and learning disabilities, are identified. Along with these, the process of BEST VALUE was developed as part of the process of modernization for local government social services.

money advice advice for people with financial difficulties, typically including advice on how to maximize income, how to manage debt and how to budget, as well as the money adviser acting as the person's ADVOCATE with creditors and the courts.

Maximizing income can include helping people to ensure that they have the best tax arrangements for their circumstances, that they are claiming all the state benefits to which they are entitled, that claims are backdated where feasible and that their wages or salaries are as high as possible (that employers are paying the statutory minimum wage for example). In addition, some advisers try to raise lump sums to alleviate immediate problems or pressing debts, sometimes from statutory sources (section 17 payments under the CHILDREN ACT 1989 or a claim for a community care grant – see WELFARE RIGHTS (8) – from the BENEFITS AGENCY) and sometimes from charitable or other sources. Maximizing income will often include 'better-off' calculations so that people can make considered judgements about whether work will pay enough or whether they will maintain a better standard of living by relying on welfare benefits.

Debt in itself does not constitute a problem as long as debtors can manage their contractual obligations to repay a creditor through agreed arrangements. It is default debt that is the problem, that is, a situation of not being able to honour contractual obligations. The management of default debt is a complex process that, first, entails working out detailed income and expenditure accounts in order to determine what sums, if any, can be used to deal with debts. In this context, it is usual to distinguish between priority and non-priority debt (priority debts are those that could ultimately entail imprisonment, fines or loss of a service, goods or dwelling), although the consumers may have their own views on which are important. There are some young men, for example, who would value a car above a home.

The next stage involves negotiating arrangements with creditors that are practicable for the debtor and are seen as sensible and fair by the creditors. In some cases it may be possible to challenge the legitimacy of a debt (for example, is it really owed by the person or is it their ex-partner's debt?) or to get a debt apportioned between people held to be jointly responsible for it. In other cases, non-priority debts may be written off by a creditor if the debtor has no long-term prospect of realistically dealing with them. Other strategies include trying to make informal arrangements with creditors to deal with default debt in the short or long term, having periods when payments might be suspended, restructuring debts or payment periods or more formal arrangements through the courts of administration orders, individual voluntary arrangements or even bankruptcy. Administration orders, in particular, can be a useful device for people with multiple non-priority debts such as hire-purchase or loans for consumer goods. As long as total debt does not exceed £5,000, courts will determine how much a debtor can pay (leaving reasonable amounts for essential living expenses), and this amount is paid to a court at intervals to be divided among debtors in accordance with each creditor's claim on the total debt. The major disadvantage of administration orders is that people are labelled as 'not credit-worthy' and will find accessing credit from reputable sources in the future very difficult.

Budgeting entails giving advice about the relative costs of fuel and how fuel might be used more efficiently, information on cheaper sources of food or on the nutritional value of cheaper foods, advice on cheaper sources of credit or help in reflecting on the economic costs of lifestyles. Frequently, budgeting includes advising consumers on how expenditure might be managed, where, for example, some bills are to be met weekly, some monthly and others at less frequent intervals. For those people who find it very difficult to budget and who have a track record of having essential services disconnected or eviction from their home threatened, other tactics such as having fuels and rent paid direct by the Benefits Agency might be usefully considered.

To be an effective debt adviser involves the ability to unravel complex financial matters, often with individuals who are themselves confused, anxious and embarrassed by their situation. The middle classes have long used solicitors and banks to advise them on financial matters, but the past 20 years have witnessed the growth of advice agencies prepared to help poor people with money difficulties. The Citizens Advice Bureaux (CAB) are pre-eminent among them, but in many areas neighbourhood offices of local authorities as well as independent ADVICE CENTRES have developed money advice services. In 1992 debt became the largest category of inquiry dealt with by the CAB (social security problems were second). The economic context of these developments includes the growth of personal consumer credit, which in 1980 was £13 billion, by 1997 was £87 billion and by 2006 was £193 billion. During 1980, 22 per cent of those in the lowest income group used credit; by 2000 this figure had risen to well over 70 per cent. Figures from the Council of Mortgage Lenders show that in 1980 about 13,500 mortgages were between six and twelve months in arrears; by 1995 the comparable figure was 178,000. Since that time the figure has fallen, reaching 29,200 in 2003; by 2005 it had risen to 32,500.

A rigorous analysis of debt and default debt has yet to be undertaken in Britain, but it is known that many people who develop problems do so as a result of unforeseen difficulties, such as unemployment, short-time working, divorce and separation, bereavement, sickness and the failure of businesses. Although there are examples of consumers whose behaviour could be construed as reckless, the vast majority seem to be those who cannot, rather than will not, pay. Indebtedness is mostly rooted in poverty, but the apparently foolhardy behaviour of some debtors still needs to be understood and advice offered. Wider social forces, such as the availability of credit, high and variable rates of interest and the general pressures to be a consumer, are critical in this context.

Contemporary research into the access to credit for very poor people has consistently found that they are obliged to use moneylenders, 'loan sharks' and other credit agencies that charge extremely high rates of interest despite the regulatory constraints of the Consumer Credit Act 1974. Often social security claimants or residents living in particular areas will be denied access to normal sources of credit such as banks and finance houses. The CREDIT UNION movement, which aims to give poor people access to relatively cheap loans based upon savings societies, is well developed in some areas but not at all in others. The Social Fund (see WELFARE RIGHTS (8)), administered by the DEPARTMENT FOR WORK AND PENSIONS, is another source of cheap loans, but the quota system with cash limits means that access cannot be guaranteed.

Most social workers now accept the connection between money problems and personal and social functioning. Stress caused by POVERTY is clearly acknowledged. Few social workers, however, develop expertise in this area of work, preferring to refer individuals to agencies like the CAB (which in many areas cannot cope with the volume of work). Yet consumers value practical help of this kind very highly. Some social services offices have their own money advice and welfare rights specialists, but these are uncommon. The part that social work has to play in ANTI-POVERTY STRATEGIES is as yet unclear and poorly developed.

M. Wolfe, *Debt Advice Handbook*, fourth edition, London, Child Poverty Action Group, 1999.

monitoring surveillance of a consumer by a social welfare or social work service or the general scrutiny of work to evaluate its effectiveness and efficiency.

In the first sense, monitoring applies to any situation where a person or family is watched in relation to some particular aspect of social functioning. For example, a child who has just started to attend school after a lengthy period of truanting may have his or her attendance monitored closely so that prompt intervention may be initiated in the event of further absences from school. Similarly, a family may be policed closely (perhaps with some form of help also being offered) following an incident of non-accidental injury to a child.

Monitoring can also apply to standards within social welfare agencies. A general duty placed upon virtually all managers is to monitor the work of all those for whom they have line management responsibility. Elected councillors have this general duty on behalf of the public. There are an increasing number of people within social welfare agencies who have specific roles to play in monitoring processes: for example, INSPECTION bodies and COMPLAINTS officers, lay visitors to prisons and police stations, and any manager with a quality assurance brief. The government has its own monitoring mechanisms, such as the SOCIAL SERVICES INSPECTORATE. Such monitoring seems to be preoccupied with value for money (efficiency), effectiveness (the evaluation function) and accountability (is work done according to standards laid down by the appropriate agency or government guidelines?).

mood an emotional state that influences a person's thoughts and behaviour.
  The basic division between 'good' and 'bad' moods refers to a number of different emotions. A good mood includes feelings of happiness, contentment, joy and cheerfulness. A bad mood can include feelings of irritability, depression, anxiety and anger. Social workers and social care workers frequently encounter people who have extreme moods – in which feelings of euphoria, excitement, anger or depression completely dominate their behaviour. These can arise from a variety of causes, such as SUBSTANCE MISUSE, MENTAL ILLNESS and BEREAVEMENT or other traumatic events.

mood swing a rapid or relatively swift change of MOOD. Common examples are changes from feelings of elation to depression or from contentment to anger. Extreme mood swings can be a symptom of MENTAL DISORDER such as bi-polar or MANIC DEPRESSION.

Moon a system of reading and writing for blind people that is based on tactile symbols.
  Moon is simpler to learn and use than BRAILLE, but the materials are considerably more bulky. It cannot be produced by hand, and the available literature is small. There is a relatively small number of Moon users, and they tend to be older people.

Motability a charity that helps disabled people and their families to become more mobile by acquiring cars or powered wheelchairs.
  Motability supplies finance for the hire or hire purchase of cars and powered wheelchairs. In return, the disabled person agrees to pay all or part of any mobility allowance received through the benefit system to Motability. Where further financial assistance is needed, or adaptations are required to the vehicle, Motability can arrange for grants to be paid either from its own funds or from funds it administers on behalf of the government.

motivation something that causes someone to do something. While motivation is easy to define in such global terms, it is harder to distinguish between potential motivators and to identify the particular cause that could be said to have led a person to behave in a particular way.
  One theory of motivation that has been influential is Maslow's 'hierarchy of needs', in which it is proposed that human needs can be placed in an order ranging from the most basic, such as thirst and hunger, to the highest, which is the need for self-actualization. According to this theory, a need further up the hierarchy becomes important as a

motivator only when more basic ones have been fulfilled. It is true that explanations for behaviour can be seen to be of different types and may fall into different levels. At the most basic level, some behaviour, such as an eye-blink, is a reflex response to stimulus, such as a puff of air. But it is possible to override even a reflex; a person picking up a precious plate that is very hot is likely to try to put it down gently rather than drop it. At the next level, biological drives, such as hunger, can be seen to motivate behaviour. Once again, the dieter or the hunger striker demonstrates that one potential motivator can be countermanded by another, so Maslow's hierarchy is not universally applicable. Beyond reflexes and biological drives, the identification of causes of behaviour becomes more problematic. Behaviourists have tried to identify secondary drives – those that, once fulfilled, could be used to satisfy a primary or biological drive. For example, money can be seen as a secondary drive that can be used to satisfy the primary drive of hunger. However, the argument becomes more circular when no obvious link between a piece of behaviour and a primary drive can be found. For example, when a child explores his or her environment, it adds little to say that the explanation for the child's behaviour is that he or she has a drive to explore.

The complexity of the subject of motivation can be seen from attempts to motivate people at work. Early researchers suggested that the way to motivate people to be more productive was to show them how to be more efficient and then pay them more for increased productivity. Later work showed, not surprisingly, that people differ: some are more affected by improvements in conditions at work, others by job satisfaction and yet others by job security. A key issue in social work is that of trying to establish how motivated service users are to try to change behaviour or circumstances that appear to be potentially within their control. Key questions are: 'can a person change?' and 'does he or she want to change?' To help service users in this regard, it is important to negotiate fully the nature both of the problems and of possible solutions. Motivation is more likely to be engaged if the person finds the issues relevant and the tasks achievable.

P. Evans, *Motivation and Emotion*, London, Routledge, 1989.

mourning the process of adapting to the loss of an attachment figure mainly, though not always , through death. Mourning is a term used to describe the often complex ways in which people express the grief they feel as a result of the loss of someone, or something, precious to them. It is both an individual and private – and therefore unique – experience in which people find their own ways of moving into a future without their loved one and also a public event in which people perhaps feel supported, although sometimes constricted, by their community and culture, which may have very clear expectations about how people should behave in such circumstances. (See also BEREAVEMENT.)

N. Thompson (ed), *Loss and Grief – A Guide for Human Services Practitioners*, Basingstoke, Palgrave, 2002.

multi-agency public protection panel (MAPPP) a meeting at which representatives of the relevant agencies plan the management of work with high-risk sexual and violent offenders.

Under the Criminal Justice and Court Services Act 2000 and the Sex Offenders Act 1997, the POLICE, PROBATION and other services are required to set up joint arrangements in the form of MAPPPs to ensure that serious sexual and violent offenders are assessed and appropriately supervised when living in the community.

The early implementation of this requirement, which came into force in 2001, has been very patchy and inconsistent. In response, the Home Office established a Dangerous Offenders Unit, which has issued detailed guidance. This makes it clear that the establishment and servicing of the panels is a joint police and probation responsibility. Community representation on panels is to be established with a view to introducing an element of community accountability. These measures do not go as far as some populist commentators have urged towards exposing offenders to community scrutiny. The community representatives will be required to keep individual cases confidential rather than acting as a conduit for 'community notification' of the presence of serious ex-offenders in neighbourhoods, as in parts of the USA under 'Megan's law'. Their presence is arguably designed to reassure worried community members and to lend legitimacy to the official agencies' decisions, not to represent punitive community views.

Indeed, the Home Office is also evaluating two experimental projects based on 'circles of support and accountability' for serious offenders in Canada. These involve community volunteers in informal supervision, support and befriending of people released from prison, with a clearly understood monitoring role. They are based upon a restorative model of criminal justice rather than a punitive one. It seems possible that the two models may in practice be required to co-exist if MAPPPs and circles of support and accountability become responsible for the same individuals in some parts of the country.

H. Kemshall and M. Maguire, 'Public protection, partnership and risk' in *Punishment and Society* 3 (2) 2001.

multidisciplinary work work undertaken jointly by workers and professionals from different disciplines or occupations.

In social work and in general social welfare provision, there is increasingly an expectation that services will be delivered collaboratively by several agencies or that a particular problem can be addressed only if professionals work together in the same organization or team. An example of the first approach is COMMUNITY CARE services involving collaboration between social services and health services in relation to vulnerable older people or those with chronic mental health problems (where social workers, health workers and housing workers in particular may need to work together). An example of the second is a CHILD

GUIDANCE clinic, where social workers may be found in the same team as a psychologist, counsellor and psychiatrist. Other examples include YOUTH OFFENDING TEAMS where a social worker will work cheek by jowl with a probation officer, a police officer, representatives from education and health services and sometimes additional professionals (such as a worker from a YOUNG OFFENDERS INSTITUTION or a careers adviser).

There are difficulties associated with multidisciplinary work. Sometimes professionals can disagree about the causes of and solutions to problems. They may have different objectives for their work (or their parent organization may have) because of differing professional paradigms. Consider, for example, the differences between the MEDICAL MODEL and the SOCIAL MODEL OF DISABILITY. There can also be relational problems because, for example, of differences in status, power and language. Multidisciplinary work requires effective decision-making and a clear allocation of roles and responsibilities. The Labour government in the early 2000s has made it clear that it wishes organizations that need to work together to do so and to bring down the 'Berlin Wall' that has characterized relationships between some agencies (in this instance Health Services and Social Services).

multi-infarct dementia DEMENTIA caused by disruption in the blood supply to the brain. The condition, which accounts for only 15 to 20 per cent of dementia, is observed as a series of minor 'strokes' that cumulatively result in an increase in mental impairment.

Munchausen's syndrome by proxy a psychological condition in which the person feels compelled to engage in frequent contact with medical authorities such as hospitals and doctors. This is done 'by proxy' – by using someone else, almost always a child, as the person who requires medical attention rather than the compulsive person.

A number of instances of CHILD ABUSE have been related to the syndrome, since the sufferer can actually harm the child in order to provide the reason for contacting the hospital or doctor. In extreme instances, protective action may have to be taken by the local authority.

N*n*

NAAPS abbreviation for NATIONAL ASSOCIATION OF ASIAN PROBATION STAFF.
NAPO abbreviation for NATIONAL ASSOCIATION OF PROBATION OFFICERS.
NASS abbreviation for NATIONAL ASYLUM SUPPORT SERVICE.
NASWE abbreviation for NATIONAL ASSOCIATION OF SOCIAL WORKERS IN EDUCATION.

National Assistance Act 1948 a legal cornerstone of the welfare state giving local authorities the duty to provide residential accommodation for vulnerable adults who need it.

This Act, introduced as part of the WELFARE STATE after the Second World War, provides the statutory mandate for the provision of residential accommodation by local authorities to those in need. Under section 21, local authorities have a duty to provide accommodation for people over 18 who 'by reason of age, illness, disability or any other circumstances are in need of care and attention which is not otherwise available to them'. The duty is owed to anyone ordinarily resident in the authority's area or who is not so resident but is in urgent need. Much accommodation so provided is found in residential and nursing homes, or special housing, but ordinary housing may be provided if this will meet a need that would otherwise have to be met by other community care services.

Charging for the care and shelter provided in such accommodation has proved a highly contentious point. Charges must be levied (section 44) for the care provided in such accommodation and local authorities must follow regulations in relation to charges made ((Community Care (Residential Accommodation) Act 1998)). In the late 1990s, however, a Royal Commission on long-term care for older people concluded that personal care should be provided without charge to individuals. Both Scotland and Wales have signalled the intention to follow this recommendation, but in England only nursing care is to be made available free of charge to recipients.

Section 29 of the National Assistance Act gives local authorities both duties and powers to make arrangements for promoting the welfare of disabled people. The duties relate to social work services, advice and support, social rehabilitation or adjustment to disability, registers, occupational, social, cultural and recreational facilities, workshops and hostels. The powers relate to holiday homes, travel, assistance in finding accommodation, warden costs, warden services, and information. Section 29 provides a definition of disability that, despite its dated terminology, remains one of the determinants of eligibility for services for disabled people:

'persons aged 18 and over, who are blind, deaf or dumb, or who suffer from mental disorder of any description, and other persons who are substantially and permanently handicapped by illness, injury or congenital deformity or such other disabilities as may be prescribed.'

Both section 21 and section 29 are in Part III of the Act, which falls within the definition of community care services developed in section 46 of the NATIONAL HEALTH SERVICE AND COMMUNITY CARE ACT 1990. Eligibility for 'Part III accommodation is thus determined through assessment of needs undertaken under section 47 of that later Act. See also WELFARE RIGHTS 6; WELFARE RIGHTS 7.

National Association of Asian Probation Staff (NAAPS) an organization for probation workers who identify themselves as Asian.

The association provides support for individual probation workers, and its practical activities include contributions to probation training programmes and to the wider debate on criminal justice issues. Asian staff who identify themselves as black join the ASSOCIATION OF BLACK PROBATION OFFICERS rather than NAAPS.

National Association of Probation Officers (NAPO) the professional association and trade union representing all grades of probation officers and other professional staff in the PROBATION SERVICE in England, Northern Ireland and Wales.

Since NAPO was founded in 1912, it has provided a forum for the discussion of professional matters and, more recently, it has also supported its members in trade union activities. It publishes a monthly newsletter and the quarterly *Probation Journal*, holds a range of conferences, and negotiates pay and conditions on behalf of its members. It also campaigns with other organizations on criminal justice and trade union issues, and is affiliated to the Trades Union Congress. NAPO has been in the forefront of campaigns about DISCRIMINATION against women, black people and lesbian and gay people in the criminal justice system and more widely. It has a national office in London and a network of local branches. Closely allied to NAPO are two autonomous professional associations, the ASSOCIATION OF BLACK PROBATION OFFICERS and LESBIANS AND GAY MEN IN PROBATION.

National Association of Social Workers in Education (NASWE) the professional association for EDUCATION SOCIAL WORKERS (education welfare officers) employed by local education authorities. NASWE represents its members' interests to the DEPARTMENT FOR EDUCATION AND SKILLS but also promotes the interests of its primary client group under the slogan 'For every child a chance'. It also promotes professional standards, training and staff development.

National Asylum Support Service (NASS) a division of the Home Office that is responsible for providing accommodation and support to asylum seekers who are destitute and who made their application after April 2000.

NASS was established under the IMMIGRATION AND ASYLUM ACT 1999. It provides accommodation and support by contracting with local authorities and private providers. Accommodation is provided in 'dispersed' locations throughout the UK on a 'no choice' basis.

National Care Standards Commission a non-departmental public body responsible to the Secretary of State for Health. It derives its authority from the Care Standards Act 2000, with the remit to set and monitor standards in the field of health and social care. Its aim is to drive up quality of care for vulnerable adults and children by ensuring greater consistency in care standards across the country. Eight new independent regional Commissions for Care Standards (CCSs) have particular responsibility for the registration and inspection of care homes, both residential and nursing, and will also inspect domiciliary social care providers.

National Health Service (NHS) the organization for the provision of state-funded health care. Established in 1948, the NHS aims to provide health care for the entire population on the basis of need.

The original intention of the NHS was the provision of health care without reference to a person's ability to pay, based on the belief that expenditure would decrease as the population became healthier as a result of the benefits of the services provided. However, a number of significant problems emerged out of the original structure of the NHS. First, the service was centred on existing hospital provision, and there was therefore an uneven geographical distribution of resources. Second, demand for services proved to be greater than anticipated and expanded as new technologies emerged. This resulted in pressures on costs that led to the intention of providing free health care being undermined and the introduction of prescription charges shortly after the creation of the service. Third, with the concentration on hospital services, other areas of provision were overshadowed by developments in surgical and other interventionist procedures. The so-called 'Cinderella' services included care for people with LEARNING DISABILITIES, MENTAL HEALTH services and provision for OLDER PEOPLE.

The NHS became subject to an increasingly frequent series of re-organizations in order to tackle its problems, including the development of health authorities to replace hospital boards and a move to change the balance in resource distribution through the establishment of the *Regional Allocation Working Party*, which channelled resources towards underfunded areas. More recently, concerns with cost containment led to a major review of the service, resulting in the publication of a government policy statement, *Working for Patients*, in 1989. The most significant changes introduced by this review included the following reforms: the introduction of an INTERNAL MARKET in which general practitioners and district health authorities purchased health services from hospitals, creating a purchaser/provider split within the NHS; the establishment of trusts in which hospitals and other services, including ambulance services and mental health hospitals, are managed independently of the health authorities; the introduction for some general practices of budgets that they had to manage themselves and from which they could purchase hospital services, screening services and sometimes the services of social workers and other carers. These changes were criticized for potentially creating a two-tier system of health care in which resources were directed towards those hospital services with trust status and general practices that are budget- or fundholders.

Partly because of these changes, the NEW LABOUR government abolished the internal market and introduced further major reforms. In 1997 the white paper *The New NHS: Modern, dependable* was published, which replaced purchasing of services by the concept of commissioning. All general practices were to be joined together in Primary Care Groups whose role is to establish local health-care needs and ensure that these are met through the commissioning of services from Hospital Trusts and other service providers. The Primary Care Groups will have representatives from social services and community nurses to ensure that issues around community-based care are taken into account as well as acute services. In 2001 a new reform paper, *Shifting the Balance of Power*, reinforced this development by establishing all Primary Care Groups as Trusts by April 2002, thus giving them greater control over their resources and provision. As part of this process, all District Health Authorities were abolished and larger Strategic Health Authorities were created with a broader role, leaving the PRIMARY CARE TRUSTS to concentrate on needs and provision.

C. Ham, *Health Policy in Britain*, fourth edition, London, Palgrave, 1999.

National Health Service and Community Care Act 1990 a watershed Act of Parliament that established the main mechanisms for providing COMMUNITY CARE services for adults.

The legal provision on community care services has developed piecemeal over many years and is spread over a number of different Acts of Parliament. It is also a constantly changing picture because of the impact of judicial interpretation in the Court of Appeal and House of Lords. From 2 October 2000 the implementation of the HUMAN RIGHTS ACT 1998 has had an impact upon this interpretation. There is a need for reform to bring all the provision under the umbrella of one Act. For the moment, piecing together the picture is rather like doing a jigsaw – it is not only necessary to know about the different provisions but also to understand how they link together.

The National Health Service and Community Care Act is an important component, providing a single gateway for access to a range of services provided under other, in many cases older, legislation. It is an Act of Parliament that was primarily concerned with the restructuring of the health service, establishing purchaser/provider arrangements between health authorities, general practices and NATIONAL HEALTH SERVICE TRUSTS, which have subsequently been overtaken by later reforms. One part of it, however, gave to local authority SOCIAL SERVICES DEPARTMENTS significant duties relating to SOCIAL CARE services, including the duty to assess people's needs in order to determine their eligibility for provision.

The Act arose from the then government's philosophy that a mixed economy of welfare was a more efficient means of delivering cost-effective services to adults with non-medical support needs arising from age, disability, mental ill-heath, drugs or alcohol, and illness. The local authority, rather than remaining the main provider of care, was to become the enabler – establishing need and eligibility through ASSESSMENT, then commissioning packages of care from a range of providers, including independent agencies. In addition to bringing cost advantages, this was intended also to promote service USERS' choice and greater flexibility in the arrangements to meet their needs.

The emphasis on care in the community was not new. There had been growing discontent with institutional care, from both professional and user perspectives, and a concern to promote more autonomous, independent lifestyles for people in need of care and support.

The guidance accompanying the Act (Department of Health 1990) clarifies the objectives for social services departments: first, to promote the development of DOMICILIARY, DAY CARE and RESPITE services to enable people to live in their own homes wherever feasible and sensible; second, to ensure that service providers make practical support for CARERS a high priority; third, to make proper assessment of need and good CARE MANAGEMENT the cornerstone of high-quality care; fourth, to promote the development of a flourishing independent sector alongside good-quality public services; fifth, to clarify the responsibilities of agencies, so making it easier to hold them to account for their performance; and sixth, to secure better value for taxpayers' money by introducing a new funding system for social care.

Despite these aims, there have remained shortcomings in community care provision in relation to the quality, consistency, flexibility and co-ordination of services. The NEW LABOUR government of the late 1990s has restated the objectives of community care as being to help people to live independently, to create fairer, more consistent services and to make sure that services fit individual needs (Department of Health 1998). Care packages should intervene in users' lives no more than is necessary to foster independence and should be constructed with the active involvement of service users and their carers.

The key to community care service provision is assessment of need. The local authority's assessment duties are contained in section 47 of the National Health Service and Community Care Act 1990. Section 47(1) states:

'... where it appears to a local authority that any person for whom they may provide or arrange for the provision of community care services may be in need of any such services, the authority:

(a) shall carry out an assessment of his needs for those services; and

(b) having regard to the results of that assessment, shall decide whether his need calls for the provision by them of any such services.'

The duty implies three decisions: Is the person someone to whom provision might be made? What are the person's assessed needs? Is it necessary to meet those needs? Case law has established that anyone to whom the local authority has the legal power to make provision must be assessed, even if services are not available.

If the person being assessed is disabled (within the definition of DISABILITY in section 29 of the NATIONAL ASSISTANCE ACT 1948) then under section 47 there are additional duties on the local authority to undertake an assessment under section 4 of the DISABLED PERSONS (SERVICES, CONSULTATION AND REPRESENTATION) ACT 1986. This is an important provision for disabled people. Section 47 requires notification to health and housing authorities by social services if a person being assessed appears to have needs that could be met by these agencies. The purpose of the notification is to invite health and housing to participate in the assessment.

Guidance on assessment, issued by the Department of Health at the point of implementation of the Act, states that assessment should: be aimed at meeting individuals' wishes, actively involve users and take their views into account, consider risk factors, health, finance, education/employment, leisure, accommodation, abilities, transport, personal care and social support needs and be needs-led, not automatic decisions on eligibility criteria. The assessment process should also establish priorities and objectives for intervention, achieve, maintain or restore social independence and quality of life, preserve or restore normal living, at home where possible, and be informed by values of dignity, fulfilment and choice.

While an assessment of need is taking place, anyone providing a substantial amount of care for the service user on a regular basis (excluding professional paid carers) is eligible for a carer's assessment under the CARERS (RECOGNITION AND SERVICES) ACT 1995. While in itself not a mandate for services directly to carers, this requires the carer's assessed needs to be taken into account when making decisions about what services might be offered to the service user. The CARERS AND DISABLED CHILDREN ACT 2000 offers a stronger mandate, providing for some services directly to carers themselves and allowing a carer's assessment to take place even when a community care assessment is not proceeding.

Once an assessment has been undertaken, professional decision-making establishes which assessed needs meet the local authority's ELIGIBILITY CRITERIA for service provision. Need is defined by the local authority, not by the service user, and the outcome of assessment is therefore a task involving professional discretion, although expressed and psychological needs must be taken into account. Once eligibility for provision has been established, service users should have choice about what particular services will meet their needs, although the ultimate decision on this again rests with the local authority.

The services available are those that fall within the definition in section 46 of the National Health Service and Community Care Act 1990. This defines community care services as those pro-vided under the following legislation:

Part 3, National Assistance Act 1948: this includes duties to provide residential accommodation and community services to disabled people. Also included are community services for disabled people provided under section 2 of the Chronically Sick and Disabled Persons Act 1970;

Section 45 of the Health Services and Public Health Act 1968: the power to make arrangements for promoting the welfare of older people;

Section 21 and schedule 8 of the National Health Service Act 1977: duties and powers to provide for the prevention of illness, the care of people who are ill, and aftercare of people who have been ill, together with home help and laundry services to expectant or nursing mothers, and people who are old, disabled or ill;

Section 117 of the Mental Health Act 1983: duty to provide aftercare services for people discharged from compulsory detention in psychiatric hospital under certain sections of that Act.

While local authorities may not charge for assessment and care management, under section 17 of the Health and Social Services and Social Security Adjudications Act 1983, they may, if they choose, charge for the services they arrange or provide. It is up to local authorities to decide what to charge, but charges must be reasonable and services must not be withdrawn because of inability to pay. Charges can be waived or reduced to what it is reasonable to expect an individual to pay. There is, however, an important exception to charging. Statutory aftercare services provided under section 117 of the Mental Health Act 1983 are exempt from charges if they are part of the section 117 package.

Instead, or as well as arranging for services to be provided, the local authority may offer the service user direct payments under the Community Care (Direct Payments) Act 1996 to enable the care arrangements to fall more within the individual's own control.

In addition to assessing and arranging services for individuals, section 46(1) of the National Health Service and Community Care Act 1990 gives local authorities the duty to produce community care plans, in consultation with other agencies and interested parties, indicating how the population needs of a locality have been determined and how local services are designed to meet them. Such plans now form only one aspect of the complex planning machinery that is imposed by central government under the health and social services modernization agenda, and it may be that they will be subsumed within the requirement for locality planning across a broad spectrum of provision.

Department of Health, *Community Care in the Next Decade and Beyond: Policy Guidance*, London: HMSO, 1990.

Department of Health, *Modernizing Social Services*, London, The Stationery Office, 1998.

Department of Health, *Care Management and Assessment: Practitioners' Guide*, London, HMSO, 1991.

National Health Services Act 1977 a statute under which certain social and health services are provided for persons who are ill or who have a MENTAL DISORDER.

This is one of several Acts of Parliament under which COMMUNITY CARE services are provided. It falls within the definition of such services in section 46 of the NATIONAL HEALTH AND COMMUNITY CARE ACT 1990 and relates primarily to people who are ill, including those with mental disorder. The Act recognizes the difficulties of delineating responsibilities between health and social services in relation to these groups of people. Section 22 requires the authorities to co-operate in providing services, a duty that has been amended, extended and updated by the Health Act 1999.

Schedule 8 of the Act outlines the services that fall within the remit of the local authority. Provision may be made for the prevention of illness, for the care of people who are ill and the aftercare of those who have been ill. This could include activity and training centres, meals, social services advice and support, night-sitting, holidays, social and recreational activities, and drug and alcohol services. In respect of most forms of illness, the services remain at the discretion of the local authority. In relation to mental disorder, however, the local authority is under a duty specifically to provide training and occupational centres, guardianship and social work services.

There is also a duty to provide home help services to households where people are ill, old or disabled, or where there is an expectant and nursing mother, and a power to provide laundry services to the same groups.

Under section 17 of the Health and Social Services and Social Security Adjudications Act 1983, local authorities may, if they choose, charge service users for the services provided.

The provisions are similar to those provided for disabled people under the NATIONAL ASSISTANCE ACT 1948 and the CHRONICALLY SICK AND DISABLED PERSONS ACT 1970, and for older people under the HEALTH SERVICES AND PUBLIC HEALTH ACT 1968.

National Health Service Trusts main provider organizations in the NATIONAL HEALTH SERVICE of health care, including hospitals and community services, established under the reforms of the 1990s as part of the development of the INTERNAL MARKET in health care. The main Trusts are the hospital services, which are largely self-governing within guidelines established by the Department of Health. Other services operating under Trust status include ambulance services and community health care, which includes community nurses, psychiatrists, occupational therapists and other allied health professionals such as physiotherapists. Since April 2002, Primary Care Groups attained Trust status as PRIMARY CARE TRUSTS, and these organizations commission services from the secondary and community care services contained in the existing trusts.

national insurance contributions (NIC) payments made by working age people, including employees (and their employers), the self-employed and those who make voluntary contributions to the National Insurance fund. National insurance contributions help to fund the NATIONAL HEALTH SERVICE and contributory benefits (see WELFARE RIGHTS 1).

National Probation Service the probation service in England and Wales became a unified national service, directly accountable to the HOME OFFICE, in April 2001.

The Criminal Justice and Court Services Act 2000 abolished the local accountability of the probation service, replacing it with a national structure in the form of the National Probation Directorate. Its director reports to the Home Secretary, and although local services remain administratively distinct, they were reorganized to ensure co-terminosity (i.e. identical boundaries) with the police. At the same time, a new national CHILDREN AND FAMILY COURT ADVISORY AND SUPPORT SERVICE took over the previous probation role in working in the family courts. Chief probation officers are now appointed by the Home Secretary and are responsible to local probation boards, which can be replaced by the Home Secretary if their performance is unsatisfactory. The boards consist of a judge appointed by the Lord Chancellor's Department and local representatives appointed by the Home Secretary.

These arrangements constitute a considerable centralization of power compared to the relative autonomy of local probation services previously. The appointment of a national director gives the service a single organizational head for the first time and should help to ensure the provision of a consistent service.

National Service Framework for Older People the structure provided by government to improve services for older people and eliminate the discrimination against older people in health and social care services.

To promote improving quality and to tackle existing variations in care, the National Service Framework sets national standards for the care of older people, defines service models, proposes strategies for implementation and sets performance measures against which to assess progress. The framework is directly linked to other policy developments such as The NHS Plan. The framework focuses on maintaining older people's independence by the development of intermediate care. It also reaffirms the push for more integrated approaches by health, social care and housing in their responses to service development and the need for greater support for informal carers.

There are eight standards:

1 *no age discrimination* – only criteria are clinical or assessed needs;
2 *intermediate care* – reduce avoidable admission to hospital or institutional care through effective rehabilitation and recovery;
3 *person-centred care* – treat older people as individuals with respect and dignity, involve them in decisions about care and develop a single assessment and integrated care;
4 *general hospital care* – shorter waiting times in Accident and Emergency, involvement in discharge planning, better trained staff and care;
5 *stroke* – action to prevent strokes, access to specialist units, coordinated rehabilitation and support for carers;
6 *falls* – improved prevention through greater access to health promotion services, specialist assessment and coordinated action to reduce risk, coordinated rehabilitation;
7 *mental health* – improvements in early diagnosis and treatment of depression and dementia, best cost-effective drug treatments;
8 *active healthy life* – promotion of health and wellbeing of older people, including smoking cessation and flu immunization, wider initiatives: exercise, healthy eating, keeping warm.

It is worth noting that the standards set by the National Service Framework are primarily focused on the physical independence of older people. While quality of life in older age is affected by physical health, the importance of social inclusion and maintaining socially valued roles does not feature; although for some older people they may be physically able to be maintained at home this may not address their psychological needs.

National Standards for Young Offenders detailed criteria for the supervision of offenders by the PROBATION SERVICE and YOUTH OFFENDING TEAMS issued by the HOME OFFICE.

Since 1989, the Home Office has issued increasingly prescriptive and detailed national standards, setting out exactly how offenders must be supervised and what action must be taken if they do not comply with court orders or post-release supervision requirements. The first national standards applied to COMMUNITY PUNISHMENT ORDERS and had little impact upon field probation staff, but further standards introduced in 1992 applied to report-writing and day-to-day supervision of offenders. Soon after the establishment of YOUTH OFFENDING TEAMS they, too, were made subject to national standards.

The stated objectives of national standards are to provide a clear framework of expectations and requirements for supervision, to facilitate professional judgement within a framework of accountability, to encourage the development of good practice and to ensure that service delivery is fair and consistent, without DISCRIMINATION.

National standards specify the frequency and promptness with which offenders must be supervised, the expected contents of PRE-SENTENCE REPORTS, the planning of supervision, record-keeping and effective enforcement. They reflect a desire by central government to ensure accountability, consistency and rigour in the work of the probation and SOCIAL SERVICES and youth offending teams. Critics argue that they have stifled initiative and creativity in work with offenders, eroded professional autonomy and institutionalized managerialist approaches.

National Vocational Qualification (NVQ) a qualification very closely related to particular areas of employment, based upon defined competences that are the result of functional analyses of jobs and occupations. Such qualifications are accredited by the *National Council for Vocational Qualifications.*

National Vocational Qualifications were originally developed as a result of dissatisfaction on the part of employers and government with traditional training and education for a wide variety of occupations. The basic concern has been that traditional preparation for work has often not reflected contemporary needs of employers. Additionally, qualifications have mushroomed, often with a lack of clarity about their value within a generally accepted framework. To prepare for NVQs, occupations have been analysed to determine what workers in particular jobs actually do or are required to do; that is, a functional analysis is completed to reveal the specific competences required for particular jobs. Training packages are then devised (underpinning knowledge) to help people acquire defined competences. A competence can be demonstrated by reference to characteristic performance criteria. Although formal courses have been devised to meet the competences required for particular jobs, it has been recognized that people can acquire knowledge and skills in other ways – for example, through practical work or even life experiences. NVQs in the social care area are currently awarded at three levels (levels 2–4). Managers of registered homes for children or for adults are supposed to have achieved competences in the relevant areas at level 4 for example. Within the areas of social work, social care and social welfare, the Care Sector Consortium developed the first awards in the 1990s. The leading body in England is now the Training Organization for the Personal Social Services (TOPSS); in Scotland it is the Scottish Social Services Council; in Wales it is the Care Council of Wales and in Northern Ireland it is the Social Care Council of Northern Ireland.

Opinion is divided about the value of NVQs as educational and training packages. Supporters have it that people can have their skills recognized, that training has become relevant, that an overall framework has been established into which many levels of activities can be fitted and that a good deal of knowledge has become 'demystified'. Those who are sceptical about NVQs argue that education has become training, that it is excessively mechanistic and that people are not encouraged to think critically or imaginatively about what they do. The past ten years have probably witnessed a greater acceptance of NVQs, especially among employers who are increasingly convinced that these qualifications are a cost-effective way of securing adequately trained personnel.

nature–nurture debate the debate concerning the extent to which individual characteristics can be attributed to the influence of biological, genetic or innate factors (*nature*) as distinct from the influence of environmental factors and family upbringing (*nurture*).

Much of the debate has centred on psychological factors such as PERSONALITY and intelligence, and it clearly may be perceived as having important repercussions for many aspects of SOCIAL POLICY such as compensatory education. If, for example, intelligence can be enhanced by having particular environments, then educationalists would want to create those environments for all children, regardless of their background.

Some psychologists argue that individual characteristics are fixed, and others argue that they can be changed. A further dispute concerns the extent of possible change, some believing that substantial change is possible while others have it that minimal change only is possible. Most agree that these issues are very difficult to unravel because most people (with the exceptions of identical twins, triplets, and so on) are both genetically unique and have a unique environmental experience. But the debate remains intense. Research over the past ten years has further affirmed the importance of genetic inheritance, whether in passing on genetically determined diseases such as cystic fibrosis or cognitive activity like perfect pitch in music. But social scientists have also established that a poor environment that gives rise to a myriad of behaviours and social problems, whether crime or mistrusting one's neighbour, even if direct causal links cannot be established. With human genome fully mapped, it can be said that there is no such thing as a 'race gene' – physical differences within a particular ethnic group, for example, are wider than those between groups. (See GENE.)

NDC abbreviation for NEW DEAL FOR COMMUNITIES.

needs the necessary requirements for maintaining life at a certain standard.

To have a need means requiring something in order to live a life to some agreed standard. This standard may be little more than subsistence living, such as provided by the 19th-century workhouse for its inmates. Or the standard may be higher and relate to a person's wellbeing or fulfilment in life. Maslow in fact suggests that needs could usefully be ordered into a hierarchical continuum beginning with very basic, but essential, needs for food, shelter and safety to 'higher order' psychological needs of belonging, approval, love and finally 'self-actualization'.

If these needs are indeed distinctive, the issue for some social thinkers is whether these needs, in part or in whole, indicate some universal functional prerequisites for all societies regardless of their complexity.

Debates over the concept of need always centre on the question of what this standard should be and who should define it. Often the standards for determining need are set by a mixture of influences, such as social consensus, Acts of Parliament, activist groups and professionals in the field. As a result, what constitutes need changes over time. A good example is provided by campaigns against DOMESTIC VIOLENCE and the need for physical safety and for safe places, such as a women's refuge (see WOMEN'S AID), where women and children can safely stay for a period. Such a need was scarcely recognized 20 years ago, although it is now widely accepted.

Needs, or what a person requires, are often distinguished in theory from 'wants', or what a person prefers or desires. In practice, however, defining what a person needs as opposed to what he or she wants is fraught with difficulty. For example, a homeless person can be said to need shelter, but shelter can mean many things: a temporary bed in a hostel, a room in BED AND BREAKFAST accommodation, a permanently rented room, a rented flat or an owner-occupied house. What are the real needs of a homeless person and who decides?

In the attempt to resolve some of the conflicts over the definition of needs, a classification has been developed by Jonathon Bradshaw consisting of: *normative needs*, that is, needs as defined by a norm or standard set by professionals; *felt needs*, which individuals declare as their needs (the same as 'wants'); *expressed needs*, that is, felt needs turned into a demand through some action; and *comparative needs*, which are defined by the fact that others, living in the same conditions, have been recognized as having a similar need and receive a service.

Most people meet their needs through their own efforts, through family or friends or through arrangements they make themselves. Social workers and social care professionals, however, often work with clients and service users who, for a variety of reasons, have many basic needs that they have not been able to meet themselves. Workers decide what these needs are through ASSESSMENT. They often have to consider a broad range of needs, such as physical care, the provision of shelter and food, cultural and religious sustenance, emotional and psychological needs arising from isolation or violent personal relationships, and social contacts. Very often clients in the same household have different needs that have to be met in different ways. Because needs are so much a matter of interpretation, it is essential that service users should participate in the process of deciding what their needs are, and that their wishes and preferences be taken into account. Welfare professionals have in the past often interpreted a person's needs in terms of the services that they could offer. Thus a frail older person might have been assessed as 'needing' a place in a day-care centre or in a residential home, rather than the worker looking at what specific care needs he or she had and then deciding how these might best be met. The only way to overcome this is to consult closely with users, to include their wishes and preferences and to think how they might be most suitably met.

When social workers define need they do so on the basis of the definitions used by their agency and from formal guidance from the Department of Health. For example, when working with children and families in general, social workers focus on the care and developmental needs of the children to ensure that each child's development is broadly in line with national averages. The needs of a child or family are assessed by a social worker and others before the family can receive services to help them look after that child. Typically these needs may include such factors as any lack of skills on the part of the child's parents, as well as any educational or health needs. When working with adults, practitioners concentrate on those needs that will allow the person to live as independently as possible. The Department of Health has outlined six broad areas of adult need that should be assessed: personal and social care; health care; accommodation; finance; education, employment and leisure; transport, mobility and access.

Needs can be met only if resources are there to enable this to be done. Because resources are so limited, social services professionals have often used a system of prioritizing needs and of developing criteria for eligibility. This invariably places greatest importance on the need to protect the health and physical safety of the client and less importance on those needs that would improve the person's wellbeing but are not essential to physical survival. At the same time, there are opportunities to widen the definitions of need. Groups of users are urging this across a number of services, including those for children and families, disabled people and people with MENTAL HEALTH PROBLEMS. Such groups can be involved in setting local policies on need, since COMMUNITY CARE reforms in particular envisage a growth of new services from the independent sector. (See also SPECIAL EDUCATIONAL NEEDS.)

A. H. Maslow, *Motivation and Personality*, second edition, New York, Harper Row, 1970.

B. Taylor and T. Devine, *Assessing Needs and Planning Care*, Aldershot Arena, 1993.

J. Bradshaw, 'The taxonomy of social need' in G. McGlachlan (ed), *Problems and Progress in Medical Care*, Oxford, Oxford University Press, 1972.

needs-led assessment an ASSESSMENT that defines an individual's real
NEEDS and not just his or her needs in terms of services that the local
authority has to offer.

One of the common failings of local authority assessments before
the introduction of COMMUNITY CARE reforms was that they viewed needs
purely in terms of the services the local authorities had to offer. Thus
a person with a LEARNING DISABILITY was declared as 'needing' a place
in a training centre, regardless of whether the centre helped such people
overcome their disability. The individual's need was defined in terms
of the service available ('Mr X needs a place in a day centre') rather than
in terms that specified the needs of the individual ('Mr X needs to learn
to recognize coins of different denominations' or 'Mr X lacks the skills
to make basic purchases at his local shop and needs to acquire those
skills').

The tendency to define need in terms of available services was heavily
criticized as a way of protecting the interests of local authority staff.
On this basis, the beds of residential units were filled, as were places at
day centres, thus apparently demonstrating need for such establishments.
One of the basic community care reforms aimed to make the assessment
function independent of providing a service (see INTERNAL MARKET)
so that an independent judgement of need could be reached, taking
into account the person's own view, instead of his or her needs being
expressed simply in terms of existing service interests. For example,
a frail, older person who is socially isolated may have a need for regular
social contact that could be met by arranging regular outings with family
or friends rather than by offering a place in a day centre.

Department of Health, *Community Care in the Next Decade and Beyond:
Policy Guidance*, London, HMSO, 1990.

neighbourhood a geographic zone or area that is continuous and small
enough for residents to have some familiarity with one another, with
local landmarks, institutions and organizations such as schools or shops.

A neighbourhood is smaller in size than other common spatial areas
such as a district, community or city. It may be based on recognized
common boundaries, whether physical, such as roads, or cultural, such
as ethnic make-up, or by social networks and local associations, income
levels or housing tenure.

Usually a person's home is often the central reference point for
determining a neighbourhood for that person. Neighbourhoods can be
defined by individuals, groups or organizations, and they may be defined
for single functions or the overall set of household activities. Often
neighbourhoods do not have precise borders but are informal
judgements about where one small area begins and another ends.

The concept of neighbourhood, like COMMUNITY, has only recently
re-emerged as a focus of social work concern. The idea that social work
should focus on a single small area fell from favour from the late 1980s,

partly because of the pressure to focus on individual risk and protection and partly because of increasing specialization around groups of users rather than geographical areas. There was also distrust within the profession of the very notion of 'neighbourhood' and 'community', which were seen as potentially repressive entities intolerant of difference or behaviour outside certain norms.

neighbourhood forum a method for bringing together the representatives of local organizations, users and residents to express their opinions on services and projects.

Neighbourhood forums in particular have become prominent as one way of achieving this. They have a semi-formal role in current regeneration initiatives and in some BEST-VALUE reviews, where they are usually organized around particular subjects of local concern – young people, community safety, job development. In Stepney, London, the New Deal for Communities project relied extensively on the work of forums to bring its delivery plan together. On the basis of the trust developed in that process, the forums' role was formalized; they received their own devolved budgets for implementation of their sector of the plan while remaining accountable to the partnership board.

neighbourhood management team a multidisciplinary team that organizes and coordinates services in a given locality or neighbourhood.

Restructuring services around a neighbourhood agenda has become the decisive element in the strategy of public services in tackling SOCIAL EXCLUSION. The concept of 'neighbourhood management' best embraces what these new developments are trying to achieve. Neighbourhood management brings together several threads in the fight against social exclusion:

1 local government decentralization – physical, administrative and political;

2 inter-agency working and joint planning;

3 community involvement.

Neighbourhood management is the most important way to follow up the special initiatives to address social exclusion (many of which we have already discussed in this volume), bringing mainstream service budgets and activity to bear on exclusionary barriers.

The Social Exclusion Unit laid out the key elements of neighbourhood management in its *National Strategy for Neighbourhood Renewal* in 2000. These include:

1 a neighbourhood board involving residents, the local authority, other public agencies, and the voluntary and private sectors to plan and steer a programme of local regeneration;

2 a multi-agency team to deliver the plan to address joblessness, community safety, poor housing and poor health, with an emphasis on building human and social capital as a way of overcoming these problems;

3 provision of accessible services that are integrated and have a continuously improving outcomes for local people;

4 services place an emphasis in their practice on prevention, drawing on evidence of 'what works';

5 building capacity through strategies that encourage and prepare residents to participate in strategy development and local control to the maximum that they are able;

6 'bending' mainstream programmes of the principal services so that they routinely target resources in areas of greatest need and in ways that have maximum impact;

7 policies at all levels of government to work to promote neighbourhood management.

The development of neighbourhood management teams inevitably means a changed relationship between frontline practitioners and management. Neighbourhood teams require devolved budgets (with which social services already has some valuable experience, as does education) to the front line, with the teams then held accountable for achieving holistic outcomes that actually show up in the improvement of quality of life and the promotion of inclusion in the locality. This can then lead to pooled budgets in which service agencies and local authority departments look at the combined resources at their disposal and then, after discussion and the creation of jointly agreed action plans, proceed to commission the services required.

To be effective, such neighbourhood teams will often deploy local 'one-stop shops' from which people can find advice for navigating the various service systems, advocates who will speak and work for their objectives as well as access to services themselves – whether family support, social care or housing. They also typically will need high levels of PARTICIPATION by local residents and users in determining service strategies and yearly action plans. (See also NEIGHBOURHOOD FORUM.)

M. Taylor, *Top Down Meets Bottom Up: Neighbourhood Management*, Joseph Rowntree Foundation, 2000.

neighbourhood offices local authority service centres for relatively small geographical areas, usually of cities. The particular mix of services offered by these offices varies but typically includes housing, social services and environmental health.

Local authorities that have taken the decision to establish neighbourhood offices have done so because of a commitment to the decentralization of services and because they believe that anti-poverty strategies can be enhanced, such as through benefit take-up campaigns and money advice services offered locally. Temporary neighbourhood offices are also sometimes established to help an area deal with major urban renewal or redevelopment – for example, when housing is to be improved or demolished but local people will resettle in the area when the work is completed.

neighbourhood renewal rebuilding both the physical and social fabric
of a NEIGHBOURHOOD.

Neighbourhoods where there are high concentrations of people living
below the POVERTY LINE have a range of social problems that impinge
on every person who lives there, whether individually poor or not. Such
neighbourhoods are generally found in the decaying owner-occupied
or privately rented terraced housing of older cities and the peripheral
housing estates that ring many of Britain's urban areas.

Social theorists use the phrase *neighbourhood effects* to describe this
impact that a neighbourhood has on the lives of residents. For instance,
decaying or abandoned homes and buildings have a severely negative
effect on the morale of residents, providing a major incentive to move
elsewhere. Highly disadvantaged neighbourhoods also frequently lack
organized activities and community facilities. As a result, residents do
not see themselves as being in control and what they want is to have
influence over regular services rather than special projects.
Neighbourhoods do matter to residents, however, and it is wrong to
characterize disadvantaged areas as lacking social cohesion and
interaction that survive in difficult places.

What cuts a neighbourhood off from the economic, social and political
activity of the city or region within which it is located? The nature of the
housing and physical layout has much to do with it. Social housing has
become a *residual service*, that is, an under-resourced basic service for
those individuals and families who could not find housing in other parts
of the housing system (in the main through home ownership). As a
result, certain low-income groups are channelled towards specific areas
within a local authority area. The consequence is a rise in the number
of people in poverty and households where no one is working. There
may also be a rise in vandalism, making housing hard to let, with
tenants wanting to stay for as short a time as possible. Shops close, and
amenities such as playgroups for children disappear. The *social fabric*
of the estate – the way people relate to each other and the strength of
local organizations such as residents' associations and clubs – is also
weakened.

To tackle many of these issues the UK government in 2001 launched
an ambitious neighbourhood renewal strategy that aims to bring
services, local people and voluntary action to repair the social fabric
of low-income neighbourhoods.

Social Exclusion Unit, *National Strategy for Neighbourhood Renewal*,
London, Cabinet Office, 2000.

neoliberalism an economic and political doctrine that believes
government should not try to manage or regulate the economy.

Neoliberals combine belief in the importance of MARKETS in the
production and distribution of goods and services with the notion
that the individual citizen is responsible for his or her own economic

and moral wellbeing. Their doctrine is so called because of the renewed influence in political and social policy discourse of 19th-century 'liberalism'. Thus, in a sense, neoliberalism is the opposite of what 'liberalism' now signifies in the USA (and to a lesser extent in the UK). That latter term stands for tolerance and acceptance of human diversity and seeks to promote government programmes to relieve poverty and counteract the impact of impersonal market forces. Nevertheless, both liberalism and neoliberalism share a belief in the importance of the individual citizen as sovereign, the need for a strong civic culture of voluntary organizations and the primacy of individual values and morality.

net widening the process by which the criminal justice and social care professions draw people in NEED into receiving statutory services, even though it may not ultimately be beneficial for them to become service users.

Net widening normally refers to the tendency of criminal justice services to label young people as offenders by failing to practise rigorous GATEKEEPING, or to the effects of social policies which demand the provision of services to minor and first-time offenders. Often with the best of intentions, social care workers fail to restrict services to those who meet allocation criteria and, in the process, service users' interests and rights can inadvertently be damaged. The fact that someone has social welfare needs does not automatically mean that it is beneficial for him or her to receive the services of official agencies.

In the case of young offenders, early use of court orders can accelerate the progress of individuals up the sentencing 'tariff': if they are given COMMUNITY SENTENCES for first or trivial offences, they are likely to be dealt with unduly severely if they re-offend during the life of the order. Similar arguments apply to women offenders: courts are prone to making COMMUNITY REHABILITATION ORDERS in respect of women committing minor offences who appear to need help. Rather than sentencing them in accordance with the seriousness of the offence, magistrates are sometimes tempted to provide them with the help they need through the statutory criminal justice services. If they then re-offend, they face punishment for breaching the order and re-sentencing for the original offence as well as the new sentence. In this way, women are up-tariffed in a similar way to young offenders.

Some provisions of the CRIME AND DISORDER ACT 1998 and the YOUTH JUSTICE AND CRIMINAL EVIDENCE ACT 1999 have been criticized for their net widening effects, such as REPARATION ORDERS, FINAL WARNINGS and REFERRAL ORDERS. The United Nations' Beijing Rules of 1985 require member states to consider diversion from formal criminal proceedings in appropriate cases and to pay attention to the principle of proportionality.

network conference a gathering of people, often family but including 'significant others' associated with a particular young person, meeting together in an attempt to solve accommodation and related problems of the young person.

The idea of a network conference was developed from that of the FAMILY GROUP CONFERENCE, a method of working adopted by New Zealand statutory child-care agencies in the mid- and late 1980s. Family conferences are rooted in Maori practices whereby extended families meet together to attempt to solve family problems. Such an approach, adopted by social workers, significantly increased the power of families to devise acceptable, and often novel, solutions to child-care issues. The same principles and procedures, with some adaptations, are being used with the problem of homelessness among young people. In this case, professional workers, in consultation with the young homeless person, convene conferences of family members and other people who are important to the young person (hence the use of the term 'network'). Network conferences are organized by workers who will provide key information (about possible resources for example) to the conference, which may help in devising solutions to the homeless person's problems; but it is the responsibility of the conference to try to find solutions. With its clear shift of power away from professionals towards individuals, families and significant others in the 'network', many see this way of working as an example of SELF-HELP and genuine PARTNERSHIP.

networking the process of linking individuals, groups and/or communities with common interests together in order to allow information and resource sharing, support and collectivity. It assumes that there is strength in numbers to challenge issues and to achieve a common aim.

networks the web of social relationships through which people are connected.

When thinking about networks it is important to remember that they exist in relation to individuals and families as well as entire NEIGHBOURHOODS. They also exist in relation to specific groups of people, for example gays or lesbians, or around the workplace or shared interests or predicaments. When working well, networks transmit certain forms of trust and commitment. *Network poverty*, on the other hand, is centrally a deficit in the means of securing trust and is strongly associated with a culture of fatalism in which people have little trust either in the reliability of systems or of other persons.

Social networks vary considerably in their impact on specific individuals and families. Networks are not confined simply to 'close personal relationships'. They may provide support or undermine, be plentiful or virtually non-existent, close and intense or far-flung and distant. The quality and purpose and functioning of networks varies dramatically whether in the numbers of people involved, the degree of interconnectedness and frequency of contact, the quality and duration of the relationships and the degree to which they are supportive or undermining.

There are various ways of describing and measuring the characteristics of networks. One helpful distinction is to think of networks for 'getting by' and those for getting ahead'. They are very different and perform very different functions. *Networks for getting by* are the close supportive networks embedded in everyday relationships of friends, neighbourhood and family. When we think of the social supports offered by extended families and friends or by close-knit communities – these are networks for getting by. They can supply gaps in child care, look after a person when he or she is ill, provide small loans and cash to make ends meet and participate in family celebrations or rites of passage.

As social workers, we are vitally interested in how these networks are viewed by the people with whom we are working. They may be seen as affirmative, nurturing or accepting or as antagonistic and inaccessible. At their very worst they can be sources of heavy responsibility, aggression and scapegoating. Understanding how natural networks function help us to better understand the distinctive characteristics of socially excluded and isolated individuals and families.

Networks for getting ahead provide crucial information for individuals and families on jobs, education, training and on a range of options for advancing one's interests. In many ways they are the opposite of networks for getting by but can achieve so much more. They are more occasional and episodic in nature and are more tenuous than a close personal relationship. They may be based on 'someone who knows someone' about a job possibility or on the links obtained through a skills agency half a city away which a person visits only occasionally. But such networks can be very powerful when finding a job.

A number of structural factors dramatically affect the kinds and quality of networks that a person has, such as income, educational background, age, gender, disability, ethnic origin and employment. Women with pre-school children at home tend to have smaller, less reliable and more localized networks, particularly if they are lone mothers. People with higher incomes, in employment and higher education tend to have richer social networks.

Networks can be crucial to families in their struggle to care for children or older dependent adults. Taking stock of these networks jointly with family members should be part of a routine ASSESSMENT, and an important part of social work practice should be to facilitate the growth of networks. Network mapping, capitalizing on existing strengths within networks for getting by, creating new networks around existing points of service, such as family centres and schools, or by using MENTORS and VOLUNTEERS are all approaches that social workers should be developing. They are particularly important when working with individuals that employment gatekeepers view stereotypically as ill-equipped for the jobs market, such as young males – black and white – disabled and older people.

Using a *social network map* helps in this work. The map collects information on the composition of the family's network and also the extent to which the networks are supportive or undermining or conflicted. By simply putting initials or first names of people into the various segments network members are recorded in any of these seven areas: household or people lived with; family/relatives; friends; people from work or school; people from clubs, organizations or religious groups; neighbours; agencies and other formal service providers.

Once the strengths and weaknesses of a family's network is clear, practitioners can use the map to ask further questions regarding the nature of the network relationships. These cover the types of supports available, for example, whether they provide information or emotional support, how critical a member of the network might be and the closeness or intensity of the relationship, or other features such as frequency of contact and length of relationship. Although any one map is constructed from the point of view of a single family, through use practitioners will become more familiar with the different characteristics of families' networks. These include the size, perceived availability of different types of support through the network, the degree of criticism that networks contain and the extent of reciprocity.

J. Pierson, *Tackling Social Exclusion*, London, Routledge, 2001.

neuroses a group of MENTAL DISORDERS with symptoms of long-term ANXIETY, nervousness, irritability and constant worry about physical health.

This group includes minor DEPRESSION, anxiety, PHOBIAS, HYSTERIA, psychosomatic disorders, eating disorders like ANOREXIA NERVOSA, obsessional compulsive disorders, POST-TRAUMATIC STRESS SYNDROME and adjustment reactions. These conditions are all distinguished from more serious mental disorders and PSYCHOSES, which involve symptoms that radically affect thinking, perception and behaviour with serious consequences for a person's ability to function. The neuroses, on the other hand, are thought to involve primarily only symptoms of MOOD disorder, such as feelings of fear (anxiety) or sadness (depression) which are similar to but more severe than ordinary fear and sadness at life's circumstances. This distinction means that people diagnosed as neurotic have been treated mainly in primary care and are not generally admitted to psychiatric hospital.

New Deal for Communities (NDC) a central government programme that provides funding for multi-agency approaches to regenerating low-income communities.

The programme has four aims: investing in people, not buildings; involving communities in their own solutions; ensuring that mainstream policies and services work for the poorest neighbourhoods and do not make problems worse; making a long-term commitment.

New Deal for Communities has departed in several respects from the cycle of urban regeneration policies developed from the 1960s through to the mid-1990s. First, it is a long-term programme with funding commitments for ten years. This allows local management boards to link the low physical and economic status of their area to individual and community development. Second, it is also notable that the areas designated under NDC are much smaller than areas of previous programmes. Many focus on a single housing estate or a spatial area with clearly defined boundaries. The target population is also smaller, embracing approximately 6,000–8,000.

The premise of NDC is that 'added value' will accrue from integrating the work of different agencies and organizations, achieving more impact from the same amount of public spending.

Social Exclusion Unit, *Bringing Britain Together: A national strategy for neighbourhood renewal*, London, The Stationery Office, 1998.

new Labour the term given to the new policy orientation that the Labour Party adopted from the mid 1990s on to underscore the changes that took place in the organization of the Party and on traditional issues such as public ownership and taxation.

The Labour Party found itself out of office for 18 years after the Conservatives gained power in 1979. A series of general election defeats and significant internal battles had led some to believe that the party had become unelectable. Battles between the left and the right of the party in the 1980s resulted in an internal split (giving birth to the Social Democratic Party), a serious conflict over the election of the Deputy Leader and efforts to exclude the far left. The leadership of Neil Kinnock, the late John Smith and then Tony Blair saw a series of victories for the centre-right of the party in their efforts to regain power. One of the most important events was the decision in the 1990s by the leadership to remove Clause 4 of the party's constitution, which committed the party to the public ownership of the means of production and tied the party in the public's mind to nationalization of key parts of the economy. However, the apparent success of the Conservative government's policy of privatization, in particular the sale of council houses to their occupants, led many at senior levels in the party to believe that Clause 4 was a key obstacle to re-election.

The combination of these events led the party to reposition itself towards the political centre, although for some in the party this was in reality a shift to the right and the acceptance of key elements of the Conservative agenda, notably an increased role for the private sector in the delivery of services, a closer relationship with employers and the business community, and a low-tax economy. These policies were seen by senior members of the party as important in their election success in 1997 and their continuation in power in 2001.

For social services and the continuation of the WELFARE STATE, the acceptance of the core features of this agenda, including an increased role for the private sector and a low-tax regime, presents a significant challenge to more traditional Labour views about the role of the state in the provision of welfare services. Increased resources are part of the New Labour policy for health and social care but only in exchange for a MODERNIZATION of these services, making increased use of PERFORMANCE MEASUREMENT and a more managerial approach. For traditional Labour supporters and many workers within the public sector, the maintenance of aspects of Thatcherite policies is seen as highly problematic and creates tensions within the Labour movement as a whole, including relations with public service workers' trades unions.

M. Temple, *How Britain Works*, Basingstoke, Macmillan, 2001.

new Right political, social and economic policies developed during the 1980s, based on a belief that the MARKET is generally the best means of enhancing human wellbeing – because individual self-reliance is fostered by reducing state welfare services and benefits – and that state intervention should be kept to a minimum. The term also refers to people and organizations holding and practising these ideas and policies.

The term 'new Right' was used to distinguish the policies of a group of economists, SOCIAL POLICY advocates and politicians who are on the right or conservative end of the political spectrum but depart radically from much of traditional Conservative policy. From the end of the Second World War, British Conservatives had largely supported the aims of the WELFARE STATE and thus were part of a broad political consensus that sought to develop it. The new Right advanced a radical set of ideas that broke with this consensus, believing that the market provided the most efficient way of producing and allocating goods and services and seeking to create conditions in which markets could function without interference. It advocated widespread deregulation and privatization of state-owned industry, such as telecommunications and public utilities, which it thought had been hobbled in their economic performance by political considerations when under state control. It also favoured reducing public expenditure (except notably on defence) and introducing tax cuts to allow consumers greater choice. In the field of social welfare, the new Right viewed the welfare state as responsible for creating a sense of dependency among claimants, arguing that claimants had little incentive to work because of the welfare benefits system. The new Right's view was that welfare institutions were bureaucratic, offered little choice and were often run to protect the special interests of the professionals employed by them. The introduction of market reforms was to be a means of overcoming these defects.

Politically, the implementation of new Right policies is largely associated with the Thatcher government in Britain and the Reagan

and Bush presidencies in the United States, but similar policies of
privatization and welfare state retrenchment can be found in many,
if not most, industrialized countries. Although such policies apparently
made a great impact throughout the 1980s, more sober assessments of
their influence have acknowledged that this was not perhaps as great as
first thought. Welfare policies and institutions continued to expand
while, even among new Right supporters, the tax cuts of the late 1980s
that they had pressed for contributed, via excessive levels of consumer
spending and debt, to the deep recession of the early 1990s. Yet, overall,
the new Right did succeed in changing the political culture. The parties
of the traditional Left, such as the Labour Party in Britain and the
Democratic Party in the USA, were able to recapture popular support
only in the 1990s by adopting some of the policy matters associated with
the new Right – tough on crime, fiscal responsibility and low taxes,
pressuring people to move off welfare and into work. (See FAR RIGHT;
NEOLIBERALISM; NEW LABOUR.)

   C. Pierson, *Beyond the Welfare State*, Cambridge, Polity Press, 1991.
NHS abbreviation for NATIONAL HEALTH SERVICE.
NIC abbreviation for NATIONAL INSURANCE CONTRIBUTIONS.
night shelter temporary accommodation for homeless, usually single,
people.

   Such accommodation is invariably very basic, organized in dormitories
and, as the name implies, unavailable for shelter in daylight hours. Meals
and bathing facilities are often available too, and some night shelters
have second-hand clothing stores. Night shelters are mostly offered by
the voluntary sector, with religious organizations like the Salvation Army
playing a prominent role. Staffing is often dependent upon VOLUNTEER
effort. A limited number of night shelters have connections with longer-
term housing projects that seek to help provide more stability in relation
to accommodation for the rootless. (See also VAGRANCY.)
non-contributory benefit see SOCIAL SECURITY; WELFARE RIGHTS 1.
non-judgmental attitude a predisposition not to regard a person as guilty
or blameworthy; the avoidance of thoughts that attach guilt or innocence
to people or their behaviour.

   This principle of social work practice is amenable to several
interpretations. To some, it comes close to the idea of acceptance,
that is, seeing people as human beings and also as they actually are.
To others, it means not judging because we cannot ever know
everything and therefore can never fully understand, rendering
judgement inappropriate. Pragmatists would argue that the line
between judgement and decisions about the need to intervene is often
fine because many behaviours are actually unacceptable to the public
or at least to legal prescriptions. Where behaviour is unacceptable in
a legal sense, judgements and interventions by social workers may be
necessary. (See also ETHICAL CODE, VALUES.)

non-means-tested benefit a kind of benefit that, unlike MEANS-TESTED
BENEFITS, is not dependent on the claimant's income or capital.
Sometimes called *universal benefits* because they are generally available,
they are regarded as an essential means of ensuring that vulnerable
groups like children are supported with minimal eligibility barriers.
Child benefit and disability living allowance are good examples.
See WELFARE RIGHTS 1.

non-molestation order see INJUNCTION.

normalization a service philosophy that emphasizes access to lifestyles
that are valued by society as a whole for people with learning disability.

Normalization is based on the assumption that integration with
non-disabled people and the adoption of societal norms of behaviour
are likely to lead to greater acceptance and respect for people with
learning disability. It arose from the recognition that the regimes in
which people with learning disability lived made it impossible for
them to live ordinary lives and therefore added to their stigmatization.
The concept was originated by Wolfensberger in Scandinavia and
further developed in North America. Wolfensberger later referred to
SOCIAL ROLE VALORIZATION (SRV), by which he meant 'the creation,
support and defence of valued social roles for people who are at risk
of devaluation'.

Challenges to normalization have come from both the SOCIAL MODEL
OF DISABILITY and from minorities using LEARNING DISABILITY
services. Both sets of challenges have identified the emphasis on
social conformity as problematic. For example, women with learning
disability may be expected to adopt behaviour based on dominant
gender stereotypes, and black and minority ethnic people may find
themselves subject to white norms. Advocates of the social model
of disability argue that the social barriers experienced by people
with learning disability should be tackled directly and that social
acceptance should not be conditional on 'normal' behaviour or roles.
Such critics point out that normalization is not a means for promoting
respect for diversity. The methods used by Wolfensberger to assess
services are known as 'pass' and 'passing'. They focus on how far
services enhance the social image and personal competence of users.
In this context, the promotion of age-appropriate behaviour is seen
as important.

Despite these reservations, normalization and SRV have been
associated with a greater recognition of dignity and choice in service
provision and integration into mainstream services and leisure
activities for people with learning disability. It has been pointed out
that normalization is managed by service providers and does not arise
out of service user activism. It has been associated, however, with
greater access to ADVOCACY and more participative forms of assessment
and planning.

notification an action on the part of medical practitioners who come into
contact with people they believe to be addicted to certain named drugs.
Medical practitioners are required to notify the chief medical officer at
the Home Office of the ADDICTION.

The most usual notifiable drugs are HEROIN and cocaine. A specially
printed form is used. The purpose of notification is twofold: first, for
statistical reasons so that annual changes in the use of different
substances can be noted; second, for general practitioners and other
doctors to check whether or not a patient is already being prescribed
medication from another source. In spite of this, some users of illegal
substances are frightened of presenting themselves to services for help
as they think notification will mean, for example, that the police or social
services will be informed. This is not so, and strict medical confidentiality
applies to all information received.

nurseries facilities providing supervised day care for pre-school children
(normally aged under five), run either by local authorities or privately.
Children may attend on a full- or part-time basis. The government funds
places for all three and four year olds.

A high proportion of nursery staff have qualifications in nursery
nursing and increasingly they are required to work in collaboration with
other social welfare workers, such as social workers, health visitors and
other medical staff. Local authority provision increasingly focuses on
children who are 'at risk' (that is, children who have been abused or
neglected), have special needs (usually meaning some kind of disability)
or are under-stimulated, or where there is some developmental delay,
or because of the particular social and economic circumstances of
parents. Care is therefore seen to be compensatory in some cases to help
with a 'deficit' in a child's life. In others it may be to help 'rehabilitate'
a child from care, while in yet others it could be to supplement the care
provided by a parent or carer that is in some sense insufficient (such as
with a parent who has a mental health problem). Private or voluntary
nurseries may be run by employers (workplace nurseries), by community
organizations and by private individuals as a business. Such provision
is much more likely to be for the children of working parents. Private
and voluntary nurseries are required to register with local authorities,
which will inspect their provision and facilities at regular intervals.

Although the bulk of the work undertaken in nurseries is with
children, some nurseries also attempt to work with parents and carers.
Here the focus is on physical care, domestic skills, PLAY and the
emotional needs of children. A few nurseries are located within FAMILY
CENTRES, where much work is done directly with children, some with
parents and children, and some with parents as individuals (that is,
activities for the enjoyment of adults or for their needs apart from
parenting needs).

B. Owen, *Caring for Children*, London, Family Policy Studies Centre, 1988.

nursing home a residential facility for the nursing care of people
experiencing sickness, injury or infirmity.

Nursing homes require registration with the secretary of state under
the REGISTERED HOMES ACT 1984. It is an offence to operate a nursing
home without registration, and the certificate of registration has to be
displayed in a prominent place. Nursing homes may offer specialized
care, as do maternity homes, homes for elderly people and homes that
offer medical treatment. Registration can be refused if the applicant is
considered unfit to run the home or if the conditions of the home are
unsatisfactory. A first-level nurse (state registered nurse or registered
general nurse) must be in charge throughout the day, but if the authority
so decides, and dependent upon the purpose of the nursing home, a
second-level nurse (state enrolled nurse) may be in charge at night with
a senior nurse on call.

The Registered Homes Act 1984 was supported by a code of practice:
Home Life. This code specifies 14 areas of good practice relevant to
nursing homes, which include inspection, registration, furniture and
equipment, services, food, facilities, provision of linen and laundry,
and the disposal of waste materials. The guidelines also cover the
control of infection and of drugs, fire safety, accident prevention,
records, notification of death, and complaints. The code recommends
that the environment should, as far as possible, be domestic in character
and enable patients to retain their individuality and self-respect, with
consideration of comfort, privacy, cleanliness and safety apparent.
Long-stay residents of nursing homes were to be encouraged to bring
personal possessions into the home with them. Guidelines for the
inspection of quality in nursing homes were issued by the Social Services
Inspectorate in 1991 and laid a duty on directors of social services to set
up and maintain specialized units for the registration and inspection
of nursing and residential care homes.

More recent government policy has introduced a raft of legislative
and policy changes with the explicit purpose of improving standards and
the quality of care. A major concern has been the considerable variation
both in access to services and in the kinds of services available across
the country. The national charter *Better Care, Higher Standards*, issued
jointly by the Department of Health and Department of Environment,
Transport and the Regions in 1999 sets out the standards that can be
expected by anyone requiring long-term care and support from local
housing, health and social services. The Care Standards Act 2000
introduced the National Care Standards Commission, which is now
responsible for the arrangements for inspection of residential and
nursing care homes. Underpinning the work of the National Care
Standards Commission will be the standards published by government
in *Care Homes for Older People. National Minimum Standards* (DoH 2001).
The standards cover: choice of home, health and personal care, daily life

and social activities, complaints and protection, environment, staffing, management and administration. There is a recognition in the standards, that different residents will have unique needs that may require specialist skills and staff training, as, for example, in the case of people with dementia.

Department of Health, *Care Homes for Older People. National Minimum Standards*, London, TSO, 2001.

NVQ abbreviation for NATIONAL VOCATIONAL QUALIFICATION.

Oo

object relations theory the theory that an infant's relationships with family members have a continuing influence throughout life.

Object relations theory was developed by a group of British psychoanalysts in the 1940s and 1950s. Within PSYCHOANALYSIS, 'object' refers to people other than ourselves, in the sense that they are the objects of our desires and sources of gratification as children. 'Object relations' then meant relations with those closest to us in infancy and early childhood, particularly mother, father and siblings. The object relations' school expanded psychoanalysis in the sense that it emphasized the importance of these relationships themselves and moved away from the view that a child uses the people close to it only for its own gratification. The theory made a huge impact on the development of social work theory and could be said to have dominated theories in the 1950s of what social work should try to achieve. As a result of this influence, work with individuals focused on their damaged early relationships and how such relationships continued to affect their adult relationships by setting up expectations and patterns that were difficult to change. Only through the relationship formed between therapist and patient, between social worker and client, were the damaged contents of the person's early relationships to be re-examined and their power reduced. Object relations theory has continued to have influence in particular strands of social work and PSYCHOTHERAPY, notably in feminist counselling.

occupational therapy a rehabilitative profession concerned to help people recover from illness or to adapt to or cope with a disability. The key objectives are optimal personal functioning and thus independent living.

Occupational therapy is one of the three rehabilitative professions recognized by the NATIONAL HEALTH SERVICE (with physiotherapy and speech therapy). It is equally represented in physical medicine and psychiatry. Occupational services are also provided by SOCIAL SERVICES DEPARTMENTS. The occupation has a practical emphasis and is concerned with the problems and activities of daily living. In hospital settings with the focus on physical problems, occupational therapy typically includes retraining for daily living skills (for example, washing and dressing), the prescription of therapeutic activities (for example, artwork, woodwork, group discussion) and provision of orthotics (for example, splints) and prostheses (for example, walking sticks and wheelchairs). In psychiatry, occupational therapy is concerned with the provision of therapeutic activities, skills training for a return to the community and possibly some aspects of PSYCHOTHERAPY. Patients within the community receive occupational therapy from social services departments. A wide range of AIDS AND ADAPTATIONS to buildings to enhance daily living and the quality of life are the major concerns for this work. Close collaboration with social workers within adult teams is necessary for the effective ASSESSMENT of needs.

R. Hagedorn, *Foundations for Practice in Occupational Therapy*, second edition, Edinburgh, Churchill Livingstone, 1997.

old age a unique experience that grows out of each individual life rather than being a fixed chronological entity.

The transitional period from mature middle age to old age is neither distinct nor precise. It is useful to think of a life course where each person's life is fluid in terms of life history and how he or she can negotiate cultural identity, personal experiences, relationships and family interactions against the backdrop of a wider social fabric. This is distinct from ageing, the normal biological process that starts at birth, continues throughout the life course and can also include a genetic component. Different individuals age physically at different rates, some ageing faster than others.

older people women and men who have usually retired from active participation in the labour market or have attained state pension age or both.

The term 'older people' is interchangeable with 'elderly', 'old persons', 'older adults', 'third age' and 'senior citizens'. There are considerable problems in defining the point at which people become 'older people'. Qualitative research studies into older people's attitudes indicated that many were concerned about *any* form of labelling based on chronological age, seeing this as stereotyping and instead wanting to affirm the homogeneity of older people and the diversity of their circumstances and values. Where respondents did have a preferred term, they chose 'senior citizen', believing the use of 'senior' denoted status while the use of 'citizen' emphasized their continuing contribution to society. The focus on 'status' and 'citizenship' by older people themselves can be seen as a challenge to alternative more negative constructions, prevalent in contemporary Western European societies, of what it means to be an older person. Ideas about what it means to be old are socially constructed and will vary over time and across cultures.

Attitudes to AGEING encompass complex cultural, economic and political/social policy issues. These are not neutral but reflect power structures that influence how collective life is ordered and the significance that is attached to the criteria used to demarcate 'old' age. These, in turn, influence decision-making about allocation of resources. Where age is used as a way of differentiating people, there is a tendency to create apparent 'natural' categories that oversimplify the reality of individual lives. The roles and norms of designated age groups create both opportunities and obstacles. At best, the common interests of similar age groups can combine to form a collective voice that can represent these interests within the competing claims of other groups. However, the norms ascribed to older age give greater emphasis to biological differences between older and younger ages rather than to social differences.

Focus on the physiological aspects of growing old serves to emphasize inevitable physical decline. Preoccupation with physical decline maintains assumptions about cognitive deterioration and promotes a stereotype of older people as having reduced conceptual ability and capacity to learn, disregarding the additional experience, perspectives and potential intellectual maturity that age can bring. As a consequence, attention is generally focused on the negative aspects of ageing, such as illness and incapacity. These stereotypes are compounded by the correlation between chronological old age and poverty, where inevitably income is reduced by enforced retirement from the workforce. While there is evidence that average incomes for older people in the UK are rising, there is also evidence of increased material inequality between some older people and the general population and a growing differentiation amongst older people themselves. Those who are materially best off in old age are those who received the greatest rewards in working life. As Vincent (see below) explains, however, a quarter of all older people in Britain are either dependent on income support or entitled to it but not receiving it.

Although created by social structures, the actual connection between ageing and poverty combines with the real increase in numbers of older people over pensionable age to sustain the belief that older people represent an economic burden and are a drain on the resources of health and social care. The number of people over pensionable age is projected to increase from 10.7 million in 1998 to 12.2 million by 2021. There is also a difference in life expectancy between men and women, with women living on average four years longer.

The term 'retirement' technically means retirement from paid work. 'Retirement from work', however, can become a synonym for 'retirement from life', reflecting the high value society puts on economic productivity. This undermines the value of alternative contributions that older people may be making as grandparents, carers, neighbours and unpaid voluntary workers and erodes their status as citizens, allowing DISCRIMINATION, which furthers social inequality. Thus, existing demarcations on the lines of race, ethnicity, class, gender and sexual orientation that influence life chances adversely combine with age to result in further disadvantage. Studies show that access to health care is more difficult for older people, and it is significant that there is no legislation to date in the UK to protect the rights of older people, as in the case of children's rights. Organizations of older people representing their own interests are not prominent.

Nevertheless, the growth in the population of older people represents a significant constituency for politicians. In 2000, 18.1 per cent of the estimated population of the UK was over pensionable age. The recognition of older people's potential to influence political outcomes has resulted in a period of significant policy and legislative change during the latter part of the last century, which builds on the cultural shift introduced by the 1989 white paper *Caring for People: Community Care in the Next Decade and Beyond* and the subsequent legislation in the NATIONAL HEALTH SERVICE AND COMMUNITY CARE ACT 1990. This policy document undertook to promote better services to enable adults to remain 'independent' in the community, upholding the principles of greater involvement of service users in shaping the development of community services, enabling 'choice' and better integration of health and social care services. This has been followed by a series of policy initiatives ostensibly seeking to further develop these principles in policy. These include *The NHS Plan* (2000), which responded to *The Royal Commission on the Long Term Care of the Elderly* (1999), *The National Service Framework for Older People* (2001). Important new legislation includes the Carers Recognition and Services Act (1995), the Community Care Direct Payments Act (1996), the Care Standards Act (2000), and the Local Government Act (2000). These changes intend to affect directly the delivery of health and social care services to older people who comprise the greatest number of users of health and social care services. In particular, the *National Service Framework for Older People* undertakes to challenge age discrimination.

There are tensions, in practice, however, in implementing these changes. The aim of improving services to older people is set within a context of low taxation and reduced public spending. There are concerns that because of the emphasis on rationing and cost effectiveness, the focus of social care services, while allowing greater numbers of older people to remain in their own home, merely maintains physical functioning and does not give enough regard to 'quality of life'. Crucial to the development of improving services will be the extent to which there are real opportunities for the voices of older people, including frail older people, to have a say in decisions that are made about the development and delivery of services.

J. A. Vincent, *Politics, Power and Old Age*, Buckingham, Open University Press, 1999.

ombudsman a government official who investigates COMPLAINTS of maladministration made by members of the public against statutory authorities, including, for example, complaints about delays in dealing with claims for a benefit or a service.

The ombudsman does not investigate any matter where there is a right of appeal. If the ombudsman finds that there has been maladministration, he or she will recommend action by the authority, including an apology and possibly compensation. There are two ombudsmen concerned with benefit administration. The Parliamentary Commissioner for Administration investigates complaints against the various executive agencies of the Department of Social Security; these complaints should be made through a constituency Member of Parliament, who will normally seek solutions direct from the agency in the first instance. The Commissioner for Local Administration investigates complaints against local authorities; these complaints should first of all be made directly to the authority, but, if still dissatisfied, the complainant can then approach the ombudsman.

one-stop shop see NEIGHBOURHOOD MANAGEMENT TEAM.

open adoption an ADOPTION in which the natural parents retain some involvement in the life of their child during and after adoption.

Historically, adoption was based on the complete anonymity of the adoptive parents, and the child's natural parents knew nothing about the family that adopted their child. The term 'open adoption' covers a number of changes in the adoption process that in one way or another break down this anonymity. This can happen in several ways. The birth parent can be actively involved in hearing about and choosing the adoptive parents through written profiles and face-to-face meetings with them, or there can simply be an exchange of non-identifying information between the two sets of parents. Most commonly an open adoption enables some form of link to be retained between the adopted child and the natural parents after the adoption is completed. Legally this is now possible in England and Wales since a court can make a CONTACT ORDER in favour of the natural parents at the same time as granting the ADOPTION ORDER on the child. Such contact might involve letters, the exchange of gifts or face-to-face meetings.

The practice of open adoption is increasingly favoured as a result of numerous studies that have highlighted the destructive impact of the secrecy and anonymity surrounding adoption. For the adoptive child, this meant not knowing the birth family's identity. The secrecy and evasiveness often required to keep the child from finding out anything about his or her origins is thought to have frequently been the source of behavioural and emotional difficulties for the child. Similarly, studies of the birth mothers of adopted children have indicated that they frequently suffered lifelong distress as a consequence of their decision. The practice of open adoption is designed to limit these painful consequences, to allow the child to retain a sense of identity and family origin and to facilitate communication between birth parent and child after the latter has reached maturity,

Mullender (ed), *Open Adoption: The Philosophy and Practice*, London, British Agencies for Adoption and Fostering, 1991.

open system a system that does not have rigid or closed boundaries, so can exchange information, concepts, resources and energy with the environment around it, allowing it to adapt to changes in the environment that ensure its survival (see SYSTEMS APPROACH).

operant conditioning learning strategies in which the person or animal must act on a stimulus to obtain a reinforcement. The reinforcement increases the likelihood of the behavioural strategy occurring again.

Operant conditioning has its theoretical origins in Thorndike's 'law of effect' (1898), which states that behavioural responses that achieve a satisfactory effect are likely to occur again, while those responses that elicit a discomforting effect are less likely to be repeated. B. F. Skinner (1904–90) is the psychologist credited with the development of theories of operant conditioning during the 20th century.

opiate any of a group of sedative drugs derived from the opium poppy and used medicinally in the treatment of extreme pain, as cough suppressants and for diarrhoea. Most are prescription-only, but some mild forms are available over the counter in combination with other constituents.

Examples of opiates include HEROIN, opium and morphine. Opiates can be both physically and psychologically addictive. People who are addicted to them will use any form of the drug that is available, often resorting to black-market adulterated supplies. Opiates that are synthetically produced are called *opioids* and include METHADONE, pethidine and dipipanane.

oppression the exploitation and marginalization of a people, social group or individuals.

Oppression is the process through which, over time, groups or individuals with power unfairly constrict and exploit the lives, experiences and opportunities of groups or individuals with less power. In the past we have tended to link oppression with authoritarian or totalitarian rule – the exercise of tyranny by a ruling group or regime that weighed down a population with harsh, unjust policies. Since the 1960s/1970s, however, the term has come to include the social disadvantages and injustices that some social groups suffer through everyday stereotypes, forms of abuse and lack of institutional power in developed democracies such as the UK. This wider notion of oppression was first developed by the 'new social movements' arising from the struggles of black and ethnic minorities, the women's movement and the gay and disability movements among others. Their experiences taught them that democratic societies were also oppressive in a certain

way that they sometimes called 'structural oppression', an oppression
that is embedded in the unquestioned norms, habits, symbols,
stereotypes and assumptions of society. As a result, whole social groups
are confined, immobilized and have far less opportunities and social
resources at their disposal.

This form of oppression cannot be got rid of by overthrowing a ruling
regime, for it is continually reproduced within our major economic,
cultural and political institutions – and in the way people relate to each
other. *Exploitation* is one aspect of oppression, but extracting profit out
of other people's work extends beyond class; it includes housework,
caring and clerical work, and other forms of what is defined socially as
'menial' labour. *Marginalization* is another way through which a whole
group is denied useful participation in social life. Violence plays a covert
but systematic part in maintaining this form of oppression – whether
in attacks on gay people, rape, racial violence or incidents of domestic
violence or child abuse. The social context makes it possible, even
acceptable, in certain localities or for certain people. It also is the context
in which forms of harassment, intimidation and threats occur so that
certain groups, such as black people, gays or women fear random,
unprovoked attack. The major oppressions that social workers have
to respond to are based on gender, 'race', disability, age and sexuality.
They also intertwine. Child sexual abuse, for example, takes place within
the wider social relations dominated by male power and adult power
over children as well as being a brutal individual act of domination.
CARERS are an oppressed group because they care for older people and
disabled people who themselves experience social, economic and
political oppression. The new understanding of oppression also implies
the view that oppressed people have a less partial and less distorted
understanding of social problems and of how society functions. Their
experiences are judged to be more authentic because they are achieved
through struggle against oppression; their aim is to get their voices
heard. (See ANTI-OPPRESSIVE PRACTICE.)

I. M. Young, *Justice and the Politics of Difference*, Chichester, Princeton
University Press, 1990.

organization theory attempts to understand how organizations work
with respect to their internal structures and processes, both formal
and informal, and their external relations.

In relation to social welfare agencies, policy-makers have been
concerned to answer several related questions. First, how can services
be organized and delivered most effectively? Second, what structures will
be most supportive of workers in what are widely recognized as stressful
occupations? Third, how are social welfare agencies to relate to service
users? Fourth, how are social welfare organizations to relate to each
other? SOCIAL SERVICES DEPARTMENTS have experimented a lot in the
past few decades. Three kinds of models have emerged. Departments

using 'functional' arrangements are organized into sections based on setting – typically fieldwork, residential and day-care services. Other functional sections might comprise research, inspection, staff development, and so on. Departments increasingly structure services around 'CLIENT groups', with the integration of all residential, fieldwork and day-care services for each client group in one section of the organization. Finally, some have a 'geographical model', dividing up the organization into smaller units that then usually employ either the functional or client group models. In practice, hybrids of various kinds are often devised. Research seems to indicate that client group models work best because all resources for a case are contained within one section of the organization. Such a model, however, is not without its difficulties: how are services to be organized, for example, when two client groups are involved in one case?

Most social welfare workers have a clear preference for flat hierarchies; that is, they appear to want few levels or tiers within the organization. Such arrangements give them access to decision-makers and make plain where the responsibilities for decisions actually lie. Similarly, they want direct access to support staff without having to go through intermediaries. For example, a worker with a case of child SEXUAL ABUSE will wish to consult with the department's adviser without complex referral systems to that adviser. 'Chains of command' vary a lot within welfare and justice agencies. Some agencies operate as collectives or with one manager only (often in the VOLUNTARY SECTOR); others may have as many as seven or eight levels (typically some social services departments), with many somewhere in between (probation departments often have only three or four tiers).

Service users will wish to have reasonable access to services. Agencies should pay attention to the siting of offices in relation to populations and to public transport routes. Many social services departments have devised outposts for isolated communities, and in large densely populated areas NEIGHBOURHOOD OFFICES may offer the first point of contact with several local government departments. Policies to promote access frequently include the provision of transport by the social welfare agency.

With the efficient coordination of services as the objective, it is clearly advantageous for welfare and justice agencies to have the same area boundaries. With some functions this has proved possible, but with others both boundaries and forms of accountability vary significantly. Some organizations are accountable to local government, others increasingly to central government or to QUANGOS. Where these organizations also have different boundaries, coordinating mechanisms are required. Not surprisingly, the service user, required to deal with two or more agencies, can be confused. (See also MULTIDISCIPLINARY WORK.)

L. Challis, *Organizing Public Services*, Harlow, Longman, 1990.

organized sexual abuse the systematic SEXUAL ABUSE of a number of children by several adults acting in a planned, coordinated way, often linked to PAEDOPHILE rings.

ouster order an order issued by county court that can require a spouse, a partner or somebody associated with the spouse or partner to leave the matrimonial home; an exclusion order issued by MAGISTRATES' courts has similar powers.

An ouster order can be issued both by a magistrates' court and by a county court. The order has as its objective the protection of people (usually women) and their children who have experienced VIOLENCE or harassment.

outreach any attempt to take a service to people who need it and who would otherwise probably not use the service.

Many social welfare agencies offer their services in a relatively passive way; their presumption often is that their service is generally well known and that those who wish to use it will do so. Similarly, it is argued that those who do not use the service do not need it or do not wish to use it. These assumptions are now known to be false. Many services if offered on an outreach basis considerably increase their usage and often bring to the service people who are different from more habitual users (sick people, people with DISABILITIES and members of ethnic minorities, for example).

Outreach workers have long been employed by the youth service (sometimes called 'detached youth workers') to work with young people who would otherwise probably not use the service (see YOUTH WORK). Such work is especially useful in relation to the young single homeless, to those involved with SUBSTANCE MISUSE and to those involved in, or who have the potential for involvement in, delinquent activity. ADVICE work is another context that has demonstrated the benefits of outreach work. Campaigns to persuade claimants to apply for a benefit that they are entitled to but are unaware of (or are reluctant to claim or are unsure about how to claim) have much higher TAKE-UP rates when advice workers leaflet an area with accessible information or undertake to contact each household, or both. Health services have also improved their uptake of services, especially around critical issues like immunization in relation to an epidemic of a serious disease and HIV/AIDS (see also COMMUNITY DRUG TEAMS). It should be remembered that poor or vulnerable people experience relative powerlessness. In this regard services have to demonstrate their relevance to people who often sorely need them but lack the will or understanding to use them. Such services have a major role to play in relation to PREVENTIVE WORK, because they have the capacity for identifying problems at an early stage of development. (See also ASSERTIVE OUTREACH).

overlapping benefits a term that refers to the general principle of social security that individuals should not be entitled to receive more than one income replacement benefit, for example retirement pension, at any one time. Where a person is entitled to more than one such benefit, such as bereavement benefit and carer's allowance, he or she can receive only the higher of the two.

If a person (usually a woman) claims an income replacement benefit in her own right, then her spouse will not be eligible to claim a dependant's increase in respect of them unless the amount of the increase is greater than the other benefit payable.

overpayment see WELFARE RIGHTS 1.

P p

paedophile a person who commits acts of a sexual nature with children under the age of 16; these involve a high degree of coercion, secrecy and cruelty, and can inflict lasting psychological and physical harm.

While the term 'paedophile' is not readily found in law, the acts associated with it are sexual offences and as such are open to criminal charges. A range of such offences are now found in law, from unwanted touching to penetrative intercourse. Recently, government activity has also focused on the commercial sexual exploitation of children, which includes the prostitution of children and young people, the production of child pornography or its distribution over the internet. The public and professional interest in paedophiles has expanded enormously in recent years. This has been prompted by several factors, including the high-profile murders of young children by known paedophiles, the arrival of the internet, which provides a means for paedophiles both to contact one another and children themselves, and the exploitation of children by paedophiles who had found employment in children's homes. The uncovering of widespread paedophile rings within residential children's homes in the northwest of England and north Wales particularly angered the public. It resulted in a long-running inquiry ending with publication of a detailed account, in the Waterhouse Report, of the extent of paedophile activity in the homes.

Despite the concern, there is continuing debate as to the nature of paedophile behaviour and whether or not it is treatable and, if not, whether the worst offenders be imprisoned for indefinite periods. Psychiatric diagnosis places paedophiles' behaviour within the range of severe PERSONALITY DISORDERS, that is, a pattern of behaviour that deviates significantly from accepted social norms and characteristically disregards the rights or safety of others and shows an incapacity to experience guilt or remorse over actions. A feminist interpretation would find a common link between paedophiles' behaviour and that of men generally in society who utilize their dominant power to assert their claim to physical gratification heedless of the harm to others. The psychiatric perspective would find a relatively smaller number of truly dangerous paedophiles in society at large while the feminist perspective tends to see the problem as part of a range of male behaviour and sees paedophiles as more numerous.

The issues of identification, treatment and incarceration of paedophiles have become explosive for practitioners, local authorities and central government itself, driven in the main by rising public concern.

Identification: there is a sharp and ongoing debate about the degree to which local residents need to know of specific paedophiles living in their area. The public's right to know, and thereby to safeguard their own children from the risk of habitual offenders, has somehow to be balanced against the rights of the individual paedophiles who, of course, may have their own families. Part I of the Sex Offenders Act 1997 obliges paedophiles (along with other sex offenders such as rapists) who have been cautioned, convicted or found not guilty by reasons of insanity of sex offences against children to notify the police of their name and address and to inform them also when they plan to travel abroad. (In 2005 there were some 44,592 sex offenders so registered in England and Wales, with some 2,800 in Scotland.) The disappearance and death of the child Sarah Payne at the hands of a paedophile in the summer of 2000 only heightened public insistence on firmer action and led the government to introduce several amendments to the Act, including five years' imprisonment for an offender's failure to register. The CRIME AND DISORDER ACT 1998 also gives police extra powers against sex offenders, allowing them to apply for a Sex Offenders Order in relation to any offender who can reasonably be deemed a public risk. The line between letting the community know and preserving the rights of the individual paedophile is still fluid and perhaps will shift back and forth for a time. Of relevance here is the High Court's decision in 2002 to refuse an application by the director of a social service department who wanted to reveal the name of a paedophile to a local landlord.

To a degree, the print media have heightened public emotions on identification. In the late 1990s local newspapers 'outed' individual paedophiles and subtly encouraged an atmosphere of vigilantism and the harassment of individual paedophiles, whether suspected or convicted and their families, sometimes undermining public order as a result. But it also clear that the public does now feel very strongly about paedophiles and wants to ensure above all that children are protected, even at the expense of civil liberties. Interestingly, this marks a sea change in public opinion on the matter. As recently as the 1970s paedophiles were regarded in a more relaxed light. At that time there was open discussion about sexual relations between adult and child as 'mutually gratifying' and as conducted with the 'child's consent'; indeed, a paedophile network, the Paedophile Information Exchange, maintained an open, public existence in a way that would be unthinkable today.

Treatment: treatment of paedophiles, as with any people with severe personality disorder, requires changing long-established beliefs and emotions about themselves and other people and the cruel or harmful antisocial behaviour that they have engaged in previously. Because paedophilia is not an illness but part of the structure of the personality, in the psychiatric perspective the notion of a 'cure' is not realistic as this would require a complete personality change. The aim is to produce more socially adaptive and constructive ways of dealing with relationships. Special units for treatment with specific regimes do seem to have had some success. In particular they have relied on forms of COGNITIVE BEHAVIOURAL THERAPY to change thinking patterns of a perpetrator as well as to improve problem solving and moral reasoning. Such programmes also aim to reduce egocentricity and to teach control of a person's own impulses more effectively. Available evidence suggests that paedophiles do not respond positively to traditional therapeutic interventions, such as individual psychotherapy.

Incarceration: under section 37 of the MENTAL HEALTH ACT 1983, as well as in proposed MENTAL HEALTH LAW REFORM, those with a severe personality disorder thought to be dangerous can be sentenced by a criminal court to detention without time limit in special hospitals, special high-security units or therapeutic prisons. But the treatment value of the special hospitals, such as Ashworth on Merseyside or Rampton in Nottinghamshire, was questioned in the late 1990s when they were shown to have severe defects in their regimes. These included lax security, abundant evidence of drugs and pornography, and inmates themselves running day-to-day affairs. Whether in special hospitals, prisons or special high-security units, the most dangerous paedophiles face indeterminate prison sentences because their risk to the public is so high. In the proposed mental health reforms there is envisaged to be a further order applying to 'high-risk patients' who could be detained on a preventative basis, that is, before a serious offence took place and perhaps without even a court appearance. Such an order raises difficult issues, such as detaining persons who have not yet done anything wrong, the indefinite nature of such detention and whether they are actually treatable or not.

Social workers are likely to be involved in work with paedophiles, predominantly within a mental health setting; work with high-risk individuals will be conducted only in highly specialist settings. Increasingly, however, there is an emphasis on preventive measures in which social workers will be working with young people who display inappropriate sexual behaviour that is not necessarily picked up by the criminal justice system. In this respect greater emphasis is now placed on young people who engage in sexual offences. The Young Abusers' Project, now run by the NSPCC, is the most familiar of several. In its work the project finds that some 10 per cent of young abusers are female.

In their attitudes to paedophiles, social workers share the public's belief that the liberties of abusers should be curtailed in order to protect children. According to a survey conducted by the weekly social care magazine *Community Care* in 2000, half of the social workers polled agreed that local people should be informed when a convicted paedophile moves into their neighbourhood and over half supported the concept of indeterminate sentences for paedophiles, that is, custody without time limit. On both issues the percentages exactly matched those of the public.

D. Howitt *Paedophiles and Sex Offences Against Children* London, John Wiley, 1995.

palliative care the approach to caring for people dying of a diagnosed incurable disease that embodies symptom control, pain relief and psychological and social support for the dying people and their relatives and loved ones.

Palliative care, sometimes referred to as *terminal care*, encourages dying people and the significant people in their lives to live in active and fulfilling ways and to participate in decisions about the management of the disease. The focus of attention is the emotional, spiritual and practical care of the dying person and his or her close relationships. This holistic approach has its origins in the HOSPICE CARE movement founded by Dame Cicely Saunders in 1967 at St Christopher's Hospice. Terminal care occurs in a number of settings. The hospice may offer short-term inpatient care on a RESPITE basis or longer-term care as death approaches. Multidisciplinary teams – doctors, nurses, social workers and occupational therapists – also use the hospice as a base for offering terminal care to patients in their own homes or in community resources. In addition, hospice teams may offer symptom control with the care of the dying in general hospital wards. Experiences from the hospice movement have in recent years led to the establishing of palliative care strategies in hospitals, COMMUNITY CARE and residential and own-home settings. Palliative care teams work alongside the patient's own primary health care workers, the general practitioner and district nurse. The distinction between hospice care and palliative care is becoming increasingly blurred. Further support to the terminally ill is offered by nurses from the Cancer Relief Macmillan Fund, who usually work from community settings in close liaison with the primary health care services.

Patients cared for by the hospice and to a lesser extent by palliative care teams are most likely to have a diagnosis of terminal cancer. Both care strategies have been reluctant to offer care to people and their relatives where the diagnosis is ALZHEIMER'S DISEASE or where a person is in the latter stages of Aids (see HIV/AIDS). While the hospice movement particularly is considering its services for Aids patients, much of the terminal care of people dying from Aids-associated illness is undertaken by friends, relatives and buddies. Buddies are people who befriend and

support those with Aids. People with Aids experience multiple losses
in addition to the diagnosis of terminal illness – friends, other family
members and their sexual partner may have already died from Aids – and
a buddy may be their only social support. Terminal care of people with
Alzheimer's disease is usually in the person's own home, supported by
health and social services' personnel and resources.

The social worker's role is a key one in the planning of care for dying
people. The patient's own concerns and wishes, and the facilitation
of patient choices in care plans, is the worker's overriding concern.
The person also has a right to choose where to die and to be supported
in this choice, although clearly the social worker will have regard for the
concerns of others affected by this choice. The social worker's emphasis
should be a maintenance of the dying person's rights, as these can all too
often be eroded by the demands of medical and social care. Institutional
arrangements in hospitals are often a barrier to patient choice. The control
of choice may be in the amount of information available to a dying
person; such information can be controlled by relatives, family and loved
ones. The social worker should be informed as to the availability of care
resources, knowledgeable in benefit provision, sensitive to possible care
needs of other family members, including OLDER PEOPLE and children,
and skilled in building confidence and trust.

Caring for dying people is stressful. Social work must therefore take
account of the needs of the carer for respite. For example, children's
hospices were established to provide relief for parents recognizing the
stress that a dying child places on a family. Children's hospices are
usually small and as homelike as possible, even to the provision of pets.

D. Clark (ed), *The future of palliative care: Issues of policy and practice*,
Buckingham, Open University Press, 1993.

paranoia a mental disorder in which the sufferer holds the unshakeable
conviction that he or she is being persecuted by others.

Intense and persistent paranoia is often diagnosed as a type of
schizophrenia. In this form the sufferer believes or perceives, where
others would be unlikely to do so, that there is a direct threat in his or
her environment. It can take the form of persecution or revolve around
a perceived injustice or belief that they will sustain a physical attack.
Anger, argumentativeness and aggression are all possible behavioural
consequences.

parental responsibility as defined in the CHILDREN ACT, the rights, duties,
powers, responsibilities and authority that in law parents have in relation
to their children.

The term is used in sections 2, 3 and 4 of the Children Act to emphasize
that parents have inescapable responsibilities when bringing up children
and should not view the relationship with their children as based solely
on PARENTAL RIGHTS. Parental responsibility is automatically conferred
on both parents of a child as long as those parents were married at the

time of the child's birth. If the parents are not married at the time of the birth, the mother of the child automatically acquires responsibility. Recent amendment to the Act also now allows the unmarried father to acquire responsibility as long as both parents have jointly registered the child's birth. If this has not happened, the father does not and can acquire responsibility only through a court order or by agreement with the mother. A parent who has parental responsibility for a child cannot lose it except through ADOPTION. It can be shared, however, delegated by a parent or acquired by others who are not the child's parents. For example, foster parents who have looked after a child for a period of time can acquire parental responsibility through a RESIDENCE ORDER, and the local authority itself acquires parental responsibility when it holds a CARE ORDER on a child. In both instances the parents do not lose parental responsibility but have to share it with the foster parents or local authority.

Knowing who does or does not have parental responsibility for a particular child is extremely important for social workers and other care professionals working with families. Although the Children Act does not define what the specific responsibilities are, people with parental responsibility have an important role in decision-making concerning a child who is being LOOKED AFTER by a local authority. They also have certain rights to maintain CONTACT with a child unless there are compelling reasons why they should not do so.

parental rights the rights, powers and duties that a parent holds in relation to his or her child.

The concept of parental rights derived originally from property law, namely that children were the property of their father, who, until the mid-19th century, almost always prevailed in any contest for custody. The term came to embrace aspects of the care and control of the child as well, but it later fell into disfavour as a more child-centred perspective in law became dominant. In GILLICK v. *West Norfolk and Wisbech Area Health Authority*, for example, the House of Lords emphasized that parental power to control a child existed not for the benefit of the parent but for the benefit of the child. The CHILDREN ACT has replaced the concept of parental rights with PARENTAL RESPONSIBILITY, which emphasizes what the old concept did not, namely that parents have certain obligations and responsibilities towards their children that they must meet and cannot easily evade even if they need to ask for help from the local authority with this task. Within social work, the concept of parental rights was often viewed as contrary to children's rights, and it was considered that if a child's welfare was to be protected the local authority had to take over parental rights from the parents. What were assumed to be opposing sets of interests provided a justification for compulsory intervention in a family's life. There is now greater realization within the profession that children's rights and parental rights are intertwined and coincide rather than oppose each other.

parent education and training services that help parents and prospective parents understand key aspects of parenting in order that they might become more effective carers of children. These services seek to help parents to understand the emotional, intellectual, physical and social needs of children as well as their own needs. Such services seek to enhance the relationship between parents (or their surrogates) and the children for whom they have responsibility. The over-arching objective is to assist parents to help their children to achieve a mature and independent adulthood.

In the past decade there have been persistent calls for the creation of a range of accessible services to assist parents with parenting. This loose movement has been driven by a number of concerns. First, many commentators have pointed out that, in the past, most adults have assumed the role of parent without any formal education or training to help them prepare for parenthood or to assist them when they encounter difficulties. Second, it is acknowledged that parenting is a complex process, especially in stressful circumstances or where children have particular kinds of problems or needs. Most parents appear to benefit from opportunities to discuss their problems and to learn from the experiences of others. Third, many have argued that statutory child-care services have been preoccupied with CHILD PROTECTION at the expense of FAMILY SUPPORT services. Family support services, it is held, are perceived as less stigmatizing than having social workers intervene in the lives of families. As a result, such services are thought capable of playing an important preventive role so that more complex and entrenched parenting and child-care problems are less likely to develop.

It is useful to distinguish between 'support for parenting' and 'support for parents'. The first refers to services that have the parent-child relationship as its focus. Such services can be generalized in nature or be concerned with problems of varying seriousness. Hardiker's typology of services is useful in this context. She distinguishes between primary, secondary, tertiary and post-crisis services. Primary services are concerned to convey basic skills in parenting, as with the health visiting service or a parenting education programme offered by the local adult education college. Such first-line services are open-access in character, designed to inform parents and would-be parents about some of the common problems and some of the solutions to successful parenting. Secondary services are designed to assist parents with some identified problem that the parent is keen to resolve, say a young exhausted lone parent is consulting a doctor because her child is very wakeful at nights and she is exhausted. Tertiary services are those designed to deal with serious problems, such as parenting in a household where there is domestic violence and emotional abuse of the child or in another household where the parents of a multiply disabled child cannot cope. Post-crisis services refer to work with parents following some critical event, such as an admission of a parent to a psychiatric hospital, a child being taken into care or a woman and child retreating to a women's refuge. Hardiker argues that parents should have reasonable access to such support services and that statutory and voluntary agencies should work together to provide them within a coherent and planned framework that takes account of local needs.

Services to 'support parents' are those that have a direct bearing upon parents as individuals but which may fundamentally affect parents' abilities to parent. Such services focus upon an adequate income, affordable and quality child-care services, family friendly employment practices, good housing, effective health and education services and reasonable play provision for children. The need for these kinds of services is located in a view that emphasizes the importance of the social and economic context to parenting. This view also underlines the need for governments to foster both kinds of services, for to emphasize parents' responsibilities for their children without providing them with the resources to do the job adequately might be regarded as oppressive.

There are many kinds of parenting problems. Some are located in special needs that children might have, such as autism, some in a parent's behaviour, condition or social context, such as a health problem or being imprisoned. Recent reports from the SOCIAL SERVICES INSPECTORATE, based upon inspections of a wide range of social services departments, have identified particular clusters of problems that have been recognized as being especially complicated. The same reports have found that social work services, both statutory and voluntary, dealing with these problems are often inadequate or poorly co-ordinated. The reports have highlighted domestic violence, mental health problems in parents, drug-abusing parents, parents with learning disabilities, teenage parents, parenting after divorce or separation (including step-parenting) and children with multiple disabilities as key areas warranting better services both to help parenting and to support parents. At least some of these difficulties in service provision arise out of the separation of children's services from adult services in social services departments.

There is now a widespread consensus that co-ordinated services to support parenting are needed. These services should take a holistic view of parents' needs, should include fathers and men yet to be fathers, should offer a range of services to deal with broad-based parent education as well as services to offer support to parents in times of stress and crisis, should be non-stigmatized and should try to promote the idea that to want to seek advice about parenting is normal rather than exceptional. All these principles are to be fostered by the new government SURE START programmes and the National Family and Parenting Institute.

P. Hardiker, K. Exton and M. Barker, *Policies and Practices in Preventive Childcare*, Aldershot, Avebury, 1991.

G. Pugh, E. De'Ath and C. Smith, 'Confident Parents, Confident Children, Policy and Practice', in *Parent Education and Support*, London, National Children's Bureau, 1994.

parenting order a court order requiring a parent to participate in activities aimed at preventing crime or disorder being committed by his or her child.

Under the CRIME AND DISORDER ACT 1998, parents can be ordered to comply with specified requirements, including compulsory counselling and guidance designed to improve their parenting skills. The requirement to undergo counselling applies for one session a week for up to three months, and additional requirements such as school attendance or being home by a certain time can be added for the total length of the order (12 months). Orders are enforced by YOUTH OFFENDING TEAMS, and parents who fail to comply with an order can be fined.

Parenting orders are increasingly being used in response to convictions under section 444 of the EDUCATION ACT 1996 where parents have failed to ensure their children's school attendance. In these circumstances they may be supervised by an officer of the EDUCATION SOCIAL WORK service of the local education authority.

Parenting Plan a document, available on the internet or from magistrates' courts, that provides practical help for divorcing parents to improve the CONTACT arrangements with their child(ren), and to ensure that arrangements are the best possible for their child(ren).

Introduced by the Lord Chancellor's Department following the FAMILY LAW ACT 1996 to help divorcing parents develop the best possible arrangements for their children, the Parenting Plan contains information, guidance and ideas on issues that need to be faced together with details of agencies that can help.

parent partnership service a service that must be provided either by a local education authority at 'arms-length or independently and that offers advice, support and information to the parents of children with SPECIAL EDUCATIONAL NEEDS (SEN).

Provision will also include procedures for resolving disagreements between schools, local education authorities and parents about the provision that is being made available for individual children as an alternative to using the more formal process of the SEN tribunal.

parliamentary select committee a committee of members of parliament that scrutinizes the implementation of government policy, including social services and social work issues.

In 1979, after an experiment in widening the role and number of parliamentary committees, a series of select committees was established to shadow each of the main central government departments. Each committee is composed of appointed MPs who have expressed a particular interest in the work of that committee. Membership is weighted in proportion to the relative strengths of the main political parties in the House of Commons, thus giving the majority party the largest number of committee places. These committees are seen, however, as being the servants of parliament and as a result they work across party lines and make serious efforts to ensure an agreed report.

Parliamentary select committees have important powers that add significantly to parliament's ability to scrutinize the actions of the government. These powers include the ability to summon ministers, civil servants and members of the public to give evidence, which enables them to question the opinions of outside experts, including local government councillors, officials and social work staff. Their investigations can take them out of the house to visit organizations in the furtherance of their inquiries. This broadens the scope of parliament to examine issues more widely and in more detail than in the traditional debate on the floor of the house. The nature of parliamentary debates and their formal structure do not permit detailed examination of ministers and do not include non-MPs. Select committees can examine issues in detail over some weeks, and this can result in lengthy questioning of ministers and others.

Reports of the committees are published, along with, in most instances, the full transcripts of hearings and the written reports of witnesses. As with the main parliamentary debates, the hearings of select committees are recorded for television and radio. Select committee reports are, however, only advisory; all too frequently the government takes only limited notice of them. The response to these reports may take place verbally on the floor of the house when the report is debated, or the government may publish a reply. Reports by the Social Services Select Committee have provided important material on both COMMUNITY CARE and the care of children. In addition, evidence has been provided on the needs of formal and informal carers, although most information is provided by organized pressure groups, such as BRITISH ASSOCIATION OF SOCIAL WORKERS and Mencap, rather than individuals. So the existence of these committees allows a more public expression of the detailed views of these organizations to parliament than would otherwise be the case.

In 1991 the structure of some committees was altered, and the Social Services Select Committee was abolished in favour of two new committees: the Select Committee on Health and the Select Committee on Social Security. This change was brought about by the reorganization of the Department of Health and Social Security into separate departments of Health and of Social Security. Further changes are made as departments change and new governments are elected but the basic principles remain the same, as do the questions concerning their effective-ness in holding governments up to scrutiny.

Since 1997 and the election of the NEW LABOUR government, disputes between select committees and the government over the content of their reports have continued. Questions over the control of membership

appointments by the party whips continue to raise issues about the role
of the select committees as servants of parliament rather than party.

parole the period of discretionary conditional release from PRISON under
licence for which certain categories of prisoner are eligible.

First introduced in 1967, parole has been altered repeatedly over the
years. In recent years, the notion of a period of time under supervision
on release, and subject to recall to prison, has been applied to shorter as
well as long-term sentences. The situation has been complicated by the
introduction of ELECTRONIC MONITORING of those prisoners released
early. The Halliday Review of sentencing is likely to lead to further changes.
Research on parole has shown that those granted early release subject to
supervision have lower reconviction rates on average than those not
granted parole, although the latter obviously represent a higher risk group.

parsimony see MINIMUM INTERVENTION.

participation the involvement of service users and local residents in
decisions that affect them.

Historically, both central and local government administered top-down
service programmes that relied on notions of infallible professional expertise
and bureaucratic procedures. Whether the NATIONAL HEALTH SERVICE,
local council housing or running residential homes for OLDER PEOPLE,
major public services gave little or no say to those who used them. Whatever
the benefits the services bestowed, the way in which they were provided
increased the powerlessness of those who used them. Social work and its
main agencies recognized this from the late 1980s onwards and began to
encourage the participation of users in services. Partly this was a result of the
pressure for greater influence by different groups. These included learning
disability advocates who urged greater service choices in the community
that were more in line with what all citizens enjoyed. Social work also received
strong criticism of its work with children and families in the mid- and late
1980s because it left parents out of the decision-making process when the
local authority social service departments were considering taking their
children into care. Adults needing some form of social care – whether a
place in a residential home or home care – were often starkly limited in
their choice and had no established means of giving opinions in any case.

Successive pieces of legislation began to require user participation
at modest levels in the assessment of need and provision of services.
The CHILDREN ACT 1989, the NATIONAL HEALTH SERVICE AND COMMUNITY
CARE ACT of 1990, and the DISABLED PERSONS (SERVICES, CONSULTATION
AND REPRESENTATION) ACT in 1996 all required local authorities to
consult more closely with users when undertaking assessments, devising
care plans and reviewing those plans. More recent government initiatives
such as QUALITY PROTECTS for children, the NEW DEAL FOR COMMUNITIES,
SURE START and the BEST VALUE framework all mandate more extensive
citizen participation. This emphasis will intensify in the future as closer
consultation and joint action with local people becomes mandatory.

Despite this general trend toward greater levels of participation, the degree of influence that service users, families or local residents actually enjoy varies considerably and depends on the attitudes of the practitioners involved, the policies of their agencies and the type of service being offered. Moreover, genuine dilemmas and real limits to participation arise when local authorities have statutory obligations to exercise authority and to provide a service that users have little choice but to accept, for example young offenders or parents strongly suspected of child abuse.

A number of principles are found in participatory social work practice. First, a social worker's investigation of problems or assessment of need should be with the explicit consent of the potential user. Second, social workers should remember that there are only two legitimate bases for intervention in an individual's life: either because the law says so or because the user has agreed. Third, social work services should be based on the views of all relevant family members and carers. Fourth, users should have the greatest degree of choice of services as possible. To help realize these principles, practitioners have developed a number of tools that provide users and their families with a greater voice in key decision-making. These include the exchange model of ASSESSMENT that gives greater weight to user opinion, WRITTEN AGREEMENTS that incorporate users' objectives for the next six months, TASK-CENTRED WORK that is based on the short-term goals defined by users themselves, and the FAMILY GROUP CONFERENCE that effectively gives the wider family important powers in cases of child protection and youth offending.

Users, local residents and community organizations also now increasingly help to shape services themselves by contributing their views, personal experiences and expertise through a variety of channels such as joint planning meetings, advisory groups, public meetings or sitting on task groups, or taking part in inspection and monitoring of a given service.

A new development is that of user-led services, which are wholly independent of the local authority and organized by committed advocates with a clear view of how society excludes users of mainstream services. Not only do they provide distinctive forms of support, they also offer powerful examples of flexibility, choice and involvement, which themselves exert wide influence.

With the increasing emphasis on SOCIAL EXCLUSION, participation as a concept can no longer be confined only to users and a particular service. Virtually all new service projects, whether originating within local authorities, community groups or voluntary services, must now give considerable attention to the kind of participation they seek and what approaches they should use. Real participation requires:

1 the availability of INFORMATION in a language and form that users can understand;

2 users' access to independent sources of advice and representation;

3 users' attendance at, contribution to, and influence on the outcome of meetings, both formal and informal, where decisions are made.

(See also ARNSTEIN'S LADDER; NEIGHBOURHOOD MANAGEMENT TEAMS.)

H. Kemshall and R. Littlechild (eds), *User Involvement and Participation in Social Care*, London, Jessica Kingsley Publishers, 2000.

partnership a working relationship that involves a number of different organizations in formal or semi-formal arrangements in which goals are agreed upon, some resources are pooled and common strategy planned.

A partner may be defined as 'one who has a share or part with others', implying that there is an overall goal or framework of which individual partners are aware although each partner may be responsible for implementing a different part of that strategy. Successive governments have invoked the concept of partnership when proposing ways that services and different professions should join together in tackling specific problems. Since 1997 the Labour government has pressed this agenda even further with its calls for NEIGHBOURHOOD RENEWAL and JOINED-UP ACTION in relation to SOCIAL EXCLUSION. Other prominent multidisciplinary solutions have been created to tackle a range of social problems, such as YOUTH OFFENDING TEAMS, EARLY YEARS forums and SURE START for children under five.

To understand the importance of partnerships in tackling social problems, it helps to see the major services as large, self-contained organizations interested only in their internal concerns. As a result, people are often 'dumped' – excluded – outside one or more service silos and hence receive no service at all. The rising exclusions from school of hard-to-teach pupils are a perfect example of dumping. Because of school performance tables, disruptive, hard-to-teach pupils are unwanted by any school and there is no other service in place for them. In social work, individuals are sometimes shuttled between hospital care and long-term residential care with neither service wanting to absorb the cost. Professional discretion in decision-making and the growing culture of managerial focus on 'core' responsibilities and competencies have only reinforced the problem of dumping.

Partners that are frequently linked together in providing services are:
1 local authorities, which are often the dominant or leading players in local partnerships and have developed experience in partnerships for delivering services;
2 public service agencies, such as the police, the health service, local schools, and social services departments;
3 voluntary sector agencies, whether large and well known or small locally based organizations representing specific groups in the community or providing specific services, for example an Asian women's refuge;
4 local community organizations, such as tenants' or residents' associations, who bring local knowledge and experience to bear on the needs of specific local constituencies and neighbourhoods;

5 the private sector, which can embrace a range of employers, job trainers, consultants and other experts.

Partnerships are required where the problems to be tackled, such as ANTISOCIAL BEHAVIOUR, are deep-rooted and have a variety of causes, making it impossible for a single professional approach or agency to resolve on their own. Partnership makes holistic solutions possible, providing the means by which practitioners can move beyond the specialisms of social work, such as CARE MANAGEMENT or CHILD PROTECTION, to create a new service with value added.

Partnerships do not automatically function well and at times they can be worse than nothing at all. They may exist on paper simply to provide a means for capturing resources. The individual organizations in a partnership may have vastly different levels of influence and power within the arrangement. While centrally imposed conditions for competitive bidding for funding requires the formation of partnerships, often the time frame is extremely short, thus giving considerable advantage to those major agencies with highly specialized workforces and the capacity to do the hours of planning and report writing that is necessary. Local organizations, users and residents usually have no such resources to fall back on. Although women often play a prominent role on partnership boards, there is a reported widespread lack of child-care arrangements during meetings. There is also often little time allowance made to read and respond to papers for those with home and care-based responsibilities.

A. McCabe, V. Lowndes and C. Skelcher, *Partnerships and Networks: An evaluation and development manual*, York, Joseph Rowntree Foundation, 1997.

pass and passing methods of determining a service's quality by measuring how far that service meets criteria associated with NORMALIZATION.

The techniques of pass and passing are proposed by their authors as suitable for assessing services for people from any devalued group, but are most commonly employed with regard to people with LEARNING DISABILITY. They focus on how far services enhance two main areas affecting service users: their social image and their personal competence. Pass and passing are similar, but passing includes only measures of normalization, while pass includes additional criteria associated with service quality. Workshops are utilized to train people in these assessment techniques.

W. Wolfensberger and S. Thomas, *Passing Program Analysis of Service Systems' Implementation of Normalization Goals*, Ontario, Canadian National Institute of Menial Retardation, 1983.

passport benefits SEE WELFARE RIGHTS 1.

pastoral support programme (PSP) a programme of support designed by a school, in consultation with parents and others, to assist a child at risk of EXCLUSION FROM SCHOOL and to promote improvement in his or her behaviour.

Guidance on the development of PSPs and the use of other supportive and preventive strategies intended to help children at risk can be found in DEPARTMENT FOR EDUCATION AND SKILLS Circular 10/99 *Social Inclusion: Pupil Support* and in procedures published by the local education authority (LEA). Other professionals should be consulted with parental permission and involved in the programme where they are working with the family. Such a package of support should normally have been attempted by the school before permanent exclusion becomes appropriate, unless the child has committed a very serious breach of the school's discipline policy, usually involving violence or supplying drugs.

patch work or **patch system** a way of delivering social welfare and especially social work services within a particular geographical area.

Patches might be worked by a single worker, by a small group of workers or by whole teams. This way of working was especially popular with GENERIC teams, that is, where a social work team undertook all the work within a designated geographical area. More recently, genericism has given way to relative specialisms, and this has discouraged or diluted the development of patch working. A patch would normally be small enough, first, for professional workers to become familiar with the other welfare agencies in the area, thus encouraging close collaborative work where needed, and, second, for workers to be able to identify and work with informal networks. Some patch systems, like that in Normanton in Yorkshire, relied heavily upon both VOLUNTEERS and DOMICILIARY care workers; these workers seemed to combine the roles of family aides, HOME HELPS and SOCIAL WORK ASSISTANTS. The experiment raised interesting questions about the numbers of professional social workers needed on a patch if their efforts are augmented by both ancillary workers and volunteers.

patriarchy a form of social system wherein men enjoy greater power over women, who are, as a direct result of the patriarchal system, confined to the private sphere of the home. Sylvia Walby (*Theorizing Patriarchy*, Oxford, Basil Blackwell, 1990) has favoured a broad definition of patriarchy. She identifies six structures as patriarchal (which operate in a manner to maintain the dominance of men); these are the family, work, the media, education, the state and male violence.

PCT abbreviation for PRIMARY CARE TRUST.

PDA abbreviation for PRACTICE DEVELOPMENT ASSESSOR.

peer group a group of people with the same social standing or status. Although peer groups are thought to be especially influential among young people, the term has general application to other age groups.

Peers may be a specific group (such as colleagues in a social work organization) or a wider group (such as the social work profession in general). Both groups can act as reference points for individuals, enabling them to make judgments about how they are faring in some particular respect. Judgment by peers is regarded as a crucial part of being a professional, in relation both to education and training and to disciplinary matters.

By far the greatest attention has been paid to adolescent peer groups and the effect they have on the behaviour of young people. While such an effect is often the source of worry for professionals, parents and the public at large, it is by no means clear that peer pressure always has a clear negative impact on adolescent behaviour. Voluminous research on the subject suggests that many young people do go through an experimental phase, partly in response to peer pressure and expectations, which may entail risky or antisocial activities. But there is also well-documented recognition that such responses increase towards mid-adolescence and then diminish as a sense of individual identity and the importance of social roles and achievement become less dependent on the affirmation of peers rather than small friendship groups.

J. Coleman and L. Hendry, *The Nature of Adolescence*, third edition, London, Routledge, 1999.

pension credit see WELFARE RIGHTS 8.

Pension Service see DEPARTMENT FOR WORK AND PENSIONS.

performance measurement a management method for quantifying output or some aspect of the performance of an organization or service.

Performance measurement is increasingly used in the public sector as a way of trying to improve efficiency and effectiveness. Central government is continuing to introduce such measures throughout most public-sector activities, and these are linked directly to the development of key aspects of BEST VALUE. The main problem in the public sector has always been the lack of a simple measure of success in the attainment of its objectives. The private sector has had the ready-to-hand measure of profitability, but the public sector frequently operates in areas where profit is an inappropriate indicator. In addition, many areas of provision may also be seen as having multiple objectives for which a simple indicator would provide little useful information. Consequently, the government is encouraging the development of performance measures by LOCAL AUTHORITIES that will enable them to identify success in the attainment of stated objectives. It believes that this will improve the efficiency of local authorities and also increase their accountability to the public. If there are specific objectives with key measures, preferably quantifiable, then the public will be able to see clearly whether the local authority is efficient and effective in its use of public money.

The AUDIT COMMISSION has played a key role in identifying performance measures for local authorities in a wide range of services, including the personal social services. The method adopted is to identify a series of objectives and then to ask questions about the processes used to attain them. These questions should relate to the identification of specific targets: for example, the number of children in care per thousand population and the direction this figure is moving in, whether up or down. Other questions may concern the number of shared rooms in a residential home or the staff-to-resident ratio. Such questions should be related very carefully to the policy objectives specified for the area of service in question and the targets for that service. A service can be broken down so that specific problems may be identified either over time or on a comparative basis. The existence of quantitative measures allows a local authority to compare the performance of different service providers to see if some are performing well or badly. The authority may also be able to compare its own service provision with that of other similar authorities. More particularly, such measures allow managers to improve service delivery by identifying more discrete areas of service where problems may exist and act as triggers for further analysis of policy implementation problems. They also help in establishing whether TARGETS have been met for service improvements.

There are, however, problems with the development of performance measures. To some extent, there is suspicion among public-sector employees and trade unions that such measures will inevitably be linked to the development of performance-related pay. Comparisons with other local authorities, or even within an authority, are difficult to use because of differences in socioeconomic factors. Also, there are major difficulties in developing reliable output measures on the quality of service provision. Input measures, such as staffing levels and financial inputs, are comparatively easy and therefore tend to dominate. To establish appropriate quantifiable output measures for issues such as quality of life and user satisfaction is much more complex and fraught with difficulties. Even so, performance measurement is increasingly utilized in service provision, and efforts will continue to improve its sensitivity.

Audit Commission, *Performance Review In Local Government: A Handbook for Auditors and Local Authorities*, London, HMSO, 1986.

permanence planning the provision of a secure, permanent home for a child LOOKED AFTER by the LOCAL AUTHORITY.

The concept of permanence planning was developed in the 1970s and early 1980s as a way of counteracting the uncertainty and drift that many children experienced in the care of the local authority. The thinking behind it stemmed from the fear that many children would move in and out of care frequently and suffer because they would not develop dependable long-term relationships with either their parents or substitute care-givers. This led to the conclusion that children in the care of the local authority should either be reunited with their families or be placed with foster parents on a long-term basis, where they would have a chance to form such relationships.

Difficulties arose over how the basic idea of permanence planning was interpreted. At the time, it was widely regarded as requiring a quick resolution of the issue of with whom the child would live. Many local authorities introduced time limits of three or six months, during which time they would attempt to reunify the child in care with his or her family. If this were not successful, the authority would look for a permanent placement for the child with foster parents, often on the understanding that the foster parents would eventually adopt the child, thereby severing all links with the natural family. In retrospect, this was a simplistic view that ignored the fact that the local authorities themselves were extremely poor at facilitating the REUNIFICATION of children with their natural families (see CONTACT). By the late 1970s, permanence planning became little more than a justification for compulsorily removing children from their own families, terminating contact between the child and family members and placing the child either for ADOPTION or for long-term FOSTER CARE.

Only later did powerful research accounts emerge to discredit this rigid and one-sided interpretation. They demonstrated that children in long-term care of the authority enjoyed anything but a 'secure' future, with placement breakdowns and moves between foster homes occurring frequently. It is now more widely recognized that often the most effective 'permanent' home for a child is with members of the child's own family, even if this means living for periods with other relations, such as grandparents, or in ACCOMMODATION provided by the local authority. Rather than being detrimental to family life, properly planned periods away from home that meet specific needs of the family can assist in the long-term stability of that family rather than undermining it.

Permanence planning for looked-after children has become central again in thinking on child placements, especially as it is linked to a renewed emphasis on adoption by central government. National standards on adoption emphasize that children who cannot return home are entitled to have adoption considered for them as a way of giving them a secure and permanent home. Decisions on permanence should be made on the basis of each child's needs and should be considered at every review of the child. In the main, a decision should be made within six months of a child becoming 'continuously looked after'; typically, such a decision would be the return of the child to his or her birth family or adoption. If the decision is for adoption, suitable parents should be identified within six months.

J. Thorburn, *Child Placement*, second edition, Aldershot, Arena, 1994.

permitted work SEE WELFARE RIGHTS 3.

personal assistant an employee who carries out specified tasks under the direction of a disabled person. This may be in order to facilitate independent living or to enable the employer to participate fully in the workplace.

Disabled people have argued that in order to gain autonomy and social participation they need to have control over their support and the way it is provided. Until recently it was assumed that they needed the services of 'carers'. The concept of personal assistance, however, better describes a relationship in which the disabled person is in charge. In the workplace, help with funding for personal assistants may be obtained from the Department for Work and Pensions. Social services departments may provide DIRECT PAYMENTS for community care services, and these may be used by disabled people to pay personal assistants. Sometimes personal assistants are employed by an organization managed by disabled people, such as a centre for INDEPENDENT LIVING, on behalf of the service user. These organizations, however, also provide support to disabled people so that they can themselves fulfil the responsibilities of being employers. Disabled people have reported that they are more able to maintain autonomy and the lifestyle of their choice when they have a personal assistant in comparison with conventional care arrangements. It is also easier to change a personal assistant if the arrangement has not worked well.

M. Priestley, *Disability Politics and Community Care*, London, Jessica Kingsley, 1999.

personal capability test see WELFARE RIGHTS 3.

personal education plan (PEP) a plan outlining educational provision for a child of COMPULSORY SCHOOL AGE who is LOOKED AFTER and deals with any necessary changes in the light of events, such as EXCLUSION FROM SCHOOL.

All children of school age in the care system should have a PEP. Standard proformas are usually available in each local authority area. The responsibility for initiating the plan lies with the appropriate social worker, in close collaboration with the child or young person's school, where a particular member of staff should have a designated role in supporting all the looked-after children. The PEP should be reviewed six-monthly in conjunction with the young person's care plan.

personality those aspects of an individual's character that remain relatively permanent across different situations.

There is a debate over the degree of permanence and how to describe an individual's personality. At one extreme, some theorists have argued that an individual differs so much between situations – for example, with friends, family or at work – that there is no element that is constant. The ways of describing personality range from classifying people according to type, such as an authoritarian personality, or according to a set of traits, such as neurotic and extrovert, to the ideographic approach that one should not try to classify people but treat them as individuals. A further debate concerns whether the structure of personality has unconscious elements. Psychoanalysts such as Freud and Jung have suggested that some parts of personality are unconscious.

Numerous methods have been employed to assess personality, ranging from clinical interviews to paper-and-pencil tests, and the method adopted reflects the theoretical position of the designer. Psychometricians such as Cattell and Eysenck utilize questionnaires containing explicit questions about a person's behaviour. These questions have been selected partly to reflect the specific structures that the designer of the

questionnaire believes to constitute personality and partly through
a statistical technique called factor analysis, which helps to identify
the most useful questions to address such structures. An alternative
approach, employing a projective test, is to give people ambiguous
pictures that they are asked to interpret. The reasoning behind this
approach is that a person will project aspects of himself or herself, some
of which may be unconscious, through the interpretations that are given.
Examples of such tests are Rorschach's inkblot test and McClelland's
'thematic apperception' test. Two questions that anyone wishing to employ
a test should ask are: how valid is the test, and how reliable is it? A valid
test is one that measures what it was designed to measure, and this is
usually checked against criteria such as the clinical judgement of a
psychiatrist. A reliable test is one that produces the same assessment of
an individual from one occasion to another. The validity and reliability of
a personality test are usually reported in the manual that accompanies it.

S. E. Hampson, *The Construction of Personality. An Introduction*, London,
Routledge, 1988.

personality disorder a MENTAL DISORDER evident in a general and
persistent pattern of maladaptive behaviour.

There are no defining characteristics of a personality disorder, but
an individual may be regarded as having such a disorder if he or she
experiences general problems of communicating with others, and of
developing and sustaining relationships, that can be traced to behaviour
rather than social factors. A brief description of the variety of personality
disorders illustrates that these behaviours are at the extremes of the spectrum
of what is generally regarded as acceptable behaviour. Such disorders
include dependency (*dependent personality disorder*); shallowness of feeling,
inability to interpret emotional cues, lack of insight (*schizoid personality
disorder*); avoidance (*avoidant personality disorder*); suspiciousness (*paranoid
personality disorder*); compulsive behaviour (*compulsive personality disorder*);
and attention-seeking and manipulative behaviour (*histrionic* or *hysterical
personality disorder*). Antisocial personality disorders may be frequently
seen by social workers as CONDUCT DISORDER in children. The profile of
this covers lying, stealing and TRUANCY in young children, developing
into drug and alcohol abuse, violent sexual behaviour and criminality.

Personality disorders are generally distinguished from the mental
illnesses (PSYCHOSES and NEUROSES) by the absence of distress. Problems
of personality can often be traced to the early relationship with parents
and other significant figures in the environment. Thus the presence of
hostility or aggression, and a lack of expressed love, human warmth and
acceptance, provide messages to the child about himself or herself, about
personal interactions and about the world in general. Personality disorder
is classed as a neurosis in the World Health Organization International
Classification of Diseases, with eight separate categories such as inadequate
personality, psychopathy and depressive personality.

I. Dewesbury, *Rights and Risk: Mentally Disturbed Offenders and Public Protection*, London, NACRO, 1998.

person-centred counselling an approach to counselling that enables the client to develop feelings of worth.

Person-centred counselling was largely developed in the work of Carl Rogers, whose terminology and concepts strongly influenced social work in the 1950s. Rogers believed that the self developed from the interaction of organism and environment. For example, a child has musical talent (organism), but parents see athleticism as of prime importance and interact with the child on that basis (self). In this case the discrepancy between organism and self may generate anxiety. Rogers viewed the organism as striving to maintain, enhance and actualize the self. For healthy development, the organism and the self need to be in harmony. However, the organism seeking to actualize may do things that are discouraged by others, bringing disapproval and possible withdrawal of affection. Thus, Rogerian theory can be seen as describing how children acquire moral standards.

The organism strives to achieve potential, Rogers suggested. This striving is the root of motivation for human beings. People may be limited by their hereditary and social environment, but this does not stop them from seeking self-fulfilment. From this striving emerges an awareness of 'I' and 'me', that is, the self. The self encompasses what a person does and what he or she is, and the maintenance of this phenomenal self becomes the individual's priority.

Rogers sees the development of the individual in terms of how one is evaluated by others and dependent on a number of factors: *positive regard*, that is, approval by others; *positive self-regard*, the child being able to give himself or herself what he or she previously needed from others; *conditions of worth*, conditions attached to regard, such as approval and attention requiring particular courses of action; and *unconditional positive regard*, genuine love and respect regardless of the child's actions. The individual also seeks to maintain a *consistency* between the self and experience. Experiences that are not consistent with a self-view are generally ignored. Such inconsistencies, however, may appear as a *threat* to the view of the self. Threats may be ignored, distorted or gradually taken into the self-view. The last strategy may bring about change in a person's behaviour as it brings change in the phenomenal field. All these activities may occur without the individual being aware of them.

Rogerian theories have their roots in the work of Jung, with its reliance on the meaning of events as a motivator for behaviour, and the person-centred approach to therapy has as its basic premise the meaning of behaviours and events for the person concerned. The therapist's strategy is to enable the client to recognize his or her feelings and behaviours in order to resolve the distortions in perception that are causing distress. The therapist uses empathic understanding, genuineness and unconditional positive regard to facilitate feelings of worth and personal growth in the client. The aim of therapy is to bring about change in the way a person sees the world, and changes in behaviour will follow.

Person-centred therapy has become increasingly popular in the past forty years, and Rogers is seen as third only to Freud and Skinner in terms of the influence of his theories. Perhaps because person-centred therapies do not prescribe specific techniques – rather, they imply an overall approach, which appears easy to learn – they also promise improvement in a shorter time than do the analytically derived therapies.

J. McLeod, *Introduction to Counselling*, Buckingham, Open University Press, 1993.

person-centred planning a planning style mainly associated with LEARNING DISABILITY services. This focuses on improving the quality of a person's life in a way that is grounded in her or his own perceptions and goals rather than those of professionals or others.

While traditional styles of planning in learning disability services tend to start with professional assessments of ability and what needs to be done to increase 'independence', person-centred planning begins with who the person is and what her or his aspirations are. This is by no means straightforward, as many people with learning disability have become used to deferring to the goals of others and some do not use traditional means of communication. An important starting point in any attempt to make planning person-centred, therefore, is to assist people to share and communicate their preferences and hopes for the future. Person-centred planning is, therefore, grounded in self-determination and SELF-ADVOCACY. It often involves bringing together those people who are important in the life of the person with learning disability, or who have the power to bring about the changes that are necessary if the identified goals are to be met. There are several styles of person-centred planning, the best known being path, personal futures planning, maps and essential lifestyle planning. Sanderson (see below) describes these as different lenses for looking at a person's life.

The white paper *Valuing People* (2001) endorses person-centred planning as the way forward in learning disability services. Guidance issued by the Department of Health stresses, however, that it is not just a new way of doing individual programme planning or care management and assessment. For example, care management and assessment might be triggered by person-centred planning where this has revealed a need for services. The Department of Health stresses that person-centred planning involves continual listening and learning about a person's aspirations and working towards these with the support of family and friends. It also stresses the importance of good facilitators, many of whom are currently found in service-providing agencies, including advocacy organizations. It is not to be seen as an end in itself, however, and current government statements suggest that the quality and outcome of person-centred plans are more important than generating large numbers of plans as a 'paper exercise'. The government has prioritized certain groups for early access to person-centred planning. It hopes this will be available for everyone still living in long-stay hospitals and for young people moving from children's to adults' services by 2003. It is envisaged that people using large day centres, living in the family home with carers, aged over 70, and people living on National Health Service campuses will be able to use person-centred planning by 2004.

Official guidance distinguishes between person-centred planning and person-centred *approaches*, which refer to service planning and commissioning that are carried out in collaboration with service users and which reflect their views and aspirations. 'Valuing People' should be implemented at local level by groups that include people with learning disability and use person-centred approaches.

H. Sanderson, 'A Say in My Future: Involving People with Profound and Multiple Disabilities in Person Centred Planning', in L. Ward (ed), *Innovations in Advocacy and Empowerment*, Lisieux Hall Publications.

phenomenology a humanistic approach to understanding people that emerged in the 1950s as a third force in PSYCHOLOGY, emphasizing people's ability to develop self-understanding. Phenomenology is based on the view that human behaviour is purposeful, governed by perceived meanings and that people have choice.

While it has its roots in the work of several writers in the first part of the 20th century, phenomenology developed rapidly after 1945. The most influential exponent of phenomenological explanations of the person has been Carl Rogers (1901–87). Phenomenology involved a move away from psychoanalytical and behavioural traditions and paid attention to the conscious aspects of the individual. Its basic theme is that behaviour is determined by the way the person perceives and understands events around him or her, that is, by his or her *phenomenal field*. It follows that changes in behaviour link to changes in perception. Phenomenology places emphasis on the concept of self, defining the self as everything a person sees as belonging to him or her: thoughts, characteristics, competency, anxieties, and so on. This perspective views people as conscious of the motives for behaviour and aware of behavioural outcomes. The phenomenological movement is diverse, embracing a number of approaches to understanding the person; it is a group of perspectives rather than a 'school of thought'. The perspectives might be humanistic, existential or holistic, but the common theme is one of focusing attention on the whole person, in the social setting.

phobia an abnormal, intense and irrational fear of a given situation, organism or object. Phobias are understood widely by the medical profession as NEUROSES and very closely linked to the condition of ANXIETY (also a neurosis).

As neuroses, phobias can be further regarded as MENTAL ILLNESS, so the person with a phobia may be referred to the psychiatric services and correspondingly may be regarded and treated negatively in society because of this label (see LABELLING THEORY). Given the understanding that phobias are forms of mental illness, the person experiencing a phobia is most likely to approach or be referred to his or her general practitioner. The person may then be treated as are people with other neuroses, receiving medication from their GP, but if the problems are long-term they may be referred to the psychiatric services (see PSYCHIATRY).

Professionals with particular training for treating phobias are clinical psychologists, but the social worker has a number of important possible roles in relation to the problem. Phobias can often arise when the person is suffering anxiety – a phobia can be understood as anxiety directed at a particular target, such that the subject when faced with that object is likely to experience a panic attack. This is very frightening and unpleasant, often leading to fears of illness, because there are powerful physiological symptoms, so the person will go to great lengths to avoid facing that object. Such a difficulty will affect the person's life to greater or lesser degrees, according to the focus of the phobia. At one end of the scale might be agoraphobia, whereby all open spaces, and indeed most situations, provoke this response; and at the other might be a phobia about spiders. The former would therefore profoundly interfere with daily living, while the latter would be occasional only and with few implications for the person's life and functioning.

Social work involvement: the social worker is likely to be involved in only those cases of phobia where there is an impact on the person's coping ability and thus on his or her life and that of others. This will very often be in situations of family conflict, typically where a woman cannot fulfil her family responsibilities of child-care and household management because of her phobia(s). As studies have shown, the community is very intolerant of neuroses, and relatives/friends of the person experiencing these are likely to expect them to 'pull themselves together'. STIGMA and criticism thus experienced can lead to further difficulties, such as depression. The usual GP intervention is to medicate, especially with women, and this may lead to additional problems – drowsiness, for example – that increase the risk of accidents to self and/or others, including children.

Women are more likely to experience phobias than men, and perhaps this is so for black people too. An explanation for this may be found in the likelihood that these groups will be vulnerable to anxiety – the underlying state from which phobias can arise – through experiences of insufficient nurturance in childhood (for white women because of their socialization into meeting the needs of others; for black people as a result of racism reducing parental resources). Other accounts are offered by BEHAVIOURISM, which regards a phobia as the result of response conditioning. PSCHODYNAMIC theories may also explain phobias as the result of projection of unacceptable painful feelings on to an aspect of the environment.

Intervention: BEHAVIOUR THERAPY involving DESENSITIZATION techniques is an approach to phobias commonly used by clinical psychologists, and social workers are not trained in these particular skills. More general approaches employed with DEPRESSION and anxiety, however, may be appropriate: anti-racist and feminist EMPOWERMENT, anxiety management, COGNITIVE BEHAVIOURAL THERAPY, assertiveness training. It is important with all these approaches, or in its own right, to remember the general 'sustaining' approach of psychosocial theory, which values the person and relieves anxiety and distress, thus facilitating his or her working towards resolving the problems by any of the above methods. The person may also be on medication or be seeing the GP or psychiatrist, which means that the social worker needs to liaise with these professionals. Additionally, intervention with long-term social difficulties such as housing and finance is important in preventing chronicity. Intervention in relation to family conflict, stigmatization, isolation and child-care concerns is also important, taking full account of different cultural and other differences in need. If the focus of the referral is the child-care situation, the best outcomes will be achieved by intervening in appropriate ways with the anxiety problems, in addition to any more child-centred strategies.

physical abuse non-accidental injuries inflicted on a person by another person. The abused person is usually in a subordinate position to the abuser.

The VIOLENCE involved in physical ABUSE often results in problems that require medical attention and can typically include fractures, bruises, burns, concussion and variable injuries to the head, abdomen and genitals (the list is not exhaustive). Historically, it is the physical abuse of children that has preoccupied both the public and social welfare agencies (see CHILD ABUSE), but more recently the abuse of vulnerable adults has received some recognition, as well as spouse abuse (see DOMESTIC VIOLENCE, ELDER ABUSE). The physical abuse of people is thought to be widespread in many societies and in all social classes. Some writers would include neglect as a form of physical abuse, at least if intention on the part of the abuser could be established; others prefer to maintain a distinction. If neglect is included, then failure to feed somebody properly, failure to provide protection from hazards and failure to secure appropriate medical care might all be included under the general term of 'physical abuse'.

There are cultural and religious differences that suggest wide variations in what might be considered to be physical abuse. The physical chastisement of children by parents would probably be regarded as acceptable by many people in many societies. Some, however, would regard such chastisement as technically an assault, although one that most law enforcement agencies would not pursue unless it was severe. There have also been changes within societies. A hundred years ago a beating with a cane by a parent would probably have been acceptable to most people; now it would bring a visit by a social worker and at least a warning to the parent. Recently, the European Court decided that corporal punishment in schools is no longer permissible.

Some cultures still practise forms of mutilation of skin, facial features or sexual organs. Although circumcision, for example, has many critics in industrialized societies, it is still one of the most frequently performed operations, sometimes conducted in ritualized ways in public places. In the extreme, infanticide is still practised in many societies with unwanted children (especially girls), with the active collusion of government bodies. In Brazil, many street children have been murdered by the police in the past decade. Tolerance of the physical abuse of children is generally widespread in societies where human rights are not valued.

The belief that children (and wives or female partners, and perhaps older people within the family) are the property and responsibility of the family – or, more specifically, the 'powerful' man – is widespread; this creates an environment in which vulnerable children and adults may not be protected. This belief is also associated with varying definitions of the public and the private. Many societies regard the family in particular as the private sphere. Those societies that seem to have made some progress in challenging abusive behaviour have had also to uphold individual human rights at the cost of PARENTAL RIGHTS and the power of men over women. (See also CHILD PROTECTION, EMOTIONAL ABUSE, SEXUAL ABUSE.)

W. Stainton Rogers *et al*, *Child Abuse and Neglect: Facing the Challenge*, London, Batsford in association with the Open University, 1989.

physical disability the restrictions associated with a physical rather than an INTELLECTUAL IMPAIRMENT.

It is argued that all disabled people experience restriction as a result of social oppression and that to describe a disability as 'physical' is to suggest that the restriction arises from impairment. The distinction between physical disability and LEARNING DISABILITY, however, is often made in practice, and the nature of the restrictions experienced by these groups may vary. Sometimes sensory impairments are included within the overall category of physical disability. Some DEAF people, however, regard themselves as a linguistic and cultural minority and would reject the labels of impairment and disability.

physician-assisted suicide where a physician supplies the means for a person, in severe and long-term pain or completely incapacitated through illness or accident and who wishes to die, to end his or her life.

The intense debate about the legitimacy of physician-assisted suicide is very similar to that about EUTHANASIA and, indeed, they are often linked in serious discussion as well as the public mind. The difference is that the person who wants to die is able, as his or her last act, to administer the means for dying. This may be pressing a button (or computer keyboard key) to begin intravenous flow of a lethal drug or taking tablets of a lethal quantity of, for example, morphine.

When there are attempts to legalize any form of euthanasia, as in Oregon in the USA or Holland, law makers usually have focused on physician-assisted suicide as the principal means. In general, such legislation has permitted physicians to prescribe life-ending drugs for terminally ill adult patients who ask for it (with 'terminally ill' meaning death within six months anyway). But such a prescription can only be made after a person makes both written and oral requests.

This suggested practice has raised certain complex issues. One has to do with the competence of the medical practitioners – are they sufficiently knowledgeable about the course of the disease or incapacity to be able to give a reliable prognosis? Are they sufficiently specialized in PALLIATIVE CARE to know what might work in reducing pain to a tolerable level? Are they able to make an accurate assessment of the patient's state of mind? And, most importantly, what requirements should there be to notify and consult the person's family?

Most contributors to this debate from either side acknowledge that there is a difference between, on the one hand, active euthanasia and on the other switching off life support machinery or providing pain relief to the point that a person's death is hastened.

pindown a method of control, involving use of compulsory baths, special clothing and systematic isolation, that was adopted by several children's homes in Staffordshire in the late 1980s and came to be regarded as dehumanizing and degrading.

The practice of pindown gave rise to the Levy-Kahan Report, commissioned by Staffordshire Social Services Department. The report perceived the regime as humiliating and the behaviour of staff as intimidating to children and young people considered to be already damaged and vulnerable. The policy was defended by some staff because they felt that they needed to be able to control children who were apt to abscond. If children could not be contained, they argued, they could not be helped. Absconding children were often at large for months and might never return to the social services for help. Once on the run, it was argued, such children are frequently forced into dangerous or immoral situations. Although these difficulties were acknowledged by the inquiry, the practice of pindown was found to be wholly unacceptable. More positively as a result of pindown, the CHILDREN ACT brought about a review of control mechanisms within children's residential facilities.

A. Levy and B. Kahan, *The Pindown Experience and the Protection of Children*, Stafford, Staffordshire County Council, 1991.

placement (1) a period spent in a social welfare agency by a student as a part of his or her education and training to achieve a social work or other qualification.

A wide range of social welfare qualifying courses require students to undertake at least one placement as an integral part of their studies. Such arrangements are to be found in the training courses of social workers, probation officers, nursery nurses, community workers and health visitors. Placements may be observational but more usually entail supervised practice. Supervisors are expected to be experienced practitioners, often with a practice teaching qualification. Their task is to assess the student's competence to practise, so they need to work closely with educational institutions in relation to the practice curriculum. Although students may have a common educational experience in college, placements may vary considerably in setting, client groups and methods. Ensuring that students are competent to practise against these varying situations can be difficult. Placements may be undertaken in either voluntary or statutory settings, with the private sector also beginning to offer placement opportunities on a small scale. Social work placements are required to be of a high standard in order to enable students to meet the required level of professional competence to practice.

placement (2) the finding of suitable care for a child being LOOKED AFTER by the local authority or where ACCOMMODATION is being provided.

Placement care is usually with foster parents, adoptive parents or residential facilities, but it may be with relatives of the child (see PERMANENCE PLANNING).

placement order see ADOPTION HEARING.

placement planning a number of essential steps in planning PLACEMENTS for children, laid down by the CHILDREN ACT and by related guidance from the Department of Health.

Historically, social work placed little emphasis on planning for children but rather put faith in the strength of relationships between child and residential staff or foster parents as the primary means by which major life decisions for the child would be taken. Plans, certainly written plans, were not deemed necessary for such objectives. Even as social workers became more involved in protective work with children, and it became increasingly clear that a child rarely remained with a single set of carers long enough to reach decisions on the child's long-term future, child-care plans, if they existed at all, were rudimentary. This lack of planning was critically highlighted in a summary of research published by the Department of Health (1986) as a chief reason why children were often the subject of erratic decision-making by local authorities.

The Children Act 1989 and the related DoH guidance now require placement planning to encompass the following:

Inquiry: the views of the child, parents and other members of the family must be obtained as to whether a placement is required and, if so, what sort of placement (for example, whether residential or short-term with foster carers); relevant information must also be collected, with the consent of the family, from other agencies and professionals involved, such as the schoolteacher, health visitor, doctor or child psychologist.

Consultation: the Act requires consultation with the child, parents and any other people with PARENTAL RESPONSIBILITY or whom the authority thinks are important to the child. Consultation should be explained and completed before the placement decision is made. The child's views must be sought in a way appropriate to his or her understanding of the situation; these views, which may differ from the parents', particularly with an older child, should be discussed at any formal meeting of professionals and recorded in writing. Both the child and the family need to be given all relevant information regarding the choices before them, together with explanations about what each involves. Having consulted, the authority must give due consideration to these views, but it is not obliged to follow them. All aspects of the consultation must be recorded in writing.

Assessment: the needs of the child – including those relating to health, development, education, disability (if any) and religious and cultural background – are identified (see ASSESSMENT).

Decision-making: the social worker, in collaboration with the child and family wherever possible, now considers what kind of placement is most fitted to meeting the child's needs and whether or not any child-protective measures are required. This decision-making entails defining the child's needs in terms of general objectives, listing and appraising the specific options available for achieving these and deciding on the preferred option.

A written placement plan, based on the information collected and decisions taken, involves both the objectives – what the needs of the child are – and what services are to be provided, including placement, to meet these. It will include, at a minimum, what sort of accommodation is needed; what other services for the child or other members of the family are to be provided; what services other professional organizations, such as the health authority or local education authority, will provide; and the likely duration of a placement. The most important element of the plan will entail arrangements for ensuring the continuing involvement of the parents and other relations in the life of the child while on placement, particularly CONTACT and when and how the child is to be reunited with the family. In the formulation of written plans for children's placement, the format devised by Bristol University and the Dartington Social Research Unit are highly recommended for practitioners.

Department of Health, *Children Act: Guidance and Regulations*, Vol. 3, *Family Placements*, London, HMSO, 1991.

play a complex set of processes undertaken by both adults and children that involve exploration and learning in many contexts and situations.

Play may be unstructured or 'free-form', as with a child playing without adult intervention in an unfamiliar situation, or highly structured, as with a well-known game with agreed rules. Play serves many purposes, including the development of motor or physical skills, the development of the intellect and the development of the person both emotionally and socially. Social workers and other social welfare workers are mostly concerned with the issue of play with respect to children and young people (although play may have a therapeutic role with mentally ill people, with REMINISCENCE THERAPY with older people and with other client groups too). Here play is regarded as a key process in socialization; without it, children will be developmentally inhibited. The ability to play is thus perceived as a significant indicator of a child's HEALTH in its broadest sense. If a child is seen as in need of help, programmes of play can be devised to promote particular skills that are seen to be lacking or poorly developed. NURSERIES, nursery schools and specialist units for play therapy are facilities where help may be available for children with such needs. Play is also a very useful tool for social workers and therapists working with abused children; it can provide a medium for revealing and understanding what has happened to a child and for therapeutic work with children who have been damaged by their experiences. (See also TOY LIBRARIES, UNDER-FIVES PROVISION.)

J. R. Moyles, *Just Playing?* Buckingham, Open University Press, 1989.

police the main civil organization devised to maintain law and order, using at least some military methods. The primary tasks of the police are to investigate alleged criminal acts, to gather evidence for the criminal justice system and to charge (in some cases to arrest and detain) alleged offenders.

A substantial and increasing amount of social work is undertaken jointly with the police or in close liaison with them. In CHILD PROTECTION, the greater proportion of initial child investigations are conducted jointly by social workers and police officers. The police also have power to remove children on EMERGENCY PROTECTION ORDERS. In some authorities, juvenile bureaux have been established, comprising seconded social workers, probation officers, youth workers, teachers and police officers, who collectively work to investigate juvenile offence behaviour and to provide cautioning schemes, diversion and sometimes REPARATION schemes too. Decisions are made within bureaux (and within juvenile liaison committees elsewhere) as to whether juveniles are to be prosecuted or not. Social workers often play the role of appropriate adult where the police are interviewing juveniles suspected of offences (see POLICE AND CRIMINAL EVIDENCE ACT 1984). The police organize attendance centres and in some areas are involved with OUTREACH work in the youth services.

An increasing area of work affecting the police is that of investigating alleged incidents of DOMESTIC VIOLENCE and, in the most progressive forces, having an active involvement in the initial work to protect women and children and to restrain and possibly charge abusing men. A further area of work concerns detaining people who are exhibiting symptoms of

MENTAL HEALTH PROBLEMS in public places, pending their assessment by social work and psychiatric services. The police are also centrally involved with CRIME AND DISORDER PARTNERSHIPS, established by the Crime and Disorder Act 1998. These partnerships are devices to mobilize key agencies in localities as well as community groups in establishing broad-based community safety strategies.

Police and Criminal Evidence Act 1984 an Act codifying POLICE powers in relation to suspected offenders and thus defining more sharply than before the rights of citizens in relation to the police.

The Act sets out clearly the powers and obligations of the police in relation to stopping and searching, entering premises, arrest, detention at a police station and interviewing. It also sets out the machinery for investigating complaints against the police, lays down rules for the admission of certain types of evidence in criminal trials and has introduced in statutory form the concept of COMMUNITY involvement in policing. For social workers and probation officers, the most important aspect of the Act is probably that relating to the role of the APPROPRIATE ADULT, and this is covered in the codes of practice issued by the Home Secretary. Social workers and (less frequently) probation officers may act as appropriate adults in relation to either juveniles or mentally disordered people who are arrested and interviewed by the police. In the absence of parents or close relatives, they are required to be present throughout the proceedings, not just to observe but also to offer advice, help communication and make representations where appropriate.

police protection provision under the CHILDREN ACT whereby a police officer may remove a child to suitable accommodation or ensure that he or she remains in a safe place, such as a hospital, if the officer has reasonable cause to believe that the child might otherwise suffer SIGNIFICANT HARM.

A child may remain under police protection for a maximum of 72 hours. During that time the child's parents and others should have reasonable CONTACT with the child if it is in the child's best interests. Having taken a child into police protection, the police officer concerned must notify the child's parents and the local authority, ensure that the child knows what is happening and take steps to find out what the child's wishes and feelings are. If it is appropriate to seek an EMERGENCY PROTECTION ORDER the police officer may do so on behalf of the local authority, even without the authority's knowledge. More usually the police will notify the local authority, which in turn will apply for the order from the court.

'political correctness' a phrase that loosely refers to a presumed set of rules that, it is claimed, prescribes the use of particular words when speaking or writing about certain subjects in public discussion.

The phrase is often used mockingly by those on the FAR RIGHT in politics who claim that issues involving race, ethnicity, disability and gender can be discussed only in a certain way and using certain words. Not to do so risks strong public criticism, so they would argue. Frequently those who use the term in this way justify their views by picking up isolated or extreme instances where terminology is insisted upon, for example by certain local authorities in discussing ethnic relations, from feminist commentators in the media or prescriptions for language on American university campuses.

The social work profession has been one of the key targets for those alleging the existence of 'political correctness'. Whether it was the rigid practice (by a few local authorities) of placing black children only with black foster or adoptive parents or the emphasis placed on 'RACE' by the now defunct Central Council for Education and Training in Social Work, such matters were regularly picked up by the news media in the 1990s, with commentators often drawing negative conclusions about the profession as a whole.

Much of the argument about 'political correctness', for and against, comes down to the use of language. Language does matter, and social work has been effective in ensuring it uses the most respectful and dignified language in relation to the people it works with. In this it has learned much from advocates and pressure groups it associates with. Over the years within social work discourse, 'disabled person' has replaced 'handicapped', 'cripple' or 'spastic'; 'black person' has replaced 'coloured' or even more derogatory phrases, 'special educational needs' has replaced 'subnormality', 'people with mental health problems' have replaced 'the mentally ill' and before that 'the insane', and so on. Some critics, both inside and outside the profession, have noted that, although certain terms generate positive images of the people referred to, social work became unduly focused on the use of language, ignoring the fact that such usage does not in itself change the quality of services or the profound inequalities that exist within society.

T. Philpot, *Political Correctness and Social Work*, London, Institute of Economic Affairs, Health and Welfare Unit, 1999.

politics and social work the interrelationship between political processes and the conduct of social work practice.

Politics is about the use and misuse of power. It can refer to one person's ability to influence another or to shape or limit his or her experience. This is the micro-perspective. Power can also refer to the influence of broader social structures upon individuals, families or communities and about the relationships between both formal and informal groups and institutions within society. This is the macro-perspective.

Within this context, there are a number of key debates. First, there are issues concerned with the power dimensions of social worker-service user relationships. Second, there are issues around social workers' abilities to bring about changes in the social contexts of service users, whether this context concerns, for example, one-to-one relationships,

families, communities or residential establishments. These issues
include problems of trying to secure resources. Finally, there are yet
other issues around the politicization of social work, including the
EMPOWERMENT of service users and the involvement of both social
workers and service users in political parties, trades unions and pressure
groups. All three debates are clearly interrelated.

Relationships between social workers and service users have attracted
close scrutiny from academics and practitioners in recent decades.
Paternalistic attitudes on the part of social workers of knowing what is
best for service users have given way to a client-centred practice that
requires openness and working relationships that rely upon consultation
and negotiation with service users. Social work methods have moved
from doing things *for* service users to doing things *with* service users.
Thus, social workers are now required to identify problems with service
users, to agree tasks, to facilitate increased autonomy of service users in
problem-solving, to keep accessible records and to be transparent in all
transactions with service users and with agencies that are involved with
service users' interests. There are, of course, contexts in which social
workers are required to compel service users. Good practice now
requires, however, that these events are kept to a minimum and that
service users are informed about resources and services that will enable
them to challenge social workers' decisions.

Social workers' interests in changing the lives of service users are
wide-ranging. They include, first, trying to improve the morale, self-
esteem and social functioning of individuals, and, second, addressing
adverse circumstances within families, small social groups and
communities. All these activities involve attempts to realign power,
confront SOCIAL EXCLUSION and secure resources. Social workers are
employed in statutory, voluntary and private sectors, sometimes acting
as agents of the state, sometimes as advocates against the state and
sometimes in more neutral roles. Social workers can be GATEKEEPERS
for resources, although more often than not they are trying to realize
resources from non-statutory sources or from other statutory agencies
such as the BENEFITS AGENCY or LOCAL AUTHORITIES. It is possible for
social workers to make a significant difference in the lives of service
users, although many have argued that in terms of the redistribution of
power and life chances, social workers' achievements are invariably modest.

Much social work is concerned with micro-issues. Many social workers
nevertheless acknowledge the influence of structural inequality upon
service users' lives and, for this reason, some encourage participation,
both for themselves and service users, in trades unions, political parties
and pressure groups (both local and national). The RADICAL SOCIAL WORK
movement, indeed, has regarded making these kinds of commitments
as essential if society is to change to ameliorate many or even most social
problems. Yet contemporary evidence suggests that an increasing

number of social workers are not engaged with this kind of political struggle. For service users, participation in service users' groups, carers' groups and community groups is probably as much as their adverse circumstances will permit, although the expectation that providers of social work services must include service users in planning, monitoring and evaluating services may increase service users' ability to shape such services according to their views of their needs.

B. Jordan and N. Parton (eds), *The Political Dimensions of Social Work*, Oxford, Blackwell, 1983.

Poor Law a system for dealing with POVERTY and UNEMPLOYMENT laid down in 1598 during the reign of Elizabeth I. With various amendments, notably the Poor Law Amendment Act 1834, the Poor Law remained the law of England until the introduction of the welfare state in 1948.

The introduction of the Elizabethan Poor Law Act arose from genuine concern to help the poor and from concern to control the numbers of unemployed people roaming the country in search of work. Under the system, parishes were empowered to raise local taxes to support sick, old, disabled and unemployed people. In general, the law recognized that poverty was a misfortune and not always within the control of the individual. Those in need could apply to their parishes of origin for assistance, but the effect was to severely curtail the migration of those looking for work.

The Poor Law Amendment Act of 1834 substantially altered a system based on recognized reciprocal duties between local society and the indigent. Following the rapid industrialization of Britain, the requirements of a market economy were articulated by political economists such as David Ricardo and reformers such as Edwin Chadwick, who saw the old Poor Law as a fetter on economic activity. They wanted to ensure that the system of poor relief allowed workers greater mobility to move to industrial urban areas and at the same time to ensure that poor relief was run as efficiently as possible. The Poor Law (Amendment) Act of 1832 (or the 'New Poor Law' as it was dubbed) introduced the 'workhouse test' to establish whether an individual was genuinely in poverty or not. Only those faced with near starvation would choose to enter the workhouse where conditions were spartan at best. A basic diet, separation of men and women and highly repetitive work, such as stone breaking, were often central to workhouse regimes, although there were many examples of humanely run establishments that sought to flout the spirit of the 1834 Act. The underlying philosophy of the Poor Law (Amendment) Act was that of deterrence: able-bodied people had to be discouraged from getting something for nothing, so were virtually compelled to obtain an income by selling their labour either inside or outside the workhouse. A guiding principle was that of 'less eligibility': that is, poor relief should not be set at a level so that people would choose it rather than paid work. In other words, the level of relief had to be lower than the lowest available wage.

Throughout the 19th century, the pace of industrialization, the ever larger numbers out of work during depressions and the continued predicaments of the old and frail placed great pressure on the system and led to a general rise in 'outdoor relief', which to some extent diluted the workhouse system. The 'deserving poor' – the sick, old, disabled and genuinely unemployed – could apply for outdoor relief, that is, payments or goods and/or parish work outside the poorhouse. Social work as a profession came into being in the 1860s to determine exactly who was deserving and undeserving. It can be said that the distinction was a cornerstone of early social work such as that practised by the Charity Organization Society and remained a touchstone of professional attitudes well into the 20th century. Behind that practice was the refusal to acknowledge that in most instances poverty was a result of personal failure. It is also important to remember that the Poor Law system operated within a framework of charity and not rights. The notion of rights did not take root until later in the 20th century and came to fruition with the introduction of the welfare state in the late 1940s.

K. Jones, *Social Policy in Britain 1830–1990*, London, Athlone.

positive action measures permitted by the RACE RELATIONS ACT 1976 and the SEX DISCRIMINATION ACT 1975 to help members of ethnic minorities and women achieve more equality (in comparison with white people and men respectively) in relation to seeking employment or promotion.

British law does not permit DISCRIMINATION at the point of selection for employment or promotion. Positive action measures mostly concern training opportunities targeted at women and members of ethnic minorities. Such training might include special attempts to equip and encourage women to apply for jobs in areas of employment hitherto dominated by men, such as in engineering. Similarly, it might be demonstrated that black people are a substantial proportion of the population within a particular area but are practically unknown within a local authority department. Training in these circumstances might be to familiarize black people with an area of work or occupation relatively unknown to them and to help them acquire the specific skills necessary to secure a job. Other measures might include NETWORKING, that is, telling particular community groups that an organization really does want to recruit more people from ethnic minorities. The use of particular newspapers and advertisements in various languages would send strong signals to particular communities about the seriousness of an organization's equal opportunities' policies. It is also possible to appoint a black person or a woman to a post (in competition with a white person or a man respectively) if he or she is considered to be equally competent to do a job and women or black people are under-represented at that level within the organization. A limited number of posts can also be 'reserved' for black people and for women where the job could be said to offer a personal service that only somebody of that ethnicity or gender could reasonably be expected to provide. Thus a woman and only a woman should be considered for a job in a rape crisis centre, and only a black person for a job as African-Caribbean advice worker.

postmodernism a theory that holds that our understanding of social reality is limited, partial and personal, depending on individual or group perspective.

'Modernism' is generally thought to originate in the scientific revolutions in Europe in the 17th century and confirmed in the rational and technical cultures that developed in Europe and North America from that point on. Modernism is characterized by notions of economic progress, the power of reason and rational thought, and hierarchical social and commercial organizations. Gender hierarchies in particular associated reason and rationality with men, and emotion and irrationality with women. Equally, modernism produced comprehensive 'world views' – whether a belief in continuous (economic) progress through the operations of the MARKET or the conviction that a socialist revolution, led by the industrial working class, was inevitable.

Postmodernism rejects such notions as well as the idea that there is a single reality or social truth that only awaits discovery. Thus it heralded the dismissal of 'grand narratives' such as Marxism and PSYCHOANALYSIS. For the social sciences it encourages a turn away from methodologies that aim to establish social truths. Rather, postmodern theorists have emphasized the need to look at the complex, interwoven patterns within society with a diversity of viewpoints and experiences. The relevance of postmodernism for social work is that it encourages the exploration and expression of multiple voices and perspectives. Under its influence, social work theory has placed greater emphasis on the importance of 'narrative' and the personal 'stories' of users. Postmodernism also favours making explicit underlying assumptions and perspectives and emphasizes the value of emotion and personal experience. Postmodernism at first seemed to place great emphasis on aspects of an individual's social identity – such as 'race', gender or disability – as virtually determining that person's view of society. By the late 1980s and 1990s, however, it played a significant part in challenging these simplistic notions of social identity by encouraging a more fluid understanding of identity and subjective experiences.

J. Gorman, 'Postmodernism and the Conduct of Inquiry', in *Social Work Affilia*, Volume 8, No. 3, 1993.

post-traumatic stress syndrome a person's reactions following an 'extraordinary' or 'catastrophic' experience that shatters his or her sense of invulnerability to harm.

Stress itself describes the state of discomfort arising in a person's emotions and mental and physical state when struggling to cope against overwhelming odds. The experiences leading to post-traumatic syndrome, in order to shatter the person's sense of invulnerability to harm, would involve a major betrayal of trust. This may mean the betrayal of trust in a particular human being (the experience of child SEXUAL ABUSE has been identified in the literature as an outstanding example of this in society); or the betrayal of trust in the government or an official agency, such as the police, if such an agency attacks the person's basic human rights through, for example, torture or imprisonment without trial; or the betrayal of trust in society through serious crime against the person, such as rape, assault, mugging or housebreaking, especially while the person is present. Devalued groups in society – black people, women, older people, disabled people, and gay and lesbian people – are particularly likely to be the victims of crime and abuse from the general population and may be treated unjustly by professionals and officials, so members of these groups are more likely than others to experience post-traumatic stress syndrome.

The feature shared by all the above experiences is that trust in a parent, in official agencies and in other people in society may be very fundamental and taken for granted as a reality to depend upon. Children trust their parents to protect them from harm in every area of life, as they have little power to do this for themselves. Members of society expect the government and official agencies, such as the police, to be active in protecting, or at least not compromising, their basic human rights, and people have a measure of trust in others also not to infringe the latter. It may be that a person has never been able to trust parents, official agencies or other people, but even so, being the victim of harm from any of these sources may still shatter the person's sense of safety and security to the degree that he or she has no other source of safety to which to retreat. It is the very fundamental nature of these sources of security that makes harm from any of them such a devastating experience, one from which it is said by some writers to be very difficult to recover.

Professional abuse from a doctor, therapist or social worker – whether it involves sexual or other forms of malpractice – may also fall into this category, if the harm is significant, because of the expectation, from professional ethics, that the professional will protect the client's interests first. Other forms of trauma betraying trust would include personal disasters, such as a house fire or involvement in a serious accident, and major disasters that again destroy or shatter the person's taken-for-granted experience of safety in his or her home or car or in a public place such as a football stadium.

All the above experiences, which are likely to lead to post-traumatic stress syndrome, are familiar to social workers, including the experiences of torture and other human rights' violations by refugees coming from abroad. Practitioners are particularly likely, however, to encounter clients who have experienced childhood sexual abuse (and perhaps other forms of child abuse) and crime, while the dangers of professional abuse also need to be borne in mind. It is therefore important to understand the effects that these experiences can have and helpful forms of intervention.

Writers on post-traumatic stress syndrome have identified two different stages of this condition: post-traumatic stress reactions, which refer to the person's immediate or short-term responses to the trauma, and post-traumatic stress disorder, referring to the longer-term responses. Post-traumatic stress *reactions* can include HYSTERIA, involving perhaps loss of memory and even consciousness, restlessness, impaired concentration and coordination, impulsiveness, weeping, confusion and perhaps psychotic experiences such as hallucinations or delusions (see PSYCHOSES). Soldiers experiencing 'shell shock' in the First World War exhibited these symptoms. The fact that psychotic symptoms are sometimes experienced may lead the worker to conclude that the person is mentally ill, or may have led to a referral for assessment under the MENTAL HEALTH ACT 1983. Workers should be aware that such symptoms may arise from other causes and assess the person's circumstances fully. Post-traumatic stress *disorder* is a continuation of these symptoms into the longer term, along with chronic disturbance of sleep, ANXIETY, DEPRESSION and impulsiveness. Lack of concentration and coordination, impulsiveness and perhaps even impaired vision or hearing may lead to accidents. In addition, there is a risk that hallucinations, 'flashbacks' of the experience, impulsiveness and depression may result in suicide attempts.

In the very long term, adult survivors of childhood sexual abuse are highly likely to suffer the MENTAL HEALTH PROBLEMS of depression, self-harm, anxiety and low self-esteem. SUBSTANCE MISUSE is also highly likely. People suffering other severe traumas may well experience similar long-term difficulties. It is important to be aware, however, that the original trauma, especially if it occurred in childhood, may be repressed from memory, but change and crises in the person's current life may trigger the memories, and this may result in all the original post-traumatic stress reactions.

CRISIS INTERVENTION alone is not sufficient to relieve the distress of the post-traumatic stress syndrome, either after the original trauma or if memories of it are triggered in later life. Long-term help is always needed, and this may often be most effective in a long-term group. This is especially so for survivors of childhood sexual abuse, where the one-to-one client–worker relationship may so painfully remind the person through transference of the abuse situation that distress, distrust and dissociation act against any benefits the therapy might provide. The main benefit that groupwork can bring is to help the person, through exploration of what has happened, to develop greater self-esteem. One of the major long-term effects of trauma, and especially of violence or abuse to the person, is a feeling of guilt and unworthiness, as if the person himself or herself had wanted such treatment.

When working, either in a group or performing other social work duties with the person, reliability and consistency are essential if the person's trust is not to be betrayed again. Nevertheless, the person may very early perceive the worker as untrustworthy, through transference, and this needs to be understood by the worker, not taken personally, and perhaps acknowledged and worked with in whatever depth is appropriate within the particular client–worker relationship. A further consideration in work with people experiencing post-traumatic stress syndrome is the likelihood that the psychiatric services, or at least the general practitioner, will be involved, and thus the worker needs to liaise with these services constructively (see MENTAL ILLNESS, MULTIDISCIPLINARY WORKING).

poverty a condition in which people are inhibited from participation in society because of a serious lack of material and social resources.

Poverty is defined in two ways: *absolute* and *relative* poverty. Absolute poverty refers to conditions that will not sustain physical life. It is defined by a fixed standard below which individuals and families experience complete destitution in which they cannot meet even minimum needs for food and shelter. The United Nations Development Programme (UNDP) uses such a standard for measuring poverty in the developing world: this is fixed at an income of one (US) dollar a day. Below that families face severe deprivation of basic human needs, including food, safe drinking water and shelter, resulting in malnutrition and dangerous levels of ill health. Absolute standards have the virtue of allowing us to calculate poverty across different countries. Thus UNDP estimates fairly accurately that within the developing world 30 per cent of all children under five are malnourished.

Relative poverty refers to the lack of resources to obtain the types of diet, participate in the activities and have the living conditions and amenities that are customary or at least widely encouraged and approved in the society to which a person belongs. Poverty cannot therefore be understood only as a subsistence threshold but can be defined more accurately *in relation* to the society of which it is a part. The basic standards of living, which most people enjoy, are implicitly defined within each society. These standards have not only to do with income but also consumer purchases, levels of health and wellbeing, and access to goods and services. Those investigating relative poverty look at the ways that individual and family life is affected by the experience of deprivation. The notion of relative poverty focuses on the degree to which people are prevented from sharing the living standards, opportunities and norms of wellbeing that society as a whole has created for itself.

The concept of relative poverty implies that as society and its norms and institutions become more sophisticated so does what an individual or family requires. Information and communication technology (ICT) presents a good example. Thirty years ago computer operations were specialized functions performed on huge, room-sized machines by small numbers of highly trained operators. In a relatively short time, skills in ICT have moved from the margin of economic activity to its core. Add its research and educative functions and its social networking value through e-mail and it becomes a central tool that impacts on individuals. Families with no access to, or knowledge about, ICT have another dimension in which they are poor – now referred to as 'information poverty'. Studies have also analysed the distribution of resources within families where there is an adequate income to reveal that the woman's share is disproportionately small. Members of ethnic minorities, similarly, are more likely than other people to be unemployed or to be in low-paid work.

The Joseph Rowntree Foundation carried out the most authoritative survey on poverty in Britain in 1999. Using a relative definition of poverty based on access to certain socially determined necessities, it found that approximately 14.5 million people, or 26 per cent of the population, were living in poverty. The survey found that between 1983 and 1999 the percentage of households living in poverty increased dramatically from 14 to 24 per cent. Since Britain has a far larger population now than in the past, the number of individuals in poverty is without historical precedent. Particularly vulnerable groups include LONE PARENTS, of whom over 60 per cent are poor, the unemployed, with 75 per cent, and the disabled or long-term sick, with 60 per cent. Other groups vulnerable to poverty include adults living in one-person HOUSEHOLDS, those who left school at 16 or under, and those living in local authority and housing association tenancies.

In general, those on the right of the political spectrum, and particularly those supporting the notion of an UNDERCLASS, believe that poor people are responsible for their own poverty through lack of work discipline and unstable family relationships. Selective coverage of poverty in some of the press compounds this with a set of negative images of poor people as lazy and welfare-dependent. The belief that the poor are responsible for their own difficulties is persistent. In the public domain, the idea of the CYCLE OF DEPRIVATION and, among sociologists, the theory of CULTURE OF POVERTY seek to explain the persistence of poverty by reference to ideas and behaviours transmitted from one generation to another. Critics of these views point to the major changes that have occurred when governments have pursued policies that seek to redistribute wealth – the clear implication being that poverty is a structural feature of society and not a question of individual behaviour.

Poor people form the largest group of consumers of social services. Poverty is a major source of stress, and although it cannot be regarded as a simple causal factor (because many who live in poverty manage to escape major personal and family difficulties), it has strong associations with MENTAL HEALTH PROBLEMS, with crime, with family problems including CHILD ABUSE and with ill-health. Yet, while social work has worked with predominantly poor people since its inception in the second half of the 19th century, it has also tended to 'pathologise' poor people, that is, to view users' poverty as the result of the poor person's perverse choices, for example, spending too much on alcohol and tobacco (or drugs) and being apathetic towards work and family responsibilities. As a result, the dominant CASEWORK tradition in social work tried to secure good personal habits, such as thrift, sobriety and hard work, through developing the personal relationship with the social worker.

Today the role of social workers in trying to alleviate the poverty of consumers of social work services is full of ambiguity. Many still do not see such work as part of their brief, preferring to perceive it as the responsibility of other agencies. Often such social workers align themselves with therapy, or at least regard helping with relationships as their major focus. Others may limit their assistance to, for example, help with second-hand clothing or a grant for a holiday. Few social workers have poverty 'centre stage' or indeed are required or permitted to develop an effective ANTI-POVERTY STRATEGY. Such an approach might entail income-maximization programmes, MONEY ADVICE, housing improvement programmes and programmes to facilitate the involvement of poor people in employment (for example, adult education services, nursery provision, and work and food cooperatives). Many such ventures would require at least a COMMUNITY focus and methods rooted in the approaches of COMMUNITY WORK and action. (See also SOCIAL EXCLUSION; POVERTY TRAP; HEALTH INEQUALITY.)

Joseph Rowntree Foundation, *Poverty and social exclusion in Britain*, York, 2000.

poverty trap the situation of people when the gains they make from increased income, typically earnings from employment, are exceeded by losses through increased payments of tax and NATIONAL INSURANCE and reductions in MEANS-TESTED BENEFITS.

The reform of means-tested benefits in 1988 reduced the extent of the POVERTY trap. Although marginal tax rates of 87 per cent are commonplace (that is, only 13p of extra income for every additional £1 received), it is only when someone with school-age children comes off income support by increasing his or her earnings or hours of work that a poverty trap arises. In practice, the phrase 'poverty trap' is used to describe any situation in which it is difficult for a person to make significant improvements in disposable income by working or increasing earnings.

power see POLITICS AND SOCIAL WORK.

practical assistance see WELFARE RIGHTS 3.

practice development assessor (PDA) a person who supervises trainee probation officers in the workplace.

PDAs are experienced probation officers responsible for the professional development of one or more trainee probation officers and for assessing their work. The PDA role was developed when probation training in England and Wales was differentiated from social work training, although many former PRACTICE TEACHERS became PDAs and the role is in many ways a similar one. Together with trainees' university tutors and line managers within the agency, PDAs have responsibility for the management of trainees' educational and professional development during the two-year training period.

practice teacher an experienced professional who, after specialized training, supervises social work students during their assessed PLACEMENTS.

Students on social work programmes are required to spend a substantial amount of time on an assessed placement in order to achieve competence in the range of skills, knowledge and practice experience laid down by the Training Organization for the Personal Social Services (TOPSS), which replaced the Central Council for the Education and Training for Social Work (CCETSW). Practice teachers are required to manage the student's learning during the placement and to liaise with agency supervisors and university/college tutors in order to maximize the learning outcomes on the placement. Some practice teachers work 'off-site' and visit the student each week for supervision and to link up with the agency supervisor who handles the day-to-day issues with the student.

B. Moss, *I've got a Student – Guidelines for Practice Teachers*, Wrexham, Prospects, 1998.

Praxis a term derived from Paulo Freire describing the community work process of reflection + action. Freire argues that reflection alone on an issue does not achieve any results, whereas action that is spontaneous rather than considered may not achieve the desired result but may have unforeseen consequences. He advocates a spiral process of problem-posing (identifying the issues), planning what action might achieve the desired outcome, taking the action and then reflecting on what the result is. The process begins again until the goal has been reached. This is the process of Praxis, which can be used by communities and community workers working together, with the worker reflecting back to the community on the achievements, issues and questions arising at each stage.

prescribed industrial disease see WELFARE RIGHTS 3.

pre-sentence report (PSR) a report prepared by a probation officer, social worker or YOUTH OFFENDING TEAM member in England and Wales to assist a court in deciding upon the most suitable method for dealing with an offender.

Courts normally obtain a pre-sentence report before passing COMMUNITY SENTENCES, and although they are no longer legally required to do so, they usually also obtain a report before passing a custodial sentence (see CUSTODY). They also often ask for reports in other cases where this may assist in sentencing decisions. Reports are normally requested after a finding of guilt in magistrates' courts. In the Crown Court, reports are required in advance, and this can present difficulties if the offender is denying the offence.

The content of PSRs is laid down in NATIONAL STANDARDS and normally includes information about the offence, especially its seriousness, the offender's attitudes and circumstances, and the effects upon the victim(s). It concludes by proposing possible appropriate sentences.

Preparation of PSRs is one of the main tasks of the PROBATION SERVICE. It usually takes a probation officer 2–3 weeks to prepare reports, although they can be written more quickly if it is considered essential to do so. Youth and magistrates' courts can also request an abbreviated form of report, known as a SPECIFIC SENTENCE REPORT, which addresses suitability for a particular sentence the court has in mind without going into much background detail.

Report writers normally interview a defendant once or twice for a PSR, with one interview at the person's home if time allows. In the reports, personal information is given and, where possible, verified, the defendant's attitude towards the offence and its victim(s) is assessed and possible sentences are discussed. The report should differentiate between verified information and opinions or impressions. Report writers are required to ensure that they conduct interviews and prepare reports in accordance with ANTIDISCRIMINATORY PRACTICE, taking account of the likely DISCRIMINATION against black people, women, people with disabilities, lesbians and gay men in the criminal justice system. Some report writers go through a process of GATEKEEPING to help them identify and eliminate any potentially discriminatory language or attitudes in their reports and to ensure that positive as well as negative factors about defendants are identified. The removal of the mandatory requirement to consider a report before passing a custodial sentence is believed by some observers to have increased the incidence of discriminatory sentencing, and the Magistrates' Association recommends obtaining a report in all such cases involving juveniles and young adults.

In Scotland, a PSR is known as a *social inquiry report*, which was the former name in England and Wales prior to 1992.

presenting problem the problem that a CLIENT or the person referring a client states as the reason for needing a social work service.

In the past, there was often a professional presumption that the presenting problem was not, or might not be, the 'real' problem; only the professionally trained practitioner could pick out the real problem. This was a presumption in particular of those approaches to social work that placed great importance on family relationships and unresolved conflicts from the client's past. This perspective devalued problems to do with housing, money or child-care that frequently lay behind a person's approach to a SOCIAL SERVICES DEPARTMENT in the first place. There is currently a wider acceptance among social workers and related professionals that the presenting problem forms the basis of work if that is the problem that matters to the client, and that a social worker proceeds to other problems only through discussion with, and with consent of, the client and others who matter to that person, such as family members or carers (see TASK-CENTRED WORK).

pressure group any of a range of organizations that may try to influence central or local government policy-making.

Pressure groups have become a significant part of the British political scene since the Second World War. The range of such groups is extraordinarily varied and often difficult to classify. Some writers, however, have tried to develop a dual classification along a variety of lines. One such writer identifies pressure groups as either interest groups or cause and promotional groups. Under this classification, groups are identified by use of a number of criteria. *Interest* groups are seen as having a limited membership, existing to promote the interest of the membership, having a long life span and being political only at the margins. For example, trade unions and professional associations such as the BRITISH ASSOCIATION OF SOCIAL WORKERS (BASW) may be characterized as interest groups. The BASW has a membership limited to qualified social workers, acts to defend and promote their interests, aims to exist as long as the profession exists and is more concerned with negotiating with employers than with entering the political arena. The other form of group, *cause or promotional* groups, may have the following characteristics: they have open-ended membership; they promote the interest of others rather than those of their own membership; their life span often last no longer than the issue they are concerned with; and they may act primarily in the political arena to change government policy on a particular issue.

Many organizations that may be identified as cause or promotional groups do not reflect all the above criteria, however, although they are certainly not interest groups as defined above. While groups such as pro- and anti-abortion campaigners can be identified as cause groups, organizations such as Mencap and the National Society for the Prevention of Cruelty to Children are less easily placed. Yet it can be argued that the latter has a largely open membership policy, is concerned with the interests of others than their members and is frequently engaged in trying to influence policy on issues affecting those interests. Both these types of organization play an important role in the development of policy in relation to social services and social work activities. While interest groups such as the BASW are obviously directly involved in social work issues, other interest groups, such as the British Medical Association and Unison, may become part of the policy-making process affecting social workers, sometimes cooperating with the BASW and sometimes in conflict with it. Cause groups such as Mencap also affect the policy process in this way but may also be involved alongside social workers through its role in providing voluntary or charitable services, including residential accommodation and advice to parents of children with LEARNING DISABILITIES. The existence of such groups is an essential part of policy-making and implementation in a modern welfare state.

D. King and G. Stoker, *Rethinking Local Democracy*, Basingstoke, Macmillan, 1998.

preventive work/prevention any work that seeks to stop a potential problem emerging or an existing problem becoming more acute, whether for individuals, families or whole neighbourhoods.

Preventive practice aims to direct resources and intervention towards addressing early signs of social difficulties or social problems before they accelerate and intensify into emergencies that require vastly greater resources in terms of time, energy and money. The notion of 'preventive work' is not wholly satisfactory, first, because it raises the question of preventing what and, second, because it suggests that it is a kind of optional extra as if social work is not really social work until it is reacting to harm or imminent catastrophe.

Child protection services provide the best example of how the heavy emphasis on risk swallows up resources for preventive work. Despite the well-known association between specific environmental stressors and child abuse, child protection systems are triggered by circumstances of imminent danger to the child or after harm has been done. While a formidable research effort has described in detail how social workers working with children and families could use resources more effectively if they got out from under the shadow of reactive protective work, the required shift in social work thinking and resource allocation proved difficult to bring about. A similar perspective applies to work with vulnerable adults. Gerald Smale and colleagues (see below) use the phrase 'development work' to distinguish the kinds of preventive work they have in mind from 'curative' or crisis work through which social work offers aid only in times of crisis.

G. Smale, G. Tuson and D. Statham, *Social Work and Social Problems*, Basingstoke, Macmillan.

P. Hardiker, 'Children Still in Need, Indeed: Prevention work across five decades', in O. Stevenson, *Child Welfare in the UK*, London, Blackwell, 1999.

Primary Care Group see PRIMARY CARE TRUST.

primary carer a person with the main responsibility of providing care for another, usually thus experiencing restriction in his or her own life. The person cared for may be physically disabled, have a mental illness or DISABILITY, or be ill or frail because of old age.

Approximately 1.7 million CARERS in Britain live in the same household as the people they care for; 1.4 million carers spend at least 24 hours a week in caring activities. Three-quarters of these people look after an old person, and about half are themselves above retirement age. Carers are usually women and men in their fifties but may be as young as 10, and spouse carers may be 70-plus. Caring is a developmental sequence over a time period – from 'semi-care', when the person cared for can be left alone at night, through part-time care, when he or she needs full-time care but the carer can attend to his or her own affairs, to full care, when it becomes impossible to leave the cared-for person alone. The primary carer is likely to be a close family relative, and up to 70 per cent of carers are likely to be daughters or daughters-in-law.

The primary carer, the person with the major responsibility for and tasks of caring, is the focal person for the implementation of COMMUNITY CARE services. The primary carer is also the person most likely to experience the physical and emotional strain that can be associated with caring, although many carers choose to care and gain great satisfaction from caring for loved ones. The differences for men and women primary carers have been noted. Men are less likely to be pressured to give up their paid employment than women, are more likely to receive support from relatives and social services and are more likely to be offered residential care for the cared-for person at an early stage. Women are often expected to give up well-remunerated work with associated pension rights to care for family members and are offered more short-stay residential and day-care support than men – but as a means of helping them to carry on longer. The NATIONAL HEALTH SERVICE AND COMMUNITY CARE ACT provides entitlement to a full ASSESSMENT for primary carers; this is a right for all carers, whether they are men, women or children.

C. Hicks, *Who Cares? Looking after People at Home*, London, Virago, 1988.

Primary Care Trust (PCT) any of the lead organizations in ensuring the delivery of health services in the NATIONAL HEALTH SERVICE.

The NEW LABOUR government published its reforms to the health services shortly after coming into office in 1997. One of the key developments was the establishment of Primary Care Groups (PCGs) to take responsibility for the delivery of primary care services and the commissioning of services from other trusts, such as hospitals and ambulance services. In addition, their role was to take the lead in ensuring that community-based services were delivered based on needs assessment of their relevant population. For the purpose of fulfilling this role, the PCGs were composed mainly of general practitioners (GPs), but in addition had representation from community nurses and social services as well as lay members. They were given the responsibility of assessing the health needs of their community and then planning and ensuring delivery of services to meet those needs.

In July 2001 the government published a document, 'Shifting the Balance of Power within the NHS', which took these developments a significant step further. The document determined that rather than an incremental process of change in which PCGs became fully fledged Primary Care Trusts (PCTs) the whole process would be completed by April 2002. The PCTs were to be the lead bodies in the development of

Health Improvement Programmes (HimPs) that would identify key TARGETS for the reduction in health inequalities in their areas as well as general improvements in health within their communities. They would take the lead in developing services for the elderly, people with mental health problems and other aspects of community care where the social services department has not been identified as the lead. However, the change includes the expansion of the role of PCTs as they develop, with new Strategic Health Authorities taking on a wider strategic remit. PCTs are to ensure the delivery of all mainline health services, from community level to secondary or hospital care.

As part of this, a key relationship is with SOCIAL SERVICES, and the rest of the local authority, with the aim of fulfilling the aims of the government's MODERNIZATION agenda. This may include an agreement with social services on the establishment of Care Trusts whose aim will be to implement the modernization of health and social care at the local level. In addition there are also changes at regional level where the REGIONAL DIRECTORS OF HEALTH AND SOCIAL CARE are now coterminous with the GOVERNMENT OFFICES OF THE REGIONS.

Department of Health, *Shifting the Balance of Power within the NHS*, London, The Stationery Office, 2001.

principles of sentencing the collective term used to describe the explanations and justifications given for imposing punishment or treatment on people who break the law.

It is usually argued that there are two broad philosophies of punishment, known as retributivism and utilitarianism. Retributivism (sometimes called the 'classical' tradition of criminal justice) maintains that the punishment of wrongdoing is a moral right and duty, an end in itself and an essential component of a civilized society. The obligations on the punisher are, first, to establish that the person to be punished is correctly identified (that is, that guilt is established) and, second, that the punishment is proportionate to the seriousness of the crime (that is, it is not excessive). Utilitarianism (whose most eloquent exponent was Jeremy Bentham, 1748–1832) maintains that punishment is itself an evil that can be justified only if it brings about a greater good, namely the reduction of wrongdoing. Punishment in this view is a means to an end, not an end in itself. The most obvious distinction between the two philosophies is that utilitarians have to demonstrate that punishment (or sentences) work, while retributivists have only to demonstrate that punishment is deserved. The main criticism of utilitarianism is that it takes insufficient account of the relationship between punishment and the seriousness of the crime, while the main criticism of retributivism is that it takes insufficient account of the harmful effects of punishment.

From the two broad philosophical approaches of retributivism and utilitarianism, a number of principles have developed that provide frameworks for sentencing. These include the following:

Just deserts: this phrase is the modern equivalent of the term 'retributivism'. It implies that the main purpose of sentencing is to denounce the crime and visit retribution on the criminal to the extent to which he or she deserves it. (Retribution may be distinguished from revenge, which is likely to be disproportionate punishment and has no acknowledged place in western philosophies of punishment.) The crucial considerations are the seriousness of the crime and the culpability of the criminal, that is, the extent to which the offender is responsible for his or her actions. There is scope to consider aggravating and mitigating factors in so far as they relate to the offence and the offender's part in it, but wider considerations of the offender's personal circumstances are less relevant.

Deterrence: this was the original concern underlying utilitarianism. It implies that the main purpose of sentencing is to deter people from committing crime. There are two main elements in this principle: *individual deterrence* and *general deterrence*. Individual deterrence refers to measures intended to impress upon the offender that the potential personal consequences of actions in the form of punishment make it 'not worth' committing crime again. The most commonly used individually deterrent sentence is the fine, but any sentence that restricts offenders' liberty or inconveniences or shames them may have a deterrent effect. General deterrence refers to measures intended to set an example to other people in the hope of deterring them from committing crime. For example, a bout of criminal damage in a particular area may result in an 'exemplary' prison sentence to demonstrate that local people have 'had enough'. One objection to deterrent sentences is that they may be disproportionate to the seriousness of the particular offence purely in order to 'make a point'. A more fundamental criticism is the underlying assumption that crime is necessarily committed as a rational choice, with the offender weighing up the possible consequences of his or her actions before deciding to offend. Although this may be true in some instances, it is by no means the only explanation for offending. Much crime is impulsive or stems from what most people would regard as irrational thoughts or feelings. Another objection to deterrent sentencing is the moral one that it treats people instrumentally: the offender who is chosen as an example is sentenced as a means to an end that has little to do with the offence or the individual.

Protection and incapacitation: another utilitarian principle, related to deterrence, is that of protecting the public from further harm from the offender. Rather than relying on the rational judgement of the offender that 'crime does not pay', a safer way of ensuring that no further crime is committed is to reduce the opportunity for crime by restricting the offender's liberty. The ultimate example of such a sentence is, of course, the death penalty. Imprisonment is less effective, since prisoners may escape or offend against each other or their guards, and they will in any case be released at some point. Giving someone a COMMUNITY PUNISHMENT

ORDER or a COMMUNITY REHABILITATION ORDER with added conditions
or subjecting them to ELECTRONIC MONITORING may seem mild measures
in comparison, but the principles of restriction and surveillance are
basically the same as with imprisonment. The extent of the restriction has
to be decided according to the seriousness of the offence, and this means
that the retributive principle of proportionality also has a part to play.

Compensation and reparation: just as deterrence may be either individual
or general, so the retributive principle of 'making good' harm done
by crime can include both the individual victim and wider society.
Compensation (predominantly financial) is usually made to the
individual victim of a rime. REPARATION is a broader concept that
involves the offender in doing something socially useful or morally
uplifting (such as unpaid service to the community), thereby
demonstrating remorse and willingness to put something back into
society. Some advocates of RESTORATIVE JUSTICE argue that reparation
offers a moral alternative to retributive justice.

Reform, rehabilitation and correction: the bringing about of fundamental
changes to the personality, attitudes and behaviour of an offender so
that he or she no longer commits offences – not because of fear of the
consequences but from an appreciation that crime is wrong – has long
been a utilitarian aim of sentencing. The distinction between reform
and rehabilitation is not an easy one. Reform tends to imply a change
of attitude or beliefs, whereas rehabilitation tends to imply a change
of circumstances (personal, social or medical) leading to a change of
behaviour, although the two concepts are very closely related. The term
'correction' is used in North America, and although for some people it
has unacceptable overtones of coercion, it has been used by some as an
alternative to 'reform' or 'rehabilitation' because it is more neutral and
implies appropriate humility about the state of our knowledge about
the reasons why people stop committing crimes.

In the past, people have viewed crime as a symptom of sin (which only
religious conversion will remedy) or of disease (which only medical
science will cure) or of an emotionally deprived childhood (which only
psychotherapeutic casework will resolve) or of poverty (which only social
and political action will resolve). While all these explanations might
provide some insight into understanding some crime, none provides a
full explanation; many people now believe that such an explanation is
neither possible nor desirable.

People commit crimes for many reasons (see THEORIES OF CRIME).
They also stop committing crime for many reasons, and the sentences
they receive may be only one among several influential factors. It would
also be a mistake to assume that sentencing is always a rational activity
based on the above principles. Sentencers' decisions can be influenced by
many factors, not all of which might be considered legitimate or relevant.
Sentencers' own backgrounds, political persuasions, occupations and

prejudices can result in sentences that appear inconsistent or unfair. Some commentators argue that sentencing practice is devoid of agreed aims and objectives and impervious to attempts at evaluation. The Court of Appeal attempts to rectify miscarriages of justice in the lower courts and the Sentencing Advisory Panel has limited powers to advise the Court of Appeal on issuing and revising sentencing guidelines under the CRIME AND DISORDER ACT 1998.

N. Walker, *Why Punish?* Oxford, Oxford University Press, 1991.

prioritizing problems a stage of TASK-CENTRED WORK in which user and practitioner draw up a list of the client's problems and decide which two or three are the most pressing and which the client would most like solved.

With some complicated problems it may be that sub-problems have to be tackled in a particular sequence – the solution to one problem may then unlock a subsequent problem. In selecting problems to work on, the MOTIVATION of the client is a key factor.

prison the most severe penalty available to UK courts, involving incarceration in a secure institution away from one's home.

Maximum prison sentences are laid down by Acts of Parliament, but within these limits courts have discretion about the length of sentences (although magistrates' courts cannot send anyone to prison for more than six months for a single offence or twelve months for more than one offence). The great majority of prison sentences are given by the Crown Courts (see CRIMINAL COURT).

Prisons are categorized according to their function and the level of security. Men's prisons are divided into local prisons (which house prisoners immediately after sentence), closed training prisons (housing relatively high-risk offenders), open prisons (for low-risk offenders) and dispersal prisons (housing the most serious, high-risk offenders). In addition, there are REMAND centres (for those awaiting sentence) and YOUNG OFFENDER INSTITUTIONS. There are two therapeutic regimes within closed prisons for men, the most famous being Grendon Underwood. Some prisons serve more than one function. Female prisons are either closed or open, but women prisoners are not formally categorized according to the level of risk they present. Some women's prisons incorporate remand centres and young offender institutions. The average prison population fluctuates considerably, but the prison population of England and Wales has in recent years been consistently among the highest in Western Europe in proportion to total population.

One of the major criticisms of prisons has for many years been the levels of overcrowding, especially in the local and remand prisons, many of which were built in Victorian times. Grossly overcrowded prisons can do little more than warehouse their inmates, often in degrading conditions. Governments have responded with a massive prison-building programme and the introduction of privately run prisons, but inmate numbers continue to rise – and many observers

2 2

argue that providing increased numbers of places will inevitably lead courts to make use of them.

Prisons as they now exist are a relatively modern form of punishment. In medieval times they were used for detention before trial (like modern remand prisons) rather than for punishment as such, which was invariably physical. During the 16th and 17th centuries, houses of correction and workhouses developed, with the general intention of containing the vagrant poor and the unemployed. Among these were some offenders, but more serious offenders received the death penalty or transportation to North America and, later, Australia. During the 18th century, however, two factors influenced the increased use of imprisonment as a punishment in its own right. First, the independence of the United States made it necessary to find alternatives to transportation (although Australia remained available initially). Second, a more enlightened attitude to the criminal law resulted in a reduction in the number of offences that attracted the death penalty. At this time, prisons were regarded as places of deterrence and retribution (see PRINCIPLES OF SENTENCING), but by the end of the 19th century they had become places for reform and rehabilitation, at least in theory. Emphasis was placed upon religious instruction, education, training and – later – psychiatric treatment for prisoners, the purpose being to encourage them to lead useful lives on release. During the second half of the 20th century, however, the gap between the rhetoric of rehabilitation and the reality of the sordid conditions and deprived regimes in most prisons became very clear. Ideologies of treatment and training have largely been replaced by more modest goals relating to secure containment and humane treatment.

Radical analysts of prison history have linked the emergence of mass imprisonment with the needs of industrial capitalist society. Prisons serve social functions, such as containing disruptive or unproductive people, minimizing these people's influence by denying them autonomy and symbolically stigmatizing deviants, which is also intended to have a deterrent effect. In addition, prison diverts attention from the 'crimes of the powerful', focusing instead on the criminals from the lower social classes who make up the majority of the prison population. Prison also serves to reassure the public that 'something is being done' about the crime problem, and although in most terms it is unsuccessful, it 'works' for politicians.

The prison service is constantly faced with serious problems that have often been characterized as 'crises', although they are arguably too chronic to merit this term. They may be summarized as problems of security (preventing escapes without undue oppression of the compliant majority), of conditions (squalid accommodation and the poverty of regimes, with inadequate work, education and time out of cells), of authority (relating to poor industrial relations, low staff morale and occasional outbursts of rioting), of control (maintaining discipline among prisoners and staff and preventing riots), and of legitimacy (maintaining a belief that the prison system is under control and that imprisonment is just).

The PROBATION SERVICE has had a presence within prisons since 1966. Initially concerned with routine 'welfare' matters, probation officers have increasingly passed this role on to prison staff through shared working arrangements, and probation officers have become increasingly involved in one-to-one and groupwork aimed at changing offenders' behaviour and attitudes. Increasingly, they have also become part of the prison management structure. Prison groups address issues such as anger management, offending behaviour, sexual offending and abuse and substance misuse. Probation staff contribute to sentence planning and risk assessment and prepare reports on prisoners' progress towards early release. Probation officers from prisoners' home areas also maintain contact and prepare reports and supervise some categories of offenders when they are released early. This is known as 'throughcare' or RESETTLEMENT.

A significant recent development in UK prisons has been privatization. The arguments in favour of privatizing prisons are both ideological (that it is compatible with a market economy) and pragmatic (the need to build more prisons quickly and to maintain them economically, to hold management more accountable and to make staff working practices more flexible). The arguments against privatization are similarly ideological (that punishment should remain a direct responsibility of the state) and pragmatic (that private security staff are not competent to contain, care for and treat prisoners, and that private prisons create a vested interest in maintaining a high prison population).

M. Cavadino and J. Dignan, *The Penal System: An Introduction*, third edition, London, Sage, 2002.

prison welfare officially an outdated term but still commonly used in prisons to refer to the work of the PROBATION SERVICE within PRISON establishments.

Probation officers working in prisons remain employed by the outside probation service but are also responsible to prison governors or directors. See the description of their role under prison and RESETTLEMENT.

private fostering a child placed for more than 28 days with a person or persons who is not a relative of the child under a personal arrangement between the child's parent (or an adult with PARENTAL RESPONSIBILITY) and the private foster carer.

Until the passage of the CHILDREN ACT 1989, private fostering was completely unregulated. Even after passage of the Act, private fostering remained outside local authority regulations and private foster carers were not vetted in any way. In fact the Children Act introduced only two modest requirements:

1 that both the carer and the child's parent notify the local authority of the intention to place a child in private foster care; and

2 the number of children whom any one carer can foster was limited to three.

The private foster carer is responsible for the day-to-day care of the child. The child's parent remains responsible for safeguarding and promoting the child's welfare, retaining financial responsibility for the child and reaching an agreement with the private foster carer on the issue of maintenance. In certain circumstances the private foster carer can claim child benefit. The child's parents and the foster carers have a legal duty to notify the local authority where the foster carer lives and where the arrangement is proposed. The local authority has a duty to satisfy itself that the arrangements are satisfactory and that the private foster carer is suitable.

Repeated investigations indicate, however, that most arrangements go unreported. As a result, there are an unknown number of children in private foster care – estimates have been as high as 10,000 – without any external oversight or basic standards in play. As a result, the children so fostered are vulnerable to exploitation and abuse. In addition, because the largest group of privately fostered children are West African, who are frequently placed with white foster carers in the UK, RACISM and separation from the child's culture are two issues intertwined. The children of refugees, unaccompanied child refugees and children privately fostered within the Chinese communities in Britain are also evident.

The abuses of children in private foster care have in part resulted from the indifference of local authority social service departments. Some local authorities, however, are now taking pro-active work in the field in which networks with connection to private fostering are cultivated and support for private foster carers developed. Following the death of Victoria Climbié in private foster care (see CHILD ABUSE INQUIRIES), there have been pressing calls for further changes in the law essentially requiring local authorities to maintain a register of private foster carers within their areas that they deem suitable. Further reforms include making it an offence to foster a child privately with an unregistered carer, to have national standards published by the Department of Health and that the 28 days' threshold for deeming an arrangement as private fostering do not have to be continuous.

T. Philpot, *A very private practice: An investigation into private fostering*, London, BAAF, 2001.

private law those aspects of family law that do not involve the state, including the local authority. Most private law proceedings that concern social workers involve matrimonial disputes.

The CHILDREN ACT contains some important private law orders called SECTION 8 ORDERS, which resolve practical matters to do with children caught up in matrimonial disputes. That Act also created a unique flexibility for courts that can draw on any of the private law orders in proceedings for a CARE ORDER if it thinks this would promote the child's welfare.

probation board a committee that is responsible for employing local
probation staff (except chief officers) and managing PROBATION SERVICE
property and policies under the direction of the Home Office and the
NATIONAL PROBATION SERVICE.

Boards replaced probation committees, which had a stronger element
of local ACCOUNTABILITY, with members nominated by local authorities
and sentencers, in 2001. Probation boards include community
representatives and a judge, but these are appointed by the Home
Secretary and the Lord Chancellor respectively. The aim is to strengthen
central control and consistency. Chief probation officers are now
appointed by the home secretary, and they sit on the probation board.

probation centre a building or part of a building, sometimes also referred
to as a rehabilitation centre, approved by the home secretary and run by
the PROBATION SERVICE, to provide GROUPWORK and other activities as
part of the requirements of COMMUNITY REHABILITATION ORDERS.

Offenders are required to attend and participate in activities for up to
60 days in an intensive programme intended to address their offending
behaviour. (The 60-day limit does not apply to sexual offenders, who can
be required to attend throughout their orders.) The activities undertaken
are approved by local PROBATION BOARDS and typically include alcohol
education groups, offending behaviour groups, anger management
groups and other social skills activities, and substance misuse groups.
Centres typically also contain some leisure facilities. Those failing to
attend as required are subject to BREACH PROCEEDINGS, and centres are
regulated by NATIONAL STANDARDS, which include provision for ensuring
ANTIDISCRIMINATORY PRACTICE.

The first probation centres (known initially as day-training centres
and later as probation day centres) were established in 1973. Most activities
in the centres are for groups of offenders, who are expected to address
their offending behaviour, which means facing up to the consequences
of their actions for themselves and their VICTIMS, trying to understand
why they offend and looking for realistic ways to stop offending. They are
also supervised individually or referred elsewhere if there are personal
problems with which they require assistance.

Probation centre users are predominantly more serious offenders
for whom attendance may be an alternative to imprisonment.

probation hostel a residential institution approved by the Home Secretary
as a place of residence for offenders either on bail or as a condition of a
COMMUNITY REHABILITATION ORDER.

Hostels are managed by the PROBATION SERVICE or by a voluntary agency.

Orders may contain conditions of residence either in an approved
probation hostel or in clinics for treatment of substance misuse. There
is also a power to require offenders to reside where directed by their
probation officers. Conditions of residence normally last for the
duration of the order, but they can be varied on application to the court.

Bail hostels provide an effective alternative to custodial remands,
but there are insufficient places to provide a consistent national network.
Probation hostels are not intended primarily for offenders with
accommodation problems: rather, they provide structured supervision
for more serious offenders regardless of whether they have secure
accommodation of their own. Hostel rules typically include a CURFEW
and a requirement to keep staff informed of the person's whereabouts
during the day. The extent to which GROUPWORK is provided on the
premises varies from place to place.

probation inspectorate a monitoring body responsible for inspecting
and enforcing standards in the PROBATION SERVICE.

The inspectorate has a statutory responsibility to ensure that the
probation service is providing high-quality advice in the form of reports
to courts, that offenders are effectively supervised and public protection
given appropriate priority, that equality and diversity are promoted
within the service and that the service provided represents value for
money. It conducts thematic inspections of particular aspects of
probation work and periodic reviews of the overall performance of
local services as well as analysing statistical returns. Its reports have
considerable influence, although they receive little publicity. It has an
additional duty to provide advice to the Home Secretary, and this appears
to arise mainly in cases where mistakes have been made or controversial
decisions have been made. Since 2001, the inspectorate has also taken
part in the inspection of initial probation training programmes.

probation order see COMMUNITY REHABILITATION ORDER.

probation service the statutory agency responsible for providing reports
to CRIMINAL COURTS, supervising offenders on community-based
programmes and working with them in a PRISON WELFARE role. It also
has some responsibilities in the area of CRIME PREVENTION and liaising
with VICTIMS.

Since 2001, the NATIONAL PROBATION SERVICE has overseen the work
of local probation services in England, Northern Ireland and Wales.
Scotland has no probation service as such, having instead a network
of criminal justice social workers. Probation workers supervise adult
offenders given COMMUNITY SENTENCES by the criminal courts and work
with offenders in PRISON to encourage them to change their behaviour
in such a way as to avoid re-offending. They also provide an information
service to VICTIMS of crime under the Victim's Charter in cases where
the offender has been sentenced to 12 months or more in prison.

Probation officers may be seconded to work in other agencies,
including YOUTH OFFENDING TEAMS and MULTI-AGENCY PUBLIC
PROTECTION PANELS. They supervise offenders on COMMUNITY
PUNISHMENT ORDERS, COMMUNITY REHABILITATION ORDERS, COMMUNITY
PUNISHMENT AND REHABILITATION ORDERS and PAROLE. They also work
with unqualified colleagues to run BAIL and PROBATION HOSTELS and

PROBATION CENTRES, and provide throughcare or RESETTLEMENT services to offenders in prison in partnership with prison staff. One of the major roles of probation officers is to prepare PRE-SENTENCE REPORTS about offenders to help courts reach the best sentencing decisions.

In each local probation area the service is supervised by a PROBATION BOARD that appoints staff and manages services and facilities, reporting through the National Probation Service to the Home Secretary. Each probation service has a chief officer with assistants and often a deputy. Deputy chief officers and assistant chief officers have specific professional areas of responsibility, and in some areas they also take responsibility for the staff and services in a geographical area. Senior probation officers act as junior managers, heading area and specialist teams of probation officers and probation service officers as well as supervising secretarial, administrative and specialist staff. Probation staff work within the NATIONAL STANDARDS issued by the HOME OFFICE, which have lessened the discretion of individual staff and reduced geographical discrepancies in the services provided.

Until the 1990s, the probation service was generally described as a social work agency, and probation officers trained alongside social workers. More recently, a specialist DIPLOMA IN PROBATION STUDIES has replaced the social work qualification, and many observers feel that the service as a whole has moved away from its social work roots. Nevertheless, the question of how closely linked the service is and should be to social work remains one that occasions lively debate, and a brief account of the history of the service will illustrate how this controversy has arisen.

The probation service has its roots in the work of the 19th-century police court missionaries, part of the temperance movement that was a major influence upon policy at the time. The first such missionary was employed by the Church of England Temperance Society in 1876 to 'reclaim' offenders charged with drunkenness and drink-related offences by encouraging them to sign a pledge of abstinence and maintaining contact in an attempt to ensure that this was honoured. The Probation of Offenders Act 1907 gave MAGISTRATES' courts the power to appoint probation officers, whose job was defined as being to advise, assist and befriend offenders placed under their supervision. Such a measure was officially deemed to be imposed instead of a court sentence, and so it remained until the 1991 Criminal Justice Act made it a sentence in its own right. The 1925 Criminal Justice Act made it a legal obligation for every court to appoint a probation officer, and during the 20th century the work of the service expanded to include working with juveniles and families as well as adult offenders. This included the role of the divorce court welfare officer, subsequently taken over by the CHILDREN AND FAMILY COURT ADVISORY AND SUPPORT SERVICE (CAFCASS). By the mid-1960s the service had also taken on responsibility for the welfare and supervision of prisoners during their sentences and on release. Over time, the evangelical mission of the service developed into a secular, professional, social work service to the courts. The distinctive professional skill developed by probation officers was in the preparation of PRE-SENTENCE REPORTS: these are assessments of offenders in their social environment, with the specific purpose of assisting courts in making sentencing decisions. Previously known as Social Inquiry Reports, these reports now emphasize risk assessment and management more, and social factors somewhat less, than in the past.

Although there had always been a degree of tension in the role of the probation officer between caring for offenders and controlling their criminal behaviour, these two aspects of the work were viewed as part and parcel of both the psychoanalytic casework and the paternalistic 'common-sense' advice that combined to characterize the typical probation officer of the early and mid-20th century. Despite its social work base, however, the probation service saw itself as to some extent distinct from other social work specialisms. For that reason, in England and Wales it did not follow Scotland's example of joining the social services departments newly created in 1971 after the SEEBOHM REPORT.

In the 1970s, probation officers became involved in supervising offenders on unpaid work in the community (see COMMUNITY PUNISHMENT ORDER). In the 1980s and 1990s, central government took increasing powers to control the work of the probation service, and a penal policy emphasizing JUST DESERTS rather than REHABILITATION came to dominate management thinking (see PRINCIPLES OF SENTENCING). Probation work became as much a matter of case management as direct work with individual offenders, with increased emphasis on groupwork and on referring offenders to partner agencies as part of supervision packages. With the publication of the VICTIM'S CHARTER in 1990, the service had to begin to find ways to reconcile its work with offenders with the interests of victims. This was reinforced with the passing of the 2000 Criminal Justice and Court Services Act, which created a statutory requirement to consult victims in certain cases. Throughout the 1990s issues of public protection, punishment and risk assessment and management became more central. In 2001, the National Probation Service was established, increasing the tendency towards central control of the work of the service and leading to greater consistency.

D. Ward, J. Scott and M. Lacey, *Probation: Working for justice*, second edition, Oxford, Oxford University Press, 2002.

probation service assistant (PSA) a member of PROBATION SERVICE staff without a formal qualification as a probation officer, working either to support a field team or to provide a specialized service.

Although not qualified as probation officers, probation service assistants may hold other professional qualifications. Some are recruited to assist qualified staff, and many such PSAs go on to train as probation officers. Some are recruited to provide specific skills not otherwise available to teams or to work either full- or part-time supervising offenders undertaking unpaid work in the community. Staff in the latter category are sometimes called Community Service Officers. PSAs are called Probation Service Officers in some areas.

probation service officer see PROBATION SERVICE ASSISTANT.

problem family a term widely used in the post-Second World War period in British social work agencies to describe families thought to have persistent problems that either were impervious to help or required constant support.

The concept of the problem family was closely associated with the idea of a CYCLE OF DEPRIVATION. Problem families were thought to have their roots in other problem families – the problems were transmitted from one generation to another through the process of socialization. Although the term is no longer used by social welfare professionals, the idea is still thought to be alive both in the public consciousness and implicitly in some social work practice. There are strong associations with the idea of the UNDERCLASS and 'scrounger'. Critics of the term argue that 'families with problems' is a more defensible idea, especially if the 'problems' are defined. The same critics have also suggested that the long-term support thought necessary for 'problem families' was actually a form of casework that cultivated in such families a form of dependence upon social work agencies.

process recording a detailed account of a piece of work conducted in a social work or social welfare setting.

Process recording may be a verbatim account of an interview or of a critical part of an interview. It may also include, in parallel, an account of the worker's reasoning or decisions in pursuing, for example, one particular line of inquiry rather than another. Thus the recording may include the aims and objectives of the interview or transaction, an evaluation of content and outcome, and an assessment of the effectiveness of the social work process. This kind of detailed recording is especially useful in social work training with student social workers and with workers in the early stages of their careers. Some see such detailed work as fruitful with very difficult cases too, especially where people are hostile or obstructive or where they find it difficult to express themselves. Process recording can be used with individual cases, with families and with GROUPWORK.

profession a group or body, of some social standing, claiming expertise in an area of work.

Features thought to characterize a profession include lengthy training in relation to some clearly demarcated area of knowledge and skill, the idea of public service or even altruistic practice, impartial service regardless of client, uniform (that is, competent) service regardless of practitioner, and a code of ethics or conduct. The classic concept of the profession, based on the medical and legal professions in the 19th century, included a scale of fees and a commitment to independence, the latter implying that none could possibly judge the individual professional except a peer or colleague.

The process of professionalization seems to involve a sequence of developments. A particular skill or area of knowledge emerges in response to changes in economic and social activity; people gather together to exchange ideas and to develop the new territory; if the 'field' has commercial or social potential, the group will increase in number; the members seek to define and set boundaries on the new activity and by so doing seek to distinguish it from associated activities; decisions are made about who can be a member and later a 'practitioner'; and the final stages involve controlling the qualifying process and the conduct of members. The state will incorporate the training of professionals into the mainstream of higher education if the activity is regarded as sufficiently important, although professional organizations will still have some measure of autonomy.

There is no doubt that social work has emerged as an occupation in the way described above. Most commentators, however, question whether social work is or can be a fully fledged profession, preferring to regard it as a 'quasi-' or 'semi-profession'. They point, first, to the roots of social work in voluntary activity and to the continuing debate about how much social work requires genuine expertise and how much of it might be undertaken by communities, in SELF-HELP activity and by volunteers. Second, they point to the lack of agreement among social workers about the knowledge and value base of the occupation. Social workers, even within the same team, may adopt quite different styles of practice based upon differing views of the social work task. Third, social workers operate within a bureaucratic context. They are part of hierarchies and, far from exercising autonomy, they are clearly accountable to a line manager on a day-to-day basis. Additionally, given that many important decisions concerning social work activities are actually made by the courts, the claim that social workers are professionally autonomous is further undermined. Indeed, there have been significant debates in recent years about the extent to which social workers are allowed to make decisions within general guidelines laid down by judges, as against a perception that judges are making many more 'casework' decisions than they did before.

Critics of the idea of profession have pointed to the self-interested behaviour of professional bodies. They may speak the language of public service and of a commitment to high-quality practice for all, but their tactics often restrict entry to the profession, discriminate against women and members of ethnic minorities and seek to maintain, if not improve, high salaries. The social class origins of the established professions are principally from the same social groups. Given these general criticisms of professions, some social workers have questioned the desirability of adopting the idea of the profession as the occupational goal. If the average social worker does accept structural inequality as the major explanation for the social problems that they have to deal with, then maybe, they argue, the occupation should aspire to a strong trade unionism. Trade unions too are interested in competent, high-quality services.

T. Johnson, *Professions and Power*, Basingstoke, Macmillan, 1972.

professional network the range of contacts that practitioners establish with other professionals in their own or other agencies and with local residents in community organizations.

A professional's own network is a critical tool in achieving certain objectives. Partnerships, for example, grow out of networks as trust and confidence in the capacity of network links deepen. Networks also generate innovative projects and multidimensional thinking. Purposeful, work-oriented networks are different in nature and purpose from users' NETWORKS and the techniques for strengthening them also differ. Practitioners should keep in mind that networks are reciprocal. Asking others for information or help in solving a problem means that similar assistance be offered in return at some point in the future.

Networks are created and maintained through the most basic moves. Shared experience and common interests are powerful glue to cement relationships. These may arise from a practitioner's personal life, shared adversity or discrimination or from simply having to knuckle under to the same set of organizational tasks. Lengthy chat with the same set of colleagues everyday while pleasant and supportive does not create the kind of network that practitioner's need for developing partnerships or a collaborative multi-agency initiative. Whether a social care worker, social worker or social services manager, you should be looking across your agency, and outside your agency for those productive links that in time may pay off. Networks also thrive on use. Depending on the nature of your relationship, some form of regular contact is probably desirable.

prohibited steps order a court order under the CHILDREN ACT that prevents a parent or any other person specified in the order from taking, without the consent of the court, a particular action that could be taken in meeting PARENTAL RESPONSIBILITY (see SECTION 8 ORDERS).

Examples of possible prohibited steps orders are an order preventing the removal of a child from the United Kingdom, an order preventing a child undergoing certain surgery or an order preventing a change in a child's schooling.

proportionality the principle that PRISON sentences should reflect the seriousness of the offence committed – see PRINCIPLES OF SENTENCING.

Proportionality requires that sentences are determinate (that is, stated by the court rather than determined by administrative decisions and of a defined duration) and that they relate to what the offender is held to deserve for the actual offence committed. See also JUST DESERTS.

PSA abbreviation for PROBATION SERVICE ASSISTANT.

PSP abbreviation for PASTORAL SUPPORT PROGRAMME.

PSR abbreviation for PRE-SENTENCE REPORT.

psychiatry the medical approach to the understanding and treatment of MENTAL HEALTH PROBLEMS.

Psychiatrists are qualified medical practitioners with a specialist postgraduate training in psychiatry and PSCHODYNAMIC theory. They operate traditionally from the hospital base.

Impact of psychiatry: psychiatry applies the MEDICAL MODEL, taken for granted in Western culture as the most scientific and effective approach to physical health problems, to mental health problems. Central to the medical model is the idea that 'disease entities' exist in the person as the cause of the symptoms of illness. These disease entities are named in the diagnosis given to the symptoms. One example of this in psychiatry is the diagnosis of schizophrenia. Disease entities can be understood as developments in the physical make-up of an individual that are defined as 'abnormal' or pathological by medical science, and, in the case of physical diseases, these developments can be detected by scientific procedures (for example, the presence of a virus in blood cells). In the case of mental health problems, however, although there is some evidence suggesting the genetic predisposition to PSYCHOSIS and NEUROSIS, this evidence is not conclusive (see MENTAL ILLNESS).

Although, therefore, physical disease entities have not been found in relation to mental health problems, the symptoms of psychoses are activated by biochemical processes in the nervous system. It has been found that the physical treatment by drugs and electroconvulsive therapy can affect these processes in many who have these conditions, with the result of reduced symptoms. The impact of these treatments was striking in the 1950s and onwards, enabling the majority of people with psychotic conditions in psychiatric hospitals to be discharged after only short stays. This meant that psychiatry could claim effectiveness in using the medical model with mental health problems. The Mental Health Act 1959 (see MENTAL HEALTH ACT 1983) consequently treated mental health problems as equivalent to physical health problems, validating the decision (on the part of psychiatrists and social workers) to admit someone compulsorily to hospital as the result of a psychiatric decision that the person was too ill to be responsible for his or her own safety and for the safety of others. Because no disease entities have been found, however, these physical treatments can only control, and do not cure, psychotic symptoms; also, more recent COMMUNITY CARE studies show that people with the most severe symptoms are least likely to be helped by medication. As a result there are people in the community with uncontrolled symptoms who may be unable to cope with settled accommodation and daily living. They may subsequently become homeless and suffer a poor quality of life, and they may also offend and end up in PRISON or secure hospitals.

The emphasis on the use of drugs by psychiatry and the compulsory powers that psychiatrists ultimately hold have led Szasz from the anti-psychiatry position, and a number of other radical writers, to regard psychiatry as a form of social control, restricting the rights and liberty of people who do not conform to the expectations of society. Anti-racist writers make this point strongly in respect of black people, who are far more likely than white people to be treated restrictively by drugs and compulsory detention.

Pathways to the psychiatrist: it is important for the worker to understand who is referred to the psychiatric services and by what routes. About 250 people in every 1,000 in the population have recognisable psychiatric problems; about 230 of these consult a general practitioner with these problems; only about 140 are recognized by the GP as having psychiatric difficulties and only 17 are referred to the psychiatric services. Many more 'drop out' once referred – at least one-third do not keep their initial appointments. This means that any help that psychiatrists can give reaches only a very small proportion of those who may be in need. The people who do get referred are those with severe symptoms, usually with a psychotic diagnosis, although about a fifth have a neurotic diagnosis (usually DEPRESSION). They will have had the symptoms for a long time and are likely to have serious social problems, possibly challenging behaviour, and may be at risk of suicide. People who see psychiatrists, therefore, have the most serious difficulties – although it could also be said that they are the people society considers to be most in need of control.

An important point about the people referred is that men, once given a psychiatric diagnosis by GPs, tend to be referred in high proportions, while women are less likely to be referred. The same pattern is found for younger as opposed to older people. This may suggest that the mental health problems of women and older people are treated less seriously than those of men and younger people. Black people are admitted to hospital in high proportions, come to the attention of psychiatrists to a disproportionate extent through the police and the courts and are more likely than white people to be placed in secure provision. Asian people, by contrast, may not be receiving a service to the extent it is needed, as they are less likely than white and black people to be referred to a psychiatrist. Members of lower socioeconomic groups who are referred to the psychiatric services with psychoses are the most likely to become 'long-term patients', that is, likely to relapse frequently, thus needing hospital admission and possibly needing medication and other help from the psychiatric services on a more or less permanent basis. This group is not large, perhaps a quarter of the 10 to 20 per cent of outpatients admitted to hospital but require specialized social work besides psychiatric help and may also have physical disabilities.

Psychiatry and community care: COMMUNITY CARE policy, which has in recent years become law under the NATIONAL HEALTH SERVICE AND COMMUNITY CARE ACT, has as a central objective the reduction of institutional care and the location of the main focus of care in the community. Consequently, psychiatric hospital beds have been massively reduced in number.

The majority of people referred to psychiatrists therefore receive care
in the community in a variety of settings. People with long-term chronic
conditions may reside in GROUP HOMES or HOSTELS, and a wider range of
people may attend day-care or community mental health centres; others
may receive visits from social workers and COMMUNITY PSYCHIATRIC
NURSES at home. Important in these services is the communication
between the different professionals: often the social worker is involved
in a MULTIDISCIPLINARY team responsible for the people needing
psychiatric services in a particular area. The team makes decisions about
the care of particular individuals and about the roles of each professional
in delivering that care, and often a psychiatrist is the head of the team.
The social worker's approach to mental health problems has been shown
in many studies to be different from that of the psychiatrist; and this,
along with the higher status of the psychiatrist in relation to the social
worker, raises many issues for the worker to deal with if they are to work
effectively within the requirements of community care policy.

Central Council for Education and Training in Social Work, *Improving
Mental Health Practice*, London, CCETSW, 1993.

psychoanalysis a theoretical perspective of the development of the
individual based on the view that the early life experiences of a person
interact with 'basic human nature' to create the adult PERSONALITY.

Psychoanalysis is both an explanation of the development of the
personality and a therapeutic process in the treatment of neurotic
disorder. Psychoanalytic theory emphasizes the *unconscious* aspects of
the individual, that is, those aspects of the personality that are below
a person's level of awareness but which have effects on behaviour,
thoughts and feelings. In 1895 Freud and Breuer introduced the concept
of the unconscious as an active force within the individual, containing
basic drives, conflicts and discomforting material, the existence of which
is unknown to the person. This inadmissible material does, however,
have a powerful impact on a person's activities and on the way the
person interacts with the world around him or her. Early psychoanalytic
explanations also referred to the presence of a preconscious – material
that is accessible but not immediately available – and the conscious –
behaviours, thoughts and feelings that the person is aware of.

In 1900 Freud presented the key concepts of psychoanalysis: the
notion of mental structure; infantile sexuality; defence mechanisms;
repression; the meaningfulness of unexplained behaviours.

Mental structure: the *id* is the most primitive part of the personality
and is wholly unconscious. It is explained as the basic structure that the
infant is born with. It has no control over its actions and seeks to gratify
the basic drives of hunger, thirst and sex. The *ego* begins to develop soon
after birth as the infant interacts with the world around it. The ego is
the control centre and is both conscious and unconscious. It is guided
by reality and attempts to meet the needs originating in the id by

negotiation with the person's environment. For example, love and work are socially acceptable ways of meeting the id's needs for sex and aggression. The *superego* is the internal judge, that is, the internalized value base of parents and society. It punishes and praises in accordance with those internalized rules.

Infantile sexuality: psychoanalysis proposes that the development of the id, ego and superego is in conjunction with an individual's progression through a number of stages in his or her early years, referred to as the *psychosexual* stages of development. Human biology interacting with environmental factors, such as parental discipline, determines a healthy or otherwise progression to adulthood. For healthy psychosexual development, the individual must progress in ways that optimize gratification and control through the *oral* stage (0–12 months), *anal* stage (12–30 months), *genital* (or phallic) stage (30 months–5 years), *latency* stage (5–12 years) and *sexual* stage (adolescent years). Throughout these stages, both boys and girls develop sexual attraction to the opposite-sex parent and wish to displace the same-sex parent. Freud termed this the Oedipus complex in boys and the Electra complex in girls. Psychoanalysis argues that the resolution of these conflicts and development through the psychosexual stages are a complicated process involving the conscious, the unconscious, longings, fears, insecurity and anxiety. The conflicts are finally resolved by the child identifying with the same-sex parent.

Defence mechanisms: throughout these stages of early life the anxiety experienced may be so intolerable that the material (memories, thoughts and feelings) is 'pushed' into the unconscious. The individual can use any number of strategies to protect the ego from anxiety, collectively referred to as *mechanisms of defence*. Psychoanalysis sees two of the major defence mechanisms, *regression* and *fixation*, as interlinked. If a person receives too little or too much gratification in any of the psychosexual stages, he or she may become fixated in that stage – that is, anxiety in later life may be managed (defended against) by regression to that stage of childhood in which the person is 'stuck'. Freud saw fixation and regression as mechanisms for enabling a person in adult life to manage stress. Anna Freud later identified and explained further the concept of defence mechanisms – for example, that denial is the refusal to acknowledge anxiety-provoking material in the environment, and reaction formation involves substituting an unacceptable emotion for one less anxiety-provoking, such as love for hate.

Repression: an ego defence mechanism in which the ego 'pushes' discomforting impulses, thoughts, feelings or memories into the unconscious. This reduces anxiety and protects a person's self-image. The process is unconscious, and in this it differs from *suppression*, which is the conscious avoidance of anxiety-provoking material. Psychoanalysis argues that residual sexual feelings for a parent are repressed as the boy or girl passes through the final psychosexual stages of growth. It is considered that the ego uses energy from the id to block (repress) anxiety-provoking material.

Meaningfulness of material: psychoanalysis has its roots in biological determinism, implicit in the view that all behaviour is caused and has meaning for the person himself or herself. The cause may lie deeply repressed in the unconscious and be unknown, but actions, behaviour, thoughts and feelings are directed by the unconscious drive of the id and the repressed material. Psychoanalysis believes that seemingly inexplicable behaviour can be explained and understood. To arrive at the cause may require a long period of analysis.

Psychotherapy: psychoanalysis as therapy relies on the technique of *free association*. The patient says whatever comes into his or her mind while under instruction from the psychoanalyst to report his or her thoughts without reservation. The aim is to give patients an insight into his or her NEUROSIS by examining the contents of the unconscious through exploration of thoughts, fantasies, dreams, slips of the tongue, mistakes, beliefs and attitudes. The psychoanalyst may or may not attempt an interpretation of the material, but the basic premise of treatment is that capricious behaviour can be explained by reference to events in a person's history. Psychoanalysis can thus reveal the motive underlying the behaviour. Psychotherapy is a prolonged and expensive form of treatment the efficacy of which has been questioned. Eysenck has suggested that, in such a lengthy treatment, symptoms are likely to remit spontaneously, regardless of any treatment. Gregory, reviewing some of the evidence for and against the value of psychotherapy, concluded that statistical research evidence confirms that 'psychotherapy in general works and its effects are not entirely due to non-specific effects such as arousal of hope nor to spontaneous recovery'.

Psychoanalysis since its early years has aroused criticism and acceptance almost in equal measures. Some of the first critics, such as Alfred Adler and Carl Jung, were themselves originally psychoanalysts. FEMINIST approaches to PSYCHOLOGY are critical of such explanations as the psychosexual stages while acknowledging the importance of early life experiences. Others have questioned whether all human behaviour can be understood as the expression of sexual and aggressive drives.

Psychoanalysis was extremely influential in social work training and practice in the postwar decades in Britain. It has been substantially replaced by more pragmatic approaches to personal and social problems but is still influential in PSYCHIATRY.

G. Pearson, J. Treseder and N. Yellowly, *Social Work and the Legacy of Freud* Basingstoke, Macmillan, 1988.

psychodynamic approach an approach to social work that uses some of the main concepts of PSYCHOANALYSIS.

Social work theory and practice were heavily influenced by psychoanalytic ideas in the 1940s and 1950s. They particularly took up the concept that children develop through a number of stages and the notion that if this development is incomplete children's behaviour can become 'fixated', remaining stuck at a certain level, or 'regress', returning to that of an earlier stage of development. The psychodynamic approach also viewed the adult PERSONALITY as a product of childhood development. Adults suffered anxiety when childhood relationship conflicts had not been fully resolved. Adults deal with anxiety by employing a number of defence mechanisms, such as regression, denial (refusal to accept that something is a problem or causes distress) or projection (an unacceptable feeling such as hatred or anger is attributed to another person).

Social work theorists developed a model using psychodynamic concepts but in a way more applicable to relatively fluid and less intensive relationships between social workers and CLIENTS. They saw clients' problems and distress as arising from childhood needs and drives (often as a result of poor relationships with parents) that persisted into adulthood because they had not been adequately dealt with at the time. The clients experience distress arising from poor ego functioning – that is, an ego that has not mastered living in the day-to-day world. Social workers used a number of techniques to help clients. Among these were: *diagnostic understanding*, understanding the precise origins of a client's distress; *ventilation*, allowing the client to express feelings; and *corrective relationship*, whereby the relationship with the social worker enabled the client to compensate for previously unsatisfactory relationships. Above all, by exploring and giving insight into the origins of conflict the practitioner helps the client to become aware of how to change.

The psychodynamic approach was widely criticized in later decades for lacking a way of addressing the social origins of problems. Indeed, a number of psychodynamically oriented theorists did introduce a social dimension into their analysis. Even so, the main legacy of the approach was a deep impact on social work terminology, which, in its crudest terms, was used to describe clients in a patronizing way. Behaviour could be described as 'infantile' or refusal to accept a social worker's point of view as 'denial'. There was also the tendency to examine a client's current difficulties as reflections of deeper problems of unsatisfactory relationships and to overlook the very real dilemmas of current relationships or environmental pressures. (See CASEWORK, LOSS, OBJECT RELATIONS THEORY.)

F. Hollis and M. Woods, *Casework: A Psychosocial Therapy*, New York, Random House, 1981.

psychology the scientific study of behaviour and of mental processes, such as perception, memory, social interaction and thinking.

Psychological theories have had considerable influence on social work practice. The application of such theoretical frameworks can improve practice and enhance workers' understanding of service users and of themselves. Psychology is now an integral part of social work training programmes. Social psychology, behaviourist theories, interactionist approaches and psychoanalytic insights are the core topics often included in the social work syllabus.

The central theme of social work is a commitment to humanely and socially based strategies to enable people to deal more effectively with the concerns and stresses of everyday life in ways that maintain dignity and self-esteem. Social workers when working with service users may need to act as counsellors, advocates, mediators and resource seekers. These complex tasks require a sophisticated approach to understanding how people react to such situations. Psychology can offer conceptual and theoretical insights that impact on the social work task to the benefit of all participants. Social work may use any one or more of a number of therapeutic strategies with service users that have their roots in psychological research: GROUPWORK, COUNSELLING, PSYCHOTHERAPY, BEHAVIOUR MODIFICATION, social interaction work, FAMILY THERAPY, SYSTEMS theory, CRISIS INTERVENTION, disaster responses, and working with the DYING and bereaved. The difficulty for social workers is that psychological knowledge is developing rapidly, and hence a reliance on particular frameworks may ultimately mean that the worker is using an outmoded approach. Thus, to use psychology appropriately in social work requires a flexibility of approach, an updating of knowledge, an evaluation of psychological theory and a willingness to review and change the way social work uses psychology. A useful example of this is that in the 1960s Freudian insights were considered of major importance in workers' one-to-one approach to problem-solving, whereas in the 1980s and 1990s phenomenological theories have come to offer a greater understanding of individuals and their social frameworks. Social workers may use only a small number of psychological insights, but these should be rooted in sound knowledge. Social workers' belief that their own therapeutic efforts can bring about change has been rooted in a commitment to a psychological framework for much of their work. Clearly, much social work attempts to address problems rooted in structural oppression; social workers in this respect are required to look beyond the individual to the social structures that shape them. Social psychology helps to some extent in this respect, but the link between broader social structures and individual functioning is properly the province, mostly, of SOCIOLOGY.

M. Herbert, *Psychology for Social Workers*, Basingstoke and London, Macmillan and British Psychological Society, 1981.

psychopathy see PERSONALITY DISORDER.

psychoses a group of incapacitating MENTAL DISORDERS that severely disrupt thinking, speech and behaviour.

Psychoses are understood broadly in Western cultures as different forms of MENTAL ILLNESS. The majority of cases are referred to the psychiatric services, as they represent the main concern of PSYCHIATRY. Psychoses include DEPRESSION, MANIC DEPRESSION and schizophrenia.

Their main distinguishing feature is that the person's responses appear to be inappropriate to his or her circumstances as defined by that person's culture and social groupings. These responses may take the form of HALLUCINATIONS, delusions, MOOD disorder, inaccurate judgements and/or unintelligible behaviour. These symptoms, which affect perception as well as a person's thoughts, emotions and behaviour, have major implications for his or her wellbeing. They profoundly change the person's ability to cope with daily living and relationships. Inwardly the sufferer experiences extreme distress and fear: as many as 10 per cent of people with schizophrenia do kill themselves. For many people with schizophrenia, 'chronic' symptoms of apathy, slowness and loss of motivation can continue long-term despite medication. Substantial numbers of people with these conditions recover, however, and the acute symptoms of many who do not can be controlled, in varying degrees, by psychotropic medication – particularly successfully in the case of manic depression.

Origins of psychosis: there is considerable debate over whether the psychoses are an illness or not. In favour of the 'illness' view, psychiatry has relied considerably upon evidence from twins' studies and studies conducted with relatives of people with diagnoses of psychosis to show that there are strong hereditary – and hence biological – influences on the likelihood of an individual developing a psychotic condition. Identical twins have a 45 per cent chance of developing schizophrenia, and a 70 per cent chance of developing either depression or manic depression. These figures contrast significantly enough with the 2 to 3 per cent chances of a member of the general population developing a psychotic condition to show that being born in the same family as someone with a psychotic condition has an influence upon the likelihood of developing the latter. It has never been shown conclusively, however, that the reasons for this lie more in physiological than environmental family factors. Recent research has furthermore shown that these studies may not have been reliable, at least in respect of schizophrenia, although other evidence is presented for the possibility that a general physiologically based sensitivity may be found among people who develop psychotic conditions. Current biological theories of psychoses – particularly of schizophrenia – focus on a general 'predisposition' and are often grouped now under the *stress vulnerability model*. In this model psychosocial stressors play a major role, with important implications for social work. A person with such a predisposition develops a psychosis only when experiencing extreme stress, such as family disruption or high levels of social deprivation; the tension results in biochemical processes in the brain becoming disordered and producing symptoms.

Other models of causation follow the SOCIAL MODEL OF DISABILITY and point to the social consequences for those with mental health problems as the prime source of difficulty. In this view, exclusion from community acceptance and employment prevents more effective recovery. There is a reality to mental ill health but this should be seen as a valued difference – part of the human condition – rather than an abnormality. The *recovery movement*, within which user perspectives are prominent, goes further. It views the psychoses not as an illness but as understandable human reactions to extreme experiences and points, for example, to the high percentage of people with psychoses as having suffered childhood physical or sexual abuse. Indeed, this perspective argues that experience of childhood sexual abuse is linked to symptoms hitherto associated only with psychoses, such as hearing voices or other hallucinations. The recovery perspective sees people with psychoses as survivors and intervention aims to help people cope and regain control. A third model of causation stems from LABELLING THEORY and some anti-psychiatry approaches, which suggests that the psychoses are no more than learned behaviour.

Impact of psychoses: about 0.3 per cent of the population are admitted to hospital each year with psychotic diagnoses, and among this group are small numbers (about 0.06 per cent of the population) who experience persistent severe symptoms not affected by medication, which may result in challenging behaviour. A third of those admitted, especially those with a diagnosis of schizophrenia, suffer severe chronic conditions with frequent relapses. A further quarter will be less disabled but still relapse. Only about a third of the people admitted with psychotic diagnoses will recover. Those who do recover are most likely to have diagnoses of depression, to live with a partner and to have been employed for significant periods of time in their lives. A model has been drawn up of the problems experienced by someone with a psychotic diagnosis, and the social work response can be related to these problems, as follows:

Primary problems: those problems associated with the 'symptoms', such as HALLUCINATIONS, and the functioning affected by these. People with 'acute' symptoms suffer fear, distress and physical discomfort as a result of these symptoms. Also, the inappropriate perceptions, feelings and beliefs involved in these symptoms can make such people liable to present risk to self and/or others. Those suffering persistent acute symptoms, beyond the control of medication, are, if discharged from hospital without adequate support, highly likely to become homeless (see MENTAL HEALTH ACT), as they cannot cope with day-to-day living, and their behaviour is not acceptable to informal or formal carers. They may often offend, although the offences are usually trivial (see MENTALLY DISORDERED OFFENDERS). Those with long-term chronic conditions may relapse and in the chronic state are still likely to be unable to cope with day-to-day living in varying degrees, especially as many in this group (and in the groups suffering persistent acute symptoms) have come from disadvantaged backgrounds and have never acquired daily living skills.

Secondary problems: problems connected with the person's psychological reactions to the effects of the illness, such as loss of confidence and apathy. Confidence and motivation can be lost as a result of battling against distressing inner experiences – the 'acute symptoms' – and from the forbidding consequences of the illness described under tertiary problems, which leave the individual with little sense of self-worth or belief in a future. Additional implications of experiencing psychosis are that the person may misuse alcohol or drugs (see SUBSTANCE MISUSE) to relieve the discomfort of the symptoms. One study found 56 per cent of patients in psychiatric hospital had misused drugs.

Tertiary problems: these arise through the societal reaction to the person's condition. Societal reaction to psychoses can take place on two fronts. First, difficulties in behaviour and functioning may present stresses for family, friends and actual or potential employers, and thus may result in tensions, rejection and unemployment (the latter in turn leading to poverty, poor housing and deprivation). Children can be seriously affected, through neglect as a result of parental psychosis, thus involving the worker in CHILD PROTECTION work; and the experience of the latter is sufficiently disturbing to lead the children themselves to develop mental health and/or behaviour problems, such as delinquency and truancy. Additional social and legal problems can result if the person is misusing drugs and/or alcohol. Second, tertiary problems for the person can arise also from lack of appropriate service provision. People with chronic psychoses who become homeless, offend, and/or use drugs are particularly unlikely to have their needs taken account of by the services.

Social work response: social work rarely plays a part in the care plan as such which focuses on medication and cognitive interventions. There are, however, several ways in which the practitioner assists the person with psychoses. First, within the CARE MANAGEMENT role the social worker should consider those social factors linked to relapse and disablement. These include the prevention of major stress events, such as eviction, and reducing long-term difficulties, for example around housing or finance. Other tasks might include negotiation with families to reduce carers' stress, misperceptions of the service users and providing good quality support, especially the opportunities for the individual with psychoses to participate in shared activities in accordance with his or her choices. This latter intervention in the recovery process will often be within a protected setting, such as a small group home, with other service users and supportive staff or volunteers.

Second, social care assessment itself provides an important role. There is evidence that many people with psychoses, placed in supported housing, lose their tenancy for a variety of reasons, often leading to homelessness, relapse and substance misuse. This breakdown arises from a poor assessment of support needs in housing and more widely in trying to live an ordinary life in the community. Thus an accurate assessment in partnership with the service user, and drawing on an OCCUPATIONAL THERAPIST's skills in assessing levels of capacity with

different daily tasks, is essential. Linking to medical staff to understand
how specific medication can affect coping is also a vital part of social
work intervention.

Third, practitioners need to have an understanding of POST-TRAUMATIC
STRESS SYNDROME and how to deal with persons who may relive these
experiences. Often social workers are simply not in a position to commit
themselves to the depth of therapeutic relationship required to work on
this kind of problem and need to be sensitive to this fact and aware of
the boundary to their professional role. A practical solution may be to
discuss with the individual user whether he or she would want specialist
counselling. Fourth, social workers liaise with health staff. Medication
can be over-prescribed, with consequences for increased rather than
reduced disability from side effects. Practitioners need to keep informed
about medication and prescription, and with that knowledge base be able
to negotiate with medical staff. Compliance with medication is a central
issue where social workers can make a difference. Often people have very
good reasons for not complying with a prescribed drug regime, such as
not being able to tolerate the side effects or having a fear that the
medication will interact negatively with other treatments for a physical
condition. By exploring such reasons with them, the practitioner may
negotiate on their behalf for a changed regime. Finally, given the link
between stress and relapse, an empowering practice needs to involve
proceeding at the user's pace to jointly establish goals, skills and tasks
that the user can comfortably work towards with appropriate supports.

C. Brooker, *Serious Mental Health Problems in the Community: Policy,
Practice and Research*, London, Ballière Tindall, 1998.

psychotherapy systematic psychological approaches undertaken by a
therapist to help people suffering from MENTAL HEALTH PROBLEMS,
difficulties in relationships, behavioural problems and other problems
of living.

Psychotherapy may be practised with individuals, with people in
relationships, including families, and with groups, although there is no
agreed conception of what it is. Psychotherapists may be social workers,
counsellors, psychologists, psychiatrists or other social or medical
professionals. The length of training to become a psychotherapist thus
varies enormously. There are also many different theoretical approaches
to psychotherapy, based on different and sometimes competing analyses
of both the nature of human beings and the means by which individual
and relational problems may be solved or ameliorated. For example,
some schools of thought stress the importance of understanding an
individual's past, whereas others place great emphasis on current
circumstances. Some therapists have it that effective work may take many
years, whereas others argue that useful work must of necessity be brief.
Some take a holistic approach, attempting to understand the whole
person, others are content to focus upon a particular aspect of behaviour,

and so on. (See also BEHAVIOURISM, COGNITIVE BEHAVIOURAL THERAPY, GESTALT, PSYCHO-ANALYSIS, TRANSACTIONAL ANALYSIS.)

public inquiry a form of inquisitorial investigation into past events where problems of public concern are evident.

These proceedings are frequently utilized to investigate failures in areas of social care and are often high-profile events involving significant expenditure of public money. The most important cases in recent years have been those involving investigations into areas of child abuse or the death of children while in care or identified as at risk. In these cases social service departments are often identified as having a responsibility for care or protection and as not having adequately executed that responsibility. In the area of care, an example was the inquiry into the operation of care homes in North Wales where significant levels of organized abuse were discovered. The Climbié Inquiry investigated the death of a child while in the care of relatives and revealed failures on the part of social services, the police and other key agencies of the state to protect a child evidently at risk of serious abuse.

These inquiries normally involve a senior member of the judiciary, who takes evidence from a wide range of interested parties, cross-examines the witnesses and then makes significant recommendations on the responsibility of the participants and for improvements in the service. The advice emerging from the inquiries are then provided to the Minister, who decides whether to act on the findings.

punishment SEE PRINCIPLES OF SENTENCING.

pupil referral unit provision made by local education authorities (LEAs) for children who cannot be educated in conventional schools, usually as a result of EXCLUSION FROM SCHOOL.

The nature and availability of the provision varies considerably. Those attending such units should still have the opportunity for a full-time education, but this may include vocational courses and other special programmes.

Qq

Quality Protects a time-limited programme, ending in 2004, of central government that aims to achieve certain objectives for children's services.

Quality Protects lays out eight objectives in relation to CHILDREN IN NEED, including LOOKED-AFTER children, disabled children and children in need of protection. These are to promote:

1 stable ATTACHMENT to CARERS with a greater range of choice of PLACEMENT, including ADOPTION;
2 protection from SIGNIFICANT HARM;
3 maximum life chances for children in need;
4 maximum LIFE CHANCES for children who are looked after, particularly in educational attainment and health;
5 social and economic inclusion of young people LEAVING CARE;
6 meeting the assessed social needs of children with a DISABILITY;
7 effective REFERRAL, ASSESSMENT and service delivery processes;
8 service delivery to ensure best value with responses appropriate to individual need and choice with high levels of participation of children, young people and their families in the planning and delivery of services.

The Quality Protects objectives are broad and relate directly to exclusionary barriers, with the emphasis on refocusing services away from CRISIS INTERVENTION. Local authorities are required to submit management action plans and have subsequent access to special funding for the service objectives.

quango a form of government agency used to provide services or carry out other duties determined by government.

The term, which is North American in origin, is subject to some dispute as to what it means. Originally an acronym for 'quasi-autonomous non-governmental organization', it referred to voluntary and non-profit organizations that had become dependent on grants and funding from government and were thus seen to be linked into government policy implementation, and questions were asked about their independence. In Britain the term more frequently became associated with agencies established by government departments, among the best-known examples being the Commission for Racial Equality and the Equal

Opportunities Commission. For this reason, the term sometimes refers to 'quasi-autonomous *national* governmental organization'.

Questions about the role of quangos were raised in the early 1980s when the Conservative government was committed to the idea of reducing the role of government. An ex-civil servant, Sir Leo Pliatsky, produced a report on the extent to which quangos were being used, with the aim of reducing their role. The main questions about quangos concerned some of the following issues: abuse of patronage by ministers who had the posts in quangos in their gift; questions of accountability in that members of quangos are non-elected appointments; the level of expenditure by quangos; and the use of quangos to depoliticise important issues.

The attack on quangos was not sustained, however, for while a number of these bodies were abolished or amalgamated, new ones were created. This was mainly because governments have found that they are very useful bodies, able to be set up at minimal cost, with appointees often paid a minimal stipend or employed on a voluntary basis. Quangos take the political heat out of a subject by removing issues such as equal opportunities from the main party political arena. They also allow the appoint-ment of experts to consider issues outside the traditional civil service hierarchies. As a result, after a brief period of decline, quangos are now as prominent as ever.

queer/queer theory part of the wider development of gay and lesbian studies within academia, queer theory emerged as an attempt to challenge essentialized and fixed definitions of sexuality by adopting a more inclusive and exploratory understanding of sexual location. Central to the idea of 'queer' is the postmodern notion of identity as fluid and changeable. Queer thinking also allows for the possibility of reinventing identity though GENDER performance. See also FEMININITY, MASCULINITY, POSTMODERNISM.

Rr

'race' a term used to describe groups considered to be biologically distinct. The biological characteristics thought to typify such groups were believed to be constant or unalterable unless 'races' intermingled. The term has effectively been discredited by physical scientists and social scientists.

Most sociologists are no longer prepared to use the term 'race' except in inverted commas, thus demonstrating that they do not accept the biological distinctness of ethnic (the preferred term) groups. 'Race' is clearly a socially constructed concept, which both currently and historically has been used to justify exploitative behaviour on the part of powerful groups. (See RACISM.)

Race Relations Act 1976 the major piece of British legislation that seeks to promote good relationships between ethnic groups and to combat racial DISCRIMINATION. The Act repealed the previous, more restrictive legislation of the 1965 and 1968 Race Relations Acts.

The Act established the COMMISSION FOR RACIAL EQUALITY to oversee its operation, and provided definitions of direct and indirect racial discrimination and of victimization. Direct discrimination is defined as 'treating one person less favourably than another on grounds of colour, race, ethnic or natural origin, in the provision of goods, facilities and services, employment, housing and advertising' (for example, always offering jobs to white candidates where black candidates have comparable qualifications). Indirect discrimination arises where certain requirements or conditions can be met differentially by different groups but where such differences are not justified (for example, a requirement to have particular English-language skills where an ethnic group's first language is not English and it can be demonstrated that these skills are not necessary for a particular job). Victimization occurs when people are treated negatively because they have complained or intend to complain about their treatment under the law.

Evidence concerning the operation of the Act in relation to individual complaints is disappointing. Few formal complaints are actually made (about 800 each year), and of these less than 10 per cent are successful. Levels of compensation are low (on average £5,000 in 2001), and the process is often lengthy. More importantly, tribunals can recommend the reinstatement of a person who has been dismissed but cannot require such reinstatement. In practice, then, complainants may lose their jobs, receive poor compensation after a long and emotionally draining experience and run the risk of being labelled as troublemakers, with the consequent danger of not being re-employed. Most complainants do not win.

The Act empowers the Commission for Racial Equality to investigate alleged discrimination and to order organizations to change their policies and practices if they are found to be illegal. The issuing of non-discrimination notices to organizations has had useful outcomes, particularly in the public sector. In relation to local authorities, the Act (section 71) requires that policies to eliminate racial discrimination and to promote equality of opportunity in all respects be pursued. The evidence in this regard is mixed (see EQUAL OPPORTUNITIES POLICIES, POSITIVE ACTION).

Race Relations (Amendment) Act 2000 an Act that strengthens section 71 of the 1976 Act by extending the protection against racial DISCRIMINATION by public authorities and placing a new, enforceable positive duty on public authorities.

The Act also introduces other important changes. It makes chief officers of police liable for acts of discrimination by officers under their direction or control. It allows complaints of racial discrimination in certain immigration decisions to be heard as part of 'one-stop' immigration appeals. It prohibits discrimination by ministers or government departments in recommending or approving public appointments and in the terms and conditions or termination of such appointments or in conferring honours, including peerages. The Act will apply to any new arrangements for appointing members of the House of Lords. It allows complaints of racial discrimination in education to be brought directly before county or sheriff courts without having to be referred first to the Secretary of State for Education. It also limits the circumstances in which 'safeguarding national security' can be used to justify discrimination.

In practice, it will mean that local authorities will need to ensure that all services are provided fairly and without discrimination, that policies and procedures do not discriminate directly or indirectly and that all their employment practices – recruitment, selection, promotion, access to training, support to staff, etc – are fair. The first priority should centre on ensuring that systems are in place to monitor both the take-up of services by different groups, and the recruitment, selection and development of staff, and to consult with different groups on service provision.

racial equality council or **race equality council** a voluntary organization, previously known as a community relations council, constituted to promote good 'RACE' relations within a particular area.

Race equality councils are registered charities. Financial support for the councils is usually from local authorities and from the COMMISSION FOR RACIAL EQUALITY, with some funding from special projects sponsored by central government departments such as the Home Office and further financial support from local industries and affiliates. Councils have as their principal objectives: first, the implementation of policies designed to promote good community relations, together with the elimination of racial DISCRIMINATION in the private, voluntary and public sectors; second, education and information services for the public; third, support and advice for ethnic communities; and fourth, support for individuals experiencing discrimination.

racially aggravated offence a specific type of crime the seriousness of which is defined by law as being increased because it is racially motivated or because the offender expresses racial hostility towards the VICTIM around the time of the offence.

The CRIME AND DISORDER ACT 1998 clarified the law on racially aggravated offences, allowing courts to sentence more severely when it is established that offences of assault, criminal damage, harassment and public disorder are racially motivated. For these purposes, the aggravation can arise from the offender's expressed hostility towards the victim's racial group (defined by reference to race, colour, nationality, citizenship, ethnic or national origins but not religion).

racism ideas, attitudes, behaviours and policies that discriminate against ethnic groups, nations and other social collectivities, where the discrimination is justified on the basis of a supposed biological superiority of the oppressing group.

Racism may be a matter of personal belief (INDIVIDUAL RACISM) or of official policy, either by design or default (INSTITUTIONAL RACISM). It seems to rest upon a number of basic assertions: first, that there are distinct racial groupings; second, that the differences between racial groupings in terms of culture and behaviour are to be explained by biological characteristics; third, that these biological characteristics can be arranged to demonstrate the relative inferiority of other racial groups in relation to northern white Europeans. The origins of racism appear to be rooted in the colonial experience: colonial powers needed a set of beliefs to justify their economic and cultural exploitation and oppression of many groups throughout the world. Such beliefs embraced a range of ideas, from paternalism to genocide. Racism would seem therefore to be the invention and practice of white Europeans. Conflicts between nations and ethnic groups have been widespread throughout history, often characterized by mutual prejudice between groups. It is the biological basis of racism that distinguishes it from mere prejudice. The attempts to establish distinct racial groups with distinct cultures scientifically have now been discredited, although racist ideas are still very much alive in Europe and in other societies with substantial

European origins. Because the ideas are discredited, many writers now refuse to use the word 'RACE' (preferring 'ethnic group' or 'origin' – such as in the expression 'a child from mixed origins') or they use the term with inverted commas: 'race' rather than race.

Some writers have argued that racism can apply only to black (that is, 'non-white') people, whereas others would include anti-Semitism and attitudes to particular ethnic groups, such as Irish people. Clearly, the treatment of Jewish people by the Nazis was influenced by a set of beliefs that included the view that Jews were somehow less than human. On a lesser scale, the 'Irish' joke, which depicts Irish people as stupid, also appears to be inspired by an attitude that implies that Irish people are somehow genetically less intelligent than the 'white Anglo-Saxons'. If racism is rooted in notions of biological inferiority, then anti-Semitism and anti-Irish attitudes must be seen as racist. Yet black people's visibility as other than white precipitates an immediate and everyday racism that seems to be different from anti-Semitism and anti-Irish attitudes, although they have a common root.

In the context of social welfare services, racism can take many forms, involving personal or institutional racism or both. Racism can occur, for example, when responsibility for tackling racism is placed on black workers alone. Tackling racism should clearly be the responsibility of all workers, especially white workers, who, after all, live in and, in a general sense, espouse white culture, which spawned racism. Racism can occur when the legitimacy of others' cultural needs is ignored or when the racism of clients is overlooked and not challenged. Another common form of racism is to assert that all clients receive equal treatment without recognizing that a service should take into account the effects of racism and the very uneven starting points that racism creates for different groups within racist societies. (See also ANTIDISCRIMINATORY PRACTICE, ANTI-RACISM, ETHNICALLY SENSITIVE PRACTICE.)

J. Rex. *Race and Ethnicity*, Buckingham, Open University Press, 1986.

radical social work an attempt to achieve a major rethink of social welfare and of social work theory and practice – either by emphasizing the degree to which personal problems are shaped by such oppressive forces as class division and racial DISCRIMINATION or by emphasizing the role of the MARKET in social welfare provision.

Britain has witnessed two loose movements regarded as radical in the field of social work over the past two decades or more. The first, springing from an unorganized socialist movement in the 1970s, held that the welfare state offered an important mechanism for sustaining and improving the conditions of poor and vulnerable people. This movement was united in the belief that social problems are socially constructed and in the main to be explained by structural inequality, notably social class. By contrast, earlier methods employed by social workers implied a view of problems as rooted in personal inadequacy or pathology, or perhaps in family dysfunction, rather than in poverty or differential life chances. Major ingredients of this movement were 'consciousness raising' (explaining to users the structural origins of their problems), user involvement in the decision-making process, and COMMUNITY WORK and GROUPWORK as legitimate methods to neutralize the dangers of CASEWORK, which tended to lay the blame for problems on individual weaknesses. It also placed greater emphasis on legal rights (including the right to free welfare services) and the creation of progressive political alliances of community and residents' groups, user groups, trade unions, pressure groups and political parties. This movement has been criticized for its omissions in relation to race and gender stratification, in particular, and for its lack of awareness of the problems of other oppressed groups, including people with disabilities, old people and gay men and lesbians.

The second movement, rooted in the NEW RIGHT of the 1980s, has sought to be radical in an anti-welfarist stance. The New Right is committed to the market, individual enterprise and initiative, and to a view that public spending should be curtailed. The New Right has attacked welfare provision because it interferes with the free working of market forces. It sees families as the principal source of moral responsibility and therefore of welfare, except where the market has encouraged the growth of welfare within a vigorous private sector. Although the notion of a welfare safety net has not been entirely eroded, it has been much reduced.

M. Langan and P. Lee, *Radical Social Work Today*, London, Unwin Hyman, 1989.

rationing controlling the allocation of services and other resources to ensure they are used as effectively as possible.

Both social services and the NATIONAL HEALTH SERVICE ration the resources that they have at their disposal, with the intention of producing the maximum effect. Whether they succeed or not, and whether the methods devised for controlling the allocation of resources are fair, are the subject of intense debate. For example, should resources be used to benefit the greatest number of people, or those, far fewer in number, who need them most?

There is general agreement that rationing has been taking place for a long time but has not been recognized as such. For example, in the National Health Service waiting lists for particular types of operation are a way of controlling the use of such medical resources as hospital beds and surgeons' time. The existence of waiting lists, therefore, is a way of rationing. Following changes in the health service and the government's pledge to guarantee speedier treatment for all patients, managers have had to devise more formal ways of rationing medical resources. To this end, they have ranked illnesses according to their severity and have stated rules as to who is and who is not eligible for treatment. Some of these have stirred considerable controversy, such as when a patient who smokes heavily is denied a heart bypass operation on the grounds that the treatment would be wasted until he or she stops smoking.

Social service agencies also have had to develop priorities as to people they regard as in the greatest NEED. As an example, highest priority is given to children who are in need of some protective action on the part of the local authority whereas far lower priority is accorded to families whose children may be in need but are not in any immediate danger. This is a form of rationing that determines that a small number of children and their families receive intensive resources in social work time, family placements and other support services, while the much larger number of children in need and their families receive little or nothing in support services.

RDA abbreviation for REGIONAL DEVELOPMENT AGENCY.

reactive depression feelings of hopelessness, sadness, tearfulness and ANXIETY that arise in response to particular circumstances, such as the death of a close family member. Such symptoms may be milder than in clinical or endogenous DEPRESSION.

A person experiencing reactive depression may recover spontaneously within a year of the trigger event, although the condition may become long-term if there are chronic problems such as financial pressures or housing difficulties. Studies of women who were depressed following specific events in their lives have shown that lack of a confidant, loss of a mother before the age of 11, lack of paid employment and caring for young children are all factors associated with prolonging such depression. The person with reactive depression may, in many cases, be receiving help, usually medication, and the social worker may therefore need to liaise with the general practitioner to judge the effects of the medication. A small number of sufferers may have been referred to psychiatric services. The worker may offer grief COUNSELLING as one way of helping the person to find an alternative response to the loss he or she has suffered.

reality orientation a therapeutic approach to maintaining memory and thinking in older people who are experiencing impairment of mental functioning.

Reality orientation uses spoken and written reminders of past and current events to enable people to maintain contact with daily life. It has developed into a philosophy of care rather than simply a set of facilitating strategies.

reasonable parent test the minimum standard of care that can reasonably be expected of parents of a particular child.

To obtain a CARE ORDER on a child, a local authority must demonstrate to the court that the SIGNIFICANT HARM the child has suffered, or is likely to suffer, is attributable to the care given to the child by the parents. It has also to be shown that the care is not up to the standard of what it would be reasonable to expect a parent to provide for that child – the reasonable parent test. In other words, if that standard were all that could be reasonably expected of hypothetical parents, the grounds for a care order would not exist.

reassessment the process of looking anew at a case in the light of developments, new information or a new emphasis to be given to old information.

Some social work ASSESSMENTS are uncomplicated, with needs identified in a straightforward way without differences of view between worker and service user. In many cases, neither worker nor service user can be clear about the nature of the problems or about the best plan of INTERVENTION. In these circumstances, short-term plans may be necessary that may solve the difficulties but may not. Any competent social welfare worker will be prepared to reassess his or her work and, in the same vein, to view past work as unsuccessful. In a sense, the best work involves constant reassessment and a willingness to see old problems in a new light. The social work process usually entails an invitation to formally evaluate work in progress at regular intervals, and this kind of reassessment is often called a CASE REVIEW.

recidivism an alternative term to 'persistent offending'. A recidivist is a person who repeatedly commits (usually relatively minor) offences and is likely to be punished disproportionately severely as a result of accumulating a lengthy list of previous criminal convictions.

A very high proportion of people in PRISON are recidivists, and this contributes greatly to prison overcrowding. In an effort to reduce the prison population and adopt a JUST DESERTS approach to sentencing, the CRIMINAL JUSTICE ACT 1991 restricted the powers of courts to take previous convictions into consideration when passing sentence. As a result of vociferous opposition, however, this particular aspect of the Act was amended in 1993 to enable courts to return to their previous practice of utilizing a TARIFF approach to sentencing, taking account of both the seriousness of the offence and the previous criminal record.

recording the process by which a social welfare agency maintains an account of its dealings with a service user. Such a record may be kept in written files or, increasingly, on computers.

The selection and recording of relevant information about service users and their families are a central task for social welfare agencies and especially for social work agencies. Recording may be understood as an expression of accountability for practitioners to their agency, but it is also, crucially, a means by which there can be accountability to the service user and, beyond, to the general public and the profession. Recording can also constitute evidence in a court of law. It is generally agreed that the overriding principle for ethical and effective recording is the service user's best interests. Good practice to the service user requires clear and purposeful recording. Competent recording facilitates an accurate account of what has actually happened and an understanding of why it has happened. This process will enhance an evaluation or a review of progress in the work. It will also help colleagues if they have to take the work on, in the absence of the responsible worker. Additionally, recording is often used by social work agencies to gather critical information about their own activities for research or monitoring purposes.

There are many interesting practice issues and dilemmas in relation to recording. Access to personal files on the part of the service user, a principle established in law with the Access to Personal Files Act 1987, can in many instances be problematic. Should, for example, a family case file be open to scrutiny by all members of that family? It may be agreed as a basic right of civil liberties that service users should see their own records, but workers may need at times to protect other people's privacy and safety and their sources of information. Similarly, the business of writing an account of an individual's or family's problems that is truthful, faces up to the considerable difficulties that some service users have but does not damage or label people in discouraging ways and may be shared with all the relevant people is patently very difficult. A related matter, which can assist in this process, is writing the record with the service user; some regard this as a major change in orientation in dealings with service users. To inform people that they may see their record if they wish is a relatively passive commitment to greater access, but to take the record to them, to invite their scrutiny and to record with them is clearly going significantly further.

Fashions have changed in relation to the fullness or brevity with which records are kept. In some critical and sensitive work, great detail helps to reveal hidden patterns; in other work areas, a detailed account of daily events is unnecessary. The depth of recording and analysis depends upon the objectives of the work. In all circumstances, however, it is important to distinguish facts from opinions, and where an opinion is ventured, the supporting evidence should always be listed to reveal the worker's thinking and analysis.

British Association of Social Workers, *Ethical and Effective Recording*, London, BASW, 1984.

recovery order a court order under section 50 of the CHILDREN ACT that compels any person who is in a position to do so to return a child who has been unlawfully removed from the care of a local authority.

A recovery order also applies to a child under an EMERGENCY PROTECTION ORDER or in POLICE PROTECTION. It authorizes a constable to enter and search premises, using reasonable force if necessary. The order is designed to stamp out the harbouring of children and young people who have absconded from the care of the local authority.

reduced earnings allowance SEE WELFARE RIGHTS 3.

re-entry order an order issued by a court ordering a person to be admitted to accommodation in which they are entitled to live.

This order is invariably issued in cases where DOMESTIC VIOLENCE has occurred and one person has been excluded as a result of an incident (see also INJUNCTION, OUSTER ORDER).

referral the process by which a social welfare agency is formally notified that a potential CLIENT or user may require access to its services.

A referral can be made by the person requesting the service or by some third party, typically members of the person's family, friends or neighbours, or by a professional within the social welfare or socio-legal systems. Some organizations label the initial contact with a user, or a person referring the would-be user, as an 'inquiry'. If the social service agency considers the inquiry suitable and that a service can be offered, then a referral is accepted. Whether a referral is accepted and becomes a live case or not can be unpredictable. Clarity of referral information, the outcome of the initial ASSESSMENT, the power and influence of the referrer, and the coherence of agencies' policies in service delivery are all major determinants as to whether a person who is the subject of a referral becomes a client.

referral order an order made by a YOUTH COURT in England and Wales, placing a young person under the jurisdiction of a referral order panel for up to 12 months.

Courts are required, under the YOUTH JUSTICE AND CRIMINAL EVIDENCE ACT 1999, to make such orders in the cases of all young people appearing before a youth court for the first time and pleading guilty (except when the offence merits an absolute discharge or is so serious that only a custodial sentence can be justified). The Referral Order Panel, made up of a member of the local YOUTH OFFENDING TEAM and lay members, devises an intervention plan with which the young person is required to comply. Its implementation is monitored by the Panel. It may include REPARATION, educational accommodation or other provisions. An order counts as a criminal conviction, but the young person appears before a court again only if breached for non-compliance (defined by NATIONAL STANDARDS).

reflective practice the ability to stand back and look critically at one's own practice.

In social work education there is an increasing emphasis being placed upon reflective practice both during basic training and also as part of a continuing professional development. The main themes include:

1 an awareness of the impact that the individual worker will have upon the service user in terms of race, gender, age, disability and class;
2 an awareness of the importance of antidiscriminatory and anti-oppressive practice and how an individual service user has been affected by an oppressive society or community;
3 an awareness of the worker's own prejudices and the impact that these will have upon practice issues;
4 the ability to apply relevant knowledge to practice.

Reflective practice is a skill in its own right and owes a lot to the seminal work of Schon but is now included in all major social work textbook discussions.

N. Thompson, *Understanding Social Work – preparing for practice*, London, Palgrave, 2000.

reframe to develop a different viewpoint or opinion regarding the same set of circumstances or events.

Reframing is used in FAMILY THERAPY, in which family members are helped to understand the actions, attitudes or behaviour of another family member in a more positive light. The term is also used widely in social work, in relation to practitioners and users alike, to mean to come to a new understanding about a person's behaviour or to reformulate a problem in a new way.

refuge a place of safety for women and children who have experienced violence from men within the home.

Refuges provide safe accommodation on a temporary basis for women and children made homeless by leaving violent homes. Refuge is also the name of the national organization that provides a network or refuges (formerly the Women's Aid Federation). There are specialist refuges for ethnic minority women, and many refuges provide additional services such as welfare rights advice, aftercare, groupwork with children and telephone help-lines. Most do not admit boys above a certain age and obtain maintenance and other services wherever possible from female workers. This is designed to create a safe environment for women and children who have been assaulted by men.

refugees see ASYLUM SEEKERS AND REFUGEES.

regeneration the economic and social revitalization of a disadvantaged area.

Regeneration conventionally has two sides. One is economic, which aims to rebuild the local economy of a particular area through tax incentives, encouraging small business and corporate investment and improving the physical environment, whether through better transport or leisure facilities. The other is social – revitalizing the social fabric or SOCIAL CAPITAL of an impoverished area as the key to improved levels of wellbeing for local residents. In the main, regeneration of either kind is associated with inner city areas and low-income social housing estates that have suffered a cycle of disadvantage over a number of years. But regeneration efforts can also be found in rural areas, such as the former coalfields where the abrupt loss of work following the mass closure of the mines produced similar levels of area-wide disadvantage.

What has become clear from the massive research effort throughout the 1990s in the USA, UK and Europe is that an effective regeneration programme will work if it tackles all the different dimensions of poverty and disadvantage at the same time. Selecting just one element – for example, economic development or physical rehabilitation of old buildings or providing better social services – will not have sufficient impact on the lives of local residents. The problems of disadvantage and SOCIAL EXCLUSION interlock. Unsafe streets, the abandonment of public places to gangs or drug dealers, poor schools, high unemployment, dilapidated housing, high levels of ANTISOCIAL BEHAVIOUR, the withdrawal of local commerce all reinforce each other. Any attempt at rebuilding such an area must have a broad enough scope and sufficient intensity to deal with a number of these problems at the same time. By concentrating and targeting scarce resources on an entire area rather than individuals has been shown to be effective. That government is now more aware of this is evident in the various regeneration programmes launched since 1997. (See NEIGHBOURHOOD RENEWAL; NEW DEAL FOR COMMUNITIES.)

PARTICIPATION by local residents has also become a major theme of all regeneration efforts. But this is easier said than done. The complexity of programmes and the demands on residents' time are enormous. Residents' participation brings with it enormous responsibilities that would test the most powerful agencies of central government. Critics say central government has in effect delegated to local actors without providing commensurate powers and resources.

J. Pierson and J. Smith (eds), *Rebuilding Community: The Policy and Practice of Urban Regeneration*, Palgrave, 2001.

Regional Development Agency (RDA) any of several bodies, established by the 1998 Regional Development Agencies Act, aimed at improving the economic position of the regions.

In particular, Regional Development Agencies are organized to help improve the competitiveness of local and regional businesses. They also have a social remit, however, in that their role is to target 'social and economic imbalances' through training programmes and efforts to reduce barriers to employment. As such, they have a role in trying to overcome aspects of SOCIAL EXCLUSION through urban and rural REGENERATION projects. Significant levels of funding are available for pump-priming development initiatives, and the RDAs are based on the successes apparent in the work of the Welsh Development Agency in creating employment and urban regeneration, particularly in South Wales.

Regional Director of Health and Social Care an official appointed to ensure the coordination of health and social care planners and providers at the regional level.

Regional directors are responsible for overseeing the developing relationship between the National Health Service and Social Services in the area of Social Care. As such, they will oversee agreements between these bodies on the development and attainment of TARGETS established within the Local Authority Local Public Service Agreement. As part of this, their staff have a role in areas of performance assessment, financial planning and monitoring. They have a key role in ensuring that health and social care are integrated, which has been a long-term ambition of many previous governments but has been an area of limited success. They also have the role of ensuring that health and social care issues are taken into full account within the work of the GOVERNMENT OFFICES OF THE REGIONS.

Registered Homes Act 1984 legislation providing for the registration, conduct and inspection of RESIDENTIAL CARE homes for adults.

The Act specifies how residential homes offering care to more than four adults are to be registered and inspected. These include homes for those who, because of old age, disability, mental disorder or drug dependency, need residential care. The Act requires all such homes to be registered with the local authority, which vets each application according to a set of standards governing physical accommodation, financial viability and, most importantly, standards of care; the last are scrutinized carefully and in detail (see NURSING HOME). The local authority is able to set conditions of operation for particular homes and can cancel registration if the standards or conditions are not met. The Act also covers nursing homes, which offer health care within a residential setting, allowing them to be dual registered and thus to provide elements of residential care at the same time.

regression see PSYCHOANALYSIS.

rehabilitation a process of restoration or recovery from an illness, accident or from some adverse circumstance or event.

The term was used widely in health settings in the latter part of the 20th century but now has much wider application in social work practice and in work in the criminal justice system. In health settings, rehabilitation has described attempts by doctors and other health professionals, such as physiotherapists and occupational therapists (see OCCUPATIONAL THERAPY) to help people recover physically, emotionally and socially from physical illness, mental illness and trauma. The term also accurately describes both social and health professionals' attempts to assist alcoholics and substance misusers (see ALCOHOLISM and SUBSTANCE MISUSE). Similarly, since the REHABILITATION OF OFFENDERS ACT 1974 became law, the concept of rehabilitation has been applied to offenders and especially those who have received custodial sentences.

In all these cases, if a holistic approach is taken with recovery from illness, accident, addiction or past offending behaviour, it is clear that interventions often need to be multi-disciplinary. Although medical assistance has an important place in many rehabilitation programmes, there is increasing recognition of the importance of social and practical support in relation to personal and social skills, relationships, employment (where appropriate), housing and income. The other key issue regarding rehabilitation is that any planned programme should be realistic, given the problems/conditions of the service user and their circumstances. Such programmes should take into account the person's motivation, personal skills and morale in order to enable him or her to feel that objectives and targets can be met.

Rehabilitation of Offenders Act 1974 an Act the underlying principle of which is that people with criminal convictions, especially if they are minor, should eventually be able to put the past behind them. The legislation assists in this process by making some offences 'spent' after a 'rehabilitation period' if the person concerned does not re-offend during that time.

After an offence legally becomes 'spent', the ex-offender no longer has to declare it (for example, when applying for a job or obtaining insurance) except in certain specified circumstances (as when applying for jobs that involve working with children or other vulnerable people). More serious convictions, such as those leading to longer periods of imprisonment, are not covered by the Act (which is under review). Rehabilitation periods for young offenders under 17 on conviction are shorter than those for adults. The National Association for the Care and Resettlement of Offenders provides information leaflets on the detailed implications of the law for individuals and employers, and the Home Office publishes a simple explanatory leaflet entitled *Wiping the Slate Clean*.

reintegrative shaming the process of respectfully encouraging offenders to express and come to terms with their shame about their behaviour, usually in a public or semi-public setting, followed by gestures or ceremonies which demonstrate that the offender's apology or remorse has been accepted and a form of rehabilitation thereby achieved.

The Australian criminologist John Braithwaite has articulated the theory of reintegrative shaming in a number of publications over the past two decades, but it has been practised in a range of cultures for centuries. It often involves a formal or ritualized process of discussion between offenders, victims and community representatives, aimed at achieving consensus about the harm done and the way forward. Shaming offenders is believed by many observers to be harmful if it is not accompanied by some symbolic process of reintegration into the offended community: it can reinforce offenders' deviant identities if mishandled. Braithwaite argues that effective crime control requires reintegrative shaming and that societies that employ it systematically can avoid creating a stigmatized group of disaffected people committed to deviant identities. Offenders who are made ashamed of their wrongdoing need to be allowed to regain the respect of the community immediately afterwards, and reintegrative shaming rituals make this possible.

Reintegrative shaming is the underlying theory behind much of the practice of FAMILY GROUP CONFERENCES with offenders, although these were developed in New Zealand and Canada prior to the publication of Braithwaite's account of the theory. Reintegrative shaming involves mobilizing community participation in criminal justice and giving a formal voice to the VICTIMS of crime. At the same time, offenders are treated with respect and their views are heard. This is achieved by involving people who are part of the community of care of both the victim and the offender in the process of resolving the offence.

Mechanisms for implementing reintegrative shaming include circles of care and accountability, family group conferences, victim-offender mediation and circle sentencing. See also RESTORATIVE JUSTICE.

G. Johnstone, *Restorative justice: Ideas value, debates,* Cullompton (Devon), Willan, 2002.

relapse in the case of people addicted to various drugs, a reversion back to the habit after a period of being drug-free.

Relapse is common with any habit, and in any work with drugs users the possibility needs to be discussed so that techniques can be developed to deal with it if and when it occurs (see ADDICTION).

religion in social work see SPIRITUALITY.

remand the process whereby CRIMINAL COURT proceedings are adjourned after an initial appearance by the defendant so that prosecution and defence cases can be properly prepared and any necessary reports obtained (including PRE-SENTENCE and medical reports).

Remands can either be on BAIL in the community, in a PROBATION HOSTEL or in PRISON. Bail is granted if the court has evidence that the defendant has a secure address, if the magistrates believe that the person can be trusted to appear in court again on the date decided and not to interfere with prosecution enquiries or commit further offences. It is an offence to commit further offences while on bail. In some courts the PROBATION SERVICE or YOUTH OFFENDING TEAMS run bail information or remand management schemes to assist defendants in obtaining bail. A bail information scheme collects verified, factual information about defendants to assist courts in making decisions about whether to grant bail, and research shows that this can prevent large numbers of unnecessary custodial remands. Remand management goes further, supplementing bail information with bail support for individuals and inter-agency negotiations to prevent unnecessary remands. Bail support involves regular supervision of (usually young) defendants and help to ensure that they meet bail conditions and attend further court appearances.

Adults who have committed very serious offences or who do not meet the conditions for bail to be granted outlined above may be sent to prison. However, the Probation Service provides hostels as an alternative. Young offenders are meant to be remanded to custodial institutions only as a last resort, and although large numbers are still sent to prison, there is a range of alternative placements available to youth offending teams through the YOUTH JUSTICE BOARD (see also SECURE ESTATE).

reminiscence therapy the process of recalling the past, a technique of memory-revival usually used with OLDER PEOPLE who have experienced memory loss.

Reminiscence work with older people has developed in the past ten years and is an important strategy for aiding them, particularly in GROUPWORK settings such as residential or day care. Reminiscence work is a form of oral history-sharing that involves older people with their peer group and with CARERS. It is easy to instigate, yet the outcomes are a rewarding and enriching experience. For example, all members of a small group of older people may be asked to bring a small object to the group that has significance for them and then to tell the group the story of that object, such as a brooch or an ornament. This in turn stimulates memories in other group participants, and a rewarding diversity of conversation topics is stimulated that may have immediate relevance to group participants. Reminiscence work thus creates 'communities' of memories that maintain and re-establish a person's place and role within the COMMUNITY.

Shared memories renew a sense of rootedness and connectedness to others that helps to anchor the person with memory difficulties in a social setting. Conventional or pre-existing relationships may change for a little while as the older person shares, with his or her carer, times from the past, giving the older person control over conversation topics. It has been shown that reminiscence group participants arrive early for sessions, greet others with enthusiasm and anticipate the events with pleasure – often wearing their best clothes and jewellery for the sessions, indicating that the group has the status of an event in the older person's life. For some people, however, reminiscence is painful, and the unavoidable recall of loss that accompanies later life may mean that sessions can be distressing for all concerned. Workers need to be genuine and skilled in supporting older people through sad memories. Involvement in reminiscence groups has been seen to help residents new to group living and to aid their transition from home and their integration into group life. It has been suggested that groups become 'safe places for sharing both joyful and sad recollections', giving participants an enhanced sense of the value and significance of their past lives and enriching their relationships with contemporaries and workers.

F. Gibson, 'Reminiscence groupwork with older people', in *Groupwork*, Volume 5, No. 3, 1992.

rent allowance, rent rebate, rent restriction see WELFARE RIGHTS 6.

reparation order a court order requiring a young person in England and Wales to make recompense to the victim of the crime or to the community in general.

Reparation – at its best – is a form of RESTORATIVE JUSTICE. It provides an opportunity for young offenders to make actual or symbolic recompense for the damage done by the offence. The reparation order is part of the CRIME AND DISORDER ACT 1998, and it requires a young offender to carry out up to 24 hours of activities, usually supervised by a member of a YOUTH OFFENDING TEAM. The work can either be for the direct benefit of an individual victim, for the community in general, or it can include activities aimed at changing the young person's attitude (such as writing a letter of apology). Direct reparation to individual victims requires the victim's (but not the offender's) consent. There is a presumption in favour of making reparation orders in cases where they are available, and courts are required to give reasons when they decide not to do so. In many other countries, reparation is voluntary on the part of both victim and offender, as it is believed that it is more effective if unforced.

reporting officer a person with a social work qualification who reports independently to a court in prospective ADOPTION cases regarding certain matters, including whether the natural parents' consent to the adoption has been fully and freely given.

The reporting officer is usually a CHILDREN'S GUARDIAN administered by the local authority or another welfare agency in each area. Panel members are independent of all other services and free to comment on cases on the basis of their professional judgement alone.

reprimand an alternative to court proceedings in relation to offences admitted by young people, introduced by the CRIME AND DISORDER ACT 1998 in England and Wales.

A reprimand is given for a first offence that is relatively minor. Reprimands may be cited in court in the same way as previous convictions. They can be given only in cases where the young person admits the offence. A reprimand is essentially a warning.

research social research is the conduct of systematic study in order to describe social behaviour or to test theories about social behaviour.

Much of the knowledge on which social workers draw in the context in which they work is the product of social research. This includes both *primary* research, in which researchers have generated new data, and *secondary* research, in which existing data is re-used for new purposes. The latter constitutes an important source of information, with researchers extracting relevant data about the health, living conditions and working lives of the population from government surveys such as the Census, the General House-hold Survey, the Labour Force Survey and the Family Expenditure Survey.

Research into social work itself, however, has until recently been more limited. There has been disagreement between those who claim that social work and its outcomes are too complex to measure and others who argue for a more scientific approach to research and for EVALUATION. This focus on evaluation and effectiveness is reflected in the work of the Social Work Research Unit at the University of Stirling among others, and is consistent with present policy, which emphasizes the importance of research in informing professionals about 'what works' in social work and social care. The integration of research-based evidence of effectiveness into practice is often referred to as *evidence-based practice* and was originally introduced in the NATIONAL HEALTH SERVICE to identify the most effective clinical practice. In social work and social care, there can be a range of different types of evidence about the effectiveness of practice and the views, feelings, behaviour and circumstances of service users. The type of evidence that is collected, and the way that social work researchers design their research studies, will depend on the nature of the research problem and also practical, theoretical and ethical issues. Social workers should be able to understand how existing research findings have been generated, to identify any weaknesses in research and to accurately identify key research findings and their implications for policy and practice. The Department of Health has therefore indicated that, in future, research methodology will be a component of qualifying degree courses.

The reasons for undertaking research can differ considerably, and research studies can be of different types. *Exploratory* research is used in order to gain an initial understanding of an issue or setting that has been little researched in the past. It is often used to identify topics that could be included in subsequent studies and can overlap with *descriptive* research, which aims to provide a picture of patterns of behaviour or the characteristics of a group of people. If researchers need to go beyond this, they may conduct an *explanatory* study that seeks to find the reasons or causes for behaviour or differences between groups. The types of explanation may vary from the discovery of the motives and frames of reference of participants to the testing of a hypothesis about associations or causal relationships between two or more variables, as in overtly *scientific* approaches to research. In *evaluative* research, which assesses a particular intervention or practice, one or more of the above approaches can be adopted depending on the type of evidence which is sought (see EVALUATION).

Whatever the purposes of the research, it is always necessary to clearly identify the research problem or question that it attempts to address. This is usually defined in relation to both empirical and theoretical issues. For example, a study about the needs of children might be framed by drawing on a theoretical approach such as ATTACHMENT theory. Researchers must also choose the settings in which to carry out their research; the choice of particular settings will, of course, have an impact on the results. For example, in research on homelessness, the number of young women affected has often been underestimated because of the practice of researching in the street or in hostels rather than in homes where they are staying temporarily.

Having framed the research problem and decided on settings, the researcher has to identify an appropriate methodology. Research strategies include *surveys*, in which standardized methods are used to collect data about a sample of respondents and comparisons drawn; *case studies*, in which a variety of methods are used to collect data about a single setting; *comparative case studies*, in which two or more settings are compared; and *longitudinal designs*, which allow for repeated data collection from the same group so as to chart change over time. An example of this is the New Child Development Survey, in which data is collected about children born in one week in 1958 at regular intervals.

Longitudinal designs can be useful for investigating the effect of interventions, although they are not as rigorous as *experimental designs* in this respect. Experiments consist of collecting relevant data from two similar groups before one of the groups receives a new service or treatment in which the researcher is interested. The two groups can then be compared after having a different type of service. However, it is often unethical to withhold a potentially effective or supportive service from one group, and it is therefore more common to use *quasi experimental designs* in which naturally occurring groups are compared. For example, services to older people may be about to change in one local authority area but not in another, which allows for before and after comparison of the two groups.

Once the strategy has been determined, a data collection method must be selected. Among the methods a researcher might choose are: in-depth interviewing; interviewing using questionnaires; participant observation; structured observation; secondary analysis of official statistics or documentary analysis. In-depth interviews can be used to collect the 'narrative' of the person being interviewed (with only a minimal list of topics for guidance), while a highly structured questionnaire can be used for either an interview or a postal survey. Observation methods can range from participation (in which the researcher takes part in the activities of the setting) through to structured observation of others using a structured checklist.

In the past, many researchers had a clear preference for either *qualitative* research methods, which generate data in the form of words describing the experience and perspectives of participants, or *quantitative* methods, which generate data in the form of numbers, allowing statistical comparisons between groups to be made. Quantitative methods have been traditionally associated with 'top-down' approaches in which the theoretical orientation, design and interpretation of research were determined by the researcher. The perspectives of research participants were more likely to permeate the design of qualitative studies. It is now increasingly recognized, however, that these methods can complement each other so as to provide a fuller understanding of social phenomena, and that both qualitative and quantitative research can reflect the perspectives of participants. Many studies therefore use a combination of qualitative and quantitative methods. There remains an ongoing debate, however, about whether researchers should 'take sides' when designing research and interpreting their findings, particularly where these might be used to promote the interests of oppressed groups. The advocates of *emancipatory research* have argued that research claiming to be objective has often been based on the erroneous assumptions of powerful groups rather than being truly objective, whereas others argue against the erosion of the scientific standards that they feel protect the credibility of social research. Recent policy has emphasized sharing the control of research with research participants and taking account of their perspectives rather than relying solely on existing academic and professional frameworks to inform the design of research. However, there should still be transparency in the way that research is conducted and findings interpreted, as it is this that distinguishes social research from less systematic forms of investigation. In quantitative research, this is often achieved through standardized procedures that are replicable, whereas detailed 'reflexive accounts' of the research process can be used in qualitative research.

Social Work Research Centre, University of Stirling, *Is Social Work Effective? Research Findings from the Social Work Research Centre, University of Stirling*, Stirling, Scottish Office, Economic and Social Research Council and University of Stirling. 1994.

resettlement or **throughcare** the arrangements made to assist and supervise a prisoner on returning to the community after leaving the institution.

'Resettlement' has recently replaced 'throughcare', which in turn replaced 'aftercare'. Aftercare was thought to be inappropriate because, all too often, it reflected the fact that resettlement was an afterthought. Many prisoners received no PROBATION contact after their release from prison or even during their sentences. 'Throughcare' is probably too redolent of social work to be acceptable to today's politicians: 'resettlement' involves surveillance as well as help, although this was always the case.

The resettlement process is now governed by NATIONAL STANDARDS, and improved arrangements are in place for liaison between the prison and probation services. A small number of prisons have been renamed as resettlement prisons with a view to improving the resettlement of lifers and other long-term prisoners. Prison and field probation officers have increasingly been required to take part in sentence planning and in the process of making decisions about EARLY RELEASE, and probation officers have considerably more involvement in post-release supervision than in the past because of changes in the early release arrangements. Nevertheless, financial constraints continue to make it difficult for field probation officers to maintain regular contact with prisoners serving their sentences a long way from home. Without such contact, it is more difficult to establish effective resettlement plans.

residence order a court order under section 8 of the CHILDREN ACT that specifies with whom the child is to live. It is used primarily in matrimonial disputes, replacing the concept of custody.

The aim of the residence order is to reduce tension between divorcing parents, because neither party any longer 'wins custody'; the issue is now merely one of the court's deciding where the child or children should live. Whatever the court's decision, both parents retain PARENTAL RESPONSIBILITY and are expected to continue to take part in decisions regarding the child. It is possible for the court to grant a residence order to each parent, with the child living alternate weeks with each. The residence order can also be used in other FAMILY PROCEEDINGS and can be applied for by people who are not parents and who do not hold parental responsibility for the child. For example, a grandparent may apply for a residence order on a grandchild in care proceedings as an alternative to the local authority's application for a CARE ORDER or SUPERVISION ORDER. Or he or she may apply for a residence order some time after a care order was made at a previous hearing; if the application is successful, the care order is automatically discharged. As another example of the order's flexibility, FOSTER CARERS may apply for a residence order on a child who has been living with them for more than three years.

Whenever an applicant is granted a residence order, it automatically gives parental responsibility for the child to the person who has applied, if he or she does not have it already. It thus provides a means by which grandparents or other members of the child's extended family, and indeed foster carers, become included in decisions regarding the child. Children may also apply for a residence order on their own behalf and have done so when they want to live with a person other than their parents. There are no specific grounds for the residence order other than the WELFARE CHECKLIST in the Children Act and the consideration that making the order should be better for the child than not making it. The local authority cannot apply but can support others such as foster carers to do so.

residential care care services provided for people living in residential homes.

Residential care embraces a number of services, some formal, some informal, that are provided for people who have left their own homes and moved to particular establishments in order to receive those services. Some of these services are basic requirements for survival, such as regular bathing to ensure physical cleanliness, meals and help with getting dressed. Other services help people to overcome isolation by providing contacts with members of staff or other residents or by facilitating continued contact with family and relations. Still other services may address specific emotional needs such as counselling or group therapy. What distinguishes residential services from DOMICILIARY care (services provided in a person's own home) and COMMUNITY CARE (services provided in the community) is that in order to receive them a person moves into a specially organized residential establishment in which he or she lives for a period of time, perhaps permanently. These establishments vary greatly in size, from large homes for OLDER PEOPLE of perhaps 30 or more residents to small CHILDREN'S HOMES of perhaps only a half a dozen. There are also homes for people who have previously lived in an institution such as a psychiatric hospital and who are getting used to living outside that institution but are not yet ready to fend for themselves, and small GROUP HOMES for adults with LEARNING DISABILITY who cooperate in preparing meals and purchasing food and other household items, and who learn to plan their own recreation and vocational training. The kind of care that each establishment has to offer depends on the needs of the residents who live there.

Many commentators have observed that certain features of residential care have a great impact on the people who live in residential establishments. People with the same difficulties living together are highly visible, and this tends to set them apart in the eyes of the community in which they live. The way in which care services are provided and the attitudes of staff working in the home have also been shown to deprive people of choice. Many residential regimes have allowed little flexibility in how residents arrange their rooms with personal effects, for example, discouraging residents from bringing with them mementos from their family homes. They have also discouraged independence, such as by not allowing residents to cook for themselves. The care in such establishments was in the past marked by rigid bedtimes and meal times, creating an atmosphere that seemed in the interests more of the staff than of the residents themselves. But with increased emphasis on choice and on CLIENTS' rights and initiatives now reflected in many aspects of residential care, practice has recently been looked upon more positively. For example, parents of children who are being LOOKED AFTER by the local authority often feel more encouraged to keep in touch with their child when that child is in a children's home than if placed with foster parents. Older people, particularly frail people with several serious physical limitations, may feel more secure than when in their own homes, and in an atmosphere of greater individuality they are now more likely to be able to personalize their rooms in ways that would not have been possible even ten years ago. The positive evidence concerning the way the best residential care is valued by residents and their relatives was extensively reported in the WAGNER REPORT.

residential rehabilitation REHABILITATION in places of residence where people experiencing problems with alcohol and drugs can stay for up to 18 months to help them with their problem of misuse and associated difficulties.

Domestic rehabilitation units vary considerably in philosophy, some being of a Christian nature, others not, with widely differing programmes available; some are very formal and hierarchical, others loosely structured. It is important to match the client to a programme that he or she can cope with to avoid failure. Sometimes it takes a person three or four attempts at a rehabilitation unit before success. RELAPSE is fairly common. The funding for residential rehabilitation units is now the responsibility of social services departments through the NATIONAL HEALTH SERVICE AND COMMUNITY CARE ACT. It is normally the responsibility of the social worker in COMMUNITY DRUG TEAMS to arrange funding.

residential work social work undertaken within units where people live,
either permanently or temporarily.

Residential provision has many purposes: an alternative home,
therapy, RESPITE CARE, CUSTODY, diagnosis and ASSESSMENT, or some
combination of these. From workhouse to orphanage, from asylum
to PRISON, residential work to some social end has existed for some
considerable time. In general terms, however, residential provision
for many client groups has contracted in the past few decades; some
has changed in character, and virtually all residential services have been
closely examined. The review of residential provision has been motivated
partly by its substantial cost and partly by fundamental criticisms of
some residential services.

In relation to children, long-stay CHILDREN'S HOMES have virtually
vanished. This change has come about principally because children's
experiences of long-term residential care have been very negative – in
effect, allowing children to drift without effective care plans. There was
a virtual absence of strategic policy for children's residential services,
alongside substantial staff turnover. Staff within such services were
invariably unqualified and, although often very committed to the children,
felt themselves to be undervalued by their employers. The concept of
'houseparent' gives a clue to the way they were viewed – as carers, and
carers can be 'ordinary' people without any special expertise but with an
ability to meet the basic physical and, to a lesser extent, emotional needs
of children. In the recent past, a number of highly publicized accounts
of children being abused by their carers have further diminished the
number (see PINDOWN). Other residential provision for children, such as
observation-and-assessment centres, has also attracted criticism because
of the problem of trying to assess children when they have been removed
from their normal environment. If a family cannot cope with a child
any more, such arrangements may still be necessary, but they are now
regarded as a measure of last resort.

For old people, the growth of local authority residential homes
(Part III of the National Assistance Act 1948) has been reversed, partly by
the growth of private provision and partly with a renewed commitment
to COMMUNITY CARE services. Cuts in public expenditure have also
contributed to this change. Some commentators have questioned the
need for social work services at all in many contemporary residential
facilities for old people, arguing that nursing care applies for some
and that the residence is an alternative to a home in the community
for people who, in the main, have no more problems than anybody else.

For people with long-term mental health problems and those with
LEARNING DISABILITIES who previously might have been long-stay
hospital patients, residential provision is being developed in sometimes
imaginative ways. A range of residential services is available in some
areas that reflects the ability of people to live more or less independently.

GROUP HOMES and are examples of such provision, with HOUSING ASSOCIATIONS particularly active in this area.

Residential provision is increasingly specialized and focused. Examples are BAIL HOSTELS as alternatives to remand in custody, units to help prepare children for LEAVING CARE, RESPITE CARE for a range of client groups to give carers a break or a holiday, SECURE ACCOMMODATION for children who are a danger to themselves or to others, and residential facilities with a very particular therapeutic focus – for example, programmes for sex offenders. Alongside such developments, the status of residential work is increasing as workers are seen to offer very specialized skills. In the light of the number of incidents of child abuse in residential homes, the government has also committed itself to a greater proportion of qualified social work staff in residential work.

R. Clough, *Residential Work*, London, Macmillan, 1982.

resource centre a central point where information, equipment, advice and sometimes training are available to a particular interest group. Resource centres tend to be specialist – for example, TOY LIBRARIES, services for disabled people and teachers' centres.

respect for persons a well-established value in social work that holds that all people are entitled to respect because of their humanity.

It follows from this principle that respect should not be contingent on any role an individual might perform nor on any trait of character this might display. Some authors have considered respect for persons to be the core value in social work from which other VALUES can be derived. In the regulations for the Diploma in Social Work, however, the Central Council for Education and Training in Social Work simply lists 'respect' among a number of values to which qualifying social workers are expected to be committed and gives equal weight to all the values listed.

respite care care for vulnerable people provided either in their own homes or, more usually, in a RESIDENTIAL or DAY-CARE setting that supplements the care provided by the main CARER – usually a family member or friend.

There is now recognition that good practice in respite care provision should ensure a stimulating and enjoyable experience for the service user as well as an opportunity for the main carer to have a break. The pattern of care depends upon need and available resources. It may be for a few weeks a year to permit habitual carers to, say, take a holiday, or it may be for a few hours a day or a week. Patterns of respite care may increase as a problem increases in severity, as with a dying person. Usually respite care is provided in residential facilities – services include short-term care beds in hostels, hospitals and small homes as well as care provided in the homes of specially recruited and trained families. In addition, respite may be provided in a service user's own home by the employment of support staff for this purpose. Most respite services are hard pressed and are unable to give as much support to carers as they or the carers would wish. Charges are levied for some of these services, and there are local variations in rates. Entitlement to benefit may be affected by respite care. If service users spend a total of 28 days away from home, they must then spend 29 days at home before more respite care away from home is provided in order not to lose benefit. Concerns about the appropriateness, quality and availability of some respite care have been raised, particularly in the case of service users from black and ethnic-minority groups. (See HOSPICE CARE.)

C. Baxter, K. Poonia, L. Ward and Z. Nadirshaw, *Double Discrimination Issues and Services for People with Learning Difficulties from Black and Ethnic Minority Communities*, London, King's Fund Centre and Commission for Racial Equality, 1990.

restorative justice an approach to criminal justice that aims to restore VICTIMS, offenders and the wider community to the position they were in before the offence was committed by involving them in the decision-making process and attempting to reconcile their conflicts through informal discussion.

According to advocates of restorative justice, the traditional criminal justice system has unhelpfully interposed the state between the parties in disputes. Restorative approaches do not remove state agencies from the process altogether, but they attempt to ensure that effective consultation arrangements enable the participants to reach their own agreed solutions to the conflicts created by crime. Informal structures can replace the need for decisions by criminal courts in some cases, or agreements reached informally can subsequently be officially endorsed by courts. The mechanisms for implementing restorative justice include VICTIM-OFFENDER MEDIATION, REPARATION, FAMILY GROUP CONFERENCES, changes to sentencing arrangements that involve wider community representation, and community involvement in supervising offenders using circles of support and accountability.

Some enthusiasts argue that restorative justice must always be preferable to retributive justice, but others suggest that this is too simplistic and that it is unlikely ever to replace formal criminal justice entirely. The recent rise in interest in and experimentation with restorative justice is connected to the rise of the victims' movement and increasing concern to make the interests of victims more central to the criminal justice process. Traditional approaches have, many argue, over-emphasized the role of the offender at the expense of the victim. The experimental introduction of family group conferences for young offenders in New Zealand in the 1980s and 1990s was successful in producing informally agreed outcomes and in diverting young offenders from courts and custody. In many cases, it also reassured victims and changed the attitudes of offenders. The process was therefore subsequently adapted for use with adults and in other countries, and has probably led to the largest expansion in experimentation with restorative approaches to criminal justice. Another influential development was victim-offender mediation, pioneered by Canadian probation officers in the 1970s and since replicated elsewhere on a much larger scale. Trained mediators (often community volunteers) prepare victims and offenders to meet and then mediate between them when they do so, aiming at a mutually satisfactory outcome. This approach has begun to be used in the case of serious offences, even including murder (where surviving relatives of the victim may wish to meet offenders to show what harm has been done and to try to encourage changed attitudes and behaviour).

The New Zealand experiment with family group conferences arose partly from dissatisfaction with the way in which colonial criminal justice disenfranchized aboriginal Maori peoples and their traditional approaches to justice. Conferencing attempted to build upon the lessons of these traditional methods (although members of Maori and other ethnic minority groups have not been well served by the new arrangements according to some researchers). Changes to sentencing practices using restorative justice also began in aboriginal communities, in this case in North America, where circle sentencing began in the early 1990s. The idea of a supportive circle of concerned individuals, including those who know the offender best, taking part in decision-making was extended subsequently in experiments with circles of support and accountability that extend community supervision of serious (often sexual) offenders released from prison as a condition of parole. Friends, family members and volunteers 'encircle' the offender with support, surveillance and help in the community but report regularly to the official authorities. Projects of this kind have been established in Canada and, more recently, in the UK. See also COMMUNITARIANISM, REINTEGRATIVE SHAMING.

G. Johnstone, *Restorative Justice: Ideas Value, Debates*, Cullompton, Willan, 2002.

retirement the transition from waged participation in the labour market to non-waged status.

Until recently, for most people retirement was a rapid process at age 65 for men and (currently) 60 for women. The disengagement from waged occupation entailed changes in daily activity, social contact and standard of living. Retirement often has considerable psychological and emotional consequences as the individual may lose a sense of usefulness. As life expectancy increases, the social consequences of creating such a rigorous divide between those who participate in the paid labour force and those who are excluded on the grounds of chronological age are being seriously questioned. There is growing awareness that many older people still have much to contribute in terms of skills and abilities and want to continue in paid work. Enforced retirement economically disadvantages older people and more flexible systems that allow gradual withdrawal from the workforce need to be created.

retirement age the age at which retirement pension is paid, regardless of other circumstances. In 1993, the retirement age for women was raised from 60 to 65, the same as for men. This will be phased in between 2010 and 2020. Women born before April 1950 will not be affected.

retirement allowance see WELFARE RIGHTS 3.

retirement pension see WELFARE RIGHTS 8.

reunification returning children to their families after they have been LOOKED AFTER by a LOCAL AUTHORITY for a period of time.

The conclusion of much research in the 1980s was that children who were looked after by the local authority away from home for a period of time easily lost touch with their families. The longer the period of separation, the greater the likelihood that the children would remain in the long-term care of the authority. To successfully reunite looked-after children means consciously planning for their return from the very beginning of PLACEMENTS. To do this, social workers and foster parents or residential care staff facilitate CONTACT such as visits and exchange of letters and gifts. The intention is to keep the parents and family involved in the life of their child and allow them to make as many decisions affecting their child as possible.

The concept of reunification therefore has to do both with the planned return as well as with the actual return of the child to members of their family. The family is understood in the extended sense – the child may be returned to relatives such as grandparents or adult siblings, for example. For many years the word 'rehabilitation' was used to denote this process of returning the child home, but this implied that parents had to overcome certain personal defects and thereby 'earn' their child's return. This approach has now been firmly discarded. 'Reunification' acknowledges a far greater responsibility resting with the local authority social worker, who often has to work intensively with parents in setting up plans, and facilitating home visits, to ensure the child's return home takes place quickly and effectively.

S. Millham, A. Bullock, K. Hosie and M. Haak, *Lost in Care*, Aldershot, Gower, 1966.

review see CASE REVIEW.

right a claim to treatment, benefit or protection that an individual can make on the basis of a law, code of practice or declaration.

There are several kinds of rights. *Political and civil rights* both protect a citizen of a particular country from the arbitrary use of power by state authorities and entitle that person to undertake certain positive actions that enable them to exert some influence, however nominal, in the political process and in influencing public opinion. *Social and economic rights* lay claims to publicly provided goods and services; these rights are not dependent on whether an individual is eligible for them or in some way is deserving. *Human rights* claim a universal status and are usually framed in global terms pertaining to all peoples. *Procedural rights* lay claim to giving people a fair hearing before any decision is made regarding a social benefit or service, such as setting a level of an individual's income support, meeting the special educational needs of a child with a learning disability or taking a child into local authority care.

Those political and civil rights that protect a citizen against abuse of state power include the right of free speech, the right to vote, the right to trial by jury, the right to personal security and the right not to be discriminated against on the basis of RACE. Such rights were established in law, often as the consequence of considerable struggle, from the 17th century onwards in Britain. They are not universal, nor can they be assumed to be permanently irreversible, as recent discussions about the right to silence of the accused in criminal trials indicate.

Social and economic rights include the right to medical care, the right to social security, the right to vocational training and the right to housing. The concept of social and economic rights does not enlist the same consensus as political and civil rights. There is fierce argument as to whether they should exist as rights at all. In general, commentators from the NEW RIGHT think that, because such claims involve a call on resources such as money and the time of those who would deliver the services or benefits, they cannot be considered as rights because the resources needed to provide them may not always be available and the concept of a right as an unconditional, automatic entitlement would be undermined. Others at the political centre and on the left argue that the difference between civil rights and social rights is not as great as it seems because they both depend on a sufficient level of resources being available. The right to personal security, for example, requires an effective police force, and the right to a fair trial requires court time and the provision of legal aid.

The best instances of global human rights provision are found in United Nations declarations regarding, for example, the right to work, education, social security and health care. Nations may have such rights enshrined in their laws, but most do not. In practice, they are often ignored even by countries that have assented to particular UN conventions. They continue to exert influence, however, by their claim to universality and through the work of many organizations, both governmental and non-governmental, such as the UN Commission on Human Rights and the World Court.

Procedural rights have a broad political consensus behind them. Increasingly, they are seen by the public as the most effective way for individuals to guard against arbitrary decisions by government bureaucracies, including those of the local authority. This trend has important implications for social work and social care. The right of a person to participate in the process of defining his or her own needs, the right to be told about the worker's role and powers in a specific situation, the right to give explicit consent or to refuse intervention (except where the worker has statutory protective duties), the right of people to receive information in their first language, the right to written agreements as the basis of any service provided are all powerful examples of procedural rights affecting how welfare professionals undertake their work with users.

The incorporation of the European Convention of Human Rights into British law came through the HUMAN RIGHTS ACT 1998. Historically, the European Convention on Human Rights has its roots in the philosophical tradition of universal rights that stretches back to the Enlightenment of the 18th century and the French Revolution, although formal adoption of the Universal Declaration of Human Rights actually came through the United Nations in December 1948.

N. Biehal, M. Fisher, P. Marsh and E. Sainsbury, 'Rights and social work', in A. Coote, *The Welfare of Citizens*, London, Rivers Oram Press, 1992.

ring-fenced budgets monies from central government provided to local government and designated for specific services areas.

Local authorities as elected bodies have powers to raise funds from charges and local taxation through the Council Tax. In addition, they receive money from central government out of general taxation, including income tax and VAT. In general, the use of this money is determined by local authorities in line with their own estimates of local needs. Consequently, in some service areas there are significant differences in charges and the amount of money allocated to various services between local authorities. Because of this, in one area clients may find they are charged for home helps while in a neighbouring authority they may not be.

One worry for providers of services is that local decisions may mean that money is moved from one budget heading to another. For example, money for mental health services may be transferred to adult or family services as a result of local political choices. This has resulted in some areas of local government budgets being ring-fenced to prevent the transfer of money away from areas favoured by central government. A key example of this was in housing where the management costs and capital expenditure on housing have to be paid for from housing income, mainly rents. The previous government prevented local government from subsidizing housing from other budget headings so that housing became self-financing with the result that rents had to rise.

risk the chance that the health or development of a person may be damaged by certain conditions or actions of others.

Care professionals use the phrase 'at risk' to indicate that a client is exposed to some source of harm and that possibly some protective measures should be taken. These sources of harm to a client may be external, such as assault by someone else, or arise from the client's own habits, such as not feeding himself or herself. For example, a 'child at risk' is regarded as vulnerable to physical or sexual ABUSE by one or more people or to other sources of harm through parental neglect. What is rarely stated is the probability that the child will suffer some harm. This is the drawback of the phrase; it is used widely but with little agreement over the actual chance that a client deemed at risk will come to some harm. Care professionals also use the word in the sense of 'risk-taking', which means making a conscious decision to put something at stake in order to make possible a worthwhile gain or benefit for the client (see RISK ASSESSMENT).

risk assessment assessing the chances of some harm occurring to a client or other person.

Risk assessment means carefully weighing the chances that particular forms of harm will happen to a client or be caused by a client in a given situation. Analysing the degree of risk is necessary, for example, when discharging from hospital a person with a mental illness who has previously been violent, when returning a child home who has been physically abused by his or her parents, or when leaving an elderly confused person who refuses to turn on the heat in the winter in his or her home. In each instance, the practitioner has to try to gauge the chance of harm occurring against the benefits. It is often necessary to accept a certain level of risk, because to try to minimize risk has its own costs and can be detrimental to the interests of the client. Although the risk could be reduced or eliminated in each of the cases above, to do that would require taking action that would be highly restrictive for the person concerned and might itself present different risks to the client's health or development. The person with mental illness, if not released, could become institutionalized, the child placed long-term with foster parents would suffer from loss of family contacts, the older person if removed to a home could become severely disoriented.

With risk assessment, the care professional must be clear as to the specific benefits and harms that may result from proposed action. Increasingly this is a joint task, discussed with the CLIENT and the client's family and carers. After both the benefits and harms are itemized, some attempt must be made to judge the probability or likelihood of each occurring. One of the most difficult examples of risk assessment concerns the level of danger to a physically or sexually abused child if left at home. To undertake risk assessment it is important to know precisely what the nature of the abuse was, whether or not it was committed by a member of the family and what the likelihood is of it happening again. Both the severity of the abuse and the probability of it happening again are important considerations. Often the assessment will be difficult, since it must try to balance the possibility of immediate harm against the long-term harm the child could suffer if removed from home for a lengthy period of time.

role expectations and obligations to behave in a particular way, arising from a recognized social position or status. Roles may carry with them specified rights as well as obligations.

People can play many roles – for example, roles of parent, worker and neighbour. People may be seen as belonging to *role sets*, that is, all the people associated with the playing of a particular role. Some people have many role sets; others have fewer, perhaps even as few as one (or none in the case of hermits or recluses). Roles can conflict in two ways. First, there can be *conflict within a role* – for example, a team leader might be expected, by members of the team, to protect them from further pressure if they are already working to capacity, but the same team leader could be expected by senior management to get workers to work harder if there are many unallocated cases. Such role conflict is referred to as *intra-role conflict.* The second kind of role conflict refers to *conflicts between roles*, that is, *inter-role conflict* – an example might be a person having to work long hours (role of worker) who is very worried about his or her children (role of parent) but feels unable to alter the situation to meet the obligations of both roles.

Roles can also usefully be seen as *ascribed* or *achieved*. Here sociologists look at the issues of whether roles are given and are unchanged (as in some traditional societies) or might be developed in later life. Some interesting problems, for example, of how first-generation Asian children adapt to both traditional expectations of them from their families and those of their peers, can be usefully analysed using role theory. Similarly, some roles might be considered to be tightly defined (*specific*) and others to be of a more general nature (*diffuse*). This typology of roles can be helpful in looking at the range of responsibilities that may be built into a role. A shift from a tightly defined role to something more diffuse, or the same process in reverse, can have interesting repercussions for the parties involved with the role-player.

ROLE THEORY has useful applications for social work and allied occupations in its attempts to make general sense of particular social problems or situations (say, women's roles in modern Britain) and in its potential for helping to understand individual problems, say, within social groups and families. FAMILY THERAPY is an area of work that has developed and applied role theory. (See also SICK ROLE.)

role-play a device or method used in the education and training of social workers and allied professionals in which participants take on specified ROLES and act out a scene or situation.

The central purposes of role-play exercises are to help students to grasp imaginatively the experience of people with problems and to help them develop their skills as workers in situations where mistakes are of little consequence. Typically, students are provided with a short case history and some indication of the personalities and personal styles of the characters in the situation. Students are then asked to develop the story in a manner that is consistent with the initial scenario. Other students can take on the roles of various workers, and students may be given the opportunity to try differing roles in the same situation. The direct observation of role-plays by trainers can provide immediate and useful feedback to students. Such devices have been found useful in developing skills for direct work with children and families, and courtroom and COUNSELLING skills.

role theory the theoretical view that a major part of observable day-to-day behaviour is simply people carrying out their social ROLES.

The theory understands role as a set of expectations with regard to the actions appropriate to a social position. For example, the role of social worker carries a set of behavioural expectations prescribed by legislation, employers and professional ethics. Role theories place a strong emphasis on understanding the individual within social networks and organizations. Thus the concept of role is useful in explaining why a person's behaviour changes when he or she changes social position. Hence if a person's social position is known, it should be possible to predict his or her behaviour. The theory maintains that attitudes and beliefs are shaped by the role a person occupies: a person brings his or her attitudes into line with the expectations of the role. For example, a soldier would be expected to develop strong attitudes of patriotism. It follows that a change in role should lead to a change in attitudes.

Role theory argues that people spend much of their lives participating in organizations and groups within which they occupy distinct positions, formally or informally assigned. Roles attach to those positions defined by expectations of behaviour, or norms. Role theory suggests that, in general, people conform to behavioural norms and to the expectations of others, and an individual is evaluated by others on his or her level of conformity to norms.

The theory has its origins in the language of the theatre: that is, people play parts in everyday life in ways that resemble actors' performances. The difference is that social roles are learned so effectively that a person *becomes* the role, such as daughter, son, soldier or doctor. People identify themselves as the role, having learned and internalized the script (expectations) through SOCIALIZATION processes. Thus roles are a key part of a person's social identity. The theory has been summarized in terms of part of people's self-concepts being based on how they think others see them, and these perceptions in turn being partially based on the roles people occupy. Some commentators have criticized role theory for seeming to imply that people are endlessly compliant to the expectations of those around them, and for suggesting that people receive information about role performance during socialization and interaction processes and then willingly set out to meet those expectations. Thus role theory, it is claimed, ignores the impact of individual determinants of behaviour: motivation and personality.

M. Barton, *Roles*, London, Tavistock, 1965.

rough sleepers that group of homeless people who literally sleep outside, often on the street itself.

Rough sleepers are by definition the most marginalized and vulnerable of the homeless, often requiring multiple forms of support in addition to shelter. The government's Rough Sleepers' Initiative offers block grant payments to agencies dealing with homeless people to explicitly target street sleepers and to offer them accommodation in shelters and to work toward their resettlement.

As a result of the Rough Sleepers' Initiative, there are smaller numbers of homeless young people than in the late 1980s and early 1990s, but those who are homeless are more vulnerable and great numbers of young people will continue to experience homelessness if only for a short period of time. For example, a high proportion of homeless young people who approach Centrepoint, an organization that offers services to homeless young people, each year are particularly vulnerable: 44 per cent are women (many under 18), 41 per cent are 16 and 17 years of age with no automatic right to benefits; 40 per cent have no income at all; 43 per cent are young black or of mixed origin; and 25 per cent have been in local authority care. Most homeless young people who arrive at Centrepoint, 68 per cent, are looking for work or training.

Projects provide temporary winter accommodation for rough sleepers with multiple problems such as alcohol and drug abuse. The Rough Sleepers' Initiative aims explicitly to make a visible impact on a specific area of London and to provide a gateway to more permanent support services. It takes a holistic view of the needs of residents and as a result adopts a multidisciplinary approach that recognizes residents as having multiple skills and interests. It offers health and psychiatric care with other services such as counselling and a drinks crisis centre. Residents can also gain from vocational guidance and various creative activities, including screen printing and computer use.

So the principal barriers to finding accommodation include lack of financial assistance, lack of any legal rights to social housing, and lack of adequate support services to make housing arrangements sustainable over time. But there is a geographical dimension to this: homeless young people come disproportionately from highly deprived neighbourhoods. Hardship payment is one means through which 16- and 17-year-olds can obtain a state benefit with no strings. Interviews for hardship payments can be intimidating, particularly when pressing for 'evidence' that abuse or traumatic cause for separation from parents. Many young people do not get as far as interview or fail to handle it well.

C. Havell, 'Homelessness: A continual problem for young people in the UK', in *Childright*, July/August 1998.

rural social work social work undertaken in low density settlements, agricultural communities, villages and small towns; social work conducted in locations other than cities and connurbations.

Various concepts or paradigms have been developed by 19th- and 20th-century sociologists (Tonnies, Sorokin and others) to suggest that there are a range of interrelated social characteristics that typify rural communities and another set of social characteristics that seem to typify urban life. Some of these thinkers have tried to use these ideas to represent a rural–urban continuum upon which might be plotted most communities or settlements. A similar continuum has been developed by theorists who have been concerned with understanding the differences between traditional societies and modern societies (Maine, Talcott Parsons). Rural–urban and traditional–modern may still be useful ways of identifying differing patterns of social organization, which may have repercussions for the way in which health, social welfare and social work services are delivered.

The key variables seem to be size, density of population, division of labour, isolation, sense of community solidarity, ROLE sets, and other factors. Rural communities are invariably much smaller in size and density than urban communities, ranging from just a few people per square mile in sparsely populated areas to many thousands of people in some inner city areas of urban locations. Rural communities are more likely to have people working in multi-faceted jobs or skills, whereas people working in urban locations are more likely to have relatively specialized occupations. This is thought to be a reflection of the need for people in rural locations to be self-sufficient, especially in agriculture in remote locations. Community solidarity is also thought to be greater in rural areas, with a much greater degree of social support and reciprocity provided by extended family, neighbours and other community members. In urban locations, social networks are more likely to be fragmented or divided, with people working with a designated group of people, pursuing leisure activities with others, indulging in political and community activities with yet others and living in particular areas with yet another group of people. Social status can also vary in each of these settings, so that a person may have, say, a low-status job, but occupy an important position in a trade union, political party or community organization. In essence, it is possible for people to achieve much more in differing social groups because of greater fluidity in urban settings and a relative lack of social constraint. Rural relationships are much narrower where there is a much greater chance of enacting all roles within the same social group. Social status is also likely to be consistent or ascribed because of the social pressure implied by the force of tradition and more or less fixed social relationships. This is most evident in the now diminishing phenomenon of tied accommodation. The landlord in these circumstances is also the employer, a position of considerable influence over an employee.

Some commentators have pointed out that the concepts of the rural and the urban are now much more fluid. First, many people can now live in the country and work in the city by commuting. Second, given the advances of technology, and in particular information technology, people can work for urban companies and work in rural areas. Third, there is the influence of urban values on rural areas promoted by the media, especially television. Finally, there is much evidence of the spread of technology and of the capitalization of much rural economic activity. Small farms are fast disappearing to be absorbed by large companies operating on highly mechanized and highly capitalized methods. There is also the possibility of rural values, of social and community supports and reciprocity, emerging in urban areas, especially where there are very settled communities and sometimes where ethnic minorities are to be found in some numbers. The extent to which extended families are living in proximity and the extent to which they offer support to each other may be a critical factor here in both rural and urban locations.

Even if the rural and the urban are becoming less distinct, there are often still residual differences that have repercussions for how social and personal needs are manifested and how services are delivered. There is evidence to suggest that it is more likely that needs will be hidden or repressed in rural locations. It is easier to keep secrets in very remote areas in regard, for example, to child and adult abuse and domestic violence. Similarly, and paradoxically given the alleged greater knowledge of neighbours in small communities, it is apparently more likely that community secrets will be kept rather than divulged to official sources. There are also some problems in meeting the needs of ethnic minorities living in rural areas, where whatever expertise is necessary to meet their needs tends to be located in cities where there are greater concentrations of such groups. The establishment of some city unitary authorities, which have been separated from their shire hinterlands, have made this problem worse because any expertise that was available in the city is no longer available to the shire.

If people in rural areas are poor or have limited resources, access to services can be a major problem. Rural public transport is scant in many areas. This can mean that the siting of health and social welfare services is critical if there can be no alternative to the service user travelling to the service. It may be that services have to think in terms of an integrated package of not only providing services but also of providing the means to access them by commissioning public or private transport for the purpose. Alternatively, or in addition, there must be some rationalization of location in order that health services can be had in the same location as social services, advice services, day or respite care, and so on. Other services, such as advice services, have been offered by the development of OUTREACH facilities, such as offering a service one day per week in a parish or village hall or the provision of a free telephone in a travelling library that can access advice from any number of public services. For very specialized needs, such as children with Asperger's syndrome or autism, it will be very hard to make the economic case to provide services locally.

An interesting alternative model is to require one professional to take on a wider assessment role in order to provide information to service users about appropriate services or make referrals to such services.

This model has already been adopted by some SURE START projects operating in both rural and urban areas. The health visitor is asked to take on an assessment role by, first, having more frequent contact with families where there is a new child than he or she normally would, and, second, for the health visitor to make an initial assessment of a family's need for other services whether it be housing, debt, respite care, welfare rights or any other problem.

The delivery of health and social welfare services to rural areas demonstrates the over-arching need to conduct periodic community audits and to require health and social welfare services to commit themselves to organizing services in the most cost-efficient way to meet identified needs. In this context, pooled budgets and/or the possibility of a service taking a lead role on behalf of others, as with the Sure Start model of health visiting described above, is clearly demonstrated.

R. Pugh, *Rural Social Work*, Lyme Regis, Russell House Publishing, 2000.

Ss

same-race placement placing LOOKED-AFTER children with foster carers or prospective adoptive parents who are of the same 'race' as the child.

The practice aims to provide children of minority ethnic background in particular with a foster or adoptive placement that will provide not only a family with the same 'race' as the child but, it is presumed, with a similar language, culture, ethnicity and even religion. The practice draws on some years of research that points to the confusion, loss of identity and self-esteem experienced particularly by black children when placed with white families. The practice is now followed generally by voluntary and local authority child-care agencies. The practice sparked some controversy, especially in the early 1990s at the height of the debate over POLITICAL CORRECTNESS, when portrayed by the media as being followed too rigidly by practitioners. High-profile instances, although few in number, in which black children were prevented from being adopted by white families were widely circulated in the press. As a result, successive governments and child-care agencies themselves underscored the fact that the goal of same race placements for each child was desirable but should not be adhered to when other elements of the child's welfare were jeopardized as a result. Most agencies now, for example, accept that if a black family cannot be found for a black child within a reasonable period of time, placement with a white family is an acceptable alternative as long as that family values the child's ethnic background and supports the child in dealing with racism.

The practice has also had to respond to the increasingly complex ethnic make-up of the UK. The inquiry into the death of Victoria Climbié uncovered the fact that while the placement was indeed 'same race', Victoria was west African and her foster parents were African-Caribbean. Victoria's black social worker, it was alleged, made an assumption on the basis of skin colour alone and on this basis decided that Victoria was in safe hands and had not seen the profound cultural difference between the child and her foster parents.

Schedule 1 a list of serious offences against children found in Schedule 1 of the Children and Young Persons Act 1933.

Those convicted of an offence contained in the list are required to notify the police of any change of address, and the prison authorities are required to inform police and social services of the address to which the offender is released. Schedule 1 offenders must also disclose their record to potential employers.

The Schedule 1 arrangements have a number of disadvantages. Courts do not usually tell offenders at the time of sentence that they will be subject to the Schedule 1 arrangements; this can be a source of considerable resentment when the requirements are explained to them at the time of release amid concern about the likely effect upon employment prospects. Some offenders 'disappear' to escape the surveillance of the authorities. Until the introduction of the MULTI-AGENCY PUBLIC PROTECTION PANELS (MAPPPS) arrangements for the most serious offenders, it was not entirely clear what the authorities in an offender's home area were supposed to do about the information disclosed under Schedule 1. The arrangements are also rigidly applied even in cases where an offence against a child was committed by someone who was also a child at the time: playground assaults and offences of unlawful sexual intercourse between young people of similar ages are treated just as seriously as predatory sexual offences. See REHABILITATION OF OFFENDERS ACT, SEX OFFENDER.

schizophrenia see PSYCHOSES.

school action and **school action plus** the two stages of in-school provision to support children with SPECIAL EDUCATIONAL NEEDS, using budgets allocated specifically for the purpose, under the leadership of the school's SPECIAL EDUCATIONAL NEEDS COORDINATOR.

All children receiving additional educational support in this way should have an INDIVIDUAL EDUCATION PLAN (IEP) that sets out the strategies being used. School action is the provision of additional and appropriate strategies to support a child's learning, over and above normal differentiation of teaching to take account of the child's needs. This may involve the deployment of additional staff, the use of specialist resources or material and focused work in groups. School action plus involves a request for additional support services from professionals outside the school, such as specialist teachers and advisers. The overwhelming majority of children with special educational needs should have their needs met in this way, without the need for STATUTORY ASSESSMENT or the provision of a STATEMENT OF SPECIAL EDUCATIONAL NEEDS.

School Attendance Order see EDUCATION ACT 1996.

school refusers or **school phobics** the term applied to a variety of children who have refused to attend school over a prolonged period.

Children may refuse to attend school for a variety of behavioural, emotional and psychological reasons, but their ANXIETY is not necessarily focused on the school experience itself. Wider issues of ABUSE or family difficulty might be relevant, and it is not normally helpful to describe this behaviour as TRUANCY. Some of these children might only be able to manage small amounts of tuition, either at home or in other settings, or may need careful programmes of reintegration if they are to return to mainstream education. School refusal is not in itself a SPECIAL EDUCATIONAL NEED, although such children often suffer educational disadvantage and are among those most at risk of SOCIAL EXCLUSION. Opinion varies about whether such behaviour should be seen as deviant, in quasi-medical terms or as an entirely normal reaction where the education on offer is not meeting the child's needs.

school transport the statutory duty of local educational authorities (LEAs) to provide transport to and from school for children who live more than two miles from their 'designated school' if a primary school or three miles if a secondary school.

If parents choose an alternative school, they are responsible for providing the transport themselves. This is sometimes a contentious issue for children who are LOOKED AFTER some distance away from their homes. Unless special arrangements have been made, the LEA will not normally be responsible for transport to the school and back to the child's home area. If the SOCIAL SERVICES DEPARTMENT or the parents wish the child to continue attending the same school as before rather than transferring to the designated school for the new address, they will usually have to finance the transport themselves. LEAs should, however, make provision where a child has been excluded from school (see EXCLUSION FROM SCHOOL) and needs to attend another that is over the specified distance.

Scotland Office the central government department representing Scotland in Whitehall.

The most significant change affecting provision of services in Scotland has been as a result of DEVOLUTION and the reintroduction of a Scottish Parliament with significant powers of decision-making. While the Scotland Office (previously known as the Scottish Office) is still a major part of the system in Scotland, its role is now determined as much from Edinburgh as from Westminster. Relations with the Scottish Executive are therefore crucial to its work. While health and education, for example, were devolved to the Scottish Executive, economic issues, including issues concerning SOCIAL SECURITY and benefits, are still the responsibility of the Scotland Office.

sculpting a technique used in experiential work to help individuals depict their thoughts and feelings about their family, their social work team or other collections of people. The technique entails individuals moving people around so that they assume particular relationships and attitudes and postures in relation to each other.

The configurations produced by sculpting are regarded both as revealing an individual's feelings about particular people and as potentially diagnostic about family, team or group functioning. Sculpting techniques can be used in such activities as FAMILY THERAPY, team-building exercises or SUPERVISION.

section 8 orders the collective name given to the four court orders described in section 8 of the CHILDREN ACT and used mainly in matrimonial proceedings: CONTACT ORDER, PROHIBITED STEPS ORDER, RESIDENCE ORDER and SPECIFIC ISSUE ORDER.

section 53 young people charged with GRAVE CRIMES and given indeterminate custodial sentences are allocated either to PRISON or to other SECURE ESTATE under section 53 of the Children Act 1933. (This provision has since been replaced by sections 90 and 91 of the Powers of the Criminal Courts (Sentencing) Act 2000 but practitioners continue to refer to 'section 53'.)

This sentence, to be detained at 'HER MAJESTY'S PLEASURE', is the equivalent of a sentence of life imprisonment for an adult. The young people concerned can serve their sentence in a local authority secure establishment or in custody, and a good deal depends upon the quality of the information involved to those making the allocation decision, particularly in the PRE-SENTENCE REPORT. Although penal reform organizations, prison inspectors, senior judges and the YOUTH JUSTICE BOARD have criticized the allocation of these often vulnerable young offenders to prison, the practice continues because of overcrowding. Even when allocated to secure establishments other than prisons, young people are liable to be transferred to the adult prison system on reaching the age of majority, often undoing any positive rehabilitative work achieved to date.

secure accommodation a residential unit for children that maintains locked doors and windows and permits only limited and closely supervised movement of residents inside and outside the premises.

To place a child in secure accommodation requires the authority to obtain a SECURE ACCOMMODATION order. Considerable debate surrounds the use of secure accommodation and whether more such units are required. Such establishments are usually run by local authorities, although the government has invited voluntary child-care organizations to run additional units in order to meet what it regards as a national shortage.

secure estate the generic term for all custodial establishments for young offenders, including secure training centres, local authority secure units and YOUNG OFFENDER INSTITUTIONS.

Under the CRIME AND DISORDER ACT 1998, the DETENTION AND TRAINING ORDER is now the only custodial sentence available to the YOUTH COURTS in England and Wales, but, once imposed, it can be served in a variety of types of establishment.

Secure training centres for young offenders are privately run, and there are relatively few of them. *Secure units*, or SECURE ACCOMMODATION, refers to local authority-run establishments, which are usually smaller than the other types of establishment and are often used for REMAND purposes.

Young offender institutions, although they at least keep younger offenders separate from adult prisoners, are large institutions that are in practice little different from adult prisons, except that they make provision for something close to full-time education for their younger inmates.

The secure estate in England and Wales is now the responsibility of the national YOUTH JUSTICE BOARD, which has tried to raise standards and bring custodial institutions under the requirements of international law. While the UK has been repeatedly criticized for failing to meet minimum standards, particularly under the United Nations Convention on the Rights of the Child, the overcrowding crisis and continued political commitment to incarcerating troublesome young people have made this aim extremely difficult, if not impossible, to put into practice.

The criticisms of PRISON apply even more forcefully to the incarceration of young offenders, who are likely both to be more vulnerable than most adults and more amenable to positive change if treated appropriately. In England and Wales, the level of incarceration of young people is massively higher than almost anywhere else in Europe, and recorded re-offending levels of those released are extremely high. Black young people are grossly over-represented in custodial institutions, not because of any greater propensity to offend but because it is here that discriminatory sentencing practices are most obvious. The rates of suicide and self-harm in these establishments are alarmingly high, and abuse and bullying are common.

The Department of Health's youth treatment centre, although part of the secure estate, no longer works with young people sentenced to detention and training orders.

Young people given custodial sentences are subject to supervision by members of YOUTH OFFENDING TEAMS, and NATIONAL STANDARDS require inter-agency working between the establishment and the fieldworker, although resource constraints can make this difficult in practice. Social workers and PROBATION officers need to be prepared to make persuasive arguments in PRE-SENTENCE REPORTS about the damage likely to be done to young people by incarcerating them.

S. Moore, 'Child incarceration and the new youth justice', in B. Goldson (ed), *The New Youth Justice*, Lyme Regis, Russell House Publishing, 2000.

Seebohm Report the report of the committee set up under Sir Frederic (later Lord) Seebohm and published in 1968. The committee was established in 1965 to examine the then fragmented state of social work services, which had been the focus of increasing criticism.

At the time of the Seebohm Committee's investigation and report, services for OLDER PEOPLE, the HOMELESS and people with physical DISABILITY were delivered by LOCAL AUTHORITY welfare departments. Services for children and families were the responsibility of children's departments, and services for people with MENTAL ILLNESS and LEARNING DIFFICULTIES were provided by health departments. The report proposed bringing these different services together into one large SOCIAL SERVICES DEPARTMENT and argued that the diverse social work tasks could be combined into the role of an all-purpose or GENERIC social worker. The report was optimistic about what it thought social work could achieve. Since the institutions of the welfare state had solved most of the major social problems, it expected social work to provide assistance to the small number of people who experienced problems in adapting to life and who perhaps needed emotional support or help in raising their children or in claiming benefit. Such a service should be non-stigmatizing and should be available from one local authority department. The hopes of the report were not realized. Social problems such as homelessness and POVERTY were not eradicated but increased, and social work's capacity to assist individuals facing major social or personal difficulties was seen to be limited. The report's major legacy was the construction of large local authority social services departments, which in the following decades received a measure of criticism as impersonal and bureaucratic.

self-advocacy a process through which service users and other devalued citizens speak up on their own behalf to promote their rights and interests. Self-advocacy is particularly associated with EMPOWERMENT and autonomy for people with LEARNING DISABILITY.

Self-advocacy is one of a range of approaches through which rights and interests can be promoted independently of service providers. It is particularly associated with group processes, but it can also be undertaken by individuals. It shares some of the features of other forms of ADVOCACY, in particular its commitment to challenging the oppression of people using welfare services by ensuring that their views are heard in decision-making settings. It has been argued, however, that self-advocacy should be the goal of all other forms of advocacy, as it is ultimately more empowering for oppressed groups to represent their own interests. Authors such as Goodley (see below) argue that citizen advocacy, in which service users' views are represented by citizen volunteers, relies upon the philosophy of NORMALIZATION, which makes it open to challenge from user-led groups.

The individual benefits of self-advocacy include improved skills, self-confidence and self-esteem. However, self-advocacy is not primarily about individual development. It has become part of the social movements through which disadvantaged groups have pressed for equality and citizenship rights, and as such it has influenced wider policy and practice in welfare services. It began as a movement of people with learning disabilities in Sweden and the USA in the late 1960s, and became firmly established in the UK following the setting up of People First in London in 1984. In the mental health field, the self-advocacy organization Survivors Speak Out grew out of the campaigning and advocacy activities of MIND at around the same time.

Self-advocacy groups and organizations are involved in representing their interests at a variety of levels. The groups that are located within service settings and represent members' views to the management of the service are perhaps the most familiar. Other self-advocacy groups exist under the general umbrella of either a general advocacy organization or an issue-based organization led by either parents or professionals. Goodley has pointed out that the facilitation of such groups can be a problem, especially when this is carried out by a professional who is in a position of power. He maintains that the notion of professional expertise is inconsistent with the SOCIAL MODEL OF DISABILITY. In self-advocacy groups informed by the social model, the members should themselves determine the nature of the assistance they require as well as the membership, agenda and policy of the group. This is easier to achieve in organizations that are financially and organizationally independent, such as People First.

Recent government policies have encouraged greater recognition of the role of self-advocacy. Both the CHILDREN ACT 1989 and the NATIONAL HEALTH SERVICE AND COMMUNITY CARE ACT 1990 have stressed that the views of service users should be taken into account in both the individual and collective planning of services. This has led to increased use of advocacy as well as self-advocacy. However, in the field of learning disability this process has gone further. Following the white paper *Valuing People* (2001), the government has endorsed PERSON-CENTRED PLANNING, which is grounded in the service user's own views and goals and strongly associated with self-advocacy. There is also a requirement to include service users directly on the inter-agency boards planning local services, which should use person-centred approaches. This has led to greater input from self-advocacy groups and also to individual service users advocating for themselves and their peers at multidisciplinary meetings. This has raised pertinent questions about the nature of the support such self-advocates need and the adjustments that might be needed in the way such planning bodies operate.

D. Goodley, *Self Advocacy in the Lives of People with Learning Difficulties*, Buckingham, Open University Press, 2000.

self-determination the making of decisions for oneself without influence or interference from others.

In social work practice, user self-determination refers to the right of service users to choose particular courses of action themselves even if that means that the person is exposed to risk. Such a right to self-determination has long been regarded as a core social work value and essential to users seeking to minimize dependence upon others (especially social workers) and encouraging personal autonomy. Yet there is a conflict between protecting a person from risk (especially a grave danger such as repeated physical abuse) and the principle of self-determination. In work with adults, and particularly older people, some commentators have argued that this principle holds even to the point of the right to refuse assessment or intervention. (Few would extend this right in its pure form to work with children.) Self-determination can be severely constrained by social circumstances (a poor person cannot choose to be rich), personal limitations (somebody with ALZHEIMER'S DISEASE may find it difficult to form a view), agency resources (accommodation for many vulnerable groups is simply not available) and the needs or wishes of others. The promotion of self-determination is a key social work task in all settings and with all client groups. (See also EMPOWERMENT, ETHICAL CODE, VALUES.)

M. Preston-Shoot, 'Evaluating Self-Determination', in B. Bytheway and others, *Understanding care, welfare and community: A reader*, London, Routledge and the Open University.

self-help a process by which individuals, groups or organizations work together with the objective of mutual aid or benefit. The focus of such activity could entail a wide range of experiences including personal and COMMUNITY problems.

If EMPOWERMENT is the process by which individuals or groups are encouraged to become more powerful, then self-help can usefully be seen as a form of empowering. Self-help activity necessarily usually involves avoiding the status of a CLIENT or user of a social work service. Other critical defining characteristics include equality of status among members, shared decision-making by individuals within the group or organization, CONFIDENTIALITY with regard to the group's or organization's activities and a common focus, interest or problem on the part of members.

Self-help encompasses a very wide range of activities, including self-sufficiency, community living, worker participation in industry and industrial cooperatives. In relation to social, health and community concerns, the list is very long indeed and includes carers' and relatives' groups, groups focusing upon some form of therapy and groups for people experiencing major problems of STIGMA. One of the best known of the large 'anonymous' self-help groups is Alcoholics Anonymous, but many more have followed this model. Over the past decade there has been a mushrooming of groups concerned with the needs of carers – for example, relatives of people with Alzheimer's disease and relatives of schizophrenics. A major commitment to self-help has developed from the community worker's perspective. COMMUNITY DEVELOPMENT and community action have both had substantial ingredients of self-help, principally because such activities have often rested upon a belief that the normal channels for getting things done are not working and that direct action is required by the people most affected by the problem. In some instances such groups have received some support from social service agencies, but in others they have managed their affairs without any external assistance from the helping professions. Some social and community workers believe that an acceptable way of working is to help establish self-help groups and then, at some later stage, to encourage the groups to 'go it alone'. Many community and interest groups have started in this way. Purists, however, would have it that this form of professional 'contamination' is unacceptable and that such intervention prevents a genuine form of self-help emerging. It is argued that, even where professionals withdraw at an early stage and where their contribution has been minimal, they may nevertheless have fundamentally determined how the group conducts its affairs. There is an obvious danger that this will be so when the 'professional' holds the purse strings for the costs of the groups' activities, as with many carers' groups.

Some commentators have been concerned that the growth of self-help groups may be a response to cuts in public expenditure. In this respect self-help may be perceived as a part of voluntary activity and perhaps a substitute for what was previously a professional welfare service. Others have argued persuasively that social work and other services have encouraged clients' dependence on professionals. Seen in this way, self-help may be a healthy antidote to professional power. The key to this debate may be in discussions about what should be guaranteed by the state and how such services are to be delivered.

R. Adams, *Self-Help, Social Work and Empowerment*, Basingstoke, Macmillan 1990.

SEN abbreviation for SPECIAL EDUCATIONAL NEEDS.

SENCO abbreviation for SPECIAL EDUCATIONAL NEEDS COORDINATOR.

Serps abbreviation for state earnings-related pension scheme (see WELFARE RIGHTS 8).

service user see USER.

settlements or **settlement houses** a movement originating in the late 19th century that established houses in poor or working class urban neighbourhoods where middle class reformers could live, mix with and share the life of local residents.

The settlements in their time were one of the mainsprings of COMMUNITY SOCIAL WORK. They were a means through which mainly young men and women from universities could experience life at first hand in the poorer districts of London and other industrial cities. They provided facilities for local people to study literature, politics, science and art, and also to engage in discussions on social problems, such as poverty, and their solutions. From the start, women played an important role in settlements and were instrumental in devising new approaches to community intervention. Settlements gained a reputation as a training ground for young reform-minded activists and civil servants and some of the most important later architects of the WELFARE STATE such as the Labour Prime Minister Clement Attlee and William BEVERIDGE passed through their ranks. Settlements also aroused fierce opposition from those who thought them vehicles for smoothing over class conflict and allowing young middle-class persons to become instant experts on social affairs.

R. Gilchrist and T. Jeffs, *Settlements, Social Change and Community Action*, London, Jessica Kingsley Publishers, 2001.

severe learning difficulty defined in the United Kingdom as affecting children with an intelligence quotient (IQ – see INTELLIGENCE TESTING) from 20 to 50 (cf. the World Health Organization's classification of IQ 20 to 35).

Categorization of severe learning difficulty by IQ has all the problems generally recognized as associated with IQ testing. Since the Education Act 1981, the emphasis has been upon the assessment of children's SPECIAL EDUCATIONAL NEEDS and the issuing of STATEMENTS that may identify additional resources required. Children with severe learning difficulty may be placed in mainstream schools with support but more usually attend special schools. Social workers' liaison with special schools can improve the service that children and their care-givers receive.

Sex Discrimination Act 1975 an Act of Parliament that seeks to eliminate DISCRIMINATION in relation to GENDER in respect of employment, education, the provision of housing, goods, facilities and services, and advertising. Specifically in relation to employment and job advertising, it is also illegal to discriminate on grounds of marital status.

The Sex Discrimination Act of 1986 has increased the scope of the earlier Act. The 1975 Act distinguishes between direct and indirect discrimination. The first might cover situations where, for example, an interview panel asks a woman about her intentions to get married and have children. The second would cover issues like length of experience. Because women on average spend less time in paid employment, they usually have less work experience than men. Good practice in these circumstances would be to express the requirements for a job in terms of the skills and knowledge needed; a woman might then compete on level terms. Victimization, where somebody is punished or dismissed because she intends to complain under the Act, is also illegal. Women who feel aggrieved and cannot solve their grievances informally or through an organization's formal procedures can take their problem to an industrial tribunal. Research has demonstrated that few such cases actually get to court. Although some women settle matters out of court, the majority do not seek redress at all, and of those who do, few are successful. Until recently financial penalties for discriminating employers, for example, were low (a maximum of £11,000), but a recent European Commission directive has forced British tribunals to abolish the upper ceiling on claims for compensation. In the past two decades there has been little evidence to indicate that the Act has improved matters for women in the areas of concern addressed by the legislation.

sex education all secondary schools must provide sex education within a moral framework that focuses on personal responsibility and respect for others. Primary schools may do so if the governors wish.

Sex education is carried out according to curriculum guidance, usually as part of a school's Personal, Health and Social Education programme for all pupils. Parents may remove their children if they wish (although not from the Science elements taught elsewhere.) In responding to any disclosure of sexual activity by older children, school staff may not necessarily follow the same guidelines as those issued by the DEPARTMENT OF HEALTH. In general, teachers are expected to involve parents wherever it is reasonable to do so except where there are allegations of ABUSE. In practice, however, young people will often seek help at school, if not from a teacher then from a school nurse who may be more able to respect their wish for CONFIDENTIALITY.

sexism the negative and unjustified treatment of any person by virtue of sex or GENDER. Sexist behaviour is regarded as discriminatory and may take personal or institutional forms.

Although men may be subject to DISCRIMINATION, it is women who experience discrimination on a major scale both within the UK and worldwide. In social work there are many examples of sexism in terms both of employment practices within social welfare organizations and of services. The majority of employees in social welfare agencies are female yet management is predominantly male. In social work departments in the pre-SEEBOHM period, women occupied a greater proportion of senior posts. In terms of equality of opportunity and employment practices, there is little evidence of progress for women. Services are clearly institutionally sexist on a grand scale. The failure of social welfare agencies to grasp and deal with the problem of violence against women can be understood only in terms of male explanations for such violence continuing to dominate both policies and practice. Social services for vulnerable people of all kinds who require care rest very clearly on an almost unquestioned assumption that women will care. In relation to mothers, social work practice often seems unable to look beyond the woman as parent to perceive the individual with individual needs. Women often face multiple problems in relation to their caring responsibilities – poverty, social isolation, poor housing and second-class citizenship – and yet still seem to attract blame for not being able to cope. The problems of black women are, of course, compounded by their additional experience of RACISM.

Different analyses and perspectives have been developed to attempt to understand the nature and origins of sexism. Some feminists perceive the problem to be rooted in an almost universal patriarchy, that is, that women are everywhere oppressed by men. This oppression takes the form of ideologies, policies and the social fabric within which men and women conduct their personal relationships. That men occupy positions of power throughout society is unquestionable, and such occupancy is a primary source of oppression. Other feminists locate the problem within an analysis of capitalism and critically in the roles they play as part of the reserve army of labour (to be taken up and put down by the economy as and when needed) and as bearers and carers of the future labour force. Some have sought to embrace both theories to achieve some kind of synthesis. It has been recognized that each theory leads to quite different anti-sexist strategies, although there is some common ground. (See also ANTIDISCRIMINATORY PRACTICE, DOMESTIC VIOLENCE, EQUAL OPPORTUNITIES POLICIES, EQUAL PAY ACT 1970, SEX DISCRIMINATION ACT 1975, FEMINISM, FEMINIST SOCIAL WORK.)

L. Dominelli and E. McLeod, *Feminist Social Work*, Basingstoke, Macmillan, 1989.

sex offender someone convicted of a sexual offence; examples include rape, incest, possession and use of certain types of pornography, indecent exposure, and serious cases of sexual harassment.

People who commit sexual offences are not inherently more dangerous than other types of offender, but they are much more unpopular, and politicians have responded accordingly in recent years. The Sex Offenders Act 1997 required certain sexual offenders to notify police of their names and addresses and any changes of these, on penalty of a fine or imprisonment, but this was not very effective. The CRIME AND DISORDER ACT 1998 created the Sex Offender Order, which requires offenders living in the community to register with the police for up to five years. Again, failure to comply can result in a fine or imprisonment. When the order was first introduced, it was unclear what the police were supposed to do with the information collected, but the introduction of MULTI-AGENCY PUBLIC PROTECTION PANELS (MAPPPs) has clarified matters, at least in respect of the most serious offenders.

There is evidence that some forms of sexual offender respond well to super-vision and treatment in the community (including PROBATION HOSTELS), and the use of PROBATION supervision has increased in such cases since the early 1990s, albeit alongside increased use of PRISON. Within custodial institutions, the Sex Offender Treatment Programme has expanded enormously since its introduction in the early 1990s.

Serious violent and sexual offenders can be given extended periods of supervision after release from prison (under the Crime And Disorder Act 1998), and this has increasingly involved the Probation Service in arranging specialist group work provision aimed at changing their attitudes and behaviour.

Practitioners who work with sexual offenders describe this as demanding work, with people who are often quite sophisticated in the ways in which they 'groom' potential victims and manipulate supervisory staff. While this is undoubtedly true, not all sexual offenders fit this stereotype, and some require help with social skills and basic education about sexuality.

Sexual offences often have a serious impact upon their VICTIMS, affecting both self-esteem and relationships with others. Many sexual offences are aimed at humiliating women and children and reinforcing the offender's sense of power over them, and this, combined with the direct physical consequences of offences, can lead to feelings of depression, self-disgust, guilt and helplessness in the victim.

Victims may turn to substance misuse, isolation from others or self-harm if not offered appropriate help. The reaction of any individual victim, however, is impossible to predict, and some victims even of serious sexual assaults rebuild their lives remarkably quickly.

HM Chief Inspector of Probation, *Exercising constant vigilance: the role of the probation service in protecting the public from sex offenders*, London, Home Office, 1998.

sexual abuse the involvement of a person or people of any age in sexual activity against their wishes, or where they do not adequately comprehend the activity, or where it is unlikely that they could give informed consent to the activity.

The phenomenon of sexual ABUSE is thought to be present in many societies and in all social groups. The evidence consistently suggests that abusers are invariably male and that the abused are primarily female, although boys constitute a smaller but nevertheless significant group of the abused. Recent evidence has revealed that women too can be abusers, but abuse perpetrated by females is rare. Sexual abuse is now accepted as a frequent component of DOMESTIC VIOLENCE. There is also increasing evidence that rape and sexual assault are much more common in many societies than previously supposed, both in married and cohabiting couples and in other relationships, and where the parties are not known to each other. The major preoccupation of social workers and health professionals in the past decade, however, has concerned child sexual abuse.

There are additional important dimensions to sexual abuse in relation to children. The Standing Conference on Sexually Abused Children described the issue in the following terms:

'Any child below the age of consent may be deemed to have been sexually abused when a sexually mature person has, by design or by neglect of their usual societal or specific responsibilities in relation to the child, engaged or permitted the engagement of that child in any activity of a sexual nature which is intended to lead to the sexual gratification of the sexually mature person(s). This definition pertains whether or not this activity involves explicit coercion by any means, whether or not it involves genital or physical contact, whether or not initiated by the child, and whether or not there is a discernible harmful outcome in the short term.'

Clearly, child sexual abuse involves many kinds of behaviour, such as non-contact sexual activity (voyeurism, provocative speech, exposure), actual contact, including fondling and masturbation, various forms of sexual penetration as well as sexual exploitation such as prostitution and pornography.

Most child sexual abuse is between two people, but it is possible for there to be more than two people involved. Again, usually the perpetrator is an adult, but sometimes both perpetrator and victim are children. The perpetrator may be adolescent and the victim a younger child, sometimes much younger; or conceivably the victim and perpetrator are the same age, but the victim is at an earlier developmental stage. Sexual abuse of almost any kind is more likely to be committed by a person known to the victim than by a stranger. Early studies suggested that the incidence of child sexual abuse was very low, but more detailed research has since revealed that the problem is on a much greater scale. The principal sources of information are statistics collected by various social work agencies that reflect upon the agencies' own work and the disclosures of adults about abuse experienced in their own childhoods. A recent study in Britain indicated that at least lo per cent of young people over the age of 15 had experienced abuse of some form at an earlier stage in their lives; 77 per cent reported that they had not experienced abuse; and the remaining 13 per cent refused to comment. Other studies in the UK and the United States have suggested much higher figures.

The dominant explanations for abusive behaviour have changed significantly over the past few decades. *Individual pathology* (the belief that it is an individual fault in some sense) and *family dysfunction* (the view that there must be something fundamentally wrong with the way family members relate to each other) were the major explanations until the 1970s. Such ideas still have wide currency in public circles and in some treatment regimes. One particularly persistent theme at this time was implicitly to blame mothers, either for not discharging their sexual obligations to their partners or for not managing to protect their children from abuse (implying that they had colluded with the abuse). Such theories have been rigorously criticized by feminists, who perceive sexual abuse in almost any form as an expression of male power and patriarchal institutions. Far from accepting the argument that sexual abuse is an aberration on the part of a small number of individuals, feminists have it that sexual abuse is an expression of the widespread abuse of power by males and that, in some sense, all men are implicated.

Treatment programmes in many places are now beginning to focus upon the offence behaviour of perpetrators, to emphasize their responsibility for the behaviour and to help them develop coping mechanisms for dealing with their attraction, for example, to young children. Few treatment programmes claim that perpetrators are cured, but the claim is that many can control their problem. Almost all workers involved with sexual offenders believe that such programmes are more effective than imprisonment. The PROBATION SERVICE is active in this field.

The major difficulties in working with the problem of child sexual abuse are those of secrecy, denial and incredulity. The major impediment to the protection of children who have been sexually abused has been the disbelief of those working in the field, including social workers, health professionals and the police. Although more abuse is perhaps being disclosed than ever before, clearly much more could be done preventively to help children disclose earlier or to prevent abuse taking place at all. (See also CHILD PROTECTION, CLEVELAND INQUIRY, EMOTIONAL ABUSE, PHYSICAL ABUSE.)

R. Coulborn Faller, *Child Sexual Abuse*, Basingstoke, Macmillan, 1989.

sexuality essentially, sexuality can be understood as generating sexual identity within contemporary society. Sexuality can therefore be seen as an expression of those socially constructed qualities, desires, roles and identity that have to do with sexual behaviour and activities. Populist notions of sexuality derive largely from the Freudian notion of libido (a biological impulse) and are commonly understood as an essential, natural and impulsive marker of sexual activity, desire and character present in all individuals. More recently, however, sociological and feminist theorists have pointed to the importance of recognizing the social significance of sexuality. A key figure in this area is the French theorist Michel Foucault (1926–84), who examined sexuality in relation to discourse, concepts of power and the social construction of sexual practices. While Foucault's work is important, however, it has been criticized, especially by feminist sociologists, for underestimating the significance of GENDER relations and the unequal power between women and men.

sexual problems and issues problems and dilemmas faced by social workers, therapists and counsellors in advising CLIENTS and service users in the matter of sexual behaviour and sexual identity.

Sexual problems and issues are a major area of work for social welfare workers that is often not acknowledged and for which professional preparation is as yet piecemeal. The issues include contraception, sexual behaviour and health risks, confronting unacceptable sexual activity and COUNSELLING around issues of sexual identity.

Work relating to contraception includes advising and providing services for prisoners, children in care and people with LEARNING DIFFICULTIES. Much of this work involves key dilemmas. For example, should contraception be offered to children under the legal age of consent and should contraception be provided in PRISON establishments when the Home Office's official policy is that sexual activity should not take place there at all? Similarly, what kinds of advice ought people with learning difficulties be given about sexual behaviour and is compulsory sterilization ever justified?

The second area of work refers to general advice about sexual behaviour and health-related matters. The focus of such work might be educational and preventive or it might be concerned with the consequences of sexual activity, such as HIV/AIDS counselling. The third area includes work with SEX OFFENDERS and with child SEXUAL ABUSE. Dealing with sex offenders in the community has become a major focus of work in recent years. Similarly, identifying child sexual abuse and helping children, or adult survivors, to work through their difficulties is also an important and growing area of work.

Counselling people on problems of sexual identity and social responses to those problems – for example, with children in care who feel themselves to be gay or lesbian – is a sensitive and difficult process. Similarly, the consequences for people 'coming out' (publicly acknowledging their homosexuality) can be substantial. Social workers may also become involved in official reports on the future care of children when families break up and one parent decides to live with another person of the same sex.

In all these areas of work there are major dimensions of ANTIDISCRIMINATORY PRACTICE.

J. Milner, *Social Work and Sexual Problems*, Birmingham, Pepar, 1986.

sheltered accommodation units of dwellings designed for vulnerable people where some measure of help is available from a paid warden who lives on the premises or nearby.

Most sheltered accommodation is purpose-built for OLDER PEOPLE. People with LEARNING DISABILITIES also live in such units, although the term 'group home' is sometimes used for this client group. Sheltered accommodation was thought to be potentially a primary service for old people. Research has revealed that although some old people move to sheltered accommodation when they become frail or less able to look after themselves independently, many do so in anticipation of future vulnerability. Wardens also prefer to have a 'mixed' group of older people, that is, some vulnerable and others relatively robust. Such findings have suggested that people in sheltered dwellings may not be significantly different from those living in their own homes in the community. Given these findings, some argue that sheltered housing may not be 'the way forward' that it once appeared to be and that a strong case can be made for supporting people in their own homes with community services such as home helps, meals on wheels and peripatetic warden schemes.

sibling abuse the inflicting of harm – sexual, physical or emotional – by a brother or sister upon another brother or sister.

Although most ABUSE occurring within families is perpetrated by adults on minors, there is a significant minority of cases where the abuse is inflicted by one minor upon another or by a young adult brother or sister upon a younger sibling. Children with disabilities are thought to be especially vulnerable to sibling abuse, as are siblings within step-families.

sick role a ROLE that can be entered by a sick person in which sickness becomes a special status, with positive and negative implications for the person concerned.

The concept was developed in the 1950s by the US sociologist Talcott Parsons, who suggested the following elements in the sick role:
1 the sick person is exempted from many usual social responsibilities;
2 it is accepted that the sick person may be unable to fend for himself or herself;

3 the sick person is expected to strive for health;

4 the sick person is expected to seek professional-advice and treatment.

The sickness role may sometimes be adopted or maintained by people who wish to escape the burden of social obligations. In these circumstances, professional agencies such as those of medicine and social work may be seen as performing a social control function in determining 'true' fitness and unfitness and thus the legitimacy of occupation of the sick role.

SIDS abbreviation for SUDDEN INFANT DEATH SYNDROME.

significant harm the degree of harm to a child that it is necessary to establish to obtain protective orders under the CHILDREN ACT.

The intention of the Children Act is to ensure that a local authority would remove a child compulsorily from his or her family only as a last resort when there is no other means to protect the child. Only when the child has suffered serious harm would such a measure find favour with the courts. Section 31 of the Children Act defines two types of harm: *ill-treatment*, which includes PHYSICAL, SEXUAL and EMOTIONAL ABUSE, and the *impairment* of HEALTH or development, which includes the effects of neglect and deprivation on the child's physical, intellectual or social development. The definition obviously includes traumatic injury such as might result from deliberate cigarette burns or an assault that causes bone fractures. It also includes types of harm at the hands of adults that are harder to define, such as repeatedly subjecting a child to sources of terror, keeping a child locked up or depriving the child of even minimal amounts of food.

The crucial question for practitioners is: what level of harm is 'significant'? Department of Health guidance suggests that 'significant' means 'considerable, noteworthy or important'. It also states that the significance of harm suffered by a child can lie either in the seriousness of the harm itself or in the effects of the harm. A physical injury such as a severe beating inflicted by a parent does not have to have longer-term effects on the physical or mental health of the child to be significant. Conversely, a physical injury – for example, to a child's genitals inflicted when he or she was being sexually abused – may be more serious in its emotional and long-term consequences. Whether a particular harm is significant depends on certain factors such as the age of the child and the length of time for which the child has suffered the harm. Overly harsh physical punishment administered to a six-month-old child leading to severe bruising would be significant, whereas the same amount of force would not necessarily be significant for a 10-year-old. A three-year-old child wandering streets late at night could be likely to suffer significant harm, whereas a 10-year-old would be less vulnerable and less likely to suffer significant harm.

As a form of harm, the impairment of health or development includes the effects of neglect and deprivation such as a very young child being left on his or her own for great lengths of time, persistent weight loss and the failure to grow over a long period of time. In addition, harm in this sense may be measured in relation to the child's overall development, including intellectual or social development. In general, social workers view the harm suffered by a child as increasing in significance if it is repeated and occurs within the context of constant parental anger, indifference or outright rejection. To establish whether the harm is significant to the particular child, the effects of the ill-treatment or neglect must be considered in detail, particularly if the case is to come to court. This is done by describing the extent of injuries inflicted by parents or other members of the family, or the extent of the neglect, such as persistently low levels of nutrition, and how the child's health and development have suffered as a result. If the harm is to the child's health and development, the Children Act requires that its significance be established by contrasting the harms that the child has suffered with a hypothetical similar child, that is, a child of the same weight, age, size and physical attributes or disabilities.

The most difficult of all forms of harm to identify is emotional or psychological abuse. Constantly criticizing the child, always blaming him or her for things, and prolonged episodes of shouting or screaming at the child may or may not do significant harm. Severe rejection of the child, refusal to speak to him or her over a long period of time and long periods of enforced isolation, depending on the age of the child, probably would be significant harm. In terms of an application to court in such cases, much would depend on the behaviour and reactions of the child; if the child showed severe behaviour problems, the harm, though not physical, could be significant. Undoubtedly, the attempt to establish this as significant harm would require a psychologist's expert opinion. (See also CHILD ABUSE, THRESHOLD CRITERIA.)

M. Adcock *et al*, *Significant Harm: Its Management and Outcome*, Croydon, Significant Publications, 1991.

signposting see WELFARE RIGHTS 1.

single assessment process a term introduced in the NATIONAL SERVICE FRAMEWORK FOR OLDER PEOPLE that aims to ensure that older people receive appropriate and timely responses to their health and social care needs and that professional resources are used effectively.

Key government objectives in introducing this framework were that:
1 the scale and depth of assessment is kept in proportion to older people's needs;
2 agencies do not duplicate each other's assessments;
3 professionals contribute to assessments in the most effective way.

The government has set out the implications of the single assessment process for older people, social workers, nurses, therapists, general practitioners, geriatricians and old age psychiatrists in a set of brief documents. Professionals are encouraged to read the documents pertaining to their interests before looking at the actual guidance.

The Guidance for Local Implementation sets out what local NHS bodies and councils have to do in order to implement the single assessment process, clarifying implementation responsibilities and time scales, the role of housing and other services, and links to the over-75s' health checks. Agencies must ensure that older people who seek help are given a copy of the implications of the process for them.

SMP abbreviation for statutory maternity pay (see WELFARE RIGHTS 7).

social action an approach to working with people which stresses empowerment and participation, often used in relation to young people.

The social action approach to practice aims to move away from 'deficit' models in which professionals step in at the outset to define the problems and to embark immediately on what they regard as the remedies. The approach spends much time probing *why* certain problems are being experienced by groups of young people. Williamson, in *Social Action*, writes: 'Only through injecting the 'why' question did the *structural* explanations for the predicaments of young people become more apparent to them, thereby sidelining the tendencies towards individualistic explanations and blame.'

The approach underscores the collective situation of young people. It seeks to explore what common experiences they share and what stories they have to tell – whether of separated parents, racial harassment, leaving care, or experiences of entry into the job market, the usefulness (or otherwise) of specific networks and channels of information.

There are several phases of the social action process: *identification* – asking what are the important issues; *explanation* – asking why are they important; *planning* – how these issues can be addressed; *action* – carrying through with the plan of action; *reflection and review* – whether the process facilitated participation and empowerment or fade-out and disillusionment.

The objective is to promote confidence and recognition in order to achieve a variety of ends that are transferrable across time. The practitioner's role is as listener and gatherer of stories, as adviser, organizer, advocate and group worker.

H. Williamson, *Social Action for Young People*, Lyme Regis, Russell House Publishing, 1995.

social capital the accumulated NETWORKS, local associations and organizations, and informal relationships that exist in a particular area that collectively are able to solve problems and ensure social norms and values are upheld.

The term 'social capital' means many things and will have different emphases depending on who is holding the discussion. Broadly it is used to distinguish the quality of social relations and the social fabric from both *economic capital*, in the form of production or financial services, and *human capital*, which are the assets that individuals have at their disposal, such as skills training or education. The concept of social capital refers to the strength and power of 'intermediary organizations', which together create 'civil society', that is, a range of non-governmental, largely local institutions that are run by the commitment and energy of local citizens (Putnam, see below). By intermediary organizations we mean local institutions, churches, trade unions, clubs, and associations. It includes things like the level of activism in civic organizations, the degree of political involvement by local citizens and the vitality of local institutions such as churches or mosques. It also includes other features such as the level of trust among residents of a neighbourhood and the amount of reciprocity built into social relations ('I will help you out on a certain matter with the expectation that you will help me at a later date').

A number of indicators have been developed by social researchers that show the strength or weakness of social capital in a given area. One such indicator is the proportion of individuals who are not involved in any civic organization – whether political party, church, mosque or temple, trade union, tenants' association, clubs or social groups. Another is data on community safety, say the total number of burglaries, access to insurance against crime, individuals expressing dissatisfaction with their neighbourhood.

Social workers perhaps rely on forms of social capital more than previously thought. Working with NETWORKS or bolstering them through MENTORING schemes, relying on a local area's capacity to provide informal care for older people, working to promote community development by encouraging local people to become engaged in the political process, all draw on forms of social capital. At the same time there is a lively debate about the implications of the concept for social policy as it can be seen to advocate an approach to low-income communities that suggests that tackling social issues successfully will happen only if they improve the quality of their local social relations.

R. Putnam, *Bowling Alone: The Collapse and Revival of American Community*, London, Simon and Schuster, 2001.

social care assistance given to people to maintain themselves physically and socially. This type of care is usually provided in residential and day-care centres or at home by DOMICILIARY staff. It is distinguished from other forms such as health care and the care given by one member of a family to another.

Social care includes a certain level of physical and personal care, such as help with bathing, help to undertake natural bodily functions and coping with incontinence. It also typically includes social support by helping people in maintaining contact with family and friends, developing social skills and skills for independent living, such as food preparation, and making social contacts both inside and outside their homes or residential establishments. Social care tasks include other such functions as collecting and giving information (for example, in contributing to the ASSESSMENT and CARE PLANS for individuals), arranging admission to and discharge from residential units, and dealing with AGGRESSION or challenging behaviour. Many observers have noted that the distinction is blurring between social care tasks and the work undertaken by staff traditionally employed in certain health-care settings such as NURSING HOMES and long-stay hospital wards for older people and people with severe learning difficulties. Residential staff in all settings are having to work across a broader range of tasks that embrace aspects of both health care and social care. Changes to social care services also give greater emphasis to ensuring the service user has a greater say in decision-making about the nature of his or her care support.

C. Davies, L. Finlay and A. Bullman (eds), *Changing Practice in Health and Social Care*, London, Sage, 2000.

Social Care Institute for Excellence an independent body set up by government to assess research and practice in social care in order to establish and disseminate good practice.

Set up as part of the government's Quality Strategy for Social Care, it will work closely with the GENERAL SOCIAL CARE COUNCIL and the National Care Standards Commission. Its priority will be the assessment of research into social care practice with the aim of identifying best practice in the delivery of social care. The development of evidence-based guidance for social workers and other carers is part of the overall aim of MODERNIZATION in social services and the establishment of national standards of care based on such research. Their work will be made available to practitioners through the internet and will help in the development of the work of the SOCIAL SERVICES INSPECTORATE in improving their assessment of providers' activities.

social class commonly defined either as a stratum within society based upon a classification of occupations or as a system based upon the distribution and ownership of property in society.

The idea of social class includes not simply economic dimensions (ownership of property, security, income and other benefits) but the social relationships that are dependent or contingent upon the economic dimensions. Although there are variations between sociologists on how they view the relationship between economic issues and other aspects of life, all agree on the overwhelming importance of the economic issues. The difference seems to be about whether the economic variables determine or simply strongly influence other aspects of life. Sociologists have been able to demonstrate a very close association between membership of a social class and other behaviours within other areas of social life. For example, class correlates closely with educational achievement, with criminal activity, with the experience of HEALTH (both mortality and morbidity), with the structure of communities and with LIFE CHANCES generally. There are also strong associations between the experiences of poor people and those of black people, although the dynamics of 'RACE' and class are by no means straightforward. The bulk of social work service users are from the working class. Such a phenomenon has to be understood as having both controlling and caring functions, partly because some service users are unwilling recipients of social work intervention and partly because some want to have contact in order to try to secure additional resources or services to meet their problems.

There is no overall ground for supposing that social work has been able to seriously embrace ANTIDISCRIMINATORY PRACTICE in relation to poor people. Most of the social work effort has appeared to be marginal or, at best, to be able to re-establish the status quo. Indeed, many commentators have perceived social work as essentially oppressive in its practices and in its association with the state apparatus. Others are more optimistic (see also EMPOWERMENT, RADICAL SOCIAL WORK).

M. Simpkin, *Trapped within Welfare*, Basingstoke, Macmillan, 1979.

social education centre a day service for people with LEARNING DISABILITY that concentrates on the development of skills and abilities in daily living.

Social education centres were introduced in many areas to replace ADULT TRAINING CENTRES, which were then regarded as outdated. Adult training centres provided workshops in which service users undertook contract industrial work for token payment. It was recognized that this did little to prepare the users for the demands of living a more independent life and that the tasks were repetitive and unrewarding. Social education centres concentrate on the skills and abilities that service users will need in order to work towards a more independent style of life. This may include communication skills, the management of money, using public transport and household management. The focus is on what people need in daily life. For example, in some settings food preparation sessions used to focus on such activities as making jam, whereas now the focus is on the preparation of everyday meals and snacks.

More recent policy is to provide day *services* rather than day *centres*. The expectation is that service users will be assisted to use mainstream leisure and educational facilities and that they will not spend most of the week within a segregated day centre site.

social exclusion a process that deprives individuals and families, groups and neighbourhoods of the resources required to flourish in society.

As a process, social exclusion is primarily a consequence of poverty and low income, but other factors such as poor housing, low educational attainment and deprived living environments also underpin it. Through social exclusion people are cut off for a significant period of their lives from institutions and services, social networks and developmental opportunities that the great majority of society enjoys.

The concept originated in France in the 1970s and was used by the European Union in the 1990s to describe the condition of certain groups on the margins of society who were cut off from regular sources of employment and the income safety nets of the welfare state as well as powerful institutions, such as trade unions, that might have given them

with whom a person identifies. If these groups do not coincide, there can be conflict as people meet pressures from their peer group to conform.

The media provide a further source of information about behaviour. This has led to fears that the norms of one culture may swamp those of another, a process sometimes called cultural imperialism. As a reaction to this, some societies have argued that the showing of films and television programmes from certain foreign countries should be rationed and that inhabitants of the country should be deliberately exposed to media that reflect the indigenous society's norms. An additional fear arises from the effect that exposure to violent or pornographic media can have, particularly on the young. Researchers disagree over the effect of such influences, some claiming that there is a detrimental effect, others that there is insufficient evidence on which to base a decision. Nevertheless, social learning theorists have demonstrated that children learn behaviour patterns from watching adults.

Socialization does not cease when a person becomes an adult. The roles a person plays when an adult can help to mould behaviour. Here the pressures are not simply from people in the same occupation but also come from other members of society who have a view about how it is appropriate for a person in a given role to behave or from STEREOTYPES about how such a person is likely to behave. (See also NATURE–NURTURE DEBATE.)

M. Hewstone, W. Stroebe, J. P. Codol and G. M. Stephenson (eds), *Introduction to Social Psychology*, Oxford, Blackwell, 1988.

social model of disability an approach to DISABILITY developed by disabled activists that explains the restrictions and exclusions experienced by disabled people as the result of social-structural, attitudinal and environmental barriers.

The social model of disability was developed by disabled people as a result of their own experiences of barriers to autonomy and full participation in society. This contrasts with previous definitions of disability, which have either focused on individual bodily deficits or on the extent to which people can carry out key 'normal' activities. In their practical application, the latter often focused on ability to carry out key tasks of self-care unaided.

The social model has not only been a new way of defining and explaining disability but also a political tool for the emancipation of disabled people. It challenges the assumption that disabled people are restricted mainly by their own IMPAIRMENT. Instead, disability is seen as the restriction arising from society's failure to take into account the requirements of people with impairments. Initially, the social model was promoted in respect of people with physical and sensory impairments. More recently, it has also been applied to the situation of people with LEARNING DISABILITY. Three types of barriers have been identified. *Social-structural* barriers include those relatively stable social arrangements that marginalize people with impairments. *Attitudinal* barriers refer to prejudice at the level of individuals or societal cultures, while inaccessible buildings and physical surroundings result in *environmental* barriers.

The social model of disability is beginning to have an impact on policy and practice in welfare services. Social workers are now encouraged to promote autonomy and independence and to have regard to the barriers that impede full participation in society. This contrasts with established approaches, which focused on assisting the service user to adjust to the limitations of her or his lifestyle. The concept of INDEPENDENT LIVING has been developed by disabled people and argues that community care policies should promote social inclusion, autonomy and service user control over arrangements for personal assistance. Advocates of the social model argue that the concepts of 'need' and 'care' have reinforced professional control over the lives of disabled people and that policy and practice would be better based on 'rights' and 'personal assistance'.

Political activism grounded in the social model has increased public awareness of both direct and indirect DISCRIMINATION against disabled people. The DISABILITY DISCRIMINATION ACT 1995, however, is based on an individual model of disability. It utilizes a definition of disability based on individual functional deficits and allows for situations in which discrimination is 'justified'. This falls short of promoting the full civil rights of disabled people.

Recent debates within the disability movement have posed the question of whether the social model should be 'renewed'. Disabled feminists such as Jenny Morris and Liz Crow have suggested that there should be more space for the personal experience of both disability and impairment. It is argued that if the restrictions and discomforts imposed by illness and impairment are not acknowledged, the movement cannot become more inclusive. These critics stress, however, the importance of the social model and argue for its renewal rather than its replacement. Other activists and academics, such as Michael Oliver, argue that the movement should concentrate on matters that are susceptible to political solutions and that by acknowledging illness and impairment the movement could be playing into the hands of those who wish to see a return to individual and medical models of disability.

M. Oliver, *Understanding Disability: From Theory to Practice*, Basingstoke, Macmillan, 1996.

social policy government policy in the area of welfare, and the academic study of its development, implementation and impact.

The area of government policy covered by the generally accepted concept of social policy encompasses education, health, housing, social security, including transfer payments such as pensions, and the personal social services. This is a wide range of policy issues but one that relates closely to the ideas embodied in the WELFARE STATE. While government played a partial role in many of these areas prior to the Second World War, the idea of an activist welfare state has come to be seen as a product of the postwar period. However, important aspects of the welfare system and social policy were in place in the early years of the 20th century, including pensions, some hospital care and state education. The commitment to full employment from the Labour government after the war and consequent legislation to support that aim resulted in a major acceleration in the development of a comprehensive system of social policy and welfare.

The academic study of social policy developed initially as part of the longer-established study of government policy associated with political science and public administration. Consequently, the field of study was originally that of social administration, which centred on the empirical examination of policy and the issues it was concerned with. This tradition is still central to the discipline, providing important information and analysis, such as by using evidence of government expenditure patterns to test assumptions about the nature of government policies. Important developments in the study of social policy have directly confronted this tradition, however. These approaches have emerged from a wide range of political perspectives and have resulted in a re-evaluation of social policy both theoretically and in its practical development. There are three main groups of critics: the NEW RIGHT, associated with 'public choice' theory; socialist theories, particularly Marxist; and feminist.

The new right has been the most influential group in practical terms because of its influence on Conservative governments since 1979, both in the UK and abroad. The essential criticism by this group has been that the main beneficiaries of the welfare state have not been those in need, the clients of welfare services, but rather the welfare professionals, including clinicians, social workers and bureaucrats. The new right argues that in the areas covered by social policy the tendency has been for budgets and services to increase as a result of bureaucrats seeking to expand their departments to enhance their status rather than to serve the needs of client groups.

Socialist critics have argued, from a different angle, that the welfare state has been concerned mainly to ensure the existence of a pool of labour to aid the accumulation of capital and to ameliorate the conditions of the working class to blunt its potential as a revolutionary social force. While welfare provision is essential to tackle the problems caused by market failure and inequality, under capitalism the needs generated are such that the economy cannot meet those needs because of their extent and prevailing priorities for expenditure.

Recent feminist writings have been concerned to show how the assumptions on which the welfare state has been built embody patriarchal attitudes to the role of women and to the position of the traditional family at the centre of society, which reinforce structural inequalities. These inequalities particularly disadvantage women through the structure of benefits, pensions and other aspects of welfare that reinforce the gender-based division of labour. Other examples frequently quoted include the consequences of moves towards COMMUNITY CARE, which place a greater reliance for the provision of care on the family and other voluntary carers. Such a change in policy tends to assume that women will take on a greater share of the caring role.

The above does not exhaust the full range of approaches that have emerged over recent years in the area of social policy. As interest in the development of government policy has widened, so too has the impact of the different social sciences with their contrasting disciplines. The challenge to the welfare state provided by Thatcherism in the practical realm of social welfare provision has inevitably encouraged a response from those concerned with the academic study of social policy. The critical appraisal of the role of New Labour and the continuation of aspects of previous Conservative policy as part of a 'modernization' agenda have presented social policy with an important new programme for study.

R. F. Drake, *The Principles of Social Policy*, Basingstoke, Palgrave, 2001.

social role valorization (SRV) a service philosophy applied mainly to LEARNING DISABILITY that emphasizes 'the creation, support and defence of valued social roles for people who are at risk of devaluation'.

Social role valorization is a further development of Wolfensberger's philosophy of NORMALIZATION. Normalization focused on the integration of people with learning disability and the development of 'normal' competencies so as to promote acceptance by the wider community. SRV takes this further by stressing that people with learning disability should have access to roles that are valued in society generally. While both normalization and SRV have been criticized as insufficiently radical, the principles with which they are associated are acknowledged to have improved practice in many settings. These are: community presence, community participation, choice, competence and respect.

social security a term used to describe financial assistance funded and regulated by the state. In Britain social security benefits are administered by one of the DEPARTMENT FOR WORK AND PENSION'S executive agencies, the Pensions Service and Jobcentre Plus. Housing benefit and council tax benefit are administered by local authorities. TAX CREDITS are treated as part of the tax system and as such are administered by HM Revenue and Customs.

The current social security system includes three types of benefit. *Contributory benefits* are still based broadly on those introduced by the BEVERIDGE REPORT to cover maternity, unemployment, sickness, widowhood and retirement. *Non-contributory benefits* include child benefit and the disability benefits attendance allowance and disability living allowance. MEANS-TESTED BENEFITS include income support, income-based jobseeker's allowance, housing benefit and council tax benefit, and was substantially overhauled in 2003 with the introduction of three new tax credits.

Spending on social security increased during the first half of the 1990s from nearly £80 billion in 1991–92 to £97 billion in 1996–97, then spending slowed so that by 1998–99 it totalled £95.6 billion. By 2004–05 it had reached £145 billion. This is equivalent to 12.8 per cent of gross domestic product (GDP) and 29 per cent of government spending. Over 30 million people, or 70 per cent of the population, receive at least one social security benefit. This includes over 10 million pensioners and nearly 13 million children. In the region of £45 billion, or 46 per cent of total benefit spending and 5.2 per cent of GDP, is spent on people over working age, mostly on retirement pension. Almost the same, nearly £44 billion, is spent on working-age people, of which three-quarters goes to people with a long-term illness or disability or non-working lone parent families.

The Department of Social Security (now the DEPARTMENT OF WORK AND PENSIONS) attributed some of the reduction on spending in the late 1990s to lower unemployment and initiatives to tackle benefit fraud (Department of Social Security, *The Changing Welfare State: Social Security Spending*, February 2000). In addition, economic improvement has resulted in less spending on the unemployed, and the transfer of tax credits to HM Revenue and Customs has resulted in a reduction in spending on people of working age. Following a comprehensive spending review, government has directed additional resources to tackle its key priorities: to reduce child poverty and to tackle low incomes among working families and pensioners. In particular, from 2003 it introduced three new tax credits: child tax credit, working tax credit and the pensions credit.

Social Security Commissioner a judge who decides appeals at the second stage of appeals on SOCIAL SECURITY, TAX CREDITS and CHILD SUPPORT appeals, but only on points of law. Other state benefits, such as statutory sick pay , statutory maternity pay and statutory paternity pay, are appealed from Tax Commissioners to the HIGH COURT. From April 2003, appeals relating to the new child tax credit and working tax credit are due to be heard by Tax Commissioners rather than the tribunals system.

There are currently (2002) 18 full-time Commissioners for Great Britain. The majority are based in London and normally hear appeals in London and Cardiff. Three are based in Edinburgh and normally hear appeals there. The commissioner looks at the tribunal's decision to see if there has been an error of law, and either gives a new decision or refers the case to a fresh tribunal. Since most errors in law concern inadequate reasons and findings of fact, the most common outcome is to refer the case back. Commissioners' decisions set legal precedents that have to be followed. All decisions are available to the public.

Appeals from Commissioners can be made to the Court of Appeal and the House of Lords, and the European Courts (one being the European Court of Justice on EU law points, the other being the European Court of Human Rights on human rights Convention matters). These are now much more common than in the past.

social services committee the committee of elected representatives in
a LOCAL AUTHORITY that is responsible for local social services policy.

Local authorities responsible for social services are at present the
shire county councils, unitary authorities and the metropolitan district
councils. They have a statutory requirement to provide personal social
services, and a group of nominated elected councillors comprise the
social services committee to oversee the work of the SOCIAL SERVICES
DEPARTMENT. The committee is accountable to the whole council for the
running of the department and for the development of policy within the
limitations imposed by central government legislation. The committee
does not technically make decisions on social services but makes
recommendations to the full council for approval. In reality, most
committees are looked to for expert decision making, with most policy
recommendations being passed by the full council. In many authorities,
before the committees' recommendations reach the full council they are
considered by a policy and resources committee, which assesses the
policy in the light of overall council priorities and resource constraints.
Central government also has an interest in these decisions and now
requires the development of a COMMUNITY CARE PLAN by each authority.
The secretary of state may intervene to overrule the council if advised
that the plan is unrealistic or out of line with government policy.

Members of the committee are elected representatives, usually with
an interest in the area of social services. They are put forward by their
respective parties, and committee membership is allocated in line with
the relative strength of the different parties on the whole council. This
gives the majority party in the council an automatic majority but also
gives minority parties a full say. Prior to recent legislation, the majority
party could form a committee made up exclusively of its supporters.
During meetings, senior full-time officers sit with the chair of the
committee to give advice on policy and management issues and also on
the constraints imposed by central government legislation and finance.
For some areas of specialist activity, committees utilize subcommittees
and working parties. These comprise members of the committee and
often appoint non-elected experts to give advice, sometimes allowing
them to vote on issues within the subcommittee. These seconded
individuals, however, do not normally have a vote on the full committee
when it meets to discuss any recommendations from the subcommittee.
The members of the committee are councillors and, therefore, in
general, part-time politicians. They bring to debates about social services
and social work issues more general and political priorities, which may
lead them into conflict with full-time officers and professional social
workers. These different criteria can, however, often bring a new light to
bear on an issue and prevent a more narrow professional viewpoint from
dominating decision-making. As elected representatives, they also have
the important task of trying to balance the needs of individual service

users with the wider concerns of the local electorate. Local government is largely about ensuring the public accountability of the actions of full-time public officials and service professionals.

L. Challis, *Organizing Public Social Services*, Harlow, Longman, 1990.

social services department the organizational structure for the delivery of personal social services in a LOCAL AUTHORITY.

Personal social services departments are the primary deliverers of social services. They are the largest employers of social workers and are the main providers of care for the main client groups. Departments are composed of full-time and part-time officials. They are accountable to elected representatives from the local authority who comprise a SOCIAL SERVICES COMMITTEE. The responsibilities of the departments include arranging care, services and support for people with LEARNING DISABILITIES, MENTAL HEALTH PROBLEMS and PHYSICAL DISABILITIES, and for OLDER PEOPLE. They also have primary responsibility for children in need and their families together with children who have been thought to be physically or sexually abused. These responsibilities are now largely determined by the NATIONAL HEALTH SERVICE AND COMMUNITY CARE ACT and the CHILDREN ACT.

The present structures of social services departments are the result of the reorganization of local government under the Local Government Act 1972 (later reformed by local government legislation in 1997), which established the county and metropolitan councils and have been influenced by the SEEBOHM REPORT, which recommended the creation of unified social services departments to replace a more fragmented and client-based structure. Organizationally, these departments are structured along a number of lines. Until recently, the major organizational arrangement was on the basis of fieldwork and residential work, with some decentralization down to local area divisions. More recently, pressures to create specialist posts have resulted in CLIENT-based approaches for the delivery of services to children and adults, or to older people, children, health and disability. Such organizational arrangements can have important consequences for the provision of services and have the potential to lead to conflict between different sectors of the departments.

After education, social services are the largest spenders of local government finance and one of the largest employers. Until the National Health Service and Community Care Act the only statutory requirement for local authorities was that they had a social services director and a social services committee. This situation led to a very wide degree of differentiation between departments, with differing structures and working practices depending on the part of the country officers worked in. Since that Act, however, these departments now require the existence of an INSPECTION process that reports to the director of social services. In addition, efforts have to be made to identify purchaser/provider roles (see MARKET) throughout the departments.

Within departments, social workers are the predominant professional group and as such are also dominant within the management structure, with directors and their deputies often qualified social workers. This, however, does not rule out disputes between managers and those social workers who have direct contact with clients. The central issue is that of resource constraints and their impact on the provision of services. Managers within the departments have a responsibility to ensure that public money is used with probity, and they are increasingly concerned with value for money. For this they are accountable to the social services committee and to central government through the district auditor, an employee of the AUDIT COMMISSION. Pressure is increasingly exerted on local authorities, including social services departments, to introduce more commercial management techniques, such as PERFORMANCE indicators, to help ensure value for money.

A. Douglas and T. Philpot, *Caring and Coping: A Guide to Social Services*, London, Routledge, 1998.

Social Services Inspectorate (SSI) an agency of the DEPARTMENT OF HEALTH that inspects SOCIAL SERVICES DEPARTMENTS and provides professional guidance on the development and implementation of departmental policy.

Established in 1985, the SSI developed from the Department of Health and Social Security's (DHSS) Social Work Service (SWS), which had been in existence since 1971. The SWS had been created as a result of the changes emerging out of the SEEBOHM REPORT and in particular the movement of children's services from the HOME OFFICE to the DHSS. The creation of large, unified personal social services departments at local level, it was believed, also required some monitoring and guidance from the centre. The SSI, while composed largely of professional social workers, is part of the DoH, and these officers are therefore civil servants. Consequently, its role is both that of a source of professional consultancy and guidance and that of a central DoH 'policeman'. It has been pointed out that the role of the SWS was from the start more than developmental because it also had a 'scanning and monitoring' role.

Further reinforcement of the monitoring role of the SWS came about with the change in its name to the Social Services Inspectorate. The change reflected the developing concern within central government departments for improvements in the management of services as opposed to a concern with good professional practice, although this was still a core concern. As with the AUDIT COMMISSION, the SSI became concerned with improving efficiency and effectiveness as well as with the provision of professional social work advice. Sometimes working with the HEALTH ADVISORY SERVICE, the SSI examines the practices of a social services department at the request of the local authority. In some reports, the SSI has emphasized the need for more specialist social workers. In addition, it has been critical of the unwillingness of some local authorities to utilize the private and voluntary sectors as service providers. This latter point is in line with its role of communicating government policy to social services departments.

The white paper *Caring for People* (1989) emphasized a more interventionist role for the SSI under the new COMMUNITY CARE policy initiative. As a result of this change of emphasis, the SSI began to provide more explicit guidance to local authorities in the run-up to the implementation of the community care legislation in April 1993. In particular, a series of publications on quality issues and quality assessment have been issued that include methods and materials for use by departments. A series entitled *Caring for Quality* has been produced, covering residential care for various client groups and guidance on quality issues in home care services. The direction of these guidelines is best summed up in the introduction to the SSI publication *Caring for Quality in Day Services* (1992), which states that the document 'encourages agencies to reflect on the future development of day services in their roles as providers, purchasers and enablers, and offers guidance on how best to provide positive packages of day services'. Such a statement reflects the DoH's policy on the role of social services departments as enablers and highlights the guidance on identifying a separation between purchaser and provider. To emphasize further the dual role of professional advice on policy development on the one hand and monitoring and inspection on the other, the SSI reorganized its formal structure in 1992. There is now an explicit division of responsibility within the agency, with an inspectorate formally separate from the policy wing.

As part of its growing importance and the key development of performance indicators, the SSI is now responsible under the Labour government for the production of league tables ranking the performances of Social Services Departments in the provision of a range of care services. This is a highly controversial process whereby the SSI examines internal documents, their own inspection documents and various measures for comparison, to produce a three-star rating system. Some departments may be given a rating of no stars and this may result in the possibility that they will be 'taken over' by inspectors for a period of time to improve their performance.

P. Day and R. Klein, *Inspecting the Inspectorates*, York, Rowntree Trust, 1990.

Social Services Select Committee a committee of Members of Parliament that scrutinizes the implementation of government policy on social services and social work issues.

In 1979 after an experiment in widening the role and number of parliamentary committees, a series of PARLIAMENTARY SELECT COMMITTEES was established to shadow each of the main central government departments. These committees are composed of appointed MPs who have expressed a particular interest in the work of the committee. Membership is weighted in proportion to the relative strength of the main political parties in the House of Commons, thus giving the majority party the largest number of committee places. However, these committees are seen as being the servants of Parliament and as a result they work across party lines and make serious efforts to ensure an agreed report. The committees have important powers that add significantly to Parliament's ability to scrutinize the actions of government. These powers allow committees to summon ministers, civil servants and members of the public to appear before them, enabling them to question the opinions of outside experts, including local government councillors, officials and social work staff. Their investigations can take them out of the House to visit organizations in the furtherance of their inquiries. As such, this broadens the scope of Parliament to debate issues that the traditional debate on the floor of the House of Commons limits; the nature of these debates and their formal structure do not permit detailed examination of ministers and do not include non-members. Select committees can examine issues in detail over some weeks, with lengthy questioning of ministers and others.

Select committee reports are usually published along with the full transcripts of hearings and the written reports of witnesses. As with the main parliamentary debates, committee hearings are recorded for television and radio. The reports are advisory only, however, and all too frequently the government takes only limited notice of them. The response to these reports may take place verbally on the floor of the House when the report is debated or the government may publish a reply. Reports by the Social Services Select Committee have provided important material on both community care and the care of children. In addition, evidence has been provided on the needs of formal and informal carers, although most information is provided by organized pressure groups, such as the BRITISH ASSOCIATION OF SOCIAL WORKERS and Mencap, rather than individuals. So the existence of these committees allows a more public expression of the detailed views of such organizations to Parliament than would otherwise be the case.

social skills training a teaching procedure designed to increase competence in social interactions.

Training people to be more effective in a variety of social situations uses particular methods drawn from social learning theory, which holds that people learn by watching the specific behaviours of another person. On this general principle a set of training methods has evolved. First, the social skill to be learned is described and instruction is given as to an appropriate performance. This often involves the instructor MODELLING or demonstrating the skill. Second, the trainee rehearses the skill with the instructor or other trainees and receives comments on how well he or she accomplished it. Third, the trainee practises the skill in more complex ROLE-PLAY that simulates real-life situations. As this is done, the instructor may coach the trainee as to what is the most appropriate or effective response. Throughout the training some form of reinforcement is used, such as praise or recognition of what has been accomplished. Fourth, the trainee is given homework by setting the skills to be performed in live situations outside the training. Care professionals often engage in social skills training with diverse groups of people such as young offenders, people with LEARNING DISABILITY or people who lack social confidence. The social skills taught are often quite specific – for example, initiating and sustaining conversation, being interviewed, making a purchase from a shop, and how to be more assertive. In training in such areas a greater emphasis is placed now on the understanding of what makes for an effective social response and on cultural values than on the simple repetitive rehearsal of a skill, which often characterized social skills training in the past.

J. and M. Collins, *Social Skills Training and the Professional Helper*, Chichester, John Wiley, 1992.

social work the paid professional activity that aims to assist people in overcoming serious difficulties in their lives by providing care, protection or COUNSELLING or through social support, ADVOCACY and COMMUNITY WORK.

From the inception of social work in the mid-19th century, there has been controversy over what in essence it seeks to achieve. The argument has been between those who believe social work is an activity that seeks to provide particular groups of people with the tools and resources to change the social structures that disadvantage them and those who believe it should assist individuals to adapt to their circumstances. The first view was promoted by SETTLEMENT HOUSES, established in low-income urban neighbourhoods from the 1880s on, which combined educative tasks, research into social conditions and mutual support for local people under one roof. The second was represented by the charity organization Society, which systematized the approach called CASEWORK, which combined home visiting, record keeping and a focus on individual conduct as the source of social problems.

This second view of social work dominated its practice from the very beginning. Social work evolved from the work undertaken by various charitable organizations in the second half of the 19th century. From its beginnings, it was based on personal contact between a largely volunteer force offering practical assistance, advice and support, and people such as abandoned or neglected children, the elderly and infirm, destitute families and the homeless who seemed to be casualties of rapid industrialization. Social work thus formed part of a broader pattern of social concern and social reform that arose as the effects of urbanization, POVERTY and deprivation on the lives of the urban poor were better documented. These early volunteer social workers were attached to hospitals, courts and prisons. Others, perhaps attached to charitable housing projects, visited people in their homes. Their legacy remains in the methods that they developed, which the profession has used to this day: systematic interviewing, record-keeping and devising rudimentary plans for improvement. They also devised the basic distinction between the 'deserving' and 'undeserving', or the helpable and unhelpable, which had lasting influence within the profession.

By the middle part of the 20th century, social work had added a strong psychological perspective to its work. Under the influence of psychoanalysis, social workers began to pay more attention to early family experiences, unconscious motivation and the roots of inconsistent or irrational behaviour. The practical consequence of this was to emphasize the relationship between social workers and the individuals and families with whom they worked. Through this relationship, users would find compensating experiences and learn strategies for overcoming their difficulties. While social work never completely abandoned its concern with the effects of poverty, it came to place great emphasis on the psychological inadequacies of clients. And for much of the 20th century it became an instrument for enforcing social norms, albeit by providing practitioners with sufficient discretion to be able to respond to an individual's or family's particular set of circumstances. But also in the course of the 20th century, a formidable array of legal powers were created to underpin that practice with people who are unwilling or unable to conform to existing social norms or standards. When working with persons whose behaviour falls outside a band of what is acceptable, it invoked its legal powers to compel them to conform.

In the late 1960s and 1970s, social work, at least in part, began again to focus on social deprivation and how the wider structures of society contributed to, and even caused, the problems of service users. RADICAL SOCIAL WORK practice in this period was intent on providing expressions of solidarity with the working class – for example, in work with unemployed centres, in joining with groups of users in community and neighbourhood action, in welfare rights work and in advice centres. When working with individual clients, radical social workers tried to heighten their awareness of the social origins of their difficulties.

Each phase in its development left its mark on social work, but each also tended to generate a number of critics both inside and outside the profession. In effect, social work came to be many different things, with large – at times grandiose – objectives, to an extent that a single summary of what it entailed became impossible. It aimed to work with 'individuals in their environment', or, from a different angle, with both the psychological and social dimensions (the 'psychosocial') of the human per-sonality. Attempts to define social work became increasingly general, such as that of the BRITISH ASSOCIATION OF SOCIAL WORKERS in 1977:

'Social work is the purposeful and ethical application of personal skills in interpersonal relationships directed towards enhancing the personal and social functioning of an individual, family, group or neighbourhood, which necessarily involves using evidence obtained from practice to help create a social environment conducive to the well-being of all.'

Partly because social work seemed to claim such a large mandate with very few tools specific to its own profession and partly because of its tradition of paternalistic attitudes toward low-income people, it became vulnerable to attacks throughout the 1980s as political forces mobilized against the very concept of the WELFARE STATE itself. The public's antipathy was spurred by high-profile instances where social services failed to remove children from parents who eventually killed them. But the media also rounded on social workers and what was regarded as overzealous and intrusive behaviour when they removed children from their families without due cause. Public perception of social work was further damaged by the widespread evidence of paedophilia throughout the residential child-care system in the 1990s, particularly in Wales and the northwest of England.

As a result, social work seemed to lose its way, with a number of competing visions as to what its principal mission should be. Some argued that the profession had been too ambitious in its claims to effect *change* both in individuals and within society at large. Social workers should aim to stabilize individuals who have acute needs and to maintain them to the highest degree possible within an environment familiar to them. Others said no, social work must press on with its mission to practise in a manner that diminishes oppression in society at large. In any case, to make it more accountable, social work practice became the subject of detailed reviews, inspection, legal statute, government guidelines and national standards throughout the 1990s and early 21st century. Vocal and assertive groups of users and their advocates also began to spell out more clearly what they expected of a social work service.

Some authorities, such as Bill Jordan in his books, argued that what distinguishes social work from other helping professions is its capacity to negotiate. Social workers are part of a bureaucracy that exerts authority over the behaviour of individuals, families and communities, often under government mandate, but unlike other professional service providers they are willing to move beyond the formality of the role and work with people in their own environment as they negotiate solutions to problems. For them, imposed, formal solutions are a last resort. Rather, they pay special attention to the way users and their families and local networks define social problems and individual needs and work within a collaborative framework to address them.

Today social work still contains many of these earlier different threads. Counselling, an area of work that attracts so many social workers to the profession in the first place, forms a diminishing but still significant part of the work even if now carried out more informally and as part of other support measures. A more clearly administrative set of tasks has taken the place of intensive face-to-face work with users. For instance, CARE MANAGEMENT, in which the social worker concentrates on the ASSESSMENT of NEED and the purchase of services, has done much to alter the nature of social work. It is arguably the greatest single source of change in social work for the past fifty years and has forced practitioners to become organizational functionaries.

One striking phenomenon in contemporary social work is how the kinds of work that it has traditionally undertaken have emerged within the new range of activities that are now associated with combating SOCIAL EXCLUSION. The personal advisers for the CONNEXIONS scheme, PASTORAL work to tackle ANTISOCIAL BEHAVIOUR and school TRUANCY among young people, the work of YOUTH OFFENDING TEAMS, all draw on what has historically been the essence of social work. Perhaps the real social work is now to be found in local VOLUNTARY organizations that combine practical supports with network development and attention to neighbourhood social problems. These range from local projects for people with disability, work with refugees, welfare organizations for a particular minority ethnic community, projects with people with mental health problems to faith-based efforts to provide community-based care for the excluded. They all build individual relationships, work with people in their personal environment, provide guidance mixed with the sensitive use of authority and are profoundly aware of local social problems.

G. Smale, G. Tuson and D. Statham, *Social Work and Social Problems: Working towards social inclusion and social change*, Basingstoke, Macmillan, 2001.

Social Work (Scotland) Act 1968 legislation that established the modern social work service in Scotland.

The Act was a product of a time of optimism, even euphoria, about what social work could achieve for the communities it served. The Act built on the recommendations of the Kilbrandon Report on young offenders but went further to establish a comprehensive social work service for all prospective client groups, including adult offenders (by bringing probation work into the new social work departments). Even more than the SEEBOHM REPORT, which was its contemporary, the Act set up the 'single door' for families and individuals seeking social work assistance. The Act's guiding principle was found in section 12, which placed the duty on the new social work departments to promote the welfare of all individuals within the communities they served by making available advice, guidance and assistance (in cash or in kind) appropriate to the area. In this sense, the values and organizational culture established within the social work departments were more closely linked to the welfare of the communities they served than was the case with the SOCIAL SERVICES DEPARTMENTS set up in England and Wales a few years later.

social work skills the range of practice-based abilities that social workers need in order to practise effectively.

These may be understood in a very broad as well as a very specific way. We could argue that in order to practise competently, a social worker needs a broad range of skills that include:

1 the intellectual skill to understand a wide range of relevant knowledge that underpins social work practice, and the capacity to apply this appropriately and effectively;

2 good skills for both oral and written COMMUNICATION across a wide variety of settings, including work with service users, inter-professional liaison and at times very formal settings such as case conferences and court work;

3 teamworking skills – social workers are required to work creatively with other colleagues in their own agency and inter-professionally;

4 information technology (IT) skills – these are becoming increasingly important for many social welfare and social work agencies which use data bases to store and record key information;

5 problem-solving skills – the daily task of social workers includes the ability to make accurate assessments and then to intervene appropriately, either from their own resources or by calling upon other agencies, or both;

6 application of number skills – social workers need to have basic numeracy skills when putting together packages of care, for example, or calculating benefit entitlements;

7 research skills – social workers need to able to access a wide range of resources and relevant information to inform their practice and to keep abreast of relevant current research in their field;

8 reflective practitioner skills – it is increasingly important for social workers to be able to reflect upon what they are doing, why they are doing it, what is the impact which they have as an individual worker upon the service user and what anti-oppressive practice means in specific situations (see REFLECTIVE PRACTICE).

These skills are broadly in line with those identified by Lord Dearing in his report on higher education and the skills that all graduates can be expected to have developed during their training and education. With social work becoming an increasingly graduate profession, this skill base has become particularly relevant.

In a more specific way, social work skills are often seen as the practical, 'hands-on' interpersonal skills without which no social worker could practise. These include the range of active listening and interviewing skills, recording skills, report-writing skills and an awareness of the importance of nonverbal communication. There are additional skills of being able to work with interpreters for people for whom English is not their first language or for people whose own communication skills are limited.

P. Trevithick, *Social Work Skills – a practice handbook*, Buckingham, Open University Press, 2000.

sociology the study of social structures and the different life experiences
of individuals within those social structures.

Sociology is, alongside PSYCHOLOGY, one of the defining academic
disciplines of social work. Social work operates within a context of law
and social policy, but the disciplines of psychology and sociology have
produced theoretical frameworks that have sought to make sense of the
relationship between the individual and the social world. If psychology
has informed the practice of social work with individuals and groups,
then sociology has provided an understanding of the social context in
which that practice is undertaken (including the basis of a radical
critique of some practice) and of differential LIFE CHANCES, affected
principally by the SOCIAL CLASS, GENDER and 'RACE' of the individual.

The early sociologists who established this new science of society –
namely, Karl Marx (1818–83), Emile Durkheim (1858–1917) and Max Weber
(1864–1920) – were preoccupied with questions such as, How does society
change? How is stability maintained? What are the bases of power in
society and how are they legitimated? All three thinkers were also
interested in the issue of social inequality and its structural determinants.
A particular major interest of Durkheim concerned DEVIANCE in society
and how individuals who do not share the social norms of the majority
can be affected by their marginality. All these concerns have been
regarded as 'grand theory', with the objective of trying to understand
the mechanisms by which whole societies function.

Subsequent theorists have sought to understand individual experience
within social structures. The interaction between biography and history,
or character and social structure, is accepted as a complex relationship.
Most individuals born into the same social conditions seem to be
constrained by those conditions in ways that seem to reveal patterns, but
others are not so constrained. Sociologists have made two points here:
first, that individuals are not simply determined by social forces outside
themselves but can act to change or limit the effect of those social forces
in some circumstances; second, that apparently similar social conditions
can mask major differences of experience for people within the same
family (to be the first child and to be a girl can be a very different
experience from that of a second child who is a boy). There is recognition
of the uniqueness of individual experience, on the one hand, but also
acceptance of the relatively persistent patterns within society. How the
particular can be understood in the context of the general continues to
be the challenge of sociology.

Within the past two decades the perspectives of 'RACE' and GENDER
have become very important to sociological analysis. Many sociologists
have accepted that they had previously conducted research in a manner
that overlooked the experiences of women and of black people.
New perspectives have thus opened up to add new dimensions to old
sociological preoccupations. The analysis of advanced capitalist society,

for example, has developed new concerns from the perspectives of women and black people in both the industrialized countries and, in the analysis of neo-colonialism, in the Third World.

Virtually every aspect of social life has been scrutinized by sociologists. Social workers have been able to draw upon studies that throw some light on the many social problems with which they have to deal. Social work training frequently uses the idea of the social construction of problems (given that individuals may need particular help too) that would appear to be suggested by a sociological analysis. Social workers work individually and are therefore invited to look inwards to relational problems and not outwards to broad social conditions that affect many service users. Because social workers also feel powerless in the face of POVERTY, UNEMPLOYMENT and HOUSING PROBLEMS, they emphasize what they feel they can achieve and run the risk of losing sight of the structural issues. It is not surprising, therefore, that sociologists have also turned their attention to the role played by welfare provision, including social work services, within societies like Britain. This analysis has revealed both empowering and liberating aspects to the role of social worker as well as more worrying oppressive practices. (See ANTIDISCRIMINATORY PRACTICE, CASEWORK, EQUAL OPPORTUNITIES POLICIES, RADICAL SOCIAL WORK.)

A. Giddens, *Sociology*, Cambridge, Polity Press, 1993.

solvents the fumes of various volatile substances that can be inhaled to give intoxicating effects. The list of products is considerable and includes glue, aerosols, cleaning fluids, paint, nail varnish, lighter fuel and petrol.

The peak age for using solvents for their effects appears to be about 14 years, although the majority of this use is short-term experimentation and is not repeated. The very small percentage of people who go on to use solvents on a regular basis probably have some underlying problem that needs to be addressed. Solvents have a similar effect to being drunk, whereby problems may be temporarily forgotten. (See SUBSTANCE MISUSE.)

special educational needs (SEN) about 20 per cent of children have particular learning difficulties to an extent that requires their identification and extra provision under the EDUCATION ACT 1996 and the relevant code of practice.

The definition includes severe, profound and multiple difficulties, general learning difficulties and specific difficulties (such as dyslexia); speech, hearing and visual disorders, behavioural and emotional difficulties, and needs arising from restricted mobility. The majority of needs will be met at school level through SCHOOL ACTION and SCHOOL ACTION PLUS. Only those children with the most severe difficulties will require a STATEMENT. Under the general principles of INCLUSION, children with SEN should be educated alongside their peers in mainstream schools wherever possible. Any problems about provision should be raised with the local education authority's PARENT PARTNERSHIP SERVICE or the school's SPECIAL EDUCATIONAL NEEDS COORDINATOR.

Special Educational Needs Code of Practice the advice given to local education authorities (LEAs) and schools by the DEPARTMENT FOR EDUCATION AND SKILLS (DfES) about provision for children's SPECIAL EDUCATIONAL NEEDS under Part IV of the EDUCATION ACT 1996.

The latest version of the code became effective from 1 January 2002. All those involved in education, health and social services must 'have regard' to it. The code is designed to help the agencies to make effective provision and contains various safeguards to ensure best practice in a general sense but does not prescribe what authorities must do in individual cases.

special educational needs coordinator (SENCO) a teacher in every maintained school who is responsible for all the children identified as having SPECIAL EDUCATIONAL NEEDS (SEN).

Under the SPECIAL EDUCATIONAL NEEDS CODE OF PRACTICE, the special educational needs coordinator should play a key role, in partnership with the head teacher and the governing body, in determining the strategic development of SEN policy and provision within the school. The SENCO takes day-to-day responsibility for the operation of the school's SEN policy and provides professional support and advice to colleagues, both in school and from other agencies, in order to ensure high quality teaching and learning for all children with SEN.

specific issue order a court order giving directions for settling a particular question that has arisen between parents or others with PARENTAL RESPONSIBILITY for the child concerned.

The order is one of four SECTION 8 ORDERS under the CHILDREN ACT. In effect, it gives the court power to settle a dispute over some aspect of raising a child, such as medical treatment or education, though stipulating what is to happen. Local authorities may apply for the order if they obtain leave from the court to do so. They could, for example, obtain an order directing that a child they are accommodating should have a particular medical operation.

specific sentence report a short PRE-SENTENCE REPORT in which a member of a YOUTH OFFENDING TEAM or a PROBATION officer can address the question of whether an offender is suitable for a particular sentence that the court has it in mind to impose.

spirituality a way of understanding the world that transcends the material and is often associated with belonging to a faith community or a religion.

Spirituality is notoriously difficult to define, even by people for whom it has some meaning and significance. People who belong to faith communities such as Christianity, Judaism or Islam would equate spirituality with a religious or devotional way of living in which prayer and meditation feature prominently as means by which they can be in communication with a divine being. Those who believe that there is something of the divine in all material things would suggest that spirituality is the art of recognizing this special dimension in all living things – Hinduism, for example. For some it has an almost mystical dimension, whereas for others it seems to mean no more, but no less, than a warm glow that comes upon them from time to time.

In social work education and training, issues to do with religion and spirituality are frequently ignored and treated with suspicion. This is partly because of the ways in which organized religions are often perceived as being oppressive to women and minority groups such as gay and lesbian people, in stark contrast to the egalitarian values underpinning social work. The militant behaviour of fundamentalist religious groups throughout the world cause many people to challenge the validity of all religions. There also remain the influential vestiges of Freudian and Marxist critiques of religion, which relegate such activities to the sidelines of emotional and political immaturity.

This is in stark contrast to both the origins of much social welfare work in the UK and the motivations of many workers in the field who saw their professional practice as being a working out of their faith and spirituality. With the increased professionalization of social work, however, issues of religion and spirituality were side-lined and seen to have perhaps as much relevance to practice as other harmless pastimes like amateur dramatics, watching sport or playing cards.

In spite of such treatment, however, religion and spirituality are still seen by many as having positive, creative and emancipatory influences both upon individuals and groups within society. Many Asian and Jewish people, for example, see their culture, religion and spirituality as being deeply interwoven. For many black people, religion and spirituality are inextricably bound up with their cultural identity and their struggles against a white supremacist majority. It is often their spirituality that motivates them in their fight against oppression. In this sense there are strong links between religious themes of being set free from oppression and the current agendas of social justice.

Alongside all this is the practice imperative for all social workers to take seriously the wide range of needs that service users bring to the social work relationship. For many people a religious faith is an important aspect of their lives, which social workers need to take into account when making their assessments.

Spirituality – and the religious commitment that sometimes, but not always, is an expression of it – needs to be part of a social worker's training agenda, even if it is not something that is influential in the worker's own life. It is worth noting, however, that in an existential sense, spirituality is seen by many people as that which gives meaning and purpose to their lives. If that definition is accepted, then spirituality is something with which everyone can identify.

B. Moss, 'Spirituality – a personal perspective', in N. Thompson, *Loss and Grief – A Guide for Human Services Practitioners*, London, Palgrave, 2002.

sponsored immigrant someone given the right to enter the UK because
a citizen or settled resident has undertaken to maintain him or her.

A sponsored immigrant is excluded from claiming means-tested
and non-contributory benefits for five years.

SPP abbreviation for statutory paternity pay. See WELFARE RIGHTS 7.

squatting living in a dwelling without the permission of the landlord
or owner.

Many people regard the problem of HOMELESSNESS as a political
problem, because in Britain it is estimated that there are more dwellings
than households. These excess dwellings may be a second home for some
people, void dwellings of local authorities awaiting repairs before being
relet, properties that are empty pending redevelopment or renewal, and
properties empty for a variety of other reasons (ex-army camps, for
example). In the face of such apparently wasted resources, squatters'
movements have appeared from time to time. Homeless families and
single people, sometimes desperate for shelter, have taken direct action
by occupying such properties. On occasions, they have succeeded in
persuading an owner to let them stay in a property for a negotiated
period. More often, disputes occur between owners and squatters,
sometimes of a violent nature and leading to the forcible eviction of
squatters. Legally a court order is required to evict squatters, but on
occasions owners have hired their own 'informal' bailiffs. Squatters can
also be accused of trespass or criminal damage if they have used force
to gain entry.

Landlords have sometimes agreed to 'short-life tenancies', whereby
a habitable property awaiting demolition is rented to a tenant on a
temporary basis – although 'temporary' has been known to be as long
as five years. Some HOUSING ASSOCIATIONS have put a lot of effort into
the renovation of short-life housing. The installation of a decent
bathroom, basic heating and some new windows can make a basically
sound dwelling habitable for a family for a temporary period and may
be preferable to BED AND BREAKFAST accommodation, although clearly
this is not a long-term solution to homelessness.

SRV abbreviation for SOCIAL ROLE VALORIZATION.

SSI abbreviation for SOCIAL SERVICES INSPECTORATE.

SSP abbreviation for statutory sick pay (see WELFARE RIGHTS 3).

stakeholder pension see WELFARE RIGHTS 8.

start point data see BASELINE.

state earnings-related pension scheme see WELFARE RIGHTS 8.

statement (of special educational needs) a written outline of the
provision being made by a local education authority to meet the needs
of a child with SPECIAL EDUCATIONAL NEEDS (SEN), (aged 2–19), following
a process of STATUTORY ASSESSMENT.

About 20 per cent of children have identified SEN but only about
2 per cent should have a 'statement'. The vast majority of children with

SEN will have their needs met at school level under SCHOOL ACTION and SCHOOL ACTION PLUS. Only children with complex or permanent and life-long needs and disabilities, many of which will be identified pre-school, are likely to need a statement unless there is a dramatic change in their circumstances. Children with a statement will not necessarily require education in a special school, although some will for at least part of their education. In accordance with the general principle of INCLUSION, even children with complex needs should be educated alongside their peers in mainstream schools wherever possible.

statutory adoption pay see WELFARE RIGHTS 7.

statutory assessment (of special educational needs) the process by which a local education authority establishes whether a child with SPECIAL EDUCATIONAL NEEDS requires a STATEMENT.

Although these assessments are primarily undertaken by an EDUCATIONAL PSYCHOLOGIST at the request of a parent or school, the input of professionals from other agencies in health and social services is often crucial in order to ensure a full picture of the child's needs. These assessments should not be confused with the assessments of children in need under the FRAMEWORK FOR THE ASSESSMENT OF CHILDREN IN NEED (although they will often involve the same children).

statutory maternity pay (SMP) see WELFARE RIGHTS 7.

statutory paternity pay (SPP) see WELFARE RIGHTS 7.

statutory sector a term describing those SOCIAL WORK agencies that by law or statute are obliged to provide certain services.

In practice, 'statutory' is another term for LOCAL AUTHORITY social work services, which by law must take certain actions to protect a child or to assist in detaining a person in psychiatric hospital. Voluntary social work agencies do not have such responsibilities and under the law may not exercise such powers even if they wish to. The fact that local authority social workers may exercise their considerable powers when working with CLIENTS often presents them with uniquely difficult decisions. Probation services are, of course, also statutory.

statutory sick pay (SSP) see WELFARE RIGHTS 3.

Stephen Lawrence Inquiry Report the report of an inquiry, chaired by Sir William Macpherson and published in 1999, which examined the investigation of the murder of Stephen Lawrence in London in 1993 and the responses of official agencies, including the police, who were condemned within the report for their INSTITUTIONAL RACISM.

The failure to provide appropriate support to Duwayne Brooks, who was with Stephen Lawrence when he died, was part of the inquiry report's argument for this finding. Instead of treating him as a traumatized witness of a racist attack, Mr Brooks was treated as a suspect. Police procedures gave priority to trying to obtain evidence and prevent it from being 'contaminated', at the expense of providing support and information to the Lawrence family and Mr Brooks. While there may have been no explicit racist intent on the part of individual officers, the cumulative effect was the same as if they had all been deliberately racist. The report also made it clear that part of the problem was ignorance and stereotyping, demonstrating that the line between institutional and intentional racism is a fine one in practice. The indignant police reaction to the report tended to concentrate upon the allegation of institutional racism rather than on the evidence provided of ignorance, prejudice and stereotyping.

What the report said was that institutional racism results in a failure to provide an appropriate professional service to the public because of prejudice, ignorance, thoughtlessness and stereotyping. This clearly applies equally to all other public services, including those in criminal justice.

Since the publication of the report, almost all of whose recommendations were accepted by the government, policies within the courts, the police and the PRISON and PROBATION SERVICES have changed substantially in order to introduce ethnic monitoring of staff grievances and of those receiving services, and to increase the representativeness of the workforce of these agencies. All public authorities have been given a legal duty to promote racial equality under the RACE RELATIONS (AMENDMENT) ACT 2000. A report by HM Inspectorate of Probation has applied the Stephen Lawrence inquiry report findings directly to probation policy and practice, reintroducing quality measures for PRE-SENTENCE REPORTS and encouraging specific new provisions for black offenders and racially motivated offenders. Local services are encouraged to develop new partnerships with black community organizations, and a programme of staff training is under way. Much of this has ben done before, however, and it remains to be seen whether the probation service can maintain its commitment to these measures.

HM Chief Inspector of Probation, *Toward race equality: a thematic inspection*, London, Home Office, 2000.

stereotype a set of biased, inflexible assumptions about an individual or group, based on physical appearance or characteristics, or social attributes or roles. These include sex, ethnicity, age, physical capacity, class, marital status, kinship, language, nationality, religion and sexual orientation.

Stereotypes differ from typifications in that typifications are flexible sets of assumptions based on individual life experiences. Typifications are open to modification through the acquisition and assimilation of additional life experiences; they are useful as building blocks to help people make sense of their social experiences and assist in the formulation of expectations of behaviour. Stereotypes, by contrast, are formulated through dominant political, social and cultural value systems and promoted by various institutions (such as through cultural traditions, religion and the media) controlled directly or indirectly by a dominant social group. They are used to justify privilege or to discriminate against individuals and groups in society in terms of access to resources or employment opportunities. Social workers often work with people who have been unfairly stereotyped, such as LONE PARENTS and people with LEARNING DISABILITY, and they may have to counter the effects of such negative stereotyping by others.

stigma a characteristic or attribute that conflicts with the expected norms or STEREOTYPES assigned to an individual or group and is therefore viewed as undesirable.

The term 'stigma' originates from the ancient Greek word for a sign branded on a person to signify something bad about him or her, for example that he or she is a traitor. The concept is now used to describe the process whereby people are allocated social identities based on stereotypes. When we first have contact with a person, we anticipate what that person is like from information that we have about him or her. Inferences are drawn from the person's visible characteristics, such as sex, ethnicity and physical capacity. As knowledge is acquired about that person, further assumptions are made on the basis of his or her name, accent, religious belief, sexual orientation, class, economic status and other invisible attributes. An attribute becomes a stigma when it is spuriously linked with undesirable behaviour or unvalued experiences: for example, an assumption that being a black man means that the person is a threat to the social order or that being female means that the person is physically weak. It is possible for some attributes to be ascribed as acceptable or desirable for some individuals but not for others; for example, it is socially acceptable for men to grow facial hair, but facial hair is stigmatizing for women.

Dominant political, social and cultural values play key roles in the operation of stigma, as they help to formulate individual value systems and reinforce the stereotypes of what is desirable for individuals and groups within society. Stigma strikes at the core of individual identity because stigmatized people either believe messages about themselves as inferior or have consciously to reject the process of stigmatization and challenge the stereotype assigned to them. The concept of stigma is useful in understanding the operation of DISCRIMINATION at all levels – from internalized racism and sexism, and so on, through individual prejudice to direct and indirect institutionalized discrimination. The process of stigmatization is particularly relevant to social work because the use of a social work service is commonly perceived as a stigmatizing experience for service users.

E. Goffman, *Stigma: Notes on the Management of Spoiled Identity*, Harmondsworth, Penguin, 1968.

subsistence level a standard of living thought sufficient to sustain life in a minimal way.

The idea of subsistence level has been used to define a minimum standard for people living in abject poverty in developing countries where life is constantly hazardous but also a minimum standard capable of supporting an individual in HEALTH. The workhouse system in 19th-century Britain attempted to define subsistence through the very spartan and at times harsh conditions it offered those who were so poor that they were forced to enter the workhouse or face slow starvation. In our own time, the United Nations Development Programme defines a global standard for subsistence as one US dollar a day income for each individual. Below that threshold families face severe malnutrition and dangerous levels of ill health.

substance misuse the non-medical use of substances that when taken into the body can substantially affect psychological and physical functions. Substances commonly misused may include legal and illegal drugs (amphetamines, cocaine, opiates, cannabis, LSD, Ecstasy), alcohol and prescribed drugs such as tranquillizers and barbiturates.

Figures for drug and alcohol misuse have increased over recent decades. Alcohol use has increased by 74 per cent since the 1950s, and heroin users registered with the Home Office have increased many times in the same period. Also, illegal drugs and alcohol are used by more and more young people and at increasingly young ages. People using illegal drugs are usually (although not exclusively) aged 20–35 and increasingly poor, unemployed, living in disadvantaged areas with poor housing and facilities, and often involved in criminal activity to sustain their habits. Alcohol users who develop problems from its use are often older, male and with families, but those with very severe problems are usually unemployed and socially isolated. Substance misuse by women, black people and older people is more hidden because these groups do not approach helping agencies (fearing stigma, racism and/or their children being taken into care) and because agencies do not recognize these groups have substance misuse problems or cater for their particular needs. Studies have shown that there may be extensive use in these groups but resulting in different problems and needs compared to those of the white male user; it is important that services take account of these differences.

Drug and alcohol misuse results in a range of serious problems for users themselves, their families and the wider society. In understanding these problems, it is important to realize there are three different types of drug and alcohol misuse – experimental, recreational and dependent use. There is no necessary progression to dependency, but people experience problems with each type of use. Experimental use can lead to intoxication and death – for example, small numbers of young people taking too large a dose of Ecstasy have died – and also to accidents through lack of control of usage because of unfamiliarity. Recreational use means controlled use in situations in which the user knows that harm is minimized. However, the physical and psychological effects of the substance still take their toll. Symptoms of psychoses and neuroses may arise – short or long term – with LSD and amphetamines; moderate use of alcohol can affect the functioning of most organs in the body, and intoxication with any substance impairs functioning for several days and may lead to accidents.

Dependent use means that the person finds it very hard to exist without the substance, and if the person is poor, crime or prostitution may be the only way of financing the habit, with criminal charges and imprisonment likely consequences. Dependent use of a substance also leads to longer-term mental and physical health problems along with problems of poor housing, homelessness, self-neglect and loss of relationships.

Social workers have a duty to intervene in all these areas of difficulty if the person is referred. In addition, there is a strong likelihood with alcohol misuse that children may be physically or sexually abused; in large proportions of CHILD PROTECTION cases, studies have shown there to be parental alcohol misuse. Neglect of children is also possible with substance misuse of all kinds, and especially when use is dependent. Thus child-care and child protection work should take full account of the issues of substance misuse if intervention is to be appropriate.

The risk of HIV/AIDS is also increased, not only through injecting substances but through the greater vulnerability to infections resulting from malnutrition and self-neglect. Social work has a responsibility to respond to the COMMUNITY CARE needs of people with HIV/AIDS in collaboration with the health service and other agencies.

There have been attempts to reduce substance misuse on a number of fronts. First, legislation making the possession and sale of illegal drugs criminal offences is intended to reduce the supply of drugs and deter use. Only specially licensed doctors are allowed to prescribe illegal drugs and opiates, and users have to be notified to the Home Office. Second, treatment programmes in general have been health-based, with drug and alcohol dependency units located in psychiatric hospitals and, more recently, COMMUNITY DRUG TEAMS and community alcohol teams funded by health authorities. The authority of licensed doctors to prescribe illegal drugs is one aspect of treatment, intended to keep the user away from the risks of the illicit market. Government policy, however, expressed in the various reports of the Advisory Committee for the Misuse of Drugs, recommends that social work should play an important role in treatment. This arose through the idea, still influential, that substance misuse was the result of the person's inability to manage his or her life, because of social or psychological pressures, and the social worker was expected to make a major contribution to the work of the medical team by helping the person to cope independently. 'Treatment' thus included rehabilitation. One important rehabilitation route has been residential rehabilitation in residential care homes provided by voluntary agencies. Social services now have the responsibility of finding these (and other) RESIDENTIAL CARE services under the COMMUNITY CARE legislation.

The third approach to reducing substance misuse involves PREVENTIVE WORK. In the 1980s the Advisory Committee for the Misuse of Drugs recommended that prevention be directed both at the risk of the person engaging in substance misuse and at the harm associated with misuse. Social work has been expected to deal with the former through the generic community work of addressing the sources of stress that bring about coping difficulties and subsequent substance misuse. There are opportunities for such work to be funded now by the Home Office drugs prevention team. A particular focus of harm reduction strategies since 1988 has been to seek to minimize the spread of Aids and HIV resulting from injecting substances. Emphasis has therefore been placed upon providing easy access to clean needles and prescriptions of substitute non-injection drugs. Other targets for harm reduction include the major problems presented by users for themselves and the wider society, through criminal activity to finance drug use, also unemployment, and distress and disruption in family and social relationships. The relative stability involved when a person receives drugs by prescription alleviates some of these problems and brings the user into contact with the services, where he or she may quickly receive support and referral if he or she is ready to try to stop using substances. In the case of people misusing drugs or alcohol, social work is involved in HARM MINIMIZATION through the community care legislation, which requires social services to include the needs of drug and alcohol users in their plans.

The fourth approach consists in the important role of social work in both prevention and treatment aspects of working with substance misuse. Traditionally, social workers have regarded the problems as more within the province of psychiatry than of social work, and they have been deterred from engaging with these issues through negative social STEREOTYPES of people misusing different substances. The Central Council for Education and Training in Social Work has, however, published guidelines for social workers that emphasize dealing with stereotypes, developing understanding of the problems and possible intervention approaches, and learning the skills of appropriately recognizing substance misuse patterns. The guidelines also encompass some of the important components of assessment and intervention, and of determining risks and needs. (See ALCOHOL, ALCOHOLISM.)

R. Griffiths and B. Pearson, *Working With Drug Users*, Aldershot, Wildwood House, 1988.

substitute family care see FOSTER CARE.

sudden infant death syndrome (SIDS) the death of an infant from no apparent cause, commonly known as 'cot death'.

While medical research has still to determine what precisely causes the swift and wholly unexpected death of an infant, it has highlighted preventive measures that can help reduce the risk. Infants should be placed on their back or side when sleeping and not on their stomach, and they should not be allowed to get too warm – parents should use lightweight blankets, adding to them or taking them away according to room temperature. Cot death seems to occur mostly to infants between one month and five months old.

suicide an intentional act of commission or omission on the part of a person that results in the same person's death. A suicidal act of commission might include self-hanging, taking an overdose of drugs or inhaling carbon monoxide fumes; an act of omission would include failing to take a life-maintaining medicine.

Statistics about suicides are notoriously unreliable and almost certainly under-represent the actual suicide rate. There are often very difficult decisions to be made by, among others, coroners and doctors about the cause of death, and strong social pressure exists, where there are doubts, to record causes other than suicide. Suicides affect all social classes. Rates are higher for men than for women, and among older people, those without children, the divorced and the widowed. Significant loss of social status is a precipitating factor. There are cultural differences, too, with pre-industrial societies usually having much lower suicide rates. Behaviour can vary a lot historically, with times of war, for example, leading to a lower incidence of suicide if group cohesiveness rises.

To determine whether an act is genuinely suicidal entails examining the problem of intent. Suicide attempts are sometimes inadvertently discovered, whereas mock-suicidal behaviour often entails careful planning in the expectation that the person will be discovered. All such behaviour must be taken very seriously, including mock attempts, because such acts are inherently risky and mock suicides usually represent profound unhappiness and major personal problems. Suicidal behaviour, if known of, usually brings about intervention from the STATUTORY SECTOR. Social work effort tends to concentrate upon the social problems that may underpin, for example, an ANXIETY state or DEPRESSION, or upon attempting to alter a person's self-perception.

supervision the overseeing of the work of SOCIAL CARE staff, social workers and student social workers by either a PRACTICE TEACHER or line manager (usually a team manager) or a consultant.

The role of supervisor includes three elements: first, to ensure that workers account for their work (the *managing* or *administrative* function); second, the professional development of workers (the *educative* or *teaching* function); and third, the personal support of workers in times of difficulty (the *supportive* or *enabling* function). The form and content of supervision vary according to the needs of the worker, the nature of the work and the abilities of the supervisor.

Qualified practitioners in any of the established professions (law, medicine, and so on) would maintain that supervision is necessary during training; thereafter the need to 'consult' with specialists would be sufficient. This pattern tends not to apply to social work and SOCIAL CARE.

There is continuing uncertainty about the status of social work as a profession and thus of the ability of even experienced and qualified practitioners to work independently. The location of much social work within bureaucratic local authorities, together with the stressful nature of the work, may also account for the widespread use of supervision, at least within fieldwork teams, for even the most experienced practitioner. Within day-care and residential settings, supervisory practices vary, with many workers continuing to receive scant support.

The predominant form for supervision continues to be the one-to-one relationship of supervisor and supervised. It is possible for experienced practitioners to be supervised by inexperienced managers, and it is common for women workers to be supervised by male team managers and black workers by white supervisors. Interesting alternative methods and arrangements for supervision continue to be rejected in favour of line management. A major initiative from the Social Care Association has, however, led to some limited experimentation on the part of some employers in supporting workers under stress, including independent counselling services that are gender- and 'race'-sensitive. A more recent trend has added appraisal of staff competence to the supervisor's role – either for the purpose of NATIONAL VOCATIONAL QUALIFICATIONS or for in-house staff appraisal systems. This has tended to dilute the supportive role of the line manager as supervisor by adding to it a watchdog function that does not always sit easily with the support function.

C. Payne and T. Scott, *Developing Supervision of Teams In Field and Residential Social Work*, Parts I and II, London, National Institute of Social Work, 1982 and 1985.

supervision order (1) in criminal cases, a sentence that places a child or young person aged 10 to 17 under the supervision of a member of a YOUTH OFFENDING TEAM or a PROBATION OFFICER for a period of up to three years.

An order may include one or more additional requirements, such as conditions of residence in a particular place, a programme of activities the young person has to participate in, restrictions on the young person leaving home at night, psychiatric treatment, school attendance and REPARATION. The conduct of staff in administering supervision orders is subject to NATIONAL STANDARDS, and young people who do not comply can be returned to court for the order to be revoked or continued. Penalties for breach include fines, CURFEWS, ATTENDANCE CENTRE ORDERS and COMMUNITY PUNISHMENT ORDERS. Community supervision creates opportunities to engage young people in discussion of their offending behaviour and the consequences for themselves, their VICTIMS and others without using damaging institutional approaches.

supervision order (2) a court order under section 35 of the CHILDREN ACT that requires a local authority social worker or probation officer to act as supervisor to the child or children named in the order.

The court may make a supervision order only when a child has suffered, or is likely to suffer, SIGNIFICANT HARM and that harm is attributable to the standard of parental care (see THRESHOLD CRITERIA). Although the grounds for making a supervision order are exactly the same as those for a CARE ORDER, it is the less intrusive of the two, since the local authority does not acquire PARENTAL RESPONSIBILITY for the child. In this sense, the court will see it as preferable to a care order, as long as it is assured that the powers under the order are sufficient to protect the child and safeguard his or her welfare. Under a supervision order, the supervisor has a duty to advise, assist and befriend the child; in practice, this often means giving guidance to parents on, for example, matters of discipline. The supervisor may have the child medically or psychiatrically examined only after seeking the court's approval and then only with the child's consent. The supervisor may also direct the child to live at a specified place for a period of up to 90 days and to participate in designated activities. These provisions are aimed at young people in their teens who may be required to attend certain activities or courses of instruction; they would apply particularly to young people who are likely to suffer significant harm through being beyond parental control. The supervisor also has powers to take all reasonable steps to see that the terms of the order are put into effect. Within the terms of the order the court may appoint a 'responsible person' – often a parent or another adult in the family – with that person's consent. The responsible person must take all reasonable steps to ensure that the terms of the order and the directions of the supervisor, such as a curfew, are met. A supervision order lasts for one year but can be extended to a maximum of three years. It can be varied or discarded by application of any of the parties involved, such as the local authority, the child or the parent.

M. Freeman, *Understanding the Children Act*, Basingstoke, Macmillan, 1994.

supported decision making an approach that regards decision making as an ongoing process rather than a 'one-off' event and acknowledges that some people may need extensive support in order to reach and convey their decisions.

Supported decision making has come to the fore in connection with access to DIRECT PAYMENTS for COMMUNITY CARE services for people with LEARNING DISABILITY. The COMMUNITY CARE (DIRECT PAYMENTS) ACT 1996 states that recipients of direct payments must be able to consent to the payments and be able (with help) to manage them. In practice, it has been the requirement for consent that has presented the greatest challenge for people with learning disability, particularly those with more complex impairments affecting their capacity to communicate their wishes. This has led some local authorities to exclude people with learning disability from their direct payment schemes, although the government has now made it clear that this is unacceptable. It has been argued that everyone can make decisions if given enough time and the right type of support. Recent research has indicated that this can be accomplished if workers spend time getting to know the way that particular service users communicate and if the decision making is treated as a process rather than a 'one-off' event. This is in contrast to approaches based on tests of mental capacity, which are more likely to reveal that service users are unable to understand the issues involved in the decision.

J. Edge, *Who's in control? Decision-making by people with learning difficulties who have high support needs*, London, Values into Action, 2001.

supported employment employment in mainstream settings that offers support for disabled people who may need additional help with learning the job or settling into the work setting.

Supported employment has developed in connection with policies to include disabled workers within mainstream work settings. This varies from sheltered employment, which involves work in separate settings designed for disabled workers, such as the Remploy factories. Supported employment is described as being for disabled people in general but is more commonly aimed at people with LEARNING DISABILITY. The Department for Work and Pensions recently changed the name of its supported employment scheme to 'Workstep'. It is described as a programme for people who face more complex barriers to getting and keeping a job and includes practical assistance to employers.

Supporting People a government programme to provide housing-related support services to vulnerable people through one funding stream. It was implemented in April 2003.

The Supporting People project draws many existing funding streams, such as Transitional Housing Benefit, Special Housing Management Grant and Probation Accommodation Grant, into a single 'pot' that is controlled by a commissioning body including local authorities, health authorities and the probation service. Local authority Supporting People Teams are responsible (through consultation with partners) for developing a strategy for the development of housing-related support services. By 1 April 2003 service providers needed to have made an 'interim contract' with the Supporting People authority in order to ensure continued funding. The contract reflects the existing service and funding levels. Thereafter has been a period of reviewing schemes, using a BEST VALUE approach, but having particular regard to the needs and gaps identified in the strategy.

The Office of the Deputy Prime Minister, which is responsible for the programme, has stated that 'the Supporting People programme offers vulnerable people the opportunity to improve their quality of life by providing a stable environment which enables greater independence. It will deliver high quality and strategically planned housing-related services which are cost effective and reliable, and complement existing care services. The planning and development of services will be "needs led". Supporting People is a working partnership of local government, service users and support agencies.'

The aim of Supporting People is to ensure that, on the basis of a common approach across the country, a comprehensive overview of the needs for support by vulnerable adults is conducted in each area. The programme also matches existing services in each area against these needs. Thus the needs and funding for support services for very different groups of users are brought together within a single framework. Among others, it covers older people in sheltered housing or those wishing to remain independently in their homes, young homeless people staying in one place for training or counselling, women escaping DOMESTIC VIOLENCE, ASYLUM SEEKERS, those with long-term mental health problems and adults with learning difficulties to live in a shared house or other supported accommodation.

The Supporting People programme is partly about rationalizing different funding schemes for supported housing, but it also has the potential for creating active partnerships between agencies (public, private and voluntary) to provide the necessary range of supported housing for vulnerable groups in localities. This could entail a significant expansion of provision for those groups mentioned above, which is currently patchy or poorly developed across the country. Supporting People also detaches support services from housing. For example, floating support services can be provided to teenage parents moving into council accommodation and in need of support or to a person with mental health problems who wishes to move back to his or her previous home. It also promotes the interlinking of care and support jointly supplied from different agencies, whether health, housing, social services or probation.

This reshaping of services could lead to a significant reconfiguring of social work in relation to supported accommodation, providing a range of services from 'floating support' to comprehensive 'on-the-premises' support. Each locality has a Supporting People multidisciplinary team that should include housing health, probation and social services. It works with other partner agencies, particularly from among the supported housing agencies. One of the principal objectives is to ensure a fuller range of support for black and ethnic users with more specialist providers available who should have a more stable funding stream to draw on as a result. In the run-up to implementation in April 2003, black and minority ethnic users and providers must be part of the consultation and planning process in each locality and services must be commissioned from providers who can address the specific needs of existing or potential black and minority users.

Sure Start a programme, funded by central government, that integrates a range of children's services in specific disadvantaged areas for all families with children under four living in those areas.

Sure Start schemes aim to improve the social and emotional development of children by helping parents to function more effectively;

to improve the ability of the children to learn by encouraging stimulating play and improving language skills; to strengthen the resources of the area to assist all families with children under four.

Sure Start schemes generally bring together a range of service projects with the intention of 'adding value' through local integration. Schemes are generally set up for areas that have between 500 and 1,000 children aged under four. They require high levels of parent involvement from the start as well as with the major service agencies such as primary schools and community organizations. The programmes are universal within their areas; that is, all families with children under four can receive Sure Start services. All schemes must strive to reach certain centrally set targets – such as increasing the number of mothers who are breast-feeding, identifying and supporting mothers who may give birth to a low birth weight baby, reducing the number of mothers smoking and reducing the number of young children on the child protection register. Sure Start is evidence-based so that research on child development and annual evaluation of specific schemes is integrated into their work.

Sure Start maternity grant see WELFARE RIGHTS 7.

survivor a term now sometimes used in preference to 'VICTIM', especially in relation to women who have experienced SEXUAL ABUSE, rape or DOMESTIC VIOLENCE.

Derived from the vocabulary of assertiveness training, the term implies that a woman who has had the strength actively to survive such an ordeal should be respected and admired rather than treated as a powerless and passive object of pity (and sometimes contempt).

suspension see EXCLUSION FROM SCHOOL.

syringe exchange scheme a system that enables drugs misusers to swap old needles and syringes for new.

Syringe exchange schemes have spread throughout Britain in the last ten years as a response to HIV/AIDS. Schemes may be offered by pharmacies or drugs agencies, whether statutory or voluntary. Schemes usually work on the basis of 'new for old', with injectors bringing back used equipment in a sharps container. The service is confidential, perhaps with initials and numbers of syringes returned and given out collected for monitoring purposes. Such schemes are usually free. The giving of clean needles, syringes and sharps containers is part of an overall HARM MINIMIZATION programme designed to prevent the spread of the HIV virus.

systems approach the undertaking of social work based on analysis and activation of the human systems around the CLIENT.

A system is a set of objects that are interdependent and interrelated so that they function as a single unit. We often refer loosely to systems in contemporary life, such as sound systems or computer systems, to indicate a grouping of components that produce something through the relationships between them that they could not produce on their own. Systems display a number of characteristics: The parts are *reciprocal*, each is related to every other so that a change affecting one will change the whole. Their *structure* endures over a period of time because systems can adapt to changes in the surrounding environment. A system copes with environmental change by receiving inputs such as information from the environment, processing that information and producing an output that enables it to adapt. Systems have a *boundary* that marks off where each system ends and the environment begins. The boundary may be open, allowing the system to interact with its environment, or closed, preventing influences, information or changes in the environment to affect its internal working. Systems strive for *equilibrium*, that is, some balance in their relationship to their environment so that they may survive with their fundamental nature intact.

In the 1970s some social work educators turned to systems theory as a basis for developing a single social work approach, or 'unitary method', that would be applicable to all social work settings. The concept of systems was applied to the way people interacted with one another. It was theorized that people depend on human systems in meeting needs. People were part of informal systems, such as family, friends and colleagues, as well as formal systems, such as clubs and trade unions, and societal systems, such as schools and employing organizations. Problems arose for people when their systems had broken down or were failing to produce sufficient resources to allow the system to continue working as before. The role of the social worker in this approach is to identify the different systems of which the client is a part (the CLIENT SYSTEM), such as family and employing organization, and to analyse how the interaction of the parts of those systems causes problems. The social worker's task is to make the client system function again by modifying the interactions between people and resources within the system. Such thinking had the benefit of requiring the social worker to see the client as a product of wider forces and to move away from the traditional concentration on the individual client. A client's problems might well be generated by relationships within his or her system so that one had to look beyond the individual to make change occur.

As a theory, systems thinking in the form of the unitary method was criticized for its difficult terminology, lack of practical guidance to social workers and tendency to exclude radical changes as options. It has, however, continued to influence social workers' understanding of families. Placing a client in relation to the various systems, now often simply understood as networks, often diagrammatically, is now a commonly used tool to allow both social worker and client to understand the range of supports present and those areas where they may have to be created. The systems approach has also provided a basis for seeing families as self-regulating systems that function according to rules established through a process of trial and error. Social workers and family therapists emphasize the capacity of family systems to adapt and change as their environment changes. Families that are closed systems, that resist change and do not evolve become 'stuck' in patterns that often place the entire blame for this on individual family members. The use of ECOMAPS is another widespread technique drawn originally from systems thinking. A whole school of FAMILY THERAPY has developed around the basic insight that family problems are a product of the relationships between all the family members and that change requires changing how all the family members behave in relation to each other rather than pinning blame on a single delinquent member. (See also ECOLOGICAL APPROACH.)

M. Payne, *Modern Social Work Theory*, London, Macmillan, 1997.

Tt

take-up the number of people claiming a benefit as a proportion of those eligible to claim it. Take-up of benefits is a matter of concern, since benefits provide at best a minimal standard of living. In particular, anyone failing to claim MEANS-TESTED BENEFITS is likely to be living in POVERTY.

Universal benefits with simple, well-known and non-stigmatizing rules are claimed by the vast majority of people who are eligible. For example, child benefit – see WELFARE RIGHTS (5) – is claimed by 98 per cent of people who are eligible. By contrast, many potential claimants feel that means-tested benefits are stigmatizing and the rules are often complex and confusing. For example, the former, rather obscurely named family credit was claimed by only about 60 per cent of those eligible, even though it was quite intensively promoted after it was introduced in 1990. Take-up rates of means-tested benefits are estimated using data from benefit administrators and from the Family Expenditure Survey. It is estimated that in total some £1,600 million in means-tested benefits is unclaimed every year.

The take-up rates of other benefits have never been systematically estimated, but it is probable that non-contributory benefits for people with disabilities, such as disability living allowance, attendance allowance and severe disablement allowance – see WELFARE RIGHTS (3) – are significantly underclaimed because of their complexity, the off-putting nature of the claims process and the isolation of many potential recipients. General take-up campaigns by local authorities to encourage claims for social security benefits were widespread during the 1980s and often enormously successful. More recently campaigns have relied more on targeting likely claimants. See also WELFARE RIGHTS 1.

targeting the selection of the most appropriate places in which to advertise the existence of particular benefits so that the maximum number of potential claimants will see them. See WELFARE RIGHTS 1.

targets the specification of outputs in terms of clear numerical improvements in services and service delivery.

These are clearly linked to PERFORMANCE MEASUREMENT and aim to give a direction to the development of services. With the establishment of health improvement programmes, targets have become a key issue for primary care trusts and their partners in social services. These include the reduction in inequalities in health by improved targeting of identifiable groups, such as the elderly and other socially excluded groups. Service providers find that the establishment of a wide range of targets can cause problems in that they are seen as too demanding or fail to take fully into account local circumstances. The government argues that targets are necessary to provide the public with evidence that services are using public money appropriately and that services are seeking to achieve a level of output in line with the best and with public expectations. As such they are part of the process of MODERNIZATION in public services.

target system the system of people or organizations that social work intervention aims to change in order to produce solutions to a CLIENT's problems.

The target system may be the same as the CLIENT SYSTEM, that is, the client's own family or immediate social network; or it may be quite different. An example is a young person who regularly truants; the school becomes the target system within which the social worker attempts to effect some change to make the school more attractive to attend.

tariff the 'menu' of sentences available to the courts and the order in which these are normally imposed upon individuals during an offending 'career'; the implications of these sentencing conventions for those who reoffend.

task-centred work a particular approach to social work that places strong emphasis on solving problems that the CLIENT considers important by completion of a series of small tasks.

Task-centred work is one of the very few approaches to social work developed by social workers themselves. It originated in the United States in the 1960s as a response to increasing criticism that long-term CASEWORK was both time-consuming and ineffective for a substantial proportion of clients. The approach is based on three key principles: first, that the social worker and user together tackle problems that the user has defined as the most important; second, that these problems are resolved through a series of small steps or tasks; and third, that the work is short-term, usually completed within three months.

Task-centred work proceeds through a number of stages. The first stage is *problem selection*. This is achieved by the social worker and user listing all the problems facing the user. From the list of problems the user and social worker agree on which are the two or three most important problems to resolve. The selected problems are written down in language that is clear to the user and expressed in as much detail as possible. For example, a problem such as 'Janice is socially isolated' is general and vague; a better way of framing the problem would be 'Janice has no opportunity to meet people during the week because she has to look after her 18-month-old twin daughters. She has no car and finds the bus service too infrequent to be of use.' It has been suggested that practitioners should use the 'five Ws' to help with problem specification: who, what, where, when and why. The social worker's role is to facilitate this process of problem selection but not to impose his or her views as to which is the most important. There is one exception to this rule: the worker may have to insist that, because of a responsibility in law such as protecting a child, a particular problem must be addressed by the user whether or not the user considers it a priority. If the social worker is unable to convince the user that the problem – say, a parent's habit of going out in the evening and leaving a young child unattended – is important to address, it means that no further task-centred work can take place, at least in respect of that particular problem. In practice, overriding the user's priorities in this way rarely happens.

The second stage is *goal setting*, that is, moving from what is wrong to what is needed. The goal is what the user wants as a way to resolve the selected problem. Goals should be realistic and achievable in a short time. Choosing goals often involves negotiation between worker and user in order to reach agreement on their feasibility or desirability. If the social worker cannot agree that a particular goal is realistic for the user, this observation is also recorded and reasons are given. As with problems, the goals are written down in the user's own words and in as much detail as possible so that everyone can agree when they have been reached. This has the merit of forcing social workers to think as specifically as possible about the user's goals. They have been notoriously vague in goal setting. 'We will work to reduce Janice's social isolation' is too woolly and does not include any way of satisfactorily measuring when the goal has been achieved. 'I want to visit my friends more often' is better but still unclear. 'Janice wants to visit her mother at least once a week and to meet her best friend two evenings a week in her local pub' is better yet. The goal as expressed is less grandiose but clear and attainable.

The third stage of task-centred work is the *setting of tasks*. Tasks are the small steps that the user, the practitioner or both undertake in order to move towards the defined goal. Tasks are jointly negotiated in a session between practitioner and user, and recorded, and a timetable for their completion is drawn up. They are often everyday activities and may seem obvious or mundane. That is their strength: they are small and achievable, but each relates to the others, often as part of a sequence. As with problems and goals, tasks are written down in a way that makes it clear whether or not they have been completed: 'Janice will ring the local bus company and note down exactly when buses call at her local bus-stop'; 'Janice will ask the driver to help her aboard with her pushchair'; 'Janice will find out what evening classes are available and will consider which one she might want to attend.' The work should emphasize the user's tasks. The whole point of task-centred work is to enhance the user's capacity to solve problems and through that to gain some control over his or her life. It makes little sense, therefore, for the practitioner to undertake tasks that the user could, with preparation or rehearsal, undertake for himself or herself. Individual tasks can be set for completion before the next meeting between practitioner and user or they can be completed during sessions. Typically session tasks rehearse with the practitioner an activity that the user wants to undertake, such as attending a job interview or writing a letter.

The fourth stage is *reviewing*. At every session, user and practitioner review whether or not the tasks set at the previous session have been completed. Both will have a written copy of what those tasks are, what they require for completion and when they should be completed. If there is little apparent progress towards the selected goals, it may be that they are inappropriate or unrealistic after all, or that user motivation is low. Whatever the reason, it may be necessary to renegotiate a new set of goals and a new time frame. But task-centred work is always short-term work, using deadlines as a spur to activity. Redefining the timetable too often inevitably undermines the work.

Task-centred work fits in closely with concepts of PARTNERSHIP and users' PARTICIPATION in decisions that affect them. It places emphasis on WRITTEN AGREEMENTS as to what work will be undertaken and by whom. The increasing requirement for partnership with users in all phases of social work makes the approach a model of considerable relevance. It is one of the few models of social work that encourages users to determine what they wish to work on rather than having to work on problems that the practitioner considers most important. It also places emphasis on user motivation, responsibility and enhancing problem-solving capacity. A significant body of research into work with a range of user groups has established task-centred work as one of the most effective of all approaches to social work.

P. Marsh and N. Doel, *Task-Centred Work*, Aldershot, Arena, 1992.

tax credit in recent years the concept of a 'tax credit' has come to mean a number of things. In one context, tax assessment, it is simply a way of enhancing income by providing allowances on which tax on earned and certain other kinds of income will not be paid. The *child tax credit* from April 2003 (see WELFARE RIGHTS 5 and WELFARE RIGHTS 9) is a form of assistance that enables taxpayers with children to retain income. As their income rises, however, the support is withdrawn so that most higher rate taxpayers do not receive it. It has been seen by some commentators as a benefit rather than a tax allowance because, unlike its predecessors, it has had to be claimed. In the SOCIAL SECURITY context, tax credit is used to describe what is more akin to a welfare benefit, so that the *working tax credit* and child tax credit, for example, bear more resemblance to a conventional benefit that is claimed and awarded, subject to a means-test. From April 2003, however, there has been no capital limits (unlike the *working families' tax credit* and *disabled person's tax credit*), and assessment is based on gross earnings, as evidenced by tax returns and P60 evidence of pay and deductions, with less reliance on separate claim forms and declarations from claimants and employers as to 'net weekly income'. Arguably, the welfare support delivered through the new tax credits represents a hybrid between more conventional welfare benefits and tax allowances and reliefs.

The rationale for these tax credits from 2003 was provided by the Chancellor and announced in the budgets (and supporting information) in 1999 (*Budget 1999 – Building a Stronger Economic Future for Britain*, HM Treasury, March 1999) and 2000 (*Budget 2000 – Prudent for a Purpose: Working for a Stronger and Fairer Britain*, HM Treasury, March 2000).

team a group of people working together to deliver a service.

Within social welfare occupations teams vary considerably in size, complexity, management structure and purpose. In social work organizations, teams may comprise GENERIC workers who carry responsibilities for all client groups within a designated area, but such teams are increasingly rare. Typically, fieldwork teams are now divided into adult services (covering principally mental health, DISABILITY and OLDER PEOPLE) and children's services. Within these two broad categories of teams there are often relative specialisms. Thus, for children there may be juvenile justice teams and teams concerned with fostering and adoption. Often there are also specialisms within teams; for example, within adult teams there are likely to be workers who have interests in mental health and others whose expertise lies with LEARNING DISABILITY.

A distinction may be drawn between a team and a network. Teams are characterized by a common goal, shared working and a high degree of consensus about how the job is to be done. Networks, by contrast, are loose entities where people work independently and where there may be substantial differences in practice from one worker to another. RESIDENTIAL WORK teams are typical of the first category Clearly, such workers are exposed to each other's practice and clients. In these circumstances several workers may have primary responsibility for one case. Fieldwork teams comparatively have their workers operating much more independently, although there may be circumstances where a case is held jointly (such as with an aggressive or potentially violent service user). Teams can be MULTIDISCIPLINARY in nature. Thus in mental health settings psychiatrists, social workers, psychiatric nurses and psychologists work together, each with his or her own particular focus. In hospital settings, psychiatrists are likely to be seen as the managers of the 'case'; in the COMMUNITY, the social worker is more likely to play the KEY WORKER role. Teamwork is enhanced by an effective team manager; few teams operate without a line manager. Effectiveness seems to be related to clear and appropriate policies, active staff support and SUPERVISION systems, and a WORKLOAD MANAGEMENT scheme that ensures both worker protection and good-quality service delivery.

A. Hey, 'Organizing teams – alternative patterns', in N. Marshall, N. Preston-Shoot and E. Wincott (eds), *Teamwork: For and Against*, London, British Association of Social Workers, 1979.

teenage pregnancy conception by a young woman or girl under the age of 20.

One of the key elements of the government's strategy to improve the health of the nation and tackle social exclusion is to prevent unwanted pregnancies across all age groups, especially among teenage women and girls. For some time Britain has had the highest teenage conception rate among Western European states. In 1997 almost 90,000 teenagers became pregnant, resulting in around 55,000 live births. Of these, 7,700 conceptions were to girls aged under 16, with 5,500 conceptions to 15-year-olds and 2,200 to girls aged 14 and under.

The chances of becoming a teenage parent (both mothers and fathers) are greatly enhanced by social and economic disadvantage. The government's SOCIAL EXCLUSION Unit has identified a number of risk factors, including poverty (girls from social class V are 10 times more likely to become pregnant than girls from social class 1), a background in care (studies have shown that as many as a quarter of females become pregnant by age 16 and nearly half had become mothers within two years of leaving care), sexual abuse (several studies have associated childhood sexual abuse with teenage pregnancies), educational problems (low educational achievement is strongly associated with teenage pregnancy), homelessness (teenage pregnancy can be both cause and effect of homelessness) and finally crime (teenagers, both females and males, who have been in trouble with the police are twice as likely to become parents as those who have had no contact with the police). Teenagers from Bangladeshi, Afro-Caribbean and Pakistani communities are also at greater risk, than the national average, of parenthood.

Explanations for high rates of teenage parenthood are complex, but a number of themes appear consistently in the research. First, teenagers are seen as lacking knowledge about key aspects of contraception, expectations of adult personal relationships and parenting. Second, low expectations seem to characterize teenage parents' aspirations for employment, housing and life in general. Thirdly, parents , the media and many public institutions provide mixed messages – or no messages at all – about sexual, personal and health-related issues. Teenagers are bombarded with sexually explicit messages and, for some, encouraged by peer groups to become sexually active. In addition, many parents, some youth services and some schools are poor at providing accurate and sympathetic information much needed by young people.

Two principal objectives currently concern government strategy: first, a reduction in teenage pregnancies and, second, improved life chances for teenagers who become parents (and by implication their children). Health services in several guises (Health Promotion Teams, Health

Action Zones, Family Planning and Contraception Services) have targeted teenagers and tried to make services more accessible. Local education departments are encouraging more robust personal, social and health education programmes through schools and youth services, including the possibility of school-based contraception services. Social services departments are active in recasting services for young people in new 'leaving care' services and FAMILY SUPPORT services. Other 'hybrid' government initiatives, such as SURE START, the Children's Fund, CONNEXIONS and FOYERS, have all included the reduction of teenage pregnancies as a key objective.

The key social work tasks in work with this group are providing advice and counselling to enhance self-esteem, increase life chances (support and encouragement to achieve educationally, be employable and to access secure and good-quality accommodation), to negotiate support from families and useful significant others and to help with parenting where a young person decides to have and keep a child. In essence, the social worker needs to help support the young people into independent maturity.

temporary admission the right to remain in the UK whilst an application for asylum, for example, is considered.

People are given temporary admission whilst their asylum claim is considered. It gives no right to claim benefit or access social housing.

terminal care SEE PALLIATIVE CARE.

theories of crime and deviance the collective term for the various explanations offered for social rule-breaking in general and criminal lawbreaking in particular.

Theories of crime and deviance vary in the extent to which they emphasize personal, cultural, social or structural factors. They assist us in understanding why people commit crime, but they do not necessarily provide prescriptions for what should be done about crime. Although there are links between theories of crime and PRINCIPLES OF SENTENCING, it is usually argued that solutions to crime reside in the attitudes and conditions in society as a whole rather than in the policies and practices of the criminal justice system.

The earliest systematic attempt to provide an explanation of crime emerged in the late 18th and early 19th centuries as a response to earlier barbaric, repressive and arbitrary legal practices. The *classical school of criminology* was based on a number of key beliefs about human nature and society, drawn from the philosophical movement known as the Enlightenment. All individuals were believed to be self-seeking and greedy by nature and therefore liable to commit crime. Nevertheless, there was believed to be a consensus in society as to the desirability of protecting private property and personal welfare. In order to prevent a 'war of all against all', individuals freely entered into a social contract with the state to preserve the peace within the terms of this consensus.

All individuals are rational and equal in the eyes of the law. The individual has free will and is responsible for his or her actions; mitigating circumstances or excuses are therefore inadmissible. (Closely allied to these beliefs were the sentencing principles of proportionality and deterrence.) Crime was therefore viewed as a matter of choice – a deliberate attempt to undermine the social contract.

Classical criminology, however, was subject to some fairly obvious criticisms. Because of differing mental capacities, not all people could be held to be equally responsible before the law. Some allowance had to be made for the very young, the 'feeble-minded' and the insane. It was also apparent that material inequalities existed in society that meant, first, that the impact and effects of punishment would differ and, second, that crime might be a rational response to inequality or poverty. Neoclassical explanations of crime, therefore, began to take account of the personal circumstances and characteristics of the criminal. Many people believe that neoclassicism is still the predominant view in the criminal justice system today.

With the development of medical science during the 19th century, there was increasing interest in the possible existence of a 'criminal PERSONALITY' that could be identified by biological or mental abnormalities. This school of thought was known as *positivist criminology*. Its basic tenets were that crime was induced or determined by factors of birth or environment; these could be studied scientifically, so that crime could be predicted and prevented by the treatment rather than the punishment of criminals. Some of the best-known positivist theories of crime include the apparent discovery of physical stigmata on criminals and the apparent preponderance among criminals of particular body builds or types, particular chromosomal make-ups, low intelligence and extrovert personalities susceptible to poor conditioning. Such theories lead to the ascendancy of REHABILITATION as a sentencing principle. They have been widely criticized, however, on technical grounds (that the so-called scientific findings are unreliable), on sociological grounds (that they provide a very narrow explanation of crime that ignores issues of power and inequality) and on political grounds (that the 'treatment' required to 'cure' a criminal personality may be out of all proportion to the seriousness of the offence, thus infringing civil liberties and notions of 'just deserts'). Despite this, the belief that criminal activity is learned, or a matter of conditioning that can be unlearned, has enjoyed a revival over the past decade with the cognitive and behavioural approaches adopted by the PROBATION SERVICE. These have involved offenders (often in groups) analysing their offending behaviour, identifying factors that trigger criminal responses and expanding their social skills to handle situations in more socially acceptable ways.

PSYCHODYNAMIC theories of crime focus on the early emotional experiences of offenders. Criminal activity is seen as an attempt to compensate for childhood (especially maternal) deprivation and for an inability to resolve – as a healthy person would – the internal emotional conflicts of growing up. Crime is viewed as disturbed, attention-seeking behaviour that requires an individual psychotherapeutic response. In the mid-20th century such theories were seen as particularly relevant in understanding juvenile crime, but their influence has declined with a return to JUST DESERTS.

Social organization theories developed in the United States from the 1920s onwards and were the first attempt to provide sociological explanations of crime. Theories of 'social space' were concerned with the influence of what would now be called town planning or building development on the attitudes and behaviour of city dwellers. The constraints of poor housing and decaying inner-city residential areas were highlighted as contributory factors to the development of a socioeconomic 'pecking order' and subcultures that condoned the commission of crime. Closely related to the 'social space' theories were those concerned with 'social (lack of) opportunity'. With increased affluence in society, people trapped at the bottom of the social structure are frustrated by the vision of success and wealth alongside the absence of legitimate opportunity for them to achieve those goals. The response to this may be the development of delinquent subcultures or a proclivity to 'drift' in and out of crime.

Social reaction and social control theories are less concerned with why people commit crime in the first place than with how criminal behaviour is perpetuated as a result of social responses to the criminal. Social reaction theory argues that official responses to crime (such as heavy policing and severe sentencing) serve to label and stigmatize criminals and thus make it more difficult for them to reintegrate into the community as law-abiding citizens. Consequently, criminals are likely to seek the company of other criminals and fulfil the negative predictions made about them. In this way, deviance is amplified, and there is a danger of moral panics being constructed by the media, which reinforce stereotypical reactions and play on public fears about the escalation of crime. Social control theories develop this idea further (and also hark back to classical criminology) by arguing that, if it were not for the strength of our socialization and our fear of getting caught, most people would commit crime at some point in their lives. Whether or not we commit crime depends on the extent to which we feel we have an investment in remaining law-abiding; the strength of this feeling may vary over time and in different situations. Being labelled and stigmatized as a criminal may be a decisive factor in continuing rather than discontinuing a life of crime.

The major criticism of all these theories is that they fail to take account of the power structure and conflicts in society. *Conflict theories* argue that it is impossible to separate individual criminals (or even local environments and responses) from the way the criminal law and the criminal justice system have been constructed and are maintained to serve the interests of powerful groups in society. Defendants are overwhelmingly drawn from the ranks of working-class and unemployed people, but some of the most serious crime (particularly financial crime) is committed by the rich and powerful. Serious class and racial conflicts are dealt with as matters of narrow criminal justice rather than as issues of broad social justice. Similarly, *feminist explanations* of crime have underlined the fact that both crime and criminal justice are overwhelmingly male enterprises and that this requires analysis of gender power relations within society.

Theories of crime and deviance provide different levels of explanation, and many people feel that they are not all necessarily mutually exclusive. Professionals working with offenders frequently adopt an 'eclectic' approach that combines elements of structural, cultural and biographical explanation.

Most PROBATION officers and YOUTH OFFENDING TEAM members would probably describe their own approaches as eclectic, but there is increasing agreement about the relevance of the research on RISK and effectiveness and its implications for practice with offenders. Specifically, these theories have led to increased use of COGNITIVE BEHAVIOURAL methods, particularly with groups of offenders, and a decline in one-to-one work. This is parallelled by a distrust of counselling and a greater emphasis upon criminogenic need.

N. Walker, *Why punish?* Oxford, Oxford University Press, 1993.

theory a set of propositions or hypotheses that seek to explain phenomena.

Theory usually implies that sets of assumptions have been formalized, published, debated and tested in some way. For example, personality theories have been defined as a 'collection of assumptions and concepts about how best to regard people and study them'. Theory provides a structure or model through which reality can be observed and predictions about events may be made. It is a way of organizing information so that it can be transmitted and added to. The concepts implicit in theories attempt to describe reality, but the theoretical concepts, the explanations, are not reality. Theories organize knowledge in a form that makes it usable and communicable, ensuring a common understanding and making for reliability and usefulness. Theories should have utility, that is, they should explain what they are intended to explain; if they do not, they may have limited application and be discarded. In social work 'good' theories offer a framework to aid an explanation of behaviour.

In social welfare it is usual to distinguish among three different sets of theories. First are those 'borrowed' from the social sciences, which have been adopted by social welfare workers such as those about the behaviour of bureaucracy or social classes. Second are those that seek to explain the nature and functions of welfare provision within societies, for example theories to do with the different types of welfare states. Third are theories that have been developed by those working in social work and allied fields such as child behaviour, for example the theory of ATTACHMENT.

There are many examples of the first group of theories because social work and social welfare services have relied very heavily upon the insights of social science, especially sociology, psychology and political science. Sociology has provided evidence of persisting patterns of inequality within society, has provided explanations of social forces that have extended our understanding of both social change and social stability and has developed interesting and suggestive ideas about the nature of deviance. Psychology has in the main looked at individual and interpersonal processes, helping us to understand how individuals develop over the course of a lifetime, how they think, feel and perceive the world, and of how relationships and group dynamics are to be understood. Political science, for its part, seeks to understand the nature of power and of how it is distributed and regulated throughout society. All the social sciences are trying to make sense of how the behaviour of individuals is to be understood in the context of wider social forces. Some theories focus on the large canvas of society seen as a whole, some on smaller entities of relationships, families and communities. All theorizing in their attempts to identify the principal ingredients of whatever they are studying and endeavouring to understand how those ingredients behave in relationship to each other. (See, for example, SOCIAL CLASS, MATERNAL DEPRIVATION, LABELLING, PRESSURE GROUPS, PSYCHOLOGY, SOCIOLOGY.)

The second set of theories seeks to explain the nature of welfare provision within society. Many writers have compared the differing manner in which welfare functions are delivered within many societies. Varying ideas about the nature of the state's responsibilities as against those of individuals and families have been noted. In general, the role of ideology in the formation of welfare provision has been regarded as most important. At a micro level social work has sometimes been regarded critically as an agent of social control and as a form of oppression as well as a helping profession. The theoretical analysis of the social work function has therefore sought to identify these ingredients of oppression and by so doing to minimize them where possible. (See MARKET, NEW RIGHT, RADICAL SOCIAL WORK, ANTIDISCRIMINATORY PRACTICE.)

The third set of theories, generated by social work academics, has been much more limited in range and indeed some would argue that they are more methodological than theoretical. These 'theories' include TASK-CENTRED methods, SYSTEMS APPROACH, COUNSELLING and CRISIS INTERVENTION. All four of these approaches lend themselves to differing theoretical interpretations. Thus, the problems defined in the task-centred methods might be differentially identified in negotiations between a worker and service user depending upon the ideas about the origins of problems that inform their views. Similarly, systems theory can be used conservatively or radically depending upon which ingredients are thought to be most important to a person's situation (that is, systems theory can be used in conjunction with a socialist view of society as well as a conservative view). Counselling, too, takes many competing theoretical forms and the manner of intervention into crises can depend very much upon other perspectives held by worker and client. A feminist, for example, might work in a very different way with a woman who has been raped or the victim of DOMESTIC VIOLENCE from another worker with more traditional views of a woman's role in society.

Many practitioners and students are worried about thinking theoretically. They might prefer to think about themselves as practical people without a need for theory. Such people do, of course, think theoretically, although they do not usually acknowledge the theory in their practice. Yet a good theory is essentially practical.

M. Payne, *Modern Social Work Theory*, Basingstoke, Macmillan, 1997.

threshold criteria the grounds for granting a CARE ORDER or SUPERVISION ORDER to a local authority under section 31 of the CHILDREN ACT.

The threshold criteria are that a child is suffering, or likely to suffer, SIGNIFICANT HARM and that this harm is attributable to the standard of care given by the parents or to the fact that the child is beyond the parents' control. A very young child left to wander streets at night, an infant losing weight because of lack of food and a child suffering fractures as a result of parental assault are all examples that meet the criteria. The grounds are referred to as threshold criteria because, even if they are established in court in respect of a particular child, the court, before making a care or supervision order, must consider other grounds as well, including the points in the WELFARE CHECKLIST and the principle that making the order must actually benefit the child in ways that would not happen if the order were not made.

throughcare see RESETTLEMENT.

time out the placing of a child for a short while in an area where he or she receives no attention.

Time out is used as a mild form of punishment within a programme of BEHAVIOUR MODIFICATION. In full, it means 'time out from positive reinforcement'. When a child engages in unwanted behaviour, he or she is immediately removed to a neutral place for a short period of three to five minutes. While there, the child has nothing to do and receives no attention for that period. Time out is used only in carefully anticipated situations, such as of refusal to comply with a request, and where positive reinforcement has failed.

The child in time out must be monitored at all times. This approach is inappropriate with children older than nine, since often the child has to be physically removed to the neutral place. On occasion, the concept has been grossly misused by residential regimes and converted into a harsh practice of deprivation and isolation over a considerable period of time. In this form, it has nothing to do with the original meaning of the term. (See also PINDOWN.)

tolerance the way the body adapts to the presence of a substance or drug being taken so that more and more is required to give the same effect.

The same drug taken by different people will have varying effects depending on how accustomed they are to taking it. This unpredictability is dangerous, making overdose a possibility, especially if the purity of the drug is higher than expected or if there has been a break from taking the drug. (See SUBSTANCE MISUSE.)

toy library a facility for people to borrow toys for their children. Such facilities are often attached to NURSERIES, nursery schools, playgroups or specialist facilities for young children.

The general purpose of toy libraries is to help poor families to have access to toys that a low income would normally not allow and, in the case of some specialist units, the use of toys specifically chosen to help stimulate a child. This may be with reference to a general understimulation or to an identified problem or need, including a DISABILITY.

tracking means by which social workers keep in touch with service users in order to monitor their behaviour and to encourage them to avoid difficulties. The concept has particular application for work in the YOUTH JUSTICE system.

Practically, young offenders, and offending adults in some circumstances (see ELECTRONIC MONITORING), are required to report regularly in the course of a day to a social worker or a support worker. The purpose of such exchanges is to help juveniles who are in situations where they seem to be offending frequently. Such close monitoring may deter them from getting into situations of temptation by means of frequent contact and encouragement from positive influences.

trait a stable predisposition in a person to behave in a particular way, such as impulsively or secretively.

Traits are intrinsic to the person and are not part of the environment, although observed behaviour may be an interaction of traits with environmental factors. Traits are presumed to be a constant within an individual; they may be mental or physical, inherited or learned. Traits cannot be observed directly; their presence can be deduced only from observable behaviours.

transactional analysis a theory that sees interactions between individuals as one of the fundamental ways in which people express and seek confirmation of their personalities.

Devised by Berne in the 1960s, the language of transactional analysis is derived from American slang. According to the theory, the structure of each person's PERSONALITY is comprised of a 'parent' and 'adult' and a 'child' ego state. In any interaction one of these ego states is in control for each person and addresses one of these ego states in the other person. As long as the two participants share the same assumptions, the interaction can continue. Thus, if a wife's 'parent' talks to her husband's 'child' about his drinking habits, the interaction can continue as long as the husband accepts the basis of the interaction and his 'child' replies to his wife's 'parent'.

Transactions can take a number of forms, the most destructive of which are 'games'. Games involve two or more people who are willing to adopt certain rules. The pay-off of a game is to confirm individuals' views of themselves, to protect them from some truth and from establishing true intimacy with others. For example, the game 'If it weren't for you' could be played by a couple whereby a woman states that if her partner had not prevented her, by his demands, she would have been a famous writer. In this way, the woman never has to confront the possibility that if she had tried to write she might have been a failure. As long as the partner accepts responsibility, the game can continue. An additional element in this system is that an individual can view himself or herself, those they interact with and other people either as OK or as not OK. In this way, a depressive view would be 'I'm not OK but you are OK and they are OK', while an arrogant view would be 'I'm OK, you're not OK and they're not OK', and a prejudiced view would be 'I'm OK, you're OK, but they're not OK'. Berne suggested that parents determine the attitude that their children will have towards themselves. The aim of transactional analysis is for individuals to recognize the games in which they habitually become involved, to stop playing them and to come to a view whereby they, those close to them and others are all OK. In this way, people should break away from the images of themselves that have been handed down to them by their parents.

E. Berne, *Games People Play: The Psychology of Human Relationships*, Harmondsworth, Penguin, 1966.

transfer summary an account of work undertaken to date, including problems solved and tasks yet to be tackled, usually completed by a social worker when a case is to be taken over by another worker.

The worker receiving the transfer summary may be either in the same team or in another area, if the service user moves from one area to another. Transfer summaries offer an opportunity for social workers to take stock or to evaluate the work completed to that point. (See also CASE REVIEW/SYSTEM.)

transracial adoption the placing of children of one 'RACE' (or of MIXED PARENTAGE) with the families of another 'race', so that, legally, the adopted children are to be regarded as it they were born to that family.

In practice, transracial ADOPTION amounts to the placing of black children with white families; the converse has rarely, if ever, taken place. Since British society regards all non-white people as effectively black, what follows utilizes that distinction. The practice of transracial adoption emerged from a number of developments in the 1970s:

first, changes in the abortion law; second, increased availability and usage of contraception; and third, major changes in social attitudes towards unmarried mothers and single parenthood. These three related developments had the effect of reducing the supply of 'healthy white babies' for adoption. Significantly, as a result of changing attitudes to adoption too, this was a time when the demand for adoptable babies was in fact growing, especially among middle-class couples. A dwindling supply of suitable babies and at the same time a growing demand for them brought to light the situation of many black babies languishing in care who had previously been regarded as unadoptable (along with children with disabilities and older children). Not only were black children considered 'hard to place', suitable black families were thought 'hard to find'. Early attempts to recruit black adopters were remarkably unsuccessful, leading to the misplaced conclusion that the idea of adoption was 'alien' to certain cultures. From these circumstances, and from the prevailing 'assimilationist' views on race of the period, the practice arose of placing black children with white families.

Until the mid-1960s the majority of ADOPTION AGENCIES operated in accordance with a strict 'matching' policy whereby the 'race' of the child was the focal issue. The concern in many policy documents of adoption societies was that children should be presentable as the biological offspring of the couple. In this context, much attention was also given to matching the religious background of the child's family of origin to that of the adopters. In the 1970s, major and wider struggles took place to determine how community relations were to be handled in Britain in the future. Opposing forces on the one hand sought the total assimilation of immigrant groups into the 'host society' and on the other supported the idea of cultural pluralism. The former position implied that 'race' in a sense did not matter, or at least should not. This broadly assimilationist view underpinned the commitment to transracial adoption. The problem of the child's identity was reduced in importance; if assimilationist policies were pursued, we would all be white in the end (so long as strict immigration policies were enforced, at least in relation to New Commonwealth citizens).

In the late 1960s a small group of black social workers provided the first critique of transracial adoption. They argued that the 'black community' might not survive because it was being 'robbed' of its most precious resource, its children. How, they asked, could the 'black community' feel any measure of pride in itself if advantage (for children taken into care) was being defined as being brought up by white families? Their second concern was the effect of transracial adoption on the psychosocial development of black children. This point raises the issue of whether white adoptive parents can grasp the problems that blacks have to face in a racist society such as Britain. Can white parents of black children create in them a pride in their blackness, in effect a positive black identity? Can such parents equip them with the necessary coping and survival skills to help them deal with racism and disadvantage? In the same vein, will such children be able to take on the social and cultural characteristics that will enable them to move freely in the 'black community'? Finally, the remaining preoccupation of the social workers was to challenge the assumption that blacks would not adopt. They were fundamentally critical of the unsuccessful methods employed to try to attract would-be black adoptive parents.

Research has been divided on the issue of whether black children adopted by white couples can meet the standards implied by the critique from the BLACK PERSPECTIVE. Some research has apparently indicated that many black children brought up by white adoptive parents are broadly well adjusted, have succeeded reasonably well at school and are able to sustain good peer relationships. Critics of this research have suggested that these children have a 'defensive' form of self-esteem, that their sense of self-worth is unlikely to stand the test of a lifetime of racism in Britain and that these children are white in all respects (including their consciousness) except their skin. The phrase 'black skins but white masks' has been widely used about these children.

In relation to the search for black families for the adoption of black children, new approaches explored by the London borough of Lambeth in 1980 proved encouraging. The recruitment of black social workers to help identify, train and support black families who were interested in adoption was only one ingredient in Lambeth's success but an important one. Other factors included combating racist attitudes in other workers, discarding stereotyped notions of the normal family and the ability to use 'black networks' in imaginative ways. These experiments have now been repeated elsewhere in Britain with at least some success.

By the mid-1980s the placement of most black children for adoption took place 'in race': that is, the children were placed with families of the same ethnic origin. Key difficulties remain. Not a few social services departments still do not have rigorous policies in relation to adoption and 'race'. There are circumstances where black or mixed-parentage children have been in long-term placements with white foster parents and where PERMANENCE has been sought with black adopters. The bonds established between white families and their black foster children can be strong; criteria must be established to determine whether in these circumstances it is in the children's best interests to be moved. Similarly, it cannot be assumed that black families necessarily have the best attitudes and values to adopt a black child. Recent discussion documents from the BRITISH ASSOCIATION OF SOCIAL WORKERS and the government suggest that a more flexible practice in relation to SAME RACE adoptions should be pursued by social work agencies, but black social workers and others have been very critical of what they see as an attempt to undermine the progress made in the past decade.

S. Ahmed, J. Cheetham and J. J. Small (eds), *Social Work with Black Children and their Families*, London, Batsford, 1986.

truancy illicit absence from school by children of COMPULSORY SCHOOL AGE; the term is often used to refer to all forms of UNAUTHORIZED ABSENCE.

'Truancy' should be used only in response to absences initiated by children that their parents are either unaware of or are unable to prevent. There are a variety of perspectives on such behaviour. Many would adopt a generally punitive approach, regarding truancy as a symptom of either poor parenting or of the child being beyond control. PARENTING ORDERS may now be made when parents are convicted, and there has been a growing tendency to see the behaviour as a YOUTH JUSTICE issue, even though it is not in itself an offence by the child. There are often links between missing school and other forms of DEVIANCE but not in every case. SCHOOL REFUSERS may owe more to emotional and psychological problems and many children miss small amounts of schooling as part of general teenage rebellion or simply because they find school boring. The enforcing authority is the local education authority, acting through the EDUCATION SOCIAL WORK (education welfare) service. At the early stages, schools are expected to address the issues with parents themselves, before involving the local education authority, in accordance with their attendance policy and as part of their pastoral system.

U*u*

unauthorized absence the correct term for the legal status applicable when children of COMPULSORY SCHOOL AGE are absent from school without the school's permission, as distinct from 'authorized absence' for an 'unavoidable cause' (EDUCATION ACT 1996, section 444).

Such behaviour is often referred to as TRUANCY, which is only one form of illicit absence. It is not the child but the parents who are legally responsible and who may themselves initiate or condone the absence. Unauthorized absence may also include taking family holidays without permission or keeping children away from school for inappropriate and trivial reasons, such as shopping or birthdays, depending on the individual school's policy.

underclass a term used both to describe and to explain the over-representation in the criminal justice system of defendants who live on state benefits and are unemployed, homeless and/or without stable family relationships.

The term is used by the FAR RIGHT in its claim that there is a class of people who are morally and criminally deviant as a result of being raised in fatherless families with a 'WELFARE STATE' mentality. Their argument runs that in adulthood the underclass is unwilling to work for a living and expects to take from, rather than contribute to, the good of society. Left-wing critics either refuse to use the term because of its judgmental connotations or insist that it should be used only in a descriptive and not an explanatory manner. According to this view, while many poor, unemployed, homeless people commit crime, this is the result of social inequality and injustice. There is no evidence to support the idea that such people have different moral values or aspirations from other people. Given the opportunity, they would also appreciate a home, a job and a settled family life. (See ANTIDISCRIMINATION, CULTURE OF POVERTY).

under-fives provision day-care facilities for pre-school children, including day NURSERIES, CHILD-MINDERS, nursery schools or nursery classes in primary schools, playgroups and other provision (nannies, au pairs, nurseries in FAMILY CENTRES).

The CHILDREN ACT places a duty on local authorities to 'facilitate' day-care provision for pre-school-age children. It also requires authorities to review such provision, including voluntary and private facilities, every three years. Acceptable standards have to be maintained, and to help providers reach and sustain these standards, authorities can provide training and guidance. In comparison with many European countries, Britain's under-fives' provision is poor and unevenly developed from one area to another. There is a clear lack of strategic thinking at both national and local levels. Comprehensive policies are needed to address the issues of child-care needs and EQUAL OPPORTUNITIES, employment and social security rights. In Britain there is a bewildering variety of complex regulations about how child day-care provision is to be regarded, costed and charged for. There is also great inconsistency in criteria for access to such provision. Urgent requirements are the development of good-quality under-fives' provision on some scale, improvements in the employment conditions for workers (especially pay) and financial help for the costs of child-care for single parents.

B. Cohen, *Caring for Children*, London, Family Policy Studies Centre, 1988.

unemployment a condition of being without paid work and of being available for such work.

Actual rates of unemployment are widely disputed because of the varying ways in which availability for work is officially acknowledged. Many people are not counted because they do not register with government agencies such as job centres. For example, women who are not entitled to any welfare benefits in their own right often do not use 'the system'. Unemployment may be redefined as working on employment training schemes. Sick and disabled people can also in some circumstances not have their wish to secure employment taken seriously. Some may be working part-time when they wish to work full-time.

The social consequences of unemployment include POVERTY, ill-health, low morale and contingent personal and family difficulties. The longer the period of unemployment, the more chronic is the poverty. In these circumstances, savings become depleted, household goods wear out and cannot be replaced, and comforts have to be given up. Unemployment is also associated with default debt, as reduced income fails to meet financial commitments incurred while the person was still in work. Not surprisingly, therefore, unemployment often leads to ill-health as morale diminishes and personal relationships become strained. The Black Report in 1980 found a very strong link between health and unemployment that could even have repercussions from one generation to the next if prolonged.

Social welfare workers mostly attempt to help with the social and personal consequences of unemployment. Thus ADVICE workers assist with benefit entitlement and debt that has got out of control, and health and social workers deal with emotional, relational and family problems.

SOCIAL SERVICES DEPARTMENTS can directly create employment through sheltered workshops for people with learning difficulties. Otherwise, efforts of social and community workers are confined to attempts to get unemployed people involved in COMMUNITY projects, which are perceived as useful in their own right and also as helpful in maintaining the morale of unemployed people. There is also the possibility that new skills might be learned that may subsequently be helpful in securing a job in the future. Adult education programmes can be integral to these efforts.

United Nations Convention on the Rights of the Child an international treaty, agreed in 1989, that applies to everyone under the age of 18. It codifies children's rights and requires countries that have signed it (including the UK) to issue periodic reports of the steps they have taken to comply with its provisions.

In addition to the convention itself, the United Nations has convened a number of international meetings at which detailed rules for its implementation have been agreed. These include the *Beijing Rules* on the administration of juvenile justice (1985) and the *Riyadh Guidelines* on the prevention of juvenile delinquency (1990). The European Convention on Human Rights has also provided additional, detailed guidance – and UK criminal law in relation to young offenders has had to be changed on a number of occasions when European courts have ruled that it breached the country's international obligations. Some of the most important aspects of European law are recognized in the UK in the HUMAN RIGHTS ACT 1998.

Some of the most important provisions of the UN Convention are:
1 that families should be provided with the support and protection they need to bring up children in a harmonious environment where their rights are respected and children are not arbitrarily or unnecessarily removed from home;
2 that the child's best interests should be paramount where there are questions of child protection;
3 the right to protection from discrimination;
4 the right to social services such as education and health.

The two sets of rules provide greater detail on matters such as the right to privacy and confidentiality in relation to contact with juvenile justice, the establishment of an official age of criminal responsibility, a separate youth justice system, the right to consideration of diversion from formal proceedings, the right to representation and to have parents participate in legal proceedings, and the parsimonious use of custodial sentences (under rule 17 of the *Beijing Rules*).

There has been considerable debate about the extent to which the legal framework set out in the CRIME AND DISORDER ACT 1998 meets the requirements of the various international treaties and rules. In some respects, the legislation brought the law in England and Wales into compliance with international standards, but in others it created potential conflicts.

R. Powell, *Child Law*, Winchester, Waterside Press, 2001.

universal benefits see NON-MEANS-TESTED BENEFIT.

unmet need a NEED identified by ASSESSMENT that is then not met, usually because the resources do not exist.

The purpose of recording unmet needs for all assessed service users is to keep track of the shortfall in resources. There has been considerable debate between central government and LOCAL AUTHORITIES as to whether the latter should compile this sort of information. In practice, most authorities do so in order to argue for more resources.

user the general term for all those who receive a social work or social care service.

The term 'service user', or simply 'user', as the generic name for the various groups of people that social workers work with has emerged only in the 1990s. In this it has come to replace CLIENT as the principal and broadest reference that embraces all the people who draw on these services. Its popularity has spread among practitioners, managers and social work educators alike because it seems to convey the more contemporary emphasis on those who receive the service having some rights and influence over that service. Brief flirtations with the words 'customer' and 'consumer', also in the 1990s, attempted to capture the same emphasis but eventually were thought to reflect excessively the ethos of purchasing goods and services. In some areas of practice, however, the term client is still widely used and often only familiarity with the specific context of the work will point toward which term is the more appropriate.

Utting Report a report commissioned in 1991 by the Department of Health in the aftermath of PINDOWN into the management, purpose and direction of CHILDREN'S HOMES after a decade of increasing incidence of ABUSE, problems of control and persistent reliance on inexperienced staff.

The report, officially entitled *Children in the Public Care*, is usually known by the name of its author, William Utting, who was head of the SOCIAL SERVICES INSPECTORATE at the time. It made a number of recommendations regarding the management, practice and resourcing of children's homes. Among these were a call for increased numbers of staff to be qualified social workers, that each staff member should have an individual development programme, and that social services departments should manage residential child-care within their overall strategy for children's services and apply the same management principles concerning information systems and quality assurance as they do to other areas of their service.

Sir William Utting, *Children in the Public Care, a Review of Residential Child Care*, London, HMSO, 1991.

V*v*

vagrancy the practice of living without permanent accommodation or of having no fixed abode.

The term is often associated with wandering, although vagrants in fact often confine themselves to particular areas. Usually vagrants are single, but families too might be vagrant. Vagrants' lifestyles may vary substantially, involving sleeping rough, using NIGHT SHELTERS, taking on temporary work with tied accommodation, and spells, often brief, of living with family or friends. Housing workers, social workers and, to some extent, probation officers have increasingly argued that the 'problem' of vagrancy should be viewed not as personal pathology or inadequacy but as an issue of HOMELESSNESS. Night shelters should therefore be seen as only a first step in trying to secure permanent accommodation for the single and mobile homeless. A recognized additional problem for vagrants is that of securing an income from the BENEFITS AGENCY. The process is usually lengthy, with benefit being given on a day-by-day basis. There are strong associations between vagrancy and a background in care and MENTAL ILLNESS.

value a belief that something is good and desirable. It defines what is important, worthwhile and worth striving for.

Social work is a distinctive profession because of the emphasis it has placed on values. Values represent the profound aspirations of professional commitment, as Chris Clark (see below) has written: 'held aloft as the ultimate and, perhaps, never wholly attainable ends of policy and practice'. While values can be thought of as attributes of persons, professions and organizations, they are less fixed than we might presume. As Clark again puts it, they are 'the ongoing accomplishments of knowledgeable and reflective human intelligences immersed in a social world'.

Social work values emerged from a wide range of beliefs, theories, religious affiliations and moral and political understandings. Although social work educators and professional associations refer to social work values as if they were well established, there are contending strands that make it difficult to find a unified set of values for the whole profession.

To make the picture more complicated, beliefs and values are very closely intertwined; indeed, values have been regarded as well-entrenched core attachments and sentiments that result in deep beliefs. This interconnection between values and beliefs means that we have to acknowledge that values may be resistant to change and immune to evidence concerning practice outcomes.

For much of the 20th century, until the 1980s at any rate, the dominant professional values arose from its CASEWORK tradition in social work. These developed at the birth of social work in the second half of the 19th century as it tried to find a set of answers to the prevailing urban poverty that it confronted. These values were tied to securing good personal habits in users, such as thrift, sobriety and hard work. This was achieved by developing personal relationships and, through that, effecting individual and family change with techniques such as counselling combined with compulsory interventions sanctioned by law (Pearson, 1989). Social work's professional values were then built up around the notion of the user as an individual and the centrality of the worker's relationship with that individual. A Catholic priest, Father Biestek, codified these in a number of principles: individualization and the uniqueness of each individual, purposeful expression of feelings, controlled emotional involvement, acceptance and a non-judgmental attitude toward the user, client self-determination, and confidentiality with regard to what the user says or reveals to the practitioner.

Since the 1980s, however, and particularly with the articulation of a newer set of values in tackling the oppressions of women and black and disabled people, the evidence for the existence of a distinctive and coherent set of normative professional social work values is now more tenuous. While there is widespread discussion within the profession about values, there is little empirical research as to what values social workers actually hold. Clark argues that, in general, the values of the profession are rooted in Christian ethics mixed with modern western secular liberal individualism. He finds four broad principles at work. First, the worth and uniqueness of every person: all persons have equal value regardless of age, gender, ethnicity, physical or intellectual ability, income or social contribution. Respect for individuals is active and needs to be positively demonstrated rather than just assumed. Second, the entitlement to justice: every person is entitled to equal treatment on agreed principles of justice that recognize protection of liberties, human needs and fair distribution of resources. Third, the claim to freedom: every person and social group is entitled to their own beliefs and pursuits unless these restrict the freedom of others. Fourth, community is essential: human life can only be realized interdependently in communities, and much of social work aims to restore or improve specific communities.

C. Clark, *Social Work Ethics: Politics, principles and practice*, Basingstoke, Macmillan, 2000.

value judgment an assessment or statement based upon one's own ETHICAL CODE or norms about the worth of a person, group or whole community, particularly about their actions or beliefs.

The very idea of having some form of social work system embodies value judgements, for it presupposes that there are certain people who need some form of support, punishment, treatment or restraint. There will be many disagreements between people about the social and moral significance of certain kinds of behaviour. Much social policy rests upon a consensus of belief, that is, value judgements. Much social work intervention is justified by reference to some value or other – there is simply no avoiding them. The task in education and in policy formation is to reveal one's own assumptions (that is, value judgements) and to be able to defend them as reasonable and just.

ventilation the expression of strong feelings to some purpose beyond personal display.

In COUNSELLING, therapy and many other situations people may need to express powerful feelings, often previously suppressed, before being able to make progress in tackling their problems. One of the skills required by workers is to recognize this need and to help the service user fully to express his or her feelings. It may be that ventilation will achieve a measure of catharsis: that is, a person may benefit directly from getting his or her feelings out into the open and acknowledged by himself or herself and perhaps by the helper. Ventilation may therefore be immediately helpful as well as contributing to the 'movement' in a problem that might otherwise have been stuck.

victim a person injured, harmed or killed either by the direct action of a third party or indirectly as a consequence of actions of negligence; the injured party in a criminal case.

Until recently, victims of crime were neglected by the criminal justice system. Although this has changed substantially, the needs of victims and witnesses continue sometimes to be met inadequately or not at all by official agencies.

The rise of the victims' movement, coupled with the increasing influence of feminist and anti-racist movements, led to increased attention being paid to victims around the world. In Britain, VICTIM SUPPORT has been a vocal critic of the inadequacies of the criminal justice system, and it has received progressively increased funding from the HOME OFFICE to provide direct assistance to individual victims. Other voluntary agencies such as Rape Crisis and Refuge have added their voices to the campaign. Since the publication of the first VICTIM'S CHARTER in 1990, official agencies in England and Wales have improved their services to victims: the Charter has given the POLICE, the CRIMINAL COURTS, the PROBATION SERVICE and the CROWN PROSECUTION SERVICE specific responsibilities in relation to victims. The Charter was revised in 1996 to strengthen these measures. It is being replaced in April 2006 by a new Victim's Code of Practice.

When asked about their needs, victims emphasize information, being treated with respect and sensitivity, compensation and support (in roughly that order of priority). It is these needs that have been targeted in the reforms mentioned above. Police training and procedures have been improved, particularly in relation to the victims of DOMESTIC VIOLENCE, sexual offences and RACIALLY AGGRAVATED OFFENCES. The procedures used by the Crown Prosecution Service and the criminal courts are gradually changing in response to the requirements of the victim's charter and the YOUTH JUSTICE AND CRIMINAL EVIDENCE ACT 1999. The Probation Service and YOUTH OFFENDING TEAMS have specific responsibilities relating to keeping victims informed and providing them with opportunities to become involved in REPARATION and VICTIM-OFFENDER MEDIATION. The government offers substantial financial subsidy to Victim Support and some help to other voluntary agencies that provide immediate support and longer-term counselling to more serious victims.

Practitioners are likely to work more often and more closely with victims and victim issues than in the past, both when involved with reparation or mediation and when preparing PRE-SENTENCE REPORTS and working with offenders. It is now a requirement of NATIONAL STANDARDS that the effect of offences upon victims be considered in court reports on both adult and young offenders, and the same applies to reports when PAROLE or EARLY RELEASE are being considered. Individual and groupwork aimed at challenging offending behaviour is likely to involve providing opportunities for offenders to consider the consequences of their behaviour for actual and potential victims.

Victims' reactions to offences are unpredictable. Some people put serious offences behind them quickly and without apparent long-term harm. Others, especially if they are vulnerable at the time of a crime, can react strongly even to relatively minor incidents. Common reactions to victimization, apart from experiencing physical harm, include feelings of shock and guilt, a loss of trust in others and in the 'just world' that people normally take for granted, heightened reactions and exaggerated vigilance, fear of being alone in the place where the offence took place or similar settings, anger and humiliation. In extreme cases, the emotional impact can be long-lasting. Where victims show signs of POST-TRAUMATIC STRESS SYNDROME (intrusive thoughts and dreams, emotional turbulence, intense and long-lasting pain, social withdrawal and avoidance of situations that might remind the victim of the offence), they may need specialized professional help.

A. Williams, *Working with victims of crime: Policies, politics and practice*, London, Jessica Kingsley, 1999.

victimless crime an offence that has no adverse consequences for the victim or has no victims.

There are those who argue that there is no such thing as a victimless crime: shoplifting and insurance fraud lead to higher prices, drug misuse may lead people to commit property crimes to fund their drug habits, and speeding offences can lead to serious accidents. If one person fails to buy a TV licence, others may have to pay more. Criminal offences are created by social and political processes, however, and definitions of crime change from time to time and from place to place. Some crimes clearly have no identifiable victim, obvious examples being the moderate consumption of some illegal drugs or certain sexual acts between mutually consenting adults in a private place.

victim-offender mediation negotiations between an offender and the victim(s) of the crime, assisted by a neutral third party, that aim to reach a mutually acceptable decision about what the offender should do to put matters right or what punishment is appropriate. See also REINTEGRATIVE SHAMING, RESTORATIVE JUSTICE.

Victim's Charter a policy document setting out the treatment victims of crime can expect from official and voluntary criminal justice agencies.

The Charter for England and Wales was first published in 1990. A revised edition was issued in 1996, and a new Victim's Code of Practice is being issued in April 2006. Its Scottish equivalent is the *Scottish Strategy for Victims* (2000). The Charter was part of a programme of citizens' charters promulgated by the Major government in the late 1980s and early 1990s. The first edition set out progress to date on improving victims' treatment by the criminal justice system, suggested some 'guiding principles', gave a 'checklist of questions' for agencies to consider and listed sources of further information. As such, it was a tentative step towards codifying victims' rights and what they could legitimately expect from the criminal justice system. Not all the agencies concerned were consulted about the Charter's contents, and no new resources were made available for its implementation. Perhaps not surprisingly, its main impact was in changing the climate of opinion rather than in leading to rapid practical changes. When it was revised, there was greater consultation and the publication of the second edition in 1996 was followed by strengthened Home Office circular instructions to local agencies that helped to ensure that it was implemented.

In the case of the PROBATION SERVICE, the 1990 Charter made suggestions about improving liaison between the service and the victims and survivors of offenders sentenced to life imprisonment. Implementation was slow and patchy, but Home Office circulars were issued in 1994 and 1995 and references to good practice with this client group were included in the 1995 NATIONAL STANDARDS. The 1996 Charter extended the requirement to liaise with victims of serious crime to the victims of all offenders sentenced to four or more years' imprisonment for violent and sexual offences. By the late 1990s, PRE-SENTENCE REPORTS prepared by probation officers routinely included at least some reference to victims' perspectives on offences, and probation services began to appoint specialist staff to support their work with victims. In 2001, when the Criminal Justice and Court Services Act 2000 came into force, the Probation Service acquired a statutory duty to consult the victims of everyone imprisoned for 12 months or more for sexual or violent offences. This represented an enormous increase in the workload, which was recognized by increased funding, and it was a significant step in terms of giving legal recognition to this area of work. The NATIONAL PROBATION SERVICE came into existence at the same time, and its director made it clear that victim work was one of the service's highest priorities.

A review of services for vulnerable and intimidated witnesses meanwhile led to substantial changes in court procedures under the YOUTH JUSTICE AND CRIMINAL EVIDENCE ACT 1999, which was implemented over a period of several years. The review of the Victim's Charter followed in 2001–02, and one outcome was a commitment to introduce further legislation to protect and codify victims' rights.

D. Ward, J. Scott and M. Lacey (eds), *Probation: Working for justice*, second edition, Oxford, Oxford University Press, 2002.

Victim Support an independent charity whose volunteers and paid workers offer help to VICTIMS of crime in the community and at court.

Victims are mainly referred to Victim Support schemes by the police, but referrals are also received from other agencies and from individual victims themselves. Founded in the 1970s, Victim Support has grown into a national network of schemes covering the whole of the British Isles and receives substantial financial support from the Home Office. In addition to the community-based schemes, Victim Support also runs Witness Support schemes in courts. These began in the crown courts and have more recently been extended to cover magistrates' courts. Although careful to maintain political neutrality and to avoid commenting on sentencing policy, Victim Support has become increasingly influential and is seen as the most representative victims' organization by government (but see REFUGE and WOMEN'S AID). In addition to a small paid staff, the organization employs the services of tens of thousands of volunteers. It began as a 'first aid' agency offering advice and non-judgmental support rather than extended counselling, but some volunteers are increasingly receiving advanced training to enable them to undertake longer-term work with victims of more serious crime and the survivors of murder victims. Women reporting rape or sexual assaults are always seen by female volunteers. Victim Support schemes usually maintain regular contact with local police, housing, health, social services, probation and other specialist agencies in order to ensure that volunteers give up-to-date and accurate information and that the victim perspective is taken into account in CRIME PREVENTION and other local strategies. The police, probation and social services are represented on local schemes' committees, and this provides a ready source of advice about difficult cases for staff and volunteers.

violence purposeful behaviour intended to hurt or damage others,
defined widely in social work to include not only physical assault but also
AGGRESSION, threatening behaviour, intimidation, and racial and sexual
harassment. Violent acts should be seen as varying combinations in the
abuse of physical, psychological and sexual power.

Most theorists regard violent behaviour as learned rather than arising
from instincts. Social welfare agencies have become concerned with
violence first in terms of internal relationships between employees,
second in the context of staff–service user relationships and third in
relation to direct work with violent clients where the concern is to help
them develop coping mechanisms and to avoid violent behaviour.

Many organizations within the field of health and social services
have now recognized that employee relationships can sometimes be very
unhappy. In particular, relationships between superiors and subordinates
can be affected by attempts to bully or harass, with sexual or racist motives
common components of such behaviour. Other motivations may include
religious discrimination, HOMOPHOBIA or simply an attempt to get
someone to leave an organization. Enlightened services have developed
grievance procedures to cover these kinds of behaviour, so that staff can
complain if they are harassed. Anti-harassment campaigns can usefully
be relaunched from time to time to ensure that the anti-harassment
culture is constantly renewed and thus kept high on the agenda.

Over the past two decades the issue of CLIENTS' violence towards social
welfare staff has come to the fore. It is now recognized as widespread,
affecting all kinds of staff (including reception and ancillary workers)
and sometimes significantly affecting how the work is done. Some social
work staff have actually lost their lives. Many have been injured or
intimidated to the point that they felt unable to continue working and
many more have testified to the great stress involved in working with
violent and aggressive service users. Social work and allied occupations
now work, in the main, in situations where it is possible to speak of their
anxieties in the expectation that practical and emotional support will be
offered and that, importantly, they will not be made to feel that their
competence is in question. This climate of trust within teams and
workplaces, which is clearly necessary, is as important to men as it is
to women.

Many social welfare agencies have recently developed policies and
procedures concerning staff safety when dealing with violent or
potentially violent clients. Such policies usually involve: first, attempts
to help staff assess the risks to themselves; second, suggestions about
how violence might be prevented or minimized; third, advice on how
to handle violent incidents; fourth, ideas about how staff might be
supported after a violent incident. The assessment of risk can usefully
include systems for noting known violent clients so that workers are
forewarned about potential difficulties. Men and boys between the ages

of 14 and 45 constitute the group with greatest risk, although violence may come from any quarter. Clearly, some social work 'set pieces' – for example, the compulsory removal of children from home, or a mental health 'section' – are also likely to lead to high emotion and to the potential for violence. Risk sometimes has to be estimated more immediately, such as in interviews where clients exhibit signs of agitation or expressive behaviour that begins to be threatening.

Attempts to prevent violence can involve tactics at many levels. Consistent policies that avoid differing practices among staff can be critical, for example, in working in a children's home. It is often helpful for staff to work in pairs in anticipated crisis situations. Similarly, careful thought about where a testing encounter is to take place could defuse a difficult interview. The layout of a room, the location of exits and the means for summoning help might all be critical. Avoidance of officious behaviour, together with a quiet, assertive and clear manner, is now generally accepted as more likely to calm than enrage.

If violence occurs, decisions have to be made rapidly about flight or containment in the light of the worker's assessment of risk, his or her willingness to use self-defence and containment techniques, and perhaps the involvement of others (the proximity both of help or of further danger from additional clients). Post-violence support should minimally involve medical attention and reports, a debriefing to try to understand what has happened, decisions concerned with immediate and future work with the offending party, possible criminal prosecution of the offender and personal support and counselling for the injured worker. Management should monitor violent incidents very closely. Analysis of the frequency and nature of such incidents might highlight, for example, the need for additional staff, different practices and staff training needs.

Programmes to help violent people develop alternative ways of dealing with situations that have in the past led to violence have been devised by both medical and various social work agencies. Approaches vary but typically include SOCIAL SKILLS TRAINING and ANGER MANAGEMENT and avoidance. Often individual COUNSELLING based upon a detailed analysis of what situations precipitate difficulties for particular clients is also offered, with many such analyses including discussions of problems around SUBSTANCE MISUSE and alcohol consumption. (See also ABUSE, DOMESTIC VIOLENCE, SEX OFFENDER.)

C. Lupton and T. Gillespie (eds), *Working with Violence*, Basingstoke, Macmillan, 1994.

visual impairment eyesight defined as defective in comparison with norms established in medical practice; this includes both lifelong and acquired impairment.

This is a general term for a wide range of visual disabilities. The wearing of glasses or contact lenses is sufficiently common to be regarded as unremarkable and does not automatically signify the difficulties and environmental barriers associated with DISABILITY. In practice, the term 'visual impairment' usually refers to people whose sight cannot easily be 'corrected' by glasses and who are likely to experience difficulties negotiating a physical environment designed for sighted people. In the UK, there are clinical criteria for BLIND AND PARTIALLY SIGHTED REGISTRATION. The World Health Organization also has definitions that distinguish between 'profound blindness' and 'severe low vision'. The former involves the inability to count fingers at a distance of ten feet or less, and the latter at 20 feet or less. Over a million people in the UK are visually impaired, and three quarters of these are aged over 75. This reflects the causes of visual impairment, which tend to be age-related. The most common causes in Britain are macular degeneration, cataracts, glaucoma and diabetic retinopathy. Over 24,000 children in Britain have visual impairments, however, and over half of these also have additional impairments.

The Royal National Institute for the Blind (RNIB) stresses that visually impaired people are 'just like everyone else' but may need aids or assistance in order to undertake some everyday tasks. Help should be offered, however, rather imposed on people. The types of challenges faced by people with visual impairments include getting out and about (often referred to as 'mobility'), and coping with everyday tasks in the home and at work, including reading and writing. In connection with these, social services departments offer mobility training, LOW-VISION AIDS and equipment. Some visually impaired people may use BRAILLE, MOON or audiotapes in order to read, but many people are also taking advantage of computer technology. Visually impaired people can work with the right support, but in reality they are disadvantaged in the labour market. This is often because of false assumptions about lack of ability and ignorance of the support and equipment that can be provided. People with serious visual impairments meet the definition of disability used in the DISABILITY DISCRIMINATION ACT 1995 and are entitled to have 'reasonable adjustments' made for them in the workplace. Some may be provided with a PERSONAL ASSISTANT to deal with any tasks for which vision is essential.

Some local authorities directly employ mobility officers and/or specialist social workers for visually impaired people, while others use local voluntary organizations to provide some services on their behalf. Registration as blind or partially sighted is not necessary in order to receive services. It is recognized that the loss of sight can be disorientating and traumatic for many people, and that the prompt provision of advice and support is essential. Many service users report delays in receiving assistance after diagnosis, however, and inspections of services for people with sensory impairments have remarked on the way these services are marginalized within local authorities.

The Improving Lives Coalition, *Improving Lives: Priorities in health and social care for blind and partially sighted people*, London, RNIB.

volatile substance abuse see VSA.

voluntary sector/independent sector following government discussion
(1990) and decision (1992), papers entitled *Partnership in Dealing with
Offenders in the Community*, the PROBATION SERVICE is required to commit
a percentage of its annual budget to developing links with voluntary
and independent organizations in the COMMUNITY to undertake work
that complements the service's statutory duties.

The main areas in which partnerships might be involved include
crime prevention, support for VICTIMS, ACCOMMODATION, supervision
projects and voluntary befriending. Partnerships have been particularly
successful in provision for YOUNG OFFENDERS, and examples include work
with National Children's Homes, Barnardo's and the Rainer Foundation.
In the area of crime prevention, the services of Crime Concern, an
independent consultancy charity, have been used. Projects have also been
developed with the National Association for the Care and Resettlement of
Offenders (NACRO). NACRO is one of a number of voluntary organizations
whose main objective is to campaign for penal reform; others include
the Howard League and the Prison Reform Trust. All these organizations
aim to educate the public by providing an information service about the
criminal justice system, publishing journals and commissioning
RESEARCH, as well as undertaking political lobbying.

volunteer a person who works for a statutory or voluntary organization
without pay. Volunteers sometimes deliver a social welfare service or
help in indirect ways so that others may deliver the service. Such activity
is considered altruistic.

Volunteers can enact many roles, including those of befriending the
vulnerable, offering support in relation to very tangible tasks such as
driving or keeping financial accounts, or directly delivering the service,
as with advice bureaux and ADVOCACY schemes. A major contribution
made by many volunteers is to the management committees of voluntary
organizations. The scale of the contribution varies too – some people
helping for a few hours a week and others working almost full-time.

Much social work and social welfare provision has its roots in
voluntary activity. Over the past century in Britain, professional social
work services have grown and in the main have been located in the
STATUTORY SECTOR. The responsibility to discharge the duties of social
welfare provision enshrined in law is mostly placed upon local
government or statutory health authorities. The contribution of the
VOLUNTARY SECTOR to social welfare remains considerable, however.
Many voluntary organizations in fact employ only paid professional
workers, sometimes to deliver, on the basis of an agency agreement,
a service on behalf of a local authority (for example, social work services
to DEAF people). Others have a mixture of the paid and unpaid, and yet
others rely wholly on unpaid volunteers. There is also considerable
variation in the extent to which organizations train, support and supervise

their volunteers. Some are rigorous in their training programmes (the Citizens' Advice Bureaux, the Samaritans and the PROBATION SERVICE, for example); others have yet to develop explicit policy on these issues.

The role of the volunteer is a matter of partisan debate, a debate located in the question of what responsibilities properly belong to the state, what to the COMMUNITY and what to the individual or family. The period between 1945 and 1975, with some fluctuations, was characterized by the growth of statutory provision. Since that time there has been encouragement for families to look after their own and for voluntary effort to replace statutory provision. There is thus considerable ambiguity in the role of the volunteer, with some seeing it as an indication of SELF-HELP and of a caring community, while others are concerned at the erosion of the minimum standards that should be guaranteed by the state.

VSA an abbreviation of the term 'volatile substance abuse', a generic definition applied to the abuse of volatile substances such as glue, gas and lighter fuel. VSA has been particularly associated in recent years with vulnerable young people, particularly those LOOKED AFTER, as identified in the 1997 Social Services Inspectorate Report *Substance Misuse and Young People*. Whilst primarily associated with adolescence, there is evidence to suggest that younger children are particularly at risk of this form of SUBSTANCE MISUSE largely because they are easy to access and affordable.

There is widespread recognition of the need for training in relation to substance misuse with social services departments. Recent research (Boylan, Braye, Worley, 2001), however, suggests that social care practitioners and carers are less aware of VSA than other forms of substance misuse.

vulnerable witness a victim or witness in criminal court proceedings who may be defined as vulnerable on the grounds of age, the nature of the offence, fear or distress at the prospect of giving evidence or because of disability. Once defined as vulnerable, witnesses are entitled to various 'special measures' that affect the way the court case is conducted.

The term 'vulnerable witness' is defined in the YOUTH JUSTICE AND CRIMINAL EVIDENCE ACT 1999. The introduction of special measures to protect vulnerable or intimidated witnesses under this legislation removed the inconsistency between courts in deciding whether to provide special facilities such as video-recorded evidence, evidence given in private, reporting restrictions, the removal of court users' wigs and gowns, and so on. Prior to the Act, preliminary hearings had to be held about such matters, and if a new judge subsequently became responsible for the case the special measures sometimes had to be discussed again. The Act also introduced new measures and clarified who should benefit from them.

Those defined as vulnerable under the legislation include everyone aged under 17, anyone with a 'mental disorder' or 'significant impairment of intelligence and social functioning' and those with physical disabilities. Others also considered vulnerable are those who would give less good evidence if they were not provided with special measures to reduce their fear or distress about testifying, those subject to intimidation by alleged offenders or their associates and those giving evidence about sexual offences.

The special measures available include screens, which prevent the accused from seeing the witness, the assistance of an intermediary to help with communication and devices that facilitate communication. Other such means are the prohibition of cross-examination of the victim by the accused in sexual offence cases, restrictions on questioning about complainants' sexual histories, waiving the requirement to swear an oath to tell the truth and cross-examination via a live video link. In addition to these legal provisions, the police provide a variety of services to vulnerable witnesses, including escorting them to and from court and providing them with a pager so that they do not have to wait in the court building to give evidence. See also VICTIM'S CHARTER.

Ww

Wagner Report the government report on RESIDENTIAL CARE services by the review committee chaired by Lady Wagner.

The Wagner Committee was set up by the government in 1985 to review residential services at a time when residential care was not only in a state of flux because of impending COMMUNITY CARE reforms but also demoralized because it was perceived by professionals and public alike as a low-status, residual service of last resort. The Wagner Report, subtitled *A Positive Choice*, intended to change that perception and through its recommendations establish residential services as part of a continuum of care in the community. It wished to see residential care as a service that people would actively choose to use because it met their needs in a way they wanted. The report focused on the rights and needs of individuals as a way of ensuring that active choice was possible. Users should have full information on the residential care options in their area as well as a number of realistic options to choose from, and they should be able to try establishments on trial. Once individuals had made a choice, it was important to protect their rights to complain about poor-quality service and to carry out those activities they were capable of, such as handling their own money. Individual capacities were not to be undermined. Other Wagner recommendations sought to ensure quality by adherence to a national set of standards and by regular inspection. The report also wished to raise the status of residential work by ensuring that all managers were professionally qualified social workers and by improvement in the pay and conditions of staff.

While the Wagner Report's recommendations were not implemented in full by the government, much of its thinking, particularly on standards and the rights of users, found its way into official guidance. Uniquely, a Wagner Development Group continued to meet after the report was published and to publicize its conclusions around the country. In this way, its objective of changing the public and professional views of residential services was achieved.

G. Wagner, *Residential Care: A Positive Choice*, London, HMSO, 1988.

Warner Report the report published in 1992 by the committee of inquiry set up by the Department of Health following the imprisonment of child-care staff for CHILD ABUSE in Leicestershire.

Chaired by Norman Warner, former Director of Kent Social Services, the committee's aim was to examine the selection, development and management of staff working in CHILDREN'S HOMES. Its report, *Choosing with Care*, urges a more rigorous staff selection procedure. Among its key recommendations are: job specifications and person specifications issued for each post and directly related to the stated purpose of the children's home; advertisements for posts offered externally; a short list of at least three candidates to be made up for each vacancy; each short-listed candidate to visit the home prior to interview; and written exercises and preliminary interviews to form part of the selection process. The report also made many recommendations concerning the management of children's homes. These included regular supervision and appraisal of all staff, ensuring children know of the complaints procedure, and an encouragement to staff to report any concerns outside their line of management if their immediate superior seems unconcerned. The committee also recommended that all staff should have a personal development contract covering their own training. Most controversially, the report called for a new diploma in the group care of children, a recommendation based on the view that the current DIPLOMA IN SOCIAL WORK cannot give sufficient attention to this complex and fraught area of work.

Choosing with Care, Report of the Committee of Inquiry into the Selection, Development and Management of Staff in Children's Homes, London, HMSO, 1992.

welfare checklist the seven points that courts must bear in mind when considering making an order under the CHILDREN ACT.

The seven points of the checklist are:

1 the wishes and feelings of the child, taken in the light of their age and understanding;

2 the child's physical, emotional and educational needs;

3 the effect of any change of circumstances on the child;

4 the age, sex and background of the child (which inevitably includes the child's racial, cultural and religious background);

5 the harm that the child has suffered or may suffer;

6 how capable each of the parents is at meeting the child's needs;

7 the range and powers of the court under the Children Act itself.

The importance of the checklist is immense. It acts as a reminder to the court that it must, above everything else, consider any order it might make in the light of the child's welfare (except the EMERGENCY PROTECTION ORDER, to which the checklist does not apply); and for the first time in child law it itemizes, however broadly, what welfare means. In particular, a court must not make an order under the Act, even if the grounds for that order exist, unless it has also taken into account the effect of making that order on each of those aspects of the child's life contained in the checklist. Although the welfare checklist is expressly for the court to consider, social workers and other professionals appearing in court in connection with an application for an order must also bear its contents in mind when presenting their arguments.

welfare rights 1 an umbrella term that broadly includes trying to maximize the income, in cash or in kind, of service USERS and their dependants. Such work requires the provision of information to claimants, the education of claimants and, where necessary, the provision of ADVOCACY and representation services to assist claimants in securing claims, reviewing and appealing against adverse decisions.

The place of welfare rights work in mainstream SOCIAL WORK services has long been contentious. Some have argued that social workers should have detailed knowledge of the complex British welfare rights system in order to be able to assist vulnerable people directly and quickly. Such a view emphasizes the importance of material circumstances to social functioning. Others have argued that it is unrealistic for social workers to have these duties, given the, usually, heavy statutory responsibilities that they carry. There is probably now a consensus that social workers should at least have direct access to welfare rights advisers. In addition, social workers should perhaps have at least an outline knowledge of the welfare benefits system in order that they might recognize a possible issue of entitlement, even if others undertake the detailed work to help service users make a claim or challenge an adverse decision (what some have called *signposting*). In some instances, of course, social workers have sole and unavoidable responsibility for determining ELIGIBILITY CRITERIA for benefits in the form of some social work services, such as HOME HELPS, MEALS ON WHEELS, AIDS AND HOME ADAPTATIONS to be used in users' own homes or charges for RESIDENTIAL CARE services.

STATUTORY SECTOR agencies will only rarely incorporate a welfare rights specialist within social work teams. More often social workers will have formal arrangements with specialist welfare rights advisers located elsewhere within a LOCAL AUTHORITY or with organizations in the VOLUNTARY SECTOR, like the Citizens' Advice Bureaux, which will provide advice to individual social workers or take REFERRALS from them. A relatively small number of local authorities dispense such services from NEIGHBOURHOOD OFFICES where welfare rights advisers might share advice functions with representatives from social services departments.

There is great complexity in the British welfare benefits system, including some variations in provision and legal framework in England and Wales in comparison with Scotland and Northern Ireland. The principal benefits are administered by the BENEFITS AGENCY, HM Revenue and Customs, local authority departments (SOCIAL SERVICES, housing and education departments in particular) and by health services.

Financial support can also be accessed from other specialist agencies, such as Job Centres (in relation to, for example, helping to support disabled people to secure work in the form of grants to adapt work-places, provide technical supports and even to subsidize wages for specified periods), from the COMMUNITY LEGAL SERVICES Commission (to help poor people with legal costs) and the CHILD SUPPORT Agency (in relation to contributions from, usually, estranged fathers to help with the financial costs of bringing up children). There are also areas of welfare rights work where issues impact upon 'private' provision, as in stakeholder pensions, for example (see WELFARE RIGHTS 8). Not surprisingly, welfare benefits' handbooks describing eligibility, rates of benefit, the relationship between benefits, appeal mechanisms and many other matters have become voluminous.

A key part of the state welfare benefits typology is the distinction, first, between contributory and non-contributory benefits and, second, between MEANS-TESTED and NON-MEANS-TESTED BENEFITS. **Contributory benefits** are those where entitlement depends upon the claimant having paid (or being treated as having paid) NATIONAL INSURANCE CONTRIBUTIONS as well as on other criteria relating to the claimant's personal circumstances – for example, age in the case of state *retirement pension* (WELFARE RIGHTS 8), or the degree of incapacity in the case of *incapacity benefit* (WELFARE RIGHTS 3). The other main contributory benefits are contributory *jobseeker's allowance* (WELFARE RIGHTS 9) and bereavement allowance (WELFARE RIGHTS 2).

Non-contributory benefits, on the other hand, are those benefits where entitlement depends only on personal circumstances and not on any means test – such benefits include *child benefit* (WELFARE RIGHTS 5) and *disability living allowance, attendance allowance* and *carer's allowance* (WELFARE RIGHTS 3).

People working in the welfare rights field, whether they be specialists or social workers, have a number of key tasks to fulfil. These tasks include trying to maximize income by determining ELIGIBILITY CRITERIA for benefits and **passported benefits**. For example, if a claimant is found to be eligible for income support (WELFARE RIGHTS 5), he or she may also be eligible (*passported*) for *housing benefit* and *council tax benefit* (see WELFARE RIGHTS 6), *free school meals* (WELFARE RIGHTS 5) and HEALTH BENEFITS. There are issues of **'better-off' tests**, where comparisons can be made about whether a claimant will be better off working rather than being reliant upon benefits. For example, a single parent with a young school-age child would have to compare the value of, say, income support, child benefit, free school meals, FREE PRESCRIPTIONS and housing benefit with a wage where there may be deductions for income tax, national insurance contributions, a contributory pension, child-care costs (for an after-school club for example) and travel costs as well as the loss of some or all of the housing benefit.

Other major areas of work concern *challenging decisions* or *appeals*, *backdating* of claims, and trying to challenge attempts by welfare agencies to reclaim funds where there is alleged to have been an *overpayment.* Research about the success rates of claims for particular benefits reveals that some benefits are very difficult to secure. For this reason, and because sometimes claimants complete forms inaccurately or fail to provide the required evidence (often because they have found it difficult to understand the claims form), a lot of the work of welfare rights workers is about challenging decisions. Such challenges can be to a designated *decision maker* in the local benefits agency office, or APPEALS to *tribunals* (a body that hears appeals about SOCIAL SECURITY matters comprising usually one legally qualified member plus one or two additional 'lay' members) or to higher bodies such as SOCIAL SECURITY COMMISSIONERS. Although such processes can be time-consuming for workers and anxiety-provoking for claimants, they can be successful. In the last quarter of 2001, 44 per cent of claimants were successful on appeal, and the figure was higher for those who attended in person and higher still for those accompanied by a welfare rights specialist.

Since the *take-up* rate of benefits varies so much (child benefit has the best rate of around 98 per cent), welfare rights workers are increasingly *targeting* (see below) particular groups of potential claimants. For example, campaigns to ensure that people with enduring MENTAL HEALTH PROBLEMS are claiming all the benefits to which they are entitled will work through many of the agencies that work directly with the mentally ill. Thus work will be done in psychiatric hospitals, supported ACCOMMODATION, DAY-CARE centres, GENERAL PRACTITIONERS' surgeries and other locations that such services users frequent. Other strategies to improve take-up include training ancillary workers, such as HOME HELPS or COMMUNITY CARE workers or family aides, so that they might become aware of potential problems of 'underclaiming'. Many agencies are systematically experimenting with OUTREACH services to take ADVICE SERVICES into communities through the use of communal facilities, mobile advice buses, or even door knocks to provide advice in people's communities or their own homes.

Targeting: a term originally borrowed from the world of advertising ('to target') by welfare rights workers to describe the intention to deliver information about particular benefits to those individuals or groups most likely to be eligible to claim them.

Because of the plethora of underclaimed benefits (see *take-up*, above), each with its own set of rules, it is difficult in general campaigns to impart enough specific information to enable individuals to be sufficiently confident about their potential eligibility to make a claim. By finding ways of targeting information, it is possible to address the potential claimant more directly and to give fuller details to allow a more informed choice to be made. Examples of targeting information would include writing to people receiving DOMICILIARY SERVICES about attendance allowance or disability living allowance, or writing to people who are registered BLIND about the lower-rate *mobility component* (WELFARE RIGHTS 3). Since the mid-1980s the word 'targeting' has been used by the government to justify an increased reliance on means-tested benefit – for example, 'targeting the most needy' – and to imply that universal provision is a waste of public expenditure. Thus a reduction in services may be described as 'better targeting'.

In a way, welfare rights' work could be regarded as an industry that is built upon the failings of welfare agencies to reach the people their services are designed to support. But while the benefits system is so complex and while there are vulnerable people who cannot easily represent their own best interests, such an industry will be much needed.

welfare rights 2 *bereavement benefits* benefits paid to men and women following the death of their spouses. Bereavement payments, widowed parents' allowances and bereavement allowances replaced widows' benefits from 9 April 2001.

Bereavement benefits: for widowers as well as widows were introduced in the UK as a response to European human rights legislation and a test case brought by the Campaign for Widows' and Fathers' Rights (*Willis and Others v United Kingdom* (1999)). This successfully challenged the philosophy that underpinned widows' benefits – that only women are financially dependent on their partners – and argued that by denying spousal benefits to males in the event of the deaths of their wives effectively denied their human rights as well as those of the surviving husbands and children. Despite this reform, benefits initially could be claimed only by the surviving partner of a *married* couple. Partners from cohabiting and same-sex couples were not eligible for bereavement benefits (see *Shakell v UK* case below). In 2006 the benefits were extended to those in a civil partnership.

Widowed mother's allowance: a contributory benefit (unless the survivor's deceased spouse died in the course of an industrial accident or from a prescribed industrial disease, in which case it is payable *without* the need for NATIONAL INSURANCE CONTRIBUTIONS). It is still paid to surviving widows in respect of bereavement before April 2001 and includes additions for children. It was replaced by the *widowed parent's allowance*, which is available for widowers as well as widows for new claimants after April 2001. As a result of the controversial decision of the European Court of Human Rights in *Shakell v UK* in July 2000, bereavement benefits are available only to a survivor who was married to the deceased partner, the court holding that a state is permitted to discriminate in ways that sustain marriage.

Widow's payment: a tax-free one-off payment to meet the immediate costs of bereavement, replaced by the *bereavement payment* from April 2001. It is payable to widowers as well as widows on a contributory basis (or on a non-contributory basis in the case of the deceased dying in an industrial accident or as a result of a prescribed industrial disease).

Widow's pension: a contributory pension for widows, payable to a woman aged over 45 until she is 65 while she remains eligible (for example for as long as she does not remarry or 'cohabit'). It was replaced by the *bereavement allowance* from April 2001, which is available to widowers as well as widows – but only for a maximum period of 52 weeks. At that point a claimant may be eligible for the bereavement category of income support (WELFARE RIGHTS 5).

welfare rights 3 *disability, incapacity, and carers' benefits* the several benefits that support those with DISABILITY and their carers:

Attendance allowance: a benefit paid to people over the age of 65 with severe disabilities who need help looking after themselves or supervision to avoid danger. It is paid at two different rates depending on the level of care needed. People under 65 claim *disability living allowance.* The higher rate is paid to people who need frequent attention with bodily functions or continual supervision to avoid danger during the day and night. It is also paid to people who are terminally ill. The lower rate is paid to people needing frequent attention or continual supervision during the day or the night. Attendance allowance is a *non-contributory* and *non-means-tested benefit* (WELFARE RIGHTS 1). It acts as a passport to higher rates of income support (WELFARE RIGHTS 5) but is not taken into account as income for any means-tested benefits. Attendance allowance often provides extra income that enables older people to remain in their homes. Many OLDER PEOPLE in receipt of attendance allowance have been forced to spend the allowance on local authority home care charges, however, which has left many older people with income close to or below POVERTY levels. The report *Charging with Care*, published by the Audit Commission in May 2000, forced the government via the Care Standards Act 2000 and associated statutory guidance to set out a broad framework to ensure that in future councils' CHARGING POLICIES are fair and operate consistently with their overall social care objectives. Local authorities should ensure that home care service users on a low income are no longer charged for services and that all those in receipt of attendance allowance or *disability living allowance* (see below) seeking support from home care services should have an ASSESSMENT of income. They should also have an individual assessment of their disability-related expenditure.

Care component: part of the *disability living allowance* (see below).

Carer's allowance: formerly known as invalid care allowance, this is a benefit paid to someone who cares for a severely disabled person. The carer must spend at least 35 hours caring for someone who gets the *attendance allowance* (see above) or *disability living allowance care component* (see below) at the higher or middle rate.

Carer's allowance can be claimed from age 16, and from October 2002 all carers can claim it after they reach the age of 65. It cannot be paid if the carer earns above a prescribed amount (£84 a week in 2005–06) or is in full-time education. TAKE-UP (see also WELFARE RIGHTS 1) of the carer's allowance is thought to be low, and non-claimers who would gain include, for example, women with partners in full-time work. Although it is taken into account as income for means-tested benefits, it gives entitlement to a *carer's premium*, which increases the value of *income support* (WELFARE RIGHTS 5), *housing benefit* and *council tax benefit* (WELFARE RIGHTS 6). Carer's allowance became payable to married women only after the European Court required this under EC SOCIAL SECURITY DIRECTIVE 79/7. It overlaps with all income replacements benefits, including *incapacity benefit* (see below), contributory *jobseeker's allowance* (WELFARE RIGHTS 9) and, most importantly, *retirement pension* (WELFARE RIGHTS 8). This means that many older carers may not actually be paid the carer's allowance although by claiming it they may qualify for the carer's premium.

Constant attendance allowance: paid as part of the *industrial injuries scheme* (see below).

Disability living allowance: a benefit paid to people with severe disabilities who need help looking after themselves or supervision to avoid danger, or who have difficulty with outdoor mobility. It includes a *care component*, paid at three different rates, and a *mobility component*, paid at two different rates.

The benefit was introduced in 1992 for people aged under 65, replacing *attendance allowance* (see above) and *mobility allowance*. People of 65 or over can still claim attendance allowance. The higher-rate *care component* is paid to people who need frequent attention with bodily functions or continual supervision to avoid danger during the day and night. It is also paid to people who are terminally ill. The middle rate is paid to people needing frequent attention or continual supervision during the day or the night. The lower rate is paid to people needing attention for a significant part of the day or who are aged 16 or over but cannot prepare a cooked meal for themselves. The higher-rate *mobility component* is paid to people aged three or over who are physically disabled and unable or virtually unable to walk, or for whom the effort needed is likely to seriously effect their health. The lower rate is paid to people aged five or more who have a physical or mental disability and who need guidance or supervision from another person to get about out of doors. Disability living allowance is a *non-contributory* and *non-means-tested benefit* (WELFARE RIGHTS 1). It acts as a passport to higher rates of *income support* (WELFARE RIGHTS 5) but is not taken into account as income for any means-tested benefits. A claim for disability living allowance includes a long self-assessment form. This was envisaged as a great improvement on the previous, often unsatisfactory, medical examinations. In practice the form has proved contentious and difficult to use.

Disabled person's tax credit: a means-tested benefit paid to people who work 16 hours or more each week and are at a disadvantage in getting jobs because of their disability. It was replaced by the working tax credit (WELFARE RIGHTS 9) from April 2003 in accordance with the Tax Credits Act 2002.

The amount paid depends on the number of people in the claimant's family (if any), the age of any children and the family income, including earnings.

Exceptionally severe disablement allowance: benefit paid as part of the *industrial injuries scheme* (see below) to people needing personal care.

Incapacity benefit: a benefit that can be claimed by people who are unable to work because of ill health or disability. It is a *contributory benefit* (WELFARE RIGHTS 1), except for young people under the age of 20 or 25 who have been in full-time education who do not have to satisfy the NATIONAL INSURANCE CONTRIBUTION conditions.

It is paid at three rates: *short-term lower rate, short-term higher rate* and *long-term rate*. People claiming the short-term higher and long-term rates can claim for adult and child dependants in specified circumstances, and those claiming long-term rate can claim an age-related addition if their incapacity began before the age of 44.

For the first 28 weeks, incapacity is usually assessed against individuals' ability to do their own jobs if they have one. Evidence for this is based on certificates from their general practitioners. After 28 weeks, or sooner if individuals do not have a regular occupation, they must satisfy the *personal capability test* (PCA). The PCA tests their ability to work. It consists of two parts: a questionnaire and usually a medical examination. The questionnaire is called an IB50; it asks claimants about their physical and mental health and is assessed using a pre-set scoring system. If the score exceeds a specified threshold, benefit can continue to be paid. In addition, most people will be required to attend a medical examination carried out on behalf of the DEPARTMENT FOR WORK AND PENSIONS by a private company that has been strongly criticized for its poor handling of medical examinations. Recent reports by the National Audit Office and the Public Accounts Committee found many shortcomings with the administration of the medical service, including unsatisfactory medical examinations, 25,000 unnecessary examinations each year, and the inability to provide interpreters and same-sex doctors when requested. As a result, 40 per cent of claimants (60 per cent where they were represented) who appealed against medical incapacity for work decisions were successful.

Industrial injuries benefits: benefits to employees who suffer personal injury through an accident arising out of and in the course of work, or who contract a prescribed disease or prescribed injury while working.

The main benefit is ***disablement benefit***, which is paid to compensate people who suffer as a result of an industrial accident or suffer from a prescribed disease involving 'loss of physical or mental faculty'. This means it can take account of the effects of trauma and disfigurement as well as inability to do things. It is normally paid only if the disablement is assessed as 14 per cent or more. Disablement benefit awards are often provisional in the first place. Final awards may be for a fixed period or for life. If the disability increases, because of deterioration in the condition or because of the interaction of some other condition, an award can be reviewed on the grounds of unforeseen aggravation.

Reduced earnings allowance: can be claimed only if the accident happened or the disease began before October 1990, when it was abolished. Reduced earnings allowance is extra benefit to provide some compensation for people who cannot earn as much as they could before the accident or disease. It can be paid provided that disablement is assessed at 1 per cent.

Retirement allowance: replaces reduced earnings allowance when people retire but is paid at a much lower rate.

Mobility component: one of the two components of *disability living allowance* (see above).

Permitted work: the amount and type of work people claiming *incapacity benefit, severe disablement allowance* (see above) and *income support* (WELFARE RIGHTS 5) (on the basis of their incapacity for work) are allowed to do and still retain benefits.

Practical assistance: one of the forms of support services available to a sick or disabled person under the CHRONICALLY SICK AND DISABLED PERSONS ACT 1970 and the NATIONAL HEALTH SERVICES ACT 1977. For some adults with LEARNING DIFFICULTIES there is considerable interplay between educational and recreational support under the 1970 Act and provision under the Education Act 1944 and other COMMUNITY CARE legislation. AIDS AND HOME ADAPTATIONS and other facilities to address DISABILITY needs come under this head. 'Additional facilities' under the 1970 Act encompasses support in the form of facilities designed to secure a person's safety, comfort and convenience. Again, there is some overlap with other disability-related services, notably the provision that may be made under the Housing Grants, Construction and Regeneration Act 1996 by way of grants.

Prescribed industrial disease: a disease that gives rise to benefits under the Industrial Injuries Scheme and is listed in detail in regulations showing the 'prescribed disease or injury' and the occupation that causes it.

Statutory sick pay (SSP): a legal minimum rate of pay, paid by employers to those with 'employee' status earning above the lower earnings limit for NATIONAL INSURANCE CONTRIBUTIONS during sickness or other incapacity. Some employers pay more or even full pay during the early weeks of sickness. Statutory sick pay is a state benefit paid by an employer to an employee for the first 28 weeks of sickness. It is no longer reimbursed, as in the past, which has tended to create problems of non-compliance by employers, in which case it may be necessary to refer disputes over *nonpayment* (see below). It is paid at one of two rates, depending on normal earnings, but is not payable to people who earn less than £84 a week (2005–06), to those who are over pensionable age or to those who have contracts of employment of less than three months. A person who does not qualify can claim *incapacity benefit* (see above) at the short-term lower rate instead. If employees are dissatisfied with decisions of their employers about their entitlement they can refer them to the Inland Revenue. Decisions can be appealed by an employer or employee to Tax Commissioners. It is now a criminal offence for an employer not to pay, or to delay payment of SSP or *statutory maternity pay* (WELFARE RIGHTS 7) without justification.

welfare rights 4 *education benefits* benefits to support children in education.
Education clothing grant: a discretionary scheme operated by some local education authorities to assist parents with the cost of school clothing.

Although school 'uniform' cannot be a legal requirement, most schools and parents prefer to have a 'dress code' as a matter of local policy. Parents are generally expected to meet the cost of required clothing, including any sports or other specialist clothing, although many schools seek to keep their expectations as simple as possible. Financial assistance may be available directly from the school, especially secondary schools, or through a scheme administered by the local education authority, usually via the EDUCATION SOCIAL WORK (or education welfare) Service. Children should not be excluded from school for breaches of the school's uniform code unless the circumstances are exceptional, such as deliberate and persistent defiance.

Educational maintenance allowance (EMA): a discretionary cash payment that may be made by local education authorities to young people who stay on in full-time education after Year 11 (post-16). Grants are usually small but more substantial schemes may be available in some areas such as Education Action Zones for deprived neighbourhoods.

The EMA scheme was started in September 1999 as part of a government pilot scheme, operating in different areas of England. It aimed to test whether extra funds will encourage more young people aged 16 to 19 to stay on in full-time education and training. The allowance is now available in England and Wales.

Free school meals see WELFARE RIGHTS 5.

welfare rights 5 *family, children and young peoples' benefits* the group of welfare benefits related to bringing up children and young people.
Applicable amount: the maximum amount of money that can be paid to people claiming *income support* (see below) – the most important of the family-related state benefits – or income-based *jobseeker's allowance* (WELFARE RIGHTS 9) as it is paid to those required to seek employment (and their family dependants). In the case of a family's welfare provision through the state benefits system, the applicable amount is an important element in MEANS-TESTED BENEFITS (see also WELFARE RIGHTS 1) given that the amount covers other members of the household for whom the claimant is claiming, that is, the partner (if she or he has one) and children. The applicable amount is then compared with the 'weekly income' available (or treated as available) to the claimant, including any income of a partner treated as available; and if income is less than the applicable amount in any week then the state makes up the difference.

Child benefit: a benefit paid in respect of a child aged under 16, or under 19 and in full-time non-advanced education, to a person with whom the child lives or who contributes to the child's maintenance to the value of the benefit.

Where two people would qualify for child benefit, special rules prioritize between claimants. It is a *non-means-tested, non-contributory benefit* (WELFARE RIGHTS 1) and is the best example of a universal benefit. People seeking to curtail public expenditure argue that child benefit is poorly targeted, because, with a TAKE-UP rate of nearly 100 per cent (unlike means-tested benefits), it is paid to all families regardless of need. Its defenders regard it, however, as an important expression of society's collective responsibility to maintain and encourage the family and see it as a way to support all children in low- and middle-income families.

Responsibility for administering child benefit (as well as *guardian's allowance*– see below) was transferred to HM Revenue and Customs in 2002, but, unlike other child-related elements of means-tested benefits, which are subsumed by *child tax credit* (see below and WELFARE RIGHTS 9) under the Tax Credits Act 2002 from April 2003, child benefit has been maintained as a benefit providing a vital floor of income on a 'universal' basis.

Child tax credit (CTC): the CTC aims to create a seamless system of income-related support for families with children. For the first time all SOCIAL SECURITY benefits (except *child benefit*, see above) and TAX CREDITS that incorporate payments for children will be brought together and paid as one child-related payment. The credit, therefore, replaces the income-related child elements currently paid in 'out of work benefits'– *income support* (see below) and *job-seeker's allowance* (WELFARE RIGHTS 9)– and the in-work *tax credits* (WELFARE RIGHTS 9)– working families' and disabled person's tax credits and the children's tax credit and the child-dependency increases paid in *non-means-tested benefits* (WELFARE RIGHTS 1) for new claims to *retirement benefit* (WELFARE RIGHTS 8), *bereavement benefit* (WELFARE RIGHTS 2), *incapacity benefit* (including residual *severe disablement allowance*) and *carer's allowance* (WELFARE RIGHTS 3). It will be paid to the main carer in families in non-working and working households.

Educational maintenance allowance see WELFARE RIGHTS 4.

Free school meals: an arrangement whereby children whose parents receive *income support* (see below) or *income-based jobseeker's allowance* (WELFARE RIGHTS 9) are entitled to a midday meal at school free of charge (Education Act 1980).

Not all schools make a hot meal available under this arrangement, but they must provide a sandwich lunch as an alternative. Application needs to be made by the relevant parent through the local education authority's EDUCATION SOCIAL WORK or education welfare service and proof of entitlement must be produced. No other benefits qualify and no cash alternative is available. The 1980 Act abolished the requirement to provide free milk, making it discretionary. Research carried out by the then Department of Employment and Education estimated that 1.8 million children were entitled to a free school meal although approximately 20 per cent did not take up their entitlement.

Social services departments have the power to provide additional assistance in response to the particular nutritional needs, special diets, etc, of children, under their general powers in the Children Act 1989, section 17. When formal assessments are made of such needs, it is now recognized as essential that the needs of a child in relation to his or her religion, culture and community are addressed adequately, and, as with other aspects of support delivered through the community care system, consultation is vital: legal requirements can dictate that a failure to do so may render the assessment unlawful. Criticism of some social services departments' approaches to this important part of the COMMUNITY CARE system were made in influential reports in 2002 entitled by Ayesha Vernon (*The User-Defined Outcomes of Community Care for Asian Disabled People*, Policy Press/J. Rowntree Foundation) – one of two important studies on the subject. The other was a study by the Leeds Involvement project, Joseph Rowntree Foundation, Joseph Rowntree Charitable Trust and the University of Leeds, *South Asian Disabled Young People and their Families* by Yasmin Hussain, Karl Atkin and Waqar Ahmad (The Policy Press).

Guardian's allowance: a benefit paid to a person looking after a child who is effectively orphaned, that is, where both parents have died or one has died and the other is in prison or cannot be found. Guardian's allowance continues as an independent child-related benefit (together with *child benefit* – see above) following the introduction of the *child tax credit* (see above) in April 2002.

Housing costs for families: the state will, in a variety of contexts, support peoples' housing needs. The state benefits system provides support for unemployed and low-income households' rental costs through the *housing benefit* (HB) system. People who are on *income support* (see below) or *income-based jobseeker's allowance* (WELFARE RIGHTS 9) will qualify automatically for maximum HB and *council tax benefit* (WELFARE RIGHTS 6); and if they have mortgage costs, the ISMI scheme (see *income support*, below) assists, although usually only after a waiting period unless the claimant or partner is over the age of 60. Also, the COMMUNITY CARE system can meet accommodation needs in a variety of contexts, including CHILDREN IN NEED (CHILDREN ACT 1989), HOMELESSNESS (Housing Act 1996), and the elderly and disabled (the NATIONAL ASSISTANCE ACT 1948, Part III). The Immigration and Asylum Act 1999 provides for those who are ASYLUM SEEKERS or subject to immigration control, who are taken, in most cases, outside the scope of state welfare unless their 'destitution' goes beyond mere financial destitution; and the Nationality, Asylum and Immigration Act 2002 (in the form of accommodation centres for asylum seekers and their families). See WELFARE RIGHTS 6.

Income support: a *means-tested benefit* (WELFARE RIGHTS 1) that is probably the most important family-related benefit, given its availability to parents who are unable to take up paid employment as a result of child-care responsibilities. It is also paid to people who are not working or who work fewer than 16 hours in a week, so in practice it enables groups like LONE PARENTS to undertake a limited amount of part-time paid work.

To receive income support, claimants must show that they fit into one of the qualifying groups, for example be carers, lone parents or people over the age of 60, or that they are incapable of work. All applicants must be interviewed at the DEPARTMENT FOR WORK AND PENSIONS' local office. Income support cannot be paid to anyone who has more than £8,000 in capital. An individual's needs under income support are called the *applicable amount* (see above), which is made up of three elements: *personal allowances*, set at fixed rates for adults and children in the family; *premiums*, designed to provide extra money for particular groups of claimants, such as pensioners, people with disabilities, carers, families and lone parent families; and *housing costs for home owners*, including interest payments for mortgages and home improvement loans. The amount paid to the claimant is the difference between the applicable amount and his or her income, with certain types of income disregarded. From April 2003 income support will be reformed so that personal allowances and premiums currently paid in respect of children will be awarded as a new tax credit called the *child tax credit* (see above and WELFARE RIGHTS 9).

Income support is frequently used to top up other benefits such as retirement pension (WELFARE RIGHTS 8). Income support paid to older people is also known as the *minimum income guarantee* (MIG). Receipt of income support acts as a passport to HEALTH BENEFITS, *housing benefit* and *council tax benefit* (WELFARE RIGHTS 6), *free school meals* (see above) and access to funding from the COMMUNITY LEGAL SERVICE fund. Income support claimants can also make claims on the *Social Fund* (WELFARE RIGHTS 8). Overall, the number of people claiming income support has decreased since 1995, but this picture is not true for all claimant groups – while the number of lone parents claiming has fallen by 12 per cent, those who are claiming because they are aged 60 plus increased by 11 per cent and those claiming who are disabled/other increased by 12 per cent.

In relation to the housing costs element of income support, the ISMI (*income support mortgage interest*) system will assist an eligible claimant with the interest element of mortgage costs, but only at a 'standard rate' (which may be less than the rate being paid to a lender). Normally, for a post-October 1995 mortgage, a claimant will have to wait 39 weeks before costs are paid (creating considerable arrears problems in situations like loss of employment, bereavement, assumption of carer responsibilities, and separation and divorce). For that reason, concessions are made to facilitate assistance. Specifically, help is brought forward in the cases of carers, partners going into prison on remand, people unable to access mortgage protection policies because of HIV, and those who have been 'abandoned' by a partner, leaving them responsible in the house for a child/young person). In these cases the 'wait' is reduced to eight weeks from the date of the income support claim (no help), 18 weeks (50 per cent of eligible costs), and then 100 per cent of costs at the end of 26 weeks. In 2002 it was confirmed that a person who has been 'constructively' abandoned, for example by violent or unreasonable behaviour, which has prompted a partner to leave the house, can be assisted by the system.

Milk tokens see WELFARE RIGHTS 7.

welfare rights 6 *housing assistance and related benefits* the group of welfare benefits related to housing.

Council tax benefit: a benefit that provides help towards the payment of council tax. It is administered by the local authority charging the tax and is credited against the account of the person liable to pay.

Council tax benefit can take two forms. *Main council tax benefit* depends on the income and circumstances of the person liable to pay council tax. *Second adult rebate* depends only on the income and circumstances of other adults in the household. Only one of these will be paid, whichever is higher. Main council tax benefit cannot be paid to anyone who has more than £16,000 in capital. People receiving *income support* (WELFARE RIGHTS 5) or *income-based job-seeker's allowance* (WELFARE RIGHTS 9) get council tax benefit to cover the full liability unless the property is in council tax bands F-H when it is restricted to the maximum amount payable for a band E house or non-dependant deductions apply. Council tax benefit for people who have income above these benefit rates is reduced at the rate of 20p in £1. The second adult rebate can be claimed where the liable person has no partner. If all the other adults are on a low income, the rebate given is of up to 25 per cent.

Discretionary housing payments: in large areas of the social security and community care services systems, decision-makers have 'discretion' rather than any clear statutory duty to meet people's welfare needs. Discretionary housing payments are payments that can be made by a local authority to help people to meet their rent or council tax liability or other exceptional housing costs – for example, if they have had their benefits reduced by a 'sanction'. Although they are administered by local authorities, like housing or council tax benefits, they have different rules.

While the payments are discretionary and can be made in a range of circumstances, including shortfall in benefits to meet rent, there are some restrictions; for example, a payment will not be made for services to meet the costs of water and sewerage or ineligible services for *housing benefit* (see below) or to cover a benefit penalty incurred because of a failure to comply with the CHILD SUPPORT Agency. Payments are made from a cash-limited budget allocated to each local authority by central government.

Housing benefit: a generic term describing benefits that provide help towards the payment of rent, administered by local authorities. *Rent allowance* is a cash payment to tenants of private landlords or HOUSING ASSOCIATIONS; *rent rebate* is a credit against a local authority tenant's rent account.

Housing benefit cannot be paid to anyone who has more than £16,000 in capital. People receiving *income support* (WELFARE RIGHTS 5) or *income-based job-seeker's allowance* (WELFARE RIGHTS 9) get maximum housing benefit. As income increases above this level, benefit is reduced, currently at the rate of 65p per £1 (2002). The maximum housing benefit is equal to the claimant's full rent but subject to certain deductions, including deductions for heating charges and for non-dependent adults (who are expected to contribute towards housing costs) and deductions if the rent is restricted. Rules allow benefit administrators to restrict rent if the accommodation is unreasonably expensive or unnecessarily large. Where housing benefit does not meet the cost of rent, the person may be able to claim a *discretionary housing payment* (see above) to cover the cost of the shortfall.

Housing benefit expenditure is substantially subsidized by central government. However, in areas where the authority has discretion – for example, to pay high rents, not to recover overpayments and to backdate benefit – the subsidy is reduced. This encourages authorities to be less generous in the exercise of their discretion.

Immigration and Asylum Act 1999 accommodation: there are powers under the Act to provide asylum seekers and those subject to immigration control with accommodation (under the NATIONAL ASYLUM SUPPORT SERVICE scheme and other arrangements under the Act). Local authorities retain residual duties and powers to provide accommodation, particularly if a person's 'destitution' goes beyond mere financial destitution – for example, if he or she is severely disabled or ill.

Income support mortgage interest (ISMI): a scheme enabling claimants to include an element of their mortgage costs (namely the interest element, at a prescribed standard rate) in their applicable amount if they are *income support* (WELFARE RIGHTS 6) or *income-based jobseeker's* claimants (WELFARE RIGHTS 9). (See, further, WELFARE RIGHTS 5: housing costs for families.)

National Assistance Act 1948 accommodation: under Part III of the 1948 Act, local authorities are under duties to provide accommodation for groups aged over 18 who 'by reason of age, illness, disability or any other circumstances are in need of care and attention which is not otherwise available to them'. There is a separate duty to provide accommodation for expectant and nursing mothers who are in need of 'care and attention', again if suitable accommodation is 'not otherwise available to them': section 21(1)(aa) of the 1948 Act. Children and young people have rights to be accommodated if they are in need and if part of their needs include accommodation. Legislative changes in 2002 have re-established such

powers in this regard following court decisions restricting the scope
of powers to rehouse under the Children Act 1989 section 17.

welfare rights 7 *maternity-related and young children's benefits*

Maternity allowance: an allowance paid to a woman off work while having
a baby, payable for up to 26 weeks when *statutory maternity pay* (see below)
is not available, for example to someone who is self-employed.

The amount of maternity allowance payable depends on the level
of a woman's earnings in the specified period before the baby is due.
It is paid at a weekly rate of £108.85 or 90 per cent of the mother's average
weekly earnings, whichever is smaller. The allowance can be claimed at
any time after the 11th week before the expected confinement.

Milk tokens: free tokens that can be exchanged for milk, available to
expectant mothers and children under five in families getting *income support*
(WELFARE RIGHTS 5) or *income-based job-seeker's allowance* (WELFARE RIGHTS 6).

Each token can be exchanged for seven 568 millilitres or eight
500 millilitres of milk a week or, for a child under one year, for 900 grams
of dried milk at a clinic. Tokens should be provided automatically by the
DEPARTMENT FOR WORK AND PENSIONS' local office to those who qualify.

National Assistance Act 1948 accommodation: an expectant and nursing
mother who is in need of 'care and attention' that is 'not otherwise
available to them' is entitled to be assessed and provided with residential
accommodation under section 21(1)(aa) of the 1948 Act.

Statutory adoption pay: a benefit payable during periods of adoption-
related leave from work, as provided for by the Employment Act 2002.

Statutory maternity pay (SMP): a legal minimum rate of pay paid by
employers during maternity leave for 26 weeks, beginning between
the 11th and the sixth week before the expected week of confinement.
Many employers pay more than this statutory minimum.

To be eligible, a woman must have been working for her employer
for at least 26 weeks and have average earnings of at least £84 per week
(2005–06). Women who have been dismissed or whose employment
ended without their consent before they are due to take maternity leave
are also eligible. For the first six weeks of maternity leave, statutory
maternity pay is paid at the rate of 90 per cent of average earnings.
For the remaining 20 weeks it is either £108.85 or 90 per cent of the
mother's average earnings if this is less than £108.85. Women who do not
qualify for statutory maternity pay may be able to get *maternity allowance*
(see above) from the DEPARTMENT FOR WORK AND PENSIONS.

Disputes over eligibility or nonpayment can be referred to the Inland
Revenue for determination, and decisions can be appealed. It is now a
criminal offence not to pay or to delay payment without justification.
In some cases nonpayment or payment at an inappropriate level may
also be a form of discrimination within the jurisdiction of the employment
tribunal, as may other actions or omissions of employers prior to, during
or after the maternity leave period.

Statutory paternity pay (SPP): a benefit payable to fathers during periods of paternity leave, as provided for by the Employment Act 2002.

Sure Start maternity grant: a payment made from the regulated *Social Fund* (WELFARE RIGHTS 8) to help meet the costs of a new baby. It is paid to an applicant who is in receipt of specified income-related benefits or tax credits and has just had a child (including adopting a baby) or expects one within 11 weeks. The payment is worth £500 for each child.

welfare rights 8 *pensioners' and older citizens' benefits*

Attendance allowance: a benefit paid to people over the age of 65 with severe disabilities who need help looking after themselves or supervision to avoid danger. See, further, WELFARE RIGHTS 3.

Graduated pension: an additional pension paid with *retirement pension* (see below). The scheme operated between 1961 and 1975 and pays limited benefits to people who contributed during that period.

Minimum income guarantee (MIG): a benefit for single pensioners or pensioner couples that supplements their incomes, particularly when they have low levels of income or reduced entitlements from benefits like the state *retirement pension* (see below). The benefit is means-tested by reference to other sources of income, and, like other MEANS-TESTED BENEFITS (see also WELFARE RIGHTS 1), there are capital limits. The MIG is superseded by the *pension credit*, under the State Pension Credit Act 2002 (see below), which consists of a guarantee credit and a savings credit, with simpler claims procedures.

Pension credit: a benefit that replaces the *minimum income guarantee* (see above), as provided in the State Pension Credit Act 2002. There are two parts to the credit – a *minimum income guarantee* and a *savings credit*. People aged 60 plus on a low income will be able to claim a 'guaranteed income top-up'. This works in the same way as income support (the current minimum income guarantee, WELFARE RIGHTS 5). It tops up low income to a specified level – £109 for a single person and £167 for a couple. Additional credits for people who are severely disabled and for carers are in the scheme.

There is also a *savings credit* for people aged 65 and over that will provide extra cash for people with incomes above the level of the basic pension – £82 for a single person and £131 for a couple in 2006. Single people with incomes of up to £151 will receive between 20p and £13.80 from the savings credit, and couples with incomes up to £221 will gain between 20p and £18.60.

There are rules regarding capital (savings). From October 2003 there is no upper capital limit and capital below £6,000 is ignored. The level of assumed income from savings will be reduced to £1 in every £500 (around 10 per cent) of savings above £6,000 and extends to housing and council tax benefit (WELFARE RIGHTS 6), except that the existing capital limit of £16,000 is retained). The Pension Service calculates entitlement to the credit when individual's claim state pension. Most people will have their credit reassessed every five years, and during this period most people will not be required to report changes of circumstances although they can ask for their credit to be reassessed if their income falls. In general, the government states that increases in income during this fixed period (known as the *assessed income period*) will be ignored.

Retirement age: the age at which retirement pension (see below) is paid, regardless of other circumstances. For women this is currently 60 and for men 65 years of age (*pensionable age*).

In 1993 the government announced plans to raise the retirement age for women to 65. This will be phased in between 2010 and 2020. Women born before April 1950 will not be affected, although they can continue to work until aged 65 if they wish. Some have argued that increased longevity will inevitably lead to a further raising of the retirement age for both men and women at some point in the future unless people can be persuaded to save much more for their retirements.

Retirement allowance see WELFARE RIGHTS 3 – *industrial injuries scheme.*

Retirement pension: the benefit payable to people over pensionable age, which is 60 years for women and 65 years for men. It can be paid even if a person continues to work. Retirement age for women will be increased to 65, to be phased in between 2010 and 2020. Women born before April 1950 will not be affected. Alternatively, retirement can be deferred for up to five years when retirement age is reached (women to 65, men to 70).

Deferring retirement for up to five years increases the value of the pension when claimed. There are four types of retirement pension. The *category A pension* is based on the claimant's contributions over his or her working life and can include additions for dependants. The *category B pension* is based on contributions paid by a spouse or sometimes a former spouse: typically, it is paid to a married woman who has either no or only reduced entitlement to a category A pension. It can only be paid once the contributor has retired. The *category C* and *D pensions* are *non-contributory* (WELFARE RIGHTS 1) and for people age 80 or over.

Stakeholder pension: schemes were introduced in April 2001 under the Welfare Reform and Pensions Act 1999 and the Stakeholder Pension Schemes Regulations 2000, SI 2000 No. 1403 as a way of providing a highly regulated, low-cost pension, including a second-tier pension for those in employment, fixed-contract workers, the self-employed and people who are not actually working but can afford to make contributions. In many cases such people might have a state *retirement pension* (see above) based on their NATIONAL INSURANCE CONTRIBUTIONS or might not (depending on their contributions record).

Most organizations are required by law to provide employees with access to a stakeholder pension – although they are not required to set up and run their own pension scheme. To qualify as a stakeholder pension the scheme must satisfy a number of criteria, including that it must be a money purchase arrangement and that management charges in each year must not exceed more than 1 per cent of the total value of the fund and are taken from the fund. The minimum contribution must not be set higher than £20. It is possible to contribute to someone else's stakeholder pension – for instance, someone can make contributions to a grandchild's or a non-working partner's stakeholder scheme on his or her behalf. Stakeholder pension schemes approved by HM Revenue and Customs are registered with Opra, the Occupational Pensions Regulatory Authority.

With the poor performance of the stock market in 2001 and 2002, concerns have grown that stakeholder pensions may not be able to deliver the benefit to retired people that was assumed when the government created them in 1999. This has not been helped by the way in which employers have started to retreat from occupational pension provision or imposing changes on pension schemes. This was the subject of a controversial report by Alan Pickering, *A Simpler Way to Better Pensions* (Alan Pickering, July 2002), which recommended deregulation of occupational pensions and the optional removal of guaranteed benefits, survivors' benefits, and other features of conventional pensions, as a means of giving employers incentives to maintain occupation pension provision. On publication, John Edmonds, General Secretary of the GMB union, reportedly said workers could be facing, by the end of 2002, 'the biggest pensions rip-off in history'.

State earnings-related pension scheme (Serps): a scheme providing an additional pension, based on individual contributions, that is paid to people claiming retirement.

State second pension (S2P): a pension introduced in April 2002 to replace the *state earnings-related pension scheme* (see above). It aims to provide a more generous additional state pension for low and moderate earners and certain carers and people with a long-term illness or disability. Research by the campaign group *Carers UK*, however, estimates that by 2050 even those who have spent the greater part of their working lifetime caring for others may receive only £50 per week extra on top of the basic state pension.

Social Fund: a fund administered by the DEPARTMENT FOR WORK AND PENSIONS that provides lump-sum payments to people in need. The Social Fund consists of two very different parts. The **Regulated Fund** provides the SURE START *maternity grant* (see also WELFARE RIGHTS 7) and *funeral expenses payments, cold weather payments* and *winter fuel payment* (see below) as of right but in closely defined circumstances. The fund's expenditure in this area is determined purely by demand and not by the judgements of individual Social Fund officers. The **Discretionary Fund** provides *community care grants, budgeting loans* and *crisis loans* (see below). Discretionary payments are made from a set budget allocated on a district basis so expenditure is therefore limited by its budget.

The Discretionary Social Fund was introduced in 1988 along with *income support* (WELFARE RIGHTS 5). It replaced 'single payments', paid as part of supplementary benefit and worth £600 million in 2000–01 with community care grants, currently worth £100 million, and repayable loans, worth £500 million.

The Social Fund has been criticized on three main grounds: first, the budget limit which requires Social Fund officers to ration payments; second, the extensive use of discretion by fund officers; and third, the absence of an independent appeal mechanism. The law on the Discretionary Social Fund is provided by the Secretary of State's directions, which broadly outline the circumstances in which a payment can be made. Fund officers who make decisions must follow the directions and take account of guidance, local priorities and the local budget. Despite an already suppressed demand for grants, only 44 per cent of community care grant applications are successful. When an applicant is refused, he or she may ask for an internal review; this includes an interview at the local office, at which a representative acting for the claimant may attend. A further review is provided by Social Fund inspectors at the Independent Review Service, but this is conducted in writing only. The inspectors check that previous decisions comply with the law, including the Secretary of State's directions. Frequently, the inspectors refer cases back for further consideration. This involves a lengthy process to deal with a claimant's needs, which are often immediate and essential.

The Regulated Social Fund:

Cold weather payment: payments from the Regulated Social Fund to cover extra domestic heating costs during exceptionally cold weather.

Cold weather payments can be made to a person receiving *income support* (WELFARE RIGHTS 5) or *income-based job-seeker's allowance* (WELFARE RIGHTS 9) that includes any pensioner premium, disability premium, severe disability premium or disabled child premium or an amount for a child aged under five. Payment will be made for any period of seven consecutive days when the average of the mean daily temperature is freezing or below. A cold weather payment should be paid automatically when temperature conditions dictate.

Funeral expenses payment: a payment from the Regulated Social Fund to which there is a legal entitlement if the applicant is receiving specified MEANS-TESTED BENEFITS (see also WELFARE RIGHTS 1) and *tax credits* (WELFARE RIGHTS 9) and has responsibility for a funeral held in the United Kingdom.

The regulations allow for the cost of a modest funeral. Costs are usually recovered from the deceased's estate.

Maternity payments: see WELFARE RIGHTS 7 *Sure Start maternity payments.*

Winter fuel payment: a lump sum paid to people aged at least 60 years to help meet the costs of winter fuel payments at the rate of £200 for those aged 60–79, and £300 for those aged 80 or over.

The government introduced annual winter fuel payments in 1997–98, initially restricted to people aged at least 60 who were also in receipt of specified qualifying benefits. This excluded men between the age of 60 and 64. In 1999 the European Court of Justice ruled that this was unlawful, and the following year the government extended the scheme to everyone over the age of 60 and paid backdated payments to anyone who had previously been excluded. It is generally paid automatically to people in receipt of retirement pension and most other social security benefits. Those not in receipt of benefits need to make a written claim.

The Discretionary Fund:

Budgeting loan: a repayable loan from the Discretionary Social Fund that people can apply for if they have been claiming *income support* (WELFARE RIGHTS 5) or *income-based jobseeker's allowance* (WELFARE RIGHTS 9) for at least 26 weeks. Loans can be paid to assist with important intermittent expenses for which it is difficult to budget.

Applications for budgeting loans are prioritized by weighting them against factual criteria laid down in the Social Fund directions. The maximum loan available is £1,000, but the amount that will be offered depends on the applicant's needs, budget and 'ability to repay' within 18 months. The loan is reduced by the value of any capital over £500 that the applicant has (or £1,000 if the person is aged over 60). Repayments can be deducted from most benefits. For those in receipt of either income support or income-based jobseeker's allowance, repayments are recovered at a rate of between 5 and 25 per cent of the *applicable amount* (WELFARE RIGHTS 5) depending on other commitments. A second loan can be given before the first one is repaid, but the Social Fund officer will restrict the amount offered in line with the directions on the maximum amount of loan available to the claimant. No interest is charged on the loan. In 2000–01 the average budgeting loan granted was £375.

Community care grant: a payment (not a loan) from the Social Fund that a person receiving *income support* (WELFARE RIGHTS 5) or *income-based jobseeker's allowance* (WELFARE RIGHTS 9) can apply for to help with a one-off expense.

The law outlines six circumstances in which payment of a community care grant may be made, subject to the Social Fund's local budget:

1 to help a person re-establish himself or herself in the COMMUNITY following a stay in institutional or RESIDENTIAL CARE;

2 to help a person remain in the community rather than enter institutional or residential care;

3 to help a person set up home in the community as part of a planned resettlement programme following a period when he or she has had an unsettled life;

4 to ease exceptional pressure on a person or his or her family;

5 to allow a person to care for a prisoner or young offender on home leave;

6 to pay travel expenses within the UK in specified circumstances, including visits to seriously ill relatives and attendance at funerals and to ease domestic crises.

These circumstances have the force of law. Guidance provided in the *Social Fund Guide*, although not legally binding on the Social Fund officer, lists 'priority groups' and 'priority items', concentrating on people deemed vulnerable by age or ill-health; however, 'absence of guidance applying to a particular circumstance, item or service does not mean that help should be refused'. A community care grant will be reduced by the value of any capital over £500 (£1,000 if aged 60 or over) that the applicant has. In 1999–2000 the majority of payments, totalling over £47 million, were made to families in order to ease exceptional pressure. *Crisis loan:* repayable loans from the Social Fund towards expenses in an emergency if this is the only means to prevent serious damage or risk to health or safety.

People can apply for a crisis loan, whether or not they receive *income support* (WELFARE RIGHTS 5) or *income-based jobseeker's allowance* (WELFARE RIGHTS 9). Loans are most commonly used to provide living expenses for short periods – in 1999–2000, 67 per cent of the expenditure was on this. Staff at the DEPARTMENT FOR WORK AND PENSIONS' local offices often decline to give people application forms, advising them that it is not worth their applying, and for this reason the success rate of applications exceeds 70 per cent.

welfare rights 9 *work and unemployment-related benefits* benefits to which people in employment and those actively seeking work may be eligible.
(1) benefits for those in work
Tax credit: in recent years the concept of a 'TAX CREDIT' has come to mean a number of things. In one context, that of tax assessment, it is simply a way of enhancing income by providing allowances on which tax on earned and certain other kinds of income will not be paid. The *children's tax credit*, which has been subsumed by the new *child tax credit* from April 2003 (see also WELFARE RIGHTS 5) is a form of assistance that enables taxpayers with children to retain income. As their income rises, however, the support is withdrawn so that most higher rate taxpayers do not receive it. It has been seen by some commentators as a benefit rather than a tax allowance because, unlike its predecessors, it has had to be claimed. In the SOCIAL SECURITY context, tax credit is used to describe what is more akin to a welfare benefit, so that the *working tax credit* and *child tax credit*, for example, bear more resemblance to a conventional benefit that is claimed and awarded, subject to a means-test. From April 2003, however, there will be no capital limits (unlike the *working families tax credit* and *disabled person's tax credit*), and assessment will be based on gross earnings, as evidenced by tax returns and P60 evidence of pay and deductions, with less reliance on separate claim forms and declarations from claimants and employers as to 'net weekly income'. Arguably, the

welfare support delivered through the new tax credits represents a hybrid between more conventional welfare benefits and tax allowances and reliefs.

There are also some special arrangements for disabled people seeking employment. The Disability Employment Advisory Service, located in Job Centres, can offer employers who are considering employing a disabled person help with adapting workplaces, providing specialist equipment such as computers or even a subsidized wage for a limited period to enable a disabled person to demonstrate his or her potential as an employee.

Earnings disregard: there are some circumstances where a person in receipt of a benefit – such as income support (WELFARE RIGHTS 5), *jobseeker's allowance* (see below), *housing benefit* or *council* tax *benefit* (WELFARE RIGHTS 6) – may be permitted to keep some of their earnings, should they have, say, a part-time job. The level of disregard varies according to the claimant's circumstances – for example, a carer, a person with disabilities, a lone parent and people in specified occupations (fire-fighter, territorial army, coastguard) can earn up to £20 per week in 2002–03 before benefit is reduced. In contrast, single people not in any of the above categories can earn only up to £5. Special arrangements for child-minders are also in place for those claiming income support where much of the income from looking after children can be retained.

(2) benefits for those seeking work

Jobseeker's allowance (JSA): a benefit paid to a person who is unemployed, 'signing on' as available for work and actively seeking work. There are two types of JSA: *contribution-based JSA*, paid to claimants who have paid or have been credited with the required NATIONAL INSURANCE CONTRIBUTIONS, and *income-based JSA*, paid to claimants who satisfy the income and capital means test. Contribution-based JSA is an individual benefit that can be paid for a maximum of 26 weeks; income-based JSA can be paid to supplement contribution-based JSA, for example, to meet the needs of a family or mortgage (interest only). It can be paid instead of contribution-based JSA to those who do not meet the national insurance contributions' conditions or who have exhausted their entitlement to the contribution-based benefit. Childless couples where one or both partners were born after 19 March 1976 are required to make a joint claim for JSA.

To claim jobseeker's allowance, all claimants must sign a *jobseeker's agreement* that specifies what steps they will take to find work and how they must demonstrate that they are 'available' for and are 'actively seeking' paid work. Those who do not comply with the regulations may be *sanctioned* (disqualified from benefit). Those who fail to comply with a direction to undertake job-search activity may be sanctioned for two or four weeks. Someone who is dismissed from his or her job for misconduct or leaves voluntarily without 'just cause' may be sanctioned for up to 26 weeks. Many cases of dismissal or of people leaving employment voluntarily include circumstances that justify only a short period of disqualification or none at all. In practice, a maximum disqualification is almost always imposed in the first instance, and claimants have to appeal to have their disqualification reviewed and to begin receiving their benefits. Jobseeker's allowance is not paid for any period covered by wages in lieu of notice. By contrast, redundancy payments do not affect entitlement.

Those in receipt of contribution-based JSA and income-based JSA are pass-ported to other benefits such as FREE PRESCRIPTIONS and possibly, for those with children, *free school meals* (WELFARE RIGHTS 5).

welfare state the organizing, financing and provision of welfare benefits and services by government.

The term 'welfare state' is used to describe the combination of benefits and services intended to increase the wellbeing of citizens and provided either directly or indirectly. The welfare state also seeks to relieve poverty and reduce inequality by guaranteeing a minimum level of financial assistance through social security or unemployment benefit. While state involvement in housing, education and social insurance occurred in Europe throughout the last half of the 19th century, the welfare state as it was constructed in Britain between 1944 and 1949 was unusually comprehensive and supported by a well-articulated philosophy that viewed it as a natural progression in social development. In Britain the welfare state became closely associated with the publicly financed services run by large institutions, such as the NATIONAL HEALTH SERVICE, local authority housing and state schools.

For some 30 years after the Second World War, the continued expansion of the welfare state was taken for granted by a broad consensus across the political spectrum. Expenditure on services and benefits took a greater share of the gross national product each year until the mid-1970s, when the government began to focus on the increasing costs of welfare. The architects of the welfare state had always linked its benefits and services to the presumption of full employment, for men if not for women. Most households, it was assumed, would have a relatively well-paid wage earner. In the mid-1970s the destabilizing effects of a sharp rise in the price of oil and the rapidly changing nature of the economy made full male employment difficult to sustain or achieve. Unemployment soared, as did inflation. At the same time, the broad consensus supporting the welfare state also began to weaken. Electorates became less willing to fund services and benefits through taxation, while politicians and commentators from the NEW RIGHT argued that welfare benefits were too generous and created a disincentive to work and a dependency on the state. Governments hostile to the welfare state were elected in both the United States and Britain.

Sober assessment of the retrenchment of welfare policies that both governments adopted, however, indicates that the welfare state has survived, if in a somewhat different form. Not until its second term did the Thatcher government attempt to cap social security spending by reducing any increase in benefits to the cost of living (previously they had been up-rated more generally with the increase in the standard of living). Other government reforms throughout the 1980s and 1990s changed the institutional arrangements of the welfare state by limiting the direct provision of welfare by state institutions. They did this by trying to separate purchasers of services from providers and by allowing schools and hospitals to manage themselves rather than be managed by local or health authorities. In effect, this introduced MARKET-like reforms into some welfare provision, channelling public money into welfare services provided through an increasing number of private and voluntary organizations rather than by public institutions and local authorities as in the past. Most analysts note that, while the form of the welfare state has changed, moving towards a greater role for private and voluntary organizations, government financing has not been cut as severely as first thought, and public support for the welfare state overall remains high. (See also ANTI-POVERTY STRATEGY, BEVERIDGE REPORT.)

H. Glennerster and J. Midgley (eds), *The Radical Right and the Welfare State*, Hemel Hempstead, Harvester Wheatsheaf, 1991.

Welsh Office the central government department responsible for most internal affairs in Wales.

Responsibility for social services was transferred to the Welsh Office in 1971. This responsibility was linked to that for the health service in Wales in the Health and Social Work Department. As a result of this development, an attempt at establishing a coherent policy in respect of social services and health was embarked upon in 1976. The most notable success is the development of a fully evaluated 'all-Wales strategy' for people with learning disabilities. The existence of an integrated department for health and social services has enabled the Welsh Office to overcome some of the departmentalism that has inhibited coordination of policies in England and Scotland. Responsibility for developing COMMUNITY CARE policy has also rested with social services rather than health services personnel, and this has allowed a social work perspective to develop rather than a MEDICAL MODEL of care. For this reason, the section of the white paper *Caring for People* (1989) on Wales is dominated by a record of achievement by the all-Wales strategy. However, the white paper formally ended specific joint funding provision by the health authorities, and responsibility has been placed more firmly with local authorities.

Devolution of powers to the elected Welsh Assembly has enabled local representatives to discuss provision of various services within the context of perceived Welsh needs. The Welsh Assembly has very limited powers, however, and the consequences for the Welsh Office and the way that it operates, including the provision of such national services, is limited when compared to the more extensive devolution to the Scottish Parliament.

D. J. Hunter and G. Wistow, *Community Care in Britain*, London, King's Fund Centre, 1987.

'What works' see EFFECTIVENESS.

whistleblowing a process of trying to make visible an abuse or misuse of power within an organization, usually by an employee of the organization, although the person may have a role other than a full-fledged employee, such as an agency worker working temporarily for an organization.

A number of public and internal enquiries within health and social welfare agencies over the past few decades have speculated about some employees' failure to report on perceived abuses in the behaviour of colleagues or about agencies' failures to respond to complaints about such abuses when they have been explicitly reported as abuses. The inability of workers to 'blow the whistle' and of agencies' unwillingness to respond to known abuses led to the devising of the Public Interest Disclosure Act 1998. This Act sought to provide protection for those who disclose abuses by discouraging employers from treating such employees in a 'detrimental manner'. Such measures included protection from unfair dismissal and other measures, such as a possible reduction in pay or failure to increase pay or failure to offer some benefit that might otherwise be provided.

The Act was designed to encourage a culture of openness. However, employers are not required to have a policy on disclosing abuses of power by their own employees, nor are there any rules about preventing employers refusing employment to an applicant on grounds that he or she was a whistleblower in a previous employment. Should an employee make a mistake, even in good faith, and an alleged abuse prove groundless or difficult to prove, then the whistleblower could find himself or herself in difficulty with a possible counterclaim of 'defamation'. These limitations have not brought about a fundamental change in the culture of health and social welfare agencies. Employees continue to feel the constraints of loyalty to colleagues or agency or a generalized wish 'not to rock the boat'. There may however be evidence of an increased use of anonymous complaints to the media or to agency INSPECTION services or encouragement to service users who wish to make formal COMPLAINTS.

P. Ells and G. Dehn, 'Whistleblowing: Public Concern at Work', in L. A. Cull and J. Roche, *The Law and Social Work*, Milton Keynes, Open University Press.

whiteness the concept denoting the ethnicity of the white population.

Little has been done to explore or understand white ethnicity, in part because anti-racist approaches in social work tended to view the needs of the white population as racist when articulated within a white perspective. As a result, there has been a lack of anti-racist initiatives responding to white working class young people who can be unsure, even fearful, over what their own racial grouping ought to signify. Indeed, research into the attitudes of white working class youth has found the view that white ethnicity was being regulated unfairly. A more positive strategy for engaging with white ethnicity can be developed around local white identities, drawing on life history and family history accounts. Settings where young people can explore and then tell their family stories, share personal biographies or trace their ethnic and social class lineage provided a way of deconstructing whiteness. Tracing their family past was a means of personalizing history, making it relevant to their life experiences to date. Once this is under way, a picture emerges of a mix of national origins and ethnicities that is more complex than previously thought.

A. Nayak, 'White English ethnicities: Racism, anti-racism and student perspectives', in *Race Ethnicity and Education*, Volume 2, issue 2, pp 177-202.

widowed mother's allowance, widow's payment, widow's pension see WELFARE RIGHTS (2).

winter fuel payment see WELFARE RIGHTS (8).

withdrawal the physical reaction to the loss of a drug that has been taken for long enough for the person to become addicted in some measure. Symptoms can include cramps, diarrhoea, shivering and nausea. In extreme cases convulsions and death may result.

witness protection see VULNERABLE WITNESS.

Women's Aid a federation of refuges for women seeking to leave or have respite from violent partners. The women's aid movement, established in 1975, is a voluntary SELF-HELP movement run by women for women.

Women's Aid is prepared to accept any woman experiencing difficulties with a violent or abusing partner. The women themselves define what is an intolerable situation: there is no 'objective' test set by the movement. The clear aims of Women's Aid in relation to women and children who have experienced violence are to help them recover from the trauma and to encourage them to take control over their own lives. The movement also has broader educational and campaigning aims in relation to social welfare and justice systems as well as the public. These are to inform about the problem of DOMESTIC VIOLENCE and the inadequacy of current policies and provision for the protection of women and children. The movement has grown rapidly in Britain. In 1975 there were 30 refuges, but by 1987 this number had grown to over 200. The under-resourcing of women's aid in general and the remarkable lack of support from local authorities in particular have dogged the movement and made it financially vulnerable. Current provision is still far short of that recommended by the Domestic Violence Select Committee in 1975.

workload management systems for determining and managing the quantity and quality of work of an individual worker and teams of workers.

Two systems of workload management are typically used; the first rests upon estimates of time allocated to identified tasks (for example, it is estimated that case A requires 5 hours a week, case B 10 hours, case C 8 hours, groupwork 6 hours, team meetings 3 hours, duty 7 hours, a training day 7 hours, and so on). Thus a worker might anticipate how the next month is to be spent. The second system is similar except that standard allowances (either points representing time or actual time slots) are given to, say, a PRE-SENTENCE REPORT, a SUPERVISION ORDER, a CHILD ABUSE investigation, a day in court and other set pieces. Systems vary in their complexity, depending upon their objectives. Some systems are also used to help management determine the range and duration of work. The principal objectives are to help protect workers from overload, thereby sustaining quality in work, and to help management determine where resources are to be allocated. Workload management can also be an aid to supervision and, if information is shared, to team functioning.

written agreement a statement written and agreed jointly by client and social worker, setting out the aims and tasks to be undertaken in any future work.

Written agreements are key tools in contemporary social work. They are designed to ensure that there is no misunderstanding over the scope and intention of any planned social work intervention and to highlight areas of cooperation between practitioner and client. They should set out clearly what specific tasks are to be undertaken and by whom. The content of any written agreement is arrived at by negotiation and should always be framed in the client's own words or in words that are readily understandable by all concerned. When working with children and families, *Guidance to the Children Act* requires that a written agreement be drawn up before a child is placed in ACCOMMODATION. In particular, such agreements will specify the length of time, the frequency and manner of contact between the child and his or her parents and the role the parents will play in the life of the child when he or she is accommodated.

Michael Preston-Shoot, 'Written agreements: A contractual approach to social work', in C. Hanvey and T. Philpot (eds), *Practising Social Work*, London, Routledge, 1994.

YOI abbreviation for YOUNG OFFENDER INSTITUTION.

YOT abbreviation for YOUTH OFFENDING TEAM.

young offender institution (YOI) a custodial institution for young offenders aged 12 to 17 that is intended to keep them separate from adult offenders and provide a rehabilitative environment.

With the formation of the YOUTH JUSTICE BOARD, young offender institutions became subject to the board's accreditation and standards and the board became responsible for commissioning and purchasing places for young offenders given custodial sentences. In the context of increased use of CUSTODY and considerable overcrowding and pressure on the system, however, this has had little short-term impact upon prison conditions.

Under the DETENTION AND TRAINING ORDER, young offenders serve half their sentence in custody and the remainder in the community under supervision. During their first few days in custody, their education, health and other needs should be assessed and a training plan compiled. This should be reviewed periodically, and a YOUTH OFFENDING TEAM member is required to visit the young person regularly in custody and to see him or her on the day of release and regularly thereafter in accordance with NATIONAL STANDARDS.

While the new arrangements under the CRIME AND DISORDER ACT 1998 succeed in keeping young offenders separate from adults, they also treat the 18–20 age group as adults and bring them into contact with more serious, older offenders. The attempt to use the SECURE ESTATE for young people more rationally by confining it to younger offenders was rapidly frustrated by courts' increased use of their enhanced powers to send young people to custodial establishments. The Youth Justice Board's ambitious plans to increase the emphasis on rehabilitation and challenging young people's offending behaviour depended upon fewer young people being imprisoned, and this has not happened.

youth court the criminal court responsible for young offenders aged 10 to 17 in England and Wales, which replaced the juvenile court in England and Wales in 1992.

Proceedings in the youth court are intended to be less formal than in an adult court. The public is excluded, and the press may not normally report young people's names and addresses (see CRIMINAL COURTS, YOUTH JUSTICE). Sentences available to the youth court but not to adult courts are the ACTION PLAN ORDER, the CURFEW, the DETENTION AND TRAINING ORDER, the REFERRAL ORDER, the REPARATION ORDER and the SUPERVISION ORDER. See also YOUTH OFFENDING TEAM.

youth culture or **subculture** a system of VALUES, ATTITUDES and behaviours shared by a group of young people and different from those exhibited by other young people or people in general within a particular society.

Sociologists have examined the idea that there are youth subcultures in Britain. The characteristics thought by some to typify a youth subculture include a degree of classlessness, particularly in relation to leisure habits, a measure of opposition to adult values and behaviour and, most important, the replacement of the family by the peer group as the key set of social relationships. Critics of this analysis have argued that for most young people, class, race and gender continue to be the most important defining characteristics rather than age. They add that society is remarkably good at reproducing itself, and in this respect attitudes and values are frequently shared by generations. Where differences are discernible, they are thought, with some exceptions, to be transitory.

Social workers and others working with adolescents and young people have it that particular PEER GROUPS can be extremely important influences upon the behaviour of individual young people. In practice, it may be difficult to distinguish between the influence of a youth culture as distinct from a more immediate peer group. It may be that a peer group is a subculture, but it is also possible, indeed usual, for the subculture to be much larger than the peer group. In some circumstances (with some offence behaviour, for example) social work with young people has to acknowledge the importance of the group in relation to an individual's behaviour and work with the group if particular problems are clearly rooted in group dynamics. Gangs, for example, can provide exclusive group membership with tightly prescribed roles and in some cases the expectation of very distinctive behaviour. Members of such groups may clearly be culturally different from other young people, but such all-embracing social groupings are rare. The values and attitudes of particular youth groups may best be understood by reference to other social phenomena such as class or race. The class origins of rockers or skinheads, for example, may be a better explanation of their behaviour than intergenerational relations. Similarly, Rastafarianism among the young in Britain may, in part at least, be understood by examining racism and relations between ethnic groups rather than through age-related explanations.

youth justice the criminal justice system as it applies to people under 18: the supervision of young offenders by the staff of YOUTH OFFENDING

TEAMS; the philosophy, policy and practice of dealing with young offenders differently and separately from the adult criminal justice system.

Since the introduction of the YOUTH COURT in England and Wales in 1991, the term 'youth justice' has replaced the previous 'juvenile justice'. From the middle of the 19th century there has been a recognition that young people cannot be held as fully responsible for their actions as adults, that it may be easier for them to change their behaviour than for adults and that they should be protected from the full force of adult punishment (see DOLI INCAPAX; THEORIES OF CRIME). At the same time, it has been acknowledged that young people commit a large proportion of all crime, which suggests a need for an official response (but see MINIMUM INTERVENTION). Since 1908, young offenders have been dealt with in a separate youth court that is closed to the public and where proceedings are meant to be less formal than in adult CRIMINAL COURTS.

The history of youth justice has been one of tension between the JUST DESERTS' model of sentencing, that of rehabilitation, in which the young person's welfare is believed to be paramount, and an approach that seeks to avoid unnecessary LABELLING by managing the youth justice system in such a way as to divert young people away from it for as long as possible (minimum intervention). The just deserts' model seems dominant in the CRIME AND DISORDER ACT 1998, but it also contains elements of REPARATION, and the YOUTH JUSTICE AND CRIMINAL EVIDENCE ACT 1999 introduced a new diversionary measure, the REFERRAL ORDER.

Youth Justice and Criminal Evidence Act 1999 the law that introduced Youth Offender Panels and REFERRAL ORDERS in England and Wales as well as new measures for the protection of intimidated and VULNERABLE WITNESSES.

Most young offenders prosecuted for the first time and pleading guilty (unless for a very serious offence) are referred by the YOUTH COURT to a Youth Offender Panel consisting of a representative of the local YOUTH OFFENDING TEAM and two lay members. The legal mechanism for this is the referral order. The panel is required to 'provide a constructive forum for the young offender to confront the consequences of crime and agree a programme of meaningful activity to prevent any further offending' (according to the short guide to the arrangements on the Home Office website). This programme will normally include an element of REPARATION and can also involve educational, accommodation or other provisions. A referral order counts as a criminal conviction, but the young person appears before a court again only if he or she is breached for non-compliance (defined by NATIONAL STANDARDS).

The court procedures for the protection of intimidated and vulnerable witnesses are intended to encourage consistency between courts in the application of such measures and to improve witnesses' willingness to give evidence. For details of the special measures and the circumstances in which they are used, see VULNERABLE WITNESS. See also YOUTH JUSTICE.

Youth Justice Board the official body set up, under the CRIME AND
DISORDER ACT 1998, to take responsibility for the management of the
SECURE ESTATE and for the implementation of government policy in
the YOUTH JUSTICE system, including the publication of NATIONAL
STANDARDS and the regulation of YOUTH OFFENDING TEAMS.

The board is intended to provide national leadership and coordination,
and to raise standards in the YOUTH JUSTICE system. It has the power to
monitor the operation of the system, to obtain and publish information
for that purpose, and to advise the Home Secretary on youth justice
policy. It has substantial funds to distribute, and carries out and
commissions research.

While the board has been active in ensuring that YOUTH OFFENDING
TEAMS are in a position to comply with NATIONAL STANDARDS and to
promote the defined aims of the youth justice system, it has been
less successful in limiting the use of CUSTODY (including SECTION 53)
by YOUTH COURTS and in promoting consistency in sentencing between
youth courts. The principal aim of the youth justice system, according
to the CRIME AND DISORDER ACT 1998, is to prevent offending by young
people. The board's other objectives are the swift administration of
youth justice ('FAST TRACKING'), confronting young offenders with
the consequences of their offending and helping them to develop a
sense of personal responsibility, intervention to tackle criminogenic
need and to reinforce protective factors, promoting proportionate
punishment, encouraging REPARATION and reinforcing parental
responsibility.

Youth Justice Plan the annual document prepared by local authorities
in consultation with YOUTH OFFENDING TEAMS and other local agencies
for the YOUTH JUSTICE BOARD, setting out their progress against their
objectives, their plans for the coming year and the funding arrangements
for their work.

youth offending team (YOT) a local inter-agency team responsible for
supervising young offenders, advising YOUTH COURTS on the sentencing
of individual young people, organizing and sitting on Youth Offender
Panels, making arrangements for REPARATION and for an APPROPRIATE
ADULT scheme and REMAND management, and participating in CRIME
AND DISORDER PARTNERSHIPS and crime prevention arrangements.

The youth offending team has a wide range of responsibilities, but
in carrying them out it draws upon the involvement of a number of
agencies that are required to contribute staff as well as the wider local
YOUTH JUSTICE system. Each team consists of at least one social worker,
probation officer, police officer and representatives of the health and
education services. In practice, most staff are seconded from social services
departments, and some teams have only one member of each of the
other disciplines. In some places, other agencies (particularly careers
advisers and prison staff) are also represented.

YOT workers supervise young people who are placed on SUPERVISION ORDERS, COMMUNITY REHABILITATION ORDERS, COMMUNITY PUNISHMENT ORDERS, COMMUNITY PUNISHMENT AND REHABILITATION ORDERS, and DETENTION AND TRAINING ORDERS. In addition, they are responsible for PARENTING ORDERS, CHILD SAFETY ORDERS, REPARATION ORDERS and ACTION PLAN ORDERS. They provide programmes in support of the FINAL WARNINGS made by the police and assist in police investigations by training and providing appropriate adults. The YOT has a responsibility for chairing and servicing REFERRAL ORDER panels and for working to implement the plans made by them. YOT members are required to provide bail support, and in most areas this is interpreted more widely as a power to undertake REMAND management (which was a particular strength of the social services-run youth justice teams in many areas prior to the establishment of YOTs). It is also YOT members who prepare PRE-SENTENCE REPORTS for the youth courts. The YOT also has an overall co-ordinating role in respect of youth justice services in its area. The detailed arrangements for funding and providing these services are agreed annually and included in a YOUTH JUSTICE PLAN submitted to the YOUTH JUSTICE BOARD, which also issues NATIONAL STANDARDS governing the detailed delivery of the orders listed above.

The guiding principles for the work of YOTs are set out in the CRIME AND DISORDER ACT 1998 and by the national Youth Justice Board. The YOT manager is directly accountable to the local authority chief executive and indirectly to the Youth Justice Board.

YOTs were created in response to the criticisms of the youth justice system contained in the Audit Commission's MISSPENT YOUTH report, and as such they represent an attempt to create a more accountable and consistent system. They came into being at a time when the Crime and Disorder Act had also increased the sentences available to youth courts, and as such they inevitably faced a growing caseload of young people in CUSTODY. They simultaneously had to make the arrangements for introducing REPARATION and working with VICTIMS of crime, which were fundamentally different from the work in which most of their staff were experienced. A few months later, they were also given responsibility for setting up and servicing referral order panels. Perhaps not surprisingly, some YOTs have struggled with the workload, reconciling the contradictions within the legislation and with the pace of change.

R. Powell, *Child Law: A guide for practitioners*, Winchester, Waterside Press, 2001.

youth work a wide range of services concerned with children and young people roughly within the age range 10 to 21, focusing upon social, recreational and educational needs and the resolution of particular problems such as homelessness and unemployment.

Youth services witnessed rapid expansion in Britain in the 1960s in both the VOLUNTARY SECTOR and the STATUTORY SECTOR. The core of these services was the youth club, offering mostly recreational provision. Clearly perceived by successive governments as a way of diverting potentially disaffected youth through constructive leisure, most localities had a youth club providing sports and leisure activities, with some weekend and holiday provision. Many clubs would additionally offer some kind of social education programme, especially the voluntary clubs located within churches. The content of social education would vary enormously depending upon the host organization, although all contended that preparation for citizenship and for adult roles was central to the task. Some youth workers were trained as social workers or had undertaken courses in teacher training colleges. A very large proportion, however, were volunteers or untrained sessional workers. An early innovation, in recognition of the fact that many young people did not attend clubs, was the unattached youth worker. Such workers were to engage with 'street-corner society', especially those young people considered to be 'at risk' of criminal activity or in moral danger. The major objective in this work was more closely akin to social work, that is, to identify problems, whether personal or in the neighbourhood, and to engage with the young people in solving them.

Over the past 20 years the youth club 'movement' has declined but not disappeared, largely because local authorities have been unable to maintain expenditure levels. Services for adolescents and young people have, however, developed in other ways to meet particular needs. Specialized work with young people who engage in ANTISOCIAL BEHAVIOUR and are at risk of being excluded from school is now more widely available in an effort to prevent them from offending (see CRIME AND DISORDER ACT). Other provision, much of it in the voluntary sector, focuses on HOMELESSNESS (see ROUGH SLEEPERS and FOYERS). Young people who are LOOKED AFTER by the local authority have long been vulnerable to homelessness, poverty and offending. The CHILDREN (LEAVING CARE) ACT 2000 places particular responsibilities on local authorities to continue to support young people they have looked after until the age of 25. Similarly, SUBSTANCE MISUSE among young people has seen the development of advisory and counselling services, again mostly in the voluntary sector, but with limited statutory provision from health and social services. A similar picture exists in relation to pregnancy advisory services and gay and lesbian helplines. General youth COUNSELLING services are offered in some localities, but provision is uneven. At the direction of the Department for Education and Employment, much attention has focused on schools and directed at young people at risk of TRUANCY or EXCLUSION FROM SCHOOL. PASTORAL SUPPORT teams draw on a range of professionals including EDUCATION SOCIAL WORKERS to help individual pupils while they complete studies for GCSEs or GNVQs.

Building relationships with many marginalized young people is not straightforward because of negative past experiences and perhaps constricted opportunities for personal and social development. Sometimes unresponsive in conversation, erratic in time planning, acting on impulse – these are common habits among adolescents. But practitioners should remember that despite the difficulties in the young person's interaction with parents, teachers, friends, mentors and social workers, relationships with adults are the crucial catalyst for marginalized young people overcoming those barriers and securing what they want.

Much practice is directly or indirectly involved in creating and strengthening such bonds. For a practitioner working with young people to help sort out their feelings is an important objective. What they value above all is their relationship with the counsellor, social worker or youth worker who is attentive and available. This goes some way towards balancing previously hurtful, unsafe experiences with adults and gives the young person a broader emotional understanding for dealing with the dilemmas they face.

One of the hardest things for a young person to learn is to distinguish between 'what's me' and 'what's not me'. The practitioner's skill in 'reflecting back' – which means listening to what the young person has to say and then repeating it so that the young person can clarify what he or she actually feels – is an important tool. A social worker or counsellor should be warm but remain non-judgmental so that young people can begin to discover their own sense of good and bad.

A principal aim of youth work is to extend the effectiveness of a young person's network through which a young person can receive informal support, advice and help in finding job training or a place in higher education. This is often achieved through MENTORING schemes; the government's CONNEXIONS aims to provide such support for all secondary school pupils. (See also ADOLESCENT SUPPORT TEAM, TEENAGE PREGNANCY, HOMELESSNESS.)

B. Goldson, *The New Youth Work*, Lyme Regis, Russell House Publishing, 1999.

Zz

zero tolerance a theory of policing that emphasizes the need to deal with all criminal offences and incivility, however trivial, first, to convey a principled position that crime ought not to be committed, and second, a conviction that minor offences, unless properly dealt with, will very likely lead to serious offences.

Although the theory refers to all crime, police authorities have been especially concerned with street crime, including robbery, drug dealing and criminal damage. In other contexts the theory has attracted significant attention in relation to the problem of DOMESTIC VIOLENCE.

Some early advocates of this view used the phrase *broken windows* to convey the idea that broken windows should be repaired and graffiti removed to prevent the creation of a perception that an area is going 'downhill', with an associated disrespect for its appearance that may lead to further vandalism and the dumping of rubbish. According to this approach, the police should intervene at an early stage in minor public order incidents in order to protect residents' quality of life and all infractions of the law merit police attention.

The original theory was developed by James Q. Wilson and George Kelling in an article published in the USA in 1982 that essentially called attention to what happens when public spaces are abandoned. They argued that broken windows and graffiti convey signals that social authority and social norms no longer prevail in a neighbourhood, thus inviting crime, particularly drug dealing, to occur. The theory was subsequently taken up by the New York Police Department in an aggressive 'zero tolerance' campaign against minor crime and incivility, which was said to lead to a spectacular reduction in the overall New York crime rate (including a reduction in the number of murders). In the nature of such claims, it is very difficult to prove a causal link between a new approach to policing and a change in the local crime rate. When the theory was applied to other US cities, it coincided with increased crime. Its application to policing has been criticized because it condones the discriminatory use of discretion and, in the New York context, led to oppressive and violent police behaviour.

Underlying the theory is a belief that even minor rule-breaking, if it is not challenged, is likely to lead on to more serious disorder and to crime. This view has been influential in wider spheres than policing and is evident in the youth justice reforms set out in the Crime and Disorder Act 1998, which favour early intervention in response to minor offending. Attempts have also been made to implement the approach in the policing of small areas in the UK, as in the removal of beggars from the streets of King's Cross in London in 1996, and the highly publicized anti-burglary initiative in Middlesborough, Cleveland, in the late 1990s.

The theory has also been adopted by campaign groups concerned with the problem of DOMESTIC VIOLENCE, initially in Edinburgh and later in other parts of the UK. In this context, zero tolerance is a wide-ranging campaign that attempts to coordinate all services that have responsibilities for the many facets of the problem. Such services, it is argued, should underline the criminal nature of domestic violence and not tolerate or overlook any expression of male power, however minor, if it leads to the abuse of women. Central to zero tolerance approaches to the issue of domestic violence is a broad-based public campaign using all available media to promote the core message that women should not be the subject of male violence. These campaigns have also held that all sections of the community are responsible for ensuring the safety of women and for holding perpetrators to account.

W. J. Bratton, 'Crime is down in New York: blame the police', in N. Dennis (ed), *Zero-Tolerance Policing: Policing in a Free Society*, London, Institute of Economic Affairs.

Finding social work resources on the internet

The internet has a vast amount of information on social work and related subjects available to students, academics, professional researchers, and practitioners alike. Finding reliable and free data should not be difficult although a few points need to be borne in mind. The material should be up to date. Small organizations and departments within academic institutions sometimes encounter funding difficulties and are unable to continue with their researches. Make sure to look at the 'Last updated' section of the main website page before using any data. Try clicking on the links to make sure that they have been maintained properly and do not result in error messages. Ideally information should be obtained from websites run by universities, government departments and agencies, research institutes, and other reputable organizations. Websites maintained by individuals may not be up to date and comprehensive. It is also possible that the prejudices of those maintaining the websites will be reflected in the content and list of links.

There is a very useful free 'tutorial' to finding and using social work information on the internet, which can be found at:

www.sosig.ac.uk/vts/socialworker

General social work and sociology sites

There are a number of gateway sites that give access to many internet sites. These are the best places to start your internet researches, as the links they contain are carefully researched and maintained.

Social Science Information Gateway

www.sosig.ac.uk/social_welfare/

This service aims to provide a trusted source of selected, high-quality internet information for researchers and students. Within the Social Welfare section of the site, there are specific categories for:

adoption; black and minority ethnic groups; carers; children; community work; disabled people; families; health services; homelessness; mental health; older people; people with learning difficulties; poverty; social policy; social security benefits; social services; social work; substance misuse; unemployment; and young people.

Within the Social Science Information Gateway, there are also major sections on:

criminal justice; psychology; public administration of social welfare; racial and ethnic minorities; research tools; social psychology; social welfare law; sociology; sociology of law; women's studies.

SocioSite

www2.fmg.uva.nl/sociosite

The SocioSite is designed to give access to information and resources which are relevant for sociologists and other social scientists. It is based at the University of Amsterdam.

SocioWeb

www.socioweb.com

The SocioWeb is an independent guide to the sociological resources available on the internet.

The Virtual Library – Sociology

socserv2.mcmaster.ca/w3virtsoclib/

The Virtual Library is the oldest catalogue of the Web, started by Tim Berners-Lee, the creator of html and the Web itself, in 1991 at CERN in Geneva, Switzerland. It is run by a loose confederation of volunteers, who compile pages of key links for particular areas in which they are expert.

BUBL Links Social Welfare and Social Work

bubl.ac.uk/link/s/socialwelfare.htm
bubl.ac.uk/link/s/socialwork.htm

Catalogue of internet resources for social work and sociology, maintained by the University of Strathclyde.

UK Government

www.direct.gov.uk

A site that gives access to all areas of government policy in one place. The section on Tax and Benefits gives summaries of the current position on many welfare benefits.

www.opsi.gov.uk

The Office of Public Sector Information website provides online access to Acts of Parliament and other official documents.

The sites that follow are for specific agencies and organizations, both official and voluntary, that are relevant to social work.

Adoption and Fostering information Line
www.adoption.org.uk/
information/page1.htm

Association of Directors of Social Services (ADSS)
www.adss.org.uk/

Association of Directors of Social Work
www.adsw.org.uk/

Audit Commission
www.audit-commission.gov.uk/

British Association for Adoption & Fostering
www.baaf.org.uk/

British Association of Social Workers
www.basw.co.uk/

British Crime Survey
www.homeoffice.gov.uk/rds/
bcs1.html

Benefits Agency online
www.beonline.org.uk

Best Value
www.bvpi.gov.uk/pages/Index.asp

The Beveridge Report
www.sochealth.co.uk/history/
beveridge.htm

British Association for Counselling and Psychotherapy
www.counselling.co.uk/

British Youth Council
www.byc.org.uk/

CAFCASS (Children and Family Court Advisory and Support Service)
www.cafcass.gov.uk/

Charity Commission
www.charity-commission.gov.uk/

Office of the Scottish Charity Regulator
www.oscr.org.uk/

Child Benefit
www.hmrc.gov.uk/childbenefit/

ChildLine
www.childline.org.uk/
Childabuse.asp

Children Act 2004
www.dfes.gov.uk/publications/
childrenactreport/
www.everychildmatters.gov.uk/
strategy/guidance/

Children's Fund
www.everychildmatters.gov.uk/
strategy/childrensfund/

Child Support Agency
www.csa.gov.uk/

Community Development Foundation
www.cdf.org.uk/

Community Legal Services
www.clsdirect.org.uk/index.jsp

Communities Online
www.communities.org.uk/

Commission for Racial Equality
www.cre.gov.uk/

Community Care
www.clsdirect.org.uk/legalhelp/
leaflet19.jsp?lang=en
www.gla.ac.uk/nuffield/index.htm

Commission for Social Care Inspection
www.csci.org.uk/

Connexions
www.connexions.gov.uk/
www.connexions-direct.com/

Criminal Defence Service
www.legalservices.gov.uk/
criminal/index.asp

Crown Prosecution Service
www.cps.gov.uk/

Department for Education and Skills
www.dfes.gov.uk/

Department for Education and Skills: adoption
www.dfes.gov.uk/adoption/
index.shtml

Department of Health
www.dfes.gov.uk/

Department for Work and Pensions
www.dwp.gov.uk/

Department of Health, Social Services and Public Safety, Northern Ireland
www.dhsspsni.gov.uk/

Disability Rights Commission
www.drc-gb.org/

Equal Opportunities Commission
www.eoc.org.uk/

European Union
http://europa.eu.int/index_en.htm

General Social Care Council
www.gscc.org.uk/Home/

Health and Social Care Advisory Service (HASCAS)
www.hascas.org.uk/

Home Office
www.homeoffice.gov.uk/

Howard League for Penal Reform
www.howardleague.org/

Independent Living Funds
www.ilf.org.uk/home/index.html

Jobseeker's allowance
www.jobcentreplus.gov.uk/JCP/

Citizen's Advice Bureau
www.citizensadvice.org.uk/

Mental Health Foundation
www.mentalhealth.org.uk/

Mental Health, Centre for Evidence-Based
www.cebmh.com/

National Association of Probation Workers (NAPO)
www.napo.org.uk/

National Asylum Support Service
www.asylumsupport.info/
nass.htm

National Association of Social Workers in Education (NASWE)
www.naswe.org.uk/

National Association for Special
Educational Needs (nasen)
www.nasen.org.uk/

National Care Standards
Commission
(Commission for Social Care
Inspection)
www.csci.org.uk/

National Children's Bureau
www.ncb.org.uk/Page.asp

National Council for Voluntary
Organizations (NCVO)
www.ncvo-vol.org.uk/

National Health Service
www.nhs.uk/
www.show.scot.nhs.uk/
www.wales.nhs.uk/

National Insurance
www.hmrc.gov.uk/nic/

National Probation Service
www.probation.homeoffice.gov.uk/
output/Page1.asp

National Society for the Prevention
of Cruelty to Children (NSPCC)
www.nspcc.org.uk/

Prison Reform Trust
www.prisonreformtrust.org.uk/

Refugee Council
www.refugeecouncil.org.uk/
index.htm

Research in Practice for Adults
www.ripfa.org.uk/

Scottish Executive
www.scotland.gov.uk/Home

Joseph Rowntree Foundation
www.jrf.org.uk/

Shelter
www.shelter.org.uk/

Social Care Online
www.scie-socialcareonline.org.uk/

Social Exclusion Unit
www.socialexclusionunit.gov.uk/

Social Policy and Social Work (SWAP)
(The Higher Education Academy)
www.swap.ac.uk/default.asp

Social Care Institute for Excellence
www.scie.org.uk/

Social Security Advisory Committee
www.ssac.org.uk/

Social Services Inspectorate
(Commission for Social Care
Inspection)
www.csci.org.uk/

Social Work Careers
www.socialworkcareers.co.uk

Special Educational Needs
www.teachernet.gov.uk/
wholeschool/sen/

Supporting People
www.spkweb.org.uk/

Sure Start
www.surestart.gov.uk/

Tax credits
www.hmrc.gov.uk/menus/
credits.htm
www.direct.gov.uk/MoneyTaxAnd
Benefits/BenefitsTaxCreditsAnd
OtherSupport/

Victims of Crime, Code of Practice
www.homeoffice.gov.uk/
documents/victims-code-of-
practice

Victim Support
www.victimsupport.org/

Welfare rights
www.direct.gov.uk/MoneyTaxAnd
Benefits/fs/en

Welsh Assembly Government
http://new.wales.gov.uk/

Women's Aid
www.womensaid.org.uk/